TEXTBOOK ON
COMMERCIAL LAW

TEXTBOOK ON

COMMERCIAL LAW

Iwan R. Davies, LLB(Cantab), LLM, PhD(Wales)

BLACKSTONE PRESS LIMITED

First published in Great Britain 1992 by Blackstone Press Limited,
9–15 Aldine Street, London W12 8AW. Telephone: 081-740 1173

© Iwan Davies, 1992

ISBN: 1 85431 195 6

British Library Cataloguing in Publication Data
A CIP cataloguing record for this book is available from the British Library

Typeset by Style Photosetting Limited, Mayfield, East Sussex
Printed by Ashford Colour Press, Gosport, Hampshire

All rights reserved. No part of this book may be reproduced or transmitted in any form or by any means, electronic or mechanical, including photocopying, recording, or any information storage or retrieval system without prior permission from the publisher.

Contents

Preface	ix
Table of Cases	xi
Table of Statutes	xxx
Table of Rules and Regulations	xxxix
Table of European and International Legislation	xl

PART 1 HISTORICAL DEVELOPMENT AND CONCEPTUAL FRAMEWORK   1

1 The *Lex Mercatoria*: The Genesis of English Commercial Law   1

Introduction — The Phenomenon of Commercial Law — The Principles of Commercial Law

2 Basic Concepts of Personal Property   15

The Distinction between Real and Personal Property — Ownership — Ownership and the Right to Possession — Property Passing and Identification — Creation of Property Interests at Common Law

PART 2 SALE AND SUPPLY OF GOODS   44

3 Definition and Nature of Contracts for the Supply of Goods   44

The Sale Contracts — Supply Contracts for Consideration other than Money — Consumer Credit — Sales and Loans on Security

4 Formalities and the Formation of Sale and Supply Contracts — 63

Formation — Exclusion and Limitation of Liability — The Doctrine of Waiver — Impossibility of Performance — Formalities

5 The Obligations of the Supplier — 79

Delivery — Implied Undertakings as to Quality and Description — Other Implied Terms — Exclusion of Liability — Manufacturers' Guarantees — Product Liability

6 Remedies of the Supplier for Misrepresentation or Breach — 121

Real Remedies: The Sale of Goods Act 1979 — Real Remedies: Contracts of Supply — Personal Remedies

7 The Transfer of Title and Security of Property — 134

The Security of Property Principle — Estoppel: The Common Law and Statutory Context — Market Overt — Voidable Title — Sellers in Possession — Buyers in Possession — Supplies of Motor Vehicles — Sale Under Common Law or Statutory Powers

8 The Obligations and Remedies of the Transferee — 161

Duty to Accept Delivery — Duty to Pay — General Principle of Risk — Transferee's Right to Reject — Loss of the Right to Reject — Action for Damages — Equitable Remedies

PART 3   CREDIT AND PAYMENT — 187

9 The Bill of Exchange — 187

Historical Development — The Function of Bills of Exchange — Characteristics of Negotiable Instruments — Requirements for a Valid Bill of Exchange — Negotiation of a Bill of Exchange — Transferability of a Bill — Forged Signatures — Enforcement of a Bill — Discharge of a Bill — Screen-based Transfers?

10 Cheques and Analogous Instruments on a Banker — 210

Cheques and Bills — The Roles of the Bank and Customer — Legal Regulation of Cheques — Other Paper Instruments — Paperless Payment Orders

Contents   vii

11 Credit Factoring and the Securitisation of Receivables 228

Late Payment of Debts — Legal Problems Associated with Credit Factoring — Securitisation of Receivables

PART 4   SECURED FINANCING   258

12 The Retention of Title Clause   258

The Principal Cases — Identification of Retention of Title Clauses — Bailment and Vertical Extension — Agency and Vertical Extension — Equitable Infiltration into Commercial Law

13 The Finance Lease   289

Problems of Definition — Legal Problems Associated with Finance Leasing — Remedies Under Lease and Hire Contracts — Leasing and the Consumer Credit Act 1974

14 Possessory Security   318

Pledge — Lien — Possession as the Base Concept — Powers of Sale

15 Non-Possessory Security Interests   327

The After-Acquired Property Interest — Fixed and Floating Charges — Unconventional Security Devices

16 Ostensible Ownership and Registration of Security Interests   358

The English Legal Response to Ostensible Ownership — Notice Filing: The US Experience — The Canadian Approach to Filing Personal Property Security Interests

17 Guarantees   374

The Substantive Law — Suretyship Contracts — Legal Presumptions — The Impact of Insolvency — Quasi-Guarantees

PART 5   CORPORATE INSOLVENCY   391

18 The Framework of Corporate Insolvency Law   391

Introduction — Historical Development of the Law — Objectives and Principles of Insolvency Law

19 The State of Insolvency and its Legal Regime — 398

The Tests for Insolvency — Voluntary Arrangements — The Administration Order — Administrative Receivership — Liquidation

20 Distribution and Ordering of Claims Following Corporate Insolvency — 425

Assets Available for Distribution — The *Pari Passu* Principle of Distribution — Exceptions to the *Pari Passu* Principle — Subordination — Distribution of Assets

21 Avoiding Powers and the Liability of Directors and Others for Improper Trading — 443

Transactions at Undervalue — Preferences — Extortionate Credit Transactions — Floating Charges — Transactions Defrauding Creditors — Dispositions of Property Made After the Commencement of Compulsory Winding Up — Non-Registration of a Registrable Charge — The Policies Behind the Avoiding Powers — Fraudulent Trading — Wrongful Trading — Prosecution and Disqualification

PART 6 RESOLUTION OF COMMERCIAL DISPUTES — 460

22 Dispute Resolution Machinery — 460

Litigation — Arbitration — Alternative Dispute Resolution Mechanisms

23 Reform and Codification of English Commercial Law — 473

Codification — The English Experience of Codification in Commercial Law — Codification: A Vehicle for Reform?

Bibliography — 481

Index — 487

Preface

One of the major difficulties in devising a textbook on commercial law is delineation of scope. The boundaries of commercial law are notoriously imprecise: contract lawyers will focus upon express and implied terms and also remedies for breach in commercial contracts; tort lawyers consider the primary functions of commercial law to be product liability and interference with goods; company lawyers categorise commercial law in terms of entitlements, registration of security interests and providing a legal framework for insolvency; property-based lawyers perceive commercial law in terms of personal property and the creation of personal property security interests. In fact, it is simplistic to compartmentalise commercial law because this ignores the dynamic business setting. Other branches of law will directly affect commercial transactions including equity, trusts and property law.

This book examines many of the conceptual and practical problems associated with modern commercial practice. It covers the subject by looking at the transactions within the distribution process: sale and supply; credit and payment; secured financing; corporate insolvency; the resolution of commercial disputes. By approaching the subject in this way, it is possible to identify common principles and themes running through the distribution process. In this regard, three 'conveyancing principles' emerge, namely, security of property, good-faith purchase and ostensible ownership. The onset of corporate insolvency collectivises what have hitherto been individual remedies operating within the framework of commercial law. It does not change the issue of pre-insolvency entitlements because this will prejudice the goal of insolvency law, that is, collective interest. We shall examine corporate insolvency because it provides a striking exception to the law's reluctance to admit class actions and is such a prominent feature of modern commercial life that it cannot be ignored. The aim of this book is to state the law as clearly as possible without prejudicing an appreciation of the commercial setting. Thus, agency is considered not as a neatly packaged subject but as one that cuts across transactional boundaries within the distribution process. In order to make the discussion manageable within the space available, the book will focus upon domestic aspects of English commercial law. Whilst consumer credit and consumer protection cannot be regarded as forming part of commercial law in the true sense, nevertheless, aspects of consumer law cannot be entirely ignored as it will so often impinge upon commercial transactions.

During the course of this book we shall draw upon primary and secondary legal materials. It should be noted that commercial case law may be more important in terms of the facts they throw out rather than any particular legal judgment: these facts provide valuable insights into the current legal problems associated with modern commercial practice.

It is a pleasure for me to record my gratitude to those who have helped in the preparation of this book, including Mrs Valerie Simpson for typing the manuscript and to Mr Tim Baker for preparing the table of cases. I should like to record my gratitude to my wife Katherine who has been a source of encouragement, and especially to our son Elidir Llŷr Dafydd who has provided a welcome distraction from the demands of academic research.

The law is stated from material available to me up to and including 17 May 1992.

Iwan Davies
Cardiff Law School
University of Wales

Table of Cases

Abbey National Building Society v Cann [1991] 1 AC 56; [1990] 2 WLR 832   261, 356
Agip (Africa) Ltd v Jackson [1990] Ch 265; [1989] 3 WLR 1367   213, 283
Aiken v Short (1856) 1 H & N 210   246
Airlines Airspares Ltd v Handley Page Ltd [1970] Ch 193; [1970] 2 WLR 163;
    [1970] 1 All ER 29   418
Akron Tyre Co. Pty Ltd v Kittson (1951) 82 CLR 477   41
Albemarle Supply Co. Ltd v Hind and Co. [1928] 1 KB 307; 138 LT 102; 71 SJ 711   136, 324
Aldridge v Johnson (1857) 7 E & B 885; 26 LJ QB 296; 119 ER 1476   32, 53, 56
Allied Marine Transport Ltd v Vale do Rio Doce Navegacao SA [1985] 1 WLR 925;
    [1985] 2 All ER 796; [1985] 2 Lloyd's Rep 18   80
Aluminium Industrie Vaassen BV v Romalpa Aluminium Ltd [1976] 1 WLR 676;
    [1976] 2 All ER 552; [1976] 1 Lloyd's Rep 443
            7, 259–60, 262, 266, 270–1, 274, 276, 280, 283, 288, 352, 355, 477–9
Amalgamated Investment and Property Co. Ltd, re [1985] Ch 349; [1984] 3 WLR 1101;
    [1984] 3 All ER 272   386
American Express International Bank Corp v Hurley [1985] 3 All ER 564; 1985 FLR 350   417
AMEV-UDC Finance Ltd v Austin (1986) 162 CLR 170; 60 ALJR 741   303, 316
Anchor Line (Henderson Bros) Ltd, Re [1937] Ch 1; [1936] 2 All ER 941   49
Andrabell Ltd, re [1984] 3 All ER 407   264–5, 270, 276–7, 435
Andrews v Hopkinson [1957] 1 QB 229; [1956] 2 WLR 732; [1956] 3 All ER 422   66
Anglo Auto Finance Co. Ltd v James [1963] 1 WLR 1042; [1963] 3 All ER 566   311–12
Anns v Merton London Borough Council [1978] AC 728; [1977] 2 WLR 1024   298
Antaios Cia Naviera SA v Salen Rederierna AB [1985] AC 191; [1984] 3 WLR 592;
    [1984] 3 All ER 229; [1984] 2 Lloyd's Rep 235   468
Anton Piller KG v Manufacturing Processes Ltd [1976] Ch 55   464
Appleby v Myers (1867) LR 2 CP 651; [1861-73] All ER Rep 452; 16 LT 669   74
Arab Bank Ltd v Ross [1952] 2 QB 216; [1952] 1 All ER 709   198, 200
Arcos Ltd v E.A. Ronaasen and Son [1933] AC 470; [1933] All ER Rep 646; 149 LT 98   87, 90
Armagh Shoes Ltd, Re [1984] BCLC 405; [1981] 9 NIJB   340
Armour v Thyssen Edelstahlwerke AG [1991] 2 AC 339; [1990] 3 WLR 810; [1990] 3 All ER 481
    267–8, 346, 353, 357
Arpad, The [1934] P 189; 50 TLR 505   177, 182
Arthur Sanders Ltd, re (1981) 17 BLR 125   389
Arthur Wheeler and Co., re (1933) 102 LJ Ch 341   278
ARV Aviation Ltd, re [1989] BCLC 664; 4 BCC 708   413
Asfar and Co. v Blundell [1896] 1 QB 123; 73 LT 648; 40 SJ 66   73
Ashington Piggeries Ltd v Christopher Hill Ltd [1972] AC 441; [1971] 2 WLR 1051;
    [1971] 1 All ER 847   72, 86, 87, 101, 103

Table of Cases

Associated Japanese Bank (International) Ltd v Crédit du Nord SA [1988] 3 All ER 902;
[1989] 1 WLR 255   64, 72, 374
Astley Industrial Trust Ltd v Miller [1968] 2 All ER 36   140
Aswan Engineering Establishment Co. (M/S) v Lupdine Ltd [1987] 1 WLR 1;
[1987] 1 All ER 135; 6 TrLR 1   94, 96, 100
Atlantic Computer Systems plc, re [1990] BCC 439; [1992] 2 WLR 367; [1992] 1 All ER 476
   408, 410
Atlas Industries Inc. v National Cash Register Co. (1975) 531 P 2d 41; 216 Kan 213   296
Attorney-General v Cohen [1937] 1 KB 478   239
Automobile Finance Co. of Australia Ltd v Law (1933) 49 CLR 1   207
Avon Finance Co. Ltd v Bridger [1985] 2 All ER 281   382
Axel Johnson Petroleum AB v MG Mineral Group AG [1992] 1 WLR 270;
[1992] 2 All ER 163; 135 SJ 60   241
Ayerst v C & K (Construction) Ltd [1976] AC 167; [1975] 3 WLR 16; [1975] 2 All ER 537   397

Babanaft International Co. SA v Bassatne [1990] Ch 13; [1989] 2 WLR 232;
[1989] 1 All ER 433; [1988] 2 Lloyd's Rep 435   464
Baden, Delvaux and Lecuit v Société Générale pour Favoriser le Developpement du
Commerce et de l'Industrie en France SA [1983] BCLC 325   213
Badische Anilin und Soda Fabrik v Basle Chemical Works, Bindschedler [1898] AC 200;
77 LT 573   53
Badische Co. Ltd, re [1921] 2 Ch 331; 126 LT 466   73
Bailey v Finch (1871) LR 7 QB 34   435
Baker v Barclays Bank Ltd [1955] 1 WLR 822; [1955] 2 All ER 571; 99 SJ 491   223
Banco di Roma SpA v Orru [1973] 2 Lloyd's Rep 505   200
Bank of Africa v Salisbury Gold Mining Co. [1892] AC 281; 66 LT 237   326
Bank of England v Vagliano Brothers [1891] AC 107; [1891-4] All ER Rep 93; 64 LT 353
   195, 196, 203, 220, 476
Bank Mellat v Nikpour [1985] FSR 87; [1982] Com LR 158   465
Banque Belge pour l'Etranger v Hambrouck [1921] 1 KB 321; 37 TLR 76   283
Barclays Bank Ltd v Quistclose Investments Ltd [1970] AC 567; [1968] 3 WLR 1097;
[1968] 3 All ER 651; 112 SJ 903   288, 435
Barclays Bank Ltd v W. J. Simms Son and Cooke (Southern) Ltd [1980] QB 677;
[1980] 2 WLR 218; [1979] 3 All ER 522; [1980] 1 Lloyd's Rep 225   220, 246
Barclays Bank plc v Bank of England [1985] 1 All ER 385; 1985 FLR 209; 135 NLJ 104   219
Barclays Bank plc v Quincecare Ltd 1988 FLR 166   214
Barclays Bank plc v Taylor [1989] 1 WLR 1066; 133 SJ 1372   214
Barclays Bank plc v Willowbrook International Ltd [1987] 1 FTLR 386; [1987] BCLC 717   340
Barker v Hargreaves [1981] RTR 197; [1981] Crim LR 262   119
Barrow, Lane and Ballard Ltd v Phillip Phillips and Co. Ltd [1929] 1 KB 574;
[1928] All ER Rep 74; 140 LT 670   72
Bartlett v Sidney Marcus Ltd [1965] 1 WLR 1013; [1965] 2 All ER 753   95–6, 97
Barton Thompson and Co. Ltd v Stapling Machines Co. [1966] Ch 499; [1966] 2 WLR 1429;
[1966] 2 All ER 222   311
Basildon District Council v J. E. Lesser (Properties) Ltd [1985] QB 839; [1984] 3 WLR 812;
[1985] 1 All ER 20   116
Bavins Jnr and Sims v London and South Western Bank Ltd [1900] 1 QB 270; 81 LT 655   192
Beale v Taylor [1967] 1 WLR 1193; [1967] 3 All ER 253   86
Bechervaise v Lewis (1872) LR 7 CP 372   380–1
Bell v Lever Bros Ltd [1932] AC 161; [1931] All ER Rep 1; 146 LT 258   64
Belsize Motor Supply Co. v Cox [1914] 1 KB 244; [1911-13] All ER Rep 1084; 110 LT 151   308, 351
Belvoir Finance Co. Ltd v Stapleton [1971] 1 QB 210; [1970] 3 WLR 530; [1970] 3 All ER 664   308
Bence v Shearman [1898] 2 Ch 582   11
Benedict v Ratner (1925) 268 US 353   247–8
Benjamin Cope and Sons Ltd, re [1914] 1 Ch 800   11, 328
Bentinck Ltd v Cromwell Engineering Co. [1971] 1 QB 324; [1970] 3 WLR 1113;
[1971] 1 All ER 33   317

Table of Cases

Benton v Campbell, Parker and Co. Ltd [1925] 2 KB 410; [1925] All ER Rep 187; 134 LT 60   76
Bentsen v Taylor, Sons and Co. [1893] 2 QB 274; 69 LT 487   67
Bentworth Finance Ltd v Lubert [1968] 1 QB 680; [1967] 3 WLR 378; [1967] 2 All ER 810   107
Bernal v Pim (1835) 1 Gale 17   322, 324
Bernstein v Pamsons Motors (Golders Green) Ltd [1987] 2 All ER 220; [1987] RTR 384
   96, 168, 170,171
Bethell v Clark (1888) 20 QBD 615; 59 LT 808   123
Beverley Acceptances Ltd v Oakley [1982] RTR 417   79
Biggerstaff v Rowatt's Wharf Ltd [1896] 2 Ch 93   433
Biggin and Co. Ltd v Permanite Ltd [1951] 1 KB 422; [1951] 2 All ER 191   181
Bishopsgate Investment Ltd (in provisional liquidation) v Maxwell and another
   [1992] 2 All ER 856   423
Billiter v Young (1856) 6 E & B 1   148
Bissell and Co. Ltd v Fox Bros and Co. (1884) 53 LT 193; 1 TLR 492   223
Blackburne, re (1892) 9 Morr 249   386
Blakely, re (1892) 9 Morr 173   386
Bloomer v Bernstein (1874) LR 9 CP 588; 31 LT 306   428
Blyth Shipbuilding and Dry Docks Co. Ltd, re [1926] Ch 494; [1926] All ER Rep 373;
   134 LT 643   52
Boardman v Phipps [1967] 2 AC 46; [1966] 3 WLR 1009; [1966] 3 All ER 721   279, 284
Bolam v Friern Hospital Management Committee [1957] 1 WLR 582; [1957] 2 All ER 118   58
Bolton v Salmon [1891] 2 Ch 48   380
Bond Worth Ltd, re [1980] Ch 228; [1979] 3 WLR 629; [1979] 3 All ER 919   186, 260–2, 266, 355
Bondina Ltd v Rollaway Shower Blinds Ltd [1986] 1 WLR 517; [1985] 130 SJ 264;
   [1986] 1 All ER 564; 1986 FLR 266   205
Booth Steamship Co. Ltd v Cargo Fleet Iron Co. Ltd [1916] 2 KB 570;
   [1916-17] All ER Rep 938; 115 LT 199   125
Borden (UK) Ltd v Scottish Timber Products Ltd [1981] Ch 25; [1979] 3 WLR 672;
   [1979] 3 All ER 961; [1979] 2 Lloyd's Rep 168   42, 260–3, 270, 280–1, 477, 478
Borrowman, Phillips and Co. v Free and Hollis (1878) 4 QBD 500; 40 LT 25   53, 161
Bostock and Co. Ltd v Nicholson and Sons Ltd [1904] 1 KB 725; 91 LT 626   181, 182
Bowes v Shand (1877) 2 App Cas 455; 36 LT 857   80, 87
Braithwaite v Foreign Hardwood Co. [1905] 2 KB 543; 92 LT 637   70, 83
Braithwaite v Thomas Cook Travellers' Cheques Ltd [1989] QB 553; [1989] 3 WLR 212;
   [1989] 1 All ER 235   225
Brandon v Leckie (1972) 29 DLR (3d) 633   154
Braude (E.) (London) Ltd v Porter [1959] 2 Lloyd's Rep 161   177
Bremer Vulkan Schiffbau und Maschinenfabrik v South India Shipping Corpn Ltd
   [1981] AC 909; [1981] 2 WLR 141; [1981] 2 All ER 289   471
Brice v Bannister (1878) 3 QBD 569   243
Bridge v Campbell Discount Co. Ltd [1962] AC 600; [1962] 2 WLR 439; [1962] 1 All ER 385
   311–12
Brightlife Ltd, Re [1987] Ch 200; [1987] 2 WLR 197; [1986] 3 All ER 673   340–1
British and Beningtons Ltd v North Western Cachar Tea Co. Ltd [1923] AC 48;
   [1922] All ER Rep 224; 128 LT 422   83
British Eagle International Air Lines Ltd v Compagnie Nationale Air France
   [1975] 1 WLR 758; [1975] 2 All ER 390; [1975] 2 Lloyd's Rep 43   430, 434, 439
British Steel Corporation v Cleveland Bridge and Engineering Co. Ltd [1984] 1 All ER 504;
   24 BLR 94; [1982] Com LR 54   460
Brooke Marine Ltd, re [1988] BCLC 546   415
Brookes v Retail Credit Cards Ltd [1986] CLY 370; [1986] Crim LR 327   103
Brown v Bateman (1867) LR 2 CP 272   334
Brown v Westminster Bank Ltd [1964] 2 Lloyd's Rep 187   203
Brown (B.S.) and Son Ltd v Craiks Ltd [1970] 1 WLR 752; [1970] 1 All ER 823   96
Browne v Carr (1831) 7 Bing 508   388
Buckley v Gross (1863) 3 B & S 566   38
Budberg v Jerwood and Ward (1935) 51 TLR 99; 78 SJ 878   139

Table of Cases

Bunge Corporation, New York v Tradax Export SA, Panama [1981] 1 WLR 711;
[1981] 2 All ER 540; [1981] Lloyd's Rep 1   67, 68, 80
Burnes v Trade Credits Ltd [1981] 1 WLR 805; 125 SJ 198; [1981] 2 All ER 122   380
Burnett v Westminster Bank Ltd [1966] 1 QB 742; [1965] 3 WLR 863; [1965] 3 All ER 81;
109 SJ 533   213
Business Applications Specialists Ltd v Nationwide Credit Corpn Ltd [1988] RTR 332;
8 TrLR 33   97
Business Computers Ltd v Anglo-African Leasing Ltd [1977] 1 WLR 578; [1977] 2 All ER 741 252
Butler Machine Tool Co. Ltd v Ex-Cell-O Corpn (England) Ltd [1979] 1 WLR 401;
[1979] 1 All ER 965   66, 460
Butterworth v Kingsway Motors [1954] 1 WLR 1286; [1954] 2 All ER 694   173

Cahn v Pockett's Bristol Channel Steam Packet Co. Ltd [1899] 1 QB 643; 80 LT 269   151
Cameron (R.W.) and Co. v L. Slutzkin Pty (1923) 32 CLR 81   106
Canadian Admiral Corporation Ltd v L. F. Dommerich and Co. Inc. (1964) 43 DLR (2d) 1   252
Candlewood Navigation Corpn Ltd v Mitsui OSK Lines Ltd [1986] AC 1;
[1985] 3 WLR 381; [1985] 2 All ER 925   298
Capital and Counties Bank Ltd v Gordon [1903] AC 240; 88 LT 574   205
Capital and Counties Bank Ltd v Warriner (1896) 1 Com Cas 314; 12 TLR 216   36
Capital Finance Co. Ltd v Stokes [1969] 1 Ch 261; [1968] 3 WLR 899   186, 355
Car and Universal Finance Co. Ltd v Caldwell [1965] 1 QB 525; [1964] 2 WLR 600;
[1964] 1 All ER 290   122, 132, 148, 151
Carlill v Carbolic Smoke Ball Co. [1893] 1 QB 256; [1891-4] All ER Rep 127   66, 255
Carlos Federspiel and Co. SA v Charles Twigg and Co. Ltd [1957] 1 Lloyd's Rep 240   53, 54
Carney v Herbert [1985] AC 301; [1984] 3 WLR 1303; [1985] 1 All ER 438   383
Carpenters' Co. v British Mutual Banking Co. Ltd [1938] 1 KB 511;
[1937] 3 All ER 811; 157 LT 329   220, 221
Carreras Rothmans Ltd v Freeman Matthews Treasure Ltd [1985] Ch 207; [1985] 1 All ER 155 288
Cebora SNC v SIP (Industrial Products) Ltd [1976] 1 LLoyd's Rep 271   190
Cehave NV v Bremer Handelsgesellschaft mbH [1976] QB 44; [1975] 3 WLR 447;
[1975] 3 All ER 739   67, 96, 476
Central Newbury Car Auctions Ltd v Unity Finance Ltd [1957] 1 QB 371;
[1956] 3 WLR 1068; [1956] 3 All ER 905   144, 158
Chandler v Webster [1904] 1 KB 493; 90 LT 217; 48 SJ 245   74
Chapman v Withers (1888) 20 QBD 824; 4 TLR 465   165
Chappel (1989) Eur Court HR, Series A, No. 152-A   464
Charge Card Services Ltd, re [1989] Ch 497; [1988] 3 WLR 764; [1988] 3 All ER 702 (CA);
[1987] Ch 150; [1986] 3 All ER 289   164, 214, 426, 436
Charles Rickards Ltd v Oppenhaim [1950] 1 KB 616   69, 70
Charnley Davies Ltd, re [1990] BCC 605   414
Chartered Trust plc v Pitcher [1988] RTR 72; 6 TrLR 97   317
Charterhouse Credit Co. Ltd v Tolly [1963] 2 QB 683; [1963] 2 WLR 1168;
[1963] 2 All ER 432   180, 310
Chase Manhattan Bank NA v Israel-British Bank (London) Ltd [1981] Ch 105   283, 428
China and South Sea Bank Ltd v Tan Soon Gin [1990] 1 AC 536; [1989] 3 All ER 839;
139 New LJ 1669   385
Christie v Taunton, Delmard, Lane and Co. [1893] 2 Ch 175   240, 252
Churchill and Sim v Goddard [1937] 1 KB 92   276
Churchill Hotel (Plymouth) Ltd, re [1988] BCLC 341; 4 BCC 112; 1988 PCC 220   458
Citicorp Leasing Inc. v Allied Institutional Distributor Inc. (1977) 454 F Supp 511   296
City Equitable Fire Insurance Co. Ltd, re (No. 2) [1930] 2 Ch 293   435
Clarke v Reilly (1962) 96 ILTR 96   56
Claydon v Bradley [1987] 1 WLR 521; [1987] 1 All ER 522; 1987 FLR 111   194
Clayton's Case (Devaynes v Noble) (1816) 1 Mer 572; [1814-23] All ER Rep 1 285-6, 379, 446, 450
Clea Shipping Corpn v Bulk Oil International Ltd (No. 2) [1984] 1 All ER 129;
[1983] 2 Lloyd's Rep 645   176

Table of Cases

Clough Mill Ltd v Martin [1985] 1 WLR 111; [1984] 2 All ER 982
  42, 126, 265–9, 346, 353, 357, 477, 479
Coggs v Bernard (1703) 2 Ld Raym 909; 92 ER 107; [1558-1774] All ER Rep 1   107, 270, 295
Cohen v Roche [1927] 1KB 169; 136 LT 219   182
Coldunell Ltd v Gallon [1986] QB 1184   382
Colehan v Cooke (1742) Willes 393   193
Coleman v Harvey [1989] 1 NZLR 723   38, 39, 272
Colin and Shields v W. Weddell and Co. Ltd [1952] 2 All ER 337; [1952] 2 Lloyd's Rep 9;
  [1952] 2 TLR 185   35
Colley v Overseas Exporters [1921] 3 KB 302; [1921] All ER Rep 596; 126 LT 58   128
Collins, re [1925] Ch 556   242, 328, 426
Commissioners of Taxation v English, Scottish and Australian Bank Ltd [1920] AC 683   223
Company, re a [1983] BCLC 492   396
Company, re a (No. 00175 of 1987) [1987] BCLC 467   404
Company, re a (No. 005685 of 1988) (No. 2) [1989] BCLC 424   444
Company, re a (No. 003079 of 1990) [1991] BCLC 235   399
Compaq Computer Ltd v Abercorn Group Ltd [1991] BCC 484   11, 248, 249, 251, 279
Comptoir d'Achat et de Vente du Boerenbond Belge SA v Luis de Ridder Ltda
  [1949] AC 293; [1949] 1 All ER 269; 65 TLR 126   31
Concorde Construction Co. Ltd v Colgan Co. Ltd (1984) 29 BLR 120   389
Condon, re, ex parte James (1874) LR 9 Ch App 609   399, 420
Connolly Bros Ltd, re (No. 2) [1912] 2 Ch 25; 106 LT 738   186, 355–6
Consumer and Industrial Press Ltd, re [1988] 4 BCC 68; [1988] BCLC 177   407
Continental Illinois National Bank and Trust Co. of Chicago v Pananicolaou
  [1986] 2 Lloyd's Rep 441   434
Cooke v Haddon (1862) 3 F & F 229   326
Cooper v Willomatt (1845) 1 CB 672   127
Core's Case (1537) 1 Dyer 20   281
Corfield v Sevenways Garage Ltd [1985] RTR 109; 4 TrLR 172   92
Corn Exchange National Bank and Trust Co. v Klauder (1943) 318 US 434; 63 SCt 679   248
Cornish v Midland Bank plc [1985] 3 All ER 513; 1985 FLR 298   383
Cornhill Insurance plc v Improvement Services Ltd [1986] 1 WLR 114; [1986] PCC 204   399
Couturier v Hastie (1856) 5 HL Cas 673; 10 ER 1065   71, 375
Craven's Estate, re [1937] Ch 423   23–4
Crédit Lyonnais v P. T. Barnard and Associates Ltd [1976] 1 Lloyd's Rep 557   202
Croftbell Ltd, re [1990] BCC 781   404, 405, 406
Crompton and Co. Ltd, re [1914] 1 Ch 954   340
Crowther v Shannon Motor Co. [1975] 1 WLR 30; [1975] 1 All ER 139;
  [1975] 1 Lloyd's Rep 382   97
Cullinane v British 'Rema' Manufacturing Co. Ltd [1954] 1 QB 292; [1953] 3 WLR 923;
  [1953] 2 All ER 1257   181
Cundy v Lindsay (1878) 3 App Cas 459; 38 LT 573   64, 147
Curtain Dream plc, re [1990] BCLC 925; [1990] BCC 341 (sub nom. Curtain Dream plc
  v Churchill Merchanting Ltd)   348
Curtice v London City and Midland Bank Ltd [1908] 1 KB 293   213
Czarnikow v Roth, Schmidt and Co. [1922] 2 KB 478   468
Czarnikow (C.) Ltd v Koufos [1969] 1 AC 350; [1967] 3 WLR 1491; [1967] 3 All ER 686;
  [1967] 2 Lloyd's Rep 457   130, 176, 180, 298

D and C Builders Ltd v Rees [1966] 2 QB 617; [1966] 2 WLR 288; [1965] 3 All ER 837   217
D and F Estates Ltd v Church Commissioners for England [1989] AC 177; [1988] 2 EGLR 213   298
Dallas, re [1904] 2 Ch 385   251
Damon Cia Naviera SA v Hapag-Lloyd Intenational SA [1985] 1 WLR 435;
  [1985] 1 All ER 475; [1985] 1 Lloyd's Rep 93   163
David Allester Ltd, re [1922] 2 Ch 211; 91 LJ Ch 797; 127 LT 434; 38 TLR 611   325
Davies v Burnett [1902] 1 KB 666; 86 LT 565   45
Davies v Customs and Excise Commissioners [1975] 1 WLR 204; [1975] 1 All ER 309   56

Table of Cases

Davies v Directloans Ltd [1986] 1 WLR 823	449
Davies v Sumner [1984] 1 WLR 1301; [1984] 3 All ER 831	91, 92, 108
Dawson (G. J.) (Clapham) Ltd v H. and G. Dutfield [1936] 2 All ER 232	56
Dawson Print Group Ltd, re [1987] BCLC 601; 3 BCC 322	458
Dearle v Hall (1828) 3 Russ 1	11, 190, 248–53, 279, 440
Debs v Sibec Developments Ltd [1990] RTR 91	143, 144, 156
Demby Hamilton and Co. Ltd v Barden [1949] 1 All ER 435; [1949] WN 73	166
Denney v John Hudson and Co. Ltd (1992) *Financial Times*, 8 May 1992	452
Denney, Gasquet and Metcalfe v Conklin [1913] 3 KB 177	239
Derby and Co. Ltd v Weldon (Nos. 3 and 4) [1990] Ch 65; [1989] 2 WLR 412; [1989] 133 SJ 83	464
Derry v Peek (1889) 14 App Cas 337	64, 465
Despina R, the [1979] AC 685; [1978] 3 WLR 804; [1979] 1 All ER 421	129
Destone Fabrics Ltd, re [1941] Ch 319	450
Diamond v Graham [1968] 1 WLR 1061; 112 SJ 396; [1968] 2 All ER 909	198
Dick Bentley Productions Ltd v Harold Smith (Motors) Ltd [1965] 1 WLR 623; [1965] 2 All ER 65	85
Dies v British and International Mining and Finance Corpn Ltd [1939] 1 KB 724; 160 LT 563	163
Diplock, re [1948] Ch 465	286
Dodd and Dodd v Wilson and McWilliam [1946] 2 All ER 691	58
Dole Dried Fruit and Nut Co. v Trustin Kerwood Ltd [1990] 2 Lloyd's Rep 309	241
Donald v Suckling (1866) LR 1 QB 585	325
Douglas Construction Services Ltd, re [1988] BCLC 397; 4 BCC 553	458
Dublin City Distillery (Great Brunswick Street, Dublin) Ltd v Doherty [1914] AC 823; 111 LT 81	35
Duke of Buccleuch v Inland Revenue Commissioners [1967] 1 AC 506; [1967] 2 WLR 207; [1967] 1 All ER 129	413
Dumas, ex parte (1754) 1 Atk 232	278
Dyer v Munday [1895] 1 QB 742; [1895-9] All ER Rep 1022; 72 LT 448	305
Eagle Star Insurance Co. Ltd v Yuval Insurance Co. Ltd [1978] 1 Lloyd's Rep 357	468–9
Eastern Distributors Ltd v Goldring [1957] 2 QB 600; [1957] 3 WLR 237; [1957] 2 All ER 525	141, 142, 150
Edwards v Edwards (1876) 2 ChD 291	363
Edwards v Harben (1788) 2 TR 587; 100 ER 315	327
El Awadi v Bank of Credit and Commerce International SA Ltd [1990] 1 QB 606; [1989] 1 All ER 242	219, 225
Elders Pastoral Ltd v Bank of New Zealand [1989] 2 NZLR 180	283
Eldon (Lord) v Hedley Bros [1935] 2 KB 1; 152 LT 507; 79 SJ 270	51
Elliott v Bax-Ironside [1925] 2 KB 301	204
Ellis v Emmanuel (1876) 1 Ex D 157	385
Elpis Maritime Co. Ltd v Marti Chartering Co. Inc. [1992] 1 AC 21; [1991] 3 WLR 330; [1991] 3 All ER 758	378
Elwin v O'Regan and Maxwell [1971] NZLR 1124	154
Esmail v J. Rosenthal and Sons Ltd [1964] 2 Lloyd's Rep 447; [1965] 1 WLR 111; [1965] 2 All ER 860	172
Esso Petroleum Co. Ltd v Customs and Excise Commissioners [1976] 1 WLR 1; [1976] 1 All ER 117	57
Esso Petroleum Co. Ltd v Mardon [1976] QB 801; [1976] 2 WLR 583; [1976] 2 All ER 5	65
Evans v Rival Granite Quarries Ltd [1910] 2 KB 979	337
EVTR Ltd, re [1987] BCLC 646	288
Exchange Travel Agency v Triton Property Trust plc [1991] BCLC 396	411
Export Credits Guarantee Derpartment v Universal Oil Products Co. [1983] 1 WLR 399; [1983] 2 All ER 205	311
Farina v Home (1846) 16 M & W 119; 16 LJ Ex 73; 153 ER 1124	33
Farnworth Finance Facilities Ltd v Attryde [1970] 1 WLR 1053; [1970] 2 All ER 774	168, 173

Table of Cases   xvii

Farquharson Bros and Co. v C. King and Co. Ltd [1902] AC 325	143
Fercometal SARL v Mediterranean Shipping Co. SA [1989] AC 788; [1988] 3 WLR 200	70, 83
Fibrosa SA v Fairbairn Lawson Combe Barbour Ltd [1943] AC 32; [1942] 2 All ER 122	74
Financings Ltd v Baldock [1963] 2 QB 104; [1963] 2 WLR 359; [1963] 1 All ER 443	309–10
Fire Nymph Products Ltd v The Heating Centre Pty Ltd (1988) 14 ACLR 274; 47 ALR 355; 61 ALR 251	341
Firestone Tire and Rubber Co. v General National Bank of Cleveland (1953) 112 NE 2d 636	246
Firestone Tire and Rubber Co. of Canada Ltd v Industrial Acceptance Corporation Ltd (1970) 75 WWR 621; [1971] SCR 357	41
Fisher v Calvert (1879) 27 WR 301	192
Fitzroy v Cave [1905] 2 KB 364; 93 LJ 499; 21 TLR 612	237
Flynn v Mackin [1974] IR 101	56
Foley v Classique Coaches Ltd [1934] 2 KB 1; [1934] All ER Rep 88; 151 LT 242	46
Foley v Hill (1848) 2 HL Cas 28; [1843-60] All ER Rep 16; 9 ER 1002	260, 283
Folkes v King [1923] 1 KB 282; [1922] All ER Rep 658; 128 LT 405	141
Ford Motor Co. Ltd v Amalgamated Union of Engineering and Foundry Workers [1969] 2 QB 303; [1969] 1 WLR 339; [1969] 2 All ER 481	376
Forster v Wilson (1843) 12 M & W 191	431
Forsyth v Jervis (1816) 1 Stark 437; 171 ER 522	56
Forth v Simpson (1843) 13 QB 680	324
Franklin v Neate (1844) 13 M & W 481; 4 LT 214; 153 ER 200	326
French's Wine Bar Ltd, re [1987] BCLC 499	452
Friend v Young [1897] 2 Ch 421	278
Frost v Aylesbury Dairy Co. [1905] 1 KB 608; [1904-7] All ER Rep 132; 92 LT 527	101
Fuentes v Montis (1868) LR 3 CP 268	138
Gallagher v Shilcock [1949] 2 KB 765; 93 SJ 302; [1949] 1 All ER 921	126
Galland, re (1885) 31 ChD 296	321
Gardiner v Gray (1815) 4 Camp 144; 171 ER 46	91, 106
Garnac Grain Co. Inc. v H. M. F. Faure and Fairclough Ltd [1968] AC 1130; [1967] 3 WLR 143	130
Garrard v James [1925] Ch 616	375–6
Geddling v March [1920] 1 KB 668; [1920] All ER Rep 631; 122 LT 775	93
Genn v Winkel (1912) 107 LT 434; 28 TLR 483	274
George Barker (Transport) Ltd v Eynon [1974] 1 WLR 462; [1974] 1 All ER 900	340, 452
George Inglefield Ltd, re [1933] Ch 1; [1932] All ER Rep 244; 147 LT 411	347–8
George Mitchell (Chesterhall) Ltd v Finney Lock Seeds Ltd [1983] 2 AC 803; [1983] 3 WLR 163; [1983] 2 All ER 737; [1983] 2 Lloyd's Rep 272	111
Gerald Cooper Chemicals Ltd, re [1978] Ch 262; [1978] 2 WLR 866; [1978] 2 All ER 49	455
Gibbons v Trapp Motors Ltd (1970) 9 DLR (3d) 742	180
Gilbert-Ash (Northern) Ltd v Modern Engineering (Bristol) Ltd [1974] AC 689; [1973] 3 WLR 421; [1973] 3 All ER 195	240
Gill and Duffus (Liverpool) Ltd v Scruttons Ltd [1953] 1 WLR 1407; [1953] 2 All ER 977	38
Gill and Duffus SA v Berger and Co. Inc. (No. 2) [1984] AC 382; [1984] 2 WLR 95; [1984] 1 All ER 438	89
Gillett v Hill (1834) 2 Cr & M 530; 149 ER 871	32
GKN Centrax Gears Ltd v Matbro Ltd [1976] 2 Lloyd's Rep 555	182
Goldsmith v Rodger [1962] 2 Lloyd's Rep 249	133
Goldsworthy v Brickell [1987] Ch 378; [1987] 2 WLR 133; [1987] 1 All ER 853	382
Goodman v J. Eban Ltd [1954] 1 QB 550; [1954] 2 WLR 581; [1954] 1 All ER 763	193
Gordon v Silber (1890) 25 QBD 491	322
Goring, The [1987] QB 687; [1987] 2 WLR 151; [1987] 2 All ER 246	323
Gorringe v Irwell India Rubber and Gutta Percha Works (1886) 34 ChD 128; 55 LT 572	242
Gough v Wood and Co. [1894] 1 QB 713	306
Government of Newfoundland v Newfoundland Railway Co. (1888) 13 App Cas 199	241
Governors of the Peabody Donation Fund v Sir Lindsay Parkinson and Co. Ltd [1985] AC 210; [1984] 3 WLR 953; [1984] 3 All ER 529	298

Graff v Evans (1882) 8 QBD 373; 46 LT 347	45
Grant v Australian Knitting Mills Ltd [1936] AC 85	85, 96
Grantham v Hawley (1616) Hob 132	332
Gray's Inn Construction Co. Ltd, re [1980] 1 WLR 711; 124 SJ 463; [1980] 1 All ER 814	452
Great Western Railway Co. v London and County Banking Co. Ltd [1901] AC 414; 85 LT 152	222
Greater Nottingham Co-operative Society Ltd v Cementation Piling and Foundations Ltd [1989] QB 71	298
Green v Baverstock (1863) 14 CB NS 204; 8 LT 360	76
Green (R. W.) Ltd v Cade Bros Farms [1978] 1 Lloyd's Rep 602	110, 111
Greenwood v Bennett [1973] QB 195; [1972] 3 WLR 691; [1972] 3 All ER 586	307
Greenwood v Martins Bank Ltd [1933] AC 51	202, 203, 215
Grenfell v E. B. Meyrowitz Ltd [1936] 2 All ER 1313	88
Griffiths v Peter Conway Ltd [1939] 1 All ER 685	101
Guaranty Trust Co. of New York v Hannay and Co. [1918] 2 KB 623	193
Gunn v Bolckow, Vaughan and Co. (1875) LR 10 Ch App 491; 32 LT 781	35
Hadley v Baxendale (1854) 9 Exch 341; [1843-60] All ER Rep 461	130, 175, 176, 178, 180, 230, 297
Hall (R. and H.) Ltd and W. H. Pim Junior and Co.'s Arbitration, re 139 LT 50; [1928] All ER Rep 763	177
Hallett's Estate, re (1879) 13 Ch D 696; [1874-80] All ER Rep 793; 42 LT 421	279, 284–6, 478
Halliday v Holgate (1868) LTR 3 Ex 299	318, 326
Hammond and Co. v Bussey (1887) 20 QBD 79; 4 TLR 95	182
Hancock v Smith (1889) 41 ChD 436	278
Hannah Blumenthal, The [1983] 1 AC 854; [1982] 3 WLR 1149; [1983] 1 All ER 34; [1983] 1 Lloyd's Rep 103	470
Hanson v Meyer (1805) 6 East 614; 102 ER 1425	32
Hardwick, re, ex parte Hubbard (1886) 17 QBD 690	319
Hardy (E.) and Co. (London) Ltd v Hillerns and Fowler [1923] 2 KB 490; [1923] All ER Rep 275; 39 TLR 189	170
Harlingdon and Leinster Enterprises Ltd v Christopher Hull Fine Art Ltd [1991] 1 QB 564; [1990] 1 All ER 737	85, 88, 89, 90, 95, 112
Harris v Nickerson (1873) LR 8 QB 286; 28 LT 410	75
Harris v Truman (1882) 9 QBD 264	278
Harris Simons Construction Ltd, re [1989] 1 WLR 368; 5 BCC 11; [1989] 5 BCLC 202	407
Harrison (W. F.) and Co. Ltd v Burke [1956] 1 WLR 419; 100 SJ 300; [1956] 2 All ER 169	239
Harrold v Plenty [1901] 2 Ch 314	320
Hartog v Colin and Shields [1939] 3 All ER 566	63
Hasan v Willson [1977] 1 Lloyd's Rep 431	198
Hatfield v Phillips (1842) 9 M & W 647	138
Hatton v Car Maintenance Co. Ltd [1915] 1 Ch 621	126, 323
Head v Tattersall (1871) LR 7 Ex 7; 25 LT 631	165, 170
Heald v O'Connor [1971] 1 WLR 497; [1971] 2 All ER 1105	375
Healy v Howlett and Sons [1917] 1 KB 337; 116 LT 591	54, 165, 167
Heap v Motorists' Advisory Agency Ltd [1923] 1 KB 577; [1922] All ER Rep 251; 129 LT 146	141, 153
Hedley Byrne and Co. Ltd v Heller and Partners Ltd [1964] AC 465; [1963] 3 WLR 101; [1963] 2 All ER 575	64, 174, 215
Helby v Matthews [1895] AC 471; 72 LT 841	60, 151, 350–1
Helstan Securities Ltd v Hertfordshire County Council [1978] 3 All ER 262	244, 245
Henderson and Co. v Williams [1895] 1 QB 521; 72 LT 98	143, 272
Hendy Lennox (Industrial Engines) Ltd v Grahame Puttick Ltd [1984] 1 WLR 485; [1984] 2 All ER 152; [1984] 2 Lloyd's Rep 422	54, 263–5, 277–8, 280, 435, 478
Henry v Hammond [1913] 2 KB 515; [1911-13] All ER Rep Ext 1478; 108 LT 729	260, 277
Henry Kendall and Sons v William Lillico and Sons Ltd [1969] 2 AC 31; [1968] 3 WLR 110	94, 98, 101, 103
Hewett v Court (1983) 149 CLR 639; 57 ALJR 211	186

Table of Cases   xix

Hewison v Guthrie (1836) 2 Bing NC 755; 2 Hodg 51; 5 LJ CP 283	321
Highway Properties Ltd v Kelly Douglas and Co. Ltd (1971) 17 DLR (3d) 710	304
Hill v Peters [1918] 2 Ch 273	250, 251
Hill and Sons v Edwin Showell and Sons Ltd (1918) 87 LJ KB 1106; 119 LT 651	131
Hilton v Tucker (1888) 39 ChD 669; 59 LT 172	23, 323
Hoare v Dresser (1859) 7 HL Cas 290; 33 LT 63; 11 ER 116	182, 183
Hobson v Gorringe [1897] 1 Ch 182; 75 LT 610; 13 TLR 139	306
Holroyd v Marshall (1862) 10 HL Cas 191; 7 LT 172 (HL); 2 De G. F. & J. 596 (LC); 2 Giff 382 (V-C)	182, 183, 328–9, 333–5, 344
Holt v Markham [1923] 1 KB 504	209
Home and Overseas Insurance Co. Ltd v Mentor Insurance Co. (UK) Ltd [1990] 1 WLR 153	469
Home Insurance Co. v Administratia Asigurilor de Stat [1983] 2 Lloyd's Rep 674	468, 469
Hongkong Fir Shipping Co. Ltd v Kawasaki Kisen Kaisha Ltd [1962] 2 QB 26; [1962] 2 WLR 474; [1962] 1 All ER 474	67
Hookway (F. E.) and Co. Ltd v Alfred Isaacs and Sons [1954] 1 Lloyd's Rep 491	106
Horn v Minister of Food [1948] 2 All ER 1036; 65 TLR 1906	73
Horne v Chester and Fein Property Developments Pty Ltd [1987] VR 913; 11 ACLR 584; 61 ALR 729	439
Houlder, re [1929] 1 Ch 205	386
Household Machines Ltd v Cosmos Exporters Ltd [1947] KB 217; [1946] 2 All ER 622	176, 177
Howard Marine and Dredging Co. Ltd v A. Ogden and Sons (Excavations) Ltd [1978] QB 574; [1978] 2 WLR 515; [1978] 2 All ER 1134	65, 109
Howell v Coupland (1876) 1 QBD 258; (1874) LR 9 QB 462; 33 LT 832	47, 48, 72, 74
Hubbard, ex parte; see Re Hardwick	
Hughes v Lenny (1839) 5 M & W 183	323
Hurst v Picture Theatres Ltd [1915] 1 KB 1; [1914-15] All ER Rep 836; 111 LT 972	306
Hyde v Wrench (1840) 3 Beav 334	460
Hyman v Nye and Sons (1881) 6 QBD 685; [1881-5] All ER Rep 183; 44 LT 919	107
Hyundai Heavy Industries Co. Ltd v Papadopoulos [1980] 1 WLR 1129; [1980] 2 All ER 29; [1980] 2 Lloyd's Rep 1	128, 163, 384
IBL Ltd v Coussens [1991] 2 All ER 133	307
IE Contractors Ltd v Lloyds Bank plc [1990] 2 Lloyd's Rep 496	387
Ind Coope and Co. Ltd, re [1911] 2 Ch 223	11
Indian Oil Corporation Ltd v Greenstone Shipping SA (Panama) [1988] QB 345; [1987] 3 All ER 893; [1987] 2 Lloyd's Rep 286	40
Ingham v Emes [1955] 2 QB 366; [1955] 2 WLR 245; [1955] 2 WLR 245; [1955] 2 All ER 740	101
Inglis v James Richardson and Sons Ltd (1913) 29 OLR 229; 14 DLR 137	37
Inglis v Robertson and Baxter [1898] AC 616	35
Inglis v Stock (1885) 10 App Cas 263; 52 LT 821	37, 166
Ingram v Inland Revenue Commissioners [1986] Ch 585; [1986] 2 WLR 598; [1985] STC 835	238
Ingram v Little [1961] 1 QB 31; [1960] 3 WLR 504; [1960] 3 All ER 332	64, 147
Inland Revenue Commissioners v G. Angus and Co. (1889) 23 QBD 579	238
Inland Revenue Commissioners v Clay [1914] 3 KB 466	413
International Banking Corporation v Ferguson Shaw and Sons 1910 182	42
Irvani v G. und H. Montage GmbH 1989 FLR 390	209
Isaacs v Hardy (1884) Cab & El 287	58
Jackson v Chrysler Acceptances Ltd [1978] RTR 474	172, 181
Jackson v Rotax Motor and Cycle Co. [1910] 2 KB 937; 103 LT 411	96
Jacobs v Morris [1902] 1 Ch 816	135
Jade International Steel Stahl und Eisen GmbH & Co. KG v Robert Nicholas (Steels) Ltd [1978] QB 917	199
Jag Shakti, The [1986] 1 AC 337; [1986] 2 WLR 87; [1986] 1 All ER 480	59
James Finlay and Co. Ltd v NV Kwik Hoo Tong Handel Maatschappij [1929] 1 KB 400; 140 LT 389; [1928] All ER Rep 62	179
James Roscoe (Bolton) Ltd v Winder [1915] 1 Ch 62	285

James Talcott Ltd v John Lewis and Co. Ltd [1940] 3 All ER 592	239
Jartay Developments Ltd, re (1982) 22 BLR 134	389
Jeffryes v Agra and Masterman's Bank (1866) LR 2 Eq 674	252
Jenney v Herle (1724) 2 Ld Raym 1361	194
Jewelowski v Propp [1944] KB 510; [1944] 1 All ER 483; 171 LT 234	132
Joachimson v Swiss Bank Corporation [1921] 3 KB 110; 125 LT 338; 65 SJ 434	217
Joe Lowe Food Products Co. Ltd v J. A. and P. Holland Ltd [1954] 2 Lloyd's Rep 71	106
Johnson v Agnew [1980] AC 367; [1979] 2 WLR 487; [1979] 1 All ER 883	82, 128, 163
Johnson v Crédit Lyonnais Co. (1877) 3 CPD 32; 37 LT 657	139
Johnson v Raylton (1881) 7 QBD 438; 45 LT 374	107
Johnson Matthey and Co. Ltd v Constantine Terminals Ltd [1976] 2 Lloyd's Rep 215	314
Jones v Gordon (1877) 2 App Cas 616; 37 LT 477	200
Jones v Jones [1977] 1 WLR 438; [1976] 242 EG 371	38
Jones v Marshall (1889) 24 QBD 269	326
Jones v Moore (1841) 4 Y & C Ex 351; 7 LT 102; 160 ER 1041	38
Jones v Page (1867) 15 LT 619	107
Jones v Tarleton (1842) 9 M & W 675; 11 LJ Ex 267	326
Jones (R. E.) Ltd v Waring and Gillow Ltd [1926] AC 670	199
Joseph v Lyons (1884) 15 QBD 280	363
Junior Books Ltd v Veitchi Co. Ltd [1983] 1 AC 520; [1982] 3 WLR 477; [1982] 3 All ER 201	298, 299
Jurgens (Ant.) Margarinefabrieken v Louis Dreyfus and Co. [1914] 3 KB 40; 111 LT 248	36
Karflex Ltd v Poole [1933] 2 KB 251; [1933] All ER Rep 46; 149 LT 140	174
Karlshamns Olje Fabriker v Eastport Navigation Corp. [1982] 1 All ER 208; [1981] 2 Lloyd's Rep 679	31–2
Karsales (Harrow) Ltd v Wallis [1956] 1 WLR 936; [1956] 2 All ER 866	86
Kayford Ltd, re [1975] 1 WLR 279; [1975] 1 All ER 604	287
Keenan Bros Ltd, re [1985] IR 401; [1986] BCLC 242	339
Keighly Maxsted and Co. v Durant [1901] AC 240	347
Kelly v Lombard Banking Co. Ltd [1959] 1 WLR 41; 103 SJ 34; [1958] 3 All ER 713	351
Kemp v Intasun Holidays Ltd (1987) 7 TrLR 161; [1987] 2 FTLR 234	181
King v Hutton (1900) 83 LT 68	275
Kings North Trust Ltd v Bell [1986] 1 WLR 119; 130 SJ 88; [1986] 1 All ER 423	382
Kirkham v Attenborough [1897] 1 QB 201; 75 LT 543; 41 SJ 141	273
Kleinwort Benson Ltd v Malaysia Mining Corporation Bhd [1989] 1 WLR 379; 133 SJ 262 (CA); [1988] 1 WLR 799; [1988] 1 All ER 714	377
Knights v Wiffen (1870) LR 5 QB 660; 23 LT 610	34
Kruger v Wilcox (1755) Amb 252	321
Kum v Wah Tat Bank Ltd [1971] 1 Lloyd's Rep 439	191
Kursell v Timber Operators and Contractors Ltd [1927] 1 KB 298; 135 LT 223; 42 TLR 435	45, 49, 75
Kwei Tek Chao v British Traders and Shippers Ltd [1954] 2 QB 459; [1954] 2 WLR 365	169, 179
Ladbroke and Co. v Todd (1914) 30 TLR 433	212
Ladbroke Leasing (South West) Ltd v Reekie Plant Ltd 1983 SLT 155	62
Lake, re, ex parte Cavendish [1903] 1 KB 151	250
Lambert v Lewis [1982] AC 225; [1981] 2 WLR 713; [1981] 1 All ER 1185	97, 112, 116, 181
Lamplugh Iron Ore Co. Ltd, re [1927] 1 Ch 308	384–5
Lancashire Loans Ltd v Black [1934] 1 KB 380	382
Landall Holdings Ltd v Caratti [1979] WAR 97	338
Lang v Jones (1990) 10 TrLR 113	146
Laurie and Morwood v Dudin and Sons [1926] 1 KB 223; [1925] All ER Rep 414	33
Lazenby Garages Ltd v Wright [1976] 1 WLR 459; [1976] 2 All ER 770; [1976] RTR 314	131
Leaf v International Galleries [1950] 2 KB 86; [1950] 1 All ER 693	65, 133
Lee v Butler [1893] 2 QB 318; 69 LT 370	60, 151, 350
Lee v Griffin (1861) 1 B & S 272; 4 LT 546	58

Table of Cases

Lee v York Coach and Marine [1977] RTR 35	96, 97
Legg v Evans (1840) 6 M & W 36	319
Leicestershire Banking Co. Ltd v Hawkes (1900) 16 TLR 317	385
Leigh and Sillavan Ltd v Aliakmon Shipping Co. Ltd [1986] AC 785; [1986] 2 WLR 902; [1968] 2 All ER 145	17, 29, 36, 298
Len Vidgen Ski and Leisure Ltd v Timaru Marine Supplies (1982) Ltd [1986] 1 NZLR 349; 2 NZCLC 99, 438	275
Levy (A. I.) (Holdings) Ltd [1964] Ch 19	452
Lewis v Averay (No. 2) [1973] 1 WLR 510; [1973] 2 All ER 229	64, 132, 147
Libyan Arab Foreign Bank v Bankers Trust Co. [1989] QB 728; [1988] 1 Lloyd's Rep 259	14
Lickbarrow v Mason (1787) 2 TR 63; 100 ER 35	156
Lilley v Barnsley (1844) 1 Car & Kir 344	323
Lind, re [1915] 2 Ch 345; [1914-15] All ER Rep 527; 113 LT 956	183, 328
Lipkin Gorman v Karpnale Ltd [1991] 2 AC 548 (HL); [1989] 1 WLR 1340; 1989 FLR 137; [1989] BCLC 756 (CA)	282
Lister and Co. v Stubbs (1890) 45 ChD 1	463
Lloyds and Scottish Finance Ltd v Cyril Lord Carpets Sales Ltd (1979) 129 NLJ 366; 130 NLJ 207	348, 351
Lloyds and Scottish Finance Ltd v Prentice (1977) 121 SJ 847	239
Lloyds and Scottish Finance Ltd v Williamson [1965] 1 WLR 404; [1965] 1 All ER 641	313
Lloyds Bank v Bank of America National Trust and Savings Association [1938] 2 KB 147; [1938] 2 All ER 63	272
Lloyds Bank Ltd v Bundy [1975] QB 326; [1974] 3 WLR 501; [1974] 3 All ER 757	382
Lloyds Bank Ltd v E. B. Savory and Co. [1933] AC 201; 148 LT 291	222, 224
Lock International plc v Beswick [1989] 1 WLR 1278; [1989] 3 All ER 373	464
Lockett v A. and M. Charles Ltd [1938] 4 All ER 170; 159 LT 547; 55 TLR 22	57–8
Lombard North Central plc v Butterworth [1987] QB 527; [1987] 2 WLR 7; [1987] 1 All ER 267	308–10
London and Globe Finance Corpn, re [1902] 2 Ch 416; 87 LT 49	321
London, Bombay and Mediterranean Bank, re (1874) LR 9 Ch App 686	386
London, Chatham and Dover Railway Co. v South Eastern Railway Co. [1893] AC 429; 69 LT 637	229, 230
London Joint Stock Bank Ltd v Macmillan and Arthur [1918] AC 777	204, 207, 215
London Wine Co. (Shippers) Ltd, re 1986 PCC 121	29–31, 34, 141
Long v Lloyd [1958] 1 WLR 753; [1958] 2 All ER 402	133
Lord Provost, Magistrates, and Town Council of Edinburgh v Lord Advocate (1879) 4 App Cas 823	286
Lumsden and Co. v London Trustee Savings Bank [1971] 1 Lloyd's Rep 114	215–6, 224
Lunn v Thornton (1845) 1 CB 379; 4 LT 417; 135 ER 587	48, 332
Lupton v White (1808) 15 Ves Jr 432; [1803-13] All ER Rep 336; 33 ER 817	40
Luxmoore-May v Messenger May Baverstock [1990] 1 WLR 1009; [1990] 7 EG 61	89
Lyle (B. S.) Ltd v Rosher [1959] 1 WLR 8; 103 SJ 15; [1958] 3 All ER 597	250, 251
Lyons (J. L.) and Co. Ltd v May and Baker Ltd [1923] 1 KB 685; 129 LT 413	122
McCrone v Boots Farm Sales Ltd 1981 SLT 103	169
Mace Builders (Glasgow) Ltd v Lunn [1987] Ch 191; [1986] 3 WLR 921; [1987] BCLC 55	450
McManus v Fortescue [1907] 2 KB 1; [1904-7] All ER Rep 707	75
McRae v Commonwealth Disposals Commission (1951) 84 CLR 377	72, 375
Madden v Kempster (1807) 1 Camp 12	324
Mahant Singh v U Ba Yi [1939] AC 601	381
Maidstone Buildings Provisions Ltd [1971] 1 WLR 1085; 115 SJ 464; [1971] 3 All ER 363	454, 457
Maillard v Duke of Argyle (1843) 6 Mac & G 40	164
Manchester Trust v Furness [1895] 2 QB 539; 73 LT 110	153, 201
Maple Flock Co. Ltd v Universal Furniture Products (Wembley) Co. Ltd [1934] 1 KB 148; [1933] All ER Rep 15	82

Table of Cases

Mareva Compania Naviera SA v International Bulkcarriers SA [1975] 2 Lloyd's Rep 509; 119 SJ 660	463
Marfani and Co. Ltd v Midland Bank Ltd [1968] 1 WLR 956; 112 SJ 396; [1968] 2 All ER 573	223, 224
Marsh v Commissioner of Police [1944] 2 All ER 392	322
Martin v World Piano Co. [1947] MULR 61	157
Martindale v Booth (1832) 3 B & Ad 498; 110 ER 180	327
Marwalt Ltd, re [1992] BCC 32	425
Mash and Murrell Ltd v Joseph I. Emanuel Ltd [1961] 1 WLR 862; [1962] 1 WLR 16; [1962] 1 All ER 77	97, 167
Matthew Ellis Ltd, re [1933] Ch 458	450
MC Bacon Ltd, re [1991] Ch 127; [1990] BCC 430; earlier proceedings [1990] BCC 78	441, 447, 457
Medina v Stoughton (1700) 1 Salk 210; 91 ER 188	25
Meesan Investments Ltd, re (1988) 4 BCC 788	409, 410
Melachrino v Nickoll and Knight [1920] 1 KB 693; [1918-19] All ER Rep 857	176
Mercantile Bank of India Ltd v Central Bank of India Ltd [1938] AC 287; [1938] 1 All ER 52	144
Mercantile Credit Co. Ltd v Waugh (1978) 32 Hire Trading (No. 2) 16	159
Metcalfe v Archbishop of York (1836) 1 My & Cr 547	330
Meux v Bell (1841) 1 Hare 73	250
Microbeads AG v Vinhurst Road Markings Ltd [1975] 1 WLR 218; [1975] 1 All ER 529	27
Miliangos v George Frank (Textiles) Ltd [1976] AC 443; [1975] 3 WLR 758; [1975] 3 All ER 801	129
Miller v Race (1758) 1 Burr 452	12, 281
Miller Associates (Australia) Pty Ltd v Bennington Pty Ltd [1975] 2 NSWLR 506; 7 ALR 144	197
Millett v Van Heek and Co. [1921] 2 KB 369; 125 LT 51; 65 SJ 355	132
Mitchell v Jones [1905] 24 NZLR 932	150
Mitchell v Winslow (1843) 17 F Cas 527 (No. 9673); 2 Story 630	328
MK International Development Co. Ltd v Housing Bank (1990) *Financial Times*, 22 January 1991	198, 199
Mogg v Baker (1838) 3 M & W 195	329
Molling & Co. v Dean and Son Ltd (1901) 18 TLR 217	168
Mondel v Steel (1841) 8 M & W 858	240
Monforts v Marsden (1895) 12 RPC 266	26
Montagu's Settlement Trusts, re [1987] Ch 264; [1987] 2 WLR 1192; 131 SJ 411	213
Moore and Co. Ltd and Landauer and Co., re [1921] 2 KB 519; [1921] All ER Rep 466	81, 87
Moorgate Mercantile Co. Ltd v Twitchings [1977] AC 890; [1976] 3 WLR 66; [1976] 2 All ER 641	144
Moralice (London) Ltd v E. D. and F. Man [1954] 2 Lloyd's Rep 526	87
Morelli v Fitch and Gibbons [1928] 2 KB 636; [1928] All ER Rep 610	93
Morley v Attenborough (1849) 3 Exch 500; 12 LT 532; 154 ER 943	25
Morris v C. W. Martin and Sons Ltd [1966] 1 QB 716; [1965] 3 WLR 276; [1965] 2 All ER 725	314
Morritt, re (1886) 18 QBD 222; 56 LT 42	343
Moschi v Lep Air Services Ltd [1973] AC 331; [1972] 2 WLR 1175; [1972] 2 All ER 393	375, 384
Moss v Hancock [1899] 2 QB 111; 80 LT 693	45
Motor Oil Hellas (Corinth) Refineries SA v Shipping Corporation of India [1990] 1 Lloyd's Rep 391	69, 70
Motor Traders' Guarantee Corpn Ltd v Midland Bank Ltd [1937] 4 All ER 90	223
Moukataff v British Overseas Airways Corporation [1967] 1 Lloyd's Rep 396	23
Mount (D. F.) Ltd v Jay and Jay (Provisions) Co. Ltd [1960] 1 QB 159; [1959] 3 WLR 537; [1959] 3 All ER 307	36
Mucklow v Mangles (1808) 1 Taunt 318; 127 ER 856	54
Mulliner v Florence (1878) 3 QBD 484; 38 LT 167	325
Multi Guarantee Co. Ltd, re [1987] BCLC 257	287
Murphy v Brentwood District Council [1991] 1 AC 398	298

Table of Cases   xxiii

Nanka-Bruce v Commonwealth Trust Ltd [1926] AC 77; 134 LT 35   52
Nanwa Gold Mines Ltd, re [1955] 1 WLR 1080; 99 SJ 709; [1955] 3 All ER 219   288
Nathan v Ogdens Ltd (1905) 94 LT 126; 49 SJ 725; 93 LT 533   192
National Australia Bank Ltd v KDS Construction Services Pty Ltd (1987) 163 CLR 668;
   76 ALR 27   448, 452
National Employers' Mutual General Insurance Asssociation Ltd v Jones [1990] 1 AC 24;
   [1988] 2 WLR 952; [1988] 2 All ER 425   155, 159
National Provincial Bank Ltd v Ainsworth [1965] AC 1175; [1965] 3 WLR 1;
   [1965] 2 All ER 472   17
National Westminster Bank Ltd v Halesowen Presswork and Assemblies Ltd [1972] AC 785;
   [1972] 2 WLR 455; [1972] 1 All ER 641   321, 434–5
National Westminster Bank plc v Morgan [1985] AC 686; [1985] 2 WLR 588;
   [1985] 1 All ER 821   382
Neste Oy v Lloyds Bank plc [1983] 2 Lloyd's Rep 658; [1982] Com LR 185   435
Nevill, re, ex parte White (1871) LR 6 Ch App 397; 24 LT 45   260
New Zealand and Australian Land Co. v Ruston (1880) 5 QBD 474   277–8
New Zealand Shipping Co. Ltd v A. M. Satterthwaite and Co. Ltd [1975] AC 154;
   [1974] 2 WLR 865; [1974] 1 All ER 1015   112
Newhart Developments Ltd v Cooperative Commercial Bank Ltd [1978] 2 All ER 896   417
Newtons of Wembley Ltd v Williams [1965] 1 QB 560; [1964] 3 WLR 888;
   [1964] 3 All ER 532   148, 151, 154
Niblett Ltd v Confectioners' Materials Co. Ltd [1921] 3 KB 387;
   [1921] All ER Rep 459   25–27, 93
Nichol v Godts (1854) 10 Exch 191; 23 LJ Ex 314; 23 LT 162   106
Nicolene Ltd v Simmonds [1953] 1 QB 543; [1953] 2 WLR 717; [1953] 1 All ER 822   63
Nippon Yusen Kaisha v Ramjiban Serowgee [1938] AC 429; [1938] 2 All ER 285; 159 LT 266   123
Noble (R. A.) and Sons (Clothing) Ltd, re [1983] BCLC 273   414
Norman Holding Co. Ltd, re [1991] 1 WLR 10; [1990] 3 All ER 757;
   [1991] BCLC 1   431, 433, 436
North and South Wales Bank Ltd v Macbeth [1908] AC 137   196
Northern Bank Ltd v Ross [1991] BCLC 504   363
Northern Regional Health Authority v Derek Crouch Construction Co. Ltd [1984] QB 644;
   [1984] 2 WLR 676; [1984] 2 All ER 175   465
Nova (Jersey) Knit Ltd v Kammgarn Spinnerei GmbH [1977] 1 WLR 713; 121 SJ 170;
   [1977] 2 All ER 463   190

O'Dea v Allstates Leasing System (WA) Pty Ltd (1983) 152 CLR 359; 57 ALJR 172   303
Oatway, re [1903] 2 Ch 356   285
Official Assignee of Madras v Mercantile Bank of India Ltd [1935] AC 53; 152 LT 170   323–4
Official Receiver v Tailby; see Tailby v Official Receiver
Offord v Davies (1862) 12 CB (NS) 748   376
Ogle v Earl Vane (1868) LR 3 QB 272   175
Old Bushmills Distillery Co., re, ex parte Brett [1897] 1 IR 488   338
Oliver v Davis [1949] 2 KB 727; 93 SJ 562; [1949] 2 All ER 353   198
Oppenheimer v Attenborough and Son [1908] 1 KB 221; [1904-7] All ER Rep 1016   140
Orbit Mining and Trading Co. Ltd v Westminster Bank Ltd [1963] 1 QB 794;
   [1962] 3 WLR 1256; [1962] 3 All ER 565   224
Orion Cia Espanola de Seguros v Belfort Maatshcappij voor Algemene Verzekgringeen
   [1962] 2 Lloyd's Rep 257   468
Ormrod v Huth (1845) 14 M & W 651; 153 ER 636   24
Oughtred v Inland Revenue Commissioners [1960] AC 206; [1959] 3 WLR 898;
   [1959] 3 All ER 623   238
Overseas Union Insurance Ltd v AA Mutual International Insurance Co. Ltd
   [1988] 1 FTLR 421; [1988] 2 Lloyd's Rep 63   468
Overstone Ltd v Shipway [1962] 1 WLR 117; [1962] 1 All ER 52   308

P & C and R & T (Stockport) Ltd, re [1991] BCLC 366 — 408
Paal Wilson & Co. A/S v Partenreederei Hannah Blumenthal [1983] 1 AC 854;
 [1982] 3 WLR 1149; [1983] 1 All ER 34; [1983] 1 Lloyd's Rep 103 — 470
Pacific Associates Inc. v Baxter [1990] 1 QB 993; [1989] 3 WLR 1150; [1989] 2 All ER 159 — 298
Pacific Motor Auctions Ltd v Motor Credits (Hire Finance) Ltd [1965] AC 867;
 [1965] 2 WLR 881; [1965] 2 All ER 105 — 150
Pagnan (R.) and Fratelli v Corbisa Industrial Agropacuaria Limitada [1970] 1 WLR 1306;
 [1970] 1 All ER 165 — 175
Palmer v Pratt (1824) 2 Bing 185; 3 LJ OS CP 250 — 193
Panama, New Zealand and Australian Royal Mail Co., re (1870) LR 5 Ch App 318 — 336
Parker v British Airways Board [1982] QB 1004; [1982] 2 WLR 503; [1982] 1 All ER 834 — 23
Parsons (H.) (Livestock) Ltd v Uttley Ingham and Co. Ltd [1978] QB 791;
 [1977] 2 WLR 990; [1978] 1 All ER 525 — 180, 298
Paterson v Tash (1743) 2 Str 1178 — 137
Patrick and Lyon Ltd, re [1933] Ch 786 — 454
Payne v Cave (1789) 3 TR 148; [1775-1802] All ER Rep 492; 100 ER 502 — 75
Payzu Ltd v Saunders [1919] 2 KB 581; [1918-19] All ER Rep 219 — 132
Peachdart Ltd, re [1984] Ch 131; [1983] 3 WLR 878; [1983] 3 All ER 204 — 262-3, 478-9
Pearl Mill Co. Ltd v Ivy Tannery Co. Ltd [1919] 1 KB 78; [1918-19] All ER Rep 702 — 162
Pearson v Rose and Young Ltd [1951] 1 KB 275; [1950] 2 All ER 1027 — 140, 153
Pennington v Reliance Motor Works Ltd [1923] 1 KB 127; 128 LT 384; 66 SJ 667 — 324
Performing Rights Society Ltd v London Theatre of Varieties Ltd [1924] AC 1 — 239, 251
Perkins v Bell [1893] 1 QB 193; [1891-4] All ER Rep 884; 67 LT 792 — 168
Perlmutter v Beth David Hospital (1954) 123 NE 2d 792 — 58
Permanent Houses (Holdings) Ltd, re [1988] BCLC 563; 5 BCC 151; 133 SJ 1001 — 341
Perrylease Ltd v Imecar AG [1988] 1 WLR 463; [1987] 2 All ER 373; 136 New LJ 987 — 11, 378
Peter Darlington Partners Ltd v Gosho Co. Ltd [1964] 1 Lloyd's Rep 149 — 90
Pfeiffer (E.) Weinkellerei-Weineinkauf GmbH & Co. v Arbuthnot Factors Ltd
 [1988] 1 WLR 150; [1987] BCLC 522 — 249, 251
Philip Head and Sons Ltd v Showfronts Ltd [1970] 1 Lloyd's Rep 140; 113 SJ 978 — 51, 58
Phillips v Huth (1840) 6 M & W 572 — 138
Phillips v Phillips (1861) 4 De G F & J 208 — 10
Phillips Products Ltd v Hyland (1984) 4 TrLR 98 — 110
Phoenix Bessemer Steel Co., Re (1876) 4 ChD 108 — 428
Photo Production Ltd v Securicor Transport Ltd [1980] AC 827; [1980] 2 WLR 283;
 [1980] 1 All ER 556 — 69, 110
Pignataro v Gilroy [1919] 1 KB 459; 120 LT 480 — 54
Pioneer Shipping Ltd v BTP Tioxide Ltd [1982] AC 724; [1981] 3 WLR 292;
 [1981] 2 All ER 1030 — 466
Pleasants v Pendleton (1828) 27 Va (6 Rand) 473; 18 Am Dec 728 — 33
Pollway Ltd v Abdullah [1974] 1 WLR 493; 118 SJ 277; [1974] 2 All ER 381 — 198
Polly Peck International plc v Nadir (1992) *The Times*, 24 March 1992; *Independent*,
 20 March 1992 — 284, 465
Porter v General Guarantee Corpn Ltd [1982] RTR 384 — 102, 172-3
Practice Direction (Commercial Lists: Manchester and Liverpool) [1990] 1 WLR 331;
 [1990] 1 All ER 528 — 462
President of India v La Pintada Compania Navigacion SA [1985] AC 104; [1984] 3 WLR 10;
 [1984] 2 All ER 773 — 229
President of India v Lips Maritime Corporation [1988] AC 395; [1987] 1 Lloyd's Rep 131;
 [1987] 3 WLR 572; [1987] 3 All ER 110 — 229
Primlaks (UK) Ltd, re [1989] BCLC 734 — 407
Pritchard v Briggs [1980] Ch 338 — 440
Procter and Gamble Philippine Manufacturing Corporation v Kurt A. Becher GmbH & Co. KG
 [1988] 2 Lloyd's Rep 21; [1988] FTLR 450 — 179-80
Proctor and Gamble Philippine Manufacturing Corporation v Peter Cremer GmbH & Co.
 [1988] 3 All ER 843 — 70

Table of Cases

Produce Brokers Co. Ltd v Olympia Oil and Coke Co. Ltd [1917] 1 KB 320; [1916-17] All ER Rep 753	166
Produce Marketing Consortium Ltd, re (No. 2) [1989] BCLC 520	455–6
Prosperity Ltd v Lloyds Bank Ltd (1923) 39 TLR 372	217
Provincial Bank of Ireland Ltd v Donnell [1934] NI 33	376
Purpoint Ltd, re [1991] BCC 121	456
R v Ford Motor Co. Ltd [1974] 1 WLR 1220; [1974] 3 All ER 489	88
R v Grantham [1984] QB 675	454–5
R v Henderson (1870) 11 Cox CC 593	272
R v Richmond (1873) 12 Cox CC 495	272
R v Secretary of State for Health, ex parte United States Tobacco International Inc. [1991] 3 WLR 529; [1992] 1 All ER 212	120
R v Thompson [1980] QB 229; [1980] 2 WLR 521; [1980] 2 All ER 102	45
R and B Customs Brokers Co. Ltd v United Dominions Trust Ltd [1988] 1 WLR 321; [1988] 1 All ER 847	92, 98, 108
Rae v Yorkshire Bank plc (1987) *The Times*, 12 October 1987; *The Times*, 16 October 1989	213
Rasbora Ltd v JCL Marine Ltd [1977] 1 Lloyd's Rep 645	111
Rawson v Samuel (1841) Cr & Ph 161	241
Reardon Smith Line Ltd v Hansen-Tangen [1976] 1 WLR 989; [1976] 3 All ER 750	86, 87
Reddall v Union Castle Mail Steamship Co. Ltd (1915) 84 LJ KB 360; 112 LT 910	124
Redler Grain Silos Ltd v BICC Ltd [1982] 1 Lloyd's Rep 435	186
Reeves v Capper (1838) 5 Bing NC 136; 8 LJ CP 44	324
Regina Chevrolet Sales Ltd v Riddell [1942] 3 DLR 159	41
Reid v Commissioner of Police of the Metropolis [1973] QB 551; [1973] 2 WLR 576; [1973] 2 All ER 97	146
Rendell v Associated Finance Pty Ltd [1957] VR 604	41
Republic of Haiti v Duvalier [1990] 1 QB 202; [1989] 2 WLR 261; [1989] 1 All ER 456; [1989] 1 Lloyd's Rep 111	464
Riddiford v Warren (1901) 20 NZLR 572	133
Robbie (N. W.) and Co. Ltd v Witney Warehouse Co. Ltd [1963] 1 WLR 1324; 107 SJ 1038; [1963] 3 All ER 613	240
Robinson v Graves [1935] 1 KB 579; [1935] All ER Rep 935	58
Robophone Facilities Ltd v Blank [1966] 1 WLR 1428; [1966] 3 All ER 128	310, 312
Rodocanachi, Sons and Co. v Milburn Brothers (1886) 18 QBD 67; 56 LT 594	176
Roe's Legal Charge, re [1982] 2 Lloyd's Rep 370	211
Rogers v Challis (1859) 27 Beav 175	331
Rogers v Parish (Scarborough) Ltd [1987] QB 923; [1987] 2 WLR 353; [1987] 2 All ER 232	95, 99
Rolfe Lubell and Co. v Keith [1979] 1 All ER 860	205
Rollason, re, Rollason v Rollason, Halse's Claim (1887) 34 ChD 495	319
Rolled Steel Products (Holdings) Ltd v British Steel Corporation [1986] Ch 246; [1985] 2 WLR 908; [1985] 3 All ER 1	417
Rolls Razor Ltd v Cox [1967] 1 QB 552	436
Roper v Johnson [1873] LR 8 CP 167	175
Rose v Hart (1818) 8 Taunt 499	435
Rother Iron Works Ltd v Canterbury Precision Engineers Ltd [1974] QB 1; [1973] 2 WLR 281; [1973] 1 All ER 394	252, 433
Routledge v McKay [1954] 1 WLR 615; [1954] 1 All ER 855; 98 SJ 247; [1954] 1 All ER 855	66
Row Dal Constructions Pty Ltd, Re [1966] VR 249	453
Rowland v Divall [1923] 2 KB 500; [1923] All ER Rep 270	27, 145, 173, 174, 178
Roxburghe v Cox (1881) 17 ChD 520	240
Royal Bank of Canada v Concrete Column Clamps (1961) Ltd (1976) 74 DLR (3d) 26	196
Royal Trust Bank v Buchler [1989] BCLC 130	410
Royscot Trust Ltd v Rogerson [1991] 2 QB 297; [1991] 3 WLR 57	65, 133, 174
Ruben (E. and S.) Ltd v Faire Bros and Co. Ltd [1949] 1 KB 254; [1949] 1 All ER 215	107
Rushforth v Hadfield (1805) 6 East 519; (1806) 7 East 224	321

Russell v Favier (1841) 18 La 585	147
Rust v McNaught and Co. Ltd (1918) 144 LT Jo 440	326
Ryall v Rowles (1750) 1 Ves Sen 348; 27 ER 1074	250
Sainsbury (H. R. & S.) Ltd v Street [1972] 1 WLR 834; [1972] 3 All ER 1127	47, 73
St Mary's, Barton-on-Humber, re [1987] Fam 41; [1986] 3 WLR 906; [1987] 2 All ER 861	153
Salomon v A. Salomon and Co. Ltd [1897] AC 22	396
Samuel Sherman plc, re [1991] 1 WLR 1070	459
Sandeman and Sons v Tyzack and Branfoot Steamship Co. Ltd [1913] AC 680; [1911-13] All ER Rep 1013	38
Sass, re [1896] 2 QB 12	379
Saunders v Anglia Building Society [1971] AC 1004; [1970] 3 WLR 1078	202, 383
Scaliaris v E. Ofverberg and Co. (1921) 37 TLR 307	107
Scammell (G.) and Nephew Ltd v Ouston [1941] AC 251; [1941] 1 All ER 14	63
Scarfe v Morgan (1838) 4 M & W 270	326
Schering Pty Ltd v Forrest Pharmaceutical Co. Pty Ltd [1982] 1 NSWLR 286	418
Scholefield Goodman and Sons Ltd v Zyngier [1986] AC 562; [1985] 3 WLR 953; [1985] 3 All ER 105	384
Scholfield v Earl of Londesborough [1896] AC 514	204, 207
Scott v Avery (1856) 5 HL Cas 811; 25 LJ Ex 308	466
Scott v Surman (1742) Willes 400	278
Secretary of State for Trade and Industry v Langridge [1991] Ch 402; [1991] 2 WLR 1343; 459[1991] 3 All ER 591	459
Sevenoaks Stationers (Retail) Ltd, re [1991] Ch 164; [1990] 3 WLR 1165	458
Shanklin Pier Ltd v Detel Products Ltd [1951] 2 KB 854; [1951] 2 All ER 471	66, 296
Shaw v Commissioner of Police of the Metropolis [1987] 1 WLR 1332; [1987] 3 All ER 405	142
Shearson Lehman Hutton Inc. v Maclaine Watson and Co. Ltd [1988] 1 WLR 946; [1989] 1 All ER 1056	470
Shearson Lehman Hutton Inc. v Maclaine Watson and Co. Ltd (No. 2) [1990] 3 All ER 723	131
Sheldon v Cox (1824) 3 B & C 420; 107 ER 789	56
Shepherd v Kain (1822) 5 B & Ald 240; 106 ER 1180	83
Shepley v Davis (1814) 5 Taunt 617; 128 ER 832	32
Sherry, re (1884) 25 ChD 692	379, 386
Shine v General Guarantee Corp. Ltd [1988] 1 All ER 911; 7 TrLR 88	96
Siebe Gorman and Co. Ltd v Barclays Bank Ltd [1979] 2 Lloyd's Rep 142	339–40, 364
Simaan General Contracting Co. v Pilkington Glass Ltd (No. 2) [1988] QB 758; [1988] 2 WLR 761; [1988] 1 All ER 791	298, 299
Simm v Anglo-American Telegraph Co. (1879) 5 QBD 188; 42 LT 37	34
Simpson v Union Oil Co. of California (1964) 377 US 13	352
Sims v Marryat (1851) 17 QB 281; 117 ER 1287	25
Sinclair v Brougham [1914] AC 398	286
Singer Co. (UK) Ltd v Tees and Hartlepool Port Authority [1988] 2 Lloyd's Rep 164; [1988] 1 FTLR 442	314
Skinner v Upshaw (1701) 2 Ld Raym 752	322
Sky Petroleum Ltd v VIP Petroleum Ltd [1974] 1 WLR 576; [1974] 1 All ER 954	184
Slingsby v District Bank Ltd [1932] 1 KB 544; 146 LT 377	216
Smit Tak International Zeesleepen Bergingsbedrijf BV v Selco Salvage Ltd [1988] 2 Lloyd's Rep 398	437
Smith, re, ex parte Bright (1879) 10 ChD 566; 39 LT 649	275
Smith v Boheme, cited in Jenney v Herle (1724) 2 Ld Raym 1361 at p. 1362	194
Smith v Eric S. Bush [1990] 1 AC 831; [1989] 2 WLR 790; [1989] 2 All ER 514	215
Smith v Hughes (1871) LR 6 QB 597; 25 LT 329	64
Snook v London and West Riding Investments Ltd [1967] 2 QB 786; [1967] 2 WLR 1020; [1967] 1 All ER 518	142
Sotiros Shipping Inc. v Sameiet Solholt [1983] 1 Lloyd's Rep 605; 127 SJ 305	132
South Australian Insurance Co. v Randell (1869) LR 3 PC 101; 22 LT 843; 16 ER 755	37, 39, 260
South Western General Property Co. Ltd v Marton (1982) 263 EG 1090; 2 TrLR 14	109

Table of Cases xxvii

Southern Livestock Producers Ltd, re [1963] 3 All ER 801; [1964] 1 WLR 24   126, 323
Space Investments Ltd v Canadian Imperial Bank of Commerce Trust Co. (Bahamas) Ltd
 [1986] 1 WLR 1072; [1986] 3 All ER 75   212, 286–7
Spellman v Spellman [1961] 1 WLR 921; 105 SJ 405; [1961] 2 All ER 498   244
Spence v Union Marine Insurance Co. Ltd (1868) LR 3 CP 427   38, 40
Stadium Finance Ltd v Robbins [1962] 2 QB 664; [1962] 3 WLR 453; [1962] 2 All ER 633   140
Staff Motor Guarantee Ltd v British Wagon Co. Ltd [1934] 2 KB 305; [1934] All ER Rep 322 150
Standard Manufacturing Co, re [1891] 1 Ch 627   335
Stanford Services Ltd, re [1987] BCLC 607; 3 BCC 326; 1987 PCC 343   458
Stanley v English Fibres Industries Ltd (1899) 68 LJ QB 839   239
Starkey v Bank of England [1903] AC 114   193
Steel v Dixon (1881) 17 ChD 825   384
Stenning, re [1895] 2 Ch 433   286
Sterling, ex parte (1809) 16 Ves Jr 258   321
Sterns Ltd v Vickers Ltd [1923] 1 KB 78; [1922] All ER Rep 126   37, 165, 261
Stevenson v Beverley Bentinck Ltd [1976] 1 WLR 483; [1976] 2 All ER 606   157
Stockloser v Johnson [1954] 1 QB 476; [1954] 2 WLR 439; [1954] 1 All ER 630   129, 303
Stoneleigh Finance Ltd v Phillips [1965] 2 QB 537; [1965] 2 WLR 508; [1965] 1 All ER 513 142
Strachan, re, ex parte Cooke (1876) 4 ChD 123   278
Street v Blay (1831) 2 B & Ad 456; 109 ER 1212   240
Stubbs v Slater [1910] 1 Ch 632   320, 343
Stumore v Campbell and Co. [1892] 1 QB 314   241
Summers v Solomon (1857) 7 E & B 879   276
Sunbolf v Alford (1838) 3 M & W 248   322

Tai Hing Cotton Ltd Mill v Kamsing Knitting Factory [1979] AC 91; [1978] 2 WLR 62;
 [1978] 1 All ER 515   176
Tai Hing Cotton Mill Ltd v Liu Chong Hing Bank Ltd [1986] AC 80   204, 216, 219
Tailby v Official Receiver (1888) 13 App Cas 523 (HL); (1886) 18 QBD 25
 (CA sub nom. Official Receiver v Tailby)   242, 328, 330–1, 334, 440
Tappenden v Artus [1964] 2 QB 185; [1963] 3 WLR 685; [1963] 3 All ER 213   307
Tasbian, re (No. 3) [1991] BCLC 792   459
Tay Valley Joinery Ltd v CF Financial Services Ltd (1987) SLT 207   253
Taylor v Blakelock (1886) 32 ChD 560   279
Taylor v Bullen (1850) 5 Exch 779; 20 LJ Ex 21   85
Taylor v Combined Buyers Ltd [1924] NZLR 627   87
Taylor v Oakes, Roncorni and Co. (1922) 27 Com Cas 261; 127 LT 267   70
Taylor v Plumer (1815) 3 M & S 562   282
TCB Ltd v Gray [1988] 1 All ER 1108   381
Teheran-Europe Co. Ltd v S. T. Belton (Tractors) Ltd [1968] 2 QB 545; [1968] 3 WLR 205;
 [1968] 2 All ER 886   103
Tesco Supermarkets Ltd v Nattrass [1972] AC 153; [1971] 2 WLR 1166; [1971] 2 All ER 127 119
Third Chandris Shipping Corpn v Unimarine SA [1979] 1 QB 645; [1979] 3 WLR 122;
 [1979] 2 All ER 972   463
Thomas v Heelas 27 November 1986 (CAT No. 1065)   148
Thomas v Kelly (1888) 13 App Cas 506   334–5
Thomas Young and Sons Ltd v Hobson and Partners (1949) 65 TLR 365   80
Todd (L.) (Swanscombe) Ltd, re [1990] BCC 125   454
Tolhurst v Associated Portland Cement Manufacturers (1900) Ltd [1903] AC 414 (HL);
 [1902] 2 KB 660 (CA)   239, 254–5
Tom Shaw and Co. v Moss Empires Ltd (1908) 25 TLR 190   242
Tool Metal Manufacturing Co. Ltd v Tungsten Electric Co. Ltd [1955] 1 WLR 761   70
Total Oil Great Britain Ltd v Thompson Garages (Biggin Hill) Ltd [1972] 1 QB 318;
 [1971] 3 WLR 979; [1971] 3 All ER 1226   304
Tournier v National Provincial and Union Bank of England [1924] 1 KB 461   214
Trade Indemnity Co. Ltd v Workington Harbour and Dock Board [1937] AC 1   388

Trans Trust SPRL v Danubian Trading Co. Ltd [1952] 2 QB 297; 96 SJ 312;
    [1952] 1 All ER 970   230
Tucker v Farm and General Investment Trust Ltd [1966] 2 QB 421; [1966] 2 WLR 1241;
    [1966] 2 All ER 508   164
Tudor Grange Holdings Ltd v Citibank NA [1991] 4 All ER 1   417
Tweddle v Atkinson (1861) 1 B & S 393; [1861-73] All ER Rep 369   297
Twyne's Case (1601) 3 Co Rep 80b; 76 ER 809   327, 336, 358

UCB Leasing Ltd v Holtom [1987] RTR 362; 7 TrLR 97   172, 178, 180, 310
Ulster Bank Ltd v Lambe [1966] NI 161   379
Underwood Ltd v Burgh Castle Brick and Cement Syndicate [1922] 1 KB 343;
    [1921] All ER Rep 515   56, 164
Underwood (A. L.) Ltd v Bank of Liverpool and Martins [1924] 1 KB 775   223
Union Transport Finance Ltd v British Car Auctions Ltd [1978] 2 All ER 385; 246 EG 131   308
Unit 2 Windows Ltd, re [1985] 1 WLR 1383; [1985] 3 All ER 647; 1986 PCC 194   437
United Dominions Trust (Commercial) Ltd v Parkway Motors Ltd [1955] 1 WLR 719;
    [1955] 2 All ER 557   244, 351
United Dominions Trust Ltd v Kirkwood [1966] 2 QB 431; [1966] 2 WLR 1083;
    [1966] 1 All ER 968   211
United Dominions Trust Ltd v Western [1976] QB 513; [1976] 2 WLR 64;
    [1975] 3 All ER 1017   64
United Overseas Bank v Jiwani [1976] 1 WLR 964; 120 SJ 329   209, 216
United Railways of Havana and Regla Warehouses Ltd, re [1961] AC 1007;
    [1960] 2 WLR 969; [1960] 2 All ER 332   129
United States of America v Dollfus Mieg et Cie SA [1952] AC 582;
    [1952] 1 All ER 572; 96 SJ 180   23
United Trading Corpn v Allied Arab Bank Ltd [1985] 2 Lloyd's Rep 554   387
Universal Guarantee Pty Ltd v National Bank of Australasia Ltd [1965] 1 WLR 691   218
Universal Thermosensors Ltd v Hibben (1992) *The Times*, 12 February 1992   464

Vacwell Engineering Co. Ltd v BDH Chemicals Ltd [1971] 1 QB 88; [1970] 3 WLR 67;
    [1970] 3 All ER 553   101
Van Lynn Developments Ltd v Pelias Construction Co. Ltd [1969] 1 QB 607;
    [1968] 3 WLR 1141; [1968] 3 All ER 824   239
Varley v Whipp [1900] 1 QB 513; 69 LJ QB 333   47, 50, 85
Vaudeville Electric Cinema Ltd v Muriset [1923] 2 Ch 74   307
Vesta, The [1921] 1 AC 774; 125 LT 621   258
Vic Mill Ltd, re [1913] 1 Ch 465; 108 LT 444   131
Victoria Laundry (Windsor) Ltd v Newman Industries Ltd [1949] 2 KB 528;
    [1949] 1 All ER 997   130, 177, 297
Vigers Bros v Sanderson Bros [1901] 1 KB 608; 84 LT 464   51
Vinden v Hughes [1905] 1 KB 795   196
Vitol SA v Esso Australia Ltd [1989] 2 Lloyd's Rep 451   69

Wadham Stringer Finance Ltd v Meaney [1981] 1 WLR 39; [1980] 3 All ER 789   303
Wadsworth v Lydall [1981] 1 WLR 598; 125 SJ 309; [1981] 2 All ER 401   230
Wait, re [1927] 1 Ch 606; 71 SJ 56; 43 TLR 150 (CA); [1926] Ch 962 (DC)
    74, 182–5, 260–1, 323, 330
Wait and James v Midland Bank Ltd (1926) 24 Ll L Rep 313; 31 Com Cas 172   31, 32
Walker v Boyle [1982] 1 WLR 495   109
Ward v Duncombe [1893] AC 369   250
Ward v National Bank of New Zealand Ltd 1883 8 App Cas 755   381
Ward (R. V.) Ltd v Bignall [1967] 1 QB 534; [1967] 2 WLR 1050; [1967] 2 All ER 449   50, 126, 127
Wardar's (Import and Export) Co. Ltd v W. Norwood and Sons Ltd [1968] 2 QB 663;
    [1968] 2 WLR 1440; [1968] 2 All ER 602   35, 53
Warde v Æyre (1615) 2 Bulst 323; 80 ER 1157   39
Warlow v Harrison (1859) 1 E & E 309; [1843-60] All ER Rep 620   76

Table of Cases

Warman v Southern Counties Car Finance Corporation Ltd [1949] 2 KB 576;
[1949] 1 All ER 711 — 178
Wates Construction (London) Ltd v Franthom Property Ltd (1991) 53 BLR 23 — 388–9
Watteau v Fenwick [1893] 1 QB 346 — 136, 137
Watts v Shuttleworth (1860) 5 H & N 235 — 385
Weiner v Gill [1906] 2 KB 574; [1904-7] All ER Rep 773 — 141
Welsh Development Agency v Export Finance Co. Ltd [1990] BCC 393;
[1992] BCC 270 — 5, 335, 347, 378, 420
White v Wilks (1813) 5 Taunt 176; 128 ER 654 — 33
White and Carter (Councils) Ltd v McGregor [1962] AC 413; [1962] 2 WLR 17;
[1961] 3 All ER 1178 — 176
White and Osmond (Parkstone) Ltd, re (1960) unreported — 454
Whitehouse v Frost (1810) 12 East 614; 104 ER 239 — 33
Whiteley Ltd v Hilt [1918] 2 KB 808; 119 LT 632 — 351
Whittington v Seale-Hayne (1900) 82 LT 49; 16 TLR 181 — 65
Williams Bros Ltd v E. T. Agius Ltd [1914] AC 510; [1914-15] All ER Rep 97 — 175–6
Williamson v Rider [1963] 1 QB 89; [1962] 3 WLR 119; [1962] 2 All ER 268 — 194
Wilson v Gabriel (1863) 4 B & S 243 — 237
Wilson v Lombank Ltd [1963] 1 WLR 1294; [1963] 1 All ER 740 — 322
Wilson v Rickett Cockerell and Co. Ltd [1954] 1 QB 598; [1954] 2 WLR 629;
[1954] 1 All ER 868 — 93, 103
Wilsons and Furness-Leyland Line Ltd v British and Continental Shipping Co. Ltd
(1907) 23 TLR 397 — 275
Wimble, Sons and Co. v Rosenberg and Sons [1913] 3 KB 743; 109 LT 294 — 166
Winkfield, The [1902] P 42; 85 LT 668 — 29
Woodar Investment Development Ltd v Wimpey Construction (UK) Ltd
[1980] 1 WLR 277; [1980] 1 All ER 571 — 296–7
Woodley v Coventry (1863) 2 H & C 164; [1861-73] All ER Rep 1839; 8 LT 249 — 34
Woodman v Photo Trade Processing Ltd (1981) 131 NLJ 933 — 111
Woodroffes (Musical Instruments) Ltd, re [1986] Ch 366 — 340
Woods v Martins Bank Ltd [1959] 1 QB 55; [1958] 1 WLR 1018; [1958] 3 All ER 166 — 212
Woodworth v Conroy [1976] QB 884; [1976] 2 WLR 338; [1976] 1 All ER 107 — 323
Woollatt v Stanley (1928) 138 LT 620 — 207
Worcester Works Finance Ltd v Cooden Engineering Co. Ltd [1972] 1 QB 210;
[1971] 3 WLR 661; [1971] 3 All ER 708 — 150
Wormell v RHM Agriculture (East) Ltd [1986] 1 WLR 336; [1987] 1 WLR 1091;
[1987] 3 All ER 75 — 93, 104, 112
Wreford, re (1897) 13 TLR 153 — 278
Wyvern Developments Ltd, re [1974] 1 WLR 1097; [1972] 118 SJ 531; [1974] 2 All ER 535 — 420

Yeoman Credit Ltd v Apps [1962] 2 QB 508; [1961] 3 WLR 94; [1961] 2 All ER 281 — 178, 310
Yeoman Credit Ltd v Gregory [1963] 1 WLR 343; 107 SJ 315; [1963] 1 All ER 245 — 208
Yeoman Credit Ltd v McLean [1962] 1 WLR 131; 105 SJ 990 — 308
Yeoman Credit Ltd v Waragowski [1961] 1 WLR 1124; [1961] 3 All ER 145 — 308
Yorkshire Woolcombers Association Ltd, re [1903] 2 Ch 284 — 336–7, 405
Young v Kitchin (1878) 3 ExD 127 — 240
Young and Marten Ltd v McManus Childs Ltd [1969] 1 AC 454; [1968] 3 WLR 630;
[1968] 2 All ER 1169 — 58, 105

Table of Statutes

Administration of Justice Act 1970
    s. 3   462
    s. 4   467
    s. 40(1)   305
    s. 40(3)   305
Administration of Justice Act 1982   229
Agricultural Credits Act 1928   331
    s. 6(2)   332
    s. 8   362
    s. 14   362
Agricultural Credits (Scotland) Act 1929
    s. 8   362
Agricultural Marketing Act 1958
    s. 15   362
Agriculture Act 1970   118
Arbitration Act 1950
    s. 12(6)(b)   468
    s. 20   468
    s. 21   466, 469
    s. 23(1)   469
Arbitration Act 1979
    s. 1   466, 468, 469
    s. 3–4   469
    s. 5   466
Auctions (Bidding Agreements) Act 1927   76
Auctions (Bidding Agreements) Act 1969   76
    s. 3   76
    s. 3(2)   76

Banking Act 1979
    s. 18   422
    s. 47   216
Banking Act 1987   211

Bankruptcy Act 1603–1914   333
Bankruptcy Act 1854   333
Bankruptcy Act 1861   392
Bankruptcy Act 1878   333
    s. 8–9   333
    s. 14   333
    s. 20   333
Bankruptcy Act 1914
    s. 31   436
Bankruptcy (Scotland) Act 1985   431
Bankrupts Act 1572   392
Bills of Exchange Act 1704   188
Bills of Exchange Act 1882   188, 212, 473, 475, 476
    s. 2   193, 197
    s. 3   194
    s. 3(1)   191, 225, 255
    s. 3(4)(a)   194
    s. 5(2)   193
    s. 6(1)-(2)   193
    s. 7(1)   195
    s. 7(3)   195
    s. 8(1)   196
    s. 9(1)(d)   194
    s. 10   194
    s. 11   193, 199
    s. 12   194, 197
    s. 16(2)   207
    s. 17(2)   192
    s. 20   195
    s. 20(1)-(2)   199
    s. 21   201
    s. 21(2)   201
    s. 23   202
    s. 23(2)   202

Table of Statutes

Bills of Exchange Act 1882 – *continued*
  s. 24   195, 197, 202, 203
  s. 25   204
  s. 26   202
  s. 26(2)   204
  s. 27(1)(b)   198
  s. 27(2)   198, 199, 200
  s. 27(3)   198
  s. 28(1)-(2)   206
  s. 29   199
  s. 29(1)(b)   201
  s. 29(2)   200
  s. 29(3)   141, 199
  s. 30(2)   197, 201
  s. 31(2)   192
  s. 31(3)   192
  s. 32   192
  s. 34(1)   197
  s. 34(4)   197
  s. 35(1)-(3)   196
  s. 36(3)   200
  s. 41(1)(a)   207, 208
  s. 41(1)(c)   207
  s. 41(1)(d)   208
  s. 41(2)-(3)   208
  s. 43   219
  s. 45   208
  s. 45(2)   208
  s. 45(4)   208
  s. 46(2)   208
  s. 48   208
  s. 48(1)(a)   207
  s. 49   208
  s. 49(2)(a)   208
  s. 49(12)   194, 208
  s. 50   208
  s. 54   197, 206
  s. 54(1)   205
  s. 54(2)(a)-(c)   205
  s. 55   197, 205, 206
  s. 55(1)   197, 206
  s. 55(1)(b)   206
  s. 55(2)   224
  s. 57   206
  s. 57(1)   206
  s. 59   209
  s. 59(2)(b)   208
  s. 60   205, 209, 220
  s. 63   209
  s. 63(1)   209
  s. 64   207, 209
  s. 64(1)   207
  s. 65-68   208
  s. 72(4)   194
  s. 73   191, 210
  s. 76   217
  s. 79(2)   218

Bills of Exchange Act – *continued*
  s. 80   220-1
  s. 81   218
  s. 81A   218
  s. 82   198, 222
  s. 83-89   224
  s. 83(1)   203, 224
  s. 88   224
  s. 89(1)-(2)   224
  s. 90   200
  s. 97(2)   190
Bills of Lading Act 1855
  s. 1   29
Bills of Sale Act   186
Bills of Sale Act 1854–1891   319
Bills of Sale Act 1854   318
  s. 7   334
Bills of Sale Act 1878   75, 361
  s. 4   325, 334
  s. 5   334
  s. 7   334
  s. 8   75
  s. 10(2)   361
  s. 19   363
  s. 49   361
Bills of Sale Act (1878) Amendment Act 1882
    75, 333, 335
  s. 1   334
  s. 3   363
  s. 5   334, 335
  s. 8   334, 362
  s. 9   62, 334, 335
  s. 17   335
Building Societies Act 1986   211
  Part IX   217
  Sch.4
    para.3   212

Charities Act 1960
  s. 30(1)   423
Cheques Act 1957   211, 212
  s. 1   221
  s. 4   222, 223
  s. 4(1)   222
Cheques Act 1992   218
Civil Aviation Act 1982   363
Civil Aviation Act 1985 (as amended)
  s. 86   362
Civil Evidence Act 1968
  s. 14(1)   464
Civil Liability (Contribution) Act 1987
  s. 3   384
Coinage Act 1870   193
Companies Act 1948
  s. 320(1)   287
Companies Act 1985   325, 393, 424
  Part VII   430

Companies Act 1985 – *continued*
  Part XII 363
  s. 35 201
  s. 36A 193
  s. 178(3)-(6) 442
  s. 196(1) 341
  s. 248(b) 411
  s. 349 204
  s. 378 421
  s. 378(1) 421
  s. 386 362
  s. 386(1)(b)-(c) 325
  s. 395(2) 356
  s. 396 231, 256, 261, 268, 339, 347, 353, 355, 356, 416, 426, 440
  s. 396(1)(c) 363
  s. 396(c)(iii) 313
  s. 399(1) 453
  s. 400 186
  s. 400(2) 453
  s. 400(3)(b) 453
  s. 402(1)-(2) 364
  s. 406 453
  s. 410 249, 253, 342
  s. 415(2)(a) 364
  s. 416(1)-(2) 363
  s. 416(3) 364
  s. 425 341, 402, 403, 406, 413
  s. 458 454
  s. 459 409, 414
  s. 618 427
  s. 651 423
  s. 711A 363
  s. 711A(2) 253
  Sch.24 454
Companies Act 1989 14, 253, 439
  Part VII 451
  s. 158(4) 431
  s. 159(1)-(2) 431
  s. 161 431
  s. 164 431
  s. 165 443
  s. 166 431
  s. 175(1) 431
Companies Winding-up Act 1844 392
Company Consolidation (Consequential Provisions) Act 1985
  s. 1 422
Company Directors Disqualification Act 1986 393, 423
  s. 1 458
  s. 3-5 459
  s. 6 400, 458
  s. 6(1) 399, 459
  s. 7(2) 459
  s. 8-13 459
  s. 15 459

Company Directors Disqualification Act 1986 – *continued*
  s. 16(1) 459
  Sch.1 458
Competition Act 1980 46
Consumer Arbitration Agreements Act 1988 470
  s. 4 470
Consumer Credit Act 1974 5, 85, 107, 151, 254, 320, 351, 377
  Part V 77
  s. 3 57
  s. 4(1) 57
  s. 8 5
  s. 8(1) 61
  s. 8(2) 314
  s. 8(3) 201
  s. 9(3)-(4) 61
  s. 10(a)-(b) 61
  s. 11(3) 61
  s. 12(a) 61
  s. 12(2) 61
  s. 13 61
  s. 13(a) 61
  s. 15(1) 59
  s. 15(2) 201
  s. 16 62
  s. 16(5)(a)-(b) 62
  s. 19(3) 78
  s. 20 61
  s. 39–40 320
  s. 56 102
  s. 56(2) 64
  s. 56(4) 102
  s. 59 129 128, 162
  s. 61(1) 46
  s. 63(1) 76
  s. 63(2) 77
  s. 65 76
  s. 67 77
  s. 67(b) 77
  s. 68 77
  s. 68(a)-(b) 77
  s. 69(1) 78
  s. 69(7) 77
  s. 70(3) 78
  s. 71(2)(a) 78
  s. 71(3) 78
  s. 72 78
  s. 72(4) 78
  s. 72(8) 78
  s. 73(2) 56, 78
  s. 73(5) 78
  s. 74 77
  s. 74(2A) 77
  s. 74(3) 77
  s. 75 102

Table of Statutes   xxxiii

Consumer Credit Act 1974 – *continued*
s. 76 316
s. 76(1) 316
s. 76(1)(a) 304
s. 87 316
s. 87(1) 314
s. 87(1)(b) 304
s. 88 314
s. 88(1)(b)-(c) 316
s. 88(2) 316
s. 88(5) 316
s. 90 59, 317
s. 90(2) 317
s. 90(5) 317
s. 91 317
s. 92(1) 317
s. 93 304
s. 94–95 315
s. 97 315
s. 98(1) 316
s. 99 315
s. 99(1) 303
s. 99(4) 315
s. 99(5) 315, 316
s. 100 59
s. 100(1) 316
s. 100(3) 316
s. 101(1) 59, 314
s. 101(7) 315
s. 105(1) 377
s. 105(3) 377
s. 105(7) 377
s. 114(1) 320
s. 115 320
s. 116(1) 326
s. 120 159
s. 121(1) 326
s. 121 159
s. 123 13
s. 123(1) 201
s. 123(3) 201
s. 127 77
s. 129–130 315
s. 130(2) 316
s. 132 59, 315
s. 132(1)-(2) 303
s. 133 316
s. 138 449
s. 138(1) 449
s. 146(1)-(4) 103
s. 169 119
s. 172 315
s. 173(2) 78
s. 183 77
s. 187(2) 61
s. 189 152, 377
s. 189(1) 61, 103, 201, 314, 316

Consumer Credit Act 1974 – *continued*
s. 192(3)(a) 157
Sch.4 27, 57, 60
para.22 157
Consumer Guarantees Bill 1990 68, 81, 84, 85, 88, 99, 106, 113, 170, 171
Consumer Protection Act 1961 119
Consumer Protection Act 1987 88, 91, 113, 114, 471
Part I 114, 115, 116, 299
Part II 114, 118
Part III 66
s. 1(2) 114
s. 2(1)(a) 114
s. 2(3) 114
s. 3 115
s. 3(2) 116
s. 3(2)(c) 115
s. 4 116, 117
s. 4(1) 116
s. 4(1)(d) 117
s. 4(1)(e) 98
s. 4(2) 117
s. 5(1) 115
s. 5(4) 115
s. 6(6) 117
s. 7 114
s. 10(7) 118
s. 11 119, 120
s. 12–14 120
s. 16 120
s. 40(2) 119
s. 41 120
s. 46 118
s. 46(2) 91, 114, 118
s. 46(3) 115
Sch.1 117
Consumer Safety Act 1978 119
Control of Pollution Act 1974 115
Copyright, Design and Patents Act 1988 360
County Courts Act 1984
s. 38 160
s. 100 160
Courts and Legal Services Act 1990 471
s. 1 462
s. 102 470
Crossbows Act 1987 75

Data Protection Act 1984 215
Drug Trafficking Offences Act 1986 213, 214

Factors Act 1823–1889 235
Factors Act 1823 136
Factors Act 1825 136
s. 2 138

Factors Act 1842   136, 138
Factors Act 1877   136, 139
  s. 3   139, 150
  s. 8–9   139
Factors Act 1889   136
  s. 1(1)   139–40
  s. 1(2)   79
  s. 1(4)   35
  s. 2   140, 150, 151, 154
  s. 2(1)   139, 140, 142, 149, 152, 154
  s. 2(2)   141, 151
  s. 8   125, 148, 149, 150, 154
  s. 9   36, 56, 59, 60, 149, 151, 153–5, 350
  s. 10   36, 55
Fair Trading Act 1973   46
  s. 132   119
Finance Act 1958
  s. 34(4)   238
Finance Act 1971
  s. 63   238
  s. 69   238
Financial Services Act 1986   14, 430
Firearms Act 1968   75
Firearms Act 1982   75
Food Safety Act 1990   118
Forgery and Counterfeiting Act 1981
  s. 1   202
  s. 9   202
Fraudulent Conveyances Act 1572   392

Health and Safety at Work Act 1974   118
Hire-Purchase Act 1964   60, 351
  Part III   157–8
  s. 27   158, 159
  s. 27(2)   158
  s. 27(3)-(4)   159
  s. 27(6)   159
  s. 28   159
  s. 29(1)   158
  s. 29(2)   157
  s. 29(3)   159
Hire-Purchase Act 1965   60
Hotel Proprietors Act 1956
  s. 1(1)   159
Human Organs Transplants Act 1989   13
  s. 1   13
  s. 2(1)   13
  s. 2(3)   13

Industrial and Provident Societies Act 1967
  s. 1   362
  s. 3–6   362
Insolvency Act 1985   393
Insolvency Act 1986   159, 255, 332, 393, 394, 398
  Part I   402
  Part II   403

Insolvency Act 1986 – *continued*
  Part XIII   421, 422
  s. 1   402
  s. 1(2)   402
  s. 5(2)(b)   403
  s. 6   403
  s. 8   399
  s. 8(1)   401, 406
  s. 8(1)(a)-(b)   407
  s. 8(2)   403
  s. 8(3)   406
  s. 9(1)-(2)   404
  s. 9(2)(a)   416
  s. 9(3)   404, 416
  s. 10   411
  s. 10(1)(a)   408
  s. 10(1)(c)   408
  s. 11   411, 416
  s. 11(1)(b)   415
  s. 11(3)(b)   415
  s. 11(3)(c)   408, 409, 410
  s. 11(3)(d)   408
  s. 12(1)   408
  s. 14(1)   411
  s. 14(2)   408
  s. 14(5)   411
  s. 14(6)   412, 420
  s. 15   412
  s. 15(1)-(2)   412
  s. 15(4)-(6)   412
  s. 18(2)   415
  s. 19(1)   415
  s. 19(1)(b)   408
  s. 19(2)   415
  s. 21   407
  s. 21(4)   399
  s. 23–24   414
  s. 27   409, 413
  s. 27(1)   413
  s. 27(1)(a)   414
  s. 27(3)   413
  s. 27(3)(b)   414
  s. 27(4)   413, 414
  s. 29(2)   405
  s. 34   417
  s. 40   339, 419
  s. 40(1)   341
  s. 42(1)   417
  s. 42(3)   420
  s. 43   417
  s. 43(1)   403
  s. 43(3)   417
  s. 44   418
  s. 44(1)(a)   418, 419
  s. 44(1)(b)-(c)   418
  s. 45(1)   415, 416
  s. 47–48   415

Table of Statutes

Insolvency Act 1976 – *continued*
  s. 74(2)(f) 442
  s. 87(1) 423
  s. 88 395
  s. 89 401
  s. 95 421
  s. 98 423, 432
  s. 107 429, 438
  s. 115 441
  s. 116 422
  s. 122(1) 422
  s. 122(1)(f) 399
  s. 123(1)(a)-(e) 401
  s. 123(2) 401
  s. 124A 422
  s. 124(1)-(2) 422
  s. 124(4)-(5) 422
  s. 127 213, 443, 451
  s. 129 451
  s. 130(2) 409
  s. 130(3) 423
  s. 130(4) 391, 396
  s. 131(2) 423
  s. 132 423
  s. 136(2) 422
  s. 137 422
  s. 139–140 422
  s. 146 423
  s. 153 396
  s. 163(4) 431
  s. 164(4) 431
  s. 165(1)-(2) 431
  s. 166(2) 423
  s. 174 339
  s. 175 423
  s. 175(2)(a)-(b) 442
  s. 178–182 427
  s. 178(2)-(3) 427
  s. 178(5) 427
  s. 186(1) 427
  s. 212(1)(b) 419
  s. 213 454, 459
  s. 214 400, 454, 459
  s. 214(3) 457
  s. 214(6) 456
  s. 214(7) 457
  s. 218–219 458
  s. 230(2) 394
  s. 233 441
  s. 234 420
  s. 234(3)-(4) 420
  s. 234(4)(a) 266
  s. 234(4)(b) 266, 421
  s. 235–236 423
  s. 238 395, 399, 443, 449, 450
  s. 238(2)-(3) 446
  s. 238(4) 444, 445, 451

Insolvency Act 1976 – *continued*
  s. 238(4)(b) 445
  s. 238(5) 445
  s. 239 287, 395, 399, 443, 448
  s. 239(4) 447
  s. 239(6) 447
  s. 240 395, 399, 443, 449
  s. 240(1)(a)-(b) 447
  s. 241 395, 399, 443, 446, 449
  s. 241(1)(c) 448
  s. 241(2) 445, 446
  s. 241(2)(b) 448
  s. 241(4) 456
  s. 242 395, 399
  s. 243 395
  s. 244 443, 448
  s. 244(2) 448
  s. 244(3)-(5) 449
  s. 245 339, 416, 443, 449, 450
  s. 245(2) 449
  s. 245(6) 449
  s. 248(b) 433
  s. 249 444
  s. 251 341, 411, 419, 442, 457
  s. 281(7) 386
  s. 283(2) 425
  s. 283(3) 342
  s. 284 213
  s. 322 441
  s. 323 432
  s. 340 443
  s. 386 423
  s. 390 394, 417
  s. 391–392 394, 417
  s. 423 443, 451
  s. 423(2) 451
  s. 423(5) 451
  s. 424–425 443, 451
  s. 425(2) 451
  s. 429(1) 341
  s. 439 444
  Sch.1 411, 417
  Sch.4
    para.5 423
  Sch.6 423
    category 5 442
  Sch.13 341
Interpretation Act 1978 193

Joint Stock Companies Act 1844 392
Joint Stock Companies Act 1856 393
Joint Stock Companies Winding-up Act 1848 393
Joint Stock Companies Winding-up Amendment Act 1857 393
Judicature Acts 1873–1875 190, 237, 239, 241, 242, 281

Land Registration Act 1925   306
Law of Property Act 1925   24
  s. 94   11
  s. 136   11, 190, 249
  s. 136(1)   237, 239
  s. 172   451
Law of Property (Miscellaneous Provisions)
    Act 1989
  s. 2   75
Law Reform (Contributory Negligence) Act
    1945   166
Law Reform (Frustrated Contracts) Act 1943
  s. 2(5)(c)   74
Limitation Act 1980   117, 144
  s. 2–3   144
  s. 11A(4)   117
  s. 14(1A)   117
Limited Liability Act 1855   393

Maritime Insurance Act 1906   475
Medicines Act 1968   118
Mercantile Law Amendment Act 1856
  s. 2   183, 184
  s. 5   384
Merchant Shipping Act   363
Merchant Shipping Act 1894
  s. 31   362
Merchant Shipping Act 1988
  Sch.3   362
Minors' Contracts Act 1987   201
  s. 2   383
Misrepresentation Act 1967
  s. 2(1)   65, 133, 174
  s. 2(2)   65
  s. 3   109
Misuse of Drugs Act 1971   118
Mock Auctions Act 1961
  s. 1(1)   76

Partnership Act 1890   475
  s. 2(3)(d)   442
  s. 3   442
Patents Act 1977
  s. 33   362
Pawnbrokers Acts 1872–1960   320
Prevention of Terrorism (Temporary
    Provisions) Act 1989   213

Registered Designs Act 1949
  s. 19   362
Resale Prices Act 1976   46
  s. 1–2   46
  s. 4   46
  s. 14–21   46
Road Traffic Act 1972   118
Road Traffic Act 1988   118, 459
  s. 75   93

Sale of Goods Act 1893   25, 62, 67, 84, 94,
    127, 133, 260, 273, 473, 474, 475
  s. 11(1)(c)   50
  s. 12   26
  s. 12(1)   25, 26
  s. 12(2)   25, 27
  s. 22   146
  s. 25(1)   139, 148
  s. 25(2)   36
  s. 47   36
  s. 52   183, 184
  s. 61(2)   2
  s. 61(4)   347
Sale of Goods Act 1979   3, 16, 24, 57, 64,
    111, 115, 116, 120, 121, 172, 273, 294,
    299, 349, 350, 357
  Part V   122, 258
  Part VI   258
  s. 2   44
  s. 2(1)   268
  s. 2(2)   45
  s. 2(5)   143
  s. 5(1)   24
  s. 6   48, 71, 72
  s. 7   48, 72, 73, 74
  s. 8   46, 52, 63
  s. 9   46
  s. 9(1)   46
  s. 10(1)   127, 162
  s. 10(2)   80
  s. 11   66
  s. 11(2)   66, 69
  s. 11(3)   66
  s. 11(4)   82, 168, 171, 172
  s. 12   24, 47, 84, 108, 146, 155
  s. 12(1)   145, 174
  s. 13   68, 73, 82, 84, 85, 86, 89, 117,
    174, 293
  s. 13(1)   85, 88–9, 90, 94
  s. 13(3)   85, 88
  s. 14   68, 84, 91, 94, 117, 167, 293
  s. 14(1)   90
  s. 14(2)   94, 98, 99, 104, 106
  s. 14(2)(b)   98–9
  s. 14(3)   101, 102, 104
  s. 14(3)(b)   102
  s. 14(4)   90, 107
  s. 14(5)   92
  s. 14(6)   93, 94, 95
  s. 15   68, 84, 90, 293
  s. 15(2)   105
  s. 15(2)(a)-(c)   106
  s. 15A   68
  s. 15A(1)(b)   84, 85
  s. 16   28, 29, 31, 35, 36, 48, 49, 52
  s. 17   28, 48, 49, 55, 258, 478, 479
  s. 17(1)   479

Table of Statutes

Sale of Goods Act 1979 – *continued*
  s. 17(2) 49
  s. 18 28, 48, 49, 55, 258, 479
    r. 1 50, 51, 73
    rr. 2–3 51
    r. 4 141, 164, 273, 352
    r. 5(1) 31, 32, 52, 53, 54
    r. 5(2) 52, 53
  s. 19 28, 55, 258, 478, 479
  s. 19(1) 55, 479
  s. 19(2)-(3) 55
  s. 20 164, 258
  s. 20(1) 28, 49, 164, 165
  s. 20(2) 166
  s. 21 10, 28, 135, 141, 142
  s. 21(1) 135
  s. 21(2)(b) 159
  s. 22 28, 135, 152
  s. 23 28, 135, 146, 152
  s. 24 28, 125, 135, 148, 149, 150–2, 156
  s. 24(1) 149
  s. 25 28, 135, 152
  s. 25(1) 36, 55, 151, 152, 153–7, 154, 155–7, 158, 283
  s. 25(2) 60
  s. 25(2)(a) 151
  s. 26 28
  s. 27 79, 123, 161, 162, 164
  s. 28 79, 80, 127, 162, 164
  s. 29 79
  s. 29(1) 79
  s. 29(3) 80, 166
  s. 29(4) 79
  s. 29(5) 80
  s. 30 80, 81
  s. 30(1)-(3) 81
  s. 30(4) 81, 171, 172
  s. 30(5) 80
  s. 31(1) 81, 82, 162
  s. 31(2) 82–3
  s. 32 79
  s. 32(1) 79, 124
  s. 32(2) 80, 166
  s. 32(3) 166
  s. 33 167
  s. 34 106, 162, 167, 169, 170, 171
  s. 35 169, 170, 171
  s. 35(1) 169
  s. 35(6) 172
  s. 36 161
  s. 37 123, 128, 168
  s. 37(1) 166
  s. 38 122
  s. 38(2) 122
  s. 39 121, 122
  s. 39(1) 122
  s. 39(1)(a) 123

Sale of Goods Act 1979 – *continued*
  s. 39(2) 123
  s. 41 28, 322
  s. 41(1) 123
  s. 42 28, 123, 322
  s. 43 28, 322
  s. 44 28, 123
  s. 45 28
  s. 45(2)-(5) 124
  s. 45(7) 124
  s. 46 28, 124
  s. 46(4) 125
  s. 47 28, 36, 152
  s. 47(2) 35, 55, 152
  s. 48 28, 125
  s. 48(1) 125
  s. 48(2) 125, 325
  s. 48(3) 80, 83, 125, 126, 162
  s. 48(4) 83, 125, 126, 128, 346
  s. 49 127, 184–5
  s. 49(1) 127–8
  s. 50 175
  s. 50(1) 128, 129 128
  s. 50(2) 130
  s. 50(3) 130, 131, 132
  s. 51 175
  s. 51(2)-(3) 175
  s. 53(1) 178
  s. 53(1)(a) 240
  s. 53(3) 179
  s. 53(4) 178
  s. 54 128, 130, 175, 178, 181
  s. 55(1) 71, 81–2
  s. 57 75
  s. 57(1)-(2) 75
  s. 57(4)-(5) 76
  s. 57(6) 75
  s. 61 72, 75, 93
  s. 61(1) 19, 35, 45, 47, 48, 66, 79, 85, 91, 122, 479
  s. 61(3) 152
  s. 61(5) 50
  s. 62(2) 2, 67, 81, 170, 184
  s. 62(4) 62, 347
Stamp Duty Act 1891
  s. 1 238
Statute of Frauds 1677 377
  s. 4 378
Statute of Frauds 1677 Amendment 1828 377
Statutes of Set-Off 432
Supply of Goods (Implied Terms) Act 1973 80, 97, 99, 105, 109, 110, 111, 115, 120, 351
  s. 8(1) 27
  s. 9(1) 85
  s. 10(2) 98

Supply of Goods (Implied Terms) Act 1973 – *continued*
  s. 10(3) 101, 102
  s. 10(5) 92
  s. 11 105
  s. 11(c) 106
  s. 14(4) 107
  s. 15(2) 93
Supply of Goods and Services Act 1982
    16, 19, 57, 58–9, 80, 84, 99, 105, 108,
    115, 116, 120, 172
  s. 1(1) 55
  s. 1(3) 105
  s. 2(2) 26
  s. 3(1) 85
  s. 4 91
  s. 4(1) 91
  s. 4(3) 98
  s. 4(4) 101, 102
  s. 4(7) 90, 107
  s. 4(8) 92
  s. 4(9) 93
  s. 5(1) 105
  s. 5(1)(c) 106
  s. 7 26, 27, 294
  s. 7(2) 26
  s. 8 294
  s. 8(1)(2) 85
  s. 9 91, 107
  s. 9(1) 91
  s. 9(3) 98, 294
  s. 9(4) 101, 102
  s. 9(4)(b) 294
  s. 9(6) 294
  s. 9(7) 90, 107
  s. 9(8) 92
  s. 9(9) 93
  s. 10(1) 105
  s. 10(2)(c) 106
  s. 12(3) 105
  s. 13 91, 105
  s. 14–15 105
  s. 16(3) 105
  s. 18 91, 93
Supreme Court Act 1981
  s. 37 463
  s. 49(2) 432
Surrogacy Arrangements Act 1985 13

Taxes Management Act 1970
  s. 20 214
Third Parties (Rights against Insurers)
    Act 1930
  s. 1 428

Torts (Interference with Goods) Act 1977
    18, 28, 39, 79, 279, 307
  s. 1 59
  s. 3 186, 305, 313
  s. 3(2)(a) 305
  s. 3(2)(c) 305
  s. 3(3)(b) 305
  s. 3(5) 305
  s. 6 145
  s. 8 59
  s. 8(1) 22
  s. 12 159, 319, 326
  s. 13 159
Trade Descriptions Act 1968 66, 88, 91, 119
  s. 20 119
  s. 24(1) 119
Trade Marks Act 1938
  s. 25 362
Trading Stamps Act 1964 57
  s. 4(1) 105

Unfair Contract Terms Act 1977 5, 57, 66,
    68, 104, 379
  Part I 109
  s. 2 112
  s. 2(1) 108
  s. 2(2) 109
  s. 3 109, 112, 226
  s. 3(2) 109
  s. 4(1) 109
  s. 5 112
  s. 5(1) 109
  s. 6 90, 103, 108, 109, 111
  s. 6(2) 82
  s. 6(2)(a) 89
  s. 7 108, 109
  s. 7(2)-(3) 108
  s. 8 109
  s. 11 109, 226, 293
  s. 11(2) 110
  s. 11(4) 109
  s. 11(4)(b) 111
  s. 11(5) 109
  s. 12 90, 91
  s. 12(1)-(3) 108
  s. 13 112
  s. 13(1)-(2) 109
  s. 14 112
  s. 26 5
  Sch.1 5
  Sch.2 100, 109, 110, 111, 226, 293
Unsolicited Goods and Services Act 1971
    57

Weights and Measures Act 1985
  s. 28(1) 119

Table of Rules and Regulations

Consumer Credit Act 1974 (Commencement No. 2) Order 1977 (SI No. 325) 61
Consumer Credit (Agreements) Regulations 1983 (SI No. 1553) 76
Consumer Credit (Exempt Agreements) Order 1980 (SI No. 52) (as amended) 62
Consumer Credit (Increase in Monetary Limits) Order 1983 (SI No. 1878) 61, 314
Consumer Credit (Rebate on Early Settlement) Regulations 1983 (SI No. 1562) 315

Insolvency Practitioners (Recognised Professional Bodies) Order 1986 (SI No. 1764) 395, 402, 417
Insolvency Practitioners Regulations 1986 (SI No. 1995) (as amended by (SI No. 2247)) 402
Insolvency Rules 1986
  r. 2.6 416
  r. 2.7(1) 416
  r. 2.10 407
  r. 2.51(1) 412
  r. 2.51(2) 412

Insolvency Rules 1986 – *continued*
  r. 4.11 437
  r. 4.43 423
  r. 4.86(1) 396
  r. 4.90 432, 435, 436
  r. 4.90(3) 436–7
  r. 4.180(1) 441
  r. 4.181 442
  r. 4.181(1) 429, 438
  r. 6.114 441
  rr. 7.4(5)–(6) 412
  r. 11.11(1) 439
  r. 11.13 396, 441
  r. 12.3 441
  r. 12.9 416
  r. 13.1 412
  r. 13.6 412

Mortgaging of Aircraft Order 1972 (SI No. 1268) 363

Rules of the Supreme Court 1965
  Ord. 14 465
  Ord. 17
    r. 6 160
  Ord. 29 465
    r. 4 160

Table of European and International Legislation

Australia
  NSW Liens on Wool Act 1843   331

Canada
  Alberta Personal Property Security Act 1988
    s. 43(8)   372
  Corporation Securities Registration Act   345
  Model Uniform Personal Property Security Act 1970   345
  Ontario Personal Property Security Act 1970   345, 369
  Repair and Storage Liens Act 1989
    s. 7   324
  Saskatachewan Personal Property Security Act   369
    s. 9   370
    s. 25   369
    s. 66(1)   372

European Community
  Bankruptcy Convention (draft)   393
  Directive on Consumer Protection
    art. 1   114
  Directive on Product Liability 1985/374   299-300
  Directive on Terms of Payment (proposed)   228
  Treaty of Rome 1957
    art. 85   288
    art. 086   288

France
  Civil Code   21-2
    art. 1118   21
    art. 1585   51
    art. 2279   22
    art. 2280   22
  Commercial Code   475

Germany
  Civil Code   21-2
    s. 242   5-6
    s. 861   22
    s. 862   22
  Commercial Code   475

India
  Contract Bill 1873 draft clause 81   137

Republic of Ireland
  Sale and Supply of Goods Act 1980
    s. 13(2)   92-3
    s. 53(2)   171

UNCITRAL Model Rules   469
UNIDROIT Convention on International Factoring 1988
  art. 5   245
  art. 5(1)   242
  art. 7   245
  art. 8   242
UNIDROIT draft rules 1985   301
  art. 10(2)   302
  art. 12(1)-(2)   302

Table of European and International Legislation

United States
 Bankruptcy Reform Act 1978 394
 Certificate of Title Acts 361
 New York Personal Property Law 1911 336
 Uniform Commercial Code 1987
  art. 2 473
  art. 2A 301
  art. 9 60, 343, 344, 346, 350, 354, 355, 364, 365, 373, 473
  s. 1-203 6
  s. 2-101 4
  s. 2-105(4) 33, 37
  s. 2-326(2) 352
  s. 2-509(2) 33
  s. 2-706 132
  s. 2A-103(1) 292
  s. 2A-211 293
  s. 2A-212 293
  s. 2A-213 293
  s. 2A-219 293
  s. 2A-407 293

Uniform Commercial Code 1987 – *continued*
  s. 2A-517
  s. 3-305 13
  s. 9-107 354
  s. 9-107(a) 354
  s. 9-107(b) 354
  s. 9-107(c) 355
  s. 9-204 336, 344, 366
  s. 9-205 13
  s. 9-208 365
  s. 9-302(1)(d) 367
  s. 9-304 369
  s. 9-312(3) 354
  s. 9-318(2) 243
  s. 9-402 370
  s. 9-402(1) 365
  s. 9-402(8) 371
 Uniform Negotiable Instruments Law 473
 Uniform Sale of Goods Act 1906 473
 Uniform Sales Act
  s. 6(2) 33

PART 1   HISTORICAL DEVELOPMENT AND
CONCEPTUAL FRAMEWORK

ONE

The *lex mercatoria*: the genesis of English commercial law?

INTRODUCTION

The history of English commercial law is intertwined with that of the law merchant (*lex mercatoria*) which developed in medieval times. During this time, the law merchant, which resulted from customary dealings of merchants throughout Europe, was applied with a reasonable degree of uniformity from town to town, fair to fair and country to country and in some sense could be described as a sort of international law of commerce. Disputes between merchants and those who dealt with merchants were adjudicated in special courts in which judge and jury were also merchants.

In England, trade was conducted largely at fairs and the law merchant developed through that medium. Merchants trading at the fairs formed part of a small community so that any disputes which arose were settled at special courts which decided cases with speed and in conformity with the customs and practices of the law merchant. The jurisdiction of such courts was limited to the time of the fair or market but extended to all civil cases (except land) and to criminal cases as well because the courts were responsible for order during that period. There were pragmatic reasons for the existence of a *lex mercatoria* which were intertwined with the fact that trade was international and this led to fairs and markets developing compatible laws throughout Europe. As Malynes put it in *Consuetudo vel Lex Mercatoria* (London: 1685), at p. 67:

> For the maintenance of Traffick and Commerce is so pleasant, amiable, and acceptable unto all Princes and Potentates, that Kings have been and at this day are of the Society of Merchants: And many times, notwithstanding their particular differences and quarrels, they do nevertheless agree in this course of Trade, because riches if the bright Star, whose height Traffick takes to direct itself by, whereby Kingdoms and Commonwealths do flourish;

Merchants being the means and instruments to perform the same, to the Glory, Illustration, and benefit of their Monarchies and States.

Many of the principles of the *lex mercatoria* differed from those of the general common law. Whilst the legal recognition of bills of lading and bills of exchange dates back to the *lex mercatoria* period, the technical rules of the common law, for example, that the consideration for a promise should not be a past consideration, did not form part of the *lex mercatoria*. Nevertheless, from the 14th century onwards the power of the merchants to influence decisions and determine the laws used diminished. Indeed, the Statute 17 Edw 4 c. 2 (1477) narrowed the jurisdiction of the special merchant courts to the area within the market or fair ground. In the 17th century, Lord Chief Justice Sir Edward Coke brought all law under the domination of the common law courts which did not adopt wholesale the *lex mercatoria* as a corpus of law for disputes between merchants. Even so, certain principles were introduced thereby refining the common law. The position was not satisfactory, which may explain why merchants often settled differences between themselves rather than submitting their disputes to what they often felt to be hostile and ignorant judges and juries.

It was not until after the appointments of Lord Chief Justices Holt and Mansfield between the late 17th and 18th centuries that the process began of developing a coherent body of commercial law. Lord Mansfield effectuated a liaison between law and commerce by creating special juries of merchants who were familiar with commercial practices. In this way, custom and usage of trade were clarified in several important areas, notably, negotiable instruments, bailment, agency and insurance. It is worth emphasising that Lord Mansfield treated mercantile usage as evidence in doubtful cases of the universal law of merchants. However, during the 19th century, under the pressure of more diversified and powerful commercial interests, mercantile custom and usage became an aspect of contract, that is, part of the intention of the parties. This was a highly satisfactory development both for commercial interests and for the judiciary since any overt attempt to give commercial custom the force of law exposed the judiciary to the charge of class legislation. Nevertheless, the synthesis of the common law and the *lex mercatoria* was completed by the end of the 19th century in the great English commercial codes (see chapter 23). Thus, under s. 61(2) of the Sale of Goods Act 1893 (now s. 62(2) of the Sale of Goods Act 1979), Chalmers, the draftsman of the Act was able to provide that 'the rules of the common law, including the law merchant . . . shall continue to apply to contracts for the sale of goods.'

During the 20th century there have been calls for a new *lex mercatoria*. This is because national laws, supplemented by rules of private international law, are often inadequate to deal with modern international commercial activity. In response to this call for an examination of the sources from which the law of international trade might be derived, the United Nations Commission on International Trade Law (UNCITRAL) was set up and, together with the International Chamber of Commerce and UNIDROIT (the International Institute for the Unification of Private Law), has sought to harmonise national laws dealing with international trade problems. The major areas of concern have been in the field of international sale of goods, international payments, international commercial arbitration and international shipping legislation. A detailed discussion of the work of international agencies in relation to international trade is beyond the scope of this book and readers are directed to more specialist texts. In this book, we shall consider English commercial law which during the course of the 20th century, has begun to lose its international flavour and has increasingly focused upon commercial problems almost entirely in terms of domestic law and trading practices. Nonetheless, impetus for change in English commercial law is likely to be provided by international and intergovernmental agencies and also, of course, from the European Community.

THE PHENOMENON OF COMMERCIAL LAW

It is sometimes argued that commercial law consists of no more than a simple aggregation of the different rules which govern particular forms of commercial contract and that there is no place for general principles of commercial law. In this vein, the American realist school of jurisprudence regarded the question of title passing as a residual principle in sale of goods to be a 'silly issue' which should not govern the modern commercial scene. This was expressed by the distinguished American commercial lawyer, Professor Karl Llewellyn, as follows in his article 'Through Title to Contract and a Bit Beyond' (1937–8) 15 NYUL Rev 157 at pp. 166–7:

> Why is a one-lump Title not determinable with certainty in Sales cases? It is because such a Title is a static concept, a something which is conceived as continuing in somebody....
> The essence of the Sales transaction is dynamic. Lump-title fits only in that rare case in which our economy resembles that of 300 years ago: where the whole transaction can be accomplished at one stroke, shifting possession along with title, no strings being left behind — as in cash purchase of an overcoat worn home. But the contract for sale on credit, the shifting of goods to market via a factor, the shipment against draft, the instalment sale, the delivery or shipment on approval, the agreement to sell goods lying in warehouse under non-negotiable receipt — these are not one-stroke transactions.... They involve a period, often an extended period, during which matters are in temporary suspension or are in active flux between the parties; over considerable periods of time there is no such Title in *either* party as the static picture of Title suggests.

As we shall see in chapter 8, it is axiomatic under the English Sale of Goods Act 1979 that risk passes with property, so, if the goods are destroyed after the buyer had acquired the property in them but they have been delivered, this is his loss irrespective of the issue of control.

The analysis favoured by the American realist school of jurisprudence entails concentrating upon the legal effects of the various stages in the process of the circulation of goods, that is, all connected problems should be solved first on their *factual* merits. A closely related argument which often accompanies this approach is that precise entitlements facilitate the efficient allocation of goods through focusing upon results of (potential) conflicts. Open-ended entitlements can be described as uncertain or 'muddy' in that they do not allow a complete identification of the parties to a transaction. Where there are 'muddy' rules, trading is so difficult that Pareto-superior moves remain unmade and goods languish in inefficient uses. Underlying this approach is that rules ought to be clearly defined so that they can influence the behaviour of the various parties. With this in mind, it is important to adopt a transactional rather than only a simple bilateral contractual approach.

This is not to say that there are no principles of commercial law because, without these, commercial law would stagnate and would be incapable of responding to changes in business practice. Where the corpus of the law consists merely of a series of rules designed to provide a practical solution to problems, the concomitant is mechanistic reasoning. Furthermore, there is an intuitive appeal to many of the principles identified below which cannot be ignored. Indeed, the intuitive appeal of ownership and title, namely, the idea of 'mine' and 'not mine', was probably underestimated by the drafters of the American Uniform Commercial Code (the UCC) which purports to abolish title from its position as the first rule of property law (UCC (1987), s. 2–101, 1 ULA 168, official comment).

THE PRINCIPLES OF COMMERCIAL LAW

In his essay, *The Death of Contract* (New York, 1974), Professor Grant Gilmore suggests that in the development of law, as in literature and the arts, there are brief classical periods characterised by orderliness which is reflected in specific legislation or codes. The reactions to the classical periods, Gilmore suggests, are romantic periods epitomised through a preference for an open-ended, improvisational approach to society. Essentially, commercial law as a whole is not well suited to either the classical or the romantic models at their extremes. The concern of commercial law should focus upon the *commercial sense* of the transaction and the parties themselves. In this regard, it is important to refer to the principles of commercial law which are essentially tools in serving the needs of the business community.

At the same time, in articulating these principles, it has to be recognised that they encapsulate values and what is entailed in the judgment process involving commercial law is the need to balance these competing values, the relative weight of which varies from legal system to legal system, and from one age to another.

The sanctity of contract
There is a philosophical attraction with the thesis that freedom under the law necessarily entails freedom to fetter one's own freedom. It follows from this that a party should be entitled to the benefit of his bargain and to the strict performance of conditions of the contract. Moreover, this is important in terms

of assessment of risk for the contracting parties and the upholding of a contract ensures predictability of judicial decisions, a crucial consideration in the business context. It is significant that much of consumer-orientated legislation encouraging intervention in contracts, notably the Consumer Credit Act 1974 and the Unfair Contract Terms Act 1977, does not apply in a pure commercial context. Thus, the Consumer Credit Act 1974 has no application to contracts with companies, or where the amount of credit exceeds £15,000 (s. 8) and the Unfair Contract Terms Act 1977 has no application to a wide range of commercial contracts (s. 26; sch. 1).

The phenomenon of legal agreement and the skill of contract draftsmanship was recognised by Sir Nicolas Browne-Wilkinson in *Welsh Development Agency* v *Export Finance Co. Ltd* [1990] BCC 393 (reversed in the Court of Appeal [1992] BCC 270) as follows at p. 403 (emphasis added):

[The contract] is very far from being a layman's document prepared by businessmen for ordinary business purposes. It is a most skilfully drawn lawyer's document, manifestly designed by its exact legal provisions to cast in the mould of agency and sale an agreement which, in commercial terms, is a financing agreement equally capable of being expressed as one by way of secured loan.... *Those who live by the sword may also die by the sword.*

Of course, whilst the freedom of contract rationale may justify the distribution of resources *inter se*, that is, between the parties to the transaction, it is otherwise where this prejudices third-party interests including creditors (see part 4) and other purchasers (see chapter 7). Even so, this does not necessarily follow where a benefit is conferred upon a third party outside of the insolvency process (see part 5). As the law currently stands, the privity of contract doctrine prevents the enforcement of a benefit by a third-party beneficiary and this is anomalous especially in the finance leasing context (see chapter 13). It is little wonder that the Law Commission consultation paper, *Privity of Contract: Contracts for the Benefit of Third Parties* (Law Com. No. 121), (London 1991), has recently suggested the abolition of the rule in this regard, and that a third party should be able to enforce a contract in which the parties intend that he should receive the benefit of the promised performance where there is an intention to create a legal obligation enforceable by him.

The sanctity of contract is also pivotal in promoting self-help mechanisms. In this regard, acceleration clauses can be invoked, contracts terminated, goods repossessed (see chapter 13), liens exercised (see chapter 14), rights of contractual set-off initiated (see chapter 11), secured collateral repossessed and an administrative receiver appointed (see chapter 19) without any need for judicial approval so long as there has been no breach of the peace. There is nothing anomalous about civilised self-help which ensures speed and cheapness of recovery, thereby facilitating the smooth running of business.

Good faith
In Continental jurisprudence the concept of good faith is pivotal, and perhaps the most notorious example is s. 242 of the German Civil Code (the BGB)

where there is a general requirement of good faith in commercial transactions. This has also found expression under the American Uniform Commercial Code (the UCC) where the so-called 'muddy' terms of 'good faith', 'commercial reasonableness' and 'unconscionability' appear. In this regard, s. 1–203 of the UCC provides that: 'Every contract or duty within this Act imposes an obligation of good faith in its performance or enforcement'. By contrast, under English law, there is no such general requirement in the enforcement of *legal* rights or the exercise of *legal* remedies. Nevertheless, the question of good faith and unconscionability is pertinent even under English law with regard to a priority dispute where an *equitable* right or remedy is involved.

It is an inevitable aspect of the judicial process that judges who see everything *ex post* really cannot help but be influenced by their *ex post* perspectives. Indeed, it could be argued that under some circumstances there is an efficiency justification for such 'muddy' rules, for example, where the costs of getting information in advance are high, or, where one party effectively blocks information to another (see Priest, 'The Common Law Process and the Selection of Efficient Rules', (1977) 6 J Legal Stud 65). Furthermore, when judges make decisions they not only try to facilitate the rational calculation of the parties, they also tell a story about the kind of society we live in. In this sense, decisions are 'constitutive' and it would corrode our moral understanding of ourselves as a society, and also commerce represented by a business 'community', if we were to permit gross unfairness to reign simply for the sake of retaining clear rules *ex ante*.

The facilitation of the creation of security interests

As between the two parties to the transaction a division of ownership is unobjectionable, resting, as it does, on the freedom of contract rationale. Since it can be assumed in a comercial transaction that the creditor and debtor are knowledgeable and capable business people who are able to determine what is in their own interests, the law should not interfere in the parties' decision as to allocation of property rights. This approach does, nevertheless, invite scrutiny on the basis of whether the taking of security *is in fact* in the economic interest of either the debtor or the creditor. A resolution of this problem will entail some discussion of micro-economic issues. Indeed, much of the American literature in this context begins with a micro-economic claim, namely, the only real justification for secured transactions ought to be empirically demonstrable economic efficiency. The argument continues that if an efficiency justification cannot be given for the preferential treatment enjoyed by secured creditors, a persuasive justification for security will be hard to find since secured creditors tend to be well informed, well represented, and powerful.

Stratification theory would suggest that there should be no cash gain to the debtor, in a world where information is perfect, from issuing secured/unsecured credit. The provision of security increases the costs to unsecured creditors by as much as it reduces the costs to secured creditors assuming that all the creditors are risk neutral. Moreover, it is simplistic from an economic perspective to refer to a 'zero-sum game', i.e., where secured credit is justified on the basis that a creditor has added to the assets 'new value' rather than taking away anything from the debtor's pool of assets, thereby, through depletion, depriving unsecured creditors. The issue still remains as to whether the lower interest rate the secured creditor charges will be offset by the higher interest rate of the debtor's other future creditors who will have to adjust to the fact of security being taken. Furthermore, the 'zero-sum' scenario is unrealistic in the sense that stock-in-trade constantly fluctuates, although, on this basis, it could be argued that subjecting the debtor's major assets to security interests inhibits the debtor from substituting riskier assets for his original assets. The reasoning here recognises the economic incentive on the debtor to increase the riskiness of a third-party loan which is based on an established assumption of risk (including the threat of perceived possible future misconduct at a given point of time) and the interest rate charge is reflected on this basis. Thus, Jackson and Kronman have argued in 'Secured Financing and Priorities among Creditors' (1979) 88 Yale LJ 1143 that the provision of secured credit decreases the monitoring or policing costs for the creditor since by focusing on one asset or group of assets (the object of the security interest), costs are less than monitoring the debtor's entire assets. The need for such monitoring is precisely to prevent the debtor from increasing the riskiness of his operation beyond that assumed in the interest charged.

The approach adopted by Jackson and Kronman envisages that the reduction in the monitoring costs attributable to the security exceeds the cost increases elsewhere. The assumption is that those creditors with high information can monitor efficiently and should, thereby, lend on an unsecured basis whilst relatively untalented monitors should have the benefit of a secured interest. Of course, the real difficulty lies in identifying creditors with high information and there is a great danger here of over-generalisation. In this respect, Jackman and Kronman argue that trade suppliers will have such information since they have continuing contact with the debtor and repeated proof in the form of payment that he is still solvent. At least in England, from the supplier's perspective, this approach is questionable given the fact that within a very short period after the decision in *Aluminium Industrie Vaassen BV v Romalpa Aluminium Ltd* [1976] 1 WLR 676 retention of title clauses proliferated in supply contracts (see chapter 12). Furthermore, the assumption made by Jackson and Kronman that banks are non-specialised creditors is open to the objection that, in the case where the debtor's general banking facilities are provided by the lending bank, the latter could learn of important changes in the debtor's affairs more promptly and in greater detail than could other creditors.

In the case of short-term loans, the incentive to monitor will not be as great as in the longer-term loans. With short-term loans, other sanctions and safeguards may be relevant, for example, the loss of goodwill. Indeed, the empirical study conducted by Beale and Dugdale, 'Contracts between Businessmen' (1975) 2 Br J Law Soc 451 showed that, in practice, many business exchanges evince little planning concerning legal sanctions and the effects of defective performance. The significance of this finding is that the interest rate reduction obtained by secured lending in these circumstances would not be offset by the increases in interest rate charges by unsecured creditors since the monitoring costs are not likely to be high in the first place.

It may be that the efficiency rationale for secured credit fails adequately to take account of the fact that, if the quest for security is an aspect of risk, whether or not a creditor demands security on a specific debt depends upon the creditor's perception of risk and this can be highly individual. Some creditors will take out security irrespective of the size or the length of the loan. Nevertheless, it could be argued that such a risk-averse creditor would, in these circumstances, prefer to buy a low-risk (perceived) debt than a high-risk debt pointing to the expense of taking a security interest. In fact, the taking of security need not necessarily involve a high cost, for example, in consumer cases the costs are small because standard-form contracts are used. Significantly, the resale value of the secured item may not be great and this factor helps to explain in large measure the abandonment by the financial services market of security taken in consumer durables. This is a market where there are numerous small loans of items of usually little resale value like 'white' and 'brown' goods including washing machines, televisions, and hi-fi systems. Revolving credit plans, unlike the instalment sale, require a payment of at least 5 per cent per month of the principal rather than the substantially smaller percentages under instalment plans. This would tend to confirm the argument that interest rates and accelerated payments can be a substitute for security. Despite this even if a creditor does not take security, a creditor who lends a large sum of money to a commercial borrower is unlikely to do so without a thorough investigation of the liquidity of the company and will demand a detailed loan agreement. Adding on a few clauses to make it a security agreement is unlikely to increase substantially transactional costs and, besides, there may be important fiscal and cash flow advantages in adopting a particular form of secured transaction as seen under the finance lease in England (see chapter 13).

There is no doubt that one element in the attempt to restrict the extent of risk exposure for the creditor is the quest for security. In this respect, the creditor, does not solely have to rely on the law recognising a particular security interest since the latter may monitor or police the debtor through the imposition of restrictive covenants in the loan contract. Although restrictive covenants can involve significant costs for the creditor, the extent of their use and survival demonstrate that they represent a contractual solution which is efficient from the standpoint of the firm. Typical covenants include restrictions on the firm's production or investment policy by specifying certain projects for which the moneys advanced have to be deployed, thereby limiting the danger of asset substitution. Where there is a flat prohibition, this may involve a considerable price for the firm because it will not be permitted to divest itself of assets whose value to others is greater than the value to itself. Other restrictive covenants could require the maintenance of assets in a particular way, which may be expensive to enforce unless the maintenance is carried out by an independent agent who reports at regular intervals to the creditor. Failure to abide by this will constitute a signal to be taken into account by the creditor either to renegotiate the loan, or to trigger the default mechanism through, for example, the crystallisation of a floating charge (see pp. 340–2), or an acceleration clause for payment (see pp. 302–4). Even if a creditor takes out an insurance policy concerning the risk of debtor misbehaviour, this will not eliminate the necessity for monitoring especially if the insurance cover does not include the entire risk. More importantly, by shifting the risk the need to monitor is not diminished since it is merely shifted on to a third party.

Effective monitoring that can supplement contract restriction often depends upon security. It should be borne in mind that the taking of security does not merely have significance on the insolvency of the debtor. By threatening to foreclose, the creditor can have up-to-date information regarding the liquidity and prospects of the debtor. The taking of security can also be regarded as important discipline on the debtor company because it represents a specific risk of the enterprise rather than merely having its assets subject to realisation in a winding up. Thus, the property interest associated with security enables the creditor to act expeditiously on default, for example, through exercising his rights of self-help principally through repossession, or through the appointment of an administrative receiver (see part 5).

An important case for secured lending is that it must expand the credit available to the debtor. Clearly, if a secured interest loan costs less than an unsecured one, a firm will grant secured credit first. In practice, however, many debtors first issue unsecured credit and turn to secured credit only when they find that they can no longer borrow unsecured. It may be then that from a micro-economic perspective, it is difficult to justify secured credit on the basis of an 'efficient credit hypothesis'. A more satisfactory approach could be to focus upon the quest for security as an aspect of risk. Whether or not a creditor demands security on a specific debt depends upon the creditor's perception of this risk. From this perspective, the function of security can be seen as enabling the creditor to influence (through leverage) the debtor's actions, especially prior to the onset of business failure.

It is important to remember that despite the superficial appeal of the 'equality is equity' or *pari passu* principle, creditors are not under a compulsion to lend and therefore the idea of 'fairness' is not overwhelming in determining whether one should adopt the *pari passu* or any other rule for determining the order of priorities (see part 5). Even if the provision for secured credit were abolished, it is unlikely that this would deter creditors and their lawyers who might, acting on the basis of self-interest and tradition, seek to devise credit and security structures. It is interesting how the financing of projects in developing countries have been secured even in legal regimes hostile to the Western approach to secured credit. Typically, in these circumstances, the first legal mortgage of land may be proscribed as local ownership of land is often conceived to be fundamental to the new nationalism of the post-colonial era. Sophisticated contractual mechanisms have emerged like the leveraged lease, or alternatively, the financier will seek assignment of debts in relation to forward contracts for sale of the product which he is helping to establish (see chapter 13). The most important element in these 'insecurity clauses' is that of control. This demonstrates the fact that often a secured party's most effective rights are not those which arise after default but rather those which occur *before* default.

The conveyancing principles and ordering of priorities

The conceptual framework underlying the English law approach to priority questions between competing claimants involves at least three conveyancing principles, namely, security of property, good-faith purchase and ostensible ownership. At the same time, it should be emphasised that *relativity of title* is the key to the understanding of property passing in personalty (see pp. 24–9) where the real issue is what principles decide *which* individuals have ownership rights over *what* things. In some respects, the weakness of the common law method of approach to this question has confused the issue. Consequently, although property rights are defined as against the entire world, the legal dispute is usually fashioned as a contest between two parties. This form of adjudication tends to postpone the interests of third persons who may have an entitlement to the *res* or property in question.

The uncertainties which often accompany the application of the conveyancing principles identified above often relate to the following factors: first, the nature of the property affected as being either tangible or intangible; second, the nature of the interests involved, that is, either legal or equitable. Nowhere is this confusion more evident than in the assignment of debts (see chapter 11). The competing claimants may be equitable assignees; one may be a legal or statutory assignee, while the other, an equitable claimant. Indeed the lack of clarity in the rules to be applied can be said to threaten the future of receivables financing (see chapter 11). We shall now examine the priority rules.

Rule 1: security of property   The first-in-time rule which is expressed at law in the Latin maxim *nemo dat quod (qui) non habet* has a certain intuitive attraction. Its equitable counterpart is *qui prior est tempore potior est iure*. The logic here, as Lord Westbury explained in *Phillips* v *Phillips* (1861) 4 De G F & J 208 at p. 215, is that the transferor disposes of only that to which he is justly entitled. At the same time, there are important legal *effects* of various stages in the circulation of goods — and these often centre around the conduct of the parties — which provide exceptions, both at common law and by statute, to the above rule (see chapter 7).

Rule 2: the good-faith purchaser   There are significant statutory exceptions to the *nemo dat* rule. Principal among these, as discussed in chapter 7, are dispositions by a mercantile agent, by a seller or buyer in possession, and by a buyer or hirer holding a motor vehicle under a hire-purchase or conditional sale agreement.

Rule 3: estoppel   Essentially what is involved here is a representation made by the owner to the disponee that the non-owner may lawfully make the disposition in question. Typically, the representation will take the form that the non-owner is acting within his authority as agent and we will consider this phenomenon in the context of s. 21 of the Sale of Goods Act 1979 (see pp. 135–45).

Rule 4: Dearle v *Hall* The priority of *successive equitable assignments* of a debt or other receivable is governed by the rule in *Dearle* v *Hall* (1828) 3 Russ 1, namely, an assignee who takes without notice of an earlier assignment and is the first to give notice of the assignment to the debtor obtains priority over the earlier assignee. If the dispute as to priority is between an earlier equitable assignee who gave notice of his assignment first to the debtor and a subsequent legal assignee without notice, it is *probable* following *E. Pfeiffer Weinkellerei-Weineinkauf GmbH & Co.* v *Arbuthnot Factors Ltd* [1988] 1 WLR 150 that the rule will apply (see chapter 12). On the other hand, it is unclear what rule applies to a priority contest between the holder of a legal or equitable tracing claim, typically a proceeds clause holder (see pp. 249–52), and a subsequent legal or equitable assignee of the *same* receivables where the assignee has given the only notice (compare *Compaq Computer Ltd* v *Abercorn Group Ltd* [1991] BCC 484).

The rule in *Dearle* v *Hall* does not apply to a negotiable instrument where payment can be made only by the holder (*Bence* v *Shearman* [1898] 2 Ch 582). Furthermore, the rule does not apply in a priority contest between a *floating* charge holder and a subsequent chargee over book debts or other receivables because the floating chargee, having *impliedly* authorised the subsequent fixed charge, cannot jump ahead by being the first to give notice to the debtor after the charge crystallised (*Re Ind Coope and Co. Ltd* [1911] 2 Ch 223).

Rule 5: the tabula in naufragio *doctrine* The basis of this rule is that a prior equitable interest can be overreached by a disposition of the legal title to a good faith purchaser for value without notice. The relevant time for the determination of notice is when the advance is made. From this it follows that the holder of a later equitable interest, in point of time, who makes an advance without notice of the prior equitable interest can be promoted by getting in the legal title. There *may* be a statutory exception to this in the guise of s. 136 of the Law of Property Act 1925 where the statutory assignee of, for example, a book debt will take *subject to the equities* (see pp. 240–1). Furthermore, the *tabula in naufragio* doctrine does not apply to the interest created by a floating charge which is easily defeated by the creation of subsequent interests other than floating charges in the same property (*Re Benjamin Cope and Sons Ltd* [1914] 1 Ch 800).

Rule 6: restriction on tacking further advances made The general rule is that there is no right to tack further advances after notice of a subsequent charge. Again the key consideration here is whether there has been *notice* of the subsequent mortgage (see below). There are special statutory exceptions regarding restrictions on tacking in respect of mortgages of *unregistered* land (see s. 94 of the Law of Property Act 1925).

Rule 7: variation of priority rules by agreement The ranking of claims *inter se* may be varied by the parties. Such a variation takes two principal forms: waiver and subordination. These are of particular significance in the insolvency context (see chapter 20).

There are two important policy factors which should be accommodated in any rational scheme for ordering priorities: first, no one should suffer loss or subordination of his rights without fault; second, no one should be affected by a prior interest of which he has neither knowledge nor the means of acquiring knowledge. A system of registration of priority claims does in large measure answer these policy issues. Where a security interest is registered in one register or another (see chapter 16), it makes it difficult for a subsequent legal purchaser to claim that he took without notice. Even so, the issue of notice can raise significant conceptual and practical problems in the context of the determination of competing priority interests (see chapter 15).

The negotiability principle
One of the features of commercial law is that it recognises the need for marketability of commercial assets sometimes, as was noted above, at the expense of the position of the true owner. In *Miller* v *Race* (1758) 1 Burr 452, the previously unquestioned assumptions of property law were overturned through the introduction of the good faith purchase doctrine. The facts involved a Bank of England bearer note which was not legal tender in 1756 but was treated by Lord Mansfield as equivalent to cash. It followed that where such a note was stolen and subsequently sold to a bona fide (good faith) purchaser, it had to belong to the purchaser rather than the previous owner because, as Lord Mansfield held at p. 457: 'the consequences to trade and commerce: which would be much incommoded by a contrary determination'. While the negotiable character of certain kinds of negotiable instruments had earlier been given some measure of protection in specialised commercial courts, this decision seems to have been the first clear-cut holding of its kind by a common law court. Following on from this, commercial law saw the development of documents of title, negotiable instruments and securities, the delivery of which passed constructive possession, in the case of goods, or, with regard to instruments and securities, legal title to the underlying rights.

It is assumed, often without examination, that the protection of the good-faith purchaser who is the embodiment of the negotiability principle, assists the free flow of commerce, and is more suited to a society which assumes exchange (contract) rather than property which assumes stability. Often the basic thrust of this approach is to draw a distinction between commercial and non-commercial transactions, and outside the commercial setting there is no compelling reason to depart from the common law which protected ownership. This may explain the common law's restrictive attitude to the question of assignment of choses in action (see chapter 11) but its championing of negotiable instruments (see chapter 9). Nevertheless, this clear-cut approach is not entirely satisfactory. In the first place, it is an oversimplification to draw an analogy between goods and negotiable instruments. The latter must circulate widely and rapidly as a medium of exchange, and it is inherent in the attribute of negotiability that the purchasers' need for costly information concerning a prior claim of defence should be minimised. Goods do not circulate in this way. Moreover, owner-risk prevention (against theft or fraud) is quite different in the case of a negotiable instrument where, for example, the risk that a note may be stolen and payment rightfully obtained by a transferee from the thief can be minimised by putting the note in order form. This is not possible in the case of goods. Secondly, there are other policy factors which have to be taken into account which may restrict transferability. Inalienability can take many forms, as where ownership is legal but sales are not permitted, or where sales are forbidden but gifts are permitted, or, alternatively, where sales are permitted at a 'fair' price but not gifts. The justifications for restraint on alienation range from protection for third parties through over-exploitation in the common pool, or protection of qualifying or disadvantaged persons which can include ordinary consumers. With regard to the latter, even negotiable instruments have been curtailed, so that s. 123 of the Consumer Credit Act 1974 makes it difficult to attain the status of a holder in due course (the good faith purchaser status) by the taking and negotiation of negotiable instruments in connection with a regulated agreement (see pp. 60–2). Similarly, in the US the use of negotiable instruments in consumer instalment transactions is forbidden (UCC (1987), ss. 3–305 and 9–205).

The policy arguments will sometimes revolve around the nature of the commodity. Thus, the inalienability of human blood is often justified on the basis of quality control. Since individuals are likely to know their own health history, a collection system which gives the depositors an incentive to reveal their past history, for example, possible exposure to AIDS, is desirable. Such an approach is not entirely convincing since the problem of quality control can be obviated by more careful selection of depositors and by more sophisticated screening. Furthermore, the altruistic argument based on quality control does not fully address the supply side of the market, i.e., where blood has been collected and then sold to patients.

The Human Organs Transplants Act 1989, which resulted from the furore surrounding the sale of kidneys by Turkish peasants, makes human organs inalienable in the market-place, but since it only precludes sale and not gifts they are not placed outside the realm of social intercourse. Indeed, the preclusion of sale here coexists with the encouragement of gifts so that the market inalienability of organs under the Act seeks to foster a transfer from one individual with a genetic link to another by gift (s. 2(1) and (3) of the Human Organ Transplants Act 1989). The point here is that human organs are put beyond advertising, marketing and valuation in terms of opportunity cost but they are not completely noncommodified. The Act criminalises all the participants in a commercial donation including the donor, doctor, donee and broker (s. 1 of the Human Organ Transplants Act 1989). Such liability is much more extensive than the Surrogacy Arrangements Act 1985 which outlaws *commercial* surrogacy arrangements by identifying the commercial actors rather than the commissioning parents or the medical staff (unless they are part of the commercial arrangements) as the proper targets for prosecution (s. 2 of the Surrogacy Arrangements Act 1985).

Usages or customs
A commercial court will often recognise established customs or usages as these will reflect business expectations. These are particularly significant in the

context of payment undertakings issued by banks which are technically unenforceable for want of consideration but are, nevertheless, recognised by the law on the basis of commercial practice, for example, the documentary letter of credit and performance bonds (see chapter 17). A further illustration of this phenomenon can be seen in the negotiability status of certain instruments (see chapter 10). A closely related phenomenon here is a continuous or consistent course of dealing between the parties to a transaction which supply an important source of implied terms in the relevant contract between the parties.

The market principle
It is often the case that lawyers categorise a market in simplistic terms, that is, as involving essentially bilateral agreement. In fact, with the advent of sophisticated telecommunication networks, the market is a vibrant phenomenon linking buyers and sellers through a network of computer terminals who would otherwise be separated in space and time. The 'market' provides the basis for determining what is a tolerable shortfall in supply by reference to its established and reasonable customs. Furthermore, the 'market' price is the reference point in computing damages for, breach and in the case of an established market, the rules requiring mitigation of damages do not normally apply (see *Libyan Arab Foreign Bank* v *Bankers Trust Co.* [1989] QB 728).

The organised market is a characteristic of London as a major international trading centre. The different markets in London may be subdivided as follows: first, physical markets where commodities are traded with a view to physical delivery; second, financial markets involving transactions of money and commercial paper, for example, the currency and interest rate swaps market, markets in Eurocurrency deposits and also Eurobonds. There has been increasing recognition that for a market to be efficient and succeed, there must not only be sound institutional structures and administrative procedures but also a legal framework within which the subject-matter of the market can operate. Of late, there has been important English legislation protecting the inviolability of market contracts in an attempt to preserve the status of London as an international commercial centre. Thus, the Companies Act 1989 contains significant provisions which apply in relation to *established* markets insulating market contracts from insolvency law (see part 5). The Financial Services Act 1986 contains an elaborate series of provisions which enable the policing of financial markets to be performed by self-regulating organisations approved by the Securities and Investments Board or under its auspices. The various exchanges and clearing houses are only permitted to operate if they have been officially recognised following a formal application together with a copy of their rules. This should ensure that members carry on their business by fairly treating their clients and also protect clients' moneys in segregated accounts.

TWO
Basic concepts of personal property

THE DISTINCTION BETWEEN REAL AND PERSONAL PROPERTY

A common-sense classification of property would distinguish between immovables and movables. In broad measure, the importance of land as a source of political power, the fact that it is permanent, that effective enjoyment of it may consist of granting rights, albeit temporarily, to others, necessarily involve a separate legal regime to other perhaps more temporary forms of property. The basis of the common law distinction was, however, linked to the different forms of action, so a real action could only be brought in respect of freehold land whilst all other actions were personal, that is, a remedy was sought against the defendant himself as opposed to property in his hands.

Certain types of property right can only exist in relation to land, for example, riparian rights or the protection afforded by the tort of private nuisance. Furthermore, the importance of land as a *phenomenon* is accompanied by a more formal legal regime, for example, where land is conveyed this has to be evidenced by a deed or other written instrument or through a registration system (see chapter 16). Nevertheless, whilst the boundary between real and personal property may be easy to state in the abstract, the definition can, in practice, be blurred, which is particularly significant where there is a personal property security registration system accompanied by a first-to-file rule (see chapter 16). Thus, where growing crops or other things attached to land are sold with a view to being severed, the question naturally arises as to whether this can be categorised as being either goods or land (see pp. 44–5). Obviously, a significant factor here will be the degree of affixation and this theme will be pursued further in the context of equipment leasing (see chapter 13). The application of equitable doctrine will also be pertinent. Thus, the maxim 'equity regards as done that which ought to be done' will be followed, so a person holding a fund of money subject to an obligation to invest it in land may be regarded as holding real property, or vice versa in the case of a person having an interest in land under an obligation to sell it.

The different types of personal property

Goods It is important to distinguish between property as a legal interest and the chose or goods themselves. The Sale of Goods Act 1979 and the Supply of Goods and Services Act 1982 use the simple term 'goods' to denote tangible personalty.

Choses in action The common law did not originally categorise a liquidated sum (debt) as a property right. However, as assignment of debts became possible in equity, it became clear that a chose in action could be regarded as being proprietary in nature. Indeed, the debt as a property right forms the basis of an important credit mechanism for British industry through invoice discounting and the factoring of receivables (see chapter 11). Examples of legal choses in action are: a debt, a right to damages, a claim on an insurance policy, a bill of exchange and the transfer of shares. Perhaps the best examples of equitable choses in action include a beneficial interest under a trust of personal property, and the right to due administration for the legatee of an interest in the estate of a person who has died.

Documentary rights In this context, a distinction may be drawn between documents of title to goods and documents of title to payment of money, for example, a negotiable instrument (see chapters 9 and 10). In the case of the former, the issue is whether the document is treated as a matter of strict law or by mercantile usage as representing the obligation. If this is so, the document can be treated as representing the goods themselves and therefore capable of transfer or pledge. Into this category fall bills of lading which, in the interests of commercial convenience, provide an easy method of transferring rights particularly in international trade where bulk cargoes are often involved including a chain of sellers and buyers (see pp. 29–36).

Intellectual property This constitutes a distinct form of chose in action, namely, the protection of ideas through copyright, patents, trade-marks and other related rights. In large measure, these rights constitute a distinct class of property and raise special issues of law and policy. The development of these interests in recent times demonstrates conclusively the inadequacy of the classification of personal property as a residuary class for non-land property rights.

The classification of property rights
The distinction between legal and equitable interests is fundamental in the classification of property rights and goes to the root of priority conflicts. In relation to personal property, the common law recognised only two property rights, namely, ownership and the bailee's special property. Of course, rights

Basic concepts of personal property   17

may arise by operation of law, for example, liens (see chapter 14). All other rights exist in equity including charges, non-possessory liens and the mortgagor's right of redemption. A careful distinction should be drawn between equitable interests and mere equities, the latter being treated for priority purposes as lesser rights. The rationale here is that a mere equity is an attempt to capture an interest that is in whole or part held by someone else. The typical scenario here is the right to rescind for fraud and the right to rectification for mistake. In this context, the principle of estoppel will be highly relevant. As Lord Wilberforce explained in *National Provincial Bank Ltd* v *Ainsworth* [1965] AC 1175, at pp. 1247–8:

> Before a right or an interest can be admitted into the category of property, or of a right affecting property, it must be definable, identifiable by third parties, capable in its nature of assumption by third parties, and have some degree of permanence or stability.

It is important to appreciate the different uses of property rights. Thus, it may be possible to classify property in terms of security rights, that is, where the primary obligation is to pay the money, so the right is effectively a subsidiary right and its exercise will be conditional upon the failure of the primary obligation. On the other hand, the rights may be ends in themselves, for example, ownership of property where the owner has the enjoyment and benefit of the property as opposed to rights to secure a right to a benefit. In the case of a bailment or trust, the enjoyment of the bailee or trustee can be described in terms of being a managerial right, namely, a beneficial right over the goods in the case of a contract of hire, or a right exercised for the benefit of another in the case of a trust, or a bailment to perform some service for another.

The nature of property rights

Property rights are rights in rem   A property right is a real right and not a purely contractual right against a specific person or body. This has profound consequences in the context of insolvency (see part 5). Indeed, one of the most powerful characteristics of property rights is the ability to bind third parties. Significant ostensible ownership problems may arise where there is a separation of possession and property (see part 6).

It is commonly said that the major characteristic of property rights is that they are good against the world. This is an oversimplification not least because the common law adjudicates the competition on a *relative* basis, that is, as between the parties to the dispute. Moreover, there are important policy issues which require the protection of possession which the tort of trespass protects although, in the case of negligence or conversion, it is important to establish a proprietary interest (*Leigh and Sillavan Ltd* v *Aliakmon Shipping Co. Ltd* [1986] AC 785). Furthermore, no property right binds everyone, for example, there are important exceptions to security of property as the first rule of priority law (see chapter 7).

Property rights are transferable   A characteristic of property rights is that they can be transferred from one person to another. An important economic justification may be given to the process of transfer. Indeed, Posner has argued that without transferability there is no incentive for an individual to invest his time and labour in the asset (see Posner, R., *Economic Analysis of Law*, 2nd ed. (Chicago, 1977)). Nevertheless, there may be some important policy reasons which affect the ability to transfer, for example, in the case of a possessory lien which is a personal proprietary right given to a person to retain possession until he is paid (see chapter 14).

It is difficult to define precisely the characteristics of a property right. We have already identified significant exceptions to defining property as being a right given against the whole world or a right that is transferable. It would appear that only general statements may be made about what constitutes property rights, for example, a right which brings the holder into a direct relationship with specific assets. The problem of identifiability of these assets will be discussed later (see pp. 29–37).

Property and other legal categories

Tort   The law of tort is an essential part of property law. Under the Torts (Interference with Goods) Act 1977, the court has a discretion whether to make an order for the delivery of the goods and, in making the order, the court may impose such conditions as seem just. Since tort is a branch of the common law, it is only relevant where a legal interest is being maintained so that equitable rights are enforced without reference to it.

It should be noted that since the basis of an action in tort is the assertion of conversion, that is, an assertion that there has been an interference with another's right to possession, in general, an action for conversion can only be maintained by one who had an immediate right to possession at the time of the act complained of.

Contract   In large measure, property rights are a creature of contract. Even so, there are difficult policy issues attendant upon the contractual allocation of property rights (see part 5).

Unjust enrichment   One of the major characteristics of the period from 1970 onwards in commercial law has been that of equitable infiltration through, especially, the trust doctrine. The precise ambit of restitutionary principles is a source of controversy and will be discussed in the context of retention of title clauses and insolvency. However, in English law, the courts treat the imposition of a constructive trust as a true property trust under which the plaintiff's interest as beneficial owner arises automatically as a substantive right. Indeed, it can be persuasively argued that the proprietary basis of such a restitutionary right prevents its scope from becoming unwieldy and unpredictable. Put simply, there has to be a *causal* link between an asset of the claimant and that asset being in the hands of the defendant. We shall see that, for our purposes, there are two main cases: first, where the asset was transferred by the plaintiff to the defendant in such circumstances that the latter never acquired an overriding right to the asset or was interfering with it; second, where the asset represents the identifiable product or proceeds of such an asset (see Goode, R.M., *Essays on the Law of Restitution*, ed. Burrows, A. (Oxford, 1991), ch. 9).

OWNERSHIP

The traditional common law analysis where a third party wishes to acquire an indefeasible interest in a chattel is to direct the latter to the 'owner'. The difficulty is that 'ownership' is an elusive concept and, indeed, Blackstone in his *Commentaries on the Laws of England* (1765) not only fails to define ownership but does not even mention it as a juridical concept. Similarly, the Sale of Goods Act 1979 fails to define 'ownership' as only the term 'property' is defined in the Act where is equated with 'general property' (s. 61(1)). It may be that 'general property' and ownership are treated as being coterminous.

A distinction is drawn in the Sale of Goods Act 1979 between the content of the right of property (general or special), the definition, creation and extinguishment of which involve questions of law, and property as the *res* or thing itself. It is obvious that the word 'property' is not used in the latter sense under the Sale of Goods Act 1979 since the word 'goods' is adopted for that purpose. Despite this, the close connection between the idea of ownership and the idea of things owned demonstrated by the use of the word 'property' to designate both has caused confusion. Thus, when the legislature thinks that an interest should be alienable and transmissible it will be reified (materialised) and capable, therefore, of ownership. This point is illustrated by the Supply of Goods and Services Act 1982, the general effect of which equates contracts of hire, work and materials and services with sale. The insistence on reification can be seen especially with regard to the problem of passing property in part of a bulk which is discussed later (see pp. 29–37).

The fact of possession in the early common law was deemed worthy of protection simply in order to discourage self-help. Significantly, the great possessory remedies of Glanvill and Bracton's time (*novel disseisin, mort d'ancestor, darrein presentment*) protected possession, untitled possession and even vicious possession. At common law, a disseissor of land joined by his tort an estate in fee simple and this also seems to be the case with respect to chattels.

Although in the early common law, *de facto* possession was protected even against a person who was prepared to prove his ownership, by the 15th century, Maitland (see 'The Beatitude of Seisin' (1888) 4 LQR 24, 286) has traced the development of titular seisin (*seisitus de libero tenemento*). The theory here is that one who is 'in by title' as contrasted with one who is 'in by tort' ought not to be ejected without process of law. Certainly by the time of Blackstone, in the 18th century, *de facto* possession was contrasted with the *right* to possession and the reality of the former as *dominion* was measured in inverse ratio to the chances of opposition. It was for this reason that possession conferred a qualified right to possess which was transmissible and valid against everyone who could not show a prior and better right.

The emphasis on the protection of possession in the early common law together with the close link between possession and ownership make it difficult to explain how, by the 15th century, English law came to recognise the transfer of ownership by agreement. This contradicts possibly the most famous maxim of Roman law which is ascribed to Diocletian in the Code, namely, in *inter vivos* transactions there must be transfer or delivery of possession in order to pass ownership (C.2.3.20). Certainly, the position of Glanvill and Bracton was that no property passed in sale until there had been delivery. The transfer of ownership by agreement has been represented by Fifoot (see Fifoot, C.H.S., *History and Sources of the Common Law* (London, 1949), p. 238) as a rationalisation of the fact that the action for delivery given to the purchaser, in contradistinction to the seller's action for the price, was an action of detinue which itself was normally brought by an owner in respect of property wrongfully detained (see also Milsom, S.F.C., 'The Sale of Goods in the Fifteenth Century' (1961) 77 LQR 257).

OWNERSHIP AND THE RIGHT TO POSSESSION

Under the early common law possession was protected independent of ownership. Indeed, no example of the word 'owner' is to be found in Old English, and in the Authorised Version of the Bible neither 'ownership' nor 'property' appears, although, 'possess' and its derivatives are fairly common. Attempts have been made, most notably by John Locke, to justify factual possession as being the basis of ownership (see Locke, J., *Two Treatises of Government*, bk 2 (1698)). On the other hand, Adam Smith considered the right of every man to his own labour was the original foundation of other property (Smith, A., *An Inquiry into the Nature and Causes of the Wealth of Nations* (1776)), whilst to Blackstone 'bodily labour bestowed upon any subject' was 'universally allowed to give the fairest and most reasonable title to an exclusive property therein' (see *Commentaries on the Laws of England*, bk 2, (1765), ch. 1). The Lockean concept of labour theory of property acquisition posits that, in the state of nature, all things are held in common. The justification for private control lies in utilitarian considerations, *viz*., all persons have claims upon the resources they need for their survival, and persons who mix their labour with commonly owned resources thereby remove them from the common. There are problems in reconciling the claims of owners and non-owners because of Locke's important caveat that appropriation is limited only when there is 'enough and as good left in common for others'. The wider question here is whether private property is inconsistent with property owners having affirmative obligations to others and, in any case, the idea of first possession as a means of establishing initial title does seem arbitrary resting as it does upon the idea of contiguity in space or time.

Possession: the root of title
Possession figures boldly in what can be regarded as the function of property law to substitute rational rules for force in the allocation of property. We will consider later the issue of possession as going towards the identification of the

goods (see pp. 29–32). In chapter 7 we shall discuss the policy factors confronted by the case of transfer of goods manifested in the struggle between the security-of-property principle (ownership) and the good faith-purchase doctrine, security in transactions, under which a purchaser for value who takes in good faith and without notice of a prior claim defeats the prior claimant. The significance of possession here is that it is at the core of the good faith exception.

The importance of the factual element of possession in the early common law has already been noted. The external relation of power (possession) was the decisive element and this was taken to coincide with right. Possession is at the root of title, that is, *beati possidentes*. It is still the case that the purchaser in good faith can acquire ownership through adverse possession in England by being in possession for six years since the Limitation Act 1980 purports to bar the 'owner's' right to bring suit to recover his property or its value after the prescribed period. Nevertheless, a possession-based rule does provide difficulties since it impedes temporal divisions of ownership of property and, in a sense, can be said to encourage theft since it makes the tracing of claims for more than one generation difficult. Moreover, as we shall see, possession can be cumbersome especially with regard to questions of identification, for example, there is no easy way of knowing *in fact* that the grain in the silo today was the same grain that was there yesterday.

Possession occupies a central place in Roman law. It is legally significant as one of the requirements of *usucapio* whilst *traditio* involves a transfer of possession. The sole requirement of *occupatio* is *possessio* and Gaius points out (G.4.148) that the possessory interdicts operate to determine which party shall be the defendant in a *vindicatio* (the claim of ownership). The interdicts, the oldest possessorial actions under Roman law, protected the possessor against violent dispossession or interruption of his possession. In fact, here we discover the paradox of Roman law which had *possessio* as a foundation of the protection granted by the interdicts. Once a possessor was dispossessed, the law had to choose between two possessions, one earlier than the other. Roman law resolved this problem through resorting to the issue of whether the earlier possession had been interrupted by violence or other unlawful means. It followed that the possessorial action was distinguished from the question of right of property. This distinction is adhered to in modern civilian codes.

The modern civilian position
The French and German civil codes evince a different emphasis with regard to the question of the extent to which possession goes towards the *right* to possession and ownership. It is generally supposed that the French Civil Code, following Savigny's possessory theory, emphasises the dual elements of *animus* and *corpus* whereas, the German Civil Code, the BGB, is more concerned with *corpus*, apparently following Jhering. Thus, the French Civil Code insists on an *animo domini* (*à titre de propriétaire*) together with factual possession, which is defined as detention or enjoyment of a thing as distinct from a detention permitted by another (C. civ., art. 1118). Possession in French law goes towards acquisitive prescription, i.e., it is *usucaptive*. This intention element is important so as to distinguish 'normal' contracts such as deposit, hire or lease

(*détenteur précaire*). In contrast, German law treats even the *détenteur précaire* as a possessor (BGB, s. 854). But this is not because German law had abandoned Savigny for Jhering; rather, the German and French codes have set themselves different tasks. The burden of German law is to protect the possessor from forcible eviction and it is conceivable, in theory, for a first thief to acquire possession against a second. An ousted possessor who is owner is allowed the right of self-help in certain circumstances by virtue of s. 859 of the BGB provided that he has been forcibly dispossessed and that he does so immediately.

Under German law, a thief or a finder can have possession inasmuch as he cannot be deprived through forcible actions (BGB, ss. 861 and 862), although he does remain subject to due process of law through a claim for recovery and/or compensation by the owner. In contradistinction the French approach views possession as a prescriptive right. The emphasis in art. 2279 of the French Civil Code is on *possession à titre de propriétaire* which must be uninterrupted, peaceful and obvious (*nec vi, nec clam, nec precario*). The difficulty with this approach is that it does not protect possession *per se*, i.e., possession which is not for the purpose of prescription. Indeed, the maxim '*en fait de meubles possession vaut titre*' (art. 2279) can lead to great problems and its legal basis is difficult to rationalise. It cannot be that it provides an example of instantaneous prescription since, by definition, prescription presupposes that a certain time has elapsed. Even if it is admitted that Article 2279 creates a method of acquiring ownership, it does not explain how the law does this and the exceptions to Article 2279 are significant. Thus, if the owner loses the movable, or it is stolen from him, he has a period of three years during which he could recover it from anyone he found in possession unless the possessor acquired the property 'at a fair or market or at a public sale, or from a merchant selling similar articles' (art. 2280). In this situation, the original owner could not demand possession except on condition of paying the person in possession the price he had paid for it.

Under English law recovery is based not on ownership, in the sense of absolute title, but rather on the better right to possess and the *ius tertii* cannot be pleaded against a possessor. Consequently, in English law there is no theoretical reason why a thief should not sue a second thief although, in practice, the first thief will probably not want to draw attention to himself. It is only in the case of market overt that an indefeasible absolute title to chattels is known to the common law (see chapter 7). The Torts (Interference with Goods) Act 1977 has instituted procedural reforms whose purpose is to resolve all claims in a single set of proceedings by allowing a defendant to ask for joinder of third parties in cases of double liability in tort. Thus, s. 8(1) of the 1977 Act relaxes the rule preventing a wrongdoer from raising the *ius tertii*, so in an action for wrongful interference with goods, the defendant can show that a third party has a better right than the plaintiff to the property in question. The third party can then be joined as a party to the proceedings and the damages awarded can be apportioned accordingly. Nevertheless, the major limitation of the 1977 Act is that it only deals with tort liability and will not extend to contractual liability.

The nature of possession

Attempts have been made to elucidate a central core idea of possession centering upon the exclusivity of control over a thing. This is not a satisfactory approach because it fails to take into account divergent authorities including the delivery of keys (*Hilton v Tucker* (1888) 39 ChD 669), and the measure of control required for a *finding* of possession. In this context, the intention to control is crucial, although the mental element of possession in criminal law has caused great difficulties (see de Meyrick, 'The Mental Element of Possession' (1984) 58 ALJ 202). The assent to control is obviously important in the case of abandonment (*Parker v British Airways Board* [1982] QB 1004) and entrustment with goods (see *Moukataff v British Overseas Airways Corporation* [1967] 1 Lloyd's Rep 396). It may not be possible, in abstract, to determine the meaning of possession. Indeed, this can be demonstrated by the ambiguity over possession under the Bills of Sale Act 1878 which examined the mortgagee's right of possession by having regard to such questions as 'actual', 'apparent' and 'formal' possession. Significantly, Professor H.L.A. Hart has suggested ('Definition and Theory in Jurisprudence' (1954) 70 LQR 37) that we should avoid seeking elucidation of single words like 'possession' and that the word should rather be considered with sentences in which it plays its characteristic role. Of course, this last approach does beg the question as to what are typical sentences.

The problems of definition of possession are particularly acute in the case of constructive possession. This expression is used in many different senses so that, for example, Salmond (*Salmond on Jurisprudence* ed. Fitzgerald, P.J. (London, 1966), p. 286) treats constructive possession as covering those cases where the law grants possession to one who is not in actual physical control whereas Pollock and Wright confine the expression to cases where there is a mere right to recover possession (Pollock and Wright, *Possession in the Common Law* (London, 1888), pp. 25–7). As Earl Jowitt put it in *United States of America v Dollfus Mieg et Cie SA* [1952] AC 582 at p.605: '. . . in truth, the English law has never worked out a completely logical and exhaustive definition of "possession".'

There are real difficulties in determining a unitary concept of possession in English law, so much so, that Stoljar has suggested that because it is such a ductile and intuitive concept, it should be rejected as even a foundation for any meaningful theory of bailment (Stoljar, S., 'The Conception of Bailment' 7 (1955–7) Res Judicatae, p. 160). This phenomenon can be illustrated in the approach of Bell who distinguishes between *immediate* constructive possession, where a person has an immediate *right* to take possession, and *qualified* constructive possession, where the person in actual possession of the goods is entitled to keep them for the present by the exercise of, for example, a lien so that the right to possession is thereby suspended (see Bell, A.P., *Modern Law of Personal Property in England and Ireland* (London, 1989), p. 53).

In some cases it will be impracticable to hand over possession and, where this is the case, there may be a transfer of symbolic possession, for example, the delivery of a key is sometimes said to give the deliveree symbolic possession of the property to which it gives access (compare *Re Craven's Estate* [1937] Ch

423, a case involving the deliverer of a key retaining a duplicate key so that it was not possible to describe the deliverer as having *given up* control over the property). Undoubtedly, a clear case of symbolic possession is where a document of title is transferred. Only certain documents enjoy such status, most notably, the bill of lading, so possession of this is equivalent to constructive possession of the property itself. The general rule, however, is that possession of a document by a warehouseman, for example, will not carry with it constructive possession of the property itself in the absence of an attornment (see pp. 33–4).

The title undertaking

English land law can be categorised as an example of a multititular system, i.e., a ranking of claims the efficacy of which depends upon the nature of the legal interest underlying it, in whom it is vested and against whom it is championed. It was not until the Law of Property Act 1925 which anticipates that title can now be registered that much of the technicality and obscurity of English land law was finally obviated. In similar fashion to the case of land, relativity of title is the key concept for the understanding of the property provisions in the Sale of Goods Act 1979, though the transient value of chattels together with the difficulty of proving title makes the chain of title short. Herein lies the rationale for the conditions and warranties found in s. 12 of the Sale of Goods Act 1979 pertaining to the seller's title where it elaborates upon the possibility of a sale of a limited interest, whilst s. 5(1) contemplates in its definition of 'goods' the transfer of only a possessory interest.

Although one can define ownership as roughly entailing exclusive possession, use and the right to transfer it voluntarily to another, a wider and perhaps more insistent question is what principles decide *which* individuals have ownership rights and over *what* things. In some respects, the weakness of the common law method of approach to this question has confused the issue. Consequently, although property rights are defined as against the entire world, the legal dispute is usually fashioned as a contest between two parties. This form of adjudication tends to postpone the interests of third persons who may have an entitlement to the property in question. To meet this problem we find the emergence of a title undertaking, a development which is intertwined with accelerating commercial activity in society. As the volume of sales increased, taking them outside the scope of fairs and market and the doctrine of markets overt (see pp. 145–6), the need for the seller to guarantee title became very pressing. However, the precise ambit of such an implied undertaking was a matter of doubt especially since it conflicted with the *caveat emptor* doctrine (see chapter 5).

The implied title undertaking: the historical position

In Blackstone's *Commentaries on the Laws of England*, book 2 (1757), the law is stated as broadly corresponding to the civil law in that it allowed recovery against one who sold as his own if the title proved deficient where there was no express warranty. In fact, no such result was adopted in England so that in *Ormrod* v *Huth* (1845) 14 M & W 651 it was suggested that in cases where there had been recovery for defective title, it was found that there was either an assertion of title embodied in the contract, or a representation of title which was false to the knowledge of the seller. The early common law sources are difficult since the meaning and effect of the warranties were canvassed most frequently in deceit. The early cases stressed that the seller *knowingly* concealed his lack of title, but in *Medina* v *Stoughton* (1700) 1 Salk 210, Holt CJ extended this in that an affirmation not known (*scienter*) to be false was a ground for liability. There were now two divergent approaches; the strict approach evidenced in the earlier cases and the less strict adopted by Holt CJ. The clash between these approaches came to a head in *Morley* v *Attenborough* (1849) 3 Exch 500, a decision which is complicated by the fact that it occurred in assumpsit and not deceit. In this case, Parke B referred to the Roman and Scottish positions but still deferred to the old English authorities establishing *caveat emptor* (see chapter 7). The position was not satisfactory and subsequently in *Sims* v *Marryat* (1851) 17 QB 281, Lord Campbell seemed to suggest that the rule in *Morley* v *Attenborough* was subject to so many exceptions that it had become obsolete.

The quiet possession guarantee
It would seem that the common law was in a confused state when Chalmers came to codify the implied undertaking regarding title under the Sale of Goods Act 1893. Consequently, it is little wonder that he looked to Benjamin's seminal 19th century treatise on *The Law of Sale of Personal Property* for clarification. Indeed, in the fifth edition of *Benjamin*, the editors claim that the Sale of Goods Act 1893 'is largely based upon and follows the lines of the treatise'. In the fourth edition treatment of implied warranty of title, Benjamin cites the relevant American law, the civil law and the French Civil Code, so the warranty of quiet possession appears prominently in the discussion. In the civil law, this is the main title undertaking and Benjamin uses this only to *support the argument that there existed a general common law warranty of title*. However Chalmers, influenced by real property concepts, made quiet possession supplementary to the general ownership guarantee, namely, the right to sell together with freedom from encumbrances. Thus s. 12(2) provides that:

(a) the goods are free, and will remain free until the time when the property is to pass, from any charge or encumbrance not disclosed or known to the buyer before the contract is made, and
(b) the buyer will enjoy quite possession of the goods except so far as it may be disturbed by the owner or other person entitled to the benefit of any charge or encumbrance so disclosed or known.

This division of title did not have a common law basis. On the other hand, the condition of right to sell in s. 12(1) did have an apparent meaning and it is little wonder that it was this concept which was used and developed.

In *Niblett Ltd* v *Confectioners' Materials Co. Ltd* [1921] 3 KB 387, Atkin LJ considered at p. 403 the warranty to resemble 'the covenant of quiet enjoyment of real property'. Furthermore the warranty, it was said, could include the tortious acts of the vendor himself but no authority was cited in support of this proposition. Such a conclusion is anomalous since s. 12(1) already gives the buyer a right to sue the seller for a failure to transfer the property in the goods irrespective of which prior seller first failed to transfer the required property rights. On the basis of the *Niblett* case, it would seem that tortious acts *within* the scope of the warranty of quiet possession are confined to those of the immediate seller, and any extension to include tortious acts of third parties would destroy the legal predictability of the warranty. This approach applies to other contracts of supply so that, for example, ss. 2(2) and 7(2) of the Supply of Goods and Services Act 1982 provide that there is an implied warranty that the goods will be free from charges and encumbrances and that the transferee will have quiet possession.

In the case of a contract of hire, s. 7 of the Supply of Goods and Services Act 1982 does not provide an implied term that the goods are free from incumbrances and charges. The only issue here relates to quiet possession. Thus in the case of a finance lease discussed in chapter 13, the lessor impliedly warrants that the hirer will enjoy uninterrupted use and enjoyment of the goods for the period of the hire. This may prove problematical for a sublessee where the intermediary lessor, the finance lessee, had no right to sublease the goods. Use of the goods by the sublessee might amount to conversion, but if the action is brought by the finance lessor after the subsidiary hiring term expired, it will be difficult to establish that such action creates an incursion upon the subsidiary hirer's quiet possession.

The general property guarantee
The precise ambit of the general property concept introduced into the Sale of Goods Act 1893 remains ambiguous. When Chalmers drafted the implied obligation to pass good title under s. 12, influenced by real property concepts, he used 'right to sell' terminology instead of, for example, 'right to pass property or title'. In this respect, s. 12(1) provides:

> In a contract of sale, there is an implied condition on the part of the seller that in the case of a sale he has a right to sell the goods, and in the case of an agreement to sell he will have such a right at the time when the property is to pass.

Initially in *Monforts* v *Marsden* (1895) 12 RPC 266, the implied condition as to title was restrictively construed. It was unlikely that Chalmers was going to depart from the previous common law and give protection to peripheral title rights. Insofar as the common law recognised any implied title obligations, these did not exceed beyond 'core' property rights and this approach was confirmed at first instance in *Niblett Ltd* v *Confectioners' Materials Co. Ltd* but the Court of Appeal ([1921] 3 KB 387) unanimously reversed this decision and resolved to read s. 12 literally and not in the light of previous authorities. The judgments of both Bankes and Scrutton LJJ equate the right to sell with freedom from legal restrictions so that, for example, Scrutton LJ said at p. 398:

The respondents impliedly warranted that they had a right to sell them. In fact they could have been restrained by injunction from selling them, because they were infringing the rights of third persons. If a vendor can be stopped by process of law from selling he has not the right to sell.

The consequence of this approach is that, whenever a seller can by legal process be restrained from selling the goods, he will not have a right to sell. However, the relationship between right to sell and quiet possession was not discussed by the majority in *Niblett*. This is unfortunate because the structure of the section with its division of title between right to sell, warranties of quiet possession, and freedom from encumbrances suggest that title interferences are divided between these undertakings, and that a distinction should be drawn between title defects of a serious and less serious nature. As Roskill LJ said in *Microbeads AG* v *Vinhurst Road Markings Ltd* [1975] 1 WLR 218 at p. 226:

> It follows that in my view these two subsections create and were intended to create independent rights and remedies for an aggrieved buyer according to whether it is the implied condition or the implied warranty which is broken.

When title encompasses lesser property rights such as trade marks, patents, as well as government legislation affecting goods, the court may more readily find breaches of the warranty envisaged under s. 12(2).

In the case of contracts for bailment, s. 7 of the Supply of Goods and Services Act 1982 provides that there is an implied condition that the bailor has a right to bail the goods and not necessarily that he is the owner of the goods. With regard to hire-purchase, s. 8(1) of the Supply of Goods (Implied Terms) Act 1973 (as substituted by sch. 4 to the Consumer Credit Act 1974) provides that there is an implied condition that the creditor-owner will have the right to sell the goods *when* the property is to pass. An important distinction may be drawn here with the contract of sale where, following *Rowland* v *Divall* [1923] 2 KB 500, a buyer can reject the goods (notwithstanding long use) if his seller had no right to sell at the time of delivery. Nevertheless, the reasoning adopted in *Rowland* v *Divall* is that the *purpose* of a sale transaction is to transfer a perfect title which is not the case with a hire contract, nor with hire-purchase at least until the time when the property is to pass. From the perspective of consumer protection, this position is unsatisfactory because the hirer under a hire-purchase contract must wait to be dispossessed before he can reject the goods. Moreover, this approach is contrary to the trend in commercial law to equate hire-purchase with sale transactions.

Property and title undertakings
The problems posed above demonstrate the difficulty of developing a clear theory of ownership or property in English law. The analytical jurist would see property in terms of *dominium* (ownership), which is often categorised as the attribution to the owner of all conceivable powers relating to the object of ownership insofar as those powers are recognised by the legal order. In this respect, property is seen as a real right, a right *in rem*, which can be transferred

only by handing over possession. Terminological problems arise with this approach by virtue of the fact that ss. 16 to 20 of the Sale of Goods Act 1979 envisage a transfer of property as between seller and buyer by agreement. It may be, therefore, that title and property terminology used in the Sale of Goods Act mean different things. Under the Act, the passing of property is said to affect only the relations of the parties *inter se* whereas title passage binds third parties. The argument here is that the section headings under the Sale of Goods Act 1979, 'Transfer of property as between seller and buyer' (ss. 16 to 20) and 'Transfer of title' (ss. 21 to 26) which contain the exceptions to the *nemo dat* doctrine in close juxtaposition support this conclusion.

It is true that if a buyer wishes to obtain possession of the goods, then framing his action in conversion, where the buyer must prove an immediate right to possession, will not provide more recovery than if he brought an action for non-delivery under the contract. However, the court's reluctance to order a decree of specific performance merely demonstrates that a violation of a right *in rem* does not necessarily give rise to an action *in rem* (see pp. 183–5). It has traditionally been the case under common law that all the writs for chattels given in the Register were set a pecuniary value. Moreover, it does not follow from this that English law has *in practice* adopted the Roman rule that delivery of possession (*traditio*) passes property in the sense that third parties would be affected. This would make English law unititular in the Roman sense, namely, that it proceeds on the view that only one claim is worthy of protection. Although there is now a statutory provision under s. 8 of the Torts (Interference with Goods) Act 1977 where a defendant in possession can set up a *ius tertii* requiring the plaintiff to prove an absolute right, this plea will cease if the owner upon being called on to intervene in the action fails to do so and is then barred from asserting his title.

Whether the property in the goods has passed to the buyer is a matter of central importance. The answer is crucial for the resolution of those issues to which property rights are normally relevant.

Effects of property passing

Risk and frustration The principle of *res perit domino* is enshrined in s. 20(1) of the Sale of Goods Act 1979 which provides that risk is transferred when property passes. This is of relevance also with regard to the doctrine of frustration. By virtue of s. 7, if there is an agreement to sell specific goods and subsequently the goods without any fault on the part of the seller or buyer perish before the risk passes to the buyer, the agreement is avoided (see chapter 4).

Insolvency of a party The courts are often called upon to determine whether property has passed when one party has become insolvent and it is necessary to decide whether the goods are assets which can be used to discharge his debts. Where property has passed, the relationship between seller and buyer is simply one of creditor and debtor. Nonetheless, ss. 41 to 48 of the Sale of Goods Act

1979 will give the unpaid seller certain real remedies such as the unpaid seller's lien and the right of stoppage in transit (see chapter 6).

Third-party claims The House of Lords decision in *Leigh and Sillavan Ltd* v *Aliakmon Shipping Co. Ltd* [1986] AC 785 emphasised that if the goods are damaged in transit between the seller and buyer, the latter will only be able to sue the carrier, in the absence of a bailment relationship between them (see *The Winkfield* [1902] P 42), if property has passed before the harm occurs. In a similar fashion, if the seller makes an unauthorised resale of the goods, the question of property location will determine the issue whether his liability is merely for breach of contract, or whether the resale amounts to conversion.

The security-of-property principle The general principle is that of *nemo dat quod non habet* which is discussed in chapter 7. However, a party who has merely a possessory title to the goods will have, in some circumstances, the power to dispose of them by virtue of statutory intervention to protect innocent third parties who are misled by appearances.

Tracing rights The infiltration of the trust doctrine into the contract of sale is highly significant especially in the light of the line of cases dealing with retention of title clauses. These are discussed in chapter 12.

PROPERTY PASSING AND IDENTIFICATION

The requirement of identification as a prerequisite for the passing of property under the Sale of Goods Act 1979 enjoys a long historical basis in the common law. However, the proprietary solution anticipated under s. 16 of the Sale of Goods Act 1979 where property passing is postponed until the goods are ascertained has proved problematic in sales of part of a bulk. Even holders of bills of lading are prejudiced since s. 1 of the Bills of Lading Act 1855 transfers the shipper's rights and liabilities to a named consignee or endorsee only when property passes (see Law Commission Report, *Rights of Suit in Respect of Carriage of Goods by Sea* (Law Com. No. 196), (London, 1991)). In recent years, developments in methods of trading in different commodities have increased the incidence of sales of part of a bulk and these have tended to highlight the major legal problems which arise in this area.

The modern commercial context
The requirement for ascertainment of goods in order for property to pass is illustrated in the decision of Oliver J in *Re London Wine Co. (Shippers) Ltd* 1986 PCC 121. It is worth setting out the facts not least because, as the eminent American commercial lawyer Karl Llewellyn pointed out, they help to focus upon the narrow legal issues which arise in a particular commercial context. The facts of the case revolved around the receivership of the London Wine Company and the issue before Oliver J was whether the debenture holder, the National Westminster Bank, had property in the stocks of wine at the relevant date (28 August 1974), which was the date of the crystallisation of the floating

charge. This case demonstrates that the passing of property involves questions of law rather than the mere intention of the parties.

The London Wine Co. dealt in wine and operated a scheme whereby customers could buy wine as an investment. The wine was sold either lying in bond, to which charges for duty, delivery and documentation together with VAT were added to the price quoted, or otherwise, such as where duty had been paid and delivered. People interested in buying wine filled in an application form. When an order was received, the company prepared an invoice subject to its usual terms and conditions which included the following condition 5:

> All goods and the documents relating thereto shall be subject to a particular lien for all moneys owing in respect of the goods and also to a general lien for all sums owing to the company either by customers or any person who has been the owner of the goods whilst in possession of the company.

The contemplation was, therefore, that the wine would belong to the purchasers who were described as 'sole and beneficial owners'. There was also a provision for the wine to be stored subject to a storage charge and an insurance payment. When the customer paid for the wine, the customer would receive a certificate of title from the company, the purpose of which was to enable the customer to establish title to the wine sold. Since the wine at issue before the judge was bought as an investment, it was clearly to the advantage of the customers to keep the wine in storage. In this respect, the warehousing policy of the company was crucial as to whether the wine bought had been ascertained, or unconditionally appropriated for the purpose of passing of property. In fact, this was found deficient because with respect to a completed sale, the company stock book would allocate the wine sold to a particular consignment reference number at a particular warehouse, but there was no notification of the sale to the warehouse concerned except where the customer wanted to mortgage or charge his wine. In this event, the company would write to the appropriate warehousemen instructing them to send the chargee a form of letter (a warehouse warrant) confirming that the appropriate quantity of wine was held in the name of the chargee. The certificate of title sent to the buyer/chargor was then cancelled.

It was generally impracticable to segregate and identify particular cases of wine and allocate them to individual purchasers or chargees. No attempt was made to do so, and in the situations referred to by Oliver J there had been no segregation or appropriation of the wine. This was primarily because large bulk orders were involved, the wine being shipped direct to the warehouse by the importer and each consignment (commonly a container load) was given a reference number. The warehousemen's stock control card only noted any physical withdrawal of the wine, for example, for consumption or sale, or a note as to how many cases in a particular consignment were held to the order of such and such a chargee or transferee without identifying the cases.

The case is important because it confronts directly the question whether property can pass where no act of appropriation had taken place at the date of receivership (see pp. 52–5). The purchasers had, however, paid for the wine and received an assurance that they had title to it. It was argued by counsel for

Basic concepts of personal property

the claimants that although the wine had not been appropriated to the contract, nevertheless, property passed as soon as the wine was ascertained through the process of exhaustion. The difficulty was that in all the case law concerned with ascertainment by process of exhaustion the location of the goods was clearly identified, but in *Re London Wine Co. (Shippers) Ltd* the undertaking given by the company was to deliver so many cases of the specified type of wine 'lying in bond' and there was no link between the wine sold with any given consignment or warehouse.

Ascertainment by process of exhaustion

In *Karlshamns Olje Fabriker* v *Eastport Navigation Corp.* [1982] 1 All ER 208, Mustill J, following *Wait and James* v *Midland Bank Ltd* (1926) 24 Ll L Rep 33, held that goods can be ascertained through a process of exhaustion where this was the intention of the parties. The facts involved four identical contracts through which the claimants purchased from S altogether 6,000 tonnes of copra c.i.f. Karlshamn (Sweden). The respondents' ship, *Elafi*, loaded 22,000 tonnes of Philippine copra in bulk, 16,000 tonnes for Rotterdam and Hamburg buyers, and 6,000 tonnes consigned to the claimants at Karlshamn who received 12 endorsed bills of lading each for 500 tonnes and paid the price. Discovering during transit that over 22,000 tonnes were shipped, the shippers sold any surplus without any bill of lading to F, who promptly resold to the claimants. After discharging at Rotterdam and Hamburg the *Elafi* delivered the remaining 6,843 tonnes, unseparated, at Karlshamn, but during discharge sea water damaged 825 tonnes owing to the respondents' neglect to make the *Elafi* seaworthy.

In this case the analysis of Mustill J proceeded by stages. First, had one c.i.f. contract covered the entire cargo, making it both ascertained and appropriated, *ab initio*, property in the whole would doubtless have passed on transfer of the shipping documents. Secondly, had two buyers each contracted for half the cargo, regardless of intentions and c.i.f. terms, s. 16 of the Sale of Goods Act 1979 would have prevented property passing until ascertainment by physical separation of the goods deliverable under each contract (*Comptoir d'Achat et de Ventre Lu Boerenbond Belge SA* v *Luis de Ridder Ltda* [1949] AC 293). Thirdly, had four parallel contracts with the *same* sellers covered the whole cargo, s. 16 must be interpreted broadly according to its purpose of determining the earliest time a buyer may acquire rights *in rem* good against everyone, so ascertainment in bulk would suffice without separation and identification of particular parts to particular contracts. Otherwise, absurdly, even delivery of the whole could pass no property unless and until the buyer separated it into parts corresponding with the several contracts. In such cases, as in *Wait and James*, the facts constituting ascertainment in bulk and so freeing property to pass also constitute appropriation in bulk for the purpose of applying the presumption in s. 18, rule 5(1), of the Sale of Goods Act 1979 (see pp. 52–5). It is otherwise in c.i.f. contracts where another intention appears. Had the claimants purchased all cargo destined for Karlshamn from the same sellers, property would have passed when completed discharge at Hamburg ascertained the goods despite the earlier transfer of documents.

The last part of Mustill J's analysis was concerned with the purchase of parts of the Karlshamn cargo from different sellers. The fact that had the excess cargo not been resold to the claimants, F would have got no title until its ascertainment by separation at Karlshamn did not prevent F sooner conferring title on the claimants. The implied obligation of a seller of unascertained goods is not to own but to have a right to sell them when the property is to pass (s. 12). Extending the reasoning in *Wait and James*, the uniting in one buyer's hands of *all* purchase contracts, even if made with different sellers, could ascertain the bulk and free the property to pass in it. Had s. 18, rule 5(1), made appropriation a precondition of property passing instead of merely rebuttably presuming such a need, difficulty could have ensued as to which seller would be responsible if the bulk delivered proved deficient, or excessive or defective. Moreover, on the basis of the facts, the parties' intentions rebutted that presumption. Regarding the part purchased from S under bills of lading, the usual c.i.f. intention that property should pass on transfer of the documents took delayed effect immediately the completed Hamburg discharge ascertained the remaining bulk. Regarding the part purchased from F, all parties to its sale and resale intended that on completion of the Hamburg discharge, property should pass in whatever excess copra remained aboard. So the claimants owned the whole Karlshamn cargo before the damage occurred and could sue in tort.

A vital distinction must be drawn between goods which are wholly unascertained in the sense that the source is not identified and those which come from an identifiable source. In the case of the latter, the seller has lost the power to substitute other goods, whereas, with regard to the former, the court is reluctant to interfere with what is considered to be acts of internal organisation of the seller in segregating goods. Thus in *Aldridge* v *Johnson* (1857) 7 E & B 885, the plaintiff had agreed to buy 100 quarters of barley out of 200 which he had seen in bulk form, and it was arranged that he should send 200 sacks for the barley which the seller would fill and dispatch to the plaintiff by rail. The seller filled 155 out of the 200 sacks, but immediately prior to his bankruptcy the seller emptied the barley out of the filled sacks and mixed it back in with the bulk. It was held that the property passed in the barley in the 155 sacks. Lord Campbell CJ said at p. 899:

> Looking to all that was done, when the bankrupt put the barley into the sacks *eo instanti* the property in each sack-full vested in the plaintiff. I consider that here was a priori an assent by the plaintiff. He had inspected and approved of the barley in bulk. He sent his sacks to be filled out of that bulk.

The common law position

The English rule is well-established; where separation is needed from a larger mass the goods are not ascertained and property cannot pass. In *Hanson* v *Meyer* (1805) 6 East 614, it was held that even though part of an order of starch had been weighed and delivered under a delivery order, since weighing had not been done for the remaining undelivered starch, the seller could countermand delivery of this starch upon the bankruptcy of the buyer. Similarly in *Shepley* v *Davis* (1814) 5 Taunt 617 (see also *Gillett* v *Hill* (1834) 2 Cr & M 530), it was held that property could not pass to the buyer since the separating and weighing of 10 tons of hemp from a mass of 30 tons had to be done before delivery. In this case, Gibbs CJ rejected the argument of Serjeant Lens for the defendants that there was a tenancy in common and that the defendant was merely trying to recover his share from the other, an approach which was based upon the authority of *Whitehouse* v *Frost* (1810) 12 East 614. In that case, the owners of 40 tons of oil in a particular cistern sold 10 tons of it to Frost who sold it to Townsend and gave him a delivery order addressed to the former owners which Townsend duly lodged with them. Townsend gave Frost a bill of exchange, but before payment he became bankrupt and the plaintiffs, his assignees, demanded the 10 tons of oil. It was held that the property in the oil had passed to Townsend and the plaintiffs were therefore entitled to recover. A comparison may be drawn here with the position in the USA. In *Pleasants* v *Pendleton* (1828) 27 Va (6 Rand) 473, it was held that the owner of fungible goods could, by use of a delivery order, convey an interest in an undivided bulk or mass without any physical appropriation or identification of specific goods. This was adopted in s. 6(2) of the Uniform Sales Act and also s. 2-105(4) of the Uniform Commercial Code (UCC). Under the UCC tender to the buyer of a delivery order when the goods are represented by a negotiable warehouse receipt does not pass the risk to the buyer until the elapsing of a reasonable time for the buyer to present the delivery order to the warehouse (see UCC (1987) s. 2-503(4) and s. 2-509(2).)

In a series of cases during the 19th century and early 20th century culminating in *Laurie and Morewood* v *Dudin and Sons* [1926] 1 KB 223, the approach taken in *Whitehouse* v *Frost* was specifically disapproved. However, if the English courts had pressed the strict approach to the rule that appropriation of fungible goods from a larger mass had to be made before property would pass to its logical extreme, the delivery note would have lost much of its practical identity. However, in *White* v *Wilks* (1813) 5 Taunt 176, the court in which Lord Mansfield presided contemplated recovery on the basis of attornment as well as estoppel, and it is by adopting this analysis that English courts have resurrected *Whitehouse* v *Frost*. By shifting the emphasis from the property/sale of goods concept to a contractual concept, the interest of the third party is protected without doing violence to the usual rule that property cannot pass between seller and buyer until the goods have become ascertained or appropriated to the contract. We shall now proceed to consider this and subsequently return to the property question by focusing upon tenancy in common.

Attornment
To a great extent, attornment represents the legal solution to a dilemma caused by the dynamic nature of trade where ownership of goods will often be transmitted along a chain of successive vendors and purchasers. Attornment arises from a change in the *character* of possession without any change in the possession itself. In a sense, attornment reflects the materialism of the common law with its emphasis on 'actual receipt'. Thus, in *Farina* v *Home* (1846) 16 M & W 119, Parke B said that there could be no actual receipt 'until the bailee has attorned so to speak'.

The traditional pattern of an attornment envisages a triangular relationship arrangement with the seller drawing upon the warehouseman by issuing the delivery order to the buyer who then presents the document to the warehouseman/bailee. It follows from this that the bailee will have no better title than his bailor. The question of attornment against the owner or the person with the better right to possess is irrelevant because there is superiority of title. Nonetheless, in order to confer a proprietary right the warehouseman must hold specific goods. It may be that the very act of attornment will constitute appropriation of goods to the contract, otherwise, the buyer can only have a personal claim against the warehouseman on the basis of estoppel. In this respect, it is irrelevant that the attornee has no title or a defective title in the goods (*Woodley* v *Coventry* (1863) 2 H & C 164), an approach which can be justified on the grounds of security in commercial transactions.

Clearly, it would be unfair to make the bailee liable for every change of ownership. In fact, attornment represents a dilemma for the bailee since, in recognising another's title in the goods, it is inconsistent with the bailee's position as against the original bailor. In the light of this, it is not surprising to find some difference of opinion among the authorities as to whether entry on the books of the warehouseman is sufficient to create an attornment.

In *Re London Wine Co. (Shippers) Ltd* 1986 PCC 121, the issue of warehouse receipts acknowledging to the reservists that the warehouse held wine to the account of their purchasers/pledgees did focus the attention of the court. On the facts, it was clear that since the goods were unascertained, no property could pass by virtue of the attornment, though there was little doubt that both the warehouseman and the vendor were estopped from denying their acknowledgement. This can be illustrated by *Knights* v *Wiffen* (1870) LR 5 QB 660, where a seller of unascertained goods was estopped by his assent to the buyer's delivery order from denying that he had appropriated the goods to the contract. A requirement that the attornee should act in reliance on the attornment was satisfied by inaction on his part in redeeming his price from an intermediate vendor on the ground that he thought that he had title in the goods. The difficulty with the estoppel theory in the *London Wine* context is that it would not bind the bank following the crystallisation of the floating charge. The wine had not been appropriated to the contract so that no interest had in fact been created which could affect a bona fide purchaser who was not 'privy' to the estoppel (*Simm* v *Anglo-American Telegraph Co.* (1879) 5 QBD 188). Interestingly, even if the issue of the bank's liability was not in question, the estoppel approach is not without difficulty since it hinges on precisely the nature of the representation made. As such it could be argued, for example, that the representation made by the vendor was an undertaking to deliver the goods for which he might have been liable to do contractually and nothing more.

Symbolic possession of goods obviating the requirement of ascertainment

It is not surprising to see the delivery order figuring largely in the problem of the passing of property in part of a bulk since one of its major functions is to facilitate the sale of a portion from a larger mass of goods prior to physical separation. Although the use of separate bills of lading describing the specified goods would obviate the need for delivery orders, the practicalities of trade, particularly the dynamic nature of a transaction which may involve a string of sellers and buyers, often makes the delivery order the only feasible way for a middle seller to break down a total shipment in order to subsell.

The law is often confronted with the dilemma of having to determine priority between two equally innocent parties, namely, the original seller and the sub-buyer. On the basis of the rule of law encapsulated in s. 16 of the Sale of Goods Act 1979 that property must be ascertained, the position of the sub-buyer would seem to be impossible. However, since one of the policies of English law is to foster trade, the inclusion of the delivery order brings into focus different policy factors than that confronted by the need to protect the owner. The basis of the sub-buyer's claim could be rather the transfer to him of a document of title. It should be noted that a delivery order is an undertaking to deliver possession and, as such, is not a document of title. Even so, s. 1(4) of the Factors Act 1889, for the purpose of that Act, defines a document of title as including, *inter alia*: '. . . any bill of lading, dock warrant, warehouse-keeper's certificate and warrant or order for the delivery of goods'. This is also the position under s. 61(1) of the Sale of Goods Act 1979. (For examples of documents which were held not even to come under the extended definition see *Gunn* v *Bolckow, Vaughan and Co.* (1875) LR 10 Ch App 491; *Dublin City Distillery Ltd* v *Doherty* [1914] AC 823.) The delivery order has no precise definition in English law having at various times been referred to as a 'delivery note', 'overside order', 'ship's release' and 'warrants' (see *Colin and Sheilds* v *W. Weddell and Co. Ltd* [1952] 2 All ER 337; *Inglis* v *Robertson and Baxter* [1898] AC 616; *Wardar's (Import and Export) Co. Ltd* v *W. Norwood and Sons Ltd* [1968] 2 QB 663).

Under s. 47(2) of the Sale of Goods Act 1979, the unpaid seller loses his lien if a document of title has been transferred to a buyer where the buyer has transferred this to a person who takes in good faith and for valuable consideration. Section 47(2) provides:

Where a document of title to goods has been lawfully transferred to any person as buyer or owner of the goods, and that person transfers the document to a person who takes it in good faith and for valuable consideration, then —

    (a) if the last-mentioned transfer was by way of sale the unpaid seller's right of lien or retention or stoppage in transit is defeated; and

    (b) if the last-mentioned transfer was made by way of pledge or other disposition for value, the unpaid seller's right of lien or retention or stoppage in transit can only be exercised subject to the rights of the transferee.

Despite this, the unpaid seller's lien or right of stoppage in transit (see chapter 6) is not affected by any subsale or other disposition unless the seller assented thereto which may, for example, take the form of attornment or estoppel. It would seem following *D.F. Mount Ltd* v *Jay and Jay (Provisions) Co. Ltd* [1960] 1 QB 159, that s. 47 is limited to the case where the buyer transfers to the sub-buyer the *same* delivery order as that issued by the original seller, although the court held that there was no such limitation with respect to s. 25(2) of the Sale of Goods Act 1893 (now s. 25(1) of the Sale of Goods Act 1979). Significantly, the court held that s. 25(2) was not confined to specific goods and that the sub-buyer, the holder of the delivery note, effectively overrode the rights of the unpaid seller (see chapter 6).

The question of ascertainment of goods and the effect of a delivery order was examined in the pre-First World War decision of *Ant. Jurgens Margarinefabrieken* v *Louis Dreyfus and Co.* [1914] 3 KB 40. In this case, an English broker entered into a contract with a merchant who did business in England and Germany to purchase 2,640 bags of mowra (or mahwa) seed on behalf of his principal. The merchant who had received a shipment of 6,400 bags of this seed in Germany, issued its negotiable delivery order on its German branch in favour of the broker in return for his cheque. The broker's cheque was dishonoured, but he sold the delivery order to a buyer who demanded delivery of the seed. The merchant refused delivery because of the dishonoured cheque. The court held that under s. 10 of the Factors' Act 1889 and s. 47 of the Sale of Goods Act 1893, the transfer of a document of title to the buyer who took in good faith and for value had the effect of defeating the seller's lien in the same way as a negotiable bill of lading would have done. In addition, the court held that the fact that the delivery order was given for unspecified goods would not have prevented this result, following *Capital and Counties Bank Ltd* v *Warriner* (1896) 12 TLR 216. Here a warehouse, in response to a delivery order given by the seller-bailor of goods, issued its negotiable warrant to the buyers of 1,500 quarters of wheat which had not been separated from 2,918 quarters of wheat in the warehouse. The buyers endorsed the warrant to the bank to cover an overdraft. However, the buyers failed to pay for the wheat, and the seller called upon the warehouse to stop delivery. It was held by Matthew J that the wording of s. 9 of the Factors Act 1889 (substantially reproduced in s. 25(1) of the Sale of Goods Act 1979) which refers to a person 'having bought or *agreed to buy* goods' this effectively means that where the buyer obtains a document of title to the goods, this is legally equivalent to having possession of the goods with the consent of the owner, *even though the goods have not been ascertained*.

The approach taken by Matthew J in the *Capital Counties* case has been criticised on the basis that s. 25(1) of the Sale of Goods Act 1979 must be read consistently with s. 16. One solution suggested (see Nicol, L., 'Passing of Property in Part of a Bulk' (1974) 42 MLR 129) to reconcile s. 16 and s. 25(1) entails casting upon the subbuyer the risk of the seller's insolvency and involves the fiction of a notional agency. Moreover, following *Leigh and Sillavan Ltd* v *Aliakmon Shipping Co. Ltd* [1986] AC 785, the subbuyer will not be able to sue the warehouseman or carrier in negligence. It may be that a more radical solution would be to focus upon the rationale of s. 16 itself and the requirement of identification. This theme will be of great significance to a prepaying financing buyer where there has been a failure to appropriate the goods to the contract of sale (see chapter 8).

Tenancy in common

In England, there has been a reluctance to admit that parties to a sale can have a proprietary interest in a certain mass as tenants according to their respective proportion. Indeed, sometimes, it is considered a misnomer to apply tenancy in common principles to sale since the purpose of a sale transaction is to transfer property in goods which have been specifically identified, in the sense of being unconditionally appropriated to the contract of sale. Unfortunately, such an argument fails to take into account that English law rarely finds that chattels are unique for the purposes of the remedy of specific performance where the courts tend to start with the assumption that damages are usually adequate. Despite this, a more fundamental objection is that focusing attention on whether property has passed is itself based upon the often fictitious intention of the parties.

It is not the case that property passage alone can adequately solve the narrow issues which arise in the context of sale of goods. These issues include: Who stands the loss if goods are destroyed without the fault of either party after the contract of sale is made but before delivery? Does the buyer have an insurable interest in undelivered goods? Who takes the risk of the buyer or seller's insolvency? These questions pose utterly different policy considerations and they appear similar only if the discussion is pitched at the level of title passing. It is significant, therefore, that some of the cases which are said to establish tenancy in common were concerned not so much with the transfer of property but rather the transfer of risk (*Inglis* v *Stock* (1885) 10 App Cas 263; *Sterns Ltd* v *Vickers Ltd* [1923] 1 KB 78; *Inglis* v *James Richardson and Sons Ltd* (1913) 29 OLR 229). The issue of the transfer of risk must have figured largely in the approach taken in *South Australian Insurance Co.* v *Randell* (1869) LR 3 PC 101. This case involved an action on a policy of insurance against fire upon the stock of wheat and other grains in a mill which contained an exemption clause concerning 'goods held in trust'. It was held that the clause was inapplicable to grain (which had not been insured separately) since it was never intended by the parties that the identical wheat delivered should be returned by the millers to the depositors. The transaction was, thereby, characterised as a sale to the millers. This conclusion contrasts with the approach taken in the USA in the so-called 'grain elevator' cases, where, if the parties can evince an intention to sell an unseparated fraction of a whole mass, they are granted a joint interest amounting to such a proportion of the whole as the indicated number, weight or measure bears to the entire amount. The grain bin may have been emptied and refilled several times before the holder demanded delivery, but it has been held that this practice does not militate against the finding of a tenancy in common. The essential issue is whether the bailee *can extract for himself at will without accounting to the others*, if so, no tenancy in common is presumed (see now UCC (1987), s. 2-105(4)).

CREATION OF PROPERTY INTERESTS AT COMMON LAW

The common law authorities mainly revolve around three scenarios which will now be discussed.

Mixture of materials belonging to different owners ('*confusio*' or '*commixtio*')

The common law has approached the mixture of fungibles in an identifiable mass from the vantage of the law of torts rather than from the point of view of the law of property. The outcome depends upon whether or not the act of confusion has taken place with the consent of the owners; where there has been accidental or inadvertent admixture, the several claimants become owners in common according to their contribution to the resultant mass. Thus in *Sandeman and Sons* v *Tyzack and Branfoot Steamship Co. Ltd* [1913] AC 680, bales of jute were shipped to various consignees. Following the discharge of the ship, some bales were missing and some others were not marked and could not be identified as belonging to any particular consignment. Lord Moulton stated the principles of law which govern the confusion of chattels when he said at pp. 694–5:

> My lords, if we proceed upon the principles of English law, I do not think it a matter of difficulty to define the legal consequences of the goods of 'A' becoming indistinguishably and inseparably mixed with the goods of 'B'. . . . if the mixing has taken place by accident or other cause, for which neither of the owners is responsible, a different state of things arises. Neither owner has done anything to forfeit his right to the possession of his own property, and if neither party is willing to abandon that right the only equitable solution of the difficulty, and the one accepted by the law, is that 'A' and 'B' become owners in common of the mixed property.

This principle has been applied in many cases. (See, for example, *Buckley* v *Gross* (1863) 3 B & S 566; *Spence* v *Union Marine Insurance Co. Ltd* (1868) LR 3 CP 427; *Gill & Duffus (Liverpool) Ltd* v *Scruttons Ltd* [1953] 1 WLR 1407. See also *Jones* v *Moore* (1841) 4 Y & C Ex 351, where the price of the salvaged oils was distributed amongst the parties concerned as owners in common.) In this respect, it is worth noting that s. 188 of the Law of Property Act 1925 empowers the court to order a division of chattels based upon a valuation or otherwise following an application by a person(s) interested in a moiety or upwards. Furthermore, a co-owner excluded from possession has the right to rent from the other (see *Jones* v *Jones* [1977] 1 WLR 438).

Mixture with consent The relationship between tenancy in common (inherent in mixture by consent) and a commodity-processing bailment is close. This was demonstrated in the recent decision of the New Zealand Court of Appeal in *Coleman* v *Harvey* [1989] 1 NZLR 723 and the facts are, therefore, worth dwelling upon. The defendant owned a company which refined silver from 'silver scrap' found in coins, X-ray film, torpedo batteries and jewellery. In 1978, a contract was concluded between the defendant on behalf of his company and the plaintiff, relating to the refining of silver coins supplied by the plaintiff, which was calculated to produce 166 kg of fine silver. In addition to the coins, the company agreed to refine materials from its own sources and, out of ingots so produced, hold in store the 166 kg for the plaintiff who, in return, agreed to supply the company with other material containing silver for a period of 12 months. The ingots were produced, but none was set aside for the plaintiff; instead the ingots were disposed of in the ordinary course of business. When the plaintiff demanded the ingots 49 kg of silver were delivered, leaving an outstanding balance of 117 kg. The defendant's company went into receivership and the question before the court was whether the plaintiff had a proprietary interest in the unrefined metal in the possession of the insolvent company capable of being converted by the defendant as a joint tortfeasor with his company.

The defendant claimed that the original delivery of the coins constituted a sale and that the coins lost their identity by chemical process, the property then passing to the company. It was held by the Court of Appeal that since the plaintiff's coins were intended to be embodied in the ingots to be set aside for him, this was not a case of sale; rather, the transaction constituted a loan of something not to be returned in its original state but to be replaced by something similar or equivalent, that is, commodity processing. A distinction was drawn with the Privy Council decision in *South Australian Insurance Co. v Randell* (1869) LR 3 PC 101 which involved the mixing of farmers' corn by a miller, great importance being attached to the fact that the farmers had no more right to claim at any time an equal quantity of corn of like quality without reference to any specific bulk from which it was to be taken. This was not the position in *Coleman*, where the New Zealand Court of Appeal held that until the company performed its contract to appropriate to the plaintiff specific ingots, the plaintiff should be treated as having a proprietary interest as a tenant in common in any silver to which his coins contributed. Accordingly, he could recover in conversion against the defendant. It is worth noting that in England, s. 10 of the Torts (Interference with Goods) Act 1977 specifically provides that co-ownership is no defence to an action founded on conversion or trespass to goods where the defendant, without the authority of the other co-owner, either:

(a) destroys the goods, or disposes of the goods in a way giving a good title to the entire property in the goods, or otherwise does anything equivalent to the destruction of the other's interest in the goods; or

(b) purports to dispose of the goods in a way which would give a good title to the entire property in the goods if he was acting with the authority of all co-owners.

Mixture without consent Where the confusion has taken place without the consent of the party with whose property the substance has been mixed, English law appears to give the property in the resultant mass to the innocent party. In this respect, as early as 1615, Coke CJ in *Warde v Æyre* (1615) 2 Bulst 323 stated the law to be, at p. 324:

> ... that if I.S. have a heap of corn, and I.D. will intermingle his corn with the corn of I.S. he shall here have all the corn, because this was so done by I.D. of his own wrong ... and if this should be otherwise, a man should be made to be a trespasser, *volens nolens*, by the taking of his goods again, and

for the avoiding of this inconvenience, the law in such a case is, that he shall now retain all.

Nevertheless, there may be important exceptions, for example, if the amount of the goods wrongfully mixed is small in comparison with the wrongdoer's goods. Such an approach is correct in principle because there is no compelling reason why the supplier should enjoy a windfall which may be at the expense of the debtor's other creditors.

The above approach is confirmed in *Indian Oil Corporation Ltd* v *Greenstone Shipping SA (Panama)* [1988] QB 345 where it was known with reasonable precision how much was contributed by the innocent party. Here the owners of a vessel on which the receivers' cargo of Soviet crude oil was shipped had mixed that cargo with other oil belonging to the owners already on the vessel. It was possible to work out with considerable precision the amounts of oil belonging to the two parties. Any doubt about the quantity would have been resolved in favour of the innocent party. Indeed, Staughton J approved a general statement of Lord Eldon in *Lupton* v *White* (1808) 15 Ves Jr 432 that in some cases, a decision has to be made 'not upon the notions that strict justice was done, but upon this: that it was the only justice that could be done'. Presumably, had there been a diversity in quality in the intermixed substances, the whole would be divided and greater allowance made to the owner whose substance was better or finer than the other. The significance of this case cannot be underestimated because the practice of commingling consignments by different shippers is accepted in many areas of commerce, for example, most of the Grain and Feed Trade Association standard contracts contain a pro rata clause.

The issue of identification Where the property can be identified, different principles will apply. Although the wrongdoer may have been liable in conversion, this should not deprive a defendant of his own identifiable property, as in *Spence* v *Union Marine Insurance Co. Ltd* (1868) LR 3 CP 427. In this case, the plaintiffs claimed from their insurers the value of 41 bales of cotton as a total loss from a ship that was wrecked. There were 2,493 bales specifically marked; 2,262 bales were saved and of those bales only 617 could be identified. The plaintiffs, who held a bill of lading for 43 bales received two as indubitably theirs. They sought compensation for the other 41 since the insurance value of the total loss was worth more than any proportionate share granted of the recovered cotton because the price of cotton had fallen. The court held that the exact size of the plaintiff's interest as co-owners could be determined and this consisted of 43/2,493 of the 231 bales entirely lost which amounted to the value of four bales. Thus, they were offered 39 bales minus two (the two bales actually delivered) which made 37.

Accession ('*accessio*' or '*adjunctio*')
The distinction between the creation of a new thing and the accession of one thing belonging to one owner on to another's property is particularly elusive. In the former, labour competes with material but in the second material competes with material. Of course, in practice, labour also enters into accession

through the act of bringing the two materials together. There must be cases where both the materials as well as labour are equally essential, especially, in the case of an artistic creation using precious materials such as diamonds. However, as a matter of principle, it is inappropriate to take into account the relative economic value of the elements involved, particularly where one of those elements is skill.

The central problem in accession is that of identification, so materials which have not acceded to or attached themselves to property may be recovered. There are two aspects to this problem: first, the question of accession to *personal* property; second, goods supplied subject to a hire-purchase or reservation of title agreement may have become so attached to *land* as to form part of the land.

Affixation as an accession to personal property This problem is particularly acute in the context of hire-purchase contracts. Much has been written about what constitutes attachment, and certain tests have been identified (see generally Goode, R.M., *Hire Purchase Law and Practice*, 2nd ed. (London, 1970), ch. 33). At one extreme is the test whether the annexation is so complete as to destroy the utility of the principal chattel. Such a test may be objected to on the basis that it is too harsh on the owner of the accessory as it involves another exception to the *nemo dat quod non habet* rule, i.e., that a transferor cannot transfer a better title than he himself has (see, for example, *Regina Chevrolet Sales Ltd* v *Riddell* [1942] 3 DLR 159). At the other extreme is the test whether the accessory is so affixed that it cannot be removed without material damage to the principal goods. Thus, in *Rendell* v *Associated Finance Pty Ltd* [1957] VR 604, a financier supplied a Chevrolet truck on hire-purchase to Pell subject to a provision for the ownership of any new accession. Pell obtained a second-hand engine for the truck from Rendell on hire-purchase. Following Pell's default under the main hire-purchase agreement, the defendants recovered the truck. The plaintiffs successfully sued in conversion for the engine and the court held that since there was no accession there was no conversion. The fact that the attached engine was obviously essential to the operation of the goods was considered irrelevant since the goods were identifiable and severable without much damage to the property (see also *Firestone Tire and Rubber Co. of Canada Ltd* v *Industrial Acceptance Corporation Ltd* (1970) 75 WWR 621). Nonetheless, where the buyer attaches his own property to the goods, the legal position may be regulated by an express term in the contract of supply. This could very well provide that title to the accessory should pass to the supplier notwithstanding the fact that the degree of annexation is not such as would satisfy the common law test for an accession (see *Akron Tyre Co. Pty Ltd* v *Kittson* (1951) 82 CLR 477). The question whether the agreement constitutes a bill of sale does not arise here since the passing of property in the accessory takes place following the occurrence of an external act (see chapter 15).

Where the goods are identifiable but not separable If a manufacturer wrongfully joins the supplier's property with his own in such a way that they are identifiable but cannot be separated without substantially damaging the supplier's property, this should not necessarily deprive the manufacturer of his property because the case is one of identifiable items and not one of confusion.

The creation of a new thing ('*specificatio*')

There is very little English authority on the commingling of two or more products in such a way as to perpetrate a loss of separate identity. It seems probable that the maker of the new thing becomes its owner irrespective of whether he has contributed any of the materials used, the former proprietors being relegated to an action in conversion or wrongful interference. This approach was confirmed by Goff LJ in the Court of Appeal in *Clough Mill Ltd v Martin* [1985] 1 WLR 111 (see pp. 265–7) where Blackstone's *Commentaries*, 17th ed. (1830), was cited as authority for the proposition that if A's material is lawfully used by B to create new goods, whether or not B incorporates other material of his own, the property in the new goods will generally vest in B, at least where the goods are not reducible to the original materials. Certainly this appears to be the position in Scotland. A dramatic example is *International Banking Corporation v Ferguson Shaw and Sons* 1910 SC 182 when A turned B's oil into lard; it was held that B was entitled only to compensation and not to the lard.

The Scottish Law Commission report, *Corporeal Moveables: Mixing Union and Creation* (Memorandum 28), (Edinburgh, 1976), has considered the problems regarding the ownership of a new product where another's materials have been used in the process of manufacture and there is neither a contract nor any question of good-faith purchase between the parties. Two alternatives are suggested. The first provides that where materials cannot be conveniently separated, *pro rata* common ownership shall be enjoyed. This alternative involves a tenancy in common and may lead to problems where the value and character of the different contributions vary considerably. The second approach attributes specific ownership to the party who has economically contributed most to the new thing. However, it is questionable whether it is possible to measure relative economic worth of labour and materials, especially, in a manufacturing environment requiring a large initial outlay in machinery and energy. Under both alternatives, it is envisaged that the court would be given a discretion where the producer is in bad faith. It is understandable that the improver should not receive any legal protection if he makes an improvement with full knowledge of the ownership rights of another. With such knowledge, the improver's conduct is little more than an effort to exact payment for work performed without the owner's consent.

Although it was not really at issue in the *Clough Mill Ltd v Martin* [1985] 1 WLR 111, both Robert Goff and Oliver LJJ in the Court of Appeal said that, at common law, property in new goods made from material supplied could vest in the supplier so long as there was an agreement to this effect. This approach was also alluded to by Judge Rubin at first instance in *Borden (UK) Ltd v Scottish Timber Products Ltd* [1979] 2 Lloyd's Rep 169 at p. 171:

> ... unless the terms of the contract of supply contained some special term I find it difficult to discover any adequate reason why a court in the exercise

Basic concepts of personal property

of a discretion should order the manufacturer of the article to deliver that article to a supplier of a raw material particularly in a case where the raw material forms only a part and not an outstandingly large part of the elements required for the manufacturing process.

The theory here is that if the parties' agreement is put into effect, the buyer does not confer on the seller an interest in the property which could then be analysed in terms of mortgage or charge: when the new goods come into existence the ownership of them automatically vests in the seller. Nevertheless, parties cannot by their contractual stipulations alone alter the application of the principles and the rules of the law of property. It follows that if the supplier qualifies his interest in the finished product in order to avoid an unintended windfall for himself, this is tantamount to a security for the debt (see part 4).

PART 2   SALE AND SUPPLY OF GOODS

THREE
Definition and nature of contracts for the supply of goods

THE SALE CONTRACT

The statutory definition of sale encapsulated in s. 2 of the Sale of Goods Act 1979 contains a number of ingredients which distinguish sale from other transactions. It is worth setting out the definition in full:

(1) A contract of sale of goods is a contract by which the seller transfers or agrees to transfer the property in goods to the buyer for a money consideration, called the price.
(2) There may be a contract of sale between one part owner and another.
(3) A contract of sale may be absolute or conditional.
(4) Where under a contract of sale the property in the goods is transferred from the seller to the buyer the contract is called a sale.
(5) Where under a contract of sale the transfer of the property in the goods is to take place at a future time or subject to some condition later to be fulfilled the contract is called an agreement to sell.
(6) An agreement to sell becomes a sale when the time elapses or the conditions are fulfilled subject to which the property in the goods is to be transferred.

In order to satisfy the Sale of Goods Act 1979, the definition requires that the following components be present:

(a) *Contract for the sale of goods*. It should be noted that within the definition of a contract of sale a distinction is drawn between an executory sale or agreement to sell, and an executed transfer. The distinction is important because the executory contract creates only personal rights between the parties themselves whereas the executed contract gives the buyer an interest in the

Definition and nature of contracts for the supply of goods   45

goods. Nevertheless, the inclusion of both the executed and executory agreement within the statutory definition does emphasise that delivery of the goods is not an essential element of a sale contract. Even so, there must be a contract, a requirement that can prove particularly problematic in supply situations where the contract element is missing, for example, drugs prescribed under the National Health Service.

The statutory definition of 'goods' in s. 61(1) includes the following:

> 'goods' includes all personal chattels other than things in action and money, and in Scotland all corporeal moveables except money; and in particular 'goods' includes emblements, industrial growing crops, and things attached to or forming part of the land which are agreed to be severed before sale or under the contract of sale.

From this definition, assignments of choses in action are excluded and this is also the case with money. Of course, where the money is no longer legal tender as seen with half-crown coins and sixpences in *R* v *Thompson* [1980] QB 229, or where it is being transferred because of its curiosity value (*Moss* v *Hancock* [1899] 2 QB 111), or because of its inherent value such as krugerrands, in these circumstances 'money' can be considered to be 'goods' for the purposes of the statutory definition. The definition of goods also embraces *fructus industriales* including industrial crops and *fructus naturales* such as grass. In *Kursell* v *Timber Operators and Contractors Ltd* [1927] 1 KB 298, a contract for timber to be felled by the buyer at a future date was treated as a sale of goods. Minerals may also be included within the definition as being things 'forming part of the land'. However, much will depend upon the circumstances so that profits à prendre cannot be considered as a contract for the sale of goods being simply a privilege to work the land in question.

  (b)   *The parties to the contract.* The two parties envisaged under the Sale of Goods Act 1979 are the seller and buyer. The seller is defined in s. 61(1) as a 'person who sells or agrees to sell goods' and the buyer is defined in similar terms. Clearly, if a person has contracted to buy his own goods from someone else, the contract can be set aside on the basis of mistake and any money paid over will be recoverable because of total failure of consideration. At the same time, s. 2(2) of the Sale of Goods Act 1979 does specifically contemplate the sale by one part owner to another (but compare *Graff* v *Evans* (1882) 8 QBD 373; *Davies* v *Burnett* [1902] 1 KB 666) and there appears to be nothing wrong, as a matter of legal principle, in treating this as a sale. In one situation the buyer, as owner of the goods, will be able to recover them from a person having a legal authority to sell them, for example, a sheriff acting in execution of a writ of *fieri facias* to which the Sale of Goods Act 1979 will apply.

  (c)   *The transfer of property.* The underlying assumption to the passing of property is the prerequisite for identification. This has a long historical lineage in the common law where great importance was accorded to specificity as seen in the Yearbooks (18 Ed 4, 14). Here the Justices all agreed that a grant to kill and take a deer in the grantor's park conferred no property in any deer. Inevitably, this requirement of identification will pose problems in English law since the passage of property is linked to agreement rather than conveyance.

The requirement of identifiability is linked in no small measure with the concept of 'goods' as the subject-matter of the contract. The categorisation here of the nature of the goods will resolve such questions as:

(i) Whether the contract is a sale or an agreement to sell.
(ii) When property in the goods passes from the seller to the buyer.
(iii) Whether specific performance of the contract may be decreed.
(iv) Whether there is a valid contract of sale.
(v) Whether the doctrine of frustration applies to the contract in question.

(d) *Price.* The statutory definition of sale requires that the transfer of property be for 'a money consideration called the price'. Open-price contracts are specifically provided for in ss. 8 and 9 of the Sale of Goods Act 1979. Where there is an agreement to sell goods on the terms that the price is to be fixed by the valuation of a third party, and he cannot or does not make the valuation, the agreement is avoided; but if the goods or any part of them have been delivered to and appropriated by the buyer he must pay a reasonable price for them. Insofar as ss. 8 and 9 represent a codification of the common law rules they will also be applicable to other supply contracts, although, in the case of regulated agreements under s. 61(1) of the Consumer Credit Act 1974 there is a requirement to state in writing the price (see sch. 6).

The determination of the price is very important since the lack of this may be an indication that the contract has not been concluded. This is especially so where such expressions as 'Our offer is made on the basis of our current price list' are used. Nevertheless, especially in the case of executed contracts, the courts are anxious to uphold contracts between business people (*Foley* v *Classique Coaches Ltd* [1934] 2 KB 1). Indeed, this approach finds statutory expression in s. 9(1) of the Sale of Goods Act 1979.

A different problem to the above concerns attempts by suppliers to control minimum resale prices where there are statutory controls under the Resale Prices Act 1976. Detailed discussion of restrictive trade practices which are regulated by antitrust laws such as the Fair Trading Act 1973 and Competition Act 1980 are beyond the scope of this work. It is sufficient to note here that under ss. 1, 2 and 4 of the Resale Prices Act 1976, collective agreement between manufacturers and dealers to withhold supplies from those who do not observe laid-down resale prices or charges for hiring, hire-purchase, or conditional sale are unlawful. There are similar provisions in relation to individual restrictions regulating minimum resale prices or charges as between a manufacturer and a retailer. Exemptions may be granted on specified grounds with respect to a particular 'class of goods' (ss. 14 to 21 of the Resale Prices Act 1976).

The categorisation of goods

Existing and future goods The goods which form the subject matter of a contract of sale may be either existing goods which are owned and possessed by the seller, or they may be future goods in the sense that they are to be manufactured or acquired by the seller. It is clear from s. 12 of the Sale of Goods Act 1979 that it is not necessary for the seller to be the absolute owner of such goods, subject to the implied statutory condition as to right to sell the goods. The mere possession of the goods will be enough for them to be categorised as 'existing' goods.

A contract for the sale of future goods can only be an agreement to sell even though the seller anticipates in the contract of sale to effect a present sale of the goods. This must be the case as a matter of logic since the statutory definition of future goods encapsulated in s. 61(1) provides that such goods are 'to be manufactured or acquired by the seller after the making of the contract of sale.' There is nothing unusual, in the absence of a misrepresentation on the part of the seller, in his offering for sale goods which he expects or hopes to acquire. Thus in *Varley* v *Whipp* [1900] 1 QB 513, all parties proceeded upon the assumption that there was a contract for the sale of 'specific goods' notwithstanding that, at the time of the contract, the reaper which was the subject-matter of the sale was owned by a third party.

Specific and unascertained goods Specific goods are defined by s. 61(1) which lays down that, subject to contrary intention, this means 'goods identified and agreed upon at the time a contract is sale is made.' The meaning of specific goods under the Sale of Goods Act 1979 may vary depending upon the context in which it is used in the Act. In *Howell* v *Coupland* (1874) LR 9 QB 462, a contract of sale of 200 tons of potatoes to be grown on a specified field was held to be a sale of specific goods, whereas, in *H.R. & S. Sainsbury Ltd* v *Street* [1972] 1 WLR 834, a contract of sale of 275 tons of barley which was believed by both parties would be the yield of the seller's farm in the summer was held to constitute a sale of unascertained goods.

One major difficulty is that the expression 'unascertained goods' is nowhere defined in the Sale of Goods Act 1979. The Sale of Goods Act 1979 does use the expression by way of contrast to specific goods. It would appear that unascertained goods must mean such goods which are not identified and agreed upon at the time the contract is made but which will become ascertained at some later stage. The distinction between 'specific' and 'unascertained' goods may therefore only be one of degree. From this, it is consistent to categorise unascertained goods into the following types:

(a) Goods to be manufactured or grown by the seller.
(b) Goods of a designated type.
(c) An unidentified part of a specific whole which, for convenience, may be categorised as quasi-specific goods.

The distinction between specific and unascertained goods is particularly acute with the passing of property in part of a bulk (see pp. 29–37).

Future specific goods The uncritical approach to future goods would be to categorise them as being unascertained. However, the definition of future goods anticipated in the Sale of Goods Act 1979 does allow for the categorisation of the goods being specific, for example, property which in the course of nature may grow from the existing property of the seller including progeny in the case of animals, or crops as seen in *Howell* v *Coupland* (1876) 1 QBD 258. In any case, the common law recognised this by allowing the legal title to after-acquired potential property to vest in the purchaser automatically upon its coming into existence without any new act or transfer. This doctrine was never applied to the fruits of manufacture where the courts relied instead on the vague 'new act doctrine' the scope of which is notoriously uncertain (*Lunn* v *Thornton* (1845) 1 CB 379).

Ascertained goods The importance of ascertainment of goods goes to the heart of identifiability. Section 16 of the Sale of Goods Act 1979 provides for the case where the contract goods are not identified at the time when the contract is made:

> Where there is a contract for the sale of unascertained goods no property in the goods is transferred to the buyer unless and until the goods are ascertained.

It is envisaged under s. 61(1) that specific goods are those identified at the time of the contract whilst ascertained goods are those which were unidentified when the contract was made but become identified subsequently as the contract goods. For the most part, ascertained goods are treated as an aspect of specific goods which is a recognition of the *fact* of identification. Two important distinctions do remain: first, the seller cannot substitute specific goods which have lawfully been rejected by the buyer since, by definition, the contract is concerned with these goods only; secondly, the frustration of a contract for the purposes of ss. 6 and 7 of the Sale of Goods Act 1979 refers only to specific goods.

Property passing as an aspect of intention
Section 17 of the Sale of Goods Act 1979 lays down the basic rule that property in specific goods only passes when the parties intend. The question of finding a common intention (express or implied) as to the passing of property has proved problematic because the parties themselves will often be more concerned with the practical side of the transaction, such as arranging delivery and payment, rather than satisfying esoteric legal criteria of property passing. Moreover, because the common law rejected an objective test of the passing of property, the courts had to lay down a series of more or less arbitrary rules for the attribution of intention which have been encapsulated in s. 18. This contains five rules dealing with the transfer of property under the contract of sale. The fourth rule in s. 18 is somewhat of an oddity since it is concerned with the delivery of goods on approval or on a sale or return basis and is not, therefore, made pursuant to a contract of sale. This phenomenon will be considered in chapter 12 which deals with reservation of title clauses.

Definition and nature of contracts for the supply of goods

Rules for ascertaining intention
The first three rules of s. 18 of the Sale of Goods Act 1979 are concerned with contracts for the sale of specific goods:

> Rule 1. — Where there is an unconditional contract for the sale of specific goods in a deliverable state the property in the goods passes to the buyer when the contract is made, and it is immaterial whether the time of payment or the time of delivery, or both, be postponed.
> Rule 2. — Where there is a contract for the sale of specific goods and the seller is bound to do something to the goods for the purpose of putting them into a deliverable state, the property does not pass until the thing is done and the buyer has notice that it has been done.
> Rule 3. — Where there is a contract for the sale of specific goods in a deliverable state but the seller is bound to weigh, measure, test, or do some other act or thing with reference to the goods for the purpose of ascertaining the price, the property does not pass until the act or thing is done and the buyer has notice that it has been done.

The meaning of the term 'specific goods' in relation to property passing was considered by the Court of Appeal in *Kursell* v *Timber Operators and Contractors Ltd* [1927] 1 KB 298. In this case, the plaintiff sold to the defendants all the trees in a Latvian forest which conformed to certain minimum specifications within a 15-year period. The buyer paid a first instalment of the price but before he could cut much timber the forest was nationalised. The Court of Appeal held that the timber had not passed to the buyer and that the risk remained with the seller because the court concluded that there was not a sale of specific goods: first, it was really a contract for the sale of a right of severance and that the trees did not become 'specific or ascertained' for the purposes of s. 17 until they were put in a deliverable state; second, the trees were held not to be specific goods until cut. This approach is overly harsh and it is submitted that contract goods need only be described by the contract in such a way that they are identifiable at the time the contract is made for them to be specific.

It should be emphasised that the s. 18 rules are merely presumptive of intention and can be displaced by contrary intention as a matter of construction of the contract, or by rule of law such as that encapsulated in s. 16. To discover the intention of the parties as required under the Act, regard must be paid to the terms of the contract, the conduct of the parties, and the circumstances of the case. The vague and general statutory language seen in s. 17(2) allows considerable latitude. Thus in *Re Anchor Line (Henderson Brothers) Ltd* [1937] Ch 1, the Court of Appeal inferred that a provision in the contract placing the risk on the buyer was an inference that property had *not* passed because under the normal rule encapsulated in s. 20(1) risk passes with property (see chapter 8). It follows from this that an obligation to insure will be an important indication of who bears the risk which, in turn, is presumptive of the fact of property passage.

Rule 1
The presumption in rule 1 is weak because it assumes that 'where there is an unconditional contract for the sale of specific goods' property passes without reference to the question of delivery or payment. Such a presumption, at least in a consumer context, is likely to be displaced as it would visit upon the consumer the risk of the contract goods being damaged or destroyed in the interim period between the conclusion of the contract and the delivery of the goods. The presumption makes little practical sense because the business seller is in a better position to insure the goods. It is little wonder, therefore, that Diplock LJ was so insistent in *R.V. Ward Ltd* v *Bignall* [1967] 1 QB 534 at p. 545:

> The governing rule . . . is in section [17] and in modern times very little is needed to give rise to the inference that the property in specific goods is to pass only on delivery or payment.

Two questions are posed by rule 1. What is an 'unconditional contract' and when are goods 'in a deliverable state'?

'Unconditional contract'   These words have proven to be particularly problematic because the expression 'condition' is used in two different senses under the Sale of Goods Act 1979. The first sense is as a major term in the contract, condition as opposed to warranty, but this cannot be the meaning here because this interpretation would almost entirely obliterate the operation of the rule. It is probable that the second interpretation is the correct one in that 'unconditional contract for the sale of specific goods' means no more than a contract of sale under which the passing of property is not made subject to a condition precedent. The courts have in a few instances, no doubt influenced by a desire to protect innocent buyers, construed this also to include a condition subsequent which is odd since, by its nature this does not suspend the operation of a contractual provision. Thus in *Varley* v *Whipp* [1900] 1 QB 513, it was held that the sale of a second-hand reaping machine which had been little used, a description which was completely inaccurate, was not an unconditional sale. Such a strained interpretation is now no longer necessary with the repeal of the original s. 11(1)(c) of the 1893 Act which provided that the buyer lost his right to reject specific goods as soon as property passed. It was understandable that the judges should give an unnatural interpretation to the words 'unconditional contract' in s. 18, rule 1, simply in order to avoid depriving a buyer of his right to reject goods.

'Deliverable state'   In addition to the requirement of specificity, the goods must be in a deliverable state. Under s. 61(5) of the Sale of Goods Act 1979, goods are in a deliverable state when they are in such a state that the buyer would under the contract be bound to take delivery of them. It follows that if something still has to be done to the goods they will not be in a deliverable state and the property will not pass. A leading decision here is *Underwood Ltd* v *Burgh Castle Brick and Cement Syndicate* [1922] 1 KB 343. The facts involved

the sale of a condensing engine weighing over 30 tons cemented to the floor of the seller's premises which had to be detached and dismantled before it could be delivered by rail as the contract specified. The seller subsequently detached the engine; but it was severely damaged whilst being loaded without any fault on the part of the seller, and, apparently, before the buyer had notice that it had been detached. The risk issue raised in this case was decided in favour of the buyers on the ground that s. 18, rule 1, did not apply because the sellers had to do something which they had not done to put the engine into a deliverable state. The key issue as to whether or not the goods are in a deliverable state depends upon whether the contract imposes an obligation to *do* something in relation to the goods. In this respect, the goods are not prevented from being in a deliverable state if, for example, there has been a serious breach of a condition entitling the buyer to reject the goods. Thus in *Lord Eldon* v *Hedley Bros* [1935] 2 KB 1, it was agreed that property had not passed under a contract by which the buyer could refuse to take delivery of or pay for mouldy or unmerchantable hay. It was held that the contract was in such terms as to show that the parties intended that property should pass to the buyer when the contract was made (compare *Vigers Bros* v *Sanderson Bros* [1901] 1 KB 608).

If the goods are to be repaired then the obligation to repair may be a condition precedent to the passing of property. Of course, this is a matter of construction of each particular contract as is illustrated in *Philip Head and Sons Ltd* v *Showfronts Ltd* [1970] 1 Lloyd's Rep 140, a case under s. 18, rule 5(1), which also contains the phrase 'deliverable state'. In this case it was held that a carpet which the sellers were to lay was not in a deliverable state mainly because it was a heavy bundle and difficult to use so that it was of little use to the buyer. It appears that if the contract anticipates a supply and installation then, as a matter of construction, property will not pass until the work of installation has been complete. The question of intention is of overriding importance so that the issue of whether or not a contract is for the sale of goods or for work and materials is itself not decisive.

Rule 2
Rules 2 and 3 of s. 18 of the Sale of Goods Act 1979 deal with the passing of property in conditional contracts for the sale of specific goods. Under rule 2 the property in goods is not to pass until the seller puts the goods in a 'deliverable state'. This contrasts with rules 1, 3 and 5 as these deal with situations where the goods are already in a deliverable state. As a matter of consistency, the phrase 'deliverable state' must have the same meaning as rule 1.

Rule 3
This rule applies only where the seller is bound to weigh, test, measure or do something with reference to the goods for the purpose of working out the price. The civilian view, as adopted in article 1585 of the French Civil Code, is that so long as the goods sold must be weighed, counted or measured the sale is not perfect. The incorporation of this principle into English law is rather odd

especially in view of the fact that ascertainment and payment of the price under s. 8 of the Sale of Goods Act 1979 are not generally prerequisites for the passing of property. Little wonder, therefore, that the rule is of slight practical importance (see *Nanka-Bruce* v *Commonwealth Trust Ltd* [1926] AC 77, PC).

Rule 5

The basic rule of law in relation to unascertained goods is contained in s. 16 of the Sale of Goods Act 1979 which requires that goods be identified or appropriated as the subject-matter of the contract of sale. Where there is a contract for the sale of unascertained goods, no property in the goods is transferred to the buyer unless and until the goods are ascertained. Unascertained goods may be goods identified by description only, for example, generic goods, or they may be a portion of a specific whole not yet identified, or they may be future goods.

Under rule 5, the presumed intention of the parties as to the passing of property is as follows:

> Rule 5. — (1) Where there is a contract for the sale of unascertained future goods by description, and goods of that description and in a deliverable state are unconditionally appropriated to the contract, either by the seller with the assent of the buyer or by the buyer with the assent of the seller, the property in the goods then passes to the buyer; and the assent may be express or implied, and may be given either before or after the appropriation is made.
>
> (2) Where, in pursuance of the contract, the seller delivers the goods to the buyer or to a carrier or other bailee or custodier (whether named by the buyer or not) for the purpose of transmission to the buyer, and does not reserve the right of disposal, he is to be taken to have unconditionally appropriated the goods to the contract.

By virtue of rule 5(1), in the case of a contract for the sale of unascertained or future goods by description, property in the goods will pass to the buyer when goods of *that description*, in a deliverable state, are unconditionally appropriated to the contract either by the seller with the assent of the buyer or by the buyer with the assent of the seller. Such an assent may be express or implied. Suffice to say that as long as the goods correspond with description the important issue is that of appropriation. If the goods do not correspond with description, as is the case where there has been a breach of s. 13, property won't pass simply because there can be no appropriation of the goods on the basis that they did not form part of the agreed subject-matter of the contract.

Appropriation In *Re Blyth Shipbuilding and Dry Docks Co. Ltd* [1926] Ch 494, the difficulties associated with the expression 'appropriation' were considered. The facts of the case were concerned with the construction and sale of a ship and the contract provided that 'materials and things appropriated' to the vessel would belong to the purchaser following the payment of this first instalment. Following the insolvency of the ship construction company, one of the issues was whether the worked and unworked material lying around the shipyard at the relevant time had been appropriated to the contract. Although the expression 'appropriation' was being used in a contract as distinct from being given its statutory use, nevertheless, the Court of Appeal read it in its proper technical sense. The word 'appropriated' was described by Sargant LJ at p. 518 as a 'term of legal art' with a definite meaning. In this respect it was held that for appropriation to take place, there had to be some definite act which in the instant case amounted to the affixing of the property to the vessel itself.

Rule 5(1) indicates that the act of appropriation may be made by the buyer. When the buyer selects the goods, he will often have appropriated them before the contract is concluded so the goods will then be specific. In certain circumstances, for example, in a mail-order business, the buyer may impliedly confer on the seller a power of selection from stock which he has not seen. This is of significance with regard to risk which would appear to be on the buyer where the article is put in the post. Nonetheless it does offer some protection against the insolvency of mail-order traders (compare *Badische Anilin und Soda Fabrik* v *Basle Chemical Works* [1898] AC 200).

One of the clearest indications of appropriation is where the seller expressly informs the buyer that he is setting aside specific goods as in the case where a notice of appropriation is sent. As soon as this has been concluded, appropriation cannot be unilaterally withdrawn by the seller. There is some weak authority which suggests that if the buyer has not yet acted on the notice of appropriation then it can be withdrawn (see *Borrowman, Phillips and Co.* v *Free and Hollis* (1878) 4 QBD 500). This will only be the case if the notice is regarded as being provisional and, in this sense, cannot therefore be truly categorised as a notice of appropriation.

In general, the question of appropriation has to be determined by reference to conduct on the part of the seller. Here, rule 5(2) operates as a presumption that delivery to a carrier or other bailee is treated as though they were agents of the buyer, irrespective of the fact that they may have been engaged by the seller. Delivery is defined in such a way as to include actual and constructive possession as well as encompassing issues of attornment (see pp. 33–4). Sale and delivery are distinct acts, though sometimes the delivery of goods may amount to appropriation of them within rule 5. Of course, actual delivery is the last opportunity for appropriation which may often occur before then, as in the case where the seller acknowledges that he holds the goods on behalf of the buyer (*Wardar's (Import and Export) Co. Ltd* v *W. Norwood and Sons Ltd* [1968] 2 QB 663).

For appropriation to be effective it must be unconditional, and if there is any equivocality about the appropriation it will be ineffective to pass property. Two contrasting cases may be cited to illustrate the difficulty of determining whether there has been sufficient appropriation. In *Aldridge* v *Johnson* (1857) 7 E & B 885, the facts of which are set out on p. 56, the court held that as soon as the seller filled some of the sacks with the barley, property passed in that quantity of barley filled. On the other hand in *Carlos Federspiel and Co. SA* v *Charles Twigg and Co. Ltd* [1957] 1 Lloyd's Rep 240, the court came to the opposite conclusion. In this case the sellers agreed to sell a number of cycles and tricycles f.o.b. a British port. They made preparations for shipping them, for example, they had arranged boxes in which the goods were packed and marked with the port of destination. The goods were never shipped and the sellers went into liquidation. The buyers claimed the goods from the liquidator on the ground that the property had passed by virtue of rule 5(1) since they had been unconditionally appropriated to the contract. Pearson J rejected this contention on the basis that it was the intention of the parties that no property in the goods should pass until shipment and that, although preparations for shipment had been made, this did not amount to an unconditional appropriation so as to pass the property.

Undoubtedly, one factor that influenced the court in *Carlos Federspiel* was the reluctance to interfere in the internal warehousing arrangements of business and to get involved in a grand stocktaking exercise. This point may be demonstrated historically in Heath J's *dictum* in *Mucklow* v *Mangles* (1808) 1 Taunt 318 at p. 319: 'A tradesman often finishes goods, which he is making in pursuance of an order given by one person, and sells them to another' (compare *Hendy Lennox (Industrial Engines) Ltd* v *Grahame Puttick Ltd* [1984] 1 WLR 485 discussed on pp. 263–4).

Sometimes the circumstances will demonstrate an intention towards unconditional appropriation. In this respect, the facts in *Healy* v *Howlett and Sons* [1917] 1 KB 337 are instructive. Here the seller contracted to sell to the buyers 20 boxes of mackerel in Valentia, County Kerry. The boxes were placed on rail, but were not marked with the buyer's name and they were sent to Holyhead along with 170 other boxes for delivery to other customers. When the fish arrived at Holyhead, the railway company allotted 20 boxes out of 190 boxes to the buyers who found that they were not in a merchantable condition. The seller sued for the price of the goods on the ground that the property had passed under s. 18, rule 5(1), since the goods had been appropriated to the contract when they were placed on rail at Valentia. It was held that there was no appropriation because none of the 190 boxes had been marked with the buyers' name so as to distinguish them from the remainder.

Whoever performs the act of appropriation, rule 5(1) indicates that assent must be given either before or after appropriation. This demonstrates that the act of appropriation by itself does no more than ascertain goods earmarked to the contract of sale. However, the courts will readily infer assent as is seen in *Pignataro* v *Gilroy* [1919] 1 KB 459. The material facts were that the sellers sold 140 bags of rice to the buyer and on 28 February 1918 the sellers gave the buyer a delivery order for a quantity at Chambers Wharf and said that the remaining 15 were available for collection at the sellers' warehouse in Long Acre. The sellers requested the buyer to take the bags away but the buyer did nothing until 25 March. When the buyer sent someone to collect the 15 bags from the warehouse, he discovered that they had been stolen a little while before. The buyer then brought an action for non-delivery, but this was denied by the King's Bench Division where it was held that the sellers had appropriated the goods to the contract with the implied assent of the buyer, so property passed by virtue of s. 18, rule 5(1). It would seem, following this case, that a refusal to give the necessary assent for appropriation would amount to a repudiatory breach unless the buyer could show good cause such as where the goods are not of merchantable quality.

It may be that the parties wish to reach the point of identifying goods without intending that property should pass immediately. This is especially important in international transactions involving c.i.f. contracts. In this situation, the buyer will want to know details of shipping, even though property will not pass until the shipping documents are in his possession and the price paid.

Conditional appropriation The s. 18 presumptions do not apply to cases of conditional appropriation, although s. 19 does provide for the specific situation where the seller has retained his ownership of the goods until conditions stipulated by him are met. It could be argued that because s. 17 already provides that property passing is an aspect of intention s. 19 is superfluous. Moreover, even if property does not pass by virtue of s. 19, this does not prevent a buyer who has obtained possession of the goods or documents of title passing a good title to a third party under s. 25(1). A particular instance of the general principle laid down in s. 19(1) is the provision in s. 19(2) where the seller is prima facie deemed to reserve the right of disposal where goods are shipped and, by virtue of the bill of lading, the goods are deliverable to the order of the seller or his agent. Property in the goods sold passes unconditionally where the bill of lading for the goods is made out in favour of the purchaser, or his agent or representative as consignee. It is common in international sales for the seller to take the bill of lading to his own order and only indorse it to the buyer against payment as is the case in c.i.f. contracts. The normal method of payment before the advent of the documentary credit was the bill of exchange, and s. 19(3) provides that property does not pass to the buyer where he has not honoured the bill of exchange. However, this should not be confused with the *power* of disposal. In *Cahn and Mayer* v *Pockett's Bristol Channel Steam Packet Co. Ltd* [1899] 1 QB 643, it was held that where the buyer negotiates the bill of lading to an innocent third party who takes without notice of the buyer's failure to pay or honour the bill of exchange, such third party will acquire property in the goods as against the unpaid seller by virtue of s. 47(2) of the Sale of Goods Act 1979 and s. 10 of the Factors Act 1889.

SUPPLY CONTRACTS FOR CONSIDERATION OTHER THAN MONEY

Exchange

Despite the fact that implicit in any definition of money is the element of exchange, English law has traditionally distinguished between sale and exchange disregarding the equivalence of economic function. When the practical rules applicable to sale and exchange are interchangeable, to distinguish between them is little more than a scholastic exercise. Under s. 1(1) of the Supply of Goods and Services Act 1982 it would seem that an exchange contract comes within its purview since it generally applies to contracts where 'one person transfers or agrees to transfer to another the property in goods'. This Act incorporates into such a contract terms almost identical to those applying in the sales contract. Following on from this, there should be no difficulty in categorising transactions where gift tokens or coupons are exchanged wholly for a product as transactions under the 1982 Act (compare *Davies* v *Customs and Excise Commissioners* [1975] 1 WLR 204). Where the price of the goods is more than the value of the token, the inclusion of a money consideration would suggest rather that the transaction is a sale of goods. In one sense, the characterisation of the transaction as being either sale or exchange may be important because the remedy for defective performance in exchange is not for the price but rather a claim for unliquidated damages for non-delivery.

In the case of a part-exchange transaction there is no difficulty in categorising the supply of new goods as a sale simply because the supplier will be receiving a composite consideration. Thus in *Aldridge* v *Johnson* (1857) 7 E & B 885, there was an agreement to transfer 32 bullocks valued at £192 in return for 100 quarters of barley valued at £215, the balance of £23 to be paid in cash; this was construed as a reciprocal sale (see also *Forsyth* v *Jervis* (1816) 1 Stark 437; *Sheldon* v *Cox* (1824) 3 B & C 420). Surprisingly, there appears to be only one English decision which deals with the trading in of motor vehicles in part exchange even though it is such a commonplace, everyday experience. The facts in this case, *G.J. Dawson (Clapham) Ltd* v *H and G. Dutfield* [1936] 2 All ER 232, are worth elaboration. The plaintiffs were dealers in second-hand lorries who agreed to transfer to the defendants two lorries for £475 and take in exchange two other lorries valued at £225 provided they were delivered within one month. The defendants paid the cash balance of £250 but did not deliver the lorries. It was held that this was a contract for sale and the plaintiff was therefore able to sue for the price. The decision would have been otherwise if no value had been assigned, as in the Irish Supreme Court decision in *Flynn* v *Mackin* [1974] IR 101.

It is a question of contractual intention whether the transaction is to be categorised as a sale or exchange. This may be important if credit finance for the new article purchased with a part-exchange is declined by the financier. In this circumstance, it is probable that both transactions will be regarded as interdependent so that the part-exchange element may be construed as a sale subject to a condition subsequent, thereby making it determinable if the financier does not accept the transaction. This analysis will have relevance as far as the passing of property and risk is concerned (see chapter 8) where the goods are damaged in the meantime (*Clarke* v *Reilly* (1962) 96 ILTR 96). Moreover the exception to the *nemo dat* principle discussed in chapter 7 will be significant here especially if the dealer is considered to have bought or agreed to buy the goods under s. 9 of the Factors Act 1889. There is also special provision under s. 73(2) of the Consumer Credit Act 1974 for a part-exchange allowance in respect of a cancelled regulated agreement where property has been transferred.

Free gifts
The requirement of consideration distinguishes a sale from a gift. Nevertheless, a wide definition is given to the term 'supply' in a contract of sale so that an insertion accompanying goods will be considered as having been supplied

under the contract, thereby attracting the implied terms under the Sale of Goods Act 1979. Sometimes, the so-called 'free gift' will constitute a collateral contract the consideration for which being the entry into the main contract of sale (see *Esso Petroleum Co. Ltd* v *Customs and Excise Commissioners* [1976] 1 WLR 1).

If the free gift is supplied as a genuine gift without the transferee being under any obligation to do anything, there will be no contractual relationship between the transferor and transferee. The significance here is that all the implied obligations under the Sale of Goods Act 1979 and Supply of Goods and Services Act 1982 will be avoided, although there may be liability in negligence. It may be that in future consumer guarantees legislation, such guarantees will be enforceable by a recipient of a free gift. Where the requirements of the Unsolicited Goods and Services Act 1971 (as amended) are satisfied, the recipient of unsolicited goods can treat those goods as an unconditional gift.

Trading stamps

The Trading Stamps Act 1964, as amended (see sch. 4 to the Consumer Credit Act 1974), is of much less importance now that trading stamps are available in so few shops. There is uncertainty as to whether the exchange of trading stamps for goods is a sale or an exchange. Notwithstanding this, the Act (as amended) grants the holder elaborate rights of redemption for cash (s. 3), as well as non-excludable implied terms under s. 4(1) against the promoter of the trading stamp scheme.

Transfers of goods and services

The law has traditionally distinguished between contracts for the supply of goods and contracts for the supply of services. With the repeal of the rule that certain sales had to be evinced in writing and, following the enactment of the Supply of Goods and Services Act 1982, the importance of the distinction is less acute. Nevertheless, there still appear to be notable differences, for example, with regard to the passing of property and also the effects of frustration.

The approach of the law is to distinguish the following transactions, namely, a contract for the sale of goods with a severable contract for services, a sale of goods, a contract for work and materials, and lastly, the supply of services. These categorisations are only important insofar as they sound in different legal treatments. Under the Supply of Goods and Services Act 1982, in any contract of supply the seller or supplier's duties will normally be strict and excludable only in limited circumstances, whereas in contracts for the supply of services, the supplier's duties will be duties of care which will be excludable subject to the reasonableness requirement of the Unfair Contract Terms Act 1977. The major difficulty is that the Supply of Goods and Services Act 1982 has not sufficiently delineated the boundary between the situation where the supply of goods was incidental to the supply of services, so liability is not strict, and the converse case. At common law, the position is that if the article in question is a standard product, like a meal in a restaurant (*Lockett* v *A. and M.*

Charles Ltd [1938] 4 All ER 170), this is a sale of goods so that liability is strict. On the other hand, the supply and installation of roofing tiles has been held to involve a contract for work and materials (*Young and Marten Ltd* v *McManus Childs Ltd* [1969] 1 AC 454; compare *Philip Head and Sons Ltd* v *Showfronts Ltd* [1970] 1 Lloyd's Rep 140). Where the article is a unique or one-off product such as the commissioning of a portrait from an artist, the court is likely to construe this arrangement as a contract of work and materials notwithstanding the incidental supply of the canvas (*Robinson* v *Graves* [1935] 1 KB 579; compare *Isaacs* v *Hardy* (1884) Cab and El 287).

Where the skill of the transferor is so important and the materials used insignificant, this is treated as a contract for the supply of services. Thus in the medical field, especially with interventionist techniques involving implantation of *human* products, for example, blood or biologics, this may be considered a supply of services because the courts will be reluctant to regard matter of human origin as 'goods' (compare *Perlmutter* v *Beth David Hospital* (1954) 123 NE 2d 792). It follows that the surgeon will not be strictly liable for the products used, his obligation being to exercise reasonable care and skill (*Bolam* v *Friern Hospital Management Committee* [1957] 1 WLR 582). On the other hand, in *Dodd and Dodd* v *Wilson and McWilliam* [1946] 2 All ER 691, the plaintiff contracted with a veterinary surgeon to inoculate his cattle with a serum, and it was held that the surgeon impliedly warranted the vaccine to be fit for the purpose for which it was supplied. This may be considered to be the more appropriate standard in *contracts* between patients and doctors where artificial products such as manufactured heart valves are used for implantation. However, it is very important to take a balanced approach here because value judgments are often made with regard to the comparative worth of the skill of the professional versus the materials used, so, for example, it is unlikely that *Lee* v *Griffin* (1861) 1 B & S 272 would be followed today. In that case the supply of dentures was considered to be a sale, and it was clear that the court paid scant regard to the dentist's skill which provides some indication of the dentist's standing in the 19th century.

Bailment and hire
Bailment is the delivery of goods to another on condition, express or implied, that they shall be returned to the bailor or dealt with according to his instructions. The purpose of bailment and sale is different because, in the case of an ordinary contract of hire, it is not intended that general property in the goods will pass to the bailor/hirer. Sophisticated credit instruments are predicated upon this legal analysis including equipment leases discussed in chapter 13. At the same time, contracts in the form of a bailment do raise interesting sale versus security issues which will be discussed in the context of retention of title clauses in chapter 12.

A contract of hire is a species of bailment and whilst it is readily distinguishable from sale in that general property is not intended to pass to the hirer, there are important public policy issues in a consumer hire context which dictate that the owner should be subject to similar liability to that visited upon the seller. This has in large measure been achieved under the Supply of Goods and Services Act 1982. Nevertheless, there are some important differences which attach to the categorisation of the transaction as a contract of hire:

(a) The hirer is not a person who has 'agreed to buy' for the purposes of s. 9 of the Factors Act 1889 (see chapter 7).

(b) Chattel mortgage legislation does not apply to a genuine contract of hire even in the case of a sale and leaseback (see chapter 15).

(c) It is not until the termination of the hiring that the owner has a sufficient interest in the goods to maintain an action for wrongful interference with goods under s. 1 of the Torts (Interference with Goods) Act 1977. This action is available if at the time of the conversion, the plaintiff was in possession of the goods (*The Jag Shakti* [1986] 1 AC 337), or had an immediate right of possession of them. One significant feature of the 1977 Act is that under s. 8 the *ius tertii* may be pleaded, thereby giving the court power to settle competing claims in one set of proceedings (see chapter 2).

(d) Because the essence of a bailment is the transfer of possession, the hiring with its obligation to pay rent does not commence until delivery and the bailee is under a prima facie duty to return the goods when the agreement comes to an end (see chapter 13).

The Consumer Credit Act 1974 applies statutory control to a regulated consumer hire agreement. This is defined under s. 15(1) of the Consumer Credit Act 1974:

> A consumer hire agreement is an agreement made by a person with an individual (the 'hirer') for the bailment or (in Scotland) the hiring of goods to the hirer, being an agreement which —
> (a) is not a hire-purchase agreement, and
> (b) is capable of subsisting for more than three months, and
> (c) does not require the hirer to make payments exceeding £15,000.

This is a wide definition and would include leasing of business equipment and vehicles, the general effect being to equate consumer hiring with instalment sales and hire-purchase agreements (see below). However, in some important respects there are differences in treatment, the most notable being as follows:

(a) The hirer is granted a more limited right of termination under s. 101(1) of the Consumer Credit Act 1974.

(b) The 'protected goods' rules (s. 90) do not apply here.

(c) The financial relief accorded to a hirer under a consumer hire agreement following the owner's recaption of the goods may be different because under s. 100 of the Consumer Credit Act 1974, there are limitations placed on recovery of money following termination in the case of conditional sale and hire-purchase. However, it is probable that under the common law a minimum payment clause stipulating for future rental payments would be void. In any case, under s. 132 of the Consumer Credit Act 1974, the court has powers to grant the defaulting hirer financial relief in respect of sums paid and payable.

Conditional sales and hire-purchase

The right of security is intimately connected with property. Herein lies the reason for the distinction drawn under the common law between credit sales (where the property in goods passes on or before delivery), conditional sales and hire-purchase. In *Helby* v *Matthews* [1895] AC 471, the House of Lords decided that a hirer under a hire-purchase agreement who was entitled to terminate the hiring agreement at any time was not a person who had agreed to buy the goods within the meaning of s. 9 of the Factors Act 1889, so confirming the *nemo dat* rule (see chapter 7). Their lordships distinguished *Lee* v *Butler* [1893] 2 QB 318, where there was a conditional sale agreement, on the basis that in that case there was a binding obligation to sell the goods to the buyer.

During the course of the 20th century, the general statutory approach has moved towards the gradual assimilation of conditional sales and hire-purchase. In this respect, although conditional sales are regulated for the purposes of the *nemo dat* exceptions in s. 25(2) of the Sale of Goods Act 1979, and hire-purchase under sch. 4 to the Consumer Credit Act 1974, the two sets of provisions are virtually identical. Moreover, the limited exception to the *nemo dat* rule created for dispositions of motor vehicles to 'private purchasers' does not distinguish between a conditional buyer or a hirer under a hire-purchase agreement. The legislature has also assimilated sale, conditional sales and hire-purchase in relation to the statutorily implied terms as to title, description, quality and fitness for purpose.

CONSUMER CREDIT

The Consumer Credit Act 1974 was inspired by art. 9 of the American Uniform Commercial Code (UCC). The Crowther committee report, *Report of the Committee on Consumer Credit* (Cmnd 4596, London, 1971), recommended that transactions should be dealt with not according to their legal form but according to their economic substance. Under the Consumer Credit Act 1974, there is a recognition that the legal rights and duties of a consumer should not necessarily turn upon whether the consumer has borrowed money to buy goods, or bought them on credit, or acquired them under a hire-purchase contract, i.e., the traditional distinction drawn between lender credit and vendor credit. Thus the Hire Purchase Acts 1964 and 1965 have been almost entirely repealed by the Consumer Credit Act 1974, and the rights and duties of the parties involved in a hire-purchase contract are similar to those of parties to a sale of goods in which the consumer has obtained credit whether from the seller or a third party.

Consumer Credit Act 1974 terminology

The Consumer Credit Act 1974 contains new functional terminology so that there are no references to hire-purchase or conditional sales. The central new terms are as follows.

Restricted and unrestricted-use credit A restricted-use credit is by definition one the debtor has no control over the use to which the credit is put. In contrast,

Definition and nature of contracts for the supply of goods 61

unrestricted-use credit is where the debtor has the *control* over the application of the loan, and this is so even if it is a term of the loan contract that he must apply the money to a specified purpose (s. 11(3) of the Consumer Credit Act 1974).

Debtor-creditor-supplier agreements This is where there is a special relationship between the creditor and the supplier who may even be one and the same person (s. 12(a)). By definition, this type of contract will always involve restricted-use credit. More difficulty is posed with third-party arrangements. In the case of restricted use credit, the Consumer Credit Act 1974 treats what under the common law would be two contracts, one of supply and the other of credit, as one composite agreement if the credit is given under pre-existing arrangements with the supplier or in contemplation of future arrangements between them, for example, credit card transactions (s. 187(2)). It is possible for there to be unrestricted-use three-party debtor-creditor-supplier agreements, but the requirements are more exacting (see s. 12(2)).

Debtor-creditor agreements All credit agreements that are not debtor-creditor-supplier agreements are debtor-creditor agreements (s. 13). Such agreements are likely to be unrestricted-use credit although this may not always be the case, for example, where a financier who has no arrangement with the seller insists on paying the money directly to him (s. 13(a)).

Fixed-sum and running-account credit This is the distinction between a hire-purchase agreement for a fixed amount (s. 10(b)) and a credit card agreement where the debtor enjoys a credit facility that he can draw upon from time to time (often) subject to a credit limit (s. 10(a)).

The ambit of the Consumer Credit Act 1974
The Consumer Credit Act 1974 applies to regulated credit agreements. In order to satisfy this four conditions must be satisfied:

(a) The transaction must have been entered into on or after 1 April 1977 (Consumer Credit Act 1974 (Commencement No. 2) Order 1977 (SI 1977/325)).
(b) The debtor must be an individual, not a company (s. 8(1)).
(c) The amount of credit given must not exceed £15,000 (Consumer Credit (Increase in Monetary Limits) Order 1983 (SI 1983/1878)). The credit here denotes not the total amount the debtor has to pay but the element of financial accommodation. The relevant formula would appear to be: Credit = Total price − any deposit payable (s. 189(1)) + the total charge for credit (s. 9(4)). In seeking to define what items are to be included as part of the total charge for credit, s. 20 emphasises that what matters is the cost to the debtor rather than the net return to the lender. In the case of hire-purchase transactions, hire rent is treated as credit by virtue of s. 9(3).
(d) It must not be an exempt transaction. A number of agreements otherwise falling within the ambit of the Consumer Credit Act 1974 are

exempted under s. 16 of the Act. Most of these relate to mortgages of land and need not detain us any further. However, of significance to the present discussion are two types of exempt agreements. The first is in relation to debtor-creditor-supplier agreements where the amount owed is to be paid off in a few instalments. Thus, the Consumer Credit (Exempt Agreements) Order 1980 (SI 1980/52) (as amended) which implements s. 16(5)(a) of the Consumer Credit Act 1974 provides, in the case of fixed-sum credit, that the agreement is exempt if no more than four payments are involved, whereas in the case of running-account credit, exemption is provided if full settlement is made at the end of each period of account. The same statutory instrument implements s. 16(5)(b) which exempts debtor-creditor agreements on the basis of the rate of interest charged. Following on from this, a debtor-creditor agreement will be exempted if the annual percentage rate does not exceed the higher of either 13 per cent or 1 per cent more than the base rates of lending banks.

SALE AND LOANS ON SECURITY

Continental law, with its emphasis upon a unitary concept of *dominium* in which possession is central (*possession vaut titre*), is reluctant to recognise a non-possessory security right except insofar as it has been introduced by statute. Therefore, it is little wonder that the Sale of Goods Act 1979's failure to reconcile 'property' and 'title' have been criticised in a Scottish context. Indeed, the extension of the Sale of Goods Act 1893 to Scotland is often portrayed as being 'hasty' and 'ill-considered' (see generally Smith, T.B., *Property Problems in Sale* (Edinburgh, 1979)). Despite this, the Sale of Goods Act 1979 does make some attempt to deal with the Scottish dilemma *vis-à-vis* non-possessory security interests through s. 62(4), a provision specifically drafted for Scotland but which also applies to England. Section 62(4) expressly excludes from the Act's application: '. . . a transaction in the form of a contract of sale which is intended to operate by way of . . . security'.

The difficulties involved in determining the 'true intentions' of the parties anticipated in s. 62(4) are particularly acute in sale and leaseback provisions (see, for example, *Ladbroke Leasing (South West) Ltd* v *Reekie Plant Ltd* 1983 SLT 155). There is no doubt that the purpose here is to evade the technical requirements of the Bills of Sale Act (1878) Amendment Act 1882 which regulates non-absolute-sale transfer transactions under which a grantee is given a licence to seize. Any mortgage bill of sale falling within the 1882 Act is void against *all* persons unless the strict form set out in the schedule to the Act is adhered to (s. 9). Nevertheless, it is the policy of the courts in England where there is security with recourse to property which can be effected by means other than a transaction of loan or charge not to treat it as being registrable. This is so even though the exact economic effect might be carried out through a transaction which in form was registrable as a security interest in the goods. This theme will be further considered in part 4 of this book.

FOUR
Formalities and the formation of sale and supply contracts

FORMATION

Whilst the contract of supply must be a complete agreement, this does not necessarily mean that every part of the contract has been worked out in meticulous detail (see *G. Scammell and Nephew Ltd* v *Ouston* [1941] AC 251). Indeed, the Sale of Goods Act 1979 has special provisions with regard to the determination of price where this is not fixed in the contract of sale (s. 8). In general, the courts are concerned to enforce contracts between business people, especially executed agreements, even where the uncertain terms may be meaningless (*Nicolene Ltd* v *Simmonds* [1953] 1 QB 543). The common law requirements of contract formation are adequately dealt with in standard works on contract. It is sufficient here merely to note the importance of the objective test for agreement, the relevant question being whether the offeree has accepted the offer in the sense in which a reasonable person would have understood it.

Contract and the doctrine of mistake
Where one party is aware that the offer or the acceptance of the other party does not represent his true intentions but still deals with the other party without disclosing the mistake, the law will abandon the objective interpretation of the first party's intentions. Thus in *Hartog* v *Colin and Shields* [1939] 3 All ER 566, it was held that the plaintiff could not sue on a contract for the sale of hare skins at so much per pound when he knew that the offeror really meant to sell at that price *per piece*. Problems with mistake have arisen with hire-purchase proposal forms where dealers have manipulated figures on proposal forms. The common law position appears to be that a dealer is not normally the agent of the finance company and a customer is bound by the terms of the document unless the finance company knows that it does not accord with the customer's intentions

(*United Dominions Trust Ltd* v *Western* [1976] QB 513). In the case of regulated consumer credit agreements (see pp. 61–2), the common law rule has been overturned, so s. 56(2) of the Consumer Credit Act 1974 provides that antecedent negotiations shall be deemed to be conducted by the dealer 'in the capacity of agent of the creditor as well as in his actual capacity'. The effect of this is that the finance company would be regarded as knowing what its agent knows, namely, the proposal form does not represent the customer's intended offer.

In cases of mistaken identity, the issue is *with whom* did the offeror actually intend to contract as seen in the famous case of *Cundy* v *Lindsay* (1878) 3 App Cas 459. Essentially, there is no real answer to this question because in most cases of fraud, the transferor actually believes that the transferee is the person he is pretending to be. The legal position appears to be (see *Citibank NA* v *Brown Shipley and Co. Ltd* [1991] 2 All ER 690 and *Lewis* v *Averay (No. 2)* [1973] 1 WLR 510; compare *Ingram* v *Little* [1961] 1 QB 31) that where a sale is made *inter praesentes*, that is, between the parties themselves, it will be treated as a voidable sale thereby championing the security of transactions principle discussed in chapter 1. Less problematic are cases of mistake relating to the quality of the goods. Of course, the relevant question here will often be the extent to which the *caveat emptor* doctrine has been abrogated through legislative intervention in contracts of supply (see chapter 5). Even so, as Lord Atkin pointed out in *Bell* v *Lever Bros Ltd* [1932] AC 161 at p. 218, a contract may be set aside for mistake as to the quality of the goods if 'it is the mistake of both parties, and is as to the existence of some quality which makes the thing without the quality essentially different from the thing as it is believed to be'. (See also *Associated Japanese Bank (International) Ltd* v *Crédit du Nord SA* [1989] 1 WLR 255.) In most cases, a mistake as to quality will be treated as a breach of one of the implied obligations under the Sale of Goods Act 1979. A distinction should be drawn here with the case where the mistake relates to the terms of the sale itself. Thus in *Smith* v *Hughes* (1871) LR 6 QB 597, it was held that the seller of oats could not hold the buyer to the contract of sale if the seller was aware that the buyer was intending to accept an offer to sell oats warranted to be old where the seller was not intending to give any such warranty.

Specific undertakings

Representations At common law, a misstatement of fact which induced a contract is a misrepresentation. The common law refused to grant damages for innocent misrepresentation but would do so in the tort of deceit if the representation was fraudulent, although, this is notoriously difficult to prove (*Derry* v *Peek* (1889) 14 App Cas 337). It was because of this that it became so important for a buyer to establish that the seller's representation amounted to a contractual term so that full damages would then be available. However, in *Hedley Byrne and Co. Ltd* v *Heller and Partners Ltd* [1964] AC 465, the House of Lords recognised that there could be liability in tort for negligent misrepresentation dependent upon the establishment of a duty of care between the parties. Inherent in this requirement is the establishment of a 'special relationship' between the parties and in *Esso Petroleum Co. Ltd* v *Mardon* [1976] QB 801, the Court of Appeal recognised that a duty of care is owed by a seller who has special expertise.

The Misrepresentation Act 1967 provides considerable protection for the buyer. Where the negligent misrepresentation induces a contract between the parties, it may be more advantageous to proceed under s. 2(1) of the 1967 Act, not least because it reverses the onus of proof by placing it upon the seller (see *Howard Marine and Dredging Co. Ltd* v *A. Ogden and Sons (Excavations) Ltd* [1978] QB 574). It also appears that the level of damages under s. 2(1) is the tortious measure, that is, recovery for any loss directly flowing from the misrepresentation (see *Royscot Trust Ltd* v *Rogerson* [1991] 2 QB 297). In the case of an innocent misrepresentation, s. 2(2) of the 1967 Act gives the court a discretion to award damages in lieu of rescission. The provision reflects the position that the normal remedy for misrepresentation is rescission, but the excessiveness of this remedy is mitigated under s. 2(2) of the Act. Here we find similarities with the position in breach of contract where the courts have recognised the innominate term as a method of reducing the hardship of categorising a term of the contract (irrespective of the consequences of the breach) as a condition (see below).

The right to rescind will be lost where *restitutio in integrum* is impossible, for example where the goods have been consumed or services provided. In addition, rescission is forfeited where the buyer has accepted the goods (see *Leaf* v *International Galleries* [1950] 2 KB 86). The principal weakness of the rescission remedy and the statutory alternative of damages in lieu of rescission is that they do not provide for consequential loss, for example, profits on resale. Even though equity together with rescission gives an indemnity, this is limited in scope to cover only expenditure *necessarily* incurred as a result of entering into the contract (*Whittington* v *Seale-Hayne* (1900) 82 LT 49). In order to get full compensation, the buyer will have to look to tort as in the case of fraudulent misrepresentation, or sue for breach of contract. It would seem from this that the issue of whether the representation has become a term of the contract cannot be avoided, especially if the buyer seeks compensation for loss of profits since expectation damages are linked to breach of contract.

Express terms Unless there is a written contract, rare in most consumer sales, there is the possibility that the parol evidence rule may prevent the successful incorporation of extrinsic evidence. Nevertheless, the rule is subject to so many exceptions that they have practically destroyed the rule. Thus, it does not apply where the evidence establishes the existence of a collateral contract, or where it can be shown that the document was not intended as a complete record of the contract terms, or where its existence or operation was dependent on some prior unexpected stipulation, or that it was procured by some illegality or misrepresentation. It is not surprising, therefore, that the Law Commission report, *Law of Contract — The Parol Evidence Rule* (Law Com. No. 154, London, 1986) has recommended no reform of the parol evidence rule, declaring that the 'rule' is not as extensive as traditionally expounded.

The question of whether a statement made during the course of negotiations remains a mere representation or becomes a contractual term turns on the intention of the parties. Such a criterion is elusive, but, in determining the precise legal status of a statement, some reliance has been placed upon the *point* during the negotiations at which the statement was made. The further away from the making of the contract it was made the more likely it is to be considered as a misrepresentation (see *Routledge* v *McKay* [1954] 1 WLR 615). Advertising by manufacturers has become notorious for the extravagant but contractually ineffective commendation of goods. The statements made which have no legal effect are often described as being mere 'puffs' (*Carlill* v *Carbolic Smoke Ball Co.* [1893] 1 QB 256). The law is concerned only with statements which take the form of remarks which are significant and are representations of present or future fact. Modern advertisements which are specific in detail, for example, advertisements for cars which specify exact performance information may sound in legal contractual liability. The scenario envisaged here is that a buyer of a car will have a contract not only with the supplier, but also a collateral contract with the manufacturer on the basis of the terms contained in a *precise* advertisement, the consideration for which being the entry into the main contract of supply (see *Shanklin Pier Ltd* v *Detel Products Ltd* [1951] 2 KB 854; *Andrews* v *Hopkinson* [1957] 1 QB 229). In the case of misleading advertisements, criminal liability is envisaged under such legislation as part III of the Consumer Protection Act 1987 and the Trade Descriptions Act 1968.

One particular problem with incorporation of terms has emerged in the context of the so-called 'battle of forms'. Classical theory, as applied in *Butler Machine Tool Co. Ltd* v *Ex-Cell-O Corpn (England) Ltd* [1979] 1 WLR 401, would suggest a mirror-image rule, namely, each proffering of standard terms is a counter-offer and it is the last document proffered which embodies the final offer when the recipient accepts by acting upon it. Of course, in theory, the mirror image rule makes printed forms matter since it encourages or even forces parties receiving documents to read them carefully. However, with standard-form contracts directed at consumers, the legislature has interfered because of the imbalance in bargaining power. The Unfair Contract Terms Act 1977 regulates the application of exemption clauses especially against consumers.

The resolution of the question whether a statement is a representation or a contractual term does not resolve the issue concerning the legal effect of the statement between the parties. Express contractual undertakings will have different consequences depending upon the significance given to the particular term ascribed by the law. There has been much confusion here mainly because the Sale of Goods Act 1979 uses the words 'condition' and 'warranty' as technical expressions, the breach of which gives the right to treat the contract as at an end in the case of a condition (s. 11(3)), but only to damages in the case of a subsidiary term like a warranty (s. 61(1)). Whether a term is a condition or a warranty depends upon the construction of the sale contract (s. 11). Moreover, s. 11(2) provides that conditions may be waived, or a breach of a condition may be treated by the buyer as a breach of warranty and not as a ground for treating the contract as repudiated, whereas s. 11(3) emphasises that a stipulation may be a condition even though called a warranty in the contract.

Formalities and the formation of sale and supply contracts 67

The binary approach to contractual obligations as anticipated under the Sale of Goods Act 1979 has provoked considerable dissatisfaction. The reason for this is that it permits buyers to set aside a bad bargain following the seller's breach of condition where only slight consequences have ensued. However, a new approach to the question of remedies available for breach was occasioned by Diplock LJ in *Hongkong Fir Shipping Co. Ltd* v *Kawasaki Kisen Kaisha Ltd* [1962] 2 QB 26 at p. 70:

> There are ... many contractual undertakings of a more complex character which cannot be categorised as being 'conditions' or 'warranties', if the late 19th-century meaning adopted in the Sale of Goods Act 1893, and used by Bowen LJ in *Bentsen* v *Taylor, Sons and Co.* [1893] 2 QB 274 at p. 280 be given to those terms. Of such undertakings all that can be predicated is that some breaches will and others will not give rise to an event which will deprive the party not in default of substantially the whole benefit which it was intended that he should obtain from the contract; and the legal consequences of a breach of such an undertaking, unless provided for expressly in the contract, depend upon the nature of the event to which the breach gives rise and do not follow automatically from a prior classification of the undertaking as a 'condition' or a 'warranty'.

This approach allows for greater flexibility by concentrating on the nature of the consequences of the breach. Nevertheless, the language used in the Sale of Goods Act 1979 does not easily admit of Diplock LJ's *tertium quid* where terms are defined as 'conditions' or 'warranties'.

In *Cehave NV* v *Bremer Handelsgesellschaft mbH* [1976] QB 44, Diplock LJ's analysis in the *Hongkong Fir Shipping* case was extended to sale of goods and this was approved by the House of Lords in *Bunge Corpn, New York* v *Tradax Export SA, Panama* [1981] 1 WLR 711. The *Cehave* case involved a sale of citrus pulp pellets where it was a term in the contract that the goods be shipped 'in good condition'. By the time the citrus pellets were delivered, the market price had fallen. The buyers argued that they were entitled to reject the goods primarily on the basis of breach of the express condition since they were slightly damaged, even though they could be satisfactorily used. The Court of Appeal indicated that the language of the Sale of Goods Act 1979, especially in view of the fact that s. 62(2) preserves the rules of the common law, did not preclude the status and effect of a term being regarded, as Ormerod LJ put it at p. 83, in the light of 'the events resulting from the breach, rather than the breach itself'. This approach was mirrored in the Law Commission working paper, *Sale and Supply of Goods* (No. 85, London, 1983), where a recommendation was made to abolish the automatic classification of statutory implied terms as conditions, the buyer in a consumer sale being given the right to reject for any breach of the implied terms unless the consequences and nature of the breach were trivial so that rejection would be unreasonable. Significantly, the Law Commission report (No. 160, 1987) did not adopt this approach preferring, in the case of consumers, to maintain the present categorisation of implied terms as conditions. This was perceived necessary so as to bolster the bargaining position of consumers. The Consumer Guarantees Bill 1990 which sought to implement the Law Commission proposals did not, therefore, eliminate the distinctions between conditions and warranties and innominate terms. Nevertheless, in one significant respect an important modification to the common law rule can be seen with the proposal for a new s. 15A of the Sale of Goods Act 1979. This part of the Bill was supported by the Government and it is reasonable to suppose that further legislative initiatives will be forthcoming. The proposed amendment was that where the buyer does not deal as a consumer, the right to reject for a breach of the statutory implied terms seen in ss. 13 to 15 of the Sale of Goods Act 1979 is limited where 'the breach is so slight that it would be unreasonable for [the buyer] to reject [the goods]'.

It is important not to take a dogmatic stance with regard to the categorisation of terms as always concentrating on the nature of the breach. The need for certainty in commercial transactions is self-evident and the parties' categorisation of terms as conditions will obviously be relevant. The House of Lords in *Bunge Corpn, New York* v *Tradax Export SA, Panama* [1981] 1 WLR 711 tabulated several factors which are relevant in the determination of the classification of a term as being a condition:

(a) There are enormous practical advantages in certainty especially in string contracts where today's buyer may be tomorrow's seller. Business people must be able to do business with confidence in the legal results of their actions.

(b) Difficulty of assessment of damages is an indication in favour of categorising a term as a condition.

(c) To make 'total loss' the only test of a condition is contrary to authority, for example, terms as to the time of shipment, delivery and payment have been traditionally regarded as conditions irrespective of the fact that failure to comply with them does not always have serious consequences. Besides, it is a cardinal principle of law that an innocent party may choose to accept repudiation and sue for damages for breach of contract, or he may choose to refuse to accept the repudiation so that the contract will remain in full effect. How could this right of election be anything other than a fiction if the breach of the term in all circumstances would deprive the innocent party of substantially the whole benefit which it was intended that he should receive?

EXCLUSION AND LIMITATION OF LIABILITY

A contract of supply may state expressly that the supplier is to be exempt from performance of some term or terms of the contract of supply, or that liability may be restricted in some way or other. The validity and application of such exclusion and limitation clauses have raised many difficult problems as well as prompting statutory intervention principally through the Unfair Contract Terms Act 1977. This legislation prohibits or restricts the exclusion of terms that would otherwise be implied in contracts of supply and is discussed in detail in chapter 5.

Where an exclusion or limitation clause is permitted, the question then arises as to its effect as a matter of law. It is not intended to give a detailed description here as there are more appropriate specialist contract texts available. For our purposes, it is sufficient merely to note that the doctrine of fundamental breach as a rule of law has finally been laid to rest by *Photo Production Ltd* v *Securicor Transport Ltd* [1980] AC 827, and it would now appear that fundamental breach is relevant only as a factor to be considered in the construction of the contract.

THE DOCTRINE OF WAIVER

An indulgence constituting a common feature of commercial life is that of waiver, that is, a substituted performance. This is embodied in s. 11(2) of the Sale of Goods Act 1979 as follows:

> Where a contract of sale is subject to a condition to be fulfilled by the seller, the buyer may waive the condition, or may elect to treat the breach of the condition as a breach of warranty and not as a ground for treating the contract as repudiated.

The efficacy of waiver is open to the technical objection that it is unsupported by consideration and, as such, it draws heavily on equitable doctrine. It is clear that a waiver is of no effect unless it is unequivocal and only where the representee acts on it to his detriment. The relationship between waiver and equitable estoppel is obvious; as Denning LJ pointed out in *Charles Rickards Ltd* v *Oppenhaim* [1950] 1 KB 616 at p.623:

> If the defendant, as he did, led the plaintiffs to believe that he would not insist on the stipulation as to time, and that, if they carried out the work, he would accept it, and they did it, he could not afterwards set up the stipulation as to the time against them. Whether it be called waiver or forbearance on his part, or an agreed variation or substituted performance, does not matter. It is a kind of estoppel. By his conduct he evinced an intention to affect their legal regulations. He made, in effect, a promise not to insist on his strict legal rights. That promise was intended to be acted on, and was in fact acted on. He cannot afterwards go back on it.

Insofar as waiver and estoppel differ, it is mainly that reliance while essential for estoppel is not important to waiver (see *Motor Oil Hellas (Corinth) Refineries SA* v *Shipping Corporation of India* [1990] 1 Lloyd's Rep 391; compare *Vitol SA* v *Esso Australia Ltd* [1989] 2 Lloyd's Rep 451). The major differences between waiver and equitable estoppel include: first, whereas waiver looks to the intention and knowledge of the waivor, estoppel does not as it is concerned with the effect on the representee; second, whilst waiver of past breaches of contract can never be revoked (although in many cases it will be impossible to restore the former position), the effect of estoppel is to suspend obligations which may be revoked with reasonable notice. The distinction was summed up by Lord Goff of Chieveley in the House of Lords who gave the principal speech in *Motor Oil Hellas (Corinth) Refineries SA* v *Shipping Corporation of India* at p. 399:

> ... the representation itself is different in character in the two cases. The party making his election is communicating his choice whether or not to exercise a right which has become available to him. The party to an equitable estoppel is representing that he will not in future enforce his legal rights. His representation is therefore in the nature of a promise which, though unsupported by consideration, can have legal consequences; hence it is sometimes referred to as promissory estoppel.

The case of *Charles Rickards Ltd* v *Oppenhaim* [1950] 1 KB 616 is a convenient illustration of the effects of the doctrine of waiver. In this case, the defendant ordered a Rolls-Royce chassis from the plaintiffs who agreed to build a body on it by 20 March. After the plaintiffs had failed to complete the work by that date, the defendant continued to press for delivery but on 29 June gave notice that, if the work was not completed within a further four weeks, he would cancel the order. The Court of Appeal unanimously held that the time of delivery was of the essence of this contract, but that this stipulation was waived by the defendant's requests for delivery after the due date which would have estopped him had there been delivery within the extended time. However, the notice given on 29 June granted a final indulgence of four weeks and constituted reasonable notice (see *Tool Metal Manufacturing Co. Ltd* v *Tungsten Electric Co. Ltd* [1955] 1 WLR 761) that time was once more of the essence of the contract, and that failure to deliver would amount to a breach of condition entitling the defendant to rescind the contract. From this it would appear that a party can be considered to have waived his rights without full knowledge of the facts. Nevertheless, the Court of Appeal in *Procter and Gamble Philippine Manufacturing Corporation* v *Peter Cremer GmbH & Co.* [1988] 3 All ER 843 pointed out that promissory estoppel may be relevant here if there is a representation which carries a strong implication that the representor did have full knowledge of the facts.

The issue of waiver is particularly important where a buyer rejects the goods for a wrong reason. The argument here is that the buyer can rely on the seller's breach as a waiver of performance so as to justify refusal to accept delivery. It is a long-established rule of law that where a contracting party refuses to perform his contractual obligations by giving a wrong reason, this does not subsequently deprive him of a justification which in fact *existed at the time* of refusal (see *Taylor* v *Oakes, Roncorni and Co.* (1922) 127 LT 267; *Braithwaite* v *Foreign Hardwood Co. Ltd* [1905] 2 KB 543; *Fercometal SARL* v *Mediterranean Shipping Co. SA* [1989] AC 788). Lastly, it should be noted that a party who reserves legal rights following breach can still, as a matter of law, be regarded to have waived the breach. The reason for this is that following the breach of condition which leads to termination, the innocent party has alternative remedies: He can either affirm the contract or terminate it.

IMPOSSIBILITY OF PERFORMANCE

The contract of supply may be set aside due to impossibility of performance. The contractual terms will be highly relevant here and it may be that, as a matter of construction, the contract will stipulate for alternative performance. In certain circumstances the supply of particular goods may be prohibited and if this prohibition is in force when the contract is made, the contract affected will be void for illegality. However, if the parties foresee that subsequent events may mean that performance is not legally possible, the loss may be determined according to the contractual allocation of risk.

Initial impossibility

The question of damage occurring in contracts of supply goes hand in hand with assumption of risk and the implied terms applicable to such contracts. Nevertheless, where the loss or damage changes the nature of the goods, it would appear that the matter is dealt with by s. 6 of the Sale of Goods Act 1979 which states:

> Where there is a contract for the sale of specific goods, and the goods without the knowledge of the seller have perished at the time when the contract is made, the contract is void.

This section is understood to confirm the *ratio* in the difficult case of *Couturier* v *Hastie* (1856) 5 HL Cas 673. Here the defendant, acting as *del credere* agent for the plaintiffs, sold a cargo of wheat thought to be on a particular ship sailing from Salonika. In fact before the contract was made, the cargo had been lawfully sold by the master of the ship because, owing to inclement weather (overheating) the cargo was unfit for further transit. The buyer refused to pay for the goods and the plaintiffs sued the defendant who, as *del credere* agent, guaranteed the buyer's performance. The House of Lords held that as the buyer was not obliged to pay neither were the defendants.

A careful analysis of the House of Lords decision in *Couturier* v *Hastie* would show that the buyer, as a matter of construction of the contract, had not assumed the risk of the non-existence of the subject-matter of the contract. This is a more appropriate basis for determining liability. With this in mind, it may be possible to argue that s. 6 is capable of being displaced by contrary agreement because s. 55(1) allows the parties to contract out of or vary 'any right, duty, or liability' which would arise by implication of law. The difficulty with this argument is that s. 6 does not impose 'any right, duty, or liability' but rather avoids them. As an alternative, it may be possible to construe any statements made as to the existence of goods as either a collateral warranty or else as a misrepresentation. If one adopts the first approach, there is the problem of finding good consideration because the main contract is treated as being void; the second approach presupposes that an express statement to the effect that the goods exist has been made, and this will not always be the case.

There is authority which suggests that, in appropriate circumstances, a seller of non-existent goods may be held liable through a strict interpretation of s. 6.

Thus in *McRae* v *Commonwealth Disposals Commission* (1951) 84 CLR 377, the defendants contracted to sell to the plaintiffs a shipwrecked tanker on a certain reef. It was held that s. 6 did not apply since the goods were not *in esse*, that is, not only was there not, and there had never been any tanker, but also the reef was non-existent. Similarly on the facts in *Associated Japanese Bank (International) Ltd* v *Crédit du Nord SA* [1989] 1 WLR 255, which involved a sale and leaseback of non-existent machinery, it is unlikely that this contract would have been caught by s. 6 of the Sale of Goods Act 1979. In adopting this approach, the Act is in danger of appearing disjointed because close parallel cases falling just within it will be void, whereas those falling just outside it will centre upon the construction of the contract. This strait-jacket approach may be inevitable as s. 6 is one of the few provisions in the Sale of Goods Act 1979 which is not expressed to give way to a contrary intention. Such an approach is unfortunate and, as a matter of principle, there is considerable appeal in Lord Diplock's dictum in *Ashington Piggeries Ltd* v *Christopher Hill Ltd* [1972] AC 441, where his lordship said at p. 501 that the Sale of Goods Act 1979 should not 'be construed so narrowly as to force upon parties to contracts for the sale of goods promises and consequences different from what they must reasonably have intended'.

The scope of s. 6 is comparatively narrow. The operation of this section, as well as s. 7 which deals with frustration, are expressed to be applicable where 'specific goods' have 'perished'. It seems appropriate, therefore, to focus upon the meaning of both of these concepts.

Specific goods Section 61 defines 'specific goods' as 'goods identified and agreed upon at the time a contract of sale is made'. It is sufficient at this stage (see pp. 46–8) merely to note that the modern tendency in the case law is to confine the scope of 'specific goods' to mean *existing* goods which have actually been identified or agreed upon (compare *Howell* v *Coupland* (1876) 1 QBD 258).

Perish The Sale of Goods Act 1979 does not define 'perish'. Clearly, it applies to cases of physical destruction and, presumably, where goods have ceased to exist in a commercial sense. In *Barrow, Lane and Ballard Ltd* v *Phillip Phillips and Co. Ltd* [1929] 1 KB 574, goods which were stolen were held to have perished. Care must be taken with this decision since it cannot be the case that all stolen goods are *per se* considered 'perished', at least until all hope has been abandoned for their recovery. The case is authority for the proposition that where a contract for the sale of specific parcels of goods (nuts in this instance) is indivisible, the perishing of part of the goods will render the contract void under s. 6. There are difficulties here because the sellers *did* deliver bags which had not been stolen when delivery was required under the contract, and the buyers paid the price without question. On the assumption that the contract was void, the buyer should only have been liable to pay a reasonable price, which would not necessarily reflect the contract price. In addition, the seller should not have been under an obligation to deliver. To consider the contract void in these circumstances does involve a legal fiction, especially in the light of the fact that the sellers delivered and the buyers paid for a substantial part of the goods (150 bags of nuts out of a parcel of 700). Moreover, at common law, it is evident, following *H.R. and S. Sainsbury Ltd* v *Street* [1972] 1 WLR 834, that the buyer may always, if he wishes, waive his right to full and complete delivery and insist on having the remainder so long as he is willing to pay the full contract price or the appropriate part of a divisible price. It is difficult to see how this can be reconciled with the statutory provision that the contract is void.

It is not possible to reconcile the case law dealing with perishability. Much depends upon the facts and the commercial sense of the transaction. Thus in *Asfar and Co.* v *Blundell* [1896] 1 QB 123, dates saturated in sewage were held to have perished, whereas, in *Horn* v *Minister of Food* [1948] 2 All ER 1036, potatoes which had so rotted as to be worthless were held not to have perished because they were still 'potatoes'. As a matter of principle, this latter approach can be supported because, taken to its logical conclusion, a seller who had sold goods in breach of their contract description under s. 13 of the Sale of Goods Act 1979 could avoid this through recourse to s. 6. In the light of advancements in technology, especially irradiation techniques, the issue of whether goods have perished will be one of degree and it may be that the question will be more intimately linked with the contract date for delivery.

Subsequent impossibility

If the risk is not on the buyer, s. 20(1) of the Sale of Goods Act 1979 presumes the risk to be on the seller. Although the rules of risk allocation determine who bears the loss of goods, they will not determine the case of subsequent impossibility, i.e., from contingencies not expressly or impliedly dealt with by the allocation of risk. In this circumstance, the contract may be set aside because of the doctrine of frustration.

The only provision in the Sale of Goods Act 1979 dealing with frustration is s. 7 which states:

> Where there is an agreement to sell specific goods and subsequently the goods, without any fault on the part of the seller or buyer, perish before the risk passes to the buyer, the agreement is avoided.

The scope of this section is comparatively narrow. We have already considered the meaning of 'specific goods' and also 'perish'. It should be noted that the presumption in s. 18, rule 1, is that a contract for the sale of specific goods passes both the property and risk at once (see pp. 50–1), so it cannot be said that the subsequent destruction of the goods can frustrate the contract. In any case, s. 7 is only a rule of construction which can be avoided by contrary agreement.

Even where s. 7 does not apply, the contract may be frustrated at common law. In the case of unascertained goods, it is unlikely that the contract may be set aside on the basis of frustration as the seller should be able to find alternative goods on the basis of *genus numquam perit* (but compare *Re Badische Co. Ltd* [1921] 2 Ch 331). Of course, where goods have been appropriated to a contract it is possible for frustration to apply, for example, damage or destruction to the contract goods as in *Appleby* v *Myers* (1867) LR 2 CP 651. Moreover there may be frustration where the goods are partially ascertained where part of a bulk is sold (compare *Re Wait* [1927] 1 Ch 606). In *Howell* v *Coupland* (1876) 1 QBD 258 it was held that an agreement to sell a crop to be grown on a particular field could be frustrated by the failure of the entire crop.

Effects of frustration   This will depend upon whether the goods are specific or not. In England, contracts for specific goods are governed by the common law because s. 2(5)(c) of the Law Reform (Frustrated Contracts) Act 1943 expressly excludes from its operation sale contracts governed by s. 7 of the Sale of Goods Act 1979. Under the common law following *Chandler* v *Webster* [1904] 1 KB 493, if the seller had been paid in advance he could keep the money irrespective of delivery, and if the price due had fallen before the frustrating event the seller could actually sue for it. This approach was tempered by the House of Lords in *Fibrosa SA* v *Fairbairn Lawson Combe Barbour Ltd* [1943] AC 32, where it was held that a buyer could recover his prepayment on the basis that there had been a total failure of consideration. The difficulty is that the seller has no claim for expenses necessarily incurred before the frustrating event, and there is no provision for the apportionment of loss. The doctrine of risk will be highly pertinent here because if the risk is on the seller, the buyer will not have to pay for goods which are not delivered to him under a contract which is subsequently frustrated. Even so, the expanding ambit of the law of unjust enrichment may ensure that benefits received by the buyer which survive the frustrating event cannot be kept without payment.

The narrow scope of s. 7 of the Sale of Goods Act 1979 should be noted. It only applies to *sale* contracts and has no application in analogous supply contracts, for example, a contract for work and materials. Moreover the frustrating event anticipated under s. 7 is confined to the perishing of specific goods so that other frustrating events including war, supervening illegality, requisitioning, or destruction of goods other than by perishing are not covered. In these situations the principles of unjust enrichment will apply insofar as they have been encapsulated in the Law Reform (Frustrated Contracts) Act 1943. Under this statute the main drawbacks of the law resulting form the *Fibrosa SA* case are remedied. The general common law rule is that frustration does not retrospectively annul the contract: it only brings the contract to an end as from the occurrence of the frustrating event. The 1943 Act provides significant rules for readjustment in the light of prepayments made or part delivery.

FORMALITIES

We have already noted that as far as contracts of supply are concerned, required formalities are the exception. Nevertheless in the following situations certain formalities have to be satisfied:

(a)   Auction sales.
(b)   Regulated consumer credit agreements.

(c) Sales of interests in land because the definition of 'goods' in s. 61 of the Sale of Goods Act 1979 as including *fructus naturales* may have to satisfy the requirements of s. 2 of the Law of Property (Miscellaneous Provisions) Act 1989. On the other hand, where severance of the subject-matter is envisaged under the contract and property is to pass at this time, it is possible to argue that this is only a sale of goods (see *Kursell* v *Timber Operators and Contractors Ltd* [1927] 1 KB 298).

(d) The Bills of Sale Act 1878 will apply to genuine sale *transactions*, so a sale of goods evidenced in writing by virtue of which the seller remains in possession is void against execution creditors and trustees in bankruptcy unless it is registered in compliance with the Act (Bills of Sale Act 1878, s. 8; compare non-absolute transfers, or sales by way of mortgage which are outside of the Sale of Goods Act 1979 but must nevertheless comply with the Bills of Sale Act (1878) Amendment Act 1882).

(e) Sales of certain capital assets like ships and aircraft which have their own registration formalities.

(f) Some dangerous goods are subject to special statutory regimes, for example, under the Firearms Acts 1968 and 1982 (as amended) and the Crossbows Act 1987.

It is sufficient for our purpose to elaborate upon the first two categories.

Auction sales

Auction sales give rise to some particular problems which are specifically regulated in s. 57 of the Sale of Goods Act 1979. Under s. 57(1), where goods are put up for sale by auction in lots, each lot is prima facie deemed to be the subject of a separate contract of sale. Section 57(2) goes on to state that a sale by auction is complete when the auctioneer announces its completion by the fall of the hammer or in some other customary manner. Until this time, any bidder may retract his bid, and this was settled in the 18th-century case of *Payne* v *Cave* (1789) 3 TR 148. Moreover, it was held in *Harris* v *Nickerson* (1873) LR 8 QB 286, an auctioneer will not be liable to a person who attends, on the strength of an advertisement, a place in the hope that an auction will take place. In these circumstances, advertisements will be construed as a declaration of intention to hold an auction and not a contract.

Where the auction is expressly advertised subject to a reserve price, s. 57(6) expressly preserves the seller's right not to sell below the reserve price. If the auctioneer, by mistake, forgets that there is a reserve price and knocks down the goods at less than the reserve price there is no sale. This is because the auctioneer has no express, implied or apparent authority as an agent to sell the goods below the reserve price (*McManus* v *Fortescue* [1907] 2 KB 1). It would seem that the bidder, in these circumstances, has no remedy either against the seller or the auctioneer because the sale was expressly subject to a reserve price and the auctioneer's authority was known to be so limited.

Where the seller instructs the auctioneer to place a reserve which is not publicised, the auctioneer may still refuse to accept any bid below the reserve since bids constitute only offers. However, in this situation the auctioneer may not accept a bid on behalf of the seller (s. 57(4) and (5)). In this case, the contract may be set aside and the buyer will be able to sue for damages. Even where a reserve price is notified, the owner is not entitled to bid unless this is specifically reserved. If, in the absence of this, he does bid and the reserve price is reached, this may be treated as fraudulent by the buyer. Furthermore, where a sale is announced to be without reserve and the seller intervenes, as distinct from withdrawing the goods from the auction, he has no right to bid so that the highest bona fide bidder will be able to treat the transaction as fraudulent (*Green* v *Baverstock* (1863) 14 CB NS 204).

If the auctioneer is a party to the seller's conduct then he may also be sued. The auctioneer may be held liable in any case on the basis that he had contracted to sell the goods to the highest bidder (compare *Warlow* v *Harrison* (1859) 1 E & E 309). Nonetheless, the auctioneer does not, in the absence of a contrary agreement, warrant the vendor's title. In *Benton* v *Campbell, Parker and Co. Ltd* [1925] 2 KB 410, it was held that the auctioneer was not liable to the purchaser for the sale of a car when it transpired that the person who put the car into the auction was not the owner. The extent of the warranty of title implied by the common law is that the possession given to the purchaser will be undisturbed by the vendor or auctioneer, and that the latter knows no defect in the vendor's title.

An attempt to conduct a mock auction is proscribed under s. 1(1) of the Mock Auctions Act 1961. Essentially, this is a consumer protection device making it a criminal offence to sell by way of competitive bidding prescribed articles. There are also statutory provisions governing undesirable auction practices by buyers under the Auctions (Bidding Agreements) Acts 1927 and 1969. At common law it appears to be doubtful whether an agreement for a 'knockout', i.e., a contract between interested bidders to refrain from bidding against each other, was illegal. These Acts apply to prevent dealers from agreeing to abstain from bidding at a sale unless there was a genuine prior agreement to purchase on joint account and a copy of this agreement lodged with the auctioneer. Section 3 of the 1969 Act provides that the seller may avoid the contract, recover the goods and, in default, any loss he has suffered, the parties to the ring being jointly and severally liable to him (s. 3(2)). The major difficulty in practice is that of proving the existence of such 'rings'.

Formation of regulated consumer credit agreement
The consumer credit agreement must contain certain information which is set forth in a prescribed manner laid down by the Consumer Credit (Agreements) Regulations 1983 (SI 1983/1553). A failure to comply with this entails that the agreement is improperly executed and cannot be enforced without a court order (s. 65 of the Consumer Credit Act 1974).

The consumer must be provided with copies of the consumer credit agreement but this requirement will vary. In the case where the consumer is accepting an offer by the creditor, the copy of the agreement must be given to him immediately (s. 63(1)). On the other hand, if the consumer is making an offer, he is entitled, for record purposes, to a copy of the agreement there and then but subsequently to a second copy which must be sent to him when the

Formalities and the formation of sale and supply contracts

creditor accepts his offer within seven days of the conclusion of the contract (s. 63(2)). Failure to comply with these rules means that the credit agreement will be improperly executed and will require a court order to be enforced under s. 127 of the Consumer Credit Act 1974.

The right to cancel A very important protection afforded by the Consumer Credit Act 1974 in the case of a regulated agreement is the right to cancel. This can be exercised during the 'cooling-off' period where the debtor did not sign the agreement at the business premises of the creditor, a party to a linked transaction, or a negotiator in antecedent negotiations (s. 67(b)). In addition, it can be exercised where, during antecedent negotiations there were oral representations made irrespective of whether they were made on or off business premises (s. 67).

The right of cancellation is subject to various exceptions which should be noted:

(a) Exempt agreements and also some small agreements in the case of credit sales where the credit does not exceed £50 (s. 74(2A)).

(b) Certain agreements secured on land, house purchase money or bridging loans (s. 67).

(c) Regulated agreements which are not caught by part V of the Consumer Credit Act 1974 as laid out in s. 74 of the Act, for example, non-commercial agreements, or small agreements (s. 17(1)), or running-account credit such as bank overdrafts, or other overdrafts exempted by the Director General of Fair Trading if this is not against the interests of debtor. This is also the case with agreements to finance payments on death (ss. 74(3) and 183).

(d) Unexecuted agreements signed by the debtor or hirer at 'business premises' which does not include the business premises of the debtor or hirer (s. 67(b)).

The cooling-off period where the debtor makes an offer allows the debtor to cancel until the end of five days from receipt of the second copy of the agreement which must be sent to him (s. 68(a)). In the case where the debtor accepts an offer made to him, a special notification of the right to cancel must be given to him and the debtor can cancel at any time until the end of the five days from receipt of that notification (s. 68(a)). A notice of cancellation sent by post is deemed to be served at the time of posting (s. 69(7)). However, in those cases where the Director General of Fair Trading has dispensed with that notice, usually in the case of mail-order consumer credit agreements, the cooling-off period runs until 'the end of the 14th day following the day on which he signed the unexecuted agreement' (s. 68(b)). The normal position is that time runs from receipt by the debtor or hirer of a second copy or notice. If this is never received, a fresh copy or notice must be served within seven days, and if this is not done, although the agreement remains binding and enforceable, it is perpetually cancellable under s. 68. It should also be noted that the right of cancellation is in addition to any common law right of rescission or statutory right of termination.

Duties following cancellation Where notice has been given, in the case of hire-purchase or conditional sale transactions, s. 72 of the Consumer Credit Act 1974 generally places upon the supplier a legal duty to redeliver the goods subject to a lien for any part-exchange goods tendered by the debtor (s. 73(5)). Under s. 73(2) the primary entitlement of the debtor or hirer is to recover the 'part-exchange allowance'. In the case of loan finance in a regulated debtor-creditor-supplier agreement, the creditor and the supplier are jointly and severally liable to him (s. 70(3)). Within a period of 10 days from the date of cancellation, the duty to pay the part-exchange allowance will be discharged by the return of the part-exchanged goods where they are in substantially the same condition as originally delivered to the negotiator (s. 73(2)). If both sides agree, any deterioration or delay regarding the return of the part-exchanged goods can be ignored (s. 173(2)). As far as the debtor's obligations are concerned, he must retain possession of the goods and make them available for the creditor to collect taking reasonable care of them in the meantime (s. 72(4)). The duty to take reasonable care is confined to the period 21 days after cancellation (s. 72(8)), thereafter, he usually becomes an involuntary bailee with a duty to refrain from wilful damage.

Where money has been paid over to the debtor before the end of the cooling-off period, the Consumer Credit Act 1974 gives the debtor the choice: first, to take a month's free credit before repaying the credit already advanced (s. 71(2)(a)); secondly, with regard to money already spent, he can repay the money with interest as provided for in the credit agreement so that the effect of the cancellation only relates to the linked supply transaction (s. 71(3)). Cancellation of a credit agreement also entails the cancellation of a linked transaction (s. 69(1)) as this has no effect until the principal agreement is made (s. 19(3)). Here again the debtor must allow the goods to be collected and take reasonable care in the meantime whilst sums paid out by him must be repaid. Cancellation of a directly financed transaction will leave the sale from dealer to financier still outstanding but this is normally covered through a contractual repurchase provision.

FIVE

The obligations of the supplier

DELIVERY

Under the Sale of Goods Act 1979, property passing is linked to contract rather than conveyance (see chapter 3). It follows that property passage and delivery may not necessarily coincide. Nevertheless, s. 27 of the Sale of Goods Act 1979 provides that it is the duty of the seller to deliver the goods. Delivery is defined in s. 61(1) as a 'voluntary transfer of possession from one person to another'. Whilst the Act does not define 'possession', it is clear from s. 1(2) of the Factors Act 1889 that actual custody is important (see *Beverley Acceptances Ltd* v *Oakley* [1982] RTR 417). In this respect, s. 32(1) of the Sale of Goods Act 1979 specifically provides that delivery to the buyer's agent may amount to transfer of possession.

It is important to determine what constitutes delivery for two reasons: first, failure to perform this act renders the supplier liable for non-delivery and allows the buyer or hirer to sue in conversion under the Torts (Interference with Goods) Act 1977; second, there is a presumption under s. 28 of the Sale of Goods Act 1979 that delivery and payment are concurrent conditions. It is for the parties to determine the method of delivery, but certain rules of delivery are set out in s. 29 of the Sale of Goods Act 1979 which are also applicable to hire-purchase transactions. According to s. 29(1) the presumption is that the buyer is to collect from the seller's place of business, or if the specific goods are situated elsewhere at that place. Section 29(4) adds that where goods are held by a third party, such as a warehouseman, unless there is an attornment or the transfer of a document of title there is no delivery (see chapter 2).

The time of delivery and acceptance

Where the seller has the contractual duty to send the goods, delivery to the carrier is by virtue of s. 32 of the Sale of Goods Act 1979 prima facie delivery to the buyer. This will not be the case where the carrier is an employee or bailee of the supplier, and neither will it apply in c.i.f. contracts since the essence of this transaction is the delivery of documentation such as a bill of lading. Where no time is fixed, the time of delivery in the case where the seller has a duty to send the goods is within a reasonable time (s. 29(3)), and within a reasonable hour (s. 29(5)). Failure to deliver within a reasonable time may amount to a breach of condition by the seller. Thus, any deviation from a time stipulated in the contract of supply may justify the other party in treating the whole contract as at an end (see *Bowes* v *Shand* (1877) 2 App Cas 455).

The seller's authority to fix the terms of the contract of transportation will be determined by the contract of supply. If the seller exceeds this authority by concluding a transit contract on terms unduly prejudicial to the buyer, he can refuse to accept delivery (s. 32(2)). Obviously, this has significance if the goods are lost or damaged in transit (see *Thomas Young and Sons Ltd* v *Hobson and Partners* (1949) 65 TLR 365). It may be that the parties agree that delivery is to be made as required by the buyer. In this instance, the buyer must require delivery within a reasonable hour and within a reasonable period. If the buyer through prevarication about delivery tries to extend the period of the contract of supply then, following some appropriate notice given to the buyer, this will justify the seller in treating the contract as being repudiated (see *Allied Marine Transport Ltd* v *Vale do Rio Doce Navegacao SA* [1985] 1 WLR 925).

Where the presumption in s. 28 of the Sale of Goods Act 1979 applies, delivery must be made in exchange for the price. Of course, time of delivery can be made of the essence of the contract (see *Bunge Corporation, New York* v *Tradax Export SA, Panama* [1981] 1 WLR 711). In the case of hire and hire-purchase contracts the tender of delivery is essential, and, insofar as the agreement does not cover delay in delivery, the rules of sale will apply by analogy. In fact, s. 10(2) of the Sale of Goods Act 1979 refrains from laying down a rule that delivery is of the essence of the contract. This is also the position regarding acceptance of delivery except where the goods are perishable, or where there is a 'spot' contract where immediate delivery is envisaged. Section 48(3) of the Sale of Goods Act 1979 enables the seller to resell perishable goods without notice to the buyer if the price is not paid when due. It is worth noting that the proposals in the Law Commission Report on *Sale and Supply of Goods* (Law Com. No. 160, London, 1987), have no application to a breach of a stipulation as to time, or any other *express* term of the contract which is classifiable as a condition.

Delivery of wrong quantity
There are no provisions under the Supply of Goods and Services Act 1982 and the Supply of Goods (Implied Terms) Act 1973 with respect to delivery of wrong quantity. The analogy provided with the approach taken under the Sale of Goods Act 1979 is an obvious one. Thus under s. 30 of the Sale of Goods Act 1979, if the seller supplies a quantity of goods different from that contracted for, the buyer can reject what is tendered subject to the *de minimis* rule and any trade usage or course of dealing between the parties (s. 30(5)). Such a strict rule is open to abuse where there is a minor discrepancy as it would seem to allow a buyer to escape from an improvidential bargain in the light of

subsequent adverse market conditions. It is for this reason that the Law Commission in their Report No. 160 recommended at para. 6.20 that, in non-consumer sales, the buyer should only be able to reject if it is reasonable to do so. Under the Consumer Guarantees Bill 1990, it was proposed to limit the buyer's right to reject for a shortfall, or his right to reject all the goods for an excess if the shortfall or excess was 'so slight that it would be unreasonable for him to do so'. Of course, this would introduce an element of uncertainty into the law, but this may be justified insofar as it will, in future, avoid technical breaches justifying rejection of the contract allowing the party to escape from an improvidential bargain where, for example, the market price has fallen.

In the case where the seller delivers too little, s. 30(1) provides that the buyer can either reject the goods, or if he accepts them he must pay for them at the contract rate. Interestingly, there is no express provision for damages even though the buyer may have suffered loss, presumably on the basis that the latter has waived the breach of contract. The exercise of the option to accept or reject assumes that the buyer knew the true facts. Moreover, the seller cannot excuse a short delivery on the ground that he will deliver the remainder in due course (s. 31(1)). The rules as to rejection for instalment delivery are more flexible and will be discussed later.

The counterpart to the delivery of too little is the delivery of too much. Under s. 30(2) of the Sale of Goods Act 1979 the buyer has the alternative of accepting the contract quantity and rejecting the surplus, or he can accept or reject the whole quantity. If the buyer accepts all the goods delivered he must pay for them at the contract rate (s. 30(3)). There is nothing anomalous about the rule which allows the buyer to reject the whole delivery in this circumstance because the buyer cannot be expected to go to the expense of separating the surplus goods. However, the implication that the seller when delivering excess goods always intends to sell the surplus is open to doubt. This is especially so when considering s. 30(4) of the Sale of Goods Act 1979 which applies to the delivery of mixed goods. In this circumstance, the buyer has only two options, namely, he may accept the goods which are in accordance with the contract and reject the rest, or he may reject the whole. It follows that the excess goods cannot be kept. Given that it is difficult to see what s. 30(4) adds to s. 30(1) which covers delivery of too much, it does seem anomalous that the buyer can keep the excess goods in all cases as is anticipated in the latter subsection. It could be argued that where a mistake is apparent in the case of excess, it is open to the courts to qualify s. 30 by reference to the common law position relating to mistake, and this is expressly provided for in s. 62(2) of the Sale of Goods Act 1979.

The interrelationship between undertakings as to quantity and quality is self-evident (see in *Re Moore and Co. Ltd and Landauer and Co.* [1921] 2 KB 519). However, there is one important distinction in legal treatment which should be noted; whereas deviation from contract description in quality points to defective performance, the tendering of a different quantity of goods amounts to a counter-offer by the supplier which gives the buyer the right to reject or accept. The rules contained in s. 30 are prima facie rules and are subject to the general proviso of contrary intention encapsulated in s. 55(1) of the Sale of Goods Act 1979. On the other hand, the requirement of description contained in s. 13 is categorised as an implied condition which automatically gives the buyer the right to reject and cannot be excluded in the case of consumer sales (s. 6(2) of the Unfair Contract Terms Act 1977).

Delivery by instalments
Unless otherwise agreed, s. 31(1) of the Sale of Goods Act 1979 provides that the buyer of goods is not bound to accept delivery of the goods by instalments. The question of whether the contract is one by instalments is a matter of construction (s. 31(2)), but it would seem that this issue is not necessarily determinative of the matter as to whether the contract is severable. If the contract is not severable, even though the goods are delivered by instalments a partial breach as we have discussed above gives rise to a right to reject all the goods. Section 31(2) of the Sale of Goods Act 1979 provides:

> Where there is a contract for the sale of goods to be delivered by stated instalments, which are to be separately paid for, and the seller makes defective deliveries in respect of one or more instalments, or the buyer neglects or refuses to take delivery of or pay for one or more instalments, it is a question in each case depending on the terms of the contract and the circumstances of the case whether the breach of contract is a repudiation of the whole contract or whether it is a severable breach giving rise to a claim for compensation but not to a right to treat the whole contract as repudiated.

It is a question in each case depending on the terms of the contract and circumstances whether the breach of contract is a repudiation of the whole contract, or whether it is a severable breach giving rise to a claim for damages. An attempt to lay down some principles to apply to s. 31(2) of the Sale of Goods Act 1979 was made in *Maple Flock Co. Ltd* v *Universal Furniture Products (Wembley) Ltd* [1934] 1 KB 148. In this case, the seller had delivered too great a quantity of rag flock in one instalment and it was held that this was not a breach which amounted to a repudiation because it was unlikely to recur. Two factors weighed heavily with the Court of Appeal: first, the quantitative ratio of the breach to the contract as a whole; second, the degree of probability that the breach would be repeated. An important distinction should be drawn between a single severable contract and a number of distinct and separate contracts. In the case of the latter, breach of one separate contract is unlikely to justify repudiation of the others. Even though s. 31(2) appears only to contemplate two remedies for the buyer, repudiation of the whole contract or damages, there is in fact a third possible course of action available to him. There is nothing objectionable in the buyer retaining the goods and rejecting the defective instalment subject to the rules governing partial acceptance under s. 11(4) of the Sale of Goods Act 1979. This appears to be correct as a matter of legal logic since termination of a contract is not equivalent to a rescission *ab initio* (see *Johnson* v *Agnew* [1980] AC 367).

A difficulty which has not yet been resolved in the case law concerns the effect of repudiation in a severable contract on the delivery of prior instalments.

A literal reading of s. 31(2) does contemplate that the buyer has the right to reject these prior instalments even though they may be in conformity with the contractual obligation. This will be of significance as a mechanism for perhaps retrospectively validating the buyer's previous wrongful rejection.

Delivery and the consequences of repudiation
The seller's duty to tender delivery and the buyer's duty to accept them are reciprocal obligations. If the buyer indicates that he will not take the delivery, the seller is entitled to accept this anticipatory breach and need not tender delivery. However, if the seller is unwilling or cannot in any case make delivery, the contract should be discharged on the basis of mutual abandonment.

In *British and Beningtons Ltd* v *North Western Cachar Tea Co. Ltd* [1923] AC 48, the House of Lords held that where there was an anticipatory breach by the buyer, the seller did not have to prove at the date of repudiation that he was ready and willing to tender delivery. Nevertheless, where the buyer can show that the seller was unable to perform his obligations this ought to be a good defence. There appears to be authority to the contrary in *Braithwaite* v *Foreign Hardwood Co.* [1905] 2 KB 543 which has caused some difficulty. This case involved the shipment of Honduras rosewood and the buyers repudiated the contract so the seller eventually resold the timber elsewhere. The defendant buyers later discovered that part of the timber did not conform to the contract, and when the plaintiff sued for damages in view of the defendants' non-acceptance, the buyers pleaded that they could not have performed their contract in any case. The buyers' defence was rejected by the Court of Appeal, but the basis of the decision has caused considerable controversy. More recently, the House of Lords in *Fercometal SARL* v *Mediterranean Shipping Co. SA* [1989] AC 788 explained the decision on the basis that the seller had accepted the buyer's repudiation. As a consequence, the contract was terminated and so was the seller's duty to deliver conforming goods. In the absence of this, it was considered in *Fercometal* that the seller could be freed from his duty to deliver where he had acted upon the representation of the buyer who was, thereby, estopped from complaining of the seller's failure to deliver. Where the buyer's own breach had induced the seller to believe that it was unnecessary to tender delivery, the doctrine of waiver could also be applied.

In practice it will be difficult to determine whether the seller has accepted the buyer's continued repudiatory conduct. This will inevitably lead to some fine distinctions. Even so, it may be that a resale of goods following a repudiation by the buyer will rescind the contract irrespective of the common law rules as to acceptance of a repudiation (see s. 48(3) and (4) of the Sale of Goods Act 1979). Despite this, the conventional position is that the buyer cannot escape liability for non-acceptance simply on the basis of showing that, had the contract continued in existence, the seller would have been unable to deliver. Even so, it is a well-established principle of law that a party is not precluded from relying upon one ground for repudiation merely because at the time he gave another and unjustified reason for repudiation. If at the time of repudiation the buyer had a good reason for repudiation unknown to himself, the fact that he gave a bad reason or even no reason for repudiation is irrelevant.

The right of the seller to sue for the price is limited to the case where property has passed to the buyer. Where the buyer refuses delivery, the seller can sue in damages for non-acceptance only (see chapter 6). If the buyer has the right to repudiate the contract then he can decline to pay the price, or if he has paid it, this can be recovered on the basis of total failure of consideration.

IMPLIED UNDERTAKINGS AS TO QUALITY AND DESCRIPTION

Historically the doctrine of *caveat emptor*, or let the buyer beware, had little place in English law. This is not surprising in a society where there was Christian influence and the concept of sin was so acute. Standards were kept in fairs and markets so that in the Assize of Bread and Beer (1256) a mechanism of complaint was instituted against poor loaves or insufficient gallons of beer. Moreover, there were customs in markets which aimed to protect standards and the emphasis was upon maintaining honesty and standards in trade.

The doctrine of *caveat emptor* with the adoption of the Latin tag does have an authentic ring to it. Even so it is alien to the spirit of the civil law. Indeed, Ulpian puts the case of a seller of a female slave who knowingly allows the buyer to believe that she is a virgin when she is not (D.19.1.11.5), a defect which is treated as incurring strict liability so that the buyer can return the slave. It is uncertain, therefore, how *caveat emptor* was adopted in English law. Certainly it could not find a place within the great authoritarian scheme by which Christian society was ordered. The emergence of *caveat emptor* is probably explained in terms of it being a shorthand expression to cover the case where no writ or redress was available and this was transmogrified into a legal principle in the 18th and 19th centuries. After all, this was the age of the triumph of the mercantile viewpoint which was quite at variance with any concept of asceticism.

The Sale of Goods Act 1893 marked the legislative beginning of the movement away from *caveat emptor* where a number of implied terms were laid down. Today s. 12 of the Sale of Goods Act 1979 provides the implied undertaking as to title which was discussed in chapter 2. Sections 13, 14 and 15 of the Sale of Goods Act 1979 include four major implied conditions which relate to conformity with description, merchantibility, fitness for purpose and conformity to any sample provided. These implied terms have been substantially reproduced in the Supply of Goods and Services Act 1982. The movement towards *caveat venditor*, at least in consumer sales, was confirmed by the Consumer Guarantees Bill 1990 which sought to implement the recommendations of the Law Commission Report, *Sale and Supply of Goods* (Law Com. No. 160, London, 1987). Here a distinction is drawn between consumer sales where the four major implied conditions remain, whilst, in non-consumer sales, a *de minimis* principle was introduced under the proposed new s. 15A(1)(b) where breach was treated as sounding only in damages. This part of the Bill had government support and it is reasonable to suppose that it will be reintroduced within the near future.

The Consumer Guarantees Bill 1990 was a private member's Bill which did not reach the statute book because it favoured legislation defining different categories of consumer guarantees and prescribing minimum provisions for each of them. Such an approach did not find favour with a Conservative government on the basis that it could lead to unnecessary bureaucracy.

Supplies by description
Section 13(1) of the Sale of Goods Act 1979 lays down that:

> Where there is a contract for the sale of goods by description, there is an implied condition that the goods will correspond with the description.

This undertaking can also be found in the case of a contract of supply (s. 3(1) of the Supply of Goods and Services Act 1982), and also in the case of a bailment (s. 8(1)(2) of the Supply of Goods and Services Act 1982) as well as a hire-purchase arrangement (s. 9(1) of the Supply of Goods (Implied Terms) Act 1973 as substituted by the Consumer Credit Act 1974).

In a sense, the inclusion of an implied term of correspondence with description is a little surprising. It was accepted quite early on that a seller would be bound by any description by which he had sold specific goods (*Shepherd* v *Kain* (1821) 5 B & Ald 240). Elementary description had a natural place, particularly where 'errors of description' had been excepted, and the courts tended to discover some measure of description *by which* the goods had been sold (see, for example, *Taylor* v *Bullen* (1850) 5 Exch 779). However, it is wrong to assume that s. 13 of the Sale of Goods Act 1979 somehow converts all statements made as to description into contractual terms, and the case of *Harlingdon and Leinster Enterprises Ltd* v *Christopher Hull Fine Art Ltd* [1991] 1 QB 564 confirms that the normal contractual principles as to incorporation of terms still subsist (see, for example, *Dick Bentley Productions Ltd* v *Harold Smith (Motors) Ltd* [1965] 1 WLR 623). The significance of s. 13 is that matters of description are treated as conditions and not as innominate terms, although this would not have been the case in non-consumer sales had s. 15A(1)(b) of the Consumer Guarantees Bill 1990 been implemented.

The meaning of description If goods sold by description are defined in terms of being identified or earmarked, in the case of a contract for the sale of specific goods, non-correspondence with description ought logically to be impossible since s. 61(1) of the Sale of Goods Act 1979 defines 'specific goods' as including those identified and agreed upon at the time of the contract of sale. In *Varley* v *Whipp* [1900] 1 QB 513, the facts concerned the sale of a second-hand reaping machine which the buyer had not seen, and the court interpreted the concept of sale by description to cover all sales of specific goods where the buyer was relying on the description. However, it also came to be recognised that a sale can be by description even though the buyer has seen the goods (*Grant* v *Australian Knitting Mills Ltd* [1936] AC 85). This is now given statutory effect by s. 13(3) of the Sale of Goods Act 1979.

The description requirement invites scrutiny of the question concerning the nature of the goods. It is important to differentiate between *which* goods are being sold and *what* they are. With regard to the former, the approach typically involves an existing subject-matter by reference to its position in time and space. Essentially, it is a process under which goods are ascertained by being identified. Nonetheless, care should be taken here to distinguish between words which can be considered to be merely useful information from words which go to the identity of the goods sold. In *Reardon Smith Line Ltd* v *Hansen-Tangen* [1976] 1 WLR 989, shipbuilders contracted to build a vessel to a certain specification at Yard No. 354 at Osaka Zosen, but the ship was in fact built at a different yard. The House of Lords did not consider these words of location as being part of the identity of the vessel. Indeed, Lord Wilberforce pointed out that only words whose purpose is to identify an essential part of the description attract the implied condition of s. 13.

There is no doubt that statements relating to the nature of the goods supplied, for example, that a car is a vintage Bentley Speed Six 'Old No. 1' is a matter of identity which goes to the heart of description. A striking case in this context is *Beale* v *Taylor* [1967] 1 WLR 1193 where the seller advertised a car as 'Herald, convertible, white, 1961'. The buyer subsequently discovered that the rear half of the car was a 1961 Herald but the front half was part of an earlier model, the two halves having been welded together. In delivering the judgment of the Court of Appeal, Sellers LJ said that even if there were no other terms as to the state of the goods, fundamentally, the seller was selling a 1961 Herald.

Most of the problems with s. 13 relate not to the question of which goods are being sold but rather what they are. Here we are concerned with essential characteristics of the goods so that, for example, in a hire-purchase case, *Karsales (Harrow) Ltd* v *Wallis* [1956] 1 WLR 936, a car was defined as being a vehicle capable of moving under its own power. In this context, we are concerned with distinguishing identity from attributes which is notoriously difficult. The leading case is *Ashington Piggeries Ltd* v *Christopher Hill Ltd* [1972] AC 441, where the facts concerned a consignment of mink food made up amongst other things of herring meal. The manufacturer of the food obtained the herring meal from a Norwegian company. Unknown to anyone, the herring meal contained DMNA, a substance which was poisonous to mink. The damage caused to the owner of minks to which the food had been given provided the basis of a counterclaim when the supplier of the food sued for the price of the food that had been sold and delivered. As between the parties themselves, the questions related to quality and fitness for purpose. However, the food supplier brought in as third party, the Norwegian company, which had provided the herring meal. One issue between these parties was whether the herring meal supplied corresponded with the description.

In discussing the meaning of s. 13, the House of Lords focused upon the question of identification so that, as Lord Hodson said at pp. 466–7:

> The language used [in s. 13 of the Sale of Goods Act 1979] is directed to the identification of goods. . . . The essential point is that identification of the goods is that with which the section is concerned.

Lord Wilberforce pointed out that the problem was not to be dealt with as though it were a philosophical question which distinguishes identity from

The obligations of the supplier

attributes. Thus, in the *Ashington Piggeries* case, it was held that herring meal containing the poison DMNA had not lost its *identity* as herring meal 'fair average quality' of the season since this was a statement of quality and not description.

If goods are sold by description, that is, by prescribing the characteristics they are to possess then, as Salmond J pointed out in *Taylor* v *Combined Buyers Ltd* [1924] NZLR 627, every element of the description, whether it relates to number, quality, kind or state, should in theory form part of the description. The reasoning here is that such goods are only capable of being identified through defining their characteristics. This phenomenon is particularly prevalent in the case of unascertained future goods where a strict approach is often evidenced. As Lord Blackburn said in *Bowes* v *Shand* (1877) 2 App Cas 455 at p. 460: 'If the description of the article tendered is different in any respect it is not the article bargained for and the other party is not bound to take it'. The leading case is *Arcos Ltd* v *E.A. Ronaasen and Son* [1933] AC 470, where the buyers agreed to buy a quantity of staves of $\frac{1}{2}$ inch thickness for making cement barrels. Only 5 per cent of the staves were of the correct thickness but the rest were nearly all less than $\frac{9}{16}$ of an inch thick. It was found, as a fact, by the arbitrator that the goods 'were commercially within and merchantable under the contract specification'. Despite this, the House of Lords rejected any concept of commercial equivalence.

An even clearer illustration of the above can be seen in *Re Moore and Co. and Landauer and Co.* [1921] 2 KB 519. In this case, tins of fruit conformed with the description in every respect except that some of them were packed in cases of 30 tins instead of 24. The packing made no difference to the market value, but the Court of Appeal held that the tins failed to comply with the description and could be rejected. In the light of the excessive technicality seen here, it is little wonder that Lord Wilberforce in *Reardon Smith Line Ltd* v *Hansen-Tangen* [1976] 1 WLR 989 and the House of Lords in *Ashington Piggeries Ltd* v *Christopher Hill Ltd* [1972] AC 441 proposed giving a narrower scope to s. 13 by confining it to matters of identification. The problem with this approach is that it begs the question concerning the nature of identification in unascertained future goods. Moreover, insofar as it suggests a commercial equivalence or *de minimis* rule this would seem to be at variance with Lord Atkin's approach in *Arcos Ltd* v *E.A. Ronaasen and Son*. In any case, the commercial context will often require strict compliance. Indeed in *Moralice (London) Ltd* v *E.D. and F. Man* [1954] 2 Lloyd's Rep 526, it was held that where the price was payable by means of a banker's commercial credit against the shipping documents, the maxim *de minimis* had no application as between the seller and the bank.

Although Lord Wilberforce in *Reardon Smith Line Ltd* v *Hansen-Tangen* called for a review of cases based upon excessive technicality, his lordship's views are *obiter* and there is no doubt that he anticipated a definitive review of the question in future cases. It may be that the mischief to which Lord Wilberforce was alluding, namely, that it allows buyers to avoid an improvident bargain, would in any case be solved if the Law Commission's proposals in the report, *Sale and Supply of Goods* (Law Com. No. 160) had been implemented as proposed by the Consumer Guarantees Bill 1990. In the case of non-consumer contracts, it was proposed that the buyer would not be allowed to reject the goods for breach of s. 13 where it was unreasonable to do so. The effect of this would be to make s. 13 an innominate term. However, in the case of consumer contracts, the right of rejection would not be lost on the basis of the recognition of the consumer's weak bargaining position. It is likely that this amendment will be implemented in subsequent legislation.

Goods sold by description and reliance If the description has a special trade usage, the goods may have to comply with the specialised meaning if this is part of the contractual intention. This is illustrated by *Grenfell* v *E.B. Meyrowitz Ltd* [1936] 2 All ER 1313, where the defendants were held not to be in breach of s. 13 when they supplied goggles of 'safety glass' which subsequently had acquired a technical meaning and the goggles conformed to this design (see *R* v *Ford Motor Co. Ltd* [1974] 1 WLR 1220 as to the meaning in the motor trade of a 'new' car). It is worth noting that under the Trade Descriptions Act 1968 and the Consumer Protection Act 1987, it is an offence to apply a false or misleading description. It is, therefore, unlikely that the *Grenfell* decision would be the same today in the light of this consumer protection legislation.

The buyer must contract to buy the goods *by* description. If there is no reliance then, notwithstanding the fact that the goods were offered for sale by description, the buyer has bought the goods on other terms. Even so, proof of reliance is not difficult especially in view of s. 13(3) of the Sale of Goods Act 1979 which provides that ordinary articles of commerce as specific goods are expressly included in the definition of sale by description. In *Harlingdon and Leinster Enterprises Ltd* v *Christopher Hull Fine Art Ltd* [1991] 1 QB 564, the Court of Appeal considered the issue of reliance on description and it is worth dwelling upon the facts. The defendants were art dealers who carried on business from a London gallery owned and controlled by the principal of the defendants, Mr Christopher Hull. In 1984, Mr Hull was asked to sell two oil paintings which had been described in a 1980 auction catalogue as being by Gabriele Münter, an artist of the German expressionist school. Mr Hull specialised in young contemporary British artists and had no training, experience or knowledge which would have enabled him to conclude from an examination of the pictures whether they were by Münter. He took the paintings to Christie's who expressed interest in them and, at the same time, he contacted the plaintiffs who carried on business as art dealers at a London gallery specialising in the German expressionist school. He told the plaintiffs that he had two paintings by Münter for sale and, accordingly, an employee of the plaintiffs visited the defendants' gallery to view the paintings. Mr Hull made it clear that he did not know much about the paintings and that he was not an expert in them. The plaintiffs' employee agreed to buy one of the paintings for £6,000 without asking any questions about the provenance of the paintings or making any further inquiries about them. The invoice for the painting described it as being by Münter, but the painting was later discovered to be a forgery. The plaintiffs claimed repayment of the purchase price on the basis that the contract was for the sale of goods by description within s. 13(1)

The obligations of the supplier

of the Sale of Goods Act 1979 which could, therefore, be avoided on the grounds of misdescription.

The leading judgment for the majority in the Court of Appeal (Stuart-Smith LJ dissenting) was given by Nourse LJ who held that there had not been a sale 'by' description (see *Gill and Duffus SA v Berger and Co. Inc. (No. 2)* [1984] AC 382). The conclusion arrived at was that the requirement 'by description' had to be determined by reference to the contract as a whole, that is, whether the characteristics had become terms in the contract. As Slade LJ put it in *Harlingdon and Leinster Enterprises Ltd* at p. 751:

> ... the fact that a description has been attributed to the goods, either during the course of negotiations or even in the contract (if written) itself, does not necessarily and by itself render the contract one for 'sale by description'.

Where there has been no reliance upon the description, it is unlikely that this can be considered an essential term in the contract. The question of reliance was determined objectively. Since Mr Hull made it plain that he was not qualified to give an opinion about the painting's authorship, the plaintiffs' employee must have realised that in proceeding with the purchase he was relying on his own skill and judgment. This argument is difficult to follow because there is no doubt that the buyer relied upon the painting being a Münter, that is, he certainly would never have bought it if he had known it was a forgery. Furthermore, the authorship of a painting is not something which can be determined before the contract is concluded in the same way that the cosmetic or mechanical condition of a consumer durable can be.

Reliance need not be total as the issue is whether the description is material in influencing the decision to buy. At the same time, it should be noted that if the description does not sound in contract, it may still have effect as a misrepresentation. In this regard, the question of *reliance* is crucial especially in the context of fine art where so-called experts' opinion may be sought. There may be little solace for potential sellers or buyers following the decision in *Luxmoore-May v Messenger May Baverstock* [1990] 1 WLR 1009, where the Court of Appeal refused to impose liability upon a firm of *provincial* auctioneers whose failure to detect the potential value of two paintings resulted in their being sold at a price substantially below their true worth. A relaxed standard of duty of care is evident in the decision, namely, there was no duty to arrive at an accurate value of an art work, rather, all that is necessary is that the valuer act honestly and diligently in the attempt to arrive at that figure. It is unfortunate that the Court of Appeal did not adopt an objective approach to competence for valuation purposes.

Exclusion of description requirement   In *Harlingdon and Leinster Enterprises Ltd v Christopher Hull Fine Art Ltd* [1991] 1 QB 564 it was argued, at first instance, that there was an actual usage or custom in the London art market which excluded the application of s. 13. Although s. 6(2)(a) of the Unfair Contract Terms Act 1977 provides that 'As against a person dealing as consumer' obligations arising from undertakings as to compliance with description cannot be excluded or restricted, the definition of 'deals as consumer' in s. 12 of the Unfair Contract Terms Act 1977 excludes a person who makes the contract 'in the course of a business'. As against a person dealing otherwise than as a consumer, as in *Harlingdon and Leinster Enterprises Ltd* v *Christopher Hull Fine Art Ltd*, exclusion of such obligations is subject to the test of reasonableness which is discussed in greater detail below (see pp. 108–12). There is no reason to suppose that in *Harlingdon and Leinster Enterprises Ltd* v *Christopher Hull Fine Art Ltd* such an exclusion clause would not have been maintained, especially since it would hardly be likely to deter art experts from using their skills in the market-place to discover masterpieces. Moreover, it is the present position that art expert buyers, in the absence of fraud or a fiduciary relationship, have no obligation to disclose information relating to the true identity of a painting.

Any clause excluding or limiting contractual description will have to be construed in the light of the common law. Obviously, if the contract goods are unascertained, an attempt to exclude *all* undertakings as to description would destroy the certainty of subject-matter in the contract. It is otherwise where the attempt is made to exclude liability for trivial breaches as in *Arcos Ltd* v *E.A. Ronaasen and Son* [1933] AC 470.

In *Harlingdon and Leinster Enterprises Ltd* v *Christopher Hull Fine Art Ltd*, by deciding that s. 13(1) of the Sale of Goods Act 1979 cannot apply because of the absence of a sale 'by description', the Court of Appeal avoided the need for the parties to exclude the term under s. 6 of the Unfair Contract Terms Act 1977 and thus expose themselves to the 'reasonableness' test. However, there is no doubt that, insofar as the seller said that he was not an expert thereby negativing reliance by the buyer on the seller, this argument comes close to an exclusion of liability, but without the common law and statutory controls that usually attach to exclusion clauses. As a consequence, s. 6 of the Unfair Contract Terms Act 1977 can be undermined simply by framing the matter of description into the general law of express contractual terms.

Undertakings as to quality
The Sale of Goods Act 1979 and the Supply of Goods and Services Act 1982 imply conditions as to fitness and quality. No other warranties or conditions to such effect may be implied except insofar as they may be annexed to the contract by custom or trade usage (s. 14(4) of the Sale of Goods Act 1979; ss. 4(7) and 9(7) of the Supply of Goods and Services Act 1982). The usage must fulfil all the normal tests of establishing a custom and it will become part of the contract so long as it is reconcilable with the terms of the contract (*Peter Darlington Partners Ltd* v *Gosho Co. Ltd* [1964] 1 Lloyd's Rep 149). However, the normal rule applicable is that of *caveat emptor* which is reflected in s. 14(1) of the Sale of Goods Act 1979:

> Except as provided by this section and section 15 below and subject to any other enactment, there is no implied condition or warranty about the quality or fitness for any particular purpose of goods supplied under a contract of sale.

This approach is also mirrored in ss. 4(1) and 9(1) of the Supply of Goods and Services Act 1982.

The *caveat emptor* doctrine has been mitigated by the implied terms as to quality. The rationale here is colourfully illustrated by Lord Ellenborough's dictum in *Gardiner* v *Gray* (1815) 4 Camp 144 to the effect that a person does not buy goods simply for the pleasure of depositing them on a dunghill. Before considering the implied terms of merchantability and fitness for purpose, some common legal themes applicable to both must first be discussed.

The supply must be in the course of business   This requirement is a common feature of consumer protection legislation and applies to both sale (s. 14 of the Sale of Goods Act 1979) and supply transactions (ss. 4 and 9 of the Supply of Goods and Services Act 1982). There is also an implied term that the supplier of a service who acts in the course of a business will supply the service with reasonable care and skill (s. 13 of the Supply of Goods and Services Act 1982). The phrase also appears in the Trade Descriptions Act 1968 and the Consumer Protection Act 1987. Moreover, under the Unfair Contract Terms Act 1977, a distinction is drawn between the effect of exemption clauses where a person acquiring the goods deals as consumer and those cases where he does not. In this respect, a person acquiring goods deals as consumer only if the supplier makes the contract to supply the goods in the course of a business (s. 12 of the Unfair Contract Terms Act 1977). This requirement reflects the policy of risk spreading.

Little guidance is given in legislation on where precisely to draw the line between business and private sales. The definitions of 'business' under the Sale of Goods Act 1979 (s. 61(1)) and the Supply of Goods and Services Act 1982 (s. 18) provide that it includes a profession and the activities of any government department or local or public authority. It would appear, therefore, that the element of profit is not a prerequisite for the finding of a business activity under this legislation. However, there must be some element of regularity of business activity, and the leading authority here is the House of Lords decision in *Davies* v *Sumner* [1984] 1 WLR 1301. This case was decided under the Trade Descriptions Act 1968, the defendant being acquitted of applying a false trade description because the sale was not in the course of a trade or business due to the absence of regularity.

It could be argued that the requirement of regularity is unduly restrictive and reflects the rationale of the Trade Descriptions Act 1968, namely, the additional duties imposed on suppliers should only fall on those who can because of the regularity of their dealings be expected to have some competence in relation to the goods supplied. Such reasoning does not easily apply to finance leasing transactions discussed in chapter 13. It is significant that under s. 46(2) of the Consumer Protection Act 1987, banks or finance companies who have only acquired goods for the purposes of supplying them on hire, hire-purchase, or conditional sale are not treated as suppliers for the purposes of liability for defective products and consumer safety. Such liability is visited upon the dealer who is considered to have introduced the goods in question into the general stream of commerce.

The view of the House of Lords in *Davies* v *Sumner* failed to take sufficient account of the variety of situations in which the phrase 'dealing in the course of a business' appears. In the case where contractual liability is strict, for example, the implied conditions under the Sale of Goods Act 1979 and Supply of Goods and Services Act 1982, the consumer protection rationale could suggest a wide interpretation of acting in the course of a business. Thus in *Corfield* v *Sevenways Garage Ltd* [1985] RTR 109, a car repairer sold a car from his garage forecourt and the Divisional Court held this to be in the course of business even though selling was an infrequent sideline. However, the Court of Appeal in *R and B Customs Brokers Co. Ltd* v *United Dominions Trust Ltd* [1988] 1 WLR 321, following the House of Lords decision *Davies* v *Sumner*, considered that the phrase 'in the course of a business' should be given a uniform interpretation in all consumer protection legislation. Unfortunately, such an approach ignores the range of situations in which the phrase appears. Nonetheless, even if it is insisted that some degree of regularity is normally required, there are situations where the first transaction entered into by a supplier can be treated as being made in the course of business, for example, one-off adventures integral to a business activity.

A significant exception to the supply in the course of a business is where a private supplier chooses to use a business agent to find a client. In this respect, s. 14(5) of the Sale of Goods Act 1979 provides:

> The preceding provisions of this section apply to a sale by a person who in the course of a business is acting as agent for another as they apply to a sale by a principal in the course of a business, except where that other is not selling in the course of a business and either the buyer knows that fact or reasonable steps are taken to bring it to the notice of the buyer before the contract is made.

A similar provision can also be found in hire and hire-purchase transactions (s. 10(5) of the Supply of Goods (Implied Terms) Act 1973, ss. 4(8) and 9(8) of the Supply of Goods and Services Act 1982). Liability is anticipated except where the seller is not, in fact, selling in the course of a business *and* prior to contracting the transferee knows this fact, or reasonable steps have been taken to bring it to his notice.

There may be important public policy issues which dictate that the implied terms as to quality should extend even to private sellers. This would essentially reverse the ordinary presumption to *caveat venditor*. Indeed in Ireland, questions of safety for road users explains the incorporation of s. 13(2) of the Sale and Supply of Goods Act 1980 (Republic of Ireland) which provides that, except where the buyer is a dealer in motor vehicles, 'there is an implied condition that at the time of the delivery of the vehicle under the contract it is free from any defect which would render it a danger to the public, including persons travelling in the vehicle'. This does not apply if the parties agree that the vehicle is not to be used in the condition in which it is when sold, and a document to this effect is signed by them and given to the buyer at the time of delivery. An important caveat to this is that the agreement must be fair and

The obligations of the supplier

reasonable. It is probable that this exception would only apply where there is a state of affairs which would make it unsafe to use the vehicle immediately. If the document is provided merely to cover the seller, it could scarcely be regarded as fair and reasonable in most cases. The Irish contractual approach is an important adjunct to action by enforcement officers. In England, the public interest is solely protected by the criminal law where s. 75 of the Road Traffic Act 1988 makes it a strict liability offence to sell an unroadworthy vehicle irrespective of the nature of the sales transaction.

The implied terms as to quality extend to the goods supplied   The undertakings as to quality extend not only to the contract goods but also to other goods supplied under the contract, for example, a defective bottle in the case of a supply of ginger beer (*Morelli* v *Fitch and Gibbons* [1928] 2 KB 636), or mineral water (*Geddling* v *March* [1920] 1 KB 668). The reference in these cases is to s. 61 of the Sale of Goods Act 1979 (s. 18 of the Supply of Goods and Services Act 1982) where the definition of 'quality of goods' covers 'their state or condition'. In the celebrated case of *Wilson* v *Rickett Cockerell and Co. Ltd* [1954] 1 QB 598, the Court of Appeal held the seller liable for damage to property caused by a detonator which was included in a consignment of Coalite. From this case, it would appear that all the goods supplied under the contract have to be of merchantable quality which is of significance with regard to 'free gifts' and promotions supplied with goods.

The protection conferred by the implied terms as to quality also extend to labels and instructions accompanying the product. Perhaps the most important case in this context is *Niblett Ltd* v *Confectioners' Materials Co. Ltd* [1921] 3 KB 387. In this case, a sale of tins of condensed milk bearing labels which infringed a registered trade mark was held to be in breach of the implied condition of merchantibility. At first instance in *Wormell* v *RHM Agriculture (East) Ltd* [1986] 1 WLR 336, it was held that accompanying written instructions were 'goods supplied under the contract'. However, this was not relied on by the Court of Appeal ([1987] 1 WLR 1091), which reversed the decision on the facts (see pp. 104–5 below).

The implied obligation of merchantable quality
The Sale of Goods Act 1979 and the Supply of Goods and Services Act 1982 provide that where goods are sold in the course of a business there is an implied condition that the goods supplied under the contract are of merchantable quality. Section 14(6) of the Sale of Goods Act 1979 which is replicated in ss. 4(9), 9(9) of the Supply of Goods and Services Act 1982 provides:

> Goods of any kind are of merchantable quality within the meaning of [the undertaking] if they are as fit for the purpose or purposes for which goods of that kind are commonly bought as it is reasonable to expect having regard to any description applied to them, the price (if relevant) and all the other relevant circumstances.

This statutory definition was originally formulated under s. 15(2) of the Supply of Goods (Implied Terms) Act 1973 which came about as a response to the demand for reform in this area. There was no definition of merchantable quality under the Sale of Goods Act 1893 because, at first, there were no problems with the definition and understanding of the concept. It was originally designed for the business community to have a broad meaning of commercial saleability in the case of unascertained goods by description.

The House of Lords in *Henry Kendall and Sons* v *William Lillico and Sons Ltd* [1969] 2 AC 31 considered the relevant authorities with respect to merchantability. The case involved sales of Brazilian groundnut extraction which proved to contain a proportion of poison. It was bought by the first buyers for the purpose of reselling in smaller quantities to be compounded into food for cattle and poultry, and was resold by them for compounding into pig and poultry food. It appeared that the extraction could still be used and would be bought at the same price for compounding into cattle food, but not for compounding into poultry food. Two tests for merchantability emerged from the survey of the old authorities by the House of Lords: The first test was whether a reasonable buyer who was acquainted with the condition of the goods would buy them without a substantial abatement of the price; the second test, favoured by the minority, was that the goods would be merchantable if they could be used by a reasonable buyer for at least one of their normal purposes. The different approaches evident in the House of Lords demonstrate the compromise which the law must seek to achieve between two extreme propositions: On the one hand, that the goods be merchantable for *every* purpose, which is harsh on the seller; and on the other, that they be merchantable for any one of the purposes, which is adverse to the buyer.

Merchantability and purpose It was a matter of speculation whether s. 14(6) of the Sale of Goods Act 1979 with its emphasis on 'purpose or purposes' had changed the law with respect to merchantability. The section could be interpreted as requiring goods to be fit for *all* of their purposes. This would have been a statutory reversal of *Henry Kendall and Sons* v *William Lillico and Sons Ltd* [1969] 2 AC 31 as well as rendering s. 14(3) which is concerned with fitness for a *particular* purpose redundant. However, the Court of Appeal in *M/S Aswan Engineering Establishment Co.* v *Lupdine Ltd* [1987] 1 WLR 1 concluded that the statutory definition in s. 14(6) had not changed the law in this respect. The facts involved the plaintiff construction company carrying on business in Kuwait which had bought a quantity of heavy-duty pails with waterproofing compound, the latter being manufactured by the first defendants. When the pails reached Kuwait they were left in the open on the quayside and the pails melted in the hot sunshine. It was held that the plaintiffs could succeed against the first defendants in contract, but in third-party proceedings the first defendants' action against the second defendants (the manufacturers of the pails) failed as the pails were merchantable under s. 14(2). The claim failed because the contract required pails suitable for export and those supplied were entirely fit for shipment to a cooler destination.

The analysis of Lloyd LJ in *M/S Aswan Engineering Establishment Co.* v *Lupdine Ltd* was an exhaustive one of previous authorities and is worth noting. His lordship maintained that s. 14(6) did not alter the law and that 'purpose or purposes' referred to the range of uses of the contract goods but not that they had to be fit for all these purposes. The question of suitability for a particular purpose was to be judged, as anticipated in s. 14(6), by reference to description and other relevant circumstances such as price. This approach is appropriate to a commercial buyer in that it forces the buyer to reveal his requirements if the purpose is over and above the most basic one for goods of that kind. Nevertheless, there is an element of incongruity here since the requirement of fitness for purpose is made the basis of s. 14(2) as well as s. 14(3).

Merchantability and quality The emphasis in s. 14(6) upon function and purpose can in one sense be regarded as undermining an important element in merchantability, namely, quality. Of course, it could be argued that purpose is not confined to use in a functional sense but also encompasses the enjoyment which the buyer can reasonably expect from his purchase. This is reflected in Mustill LJ's approach in *Rogers v Parish (Scarborough) Ltd* [1987] QB 933 where his lordship maintained at p. 944 that the purpose of buying a car was:

> . . . not merely the purpose of driving it from one place to another but of doing so with the appropriate degree of comfort, ease of handling, reliability and . . . pride in the vehicle's outward and interior appearance.

His lordship specifically rejected the argument that drivability was the sole test of merchantability and overturned the decision at first instance ([1987] 2 WLR 353) where it is held that the vehicle was merchantable as its defects did not destroy 'the workable character' of the machine. The facts involved the sale of a Range Rover sold as new which had a defective engine, gearbox, bodywork and oil seal, but which was still drivable and roadworthy. The Court of Appeal in finding against merchantability laid emphasis upon the reasonableness of the degree of fitness to be expected. This was determined by the price range, the fact that the vehicle was sold as new and by the expectations raised by the description 'Range Rover'. The fact that the car had been sold with a manufacturer's warranty was irrelevant.

It is important to remember that the question of merchantability cannot be divorced from the contract description. Indeed, this was recognised by Slade LJ in *Harlingdon and Leinster Enterprises Ltd v Christopher Hull Fine Art Ltd* [1991] 1 QB 564 at p. 586:

> The complaint, and only complaint as to the quality of the picture, relates to the identity of the artist. There is no other complaint of any kind as to its condition or quality. If the verdict of the experts had been that the artist was in truth Gabriele Münter, the claim would not have arisen. Having concluded that this was not a contract for the sale of goods by description . . . I see no room for the application of section 14. If the plaintiffs fail to establish a breach of contract through the front door of section 13(1), they cannot succeed through the back door of section 14.

This explains the approach in *Bartlett v Sidney Marcus Ltd* [1965] 1 WLR 1013 which was a pre-1973-definition case. In this case, a plaintiff bought a used car and was told it had something wrong with the clutch and oil-pressure gauge but that neither would be serious. After a few weeks, other problems appeared and the plaintiff sued for the cost of repairing them. At first instance, the judge held that the car was not of merchantable quality. This was overturned on appeal where Lord Denning held at p.1015:

> ... a buyer should realise that, when he buys a second-hand car, defects may appear sooner or later and in the absence of an express warranty, he has no redress ...

Even if a car is sold as new this does not necessarily mean that it should be perfect. Thus in *Bernstein* v *Pamsons Motors (Golders Green) Ltd* [1987] 2 All ER 220, Rougier J held that although a purchaser of a new car was entitled to expect a better-quality vehicle than the buyer of a second-hand car, nevertheless, teething problems had to be expected. The defect in this case, a drop of sealant had got into the lubrication system, went beyond mere teething trouble. A buyer was entitled to a car, not a running fight with a defective machine.

Merchantability and price The issue of price may also be relevant in the determination of merchantability. In the pre-1973-definition case of *B.S. Brown and Son Ltd* v *Craiks Ltd* [1970] 1 WLR 752 which was accepted as authority in *M/S Aswan Engineering Establishment Co.* v *Lupdine Ltd* [1987] 1 WLR 1, the House of Lords held that goods will be unmerchantable if they can only be resold at a substantially reduced price. Such an approach is also mirrored in *Shine* v *General Guarantee Corp. Ltd* [1988] 1 All ER 911. In this case, the Court of Appeal held that there had been a breach of s. 14(2) as the plaintiff had thought he was buying a second-hand enthusiast's car in good condition at a fair price when, in fact, he was buying at the same price a car which no one, knowing its history (a car insurance write-off because it had been submerged in water for over 24 hours) would have bought at other than a substantially reduced price. At the same time it has to be admitted that pecuniary considerations are only a guide, and there is authority that defective goods can be unmerchantable *per se*, for example as in the case of underpants impregnated with sulphate (*Grant* v *Australian Knitting Mills Ltd* [1936] AC 85). Similarly in *Lee* v *York Coach and Marine* [1977] RTR 35, a second-hand Morris car that was unsafe to drive was held unmerchantable even though the cost of repair was small. With manufactured goods, trivial defects have sometimes been held to render the goods unmerchantable as in the case of *Jackson* v *Rotax Motor and Cycle Co.* [1910] 2 KB 937 where motor horns bought for resale were slightly dented. This approach would seem to be correct because goods in that condition were unsaleable by the buyer under the contract description (but compare *Cehave NV* v *Bremer Handelsgesellschaft mbH* [1976] QB 44).

Durability and determination of merchantability It was clearly established in the pre-1973 cases that where goods are entrusted to a carrier for transmission to the buyer, they must be capable of remaining fit throughout the normal incidents of carriage (*Mash and Murrell Ltd* v *Joseph I. Emanuel Ltd* [1961] 1 WLR 862, reversed [1962] 1 WLR 16). By itself, this approach does not establish a concept of durability since, in the case of perishables, it is self-evident that if at the time of delivery to the carrier the natural produce are in such peak condition that they are likely to arrive in a deteriorated state, the requirement of merchantability at the time of delivery to the buyer has not been satisfied.

Following the passage of the Supply of Goods (Implied Terms) Act 1973, the requirement of reasonable durability has received some explicit recognition. This can be illustrated by Lord Denning's approach in *Crowther* v *Shannon Motor Co.* [1975] 1 WLR 30 where a used Jaguar car with over 82,000 miles on the clock was driven for three weeks covering 2,300 miles before it broke down with engine seizure. In this case, Lord Denning distinguished *Bartlett* v *Sidney Marcus Ltd* [1965] 1 WLR 1013 by explaining that if a car does not go for a reasonable time and the engine breaks up, this is evidence to show that the car was not fit for its purpose when sold. Similarly in *Lee* v *York Coach and Marine* [1977] RTR 35, the requirement of reasonable durability in the case of a second-hand car was recognised the court drawing strongly upon the approach of the House of Lords in *Lambert* v *Lewis* [1982] AC 225. A decision which seems to be on the borderline in this respect is *Business Applications Specialists Ltd* v *Nationwide Credit Corpn Ltd* [1988] RTR 332. The facts involved the sale of a second-hand Mercedes car which developed unusual faults requiring repair for a Mercedes of that age and mileage. It was held that the car was merchantable because some defects and some ordinary wear and tear should be expected with a second-hand motor car. Clearly, this is a matter of degree especially with an expensive second hand car. In order to remove all doubt, the Law Commission in their report, *Sale and Supply of Goods* (Law Com. No. 160, London, 1987), recommended that the concept of merchantability should explicitly include reasonable durability *as measured from the time of supply* and this was included in the Consumer Guarantees Bill 1990. Certainly, where the manufacturer prints advice as to shelf life on the product, this can be analysed as an express term incorporating durability.

Where goods are not durable, the mischief lies not in the fact that they ceased to perform adequately but rather at the date of supply they did not have the capacity to endure. This is important for limitation purposes so that time runs from the sale of the goods. The same approach would also apply to contracts of supply, for example, bailments and contracts of hire. It does not necessarily entail that goods supplied must be fit for the whole hire period, especially where extended hire periods are envisaged. Nevertheless, in the case of 'contract hire' of motor vehicles, the requirement of durability for the whole contract period is often expressly incorporated in the contract where, of course, the hirer pays extra in terms of rentals for facilities such as servicing and the provision of a replacement vehicle.

The determination of merchantability is at the point of delivery. However, there are difficulties with latent defects including characteristics not known to be harmful at the time of delivery, or immunities to harmful substances being subsequently discovered. These issues were considered by the House of Lords in *Henry Kendall and Sons* v *William Lillico and Sons Ltd* [1969] 2 AC 31 where the majority held that subsequent knowledge should be taken into account as otherwise, Lord Guest argued at p. 108, it would be 'to approach the true situation with blinkers'. With respect, there is much to be said for the minority view expressed by Lord Pearce which is based upon certainty in transactions and would not expose the parties to shifts in scientific knowledge right up to the time of trial. It is surely reasonable to maintain that the parties assumed to contract in the light of the scientific knowledge prevailing at the time of delivery.

Henry Kendall and Sons v *William Lillico and Sons Ltd* demonstrates that liability for merchantability is strict and it is no defence that the seller took all reasonable care that the goods were merchantable. As such, the issue of fault is irrelevant which is beneficial to a buyer especially since s. 4(1)(e) of the Consumer Protection Act 1987 restricts recovery in tort with its development risks or state of the art defence.

Excepted defects There is no condition as to merchantability where defects have been drawn to the buyer's attention before the contract is made, or if the defects should have been obvious from examination. Thus s. 14(2) of the Sale of Goods Act 1979 (replicated in s. 10(2) of the Supply of Goods (Implied Terms) Act 1973 and ss. 4(3) and 9(3) of the Supply of Goods and Services Act 1982) provides:

> Where the seller sells goods in the course of a business, there is an implied condition that the goods supplied under the contract are of merchantable quality, except that there is no such condition —
> (a) as regards defects specifically drawn to the buyer's attention before the contract is made; or
> (b) if the buyer examines the goods before the contract is made, as regards defects which that examination ought to reveal.

Proviso (a)
It is difficult to understand this defence because it is already included within the statutory definition of merchantibility as it will affect the description under which the goods are sold. The requirement that the defects be disclosed to the buyer is one of degree and it is probable that some positive act of drawing attention seems to be required.

Proviso (b)
There is no requirement that the buyer examines the goods. At common law, the merchantability undertaking was excluded by the mere opportunity for pre-contract examination which is retained in the case of sales by sample (see pp. 105–6). Under the present s. 14(2)(b), the crucial issue is what defects the examination *actually* carried out *ought* to have revealed. The standard applied here is an objective one based upon the reasonable man in the seller's position ignoring any peculiar idiosyncrasies of the buyer. In *R and B Customs Brokers Co. Ltd* v *United Dominions Trust Ltd* [1988] 1 WLR 321, a car bought on

The obligations of the supplier

conditional sale was delivered to the customer before the relevant documentation was completed. The customer discovered during this period that the car had a roof that was leaking and it was argued that, as a result of the customer's examination of the car before the contract was made, he had knowledge of the defect so as to exclude liability under s. 14(2)(b). Undoubtedly, such an approach will prejudice any buyer who takes delivery before concluding the contract of supply.

Purpose versus quality and law reform It may be that judicial ingenuity has already introduced into the law, irrespective of its emphasis upon purpose and function, a requirement that the goods supplied should be free of cosmetic defects, thereby, introducing an acceptability test. This is clearly illustrated by Mustill LJ's approach in *Rogers* v *Parish (Scarborough) Ltd* [1987] QB 933, discussed above, which gave a wide scope to s. 14(6) by bringing in defects that are, comparatively speaking, minor ones. It is submitted that this approach inhibits the development of an appropriate standard and definition of merchantable quality especially in a non-consumer setting. The matters listed by Mustill LJ, such as comfort, handling, appearance and reliability, are the concerns of a relative standard of *quality* rather than purpose. The point here is that merchantability, as a commercial concept, is unsuited in its application to consumer supply contracts, a fact which was recognised under the ill-fated Consumer Guarantees Bill 1990. This stipulated that products had to be fit for their purpose and meet standards of appearance and finish being free from minor defects, as well as safe and durable. The Consumer Guarantees Bill 1990 would have included in the present s. 14(2) of the Sale of Goods Act 1979 and its equivalent provisions under the Supply of Goods (Implied Terms) Act 1973 and the Supply of Goods and Services Act 1982 the following provision which is worth setting out in full since it received government approval and is likely to be reintroduced in the near future:

(2A) For the purposes of this Act, goods are of satisfactory quality if they meet the standard that a reasonable person would regard as satisfactory, taking account of any description of the goods, the price (if relevant) and all the other relevant circumstances.

(2B) For the purposes of this Act, the quality of goods includes their state and condition and the following (among others) are in appropriate cases aspects of the quality of goods—
  (a) fitness for all the purposes for which goods of the kind in question are commonly supplied,
  (b) appearance and finish,
  (c) freedom from minor defects,
  (d) safety, and
  (e) durability.

(2C) The term implied by subsection (2) above does not extend to any matter making the quality of goods unsatisfactory—
  (a) which is specifically drawn to the buyer's attention before the contract is made,

(b) where the buyer examines the goods before the contract is made, which that examination ought to reveal, or

(c) in the case of a contract for sale by sample, which would have been apparent on a reasonable examination of the sample.

The Law Commission in their report No. 160 recognised many of the weaknesses in the present law on merchantable quality (paras 3.4 to 3.6) and recommended a new definition to be adopted in all contracts involving supply of goods. Unfortunately, the Law Commission thought that it was not appropriate to provide different standards according to the *nature* of the transaction (para. 3.8). In this respect, the report is inconsistent since it later recommends that there should be different remedies separating consumer and business transactions. The basic principle encapsulated in the report is that goods must be of an acceptable quality: the word 'merchantable' is dropped. Goods must meet the standard that a reasonable person would regard as acceptable taking into account any description of the goods, the price (if appropriate) and all other relevant circumstances. This was considered preferable by the Law Commission to using a single word to denote either a qualitative standard, such as 'good', or a neutral standard, such as 'proper'. The new test replaces the usability test with an acceptability one which makes clear that breaches will not be confined to those which impair the use or function of the product, but extend to other factors that a reasonable person would take into account. The definition also removes the present reference to expectation and, with it, the possible argument that goods which are generally of low quality generate low expectations. The government has accepted the recommendations of the Law Commission but with the substitution of the word 'satisfactory' for 'acceptable'. There is no doubt that this substitution sounds in semantics rather than substance (see DTI consultation paper, *Consumer Guarantees* (London, 1992), para. 5).

The use of a non-exhaustive list of examples has been usefully employed elsewhere to put flesh on the bones of a general standard (see for example, Unfair Contract Terms Act 1977, sch. 2). The list covers fitness for purpose, state, condition, appearance, finish, minor defects, safety and durability (paras 3.28 to 3.65). A few specific points need to be made about some of these examples. First, the fitness of purpose envisaged is a fitness not just for one or some of the purposes to which the goods are commonly put, but a fitness for all such purposes. This reverses the present position as established in *M/S Aswan Engineering Establishment Co.* v *Lupdine Ltd* [1987] 1 WLR 1. Second, as regards durability, the goods should last for a reasonable time and any breach should be regarded as occurring at the time of supply rather than when the lack of durability became apparent. Finally, apart from demoting the status of fitness for purpose and reversing the *Aswan* case, this list does not change the present law, but merely removes uncertainty and renders the implied term easier and less uncertain in application. For practical reasons, the Law Commission decided not to include suitability for immediate use, spare parts and servicing facilities in the list. However, this does not mean that, in an appropriate case, they will not be relevant matters for a court to take into

The obligations of the supplier

account, especially where items of equipment are complex and require specialist knowledge and materials for repair.

The implied obligation of fitness for purpose
The implied condition of merchantability is supplemented by the fitness for purpose provision found in s. 14(3) of the Sale of Goods Act 1979 and is replicated in other supply contracts (see s. 10(3) of the Supply of Goods (Implied Terms) Act 1973, ss. 4(4) to (6) and 9(4) to (6) of the Supply of Goods and Services Act 1982). It would seem that two factors are especially relevant: first, knowledge on the part of the seller, bailor, transferor or their agent of the purpose for which the goods are sought; secondly, reliance upon the skill or judgment of the seller, bailor or transferor.

The statutory undertaking requires that the goods be 'reasonably fit' for the normal purpose or special purpose as communicated to the supplier (see below). This is the case irrespective of whether the supplier himself has exercised all reasonable care and skill and has not been careless, so liability is strict. Thus in *Frost* v *Aylesbury Dairy Co.* [1905] 1 KB 608, the supplier was held liable under this section for the supply of milk for household purposes contaminated with typhoid. This should be contrasted with the decision of the Court of Appeal in *Griffiths* v *Peter Conway Ltd* [1939] 1 All ER 685 where it was held that a buyer could not rely on this section when she contracted dermatitis from a Harris tweed coat supplied because of her unusually sensitive skin (see also *Ingham* v *Emes* [1955] 2 QB 366).

Sometimes the question of fitness under s. 14(3) relates to issues of remoteness of liability. This can be demonstrated in *Vacwell Engineering Co. Ltd* v *BDH Chemicals Ltd* [1971] 1 QB 88 where a chemical supplied by the defendants, although fit for the plaintiffs' purposes, exploded on contact with water, though this was unknown to the plaintiffs. It was held that the defendants were liable because they ought to have foreseen the possibility of the chemical coming into contact with water and they had not warned the buyers of this danger. The extent to which instructions and warnings can limit liability will be discussed below (see pp. 104–5).

The question of knowledge The problem of ascribing knowledge to the supplier of the purpose for which goods were intended is complicated by the fact that the goods may sometimes have more than one purpose. The overlap here with the merchantability provision is obvious and often the two will coincide. However, s. 14(3) comes into its own where the purpose in question is not a common one, or, even if it is a common one, the goods are fit for some other common purpose thereby making them merchantable. This was the case in *Ashington Piggeries Ltd* v *Christopher Hill Ltd* [1972] AC 441 where cattle food suitable for animals generally was bought for the particular purpose of being fed to mink and turned out to be poisonous to mink.

The meaning of the requirement of specificity for a particular purpose was considered in *Henry Kendall and Sons* v *William Lillico and Sons Ltd* [1969] 2 AC 31. This case involved the sale of 'Brazilian groundnut extractions' required for compounding as food for cattle and poultry by the first buyers.

They sold to the second buyers for the purpose of compounding into food for pigs and poultry. The second buyers compounded the goods into food for birds and the third buyers bought the compound and fed it to poultry which died because, unknown to anyone at the time of supply, the compound included minute traces of poison rendering it unfit for poultry. It was held that there had been a breach of the implied condition as to fitness for purpose, the court refusing to read the word 'particular' in s. 14(3) in the sense of special as opposed to general purpose.

Communication of knowledge to agent or credit broker Section 14(3) of the Sale of Goods Act 1979 makes specific provision for the situation where goods are taken on credit terms. This solves the common law problem where a particular purpose is made known by a consumer to a dealer who may not have had ostensible or actual authority to receive such communication on the part of the financing institution. Similar provisions are also found in relation to other supply situations (see s. 10(3) of the Supply of Goods (Implied Terms) Act 1973, ss. 4(4) and 9(4) of the Supply of Goods and Services Act 1982).

The statutory agency anticipated under s. 14(3)(b) of the Sale of Goods Act 1979 is in line with the trend towards consumer protection. It reflects the business reality of the situation in that for the consumer there is no distinction between vendor credit and lender credit. The logic here is carried a stage further in s. 75 of the Consumer Credit Act 1974 which applies in three-party debtor-creditor-supplier agreements as it allows the debtor a 'like claim' against the creditor as he has against the transferor. In *Porter* v *General Guarantee Corpn Ltd* [1982] RTR 384, s. 75(2) of the Consumer Credit Act 1974 was clearly misapplied. This case involved an unroadworthy car sold by a dealer to the finance company to the debtor on hire-purchase. A hire-purchase agreement is a *two-party* debtor-creditor-supplier agreement to which s. 75 does not apply. In this situation, the dealer's liability to the finance company should have been founded on the sale contract between them.

Section 56 of the Consumer Credit Act 1974 provides that in antecedent negotiations the supplier is deemed to act as agent for the creditor. In particular, the effect of s. 56(4) is very wide since this defines antecedent negotiations in the following way:

> For the purposes of this Act, antecedent negotiations shall be taken to begin when the negotiator and the debtor or hirer first enter into communication (including communication by advertisement), and to include any representations made by the negotiator to the debtor or hirer and any other dealings between them.

Thus, negotiations will include representations and 'other dealings' which extend back in time to when the debtor or hirer reads an advertisement inserted by the negotiator. Antecedent negotiations terminate on the formation of a regulated agreement. It should be noted that the definition of credit-broker under the Sale of Goods Act 1979, the Supply of Goods (Implied Terms) Act

1973 and the Supply of Goods and Services Act 1982 refers to a person acting in the course of a business of credit brokerage and effecting *introductions* of 'individuals' which would appear to exclude a registered company as a single consumer (see s. 189(1) of the Consumer Credit Act 1974). It follows also that it is not credit-broking merely to advertise credit facilities or even carry application forms. The key issue is the forwarding of a completed proposal form to the creditor or owner (see *Brookes* v *Retail Credit Cards Ltd* [1986] Crim LR 327). At the same time, the Consumer Credit Act 1974 exempts certain categories from liability here: first, lawyers involved in contentious business (s. 146(1) to (4)); second, where introductions are not effected by someone acting in the capacity of an employee canvassing off trade premises (s. 146(3)). The sense of this second exception is to apply (especially) to ladies who solicit business for friends from mail-order catalogues.

The question of reliance It is not enough that the seller knows of the particular purpose of the goods sold, the buyer must also have relied upon the credit broker or seller's skill and judgment at the date of the contract. It is not necessary to show exclusive reliance. Thus, in *Ashington Piggeries Ltd* v *Christopher Hill Ltd* [1972] AC 441 it was recognised that both the seller and buyer had their own areas of expertise, and the issue was whether the defect fell within the area of expertise of the buyer in that case. The onus of showing reliance has now shifted away from the buyer and it is for the seller to prove that there was no reasonable reliance.

There is no doubt that the shift in the burden of proof means that reliance will now be assumed. If the supplier is on an equal footing with the buyer there will be no implied undertaking. In *Teheran-Europe Co. Ltd* v *S.T. Belton (Tractors) Ltd* [1968] 2 QB 545, the facts involved the sale of machinery to a Persian company and it was held that there was no reliance on the seller's skill or judgment since the seller was ignorant of the foreign market where the goods were destined for resale. At the same time, the fact that both buyers and sellers are members of the same commodity market does not, of itself, show that the buyer does not rely on the seller. Indeed, it was pointed out in *Henry Kendall and Sons* v *William Lillico and Sons Ltd* [1969] 2 AC 31 that if the seller is himself the manufacturer of the goods the implied condition will normally apply.

Even if the buyer relies on the seller's skill or judgment the implied condition cannot be invoked where this reliance is unreasonable. Thus, a sale of 'Coalite' in *Wilson* v *Rickett Cockerell and Co. Ltd* [1954] 1 QB 598 was a sale under a trade or patent name which the Court of Appeal considered to preclude reliance. Nonetheless, the mere fact that the buyer has inspected the goods does not necessarily preclude reliance. Certainly, undertakings in the contract that the buyer has not relied upon the seller's skill and judgment will not be conclusive, especially in consumer sales where s. 6 of the Unfair Contract Terms Act 1977 precludes contracting out of the implied condition of fitness. Of course, it is still a matter of degree because the contract may be concluded specifically on the basis of non-reliance. Even so, the obligation of merchantability will still remain.

The significance of instructions and warnings Instructions placed on the goods may indicate unreasonableness of reliance. In principle, a careful approach should be adopted here since the seller should not be able to avoid the strictures of the Unfair Contract Terms Act 1977 merely by expressly stating no reliance. The only modern English case concerning instructions is that of *Wormell* v *RHM Agriculture (East) Ltd* [1987] 1 WLR 1091 (reversing [1986] 1 WLR 336). In this case, the plaintiff farmer was prevented from getting on to his land to spray his crops in order to kill wild oats until much later than normal during the wet spring of 1983. He therefore consulted the defendant sellers of agricultural products and asked them to recommend a herbicide that could be used later than usual. Their recommendation was a Shell weedkiller called 'Commando', and, accordingly, the plaintiff purchased some to the value of £6,438. The full technical instructions on the can stated that the contents ought not to be applied beyond a recommended stage of crop growth as damage might result to the crop. The plaintiff understood this to mean that, although damage to the crop might result, the 'Commando' would nevertheless be effective to kill the wild oats; and, as the weed infestation was so serious, he was prepared to run the risk of some loss to his crop of winter wheat. The 'Commando' was thus applied later than normal. However, although there was no damage to the crop, the herbicide was almost totally ineffective in killing the weeds. The plaintiff sought damages from the defendants for breach of the implied terms of s. 14(2) and (3) of the Sale of Goods Act 1979. At first instance the judge found, as a matter of fact, that the instructions were misleading and ambiguous. One of the defendants' arguments was that there was no reliance on the sellers' skill and judgment, but rather a reliance by the buyer on his own understanding of the manufacturer's instructions. The judge found that the manufacturer's misleading instructions attached to the goods sold by a retailer was a breach of s. 14(3) even though the sellers themselves did not have sufficient technical expertise to know whether the instructions were accurate.

The Court of Appeal reversed this decision, but it was held that instructions were relevant in deciding fitness for purpose. Since the 'Commando' had a clear warning that the contents should not be used after a certain time, this was deemed to put the plaintiff on notice not to use the herbicide, and he could not complain that his own misunderstanding of the consequences of ignoring the warning had rendered the herbicide unfit for the purpose for which it was supplied. It would seem, following this case, that the importance of instructions cannot be underestimated. Where they are unduly complicated they themselves may be subject to scrutiny for fitness for purpose as they could be considered to be part of the goods supplied under the contract. Indeed, it could be argued that where instructions are not adequate then there may be a breach of the merchantability provision.

It is worth noting that there is a substantial body of scientific research which demonstrates that warnings on labels simply do not work under many circumstances. There are a number of factors which control the effectiveness of a warning including whether the person is looking for the information; whether the warning is perceived as being relevant to the consumer; the degree of difficulty or inconvenience associated with following a warning. These factors help to explain why warnings are ineffective with regard to familiar consumer products simply because consumers are not usually seeking such information, that is, past experience rather than the label is the controlling factor (see Robinson, J.N., and Brickle, B.V., 'Warning Labels: Science and the Law' (1992), 142 NLJ 83).

Implied obligations in supply and services contracts

The general effect of the Supply of Goods (Implied Terms) Act 1973 and the Supply of Goods and Services Act 1982 is to equate the implied conditions applied to sale in transactions of supply. This phenomenon can also be seen in trading stamp transactions (see s. 4(1) of the Trading Stamps Act 1964).

In the case of the supply of services, s. 13 of the Supply of Goods and Services Act 1982 states that where the supplier is acting in the course of a business 'the supplier will carry out the service with reasonable care and skill'. This is the common law position and s. 16(3) provides for the possibility of a court implying stricter terms, so the reasonable care provision may be regarded as the minimum legal requirement. At the same time, the reasonableness provision under ss. 14 and 15 of the Supply of Goods and Services Act 1982 extends to time of performance and price where these are not stipulated in the contract. Obviously, these are questions of fact to be decided in each case.

Problems may arise with regard to hybrid contracts containing both a service and supply element. Section 1(3) of the Supply of Goods and Services Act 1982 states that a contract is a contract of transfer notwithstanding that services are also provided, whilst s. 12(3) states that a contract is a contract for the supply of services even though goods are also transferred. It follows that the materials element will be governed by s. 4 which refers to merchantability and fitness for purpose (see *Young and Marten Ltd* v *McManus Childs Ltd* [1969] 1 AC 454) whilst the services element will be governed by the reasonableness provision as a minimum standard laid down in s. 13. With regard to the *end-product* following a supply of materials and services, it is a question of the intention of the parties as to whether the service or materials element is the most important factor.

Implied obligations in contracts by sample

The most common situation associated with contracts by sample is where the seller abstracts a small quantity from a larger bulk, or where the buyer is sent a small representative quantity in advance. The special conditions contained in s. 15(2) of the Sale of Goods Act 1979 replicated in other supply contracts (s. 11 of Supply of Goods (Implied Terms) Act 1973; and ss. 5(1) and 10(1) of the Supply of Goods and Services Act 1982) do not apply to every case in which a sample is exhibited, for example, in a shop, but only to sales by sample. In shop sales it may still be possible to imply as a matter of general contract law that the goods supplied, in the absence of representation to the contrary, correspond to the goods displayed in the shop.

Essentially, a sample is a non-verbal description and whether or not a sale is by sample depends upon the intention of the parties. Thus, it may be that the only undertaking being made is that the sample was honestly and properly taken from the bulk as was the case in *Gardiner* v *Gray* (1815) 4 Camp 144. However, the vast majority of cases in which samples are exhibited are, in any case, likely to be sales by description. In *Nichol* v *Godts* (1854) 10 Exch 191, a sale of 'foreign refined rape oil, warranted only equal to samples' was held to be a sale by description so that a seller could not deliver something which although equal to sample could not match the contract description. Of course, this presupposes that the description is a meaningful one (see *R.W. Cameron and Co.* v *L. Slutzkin Pty Ltd* (1923) 32 CLR 81).

It is well-established that a buyer may reject goods which do not conform to a contractual sample. Strict compliance is needed so that in the case of *E. and S. Ruben Ltd* v *Faire Bros and Co. Ltd* [1949] 1 KB 254, the buyers were held entitled to reject rolls of rubber which unlike the sample shown were crinkly and hard. It was irrelevant that the rubber would correspond with the contract sample by the simple process of warming the rubber, and it would seem that the only relaxation of this strict rule is the *de minimis* principle (see *Joe Lowe Food Products Co. Ltd* v *J.A. and P. Holland Ltd* [1954] 2 Lloyd's Rep 71). Nevertheless, conformity with sample depends upon the nature of the investigation carried out. If the normal trade practice is that a sample be subjected only to visual examination, there is no breach of s. 15(2)(a) if the bulk does not correspond with the same in some manner not discoverable by such visual examination (*F. E. Hookway & Co. Ltd* v *Alfred Isaacs and Sons* [1954] 1 Lloyd's Rep 491).

The buyer is given an opportunity to inspect the goods by virtue of s. 15(2)(b). This is a specific application of ss. 34 and 35 where the buyer is given the right to examine the goods for the purpose of ascertaining whether they are in conformity with the contract determined at the contractual delivery point. The Law Commission in their report No. 160 recommended that s. 15(2)(b) should be deleted and, instead, a reference to the buyer having a reasonable opportunity to compare the bulk with the sample should be inserted into s. 34. This provision was indeed included in the ill-fated Consumer Guarantees Bill 1990.

The requirement of merchantability under s. 15(2)(c) is part of the wider principle applicable to contracts of supply (see also s. 11(c) of the Supply of Goods (Implied Terms) Act 1973; ss. 5(1)(c) and 10(2)(c) of the Supply of Goods and Services Act 1982). Despite this, there are important differences, for example, there is no requirement to supply in the course of a business, and there is no express defence of defects specified. Perhaps the most important difference is that the buyer cannot complain of defects that a reasonable examination ought to reveal. Thus, whereas a buyer by sample can complain only of latent defects, a buyer 'by description' can complain of any defects except those which his *actual* examination (if any) ought to have brought to light. This less generous treatment does not seem unreasonable because it can surely be expected that the sample should be examined. Be that as it may, the buyer can still rely on the general merchantability provision in s. 14(2). In this respect, the Law Commission in their report No. 160 proposed at para. 6.27 that reliance should no longer be possible and that s. 14(2) should be made subject to s. 15(2)(c). This proposal also extends to corresponding sections in the Supply of Goods and Services Act 1982 and was included in the Consumer Guarantees Bill 1990.

OTHER IMPLIED TERMS

The statutory undertakings discussed above are perhaps the best-known examples of the implied terms recognised in the common law and have been codified as such. Nevertheless, s. 14(4) of the Sale of Goods Act 1979 which is replicated in other supply contracts (s. 10(4) of the Supply of Goods (Implied Terms) Act 1973 as substituted by the Consumer Credit Act 1974; ss. 4(7) and 9(7) of the Supply of Goods and Services Act 1982) provides:

> An implied condition or warranty as to quality or fitness for particular purpose may be annexed to a contract of sale by usage.

The general rules apply that the usage or custom must be reasonable, universally accepted by the particular trade, certain, not unlawful and not inconsistent with the express or implied terms of the contract. An example of terms routinely implied in contracts of sale are where goods are ordered from a manufacturer who makes such goods, it is implied that the goods are the manufacturer's own make and also supplied under his normal label for the brand (see *Johnson* v *Raylton* (1881) 7 QBD 438; *Scaliaris* v *E. Ofverberg and Co.* (1921) 37 TLR 307). It can be argued that a car dealer has an implied obligation to make pre-delivery checks on a new car to ensure that it meets the manufacturer's specification. In this respect, voluntary codes of practice applied in a particular trade are highly relevant.

It is still possible to refer to the common law position. Sometimes this is difficult to state so that, for example, although the common law did refer to the owner being under an obligation to hire out goods of a reasonable fitness, the level of care associated with this obligation was uncertain being mainly the product of dictum rather than decision. Indeed the Law Commission working paper, *Implied Terms in Contracts for the Supply of Goods* (No. 77, London, 1977), recognised three possible approaches: first, the bailor is strictly liable (*Jones* v *Page* (1867) 15 LT 619 per Kelly CB at p. 621); secondly the goods must be a fit as care and skill can make them (*Hyman* v *Nye and Sons* (1881) 6 QBD 685 per Lindley J at p. 682); thirdly, the bailor is liable only if he fails to take reasonable care to ensure that the goods are fit which, as the *via media* of the two other approaches, was eventually adopted in s. 9 of the Supply of Goods and Services Act 1982. Other implied terms seen in the context of hire include an obligation to deliver the goods in substantially the same condition as they were inspected by the hirer. In the case of hire-purchase contracts, the supply of documentation including a logbook or registration document has been considered necessary (*Bentworth Finance Ltd* v *Lubert* [1968] 1 QB 680). The bailee's implied duties normally include not to convert the goods nor to deviate in the case of a carrier's obligation to follow his stipulated route. Different standards of care are applicable to the various types of bailment recognised in the seminal case of *Coggs* v *Bernard* (1703) 2 Ld Raym 909 (discussed on p. 295). The extent of the duties will normally be settled by agreement as seen in the case of finance leasing contracts discussed in chapter 13.

EXCLUSION OF LIABILITY

Far-reaching controls on attempts to exclude contractual and tortious liability were introduced by the Unfair Contract Terms Act 1977. In s. 6 of the Act, there are certain special provisions which relate to the statutory implied terms in contracts of sale and s. 7 (as amended by the Supply of Goods and Services Act 1982) contains analogous provisions with regard to other contracts for the transfer of goods. As against a person dealing as consumer, liability in respect of the goods' correspondence with description or sample, or their quality or fitness for any particular purpose, cannot be excluded or restricted by reference to any such term. There can be no exclusion of the implied title undertaking, but this is somewhat misleading since it is possible under s. 12 of the Sale of Goods Act 1979 to sell only a limited interest in the goods. The effect of s. 7(2) and (3) is that the other implied terms cannot be excluded or restricted at all where the buyer deals as a consumer; they can be excluded outside of consumer supply transactions so long as the supplier can show that such an exclusion is fair and reasonable.

Whether a person acts in the course of a business is a key element in establishing whether a person 'deals as consumer'. The Court of Appeal in *R and B Customs Brokers Co. Ltd* v *United Dominions Trust Ltd* [1988] 1 WLR 321 applied the criteria identified in cases under the Trade Descriptions Act 1968 including *Davies* v *Sumner* [1984] 1 WLR 1301 in resolving this question (see pp. 91–2). It was held that a private company which was buying a car for a director did not acquire the vehicle 'in the course of a business'. The acquisition of a car for the private and business use of a director was not considered by both members of the Court of Appeal (Neill and Dillon LJJ) to be an integral part of the company's business. Furthermore, there was an insufficient degree of regularity to make the purchase of the car by the plaintiffs something which was done in the course of their business.

The requirement in s. 12(1) of the Unfair Contract Terms Act 1977 that the goods must be of a type ordinarily supplied for private use or consumption is obviously problematic. This is illustrated by the facts in *R and B Customs Brokers Co. Ltd* v *United Dominions Trust Ltd* discussed above where a car can be used both for business and private use. It is surely a matter of degree whether the goods are 'ordinarily' supplied for private use, but s. 12(3) of Unfair Contract Terms Act 1977 provides that the onus is upon the supplier to prove that the buyer is not a consumer. The two special cases in s. 12(2) should also be noted, namely, a buyer is not to be treated as a consumer where he buys at auction, and neither is he where the sale is by competitive tender.

Exemption clauses affected by the Unfair Contract Terms Act 1977
The ambit of the Unfair Contract Terms Act 1977 in relation to exclusion clauses includes attempts to disclaim by notice liability in tort for negligence. Thus s. 2(1) of the Unfair Contract Terms Act 1977 nullifies contractual

provisions and notices excluding or restricting liability for negligence resulting in death or injury. Where a party to a contract deals as consumer or on the other's written standard terms of business (*McCrone* v *Boots Farm Sales Ltd* 1981 SLT 103), that other cannot by reference to a contract term limit, exclude or restrict his liability (ss. 3 and 13(1) of the Unfair Contract Terms Act 1977), and this applies to terms and notices (s. 13(2) of the Unfair Contract Terms Act 1977). Such an approach also applies to product guarantees which attempt to exclude or restrict the consumer's rights (s. 5(1) of the Unfair Contract Terms Act 1977).

The requirement of reasonableness Part I of the Unfair Contract Terms Act 1977 permits a party to restrict or exclude liability by reference to the requirement of reasonableness in the following cases:

(a) negligent damage to property (s. 2(2));
(b) standard form contracts (s. 3(2));
(c) indemnity clauses (s. 4(1));
(d) implied terms in supply contracts (ss. 6, 7);
(e) misrepresentation (s. 3 of the Misrepresentation Act 1967 as amended by Unfair Contract Terms Act 1977).

Except for (a), the requirement of reasonableness can only be invoked outside a consumer context.

The reasonableness test is set out in s. 11 of the Unfair Contract Terms Act 1977 with further guidelines provided in sch. 2. The requirement of reasonableness is determined at the time of contracting which is an important difference from the Supply of Goods (Implied Terms) Act 1973, under which the test of reasonableness was to be applied taking account of all the circumstances including those which occurred after the making of the contract, whereas under the Unfair Contract Terms Act 1977, the test is to be applied to the terms of the contract at the *time* of contracting. In this respect, s. 11(4) provides that where an exclusion clause seeks to restrict liability, regard should be had to the availability of resources and insurance to meet the liability. Of great practical importance is s. 11(5) which provides that the onus is upon the party who claims that an exclusion clause is reasonable to satisfy the court that it was. Thus in *Walker* v *Boyle* [1982] 1 WLR 495, a clause was held unreasonable although Dillon J listed no reasons why this was so.

The Unfair Contract Terms Act 1977 also deals with clauses exempting a party to a contract from liability for misrepresentation (s. 8). In *Howard Marine and Dredging Co. Ltd* v *A. Ogden and Sons (Excavations) Ltd* [1978] QB 574, a case decided under s. 3 of the Misrepresentation Act 1967, Lord Denning considered the following factors to be relevant: the parties were of equal bargaining position, the representation made was innocent and, in any case, the plaintiffs had failed to prove that they had reasonable grounds for believing the truth of the statement.

The question of reasonableness is determined as between the actual parties. Hence in *South Western General Property Co. Ltd* v *Marton* (1982) 263 EG

1090, a clause in an auctioneer's catalogue attempting to avoid the effects of the Misrepresentation Act 1967 was held unreasonable. The other party was a builder who bought a plot of land at auction to build a house for himself and his family. He had obtained the auctioneer's catalogue only a day before the sale and the purported effect of the clause was to relieve the sellers from telling more than a part of the material facts, thereby obliging the buyer to check the remainder for himself. There are suggestions in the judgment that the decision would have been otherwise had the buyer been a property speculator. This allows a court to adjust its decision according to the other party involved (see also *Phillips Products Ltd v Hyland* (1984) 4 TrLR 98).

A clause that is otherwise unreasonable will not necessarily be saved because it is a clause of long standing in a widely used standard form. Nonetheless, a standard form drafted by both parties or by bodies representing both parties is more likely to be considered reasonable. Thus in *R.W. Green Ltd v Cade Bros Farms* [1978] 1 Lloyd's Rep 602, a clause in a contract used for many years with the approval of bodies representing both sides was held to be reasonable.

Statutory guidelines Supplementary guidelines to the reasonableness test are included in sch. 2 the Unfair Contract Terms Act 1977. These guidelines are similar to those Supply of Goods (Implied) Terms Act 1973 and apply to sale and supply contracts by virtue of s. 11(2) of the Unfair Contract Terms Act 1977. Even so, the guidelines have been used in other cases as factors to be considered where the statute applies. These guidelines, although not exhaustive of the factors to be considered, include the following:

(a) the strength of the bargaining positions of the parties relative to each other, taking into account (among other things) alternative means by which the customer's requirements could have been met;

(b) whether the customer received an inducement to agree to the term, or in accepting it had an opportunity of entering into a similar contract with other persons, but without having to accept a similar term;

(c) whether the customer knew or ought reasonably to have known of the existence and extent of the term (having regard, among other things, to any custom of the trade and any previous course of dealing between the parties);

(d) where the term excludes or restricts any relevant liability if some condition is not complied with, whether it was reasonable at the time of the contract to expect that compliance with that condition would be practicable;

(e) whether the goods were manufactured, processed or adapted to the special order of the customer.

If one party freely consents to a clause, a court is unlikely to hold it unreasonable. Paragraphs (a) to (c) and perhaps (d) of sch. 2 reflect this fact. Clearly a pertinent factor in the determination of the free-consent issue is whether one party has exercised superior bargaining strength to impose terms on the other. The central theme of the House of Lords decision in *Photo Production Ltd v Securicor Transport Ltd* [1980] AC 827 is that the parties' arrangements will stand if there is no inequality. In this respect, alternative courses of action available to the party will be relevant. Thus in *R.W. Green Ltd* v *Cade Bros Farms* [1978] 1 Lloyd's Rep 602, farmers bought seed potatoes under a contract which limited the supplier's liability to the cost of the seed. Nonetheless, the farmers could have bought at a slightly higher price certified seed, which, being certified, was less likely to be suffering from the virus which affected the seed actually bought.

Only *genuine* alternative courses of action available will be relevant to the reasonableness question. This is illustrated in *Woodman* v *Photo Trade Processing Ltd* (see Lawson (1981) 131 NLJ 933) where insurance was said not to be a suitable alternative to cover the loss of a precious film. What was needed was a guarantee that extra care would be taken not to lose the film. Insurance is only mentioned in the Unfair Contract Terms Act 1977 (s. 11(4)(b)) with regard to clauses which seek to restrict liability to a specified sum. In this respect the court has, in holding a clause unreasonable, pointed to the facts that a seed merchant seeking to rely on the clause could have insured against the risk of crop failure caused by supplying the wrong variety of seed and that such insurance would not materially have increased the price of the seed (see *George Mitchell (Chesterhall) Ltd* v *Finney Lock Seeds Ltd* [1983] 2 AC 803).

The criteria identified in sch. 2 operate within the normal principles of incorporation of exclusion clauses under the common law. Under sch. 2, para. (c), a clause is more likely to be held reasonable if the party knew or should have known of it when he entered into the contract. A distinction should be drawn here with the reasonableness of a clause which is the main test under Unfair Contract Terms Act 1977. The wider the purported exclusion the more likely it is to be held unreasonable. In *Rasbora Ltd* v *JCL Marine Ltd* [1977] 1 Lloyd's Rep 645, which was a case decided under the Supply of Goods (Implied Terms) Act 1973, the builders of a power boat purported to exclude liability for breach of s. 14 of the Sale of Goods Act 1979. The only undertaking made was to repair or replace defective parts as a result of the use of faulty materials or of faulty workmanship. Obviously, this undertaking was of no use when, as happened, the boat caught fire and sank. In such a case, Lawson J held that the sale was a consumer sale so that the exclusion clause was void insofar as it excluded the implied conditions under the Sale of Goods Act 1979. However, he went on to say that even if the sale had not been a consumer sale, the exclusion clause was unreasonable since the buyer would be left with no remedy insofar as it purported to exclude the merchantability provision.

Limited contracting out
It may still be possible to contract out of the implied obligations owed under supply contracts. In this respect, s. 6 of the Unfair Contract Terms Act 1977 provides that liability for breach of the obligation arising under the implied terms cannot be excluded or restricted by 'reference to any contract term'. This provision has a narrow ambit and it does not prevent a supplier attempting to shrink the core of the obligations rather than excluding the implied terms. Thus, for example, the seller may argue that a sale is not by description but is rather a contract for the sale of a specific unique chattel. Alternatively, a seller

may state expressly that he is not an expert and no reliance should be placed upon any opinion he expresses (see *Harlingdon and Leinster Enterprises Ltd* v *Christopher Hull Fine Art Ltd* [1991] 1 QB 564 discussed earlier).

A fine balance has to be achieved between the definition of obligations and exclusion of liability. This can be illustrated through the increasing trend of restricting liability by reference to labelling and the insertion of instructions for use. The general approach of the Unfair Contract Terms Act 1977 relating to contractual liability is confined to contractual terms and it is, therefore, desirable that instructions and labels should be regarded as terms if they are to be controlled by the Unfair Contract Terms Act 1977. Nevertheless, s. 13 also covers 'notices' which exclude or restrict the relevant duty. 'Notice' is defined in s. 14 as including 'an announcement, whether or not in writing, and any other communication or pretended communication'. This is a wide definition which should cover pre-contractual labels or post-contractual instructions included, for example, in sealed goods. Failing this, if a consumer buyer is effectively denied the protection of the implied terms because the instructions or labels have shrunk the central obligations, recourse will have to be made to the common law rules on incorporation and the general controls of reasonableness found in ss. 2 and 3 of the Unfair Contract Terms Act 1977.

MANUFACTURERS' GUARANTEES

In *Lambert* v *Lewis* [1982] AC 225, the Court of Appeal declined to hold that statements made in advertising literature constituted a collateral warranty on the basis that they were not 'intended' to create contractual liability (this decision was reversed on other grounds in the House of Lords [1982] AC 225). Such an approach is anomalous especially since buyers will often rely upon promotional literature, and the collateral contract device may be relevant here with regard to express statements made. Of course, in order for the label or promotional literature to constitute a representation, it would have to induce the representee to enter the main contract of sale and he would have to know of it *prior* to the contract.

We have already noted that s. 5 of the Unfair Contract Terms Act 1977 restricts the ability of a manufacturer in the case of goods ordinarily supplied for private use or consumption to exclude liability for negligence. There are important limitations here so that a guarantee could provide a defence to a manufacturer in respect of damage to *property* caused by defective goods which is not due to negligence (personal injury and death being excluded by s. 2 of the Unfair Contract Terms Act 1977). Additionally, s. 5 does not apply to goods manufactured for commercial use, as in the case of commercial weed-killer bought by a farmer in *Wormell* v *RHM Agriculture (East) Ltd* [1987] 1 WLR 1091 discussed earlier. There may be circumstances where an exclusion of liability clause included in the guarantee for the benefit of a retailer may be incorporated *outside* a consumer sale context into the main contract of sale where it is read pre-contractually (see *New Zealand Shipping Co. Ltd* v *A.M. Satterthwaite and Co. Ltd* [1975] AC 154).

It would appear that the current legal status of manufacturers' guarantees is somewhat ambiguous and much will depend upon the individual circumstances of each case. It is for this reason that the National Consumer Council (the NCC) in their report, *Competing in Quality* (1989), favoured the introduction of statutorily enforcing manufacturers' guarantees. This also found expression in the ill-fated Consumer Guarantees Bill 1990 which, had it been implemented, would have defined different categories of guarantee and prescribe minimum provisions for each. Typically, where a manufacturer chose to offer a guarantee, this would have been stautorily recognised to cover the whole product and last at least 12 months. If the product then developed a 'defect' it would have had to have been repaired at no cost to the purchaser. If there was no successful repair within five days, for normal consumer items, or three days, in the case of a car, then the purchaser would have had the right to a loan of a similar item or to be compensated for any loss or expense. Further, where the defect could not have been put right in three attempts, or where the product was out of use for 30 days during a 12-month period, the purchaser would have been given the choice of refund or a replacement. This approach was rejected by the government ostensibly because, as the DTI consultation paper, *Consumer Guarantees* (1992), noted at para. 7, it ran 'the risk of creating loopholes that could be exploited by manufacturers seeking to avoid taking responsibility for the quality of their product'. Equally it could be argued that such a reform could be abused by consumers to obtain free use of products, that is, a form of 'consumer terrorism'. Nevertheless, to make the manufacturer directly responsible to the consumer for poor-quality products has been recognised for several decades (see Jolowicz, 'Protection of the Consumer and Purchaser of Goods under English Law' (1969) 32 MLR 1) and it is for this reason that the government has proposed legislation on the substance of the manufacturer's promise. Significantly, in the DTI consultation paper, consideration is also being given to extending the net of liability to *all* those involved in the chain of distribution and this accords with the position under the Consumer Protection Act 1987. Of course, one obvious effect of such legislation would be the further circumvention of the doctrine of privity by the creation of a 'statutory contract' between the consumer and manufacturer or importer of the goods.

Under the Consumer Guarantees Bill 1990, it was open to the manufacturer not to offer a consumer guarantee. By refusing to offer such a guarantee, this would constitute a signal of the manufacturer's lack of confidence in the product. Those manufacturers which did offer such a guarantee would enjoy a high reputation, thereby increasing the general demand for the goods. In practice this legislation could affect prices although, ultimately, this would depend upon whether the increase in demand was outweighed by the cost of improving product quality (see Shapiro, 'Premiums for High Quality Products as Returns to Reputations' (1983) 93 Q J Econ 1).

PRODUCT LIABILITY

In recent years there have been significant statutory interventions protecting the consumer. The most important of these relate to the quality and fitness of goods under supply contracts. Major new legislation in the Consumer

Protection Act 1987 has changed the basis on which a victim can sue a producer, introduced new criminal offences, and extended the powers of the safety enforcement authorities. It is clearly not appropriate in a work of this length to consider fully all the implications of such consumer protection legislation. All that is attempted is to focus upon a number of questions and recurrent themes.

Statutory product liability under part I of the Consumer Protection Act 1987
Part I of the Consumer Protection Act 1987 is the response of English law to the European Community Directive on the approximation of the laws of the member States relating to liability for defective products. The basic principle of the Consumer Protection Act 1987 is stated in art. 1 of the Directive, namely: 'The producer shall be liable for damage caused by a defect in his product'. Strict liability has become a basis on which a victim can sue a producer. Although the burden of proof is still on the victim to show the damage, the defect, and the causal link between them, it is no longer necessary to establish negligence. Furthermore, liability cannot be limited or excluded by virtue of s. 7 of the Consumer Protection Act 1987 by any contract term, notice or otherwise. Given the far-reaching nature of this legislation the different elements will now be considered.

The ambit of the Act: liability The basic liability under s. 2(1)(a) of the Consumer Protection Act 1987 is upon 'the producer of the product'. Although primary liability for breach is laid upon the producer of the product, the principle of joint and several liability is introduced into the Consumer Protection Act 1987 in order to ensure that the person injured can find a defendant within the jurisdiction. Thus, three other categories of persons who are not involved in any manufacturing are treated as if they were producers, namely, own-branders, importers and suppliers. Even so, the general approach is that a supplier is not liable under part I of the Consumer Protection Act 1987 for defective goods, but he may be liable in contract or negligence, or perhaps be criminally liable under part II of the Consumer Protection Act 1987 discussed below. However, s. 2(3) of the Consumer Protection Act 1987 enables the persons injured to hold an *effective* supplier liable where, for example, the product is anonymous. The reference to an effective supplier is in the case of a directly financed transaction to the dealer rather than the financier (s. 46(2) of the Consumer Protection Act 1987) and this will be relevant in our discussion of finance leasing in chapter 13.

The ambit of the Act: product Under s. 1(2) of the Consumer Protection Act 1987, 'product' is defined to mean:

> any goods or electricity and . . . includes a product which is comprised in another product, whether by virtue of being a component part or raw material or otherwise.

The obligations of the supplier 115

This is a wider definition that that of goods under the Sale of Goods Act 1979. Even fixtures can be goods for the purposes of the Consumer Protection Act 1987. The point here is that materials incorporated into buildings will be covered if they turn out to be defective (s. 46(3)). Waste can also be a product, for example, where it is sold as a by-product or if it is disposed in a supply situation rather than a mere discharge where it may be covered under the Control of Pollution Act 1974.

A product is defective under the Consumer Protection Act 1987 when it does not provide the safety which persons generally are entitled to expect taking into account all the circumstances. It would seem that if the real complaint is about shoddiness or unsuitability of the goods, the course of action is still by reference to the implied terms under the Sale of Goods Act 1979, Supply of Goods and Services Act 1982 and Supply of Goods (Implied Terms) Act 1973. An objective test is adopted for the determination of the issue of safety. To assist in the application of criteria, s. 3 of the Consumer Protection Act 1987 requires the courts to take all the circumstances into account and, in this respect, sets out three non-exclusive factors to be considered:

(a) Marketing circumstances and instructions.

(b) Use. The producer should reasonably foresee what might be done with the goods such as predictable misuse by a child. If it is not possible to remove the hazard, adequate warnings or instructions will be relevant here.

(c) Time of supply. Section 3(2)(c) states that the precise time to which reference should be made is when 'the product was supplied by its producer to another'. Obviously this will be of significance for producers where there is a long shelf life.

The ambit of the Act: damage Pure financial loss is not covered under the Consumer Protection Act 1987 where 'damage' is defined under s. 5(1) to mean 'death or personal injury or any loss of or damage to any property (including land)'. The damages recoverable (including damages for congenital disability) are as in any other civil case subject to the following:

(a) Damage to the product itself is not recoverable and in this situation the buyer must pursue a claim under the Sale of Goods Act 1979 for his money back or any other settlement. Of course, recovery is still possible under the general damage heading in s. 5(1) against the manufacturer of either the appliance or the manufacturer of the component.

(b) Damage to business property. Producers who supply products solely for business use where the only likely consequence of a defect is damage to business property or financial loss are unaffected by part I of the Consumer Protection Act 1987. Essentially, part I of the Act is designed as a *consumer* protection measure.

(c) Damage which is trivial. Under s. 5(4), no damages are awarded in respect of trivial property damage which is defined as where the total capital loss does not exceed £275. This lower threshold applies only to property, not personal injury. Claims for property losses under £275 will therefore have to be pursued in contract and negligence. It should be noted that the £275 minimum takes account of any reduction in damages through contributory negligence.

The ambit of the Act: defences The burden of proof of causation under the Consumer Protection Act 1987 is upon the victim. Damages may be reduced by his contributory negligence and, in this respect, it could be argued that disregard of instructions breaks the chain of causation. This was a position taken by the House of Lords in *Lambert* v *Lewis* [1982] AC 225. Here it was held that the chain of causation was broken where the buyer continued to use the goods with actual knowledge of the breach as regards subsequent consequential loss (compare *Basildon District Council* v *J.E. Lesser (Properties) Ltd* [1985] QB 839).

The Consumer Protection Act 1987 specifically provides in s. 4 for defences available with respect to 'the person proceeded against' for defects in a product supplied. These defences are enumerated in s. 4(1) as follows:

(a) that the defect is attributable to compliance with any requirement imposed by or under any enactment or with any Community obligation.

The essential point here is that the producer must show that the defect was the *inevitable* result of compulsory compliance with domestic or Community law. Where standards followed by manufacturers are voluntary rather than mandatory, such as a British Standard, this is not within the defence anticipated here.

(b) that the person proceeded against did not at any time supply the product to another.

The defence is confined to absence of supply, for example, where the goods are stolen from the manufacturer or scrapped by him.

(c) ... (i) that the only supply of the product to another by the person proceeded against was otherwise than in the course of a business of that person's; and
 (ii) that section 2(2) above does not apply to that person or applies to him by virtue of things done otherwise than with a view to profit.

The Consumer Protection Act 1987 is similar to the Sale of Goods Act 1979 and the Supply of Goods and Services Act 1982 with respect to merchantibility and fitness for purpose as it imposes liability only on those acting 'in the course of a business'. A private supplier will not face strict liability under part I of the Consumer Protection Act 1987 unless the supply is with a view to a profit in the course of a business

(d) that the defect did not exist in the product at the relevant time.

This in practice is the most important defence. The relevant time is when originally supplied (s. 4(2)). Where there has been malicious tampering with a product, if this occurs before the time of supply by, for example, an employee of the manufacturer, the latter will be strictly liable. If it occurs after the time of supply then he will have a defence, although the retailer will be liable for breach of the implied terms under ss. 13 to 14 of the Sale of Goods Act 1979 and analogous provisions in contracts of supply.

    (e)   that the state of scientific and technical knowledge at the relevant time was not such that a producer of products of the same description as the product in question might be expected to have discovered the defect if it had existed in his products while they were under his control.

This defence can be best described as 'development risks'. The Directive made the adoption of this defence optional and despite strenuous attempts by the consumer lobby to have it rejected, the government included it in the Act. The test adopted is objective, based on the reasonable producer so that the resources and experience of the particular producer will not be relevant. The determining time, as defined under s. 4(2), is when the product was *supplied* and not when it was manufactured. It follows from this that the producer must keep abreast of developments until the product leaves his control. However, merely because safer products are subsequently produced this does not necessarily mean that a product was defective when put into circulation (s. 4(1)(d)).

    (f)   that the defect—
        (i)   constituted a defect in a product ('the subsequent product') in which the product in question had been comprised; and
        (ii)   was wholly attributable to the design of the subsequent product or to compliance by the producer of the product in question with instructions given by the producer of the subsequent product.

To qualify for this defence, the component producer must have no responsibility for the design of the finished product or be simply following specifications which prove to be unsuitable.

The Consumer Protection Act 1987 amends the Limitation Act 1980 with respect to time-limits for bringing an action (see s. 6(6) and sch. 1). There is an overall cut-off point for any proceedings to be brought which is 10 years after the 'relevant time'. The 'relevant time' is defined in s. 4 of the Consumer Protection Act 1987 as discussed above. A second limitation on actions contained in s. 11A(4) of the Limitation Act 1980 is that claims for personal injuries or property damage cannot be brought more than three years after becoming aware of the damage, the defect, and the identity of the defendant, subject to the ultimate cut-off of 10 years. For latent damage the three-year period commences on the 'date of knowledge' of the plaintiff (s. 14(1A) of the Limitation Act 1980). The reason for the overall cut-off point of 10 years is to prevent the threat of legal action stretching out for an unlimited period. Of course, many products will not have a 10-year life span, but in this situation the definition of 'defect' takes into account consumption, perishability, and wear and tear as part of what 'persons generally are entitled to expect'.

Undoubtedly, the Consumer Protection Act 1987 does simplify the plaintiff's task in establishing liability since a victim no longer has to show that the producer was negligent or be party to a contract. Nevertheless, there are important difficulties which still remain, for example, the level of safety that persons are generally entitled to expect, problems with causation, contributory negligence and the development risks defence. Moreover, part I has other limitations in that it does not in any case apply to all products, neither does it cover damage to business property or to personal property below £275. Lastly, the Consumer Protection Act 1987 is not retrospective so that products supplied before 1 March 1988 are not covered.

Criminal liability under part II of the Consumer Protection Act 1987
Under part II of the Consumer Protection Act 1987, 'consumer goods' must comply with a general safety requirement. This is a catch-all provision which contrasts with piecemeal safety legislation covering specific products, such as food, drugs, motor vehicles, and specific places including factories and mines. Under the general safety requirement, retailers are criminally liable if they knowingly expose an unsafe product for sale, whereas in civil law under the product liability regime, retailers are liable to third-party victims only if they present themselves as the producer or cannot identify the person who supplied them with the product.

The general safety requirement Criminal liability is not confined to producers as is the case with civil liability but extends to any supplier. 'Supply' is defined under s. 46 of the Consumer Protection Act 1987 as sale, hire, loan, hire-purchase, exchange and providing goods in connection with a statutory function (for example, electricity), giving a prize or gift. The 'person' need not be a trader nor a trader supplying the goods he normally supplies. In direct financing the ostensible supplier, the financier, is not treated as supplier for liability purposes (s. 46(2)). It should be noted that liability is confined to 'consumer goods' intended for private use in the course of a business. Under s. 10(7) the following are excluded: growing crops and emblements, water, food, feed or fertiliser, gas, aircraft or motor vehicles, drugs, tobacco. This is a much narrower definition than 'product' in part I of the Consumer Protection Act 1987. However, when one takes into account other safety legislation such as the Food Safety Act 1990, Agriculture Act 1970, Medicines Act 1968, Misuse of Drugs Act 1971 and the Road Traffic Acts 1972 and 1988, these limitations are not significant. The exception in relation to tobacco recognises the difficulty of making the supply of tobacco a criminal offence. The limitation that 'consumer goods' must be for private use or consumption, whilst a 'product' can be supplied for any use does not mean that suppliers of industrial or business products can escape their responsibilities because the Health and Safety at Work Act 1974 will apply.

'Safe' is defined in s. 19(1) in terms of risk of causing death or personal injury only, whereas under part I, liability also arises for damage to personal property exceeding £275. Compliance with a Community obligation is a defence (s. 10(3)(a)). This is identical to the defence seen in part I, but the risk must be directly attributable to compliance. Meeting the minimum requirements of safety legislation or standards is a complete defence to criminal liability. Contrastingly, it is not a defence to a civil claim where legislative standards are regarded as minimum which should, in some circumstances, be exceeded by the reasonably prudent producer.

The 'due diligence' defence The 'due diligence' defence represents a crucial difference between the idea of strict civil liability under part I and criminal liability under part II of the Consumer Protection Act 1987. There is a natural reluctance to make criminals of suppliers who have taken reasonable steps to ensure that their goods accord with modern standards. The emphasis is upon reasonableness of procedures. Buying goods from a reputable source is not enough as the supplier will be required to entertain elementary precautions, for example, sampling or checking the weight of the goods supplied (s. 28(1) of the Weights and Measures Act 1985) and ensuring that the system can cope with mistakes.

The defence of 'due diligence' is an ameliorating feature of most consumer protection strict liability statutes (see for example, s. 24(1) of the Trade Descriptions Act 1968). As Lord Reid put it in *Tesco Supermarkets Ltd* v *Nattrass* [1972] AC 153 at p. 174, if a defendant has done all that can reasonably be expected of him, how can he do more? Thus in *Barker* v *Hargreaves* [1981] RTR 197, it was held that excusable ignorance could be a defence in the case of latent defects under the Trade Descriptions Act 1968. Where a 'due diligence' defence is relied upon the burden of proof is on the accused who must show that the transgression was due to the act of another, and the general rule for criminal liability is that an employer will not be vicariously liable for his employee's crimes. In *Tesco Supermarkets Ltd* v *Nattrass*, a shop manager of a large supermarket chain with considerable managerial powers was held to be 'another person', thereby allowing the company to escape liability for a breach of the Trade Descriptions Act 1968 when a misleading price offer was displayed due to his failure to check it. It is otherwise where the employee can be considered to be part of the 'brains' of the company, i.e., sufficiently senior for his acts to be regarded as those of the company. Moreover under most consumer protection legislation, senior corporate officers will be vicariously liable where a corporation has been found criminally liable under such legislation (see s. 20 of the Trade Descriptions Act 1968; s. 132 of the Fair Trading Act 1973; s. 169 of the Consumer Credit Act 1974 and s. 40(2) of the Consumer Protection Act 1987).

Safety regulations Under s. 11 of the Consumer Protection Act 1987, the Secretary of State has comprehensive powers to issue regulations covering all aspects of product safety but subsuming the regulations already made under the Consumer Protection Act 1961 and Consumer Safety Act 1978. Given the catch-all general safety requirement under the Consumer Protection Act 1987, it is in the interest of retailers that these regulations be made since they will provide a shelter from liability. Moreover, the Minister has a statutory duty to consult organisations he considers are representative of interests which will be affected by a proposed regulation and, in his dealings, demonstrate a high degree of fairness and candour (see *R* v *Secretary of State for Health, ex parte United States Tobacco International Inc.* [1991] 3 WLR 529).

A person who buys goods not complying with the regulations will have an action for breach of a statutory duty. However, the defendant may be able to escape liability if he can prove that he took all due diligence to avoid the commission of an offence (s. 12 of the Consumer Protection Act 1987). By virtue of s. 41 of the Consumer Protection Act 1987, breach of a safety regulation, as distinct from the general safety requirement, is also grounds for a civil action by any person affected which cannot be excluded or limited by any contract term or notice. In effect, safety regulations become part of the definition of 'defective' in respect of personal injuries and have the great advantage of being self-enforcing.

In addition to the general power under s. 11 to make regulations, the Secretary of State and enforcement authorities have further powers to restrict the circulation of unsafe goods, for example, the Minister can issue a prohibition notice (s. 13), and the enforcement authority can issue a suspension notice (s. 14) or order forfeiture of unsafe goods (s. 16).

The majority of consumer complaints concern defective goods and centre upon claims for pure economic loss. As we have seen, the approach taken under the Sale of Goods Act 1979, Supply of Goods and Services Act 1982, and the Supply of Goods (Implied Terms) Act 1973 is to make the supplier in the ordinary course of business strictly liable with regard to the merchantability provisions. Such an approach may be justified on the basis of risk allocation since the business supplier is in a good position to bear the risk. The major difficulty with this contract-based approach is the doctrine of privity of contract. The purchaser must be the person suffering loss unless it can be shown that the purchaser was acting as agent for the injured customer. Even here, unless the purchaser was expressly authorised to contract for the principal, such a contract can only be ratified if the purchaser at the time of making the contract professed to contract on the principal's behalf. Nevertheless, the courts have been remarkably inventive in circumventing the privity doctrine through the development of the collateral contract device and negligent misrepresentation. The Consumer Protection Act 1987 represents a major statutory shift by changing the basis on which a victim can sue a producer and through the introduction of new criminal offences and extending the powers of the safety enforcement authorities.

SIX
Remedies of the supplier for misrepresentation or breach

One effect of property passing is that the relationship between the seller and the buyer becomes that of debtor and creditor. Over a period of time, sophisticated contractual mechanisms have emerged to avoid this consequence, most notably, retention of title clauses, finance leasing, contracts of hire and hire-purchase (see part 4). In this chapter we shall consider the statutory remedies available to an unpaid seller under the Sale of Goods Act 1979 as well as discussing the position of the ordinary supplier. The significance here is that, in appropriate circumstances, a buyer will not be entitled to possession of the goods by delivery irrespective of whether property has passed as an aspect of contract. The real remedies of the seller can only be exercised when the buyer has not paid the price for the goods and contain important innovative elements peculiar to the Sale of Goods Act 1979. We shall then proceed to consider the personal remedies available to the seller which are not restricted in their application to non-payment of the price. The remedies available to the owner or lessor following the default of the hirer or lessee are discussed in chapter 13.

REAL REMEDIES: THE SALE OF GOODS ACT 1979

The Sale of Goods Act 1979 confers upon the unpaid seller the following rights encapsulated in s. 39:

(1) Subject to this and any other Act, notwithstanding that the property in the goods may have passed to the buyer, the unpaid seller of goods, as such, has by implication of law—
    (a) a lien on the goods or right to retain them for the price while he is in possession of them;
    (b) in case of the insolvency of the buyer, a right of stopping the goods in transit after he has parted with the possession of them;

(c) a right of resale as limited by this Act.

(2) Where the property in goods has not passed to the buyer, the unpaid seller has (in addition to his other remedies) a right of withholding delivery similar to and coextensive with his rights of lien or retention and stoppage in transit where the property has passed to the buyer.

The three rights enumerated above arise by implication of law, but they may be excluded by the express terms of the agreement between the parties.

Care should be taken to distinguish between the powers of the unpaid seller and his rights as against the first buyer. Thus, it is easy to see that s. 39(1) is geared towards conferring upon the seller not merely the power to deal with the goods, but also the right to do so as against the buyer. More difficulty is posed by s. 39(2) which seems superfluous since the owner of goods has the power in any case of withholding delivery. Moreover, it does not confer upon the unpaid seller a right to resell as against the buyer. Remarkably, an unpaid seller could, on this basis, resell where property had passed to the buyer, but could not do so where the property had not passed. The better view here is that s. 39(2) ensures that a seller who has retained the property in the goods will be no worse off than one who has not done so with regard to his rights of lien and stoppage.

The real remedies afforded by the Sale of Goods Act 1979 are not of great practical importance for commerce. In large part this is due to the rise of the documentary letter of credit and also the utilisation of the simple expedient of stipulating for prepayment in commercial relations. Often sales will be on credit terms so that both possession and property will pass to the buyer before payment. Section 38 of the Sale of Goods Act 1979 makes it clear that the seller qualifies as being unpaid, and therefore entitled to exercise the real remedies under s. 39, where the whole of the price has not yet been paid or tendered, or where conditional payment has been made by a negotiable instrument which has been dishonoured. Clearly, the real rights are not exercisable where both property and possession have passed unless the contract can be rescinded for misrepresentation. However, this will all too often be barred because of a resale by the buyer to an innocent third party (compare *Car and Universal Finance Co. Ltd v Caldwell* [1965] 1 QB 525).

A wide definition is given to the term 'seller' for the purpose of exercising the unpaid seller's rights under part V of the Sale of Goods Act 1979. The conventional definition under s. 61(1) defines a seller as 'a person who sells or agrees to sell goods' but, by virtue of s. 38(2) the concept is extended to include any person in the position of the seller, for example, his agent or assignee. Nonetheless, the definition does not extend to a buyer who has justifiably rejected the goods for non-compliance after paying the price (see *J.L. Lyons and Co. Ltd v May and Baker Ltd* [1923] 1 KB 685). In this circumstance, the buyer should only reject the goods and sue for the price if he is satisfied as to the solvency of the seller.

The unpaid seller's lien and right of retention

At common law, a lien is possessory and presupposes that property in the goods has passed so a person cannot have, as Lord Wright pointed out, a lien over his

Remedies of the supplier for misrepresentation or breach 123

own goods (see *Nippon Yusen Kaisha* v *Ramjiban Serowgee* [1938] AC 429 at p. 444). However the purpose of s. 39(2) is that an unpaid seller who has retained both property and possession should not have any less right than one who has merely retained possession. Thus, the unpaid seller's lien is a particular lien arising under the Sale of Goods Act 1979. It may be exercised only in respect of the price of the goods which are being retained (ss. 39(1)(a) and 41(1) of the Sale of Goods Act 1979). No other charges are included within the scope of this lien, for example, charges for storing the goods which are only recoverable in a claim for damages (s. 37). Of course, storage charges fall within the seller's lien if bargained for in the price.

The unpaid seller's lien is a qualification of the seller's obligation to deliver the goods found in s. 27 of the Sale of Goods Act 1979. Particular problems are posed by part delivery of the goods. The principle applied to this situation is s. 42 of the Sale of Goods Act 1979 where the issue is whether delivery of the part was made in circumstances which showed an agreement to waive the lien. There is some difficulty because a waiver is not dependent upon an agreement but is a unilateral act. Clearly, where there is a series of contracts, a seller cannot claim a lien over part of the goods to be separately paid for and delivered. This would be equivalent to a general lien and although this may be conferred by contract, the Sale of Goods Act 1979 anticipates only a particular lien (see chapter 14). Nevertheless, it does not follow that where goods are to be delivered and paid for by instalments that there is a series of contracts. On the contrary, the common law rule is that a contract for the sale of goods by instalments is one contract and the lien may be exercisable over the remainder of the goods.

The unpaid seller's right of stoppage in transit
An unpaid seller has the right to resume possession of the goods by preventing delivery to the buyer when they are still in the course of transit, and the buyer has become insolvent (s. 44 of the Sale of Goods Act 1979). The right of stoppage is mostly of theoretical interest as being an example of a right of recaption arising by operation of law. For obvious reasons, this right is only important where the transit is a long one and is therefore mostly confined to international sales. Even here, it has greatly reduced significance now because of the widespread use of bankers' confirmed commercial credits where there is little prospect of non-payment.

It makes no difference whether or not property has passed to the buyer (s. 39(2)) so that the right of stoppage, as a matter of principle, is an extensive one, given that it entitles the unpaid seller to interfere not only in the possession of goods, but also with the property in goods vested in another. The right of stoppage does appear to be contrary to the *pari passu* principle of distribution on bankruptcy, especially in the light of Lord Esher MR's remark that the doctrine is always construed favourably to unpaid sellers (see *Bethell* v *Clark* (1888) 20 QBD 615 at p. 617).

The exercise of the right The seller must be unpaid and the buyer must be insolvent (s. 44 of the Sale of Goods Act 1979). If the buyer is not insolvent and the seller delays delivery by stopping the goods in transit, the seller will be liable to the buyer for loss resulting from the delay in delivery caused by the stoppage.

There is no doubt that the course of transit is one of the most thorny questions in this context. The right of stoppage only exists where the goods are in the hands of a third party and although it is presumed that there has been constructive delivery when the goods are in the hands of the carrier (s. 32(1)), for the purpose of stoppage, the carrier is generally deemed to be neutral. Of course, where the carrier is the seller's agent, the seller can rely on his unpaid seller's lien and does not need to invoke the less extensive right of stoppage. On the other hand, if the buyer can show that the carrier was his agent, there can be no right of stoppage simply because the transit has never started (s. 45(5)). Nevertheless, the mere fact that the buyer is responsible for arranging shipping space, as in the case of an f.o.b. contract, transit does not end and continues until the buyer or his agent acquires possession.

The right of stoppage terminates following the carrier's attornment to the buyer (s. 45(3)). This may be implied from the carrier's conduct, for example, where he follows instructions given to him by the buyer to carry the goods to a new destination. Even so, the seller retains his right to stop the goods until they reach their ultimate destination (see *Reddall* v *Union Castle Mail Steamship Co. Ltd* (1915) 84 LJ KB 360). If the buyer rejects the goods, the carrier or bailee is treated as if he were in continued possession of the goods by virtue of s. 45(4). There is no difficulty in reconciling attornment and subsequent buyer rejection of the goods because, clearly, the attornment will only operate to transfer possession to the buyer provided that he has assented to this. Where there has been part delivery, this may amount to a constructive delivery of the whole, but s. 45(7) of the Sale of Goods Act 1979 provides that the presumption is that it does not, and so the seller is enabled to stop what remains in the carrier's possession.

Interception of the goods before they reach their ultimate destination brings the transit to an end (s. 45(2)). Thus in *Reddall* v *Union Castle Mail Steamship Co. Ltd*, the buyer intercepted the goods at the end of one stage of their transit. The goods were in the custody of a carrier who charged the buyer rent for warehousing costs, and Bailhache J held at p. 362: 'Where the original *transitus* is interrupted by the buyers, the test is whether the goods will be set in motion again without further orders from the buyers; if not the transit is ended and the right to stop lost'. This exception recognises the fact that a carrier and buyer can agree to a different destination or form of disposal than that established by the seller and carrier. It may be, in this circumstance, that the seller will have recourse against the carrier for breach of the contract of carriage by his compliance to the buyer's request.

The exercise by the unpaid seller of his right of stoppage may be through regaining possession, or by giving notice to the carrier or bailee in possession (s. 46). If, following this notice, the carrier or bailee in possession delivers the goods to the buyer he will be liable in conversion. On the other hand, if there is no right of stoppage, failure to deliver to the buyer will be wrongful and both seller and carrier or bailee in possession will be liable to the buyer in conversion. Clearly this is unsatisfactory for the carrier who, in an attempt to protect his position, may seek to be indemnified against the buyer for wrongful delivery, or against the seller for refusal to deliver.

When a notice of stoppage is given to the carrier or bailee in possession, the goods must be redelivered to or at the direction of the seller (s. 46(4)). The expenses of such redelivery must be borne by the seller, and the carrier has a particular lien on the goods for his freight which prevails over the seller's lien. In addition, an unpaid seller who stops the goods in transit must provide the carrier with instructions as to their disposal or return, otherwise the carrier will be exonerated from any liability in this respect (see *Booth Steamship Co. Ltd* v *Cargo Fleet Iron Co. Ltd* [1916] 2 KB 570).

The exercise of the right of stoppage does not itself rescind the contract of sale. It follows that tender of payment by the buyer's personal representative obliges the seller to redeliver the goods in the absence of there being a repudiatory breach.

The right of resale

We have already seen that the effect of the unpaid seller's exercise of his right of lien or stoppage does not rescind the contract of sale (s. 48(1) of the Sale of Goods Act 1979). Therefore, the seller may elect to rescind the contract and sue for non-acceptance damages. In this case, if property has passed to the buyer it will revert to the seller who can then transfer a good title to the subbuyer. However, if the unpaid seller elects to affirm the contract then property will pass to the buyer, and the seller can sue for non-payment of price and damages for non-acceptance while, perhaps, maintaining his unpaid seller's lien. Where the seller subsequently resells the goods, s. 48(2) of the Sale of Goods Act 1979 confers a *power* of resale; the resale confers a good title on the new buyer though it does constitute a breach of the original sale contract. This remedy enables the seller to get rid of unwanted possession of goods and it is for this reason, unlike s. 24 of the Sale of Goods Act 1979 and s. 8 of the Factors Act 1889, there is no requirement that the buyer acted in good faith and without notice of the original sale.

Where goods have been delivered and property passed, the seizure and resale of the goods will be a tortious act. In the absence of one of the exceptions to the *nemo dat* doctrine applying, good title will not pass (see chapter 7). Section 48 of the Sale of Goods Act 1979 deals with two situations in which the unpaid seller may resell the goods without breaking his contract with the original buyer. Section 48(3) states:

> Where the goods are of a perishable nature, or where the unpaid seller gives notice to the buyer of his intention to resell, and the buyer does not within a reasonable time pay or tender the price, the unpaid seller may resell the goods and recover from the original buyer damages for any loss occasioned by his breach of contract.

No mention is made as to whether the effect of resale is to rescind the original contract. This situation contrasts with s. 48(4) of the Sale of Goods Act 1979 which provides:

Where the seller expressly reserves the right of resale in case the buyer should make default, and on the buyer making default resells the goods, the original contract of sale is rescinded but without prejudice to any claim the seller may have for damages.

It was suggested in *Gallagher v Shilcock* [1949] 2 KB 765 that the effect of s. 48(3) where property had passed to the buyer was that the seller was reselling the buyer's goods as a quasi-pledgee and would, therefore, have to account to the latter. This approach was rejected by the Court of Appeal in *R.V. Ward Ltd v Bignall* [1967] 1 QB 534. The argument here is that the seller in reselling the goods is accepting the buyer's repudiation of the contract. The effect of s. 48(3) is to make the time-of-payment stipulation of the essence of the contract where goods are perishable or when notice of resale has been given. In this respect, the right of resale is an aspect of the seller's ownership which revests on termination. Such a right arises by operation of law, but if the seller had stipulated in the contract of sale that he should have a right of resale, the effect of s. 48(4) is to make clear that the contract is brought to an end. It follows that the reason for the contrast between s. 48(3) and (4) is not because the former subsection is intended to have a different result, rather, the express provision of rescission, in the sense of termination of the contract, is not necessary under s. 48(3).

The effect of resale under s. 48(3) and (4) is that the seller is acting in his own capacity and should, therefore, be entitled to any profits which accrue on resale. Thus, where there is a retention of title clause linking property passage with payment of the price, if the supplier recovers the goods for failure of the contract, it is clear that the buyer cannot claim any surplus profit made on resale. However, the Court of Appeal in *Clough Mill Ltd v Martin* [1985] 1 WLR 111 suggested that it was possible for such a resale to take place without rescission. This approach is anomalous in the light of s. 48(4) which would appear to insist that such a *sale* contract will be rescinded in this circumstance. Of course, where the transaction is categorised as creating a security interest for the seller, it is perfectly proper for the buyer to be entitled to any surplus gained on resale on the basis that property will have passed to him.

REAL REMEDIES: CONTRACTS OF SUPPLY

The transferor may have real remedies like those of the unpaid seller under the Sale of Goods Act 1979. In the case of work and materials contracts, the lien is analogous to that of the artificer's lien which applies by operation of law so long as the work done *improves* the goods (*Re Southern Livestock Producers Ltd* [1964] 1 WLR 24). Sometimes, particularly fine distinctions arise which, as a matter of legal logic, may be criticised. In this respect, whilst maintenance work on cars is not considered to amount to an improvement, a lien can attach when a car is actually repaired since this is considered to constitute an improvement (see *Hatton v Car Maintenance Co. Ltd* [1915] 1 Ch 621). As a species of particular lien, it entitles the lienee to retain the goods against payment for services provided only in relation to them (see chapter 14).

Remedies of the supplier for misrepresentation or breach 127

One important difference between unpaid transferors and sellers is that s. 48(2) of the Sale of Goods Act 1979 empowers the unpaid seller to sell the goods without terminating the contract and confer a good title upon the third party. This power was an innovation of the Sale of Goods Act 1893. It follows that an unpaid transferor has no power of sale as opposed to a right of resale on termination of the contract. However, the sophisticated argument applied by the Court of Appeal in *R.V. Ward Ltd* v *Bignall* [1967] 1 QB 534 discussed above will be pertinent in this context with respect to products of a perishable nature. In other cases, the general position is that a disponee will be held liable in tort for conversion if the transferee subsequently tenders performance and, by doing so, obtains an immediate right to possession. Of course, in the case of a bailment at will, the very act of disposition will go to the root of the bailment thereby entitling the bailor to repossess the goods (*Cooper* v *Willomatt* (1845) 1 CB 672).

PERSONAL REMEDIES

In addition to the real remedies over the goods discussed above, the unpaid seller has personal contractual remedies against the transferee himself.

Action for the price under the Sale of Goods Act 1979

It is the duty of the buyer to pay for the goods according to the terms of the contract of sale. Payment must usually be made at the seller's place of business subject to a contrary intention expressed in the contract. It is normally the duty of the buyer, as any other species of debtor, to ensure that payment is tendered to the seller and he will take the risk of this failing to occur. We have already seen that time is not normally of the essence in a contract of sale (s. 10(1) of the Sale of Goods Act 1979). This reflects the fact that, in a commercial transaction, the most the seller is likely to lose is his interest payment on moneys received, and repudiation here would be a penalty disproportionate to the loss suffered by the seller through non-payment.

Unless otherwise agreed, delivery of the goods and payment are concurrent conditions (s. 28 of the Sale of Goods Act 1979). The duty to pay the price is remediable by an action for the price. Breach of the duty to pay the price can result in the exercise by the seller of both real and personal remedies where the goods are still in the possession of the seller, i.e., before acceptance. If there has been acceptance by the buyer followed by non-payment, only a personal remedy may be pursued. The basic remedy with respect to the action for the price is dealt with in s. 49 of the Sale of Goods Act 1979. The analogy here is with the remedy of specific performance which has significance for two reasons: first, there will often be a difference between the price of goods and damages received for breach; secondly, in an action for the price, the seller is under no obligation to mitigate his loss.

Complications arise because property passing in English law is linked to contract rather than conveyance. Section 49(1) of the Sale of Goods Act 1979 states:

Where, under a contract of sale, the property in the goods has passed to the buyer and he wrongfully neglects or refuses to pay for the goods according to the terms of the contract, the seller may maintain an action against him for the price of the goods.

On the other hand s. 50(1) of the Sale of Goods Act 1979 provides:

Where the buyer wrongfully neglects or refuses to accept and pay for the goods, the seller may maintain an action against him for damages for non-acceptance.

It appears to be essential that property should have passed, and it is not enough that property would have passed if the buyer had cooperated unless the buyer is estopped by his conduct from denying that property has passed (see *Colley v Overseas Exporters* [1921] 3 KB 302).

The seller is placed in a somewhat invidious position where the goods have not been delivered. If he maintains that property had passed and sues for the price, the court could maintain that, on the facts, property has not passed and restrict the seller to damages for non-acceptance where he will have a duty to mitigate his loss. On the other hand, if the seller does attempt to resell the goods, the court could take the view that this is an acceptance by the seller of the repudiation of the contract by the buyer so that an action for the price will no longer lie. The requirement that property should have passed is dispensed with where the contract separates payment from delivery. The assumption here is that the parties are impliedly making payment independent also of the passing of property.

In the case of advance payments made to the seller, there may be difficulties with the application of the strict distinction drawn by the House of Lords in *Johnson v Agnew* [1980] AC 367 between mere termination as a result of breach, and rescission of a contract *ab initio*. It has been suggested that if the price is payable before termination, this can be retained or recovered by the seller even if he has not delivered the goods (see *Hyundai Heavy Industries Co. Ltd v Papadopoulos* [1980] 1 WLR 1129). This approach cannot be correct insofar as it applies to sale of goods contracts because the duty to pay will normally be conditional on the other party's performance. Moreover, the effect of termination in sale of goods does have a retrospective element in that, if property has already passed to the buyer, it will revert to the seller (s. 48(4)). Equally, it could be said that the non-delivery amounts to a total failure of consideration.

Special damage claims
Where the buyer neglects to take delivery, the seller in addition to his right to claim damages for non-acceptance or an action on the price, can sue under s. 54 of the Sale of Goods Act 1979 for any special loss incurred. Furthermore, s. 37 allows the seller to claim for further loss resulting from incidental costs such as care and custody of the goods. In any case, these costs will figure in a damages action as a matter of course.

As a matter of principle, linking the action for the price with the question of whether property has passed is too simplistic. The spectre of property passing covers too many classes of buyer and seller for it to be a meaningful concept in this context. The issue would be better resolved by reference to whether, as a matter of commercial practice, the buyer or the seller should have the responsibility of reselling or otherwise disposing of the goods.

Termination and damages

Once property and possession have passed to the buyer, the seller cannot terminate the contract for non-payment because this is not repudiatory conduct. The reasoning here is that if the buyer has received the full benefit of the contract and wants to keep the goods, this can only be treated as an affirmation rather than a repudiation of the contract. Conversely, if the buyer wants to give up the goods and is unwilling to pay for them, this is a repudiation which the seller can accept by repossessing the goods.

We have already seen that by virtue of s. 50(1) of the Sale of Goods Act 1979, where the buyer wrongfully neglects or refuses to accept and pay for the goods, the seller may maintain an action against him for damages. This action can be brought irrespective of whether or not property has passed. Damages for non-acceptance can now be awarded in a foreign currency where this is appropriate (*The Despina R* [1979] AC 685). The rule is applied in such a way as to produce a just and appropriate result. In *Miliangos* v *George Frank (Textiles) Ltd* [1976] AC 443, the House of Lords, reversing its earlier decision in *Re United Railways of Havana and Regla Warehouses Ltd* [1961] AC 1007, held that an English court did have the power to order that a defendant in an action of debt should pay the sum owing in a foreign currency (Swiss francs) rather than in pounds sterling. In determining the date for payment, the House of Lords settled for the date when the court authorises enforcement of the judgment in terms of sterling. Such an approach favours the creditor in the face of swift changes in the value of sterling.

The buyer's misconduct may amount to repudiation entitling the seller to rescind the contract, and he will be absolved from liability for failure to deliver. Although the buyer is entitled to the return of a part payment made, a deposit is not returnable even if the seller has suffered no damage following the resale because it is in the nature of a preliminary contract guaranteeing completion. Nonetheless, equity may offer relief against forfeiture (*Stockloser* v *Johnson* [1954] 1 QB 476). In the case of a prospective regulated consumer credit agreement, a preliminary contract will be void under s. 59 of the Consumer Credit Act 1974 so that the deposit will be recoverable for total failure of consideration.

Measure of damages for non-acceptance

Non-acceptance denotes rejection of the goods which is repudiatory conduct at least as to the part of the contract relating to the goods in question. A careful distinction should be drawn between non-acceptance and refusal to take delivery since the latter may simply denote that the buyer is not *yet* ready to receive the goods.

The measure of damages for non-acceptance is provided by s. 50(2) and (3) in the following terms:

> (2) The measure of damages is the estimated loss directly and naturally resulting, in the ordinary course of events, from the buyer's breach of contract.
>
> (3) Where there is an available market for the goods in question the measure of damages is prima facie to be ascertained by the difference between the contract price and the market or current price at the time or times when the goods ought to have been accepted or (if no time was fixed for acceptance) at the time of the refusal to accept.

The object of s. 50(2) is the statutorifying of the first rule in *Hadley* v *Baxendale* (1854) 9 Exch 341. The effect is to distinguish normal, foreseeable consequences of a breach for which damages are recoverable, from abnormal, special or particular loss which does not come within the scope of recoverable damages. It would seem that the underlying test for recoverable damages, as in *Victoria Laundry (Windsor) Ltd* v *Newman Industries Ltd* [1949] 2 KB 528, is that of reasonable foresight. This approach was generally approved by the House of Lords in *C. Czarnikow Ltd* v *Koufos* [1969] 1 AC 350, although a higher degree of probability of occurrence was anticipated in this case. The second rule in *Hadley* v *Baxendale* finds expression in s. 54 which applies where the guilty party has knowledge of some special circumstance which is such as to increase the loss naturally arising from his breach.

Having set out in s. 50(2) the general rule for calculating the measure of damages in actions for non-acceptance, the Sale of Goods Act 1979 provides in s. 50(3) a prima facie rule for the computation of damages. There are several problems flowing from this which we shall now proceed to discuss.

Available market Where there is an available market, the presumption is that the seller will go into that market and resell the goods. The question of whether there is an available market is a question of fact and also of degree. Thus in *Garnac Grain Co. Inc* v *H.M.F. Faure and Fairclough Ltd* [1968] AC 1130, it was held that there was a market even though it was not possible to buy the contract quantity in one amount for immediate delivery. Evidence that similar goods are disposable will suggest that there is an available market. In general, the courts adopt a broad view of this question.

The significance of the market price attached to the available market concept should not detract from the fact that the supplier will be compensated for any special damage incurred (s. 54 of the Sale of Goods Act 1979). An example of this would be the cost of return carriage, although this must be offset against any rise in the market price after the due date for acceptance. The onus of proving the price obtainable in the market at the time of acceptance is on the seller so that, if this is below the contract price, the seller is prima facie entitled to the difference between the two (s. 50(3)). Where the market price or value is difficult to establish, the actual resale price may be evidence of it.

The market rule is really an abstract concept since it is based upon the supposed activity of reselling by the seller *at the time* of non-acceptance as part of his duty to mitigate his loss. Thus, if the seller delays the resale, he can still only recover the difference between the contract price and the market price at the time of non-acceptance. It was held in *Shearson Lehman Hutton Inc.* v *Maclaine Watson and Co. Ltd (No. 2)* [1990] 3 All ER 723 that the measure of damages payable by the defaulting buyer is the difference between the contract price and the market price at the date of breach, irrespective of any characteristics of the seller which may have led to a lower price being obtained. This approach stresses the element of certainty and objectivity in s. 50(3) which does not require scrutiny of whether the seller has behaved reasonably. The question of 'available market' was linked to whether there was, in the case of an actual sale, one actual buyer at the date of breach at a fair price. On the other hand, in the case of a hypothetical sale, the test is whether, on the relevant day, there were in the market sufficient traders to enable the seller, if he so wished, to sell the goods. In determining a fair price where there is no actual sale, this is not confined to the price obtainable assuming that the seller sold them on the relevant date; rather, in large-scale commodity contracts, the court can take into account the price which would be negotiated within a few days with persons who were members of the market on that day, and who could not be taken into account as potential buyers on the day in question only because of difficulties of communication.

No available market There may be no available market for the seller where the supply exceeds demand. Where a chattel is unique, the rule in s. 50(3) is not applied as seen in *Lazenby Garages Ltd* v *Wright* [1976] 1 WLR 459. In this case, the contract was for the sale of a second-hand car which the buyer later wrongfully refused to accept. It was held by the Court of Appeal that the 'available market' rule was not one to invoke as there was no market for second-hand cars. In contrast, where the seller could show, as in the case of a new car, that he had sold one car less than he would otherwise have done, the seller would then be allowed the loss of profit on the car.

The problem of how to assess damages where there is no available market was considered by the Court of Appeal in *Re Vic Mill Ltd* [1913] 1 Ch 465. In this case a company ordered machines which it later did not accept, but parts had been purchased by the seller in preparation for the manufacture of the machines. Following the repudiation of the contract by the buyer, the seller modified these parts and sold them to another customer. The Court of Appeal held that the seller had lost the opportunity of making two sets of profit; one from the defaulting buyer and the other from the actual buyer. If no such opportunity had existed, the seller could not have claimed loss of profit on the sale since the sellers would have made that profit through a substituted customer. The Court of Appeal held that the customer in this case was an additional and not a substituted customer. It is for this reason that the House of Lords in *Hill and Sons* v *Edwin Showell and Sons Ltd* (1918) 87 LJ KB 1106, permitted a buyer to show that the seller could not have earned more as a result of acceptance by the buyer because the seller could not have dealt with more than one order at a time.

As a matter of principle, the rule allowing recovery for loss of profit on the extra sale can be criticised. For example, although it can be shown that the seller had the capacity to meet the different orders, this should not be determinative of the issue, especially since the manufacture of the two orders may have been prevented by other factors, for example, industrial action. Moreover, it is simplistic to equate the loss sustained with the full profit given up from the defaulting sale because each unit of stock carries its own overhead expenses for the supplier, and there may be considerable savings here resulting from the buyer's termination. At least some discount should be considered in order to take into account the possibility that the second sale would have been less profitable than the broken contract.

The duty to mitigate loss Where the buyer is in default, it is the duty of the seller to mitigate his damages. Generally, the standard required for mitigation is a low one, although it has been held to be unreasonable for a plaintiff to decline an offer by the defendant to enter into a fresh contract on cash instead of credit terms (*Payzu Ltd* v *Saunders* [1919] 2 KB 581), or to refuse an offer for late delivery (*Sotiros Shipping Inc.* v *Sameiet Solholt* [1983] 1 Lloyd's Rep 605). A problem which has arisen is whether a seller is obliged, in fulfilment of his duty to mitigate, to spend money upon goods in order to render them fit for resale. In this respect, it was held in *Jewelowski* v *Propp* [1944] KB 510 that where the expenditure is speculative, a plaintiff's duty to mitigate cannot be taken so far as to make it necessary for him to spend money.

The overriding issue concerning the duty to mitigate loss is whether or not the seller's conduct is reasonable having regard to the character of the goods and the demand for them. This is also pertinent in determining where there is an available market for disposal of the goods. The relevant criterion is not where a substitute sale is to be made, but whether a seller can reasonably find a substitute purchaser. It is for this reason that English courts take a broad and common-sense view of what is an available market.

One problem that emerges with respect to mitigation is that of anticipatory breach. The seller may elect to accept the anticipatory breach and will be under the ordinary duty to mitigate, or alternatively affirm the contract and so increase his loss. With regard to the former, the assumption is that the seller will wait until the due date of acceptance before reselling the goods and thereby mitigate his loss (*Millett* v *Van Heek and Co.* [1921] 2 KB 369). Any profit or loss made by the seller through selling the goods before the due date is ignored. Such an approach is odd and seems inconsistent with the literal words used in s. 50(3) which refer to the relevant time as being when the buyer refuses to accept the goods (compare s. 2-706 of the US Uniform Commercial Code).

Rescission of the contract
When a contract has been induced by misrepresentation, the innocent party may be able to rescind the contract *ab initio*. The most common event giving rise to a right of rescission in this context will be the buyer's fraud, for example, where he misrepresents his identity (*Lewis* v *Averay* [1972] 1 QB 198; compare *Ingram* v *Little* [1961] 1 QB 31). The right to rescission will be lost if an innocent third party acquires an interest in the goods, so the seller will have to act swiftly if rescission is to be effective (see *Car and Universal Finance Co. Ltd* v *Caldwell* [1965] 1 QB 525).

There has been some discussion in the case law as to whether the remedy of rescission of a contract of sale of goods for innocent misrepresentation has survived the Sale of Goods Act 1893. Despite some Commonwealth authority to the contrary (see *Riddiford* v *Warren* (1901) 20 NZLR 572), the Court of Appeal has, in recent years, on several occasions assumed that rescission is available for contracts of sale of goods (see *Leaf* v *International Galleries* [1950] 2 KB 86; *Long* v *Lloyd* [1958] 1 WLR 753; *Goldsmith* v *Rodger* [1962] 2 Lloyd's Rep 249). The remedy of rescission is a powerful one and is available even if both property and possession have passed to the buyer irrespective of the latter's solvency.

Damages for misrepresentation
It was held in *Royscot Trust Ltd* v *Rogerson* [1991] 2 QB 297 that a supplier of finance who was induced into entering a hire-purchase agreement with a customer through the misrepresentation of a dealer was entitled to damages on the basis of the tortious measure under s. 2(1) of the Misrepresentation Act 1967. Thus, the Court of Appeal held that damages under s. 2(1) should seek to put the representee into the position which he would have been in if the misrepresentation had not been made. In this way, the award of damages protects the representee's reliance interest without seeking to elevate what is no more than a mere representation into a contractual promise.

SEVEN
The transfer of title and security of property

THE SECURITY OF PROPERTY PRINCIPLE

The concept of *nemo dat quod (qui) non habet* (see p. 10) was firmly rooted in classical Roman law which provided for absolute ownership limited only by the very narrow exception of the bona fide possessor with a *titulus*. The *nemo dat* doctrine has a long history in the common law. It appeared in Perkins's *Profitable Book* which was published in 1532 in law French citing the Yearbooks as authority. Although Noy's *Maxims*, first published in 1641, also has the rule, no authority is cited. It appears to have become fashionable to quote the rule in one of its Latin versions only in the 19th century, and this may have been due to the use of Latin as being more respectable and impressive, and possibly more comprehensible than Perkins's law French.

There is a certain logic in the proposition that one cannot transfer what one does not have. Even so, a historical hypothesis given by Professor Milsom for the severity of English law towards a bona fide purchaser of corporeal movables involves the fictitious allegation, in actions of detinue and conversion, that the plaintiff had lost the article in question, the defendant had found it (trover) and had either refused to return it or had converted it to his own use (Milson, S.F.C., *Historical Foundation of the Common Law*, 2nd ed. (London, 1981) at pp. 264–6). It was not until the 18th century that the judges began questioning the previously unquestioned assumptions of property law in the context of negotiable instruments with the introduction of the 'good-faith purchaser' principle. By the 18th century, the law merchant had been absorbed into the common law and the attention of the King's courts began to be concentrated upon the development of a body of doctrine to encourage the free circulation of goods and commercial paper (see chapter 1). The emphasis was now on 'good-faith purchase' and not upon 'good-faith performance'. The latter refers to the influence of canon law and religious and moral ideas which characterised

The transfer of title and security of property 135

the English law merchant and contributed to enforcing high standards of good faith and fair dealing.

It is significant that the Sale of Goods Act 1979 retains the primacy of the *nemo dat* principle and the exceptions are contained in ss. 21 to 25 of the Act. It is important to bear in mind that since title under English law is relative, even the exceptions to the *nemo dat* rule which must be treated as curing the seller's defective title do not necessarily mean the granting of an absolute indefeasible title. Several policy factors emerge: estoppel of the true owner, ostensible ownership and possession, the significance of negotiability in order to stimulate trade. These factors will now be discussed.

ESTOPPEL: THE COMMON LAW AND STATUTORY CONTEXT

Section 21(1) of the Sale of Goods Act 1979 provides:

> subject to this Act, where goods are sold by a person who is not their owner, and who does not sell them under the authority or with the consent of the owner, the buyer acquires no better title to the goods than the seller had, unless the owner of the goods is by his conduct precluded from denying the seller's authority to sell.

Although the Sale of Goods Act 1979 adopts the term 'precluded' rather than 'estoppel', s. 21(1) is usually classed as an example of the doctrine of estoppel, the rationale of which according to Coke is: 'because a man's own act of acceptance stoppeth or closeth up his mouth to allege or pleade the truth' (Co Litt 352a). It is important, in the statutory context, to distinguish between authorised dispositions carried out in an improper way by an agent and an improper disposition by a non-owner. This distinction goes to the heart of the good-faith purchase exception to the *nemo dat* rule because whereas the former will normally bind the owner, the latter will only do so exceptionally.

Agency: the dilemma of unauthorised dispositions

Whilst the essential legal characteristic of agency is easy to describe, namely, that it involves the ability of the agent to affect the legal relations of the principal to a third party, the juridical rationale of this is not easy to explain. It is sometimes maintained that the power of the agent to bind his principal rests entirely upon contract. Undoubtedly, actual authority may be express or implied and the rules of construction of the contract are highly relevant. Thus, if an agent is given authority to do particular acts and this is expressed in general words, the words will be restricted to what is absolutely necessary for the performance of the acts in question (*Jacobs* v *Morris* [1902] 1 Ch 816). Furthermore, agents who practise a particular trade, business or profession are normally authorised to do everything which is usually or ordinarily done in such a trade. The rationale of this is that it makes express actual authority more effective since such power will almost invariably include 'median powers' which are not expressed, that is, they are necessary to accomplish the object of the express actual authority.

The consensual model as the basis for explaining the power of the agent to bind his principal is defective for at least two reasons: first, in the case of a gratuitous agency, for example, an 'agency of necessity' arising out of an emergency situation, the agent has the right to be indemnified for any losses he has sustained and also expenses. This indemnity, however, cannot be regarded as consideration moving from the principal because it is a duty which is one of the normal incidents of agency arising by operation of law quite independently of any agreement between the parties. Second, the consensual model does not explain the cases of apparent and presumed authority which we shall now proceed to consider in greater detail.

Usual or presumed authority: unauthorised mode of making a disposition
Complications arise when the principal has expressly deprived his agent of powers which are considered 'usual' in the conduct of the business with which he has been entrusted. The case in point here is *Watteau v Fenwick* [1893] 1 QB 346, where an agent was employed as manager of a public house conducting the business in his own name. The principal had expressly prohibited his manager from buying cigars on credit from certain third parties but, nevertheless, he did so. When later the principal was discovered and sued, he was held liable for the purchase money on the basis that the purchase was within the usual authority of a manager. In a short judgment, the court rejected the argument that an undisclosed principal is only bound by contracts he has actually authorised. Clearly, the juridical rationale for this decision cannot, therefore, be based upon contract. It is best understood as an aspect of apparent ownership, that is, the principal had invested the agent with all the external signs of ownership and should accordingly bear all the consequences. No question of the precise ambit of the agent's authority can arise when the extent of the agent's authority apparently is such that it allows him to appear as sole principal. Of course, where the agent's status is not clear, the question of the scope of his authority will be highly relevant. Herein lies the explanation for statutory intervention in the guise of the Factors Acts 1823 to 1889 which attempted to regulate the effects of the various dispositions made by factors upon third-party purchasers including pledgees.

Apparent authority: unauthorised mode of making a disposition   In reality, this is a particular application of the doctrine of estoppel where a principal allows his agent to give the impression that he has more authority than he actually enjoys. Ultimately, in all of the cases, what is essential is the principal's own conduct by way of a representation and the third party's reliance or change of position or detriment in response to this representation. There must be some positive act by the principal although this does not include acquiescence. Mere delivery of possession to the hirer under a hire-purchase agreement does not constitute an implied representation either of authority or of ownership, but in *Albemarle Supply Co. Ltd v Hind and Co.* [1928] 1 KB 307, it was held that a bailor who had expressly prohibited the creation of a lien was estopped from denying its validity after a lengthy period of acquiescence in the bailee's practice of garaging the relevant vehicles (taxis) with an artificer for the purpose of repair. Further difficulties arise where the third party does not actually know, but ought to have known, of restrictions in the agent's authority. Where the agent is acting within the ambit of the usual authority which agents of his kind possess, there will be no duty to inquire unless the circumstances are suspicious. It follows from this that a duty will exist if the agent is performing acts which lie outside the scope of his usual authority.

The main distinction between presumed authority and apparent ownership is that it is only in the case of the former that the principal can be sued as owner. Apparent ownership, on the other hand, does not involve any assertion that the non-owner acted in a representative character. In practice, apparent ownership is easier to establish and does not depend upon controversial rules. Indeed, the difficulty of finding a theoretical basis for *Watteau* v *Fenwick* [1893] 1 QB 346 has led to calls for its overruling and, if this occurred, it would rid the law of agency of the independent heading of 'usual authority'.

Statutory intervention: the Factors Acts 1823 to 1889

During the 19th century, there were a series of statutory interventions in England through the Factors Acts, the purpose of which was to accommodate the perceived requirements of trade. This legislation grew up in the wake of increasing trade in the 19th century, particularly in the practice of the English consignee/factor in making advances on goods to a foreign consignor. The Select Committee of the House of Commons of 1823 on the Law Relating to Merchants, Agents or Factors upon whose report the various Factors Acts were based, contended that the practice of the consignee himself treating the goods of all his consignors as his own and borrowing upon them *en bloc* was a practice which was beneficial to commerce, and that the lender should be given good title against the consignor. The advantage of this practice, according to the report, was that the consignee was relieved of the necessity of selling in a falling market and could postpone the sale until a good price could be obtained. Instances were given of the sale in some trades being postponed for six, nine or 12 months, and a great rise in price being taken advantage of. This was very popular for foreign consignors and there are examples of goods being described as shipped to the UK and then, when the price was right, re-exported to Continental ports.

Often the British consignees would not have sufficient capital to provide financing. They would then turn to brokers and bankers, pledging the consignee's various correspondents' securities *en bloc* in order to secure a lump sum. Although it was well-established that a factor was given a lien against the consignor's goods for moneys advanced, the difficulty was that the rule in *Paterson* v *Tash* (1743) 2 Str 1178 appeared to preclude the factor from affecting the property of the goods by pledging them for his own debt. This rule tended to jeopardise the credit structure on account of the increase in importance of the commission merchant as a financier of overseas trade. Interestingly, to combat this mischief, one of the suggestions of the committee was to introduce into English law the civilian concept of *possession vaut titre* (see pp. 21–2). In a similar vein in 1873, the Indian Law Commissioners in the draft clause 81 of the Indian Contract Bill proposed:

The ownership of goods may be acquired by buying them from any person who is in possession of them provided that the buyer acts in good faith and under circumstances which are not such as to raise a reasonable presumption that the person in possession has no right to sell them.

As in 1823, this approach was rejected on the basis that it would make British India an 'asylum for cattle stealers from Indian States'. Nevertheless, it does demonstrate the fluidity of the property-passing concept during the 19th century.

The factors legislation incorporated the principle of apparent ownership. Although by 1825 the right of the pledgee to the entire interest in the goods themselves and not just the pledgor's interest as under the 1823 legislation was provided, no power was in fact given to a known agent for sale. The financier was not to have notice that the person pledging the documents was not the actual owner, and the notice requirement was an onerous one as it was extended to cover the case of a reasonable man. Since at the beginning of the 19th century the consignment pattern of dealing in overseas trade had taken on considerable importance, it was virtually impossible for a reasonable man to be unaware that the goods and documents offered to him as security were more likely to be the property of someone other than the party seeking the advance. Furthermore, the documents of title under s. 2 of the 1825 Factors Act had to be 'entrusted with and in possession' of the factor which the courts construed as entrustment *qua* agent. The burden of proving entrustment was placed on the financier and the courts distinguished 'goods' from 'documents of title'. This explains why in *Phillips* v *Huth* (1840) 6 M & W 572 and *Hatfield* v *Phillips* (1842) 9 M & W 647 the courts insisted that possession of the goods themselves by the factor did not bring the latter within the Act. It was held that the Act only applied where the factor had in his hands some document which showed title to the specific goods.

The 1842 Factors Act aimed to amend the *Phillips* v *Huth* interpretation so that both documents of title and goods were covered by the Act. Unfortunately, the 'entrusting' terminology was still adopted which gave the court an opportunity in *Fuentes* v *Montis* (1868) LR 3 CP 268, affirmed (1868) LR 4 CP 93 to reassert the previous authorities and place upon the banking community the burden of inquiry. In this case, the plaintiffs had consigned a quantity of wine to a factor for sale. Having become dissatisfied with him as their agent, the plaintiffs terminated his authority and entrusted him to turn over the wines to another agent. Instead, the factor wrongfully pledged the dock warrants representing the wines to the defendants. The court held that as soon as the owner demanded his goods back, the factor ceased to be 'entrusted' and the subsequent pledge failed. This approach may have been predicated on policy reasons, that is, an attempt by the Bench to introduce a measure of prudence in commodity dealings. More likely, the approach demonstrated judicial attitudes to statutory interpretation.

By the 1850s and 60s the factor's pre-eminence as a purveyor of credit and a buying and selling agent diminished in the wake of the emergence of trading to order. The question of the factor's 'authority' and 'entrusting' was not of

The transfer of title and security of property 139

such crucial significance for international trade and it was not until the 1877 Factors Act that the decision was overturned. The 1877 Act did go further since it was also concerned with removing the anomaly presented in *Johnson* v *Crédit Lyonnais Co.* (1877) 3 CPD 32. In this case, a buyer had innocently left goods in the seller's possession and, not knowing that there were documents of title left those in his possession too. The seller pledged these documents of title to the bank for an advance, and in a priority contest between the bank and the buyer the court decided in favour of the latter. This decision was reversed in s. 3 of the Factors Act 1877 where a provision was inserted giving a seller in possession of documents of title to goods power to dispose of the goods to a bona fide purchaser, and a corresponding solution was adopted where documents of title had come into the possession of the buyer with the consent of the seller. It is these provisions which became encapsulated in ss. 8 and 9 of the Factors Act 1889 and were further substantially reproduced in s. 25(1) and (2) of the Sale of Goods Act 1893 (see below pp. 151–7).

The emergence of the mercantile agent
In the Factors Act 1889 the 'entrusting' provisions were formally scotched. Even so, the 1889 Act does incorporate the principle of apparent ownership so that s. 2(1) provides:

> Where a mercantile agent is, with the consent of the owner, in possession of goods or of the documents of title to goods, any sale, pledge, or other disposition of the goods, made by him when acting in the ordinary course of business of a mercantile agent, shall, subject to the provisions of this Act, be as valid as if he were expressly authorised by the owner of the goods to make the same; provided that the person taking under the disposition acts in good faith, and has not at the time of the disposition notice that the person making the disposition has not authority to make the same.

In a sense, the Factors Act 1889 is curiously named since it deals with classes of agent other than the factor.

Who is a mercantile agent? The broad definition of mercantile agent makes it no longer necessary to distinguish between factors and brokers so, according to s. 1(1) of the Factors Act 1889 mercantile agent means:

> a mercantile agent having in the customary course of his business as such agent authority either to sell goods, or to consign goods for the purpose of sale, or to buy goods, or to raise money on the security of goods.

The essential issue is that a 'mercantile agent' is one who by way of business is customarily entrusted with goods as agent. In this respect, a person who induces another to let him have goods on the representation that he can sell them to another is not, without more, a mercantile agent. Quite often the presence of a commission will help to assert his status. Thus in *Budberg* v *Jerwood and Ward* (1935) 51 TLR 99, it was held that the Act did not apply to defeat the title of an owner who entrusted her jewellery to a friend for the purposes of sale because of the absence of a commission which negatived any suggestion of a business relationship. There is an apparent conflict between s. 1(1) which refers to 'customary course' and s. 2(1) which alludes to 'the ordinary course of business of a mercantile agent'. In *Oppenheimer* v *Attenborough and Son* [1908] 1 KB 221, the question arose whether the agent for sale is authorised to pledge. The court expressed the opinion that the 1889 Act made no difference to the pre-existing law. With respect, this approach cannot be sustained especially in view of the inclusion of 'ordinary course of business'. Moreover, the definition of mercantile agent stipulates four kinds of activity and it is obvious that the ordinary kind of business of each will be different. Indeed, it appears from *Hansard* that the clause as originally drafted contained the words 'such a mercantile agent' which shows what the intention of the draftsman was (see *Hansard*, 3rd series, vol. 339, p. 230).

The disposition must be made in the ordinary course of business The Factors Act 1889 is a compromise reached by the instigators of the legislation, namely, the Institute of Bankers and the London Chamber of Commerce, bodies which represented the rival interests of the bankers and the merchants. The entrusting concept found in previous factors legislation is incorporated in the 1889 Act through the provision in s. 2 that the sale or pledge must be 'in the ordinary course of business of a mercantile agent'. A degree of illogicality has entered into English law because the courts although recognising, for example, that a car logbook and registration certificates are not documents of title, nevertheless have given them some special status in relation to 'ordinary course of business of a mercantile agent'. Thus in *Pearson* v *Rose and Young Ltd* [1951] 1 KB 275, the Court of Appeal unanimously held that a disposition of a car with its logbook was not in the ordinary course of business because the mercantile agent was in possession of the logbook without the consent of the owner. The fact of physical possession was ignored for the purpose of the disposition.

This decision was taken a stage further in *Stadium Finance Ltd* v *Robbins* [1962] 2 QB 664. In this case a dealer had been given possession of the owner's Jaguar car in order that he should find a buyer. The owner kept the ignition key, clearly intending to control the sale himself. Inadvertently, he left the registration book in the locked glove compartment. It was held by the Court of Appeal that as the dealer had not been given possession of the registration book and ignition key, a subsequent sale could not be in the ordinary course of business even though he obtained a duplicate key and was able to hand a key and the registration book to the hirer. However, it is difficult to accept such reasoning, and perhaps the best approach is to draw a distinction between the possession of the car itself, which must require the subjective consent of the owner, and the subsequent disposition which objectively requires, for the sale to be within the ordinary course of business, a logbook or registration document. Significantly in *Astley Industrial Trust Ltd* v *Miller* [1968] 2 All ER 36, Chapman J considered that the Court of Appeal decisions were wrong on this latter point. He did distinguish the two cases on the ground that with brand

The transfer of title and security of property 141

new cars, the registration document is by no means so important regarding title, and that the sale of a new car without the document can apparently be in the ordinary course of business.

The disposition must be made with the consent of the owner The English courts have adopted a wide approach with regard to the question of the consent of the owner. Thus in cases involving jewellers, the courts would point to evidence of a contrary intention which overrode s. 18, r. 4, of the Sale of Goods Act 1979 (*Weiner* v *Gill* [1906] 2 KB 574). While there must be actual consent to the agent's possession by the owner, it is irrelevant that this consent was obtained by a trick. In *Folkes* v *King* [1923] 1 KB 282, a motor agent was given possession of the owner's car and authorised to sell it for him for not less than £575, but in fact he sold it for £340. The buyer knew nothing of the cash restriction which the owner had placed upon the agent's actual authority and bought it in good faith. The agent was a mercantile agent and the buyer, therefore, obtained a good title. Moreover, so long as possession was originally given by the owner, withdrawal of that consent is immaterial (s. 2(2) of the Factors Act 1889) unless the buyer knew that it had been withdrawn, in which event he might no longer take in good faith in any case. The burden of proof is upon the buyer that he took in good faith and without notice that the sale was made without the owner's authority (*Heap* v *Motorists' Advisory Agency Ltd* [1923] 1 KB 577).

Improper dispositions by non-owners: limitations of the estoppel doctrine

The question of whether a purchaser acquires title as a consequence of estoppel has taken on significance in the wake of the *London Wine* débâcle (*Re London Wine Co. (Shippers) Ltd* 1986 PCC 121, discussed earlier (see pp. 29–31). In this case it was held that since the wine had not been ascertained, no property in any event could pass to the claimants, and the bank, as a debenture holder, could prevail since it was not 'privy' to the estoppel of the company and the warehouse. Inasmuch as it is true to say that a rule which prevents the owner from asserting his rights in effect takes them away from him, it cannot be the case that the estoppel of such a person can bind another (in the absence of being privy to the estoppel) with a title paramount. It has sometimes been maintained, drawing upon the approach taken by Devlin LJ in the Court of Appeal in *Eastern Distributors Ltd* v *Goldring* [1957] 2 QB 600, that the effect of s. 21 is to transfer to the buyer a real title and not a metaphorical title by estoppel. In this case, a van owner signed hire-purchase proposals which made a dealer appear to be the owner. This was part of a scheme to enable the customer to obtain another vehicle on credit without having to pay the deposit required by the then current credit regulations. The scheme failed, but the dealer, using the documents which the owner had given him, was able to sell the van to a hire-purchase company although having no right to do so. The hire-purchase company acquired a good title because, although the dealer had no right to sell, the owner's conduct in completing false forms estopped him from asserting this. It was held by Devlin LJ at p. 611:

that apparent authority to sell is an exception to the maxim *nemo dat quod non habet*; and it is plain from the wording that if the owner of the goods is precluded from denying authority, the buyer will in fact acquire a better title than the seller.

Subsequent case law has experienced difficulty in determining the exact basis of the decision. In *Stoneleigh Finance Ltd* v *Phillips* [1965] 2 QB 537, Davies LJ referred to an 'ostensible title to sell' in connection with *Eastern Distributors Ltd* v *Goldring*, while in *Snook* v *London and West Riding Investments Ltd* [1967] 2 QB 786, Russell LJ stated at pp. 803–4 that the plaintiff in that case was estopped by his own conduct. Other decisions have referred to the *Eastern Distributors* case as being based on ostensible ownership and not ostensible agency. It appears that the position is very confused especially since, on the facts, the decision in *Eastern Distributors Ltd* v *Goldring* could have been justified on more conventional agency principles because the owner had consented to give the van to a mercantile agent for the purpose of sale as well as relevant documentation relating to the van. This scenario seems to be on all fours with the mischief contained in s. 2(1) of the Factors Act 1889 (see above).

There are real difficulties in reconciling the proprietary estoppel doctrine with statutory interpretation since the Sale of Goods Act 1979 adopts the rule that property passes by agreement and not by conduct. Moreover, the proprietary estoppel approach fails to take into account the dynamic nature of the sale transaction as it concentrates on the assumption that there are three parties, namely, an owner, a rogue and a good-faith purchaser. In fact, the goods may have passed through several hands and the innocent purchaser may have been persuaded to enter into the sale transaction by a rogue who knew the extent of an agent's authority. If title is a rule of evidence or impressed with an equity and not of absolute conveyance, the rogue, as subpurchaser, will not prevail against the owner. The essential issue is whether goods are *freely* negotiable. Certainly, in the case of the bill of exchange, a person with notice of fraud or illegality may acquire a perfect title provided he acquires it from a holder in due course (s. 29(3) of the Bills of Exchange Act 1882). However, the development of the doctrine of estoppel in the context of chattels has stressed the need for a *representation* either by words or by conduct.

Estoppel and the requirement of a representation The limitations of the estoppel doctrine can easily be illustrated by reference to two comparatively recent cases. In *Shaw* v *Commissioner of Police of the Metropolis* [1987] 1 WLR 1332, the owner of a Porsche motor car entrusted it to a rogue to find a buyer. Unfortunately, the owner signed a letter stating that he had sold the car to the rogue. Relying on that letter, a good-faith purchaser agreed to buy the car under a conditional contract which did not pass property until the rogue vendor was paid. The Court of Appeal held that the owner of goods was precluded by s. 21 of the Sale of Goods Act 1979 from denying an intermediate seller's authority to sell goods of which the seller was not the owner, only if the goods were 'sold' by the intermediate seller. Statutory estoppel did not apply where there was merely an agreement to sell since, under s. 2(5) of the Sale of Goods Act 1979, an agreement to sell does not involve a transfer of property.

The facts of the more recent case of *Debs v Sibec Developments Ltd* [1990] RTR 91, provide an excellent illustration of the estoppel doctrine. In August 1987, the plaintiff bought a Mercedes-Benz car for £57,100. He was robbed of this car and, during the robbery, his life was threatened unless he signed a document containing his name and address, together with an acknowledgement that he had received a sum of money in full and final settlement for it. The robbers in taking the ignition key and registration document maintained the threat (through subsequent phone calls) not to go to the police and report the incident, by promising to kill his children on the occurrence of this eventuality. A month passed by before the plaintiff was persuaded to go to the police. In the meantime, the car was sold to a dealer merely on the production of the 'receipt' and the top half of the registration document. The dealer checked with Hire Purchase Information Ltd (HPI) that the car was not stolen or on hire-purchase and agreed to buy it for £46,950. This was done without either securing the address of his immediate seller or through making contact with the plaintiff. The car was then sold to a second dealer and then, at the defendants request, to Forward Trust Ltd for £51,000 who also had checked with HPI. Soon afterwards, the police traced the car to the defendants. The plaintiffs in this action before Simon Brown J succeeded in their claim for damages for conversion against the defendants. The arguments based on estoppel are especially significant. One argument was that there had been an estoppel by representation by virtue of the written receipt. This was rejected quite properly on the basis that the representation was not a voluntary one in that it was induced by force. The impact of the facts of this case is that they neatly illustrate the narrowness of the estoppel-by-negligence doctrine.

When the owner has enabled the representation to be made, the question of whether he owed a duty of care and, if so, whether he has broken that duty, must be material. The leading authority here is *Henderson and Co. v Williams* [1895] 1 QB 521, the facts of which are as follows. Bags of sugar belonging to O (the original owner) were stored in Williams's warehouse. O was defrauded by a rogue into 'selling' the goods to the rogue and in this respect, O instructed Williams to hold the goods on behalf of the rogue. This enabled the rogue to sell the goods to Henderson. Before buying, Henderson enquired from Williams who assured him that the rogue did have a right to the goods. The fraud was then discovered. The first contract between O and the rogue was held void for mistake. The warehouseman, therefore, refused to deliver up the goods to Henderson, the innocent buyer. It was held that both the warehouseman and O were estopped from denying the rogue's title because they had held him out as having a right to the goods. This case may be contrasted with *Farquharson Bros and Co. v C. King and Co. Ltd* [1902] AC 325. The facts involved a clerk employed by the plaintiffs who had authority to send delivery orders to the dock company with whom timber belonging to the plaintiffs was lodged. The clerk fraudulently transferred the timber to himself through the dock company under a fictitious name, and, using that name, he purported to sell the timber to the defendants. The House of Lords held that the plaintiffs were not estopped from denying the title of the defendants on the grounds that the plaintiffs had made no representation of any kind to them. Their lordships were clearly of the opinion here that the plaintiffs owed no duty of care to the defendants in this situation.

Estoppel and negligence   The extent of the duty of care in negligence occupied Simon Brown J in *Debs* v *Sibec Developments Ltd* [1990] RTR 91. In this respect, he adopted a suppositive argument; even if the plaintiff had been negligent in failing to report the theft, supposing he had reported it, this would not have been included on the HPI register when the first dealer checked the records. It followed that if the defendant was to succeed, the scope of the duty of care would have to extend to *each* purchaser in a chain of purchasers with the result that protection would or would not be gained according to when an inquiry of HPI would reveal the theft. This was rejected by Simon Brown J and reference was made to *Moorgate Mercantile Co. Ltd* v *Twitchings* [1977] AC 890. In that case it was held that even where a hire-purchase company, a member of HPI, failed to notify the HPI register of its interest in a vehicle under a hire-purchase agreement with the result that loss was caused to another dealer, a member of HPI, who, after checking the register subsequently acquired the vehicle, that dealer had no claim against the hire-purchase company.

The scope of the estoppel doctrine is extremely limited and it is well to recall the statement of Lord Wright in *Mercantile Bank of India Ltd* v *Central Bank of India Ltd* [1938] AC 287 at p. 302: 'There are very few cases of actions for conversion in which a plea of estoppel by representation has succeeded'. The emphasis on wilful conduct means that common law doctrine does not go very far in entrustment cases since it is settled that mere possession of property does not convey a title to dispose of it (*Central Newbury Car Auctions Ltd* v *Unity Finance Ltd* [1957] 1 QB 371). At the same time it should not be forgotten that possession is at the root of title, i.e., *beati possidentes*. It is still the case that the purchaser in good faith can acquire ownership through adverse possession in England by being in possession for six years (see pp. 20–1). The Limitation Act 1980 purports to bar the owner's right to bring suit to recover his property or its value after the prescribed period (Limitation Act 1980, ss. 2 and 3).

Estoppel and a 'right' to cure?
One further aspect of the doctrine of estoppel will be considered; the possibility of estoppel on the part of the seller 'curing' an initial defective title. There appears to be nothing wrong in legal logic with the idea that a seller can cure a defective title. As the number of encumbered goods in the economy increases, it may be unfair to shift all of the credit and crime risks with regard to the title to chattels on the seller. One way of doing this is through adopting a limited notion of 'cure'. Just as the vendor selling goods to which he has no title is estopped from denying the validity of the transfer, so also where the seller subsequently acquired a good title the buyer is protected by the estoppel, i.e., the estoppel is 'fed'. The basic problem here is determining at what stage the estoppel arises in the absence of waiver by the buyer. This is especially

problematic in view of the fact that s. 12(1) of the Sale of Goods Act 1979 envisages that a seller who does not have a right to sell at the time of the sale commits a breach of condition. It may be that a way of avoiding this dilemma is through s. 11(4) which relegates a breach of condition to that of a warranty in a non-severable contract where the buyer has accepted the goods. The main difficulty here is that Atkin LJ's judgment in *Rowland* v *Divall* [1923] 2 KB 500 would seem to preclude this possibility at pp. 506–7:

> The whole object of a sale is to transfer property from one person to another, and I think that in every contract of sale of goods there is an implied term to that effect that a breach of the condition that the seller has a right to sell the goods may be treated as a ground for rejecting the goods and repudiating the contract notwithstanding the acceptance within the meaning of the concluding words of [the subsection].

In fact, there is no warrant for this view in the Act itself, and it is doubtful whether Atkin LJ contemplated that his proposition would apply in cases where the seller had been able to remedy the breach before the repudiation by the buyer. It is noteworthy that in *Rowland* v *Divall* the seller never acquired the right to sell the car which was recovered from the buyer after four months' usage and it follows, therefore, that the buyer could not be regarded as having accepted the goods.

It does seem harsh that if the seller can and does cure his defective title *before* the buyer's repudiation, the latter can nevertheless repudiate the contract despite prolonged use and perhaps depreciation of the asset. The Law Reform Committee, 12th Report, *Transfer of Title to Chattels*, (Cmnd 2958, 1966) at para. 36 recommended that the buyer should not be able to recover the price in full in the situation where he had use of the goods. This approach has been echoed in subsequent Law Commission reports, but interestingly in the most recent Law Commission report, *Sale and Supply of Goods* (No. 160, 1987), at para. 6.4, the problems of quantifying the buyer's unjust enrichment have precluded any recommendation for reform in this area. Although it may be the case, as the Law Commission Report No. 160 points out at para. 6.5, the valuation of the buyer's unjust enrichment on termination through his prolonged use of the goods will be uncertain, nonetheless, if there has been a subsequent acquisition of title there can be no objection in principle to this feeding the title of the buyer if the latter had not, by that time, elected to treat the contract as repudiated. Under English law, the buyer would be subject to a claim in conversion by the true owner. In this circumstance, an allowance must be made against the tortfeasor's liability in damage to the extent of the value of the improvements made to the chattel in good faith (see s. 6 of the Torts (Interference with Goods) Act 1977).

MARKET OVERT

Under English law, recovery is based not on ownership, in the sense of absolute title, but rather on the better right to possess and the *ius tertii* cannot be pleaded against a possessor. Consequently, there is no theoretical reason why a thief should not sue a second thief although, in practice, the first thief will probably not want to draw attention to himself. It is only in the case of market overt that an indefeasible absolute title to chattels is known to the common law. Even the importance of this must not be overemphasised. Significantly, the present market overt provision incorporated in s. 22 of the Sale of Goods Act 1893 was deleted by the select committee of the Commons and the principle of relativity of title was substituted. However, later, market overt was restored on the ground that such an important change in the law endangered the passing of the Bill, and since then, the 12th Report of the Law Reform Committee (1966) has recommended at para. 11 that the rule should be extended to the sale of goods in all retail establishments. The effect of this recommendation is to shift the right of action available to the bona fide purchaser of goods under s. 12 of the Sale of Goods Act 1979 to the owner.

It would be simplistic to assert that market overt has overturned the security-of-property principle. There are strict rules, so sales in 'privy places' are not in market overt, nor is a sale by candlelight or after sunset as confirmed in *Reid v Commissioner of Police of the Metropolis* [1973] QB 551. The area of operation of market overt is small and is confined to ancient markets. Thus in *Lang v Jones* (1990) 10 TrLR 113, a sale in a private market held on property adjacent to a properly constituted market at Bermondsey was held not to be in market overt so that absolute title did not pass to the purchaser. Perhaps the most famous market overt is the City of London where every shop in which goods are exposed publicly for sale is a market overt for such things as the owner professes to deal in, every-day being a market overt except Sundays and holidays. Auction rooms are not shops. Of course there are difficulties in applying the ancient concept of market overt to modern retailing situations.

It is worth emphasising the significant historical exceptions to the full rigours of the market overt doctrine. In the first place, if a thief was prosecuted to conviction, the owner was entitled to the return of his goods. Secondly, there were statutory formalities that had to be complied with in order to pass title to horses. These exceptions may be indicative of sophisticated reasoning in that owners were expected to minimise the risk that stolen goods might pass into the hands of bona fide purchasers by reclaiming them before they were sold. The public policy issue here seemed to favour the prosecution of thieves by giving the owner an incentive to recover the goods. However, the rule and its rationale were somewhat suspect especially in view of the fact that it did not matter whether the owner *himself* had brought the prosecution.

VOIDABLE TITLE

Since English law fails to distinguish between contract and conveyance, no property can pass if the contract of sale is void. The emergence in England of voidable title theory in the 19th century included in s. 23 of the Sale of Goods Act 1979 may indicate a judicial propensity towards sophisticated allocation of risk since it enabled the courts to protect some good-faith purchasers without overturning the security-of-property principle.

The formalistic position adopted depends upon the intention of the parties: whether the owner intends to transfer possession only, or whether he intends to transfer title to the wrongdoer. However, the fundamental flaw with the voidable title approach is, how can the owner's subjective intent supply the innocent purchaser with realistic criteria for judging the legitimacy of the transaction? In addition, the owner-intent cases can be seen as an example of inductive judicial reasoning (see, for example, *Ingram* v *Little* [1961] 1 QB 31; *Lewis* v *Averay* [1972] 1 QB 198).

One of the most celebrated cases in this context is *Cundy* v *Lindsay* (1878) 3 App Cas 459. A rogue persuaded Lindsay to 'sell' linen to him on credit by pretending to be Blenkairon and Co, a known and reputable customer. The rogue then resold to Cundy whilst Lindsay, unpaid by the rogue, sued Cundy for conversion. In this case, a risk analysis based on fault may have stressed that, in the supply of cotton, there was a rapid turnover unlike the slower legal mechanism for the transfer of realty which often involves noting a property interest on a register, and that the owners having been tricked acted quickly and tried to reduce the risk to third parties. On the other hand, it is possible to argue that the owners were negligent by not spotting the discrepancy on the letter heading, which they should have done given the fact that the degree of commercial pressure was less than in an *inter praesentes* shopping situation. The House of Lords rejected any analysis based on fault, preferring a formalistic approach. Interestingly in *Cundy* v *Lindsay*, the unsuccessful third party was represented by Benjamin, the Louisiana lawyer who had fled to England after the US Civil War. It was Benjamin who sharpened the 'title' concept both in Louisiana and in England where, on at least two occasions, he unsuccessfully presented the point of view of security of transactions. Thus in *Russell* v *Favier* (1841) 18 La 585, Benjamin, a young man of 30, unsuccessfully represented a purchaser of a slave from a lessee who had improperly sold it. He argued at p. 587:

> A purchaser of movable effects at public auction who buys bona fide from an individual to whom the real owner has intrusted the possession, acquires a good title even though the owner had given the possession without authority to sell — or in other words, possession is such proof of title to movables as to enable the possessor to convey a good title to bona fide purchasers in ordinary course of business, unless the possession has been feloniously obtained [citing New York cases]. The distinction is this: if possession be obtained feloniously as by theft, the possessor can pass no title; but if obtained fraudulently, it suffices to enable him to pass title to third persons.

But this position failed because the court held that 'title' had not passed to the wrongdoer. Thirty-seven years later in *Cundy* v *Lindsay*, Benjamin argued that 'title' had gone to the impersonator and so could be passed on free of the 'equity'.

The issue of the 'equity' of the original owner envisaged by Benjamin in *Cundy* v *Lindsay* is very important. For example, if a wrongdoer transferred to an innocent purchaser who subsequently transferred to a purchaser with notice of the initial wrongdoing, the second purchaser's right or duties would depend on the definition of voidable title used by the courts. If voidable title is defined as an inferior title, it would include no power to cut off the rights of the original owner (security of property). This was the approach of Cresswell J in *Billiter v Young* (1856) 6 E & B 1 at p. 25 in holding that the voidable title rule was based upon the fact 'not . . . that the second vendee had a good title, and therefore the first sale was not void, but that the first sale was not void, and therefore the second vendee had a good title'.

Another interpretation, which is traditionally adopted in England, is that the title transferred is a perfect one subject to a condition subsequent based on rescission. This approach coheres with security in transactions. However, it is interesting how the courts have ensured the primacy of the security of property principle not by reference to the 'equity' of the original owner but rather by taking a wide approach to the question of notice of rescission. Thus in *Car and Universal Finance Ltd v Caldwell* [1965] 1 QB 525, the owner of a car sold it to a plausible rogue and allowed the rogue to take it away in return for a cheque. The cheque was dishonoured and the seller immediately informed the police requesting them to try to get his car back. After this, the rogue resold the car to X who took it in bad faith knowing of the fraud. X then resold it to the plaintiffs who bought in good faith. It was held that since the rogue could not have been contacted, the original seller had rescinded the contract by informing the police and doing everything practicable to make public his intention to rescind, for example, by informing the AA. Subsequently in *Newtons of Wembley Ltd v Williams* [1965] 1 QB 560, it was held that informing the police and a motorists' organisation like the AA or RAC was sufficient to rescind the contract when the rogue could not be found. Of course, this is of little comfort to the innocent buyer and it is for this reason that the Law Revision Committee's 12th Report, *Transfer of Title to Chattels* (Cmnd 2958, 1966), recommended that the rule as to avoidance laid down in *Car and Universal Finance Ltd v Caldwell* should be reversed and actual communication required. Nevertheless, the approach taken in *Car and Universal Finance Ltd v Caldwell* has more recently been endorsed in *Thomas v Heelas* 27 November 1986 (CAT No. 1065). In this case, the court held that when an owner sought to recover goods in the possession of somebody who was not a party to the voidable transaction, the onus was on the possessor to show that he had good title. Clearly, this is an onerous task especially where the chain of title is long. On the facts of this case, over six months had elapsed between the owner's original rescission by informing the police and the eventual discovery of the car.

SELLERS IN POSSESSION

Section 8 of the Factors Act 1889 deals with the case of a seller under a sale or agreement to sell remaining in possession of goods, or of the documents of title to the goods. This was virtually duplicated in s. 25(1) of the Sale of Goods Act 1893 (now s. 24 of the Sale of Goods Act 1979) which provides as follows:

Where a person having sold goods continues or is in possession of the goods, or of the documents of title to the goods, the delivery or transfer by that person, or by a mercantile agent acting for him, of the goods or documents of title under any sale, pledge, or other disposition thereof, [or under any agreement for sale, pledge, or other disposition thereof,] to any person receiving the same in good faith and without notice of the previous sale, has the same effect as if the person making the delivery or transfer were expressly authorised by the owner of the goods to make the same.

The words in brackets are additional words included in the Factors Act 1889, s. 8.

A literal construction of s. 24 of the Sale of Goods Act 1979 would suggest that although the owner is deemed to authorise the delivery of the goods or the transfer of the documents of title, he is *not* deemed to have given his authority to the sale, pledge or other disposition. This contrasts with the 'notional mercantile agency' device adopted in s. 9 of the Factors Act 1889 where the buyer in possession is treated as if he were such a mercantile agent. The significance of this is that s. 2(1) of the Factors Act 1889, the main mercantile agency provision, allows the mercantile agent within certain constraints to pass title by delivery of goods unaccompanied by documents. As a result of this notional mercantile agency, the effect of s. 9 is wider than s. 8.

The approach taken in s. 8 of the Factors Act 1889 is consistent with the multititular characteristic of English law. Prior to the amendment made in s. 8, any purchaser of goods from a seller in possession who did not transfer documents of title would have been liable to the true owner in conversion. There is now a statutory defence to such an action because by virtue of s. 24(1) of the Sale of Goods Act 1979, the true owner is deemed to have authorised the delivery of the goods to the buyer and must, therefore, have waived his right to immediate possession. It is odd that s. 8 does not include a notional mercantile agency as seen in s. 9 of the Factors Act 1889. The reason for the difference in treatment may be due to the legacy of the historical function of the factor who was a *buying* and selling agent. Up to the mid-19th century, the factor enjoyed a dominant financial role in domestic and international trade and would sell in his own name, and the foreign merchant trusted him with actual possession of the goods. The new classes of agent as well as buyers and sellers may have been grafted on to the same mischief which was covered by earlier factors legislation. Consequently, since the factor was never a seller *qua* owner in possession, there was no need to incorporate the notional mercantile agency provision since the factor's possession would be as a mercantile agent in any case.

Sellers in possession and notice requirement for good faith purchase
The question of the notice requirement for good-faith purchase is particularly pertinent under a literal interpretation of s. 24 of the Sale of Goods Act 1979. This section provides that goods may be delivered 'under any sale, to *any person*'. Thus, delivery need not be to the first purchaser from the seller but to a subpurchaser direct from the original seller. The problem revolves around

the question concerning the obligation to act in 'good faith and without notice of the previous sale' which is required in s. 24. The material words read as follows: '... the delivery ... of the goods ... under any sale ... to any person receiving the same in good faith and without notice of the previous sale'. This suggests that only the subpurchaser needs to be in good faith, and even if the latter is in bad faith he will acquire title by virtue of the buyer's good faith. The approach taken under s. 8 of the Factors Act 1889 differed from its forerunner, s. 3 of the Factors Act 1877. This provided that title passed to 'any other person who ... purchases such goods' so that title is linked to any person who purchased the goods without notice of the previous sale. The present rule, however, requires not only sale but also a delivery. So long as the delivery is to a person (not necessarily a purchaser) who is acting in good faith, the buyer in bad faith may acquire title by virtue of a delivery to a person who takes delivery in good faith. In contrast, under the doctrine of estoppel, or s. 2 of the Factors Act 1889, the second buyer is protected as from the moment of sale which does not necessarily coincide with delivery.

The possession of the seller and section 24
The capacity in which the seller retains possession has engaged the attention of the courts. Some of the cases have suggested that if the seller retains possession but acts in relation to the goods as a hirer, the subpurchaser will not be protected (see *Staff Motor Guarantee Ltd* v *British Wagon Co. Ltd* [1934] 2 KB 305; *Eastern Distributors Ltd* v *Goldring* [1957] 2 QB 600). The modern position is that the *capacity* in which the seller remains in *continuous* possession is immaterial. Thus in *Pacific Motor Auctions Ltd* v *Motor Credits (Hire Finance) Ltd* [1965] AC 867, a dealer unsuccessfully attempted to achieve a stocking plan by way of a sale and rehiring, and the Privy Council held that the words 'continues ... in possession' referred to the continuity of physical possession, notwithstanding any private transaction between the seller and the first buyer which might have altered the legal capacity under which the possession was held. Of course, where physical possession has been given up, as in *Mitchell* v *Jones* (1905) 24 NZLR 932, the second buyer is not protected because of the break in the continuity of possession.

The transactional extent of section 24
Section 24 of the Sale of Goods Act 1979 does not only apply to resale but extends to any 'sale, pledge or *other disposition*'. The words 'other disposition' have been held to cover any transaction which, like sale or pledge, transfers some proprietary interest in the goods. This can be illustrated by the facts in *Worcester Works Finance Ltd* v *Cooden Engineering Co. Ltd* [1972] 1 QB 210, where X bought a car from the defendants but paid with a cheque which was dishonoured. He then sold the car to the plaintiffs, although he retained possession for the time being. Meanwhile the defendant, the original owner, sought to rescind the contract because X's cheque had not been honoured. X agreed to this and allowed the defendants to retake the vehicle. When the plaintiffs pointed out that the car now belonged to them and claimed the vehicle or its value from the defendants, the action failed. As against the plaintiffs, X

The transfer of title and security of property 151

was still a seller in possession, and when X accepted the defendant's rescission of the original contract and returned the car, this was held to be a 'disposition' within s. 24 so that title had passed. The effect of this decision was that the plaintiffs had recourse only to X, if this was indeed a worthwhile remedy.

BUYERS IN POSSESSION

Section 9 of the Factors Act 1889 and s. 25(1) of the Sale of Goods Act 1979 provide for property passing by virtue of the buyer's possession:

> Where a person having bought or agreed to buy goods obtains, with the consent of the seller, possession of the goods or the documents of title to the goods, the delivery or transfer by that person, or by a mercantile agent acting for him, of the goods or documents of title, under any sale, pledge, or other disposition thereof, [or under any agreement for sale, pledge, or other disposition thereof,] to any person receiving the same in good faith and without notice of any lien or other right of the original seller in respect of the goods, has the same effect as if the person making the delivery or transfer were a mercantile agent in possession of the goods or documents of title with the consent of the owner.

The words in brackets are omitted in s. 25(1) of the Sale of Goods Act 1979.

If good title has passed to the buyer then s. 25(1) will rarely apply. The section refers to a contract of sale where the buyer has 'bought' the goods, which appears to be surprising for the simple reason that, in any case, the *nemo dat quod non habet* principle will apply. However, the subsection may be important where the buyer has obtained both property and possession of the goods but title has subsequently been avoided by the seller. In this respect, s. 25(1) renders the decision in *Car and Universal Finance Co. Ltd* v *Caldwell* [1965] 1 QB 525 redundant. Thus s. 2(2) of the Factors Act 1889 specifically states that the subsequent withdrawal of the consent by the seller does not prevent the application of the Act. It is clear from *Cahn* v *Pockett's Bristol Channel Steam Packet Co. Ltd* [1899] 1 QB 643 and *Newtons of Wembley Ltd* v *Williams* [1965] 1 QB 560 that the issue of consent in s. 9 of the Factors Act 1889 and s. 25(1) of the Sale of Goods Act 1979 is subject to the treatment of the seller's consent in s. 2 of the Factors Act 1889.

The limitation imposed by the words 'agreed to buy' should not be underestimated. This is the distinction between hire-purchase (*Helby* v *Matthews* [1895] AC 471) and conditional sale (*Lee* v *Butler* [1893] 2 QB 318) which is excessively technical concentrating on legal form rather than economic substance (see pp. 346–54). It is significant that in accordance with the general assimilation of conditional sale agreements to hire-purchase agreements, it is now provided that for the purposes of s. 9 of the Factors Act 1889 and s. 25(1) of the Sale of Goods Act 1979 'the buyer under a conditional sale agreement is to be taken not to be a person who has bought or agreed to buy goods' (s. 25(2)(a) of the Sale of Goods Act 1979). It would appear that such conditional sales are governed by the Consumer Credit Act 1974.

However, with respect to other conditional sales not covered by the 1974 Act, for example, if the total credit provided is in excess of £15,000, or if the buyer is a body corporate (s. 189 of the Consumer Credit Act 1974), s. 25(1) still applies. Moreover, consignment sales, including sale or return transactions, are not covered by s. 25(1) of the Sale of Goods Act 1979 because the possessor is not a person who has agreed to buy goods even though, in a certain sense, he has made a conditional contract of sale. This emphasises the continued existence in English law of legal form as a phenomenon triumphing over economic substance.

Documents of title

Section 25(1) of the Sale of Goods Act 1979 applies equally where the buyer is in possession of documents of title to the goods with the seller's consent. What if an unpaid seller transfers a bill of lading or other document of title before the buyer gets physical possession of the goods? In this event, s. 25(1) would appear to allow the buyer to resell the document of title so as to defeat any unpaid seller's lien or right of stoppage (see chapter 6).

Good faith and notice

The third party under s. 25(1) must take the goods 'in good faith and without notice of any lien or other right of the original seller in respect of the goods'. This provision is repeated in s. 2(1) of the Factors Act 1889 and ss. 22 to 25 of the Sale of Goods Act 1979. It is sometimes said that s. 47(2) is more favourable to the third party because it does not say anything about notice of the rights of the original seller (see pp. 35–6). Before considering this point, it is important to draw a clear distinction between notice and knowledge. Notice is not necessarily knowledge since essentially the former is a mechanism by which the latter is attributed. Thus, the terms are not interchangeable since knowledge is a question of fact, whereas notice is a more expansive concept as it can anticipate knowledge being attributed to a person.

Although in its extreme form actual notice is coextensive with knowledge in that the person with such notice has, as a matter of fact, conscious awareness, it should be recognised that notice is an aspect of a continuum and at the other extreme, constructive notice is *treated* as being knowledge. Great difficulties have emerged in distinguishing actual notice from constructive notice. The modern approach is to eschew the evidence-orientated approach and concentrate rather on the question of *whose actions* are relevant. If the state of mind of the party to be charged is relevant then this is a question of actual notice. Such is the case with s. 47, and it is doubtful whether the absence of notice under this provision adds much to the good faith requirement. On the other hand, if the state of mind is irrelevant then the issue is whether a formal act has been properly performed by the party seeking to protect the prior rights. It follows that constructive notice is a matter for form, whilst actual notice rests upon the consciousness of the relevant party.

The question of 'good faith' is defined in s. 61(3) of the Sale of Goods Act 1979 as follows:

A thing is deemed to be done in good faith within the meaning of this Act when it is in fact done honestly, whether it is done negligently or not.

It is clear that negligence when surrounded by other circumstances will go to the question of knowledge. For the sake of convenience, knowledge may be categorised as actual, 'Nelsonian', i.e., wilfully shutting one's eye to the obvious, and 'naughty' knowledge where there has been an element of recklessness concerning circumstances which would indicate the facts to an honest and reasonable man (see *Heap* v *Motorists' Advisory Agency Ltd* [1923] 1 KB 577; *Pearson* v *Rose and Young Ltd* [1951] 1 KB 275). Nonetheless, the doctrine of constructive notice does not normally apply to commercial transactions (*Manchester Trust* v *Furness* [1895] 2 QB 539), and there is no general duty on the buyer of goods in an ordinary commercial transaction to make inquiries as to the right of the seller to dispose of the goods. Certainly, it would be anomalous to punish knowledge by the subbuyer of the buyer's non-payment, especially since it is a common business occurrence for a seller to be paid for goods before he himself can pay for them. It would be unreasonable, in this respect, for a subbuyer to be put on notice merely because of his knowledge of a retention of title clause, not least because there are so many types of retention of title clauses, many of which include proceeds provisions (see pp. 268–70). In the case where property has passed to the buyer, the subbuyer's knowledge of non-payment cannot be described as bad faith because this can hardly be considered a right 'in respect of the goods'; it is merely a personal right in respect of the contract of sale.

There may be some situations where the property in the goods sold will have passed to the buyer by virtue of documents of title having been delivered where the seller could still have a lien over the goods. With this in mind, the third party could invoke the good-faith provision in s. 9 of the Factors Act 1889 which refers to 'good faith and without notice of any lien'. Moreover, it seems that an unpaid seller might still retain his lien over the goods if possession has been given to the buyer for a limited period or temporarily. Even though possession of the goods may terminate the unpaid seller's statutory lien (see pp. 122–3), the contract itself may create a special right in the seller analogous to a lien.

The effect of section 9 of the Factors Act 1889 and section 25(1) of the Sale of Goods Act 1979

There are bound to be real difficulties in a section which uses four terms of identification, 'seller', 'buyer', 'original seller' and 'owner'. Essentially the problem is one of construction of this section and it could be argued that a literal approach would allow a thief to pass good title by virtue of a strict interpretation of s. 25(1). Such an approach would not be confined to thieves as it would naturally extend to situations where initial disposals of property were improper. An example of this phenomenon is the removal of property from a church achieved without going through the proper procedure, for example, the confirmatory faculties heard before a Consistory Court. This was the case in *Re St Mary's, Barton-on-Humber* [1987] Fam 41.

The argument is that the thief's consent to his purchaser's possession could be treated as being equivalent to the consent of the owner. Nevertheless over the past 20 years, certain Commonwealth decisions have equated 'seller' with 'owner' so that there can never be a 'seller' or at least 'original seller' where there has been a theft (*Elwin* v *O'Regan and Maxwell* [1971] NZLR 1124; *Brandon* v *Leckie* (1972) 29 DLR (3d) 633). This approach can be criticised on the basis that it departs from ordinary principles of construction in a way that the Court of Appeal refused to do in *Newtons of Wembley Ltd* v *Williams* [1965] 1 QB 560. In this case, the owners of a car sold it in return for a cheque, but it was expressly agreed that ownership should remain in the seller until the cheque was cleared. The rogue resold the car in Warren Street, London, a recognised market for second-hand cars. It was held that the subbuyer prevailed since the rogue, as a buyer in possession, could transfer a good title by virtue of s. 25(1) of the Sale of Goods Act 1979. The Court of Appeal took a literal approach to the requirement of acting in the capacity of being a mercantile agent. In this respect, the resale by the rogue had been in circumstances (i.e., an established second-hand car market) such that the subbuyer could reasonably assume that he was buying from a mercantile agent in the ordinary course of business. Thus Pearson LJ pointed out at p. 578:

> When the provisions of section 2 are applied to the section 9 position . . . this is the prima facie result: if the transaction is made by the person concerned when acting in the ordinary course of business of a mercantile agent, the transaction is validated: on the other hand, if the transaction is made by him when not acting in the ordinary course of business of a mercantile agent, the transaction is not validated.

This *obiter* approach would, if unrestricted in its application, severely limit s. 9 of the Factors Act and s. 25(1) of the Sale of Goods Act 1979. Moreover, it is difficult to understand the development of the hire-purchase mechanism as a device to avoid s. 9 if this indeed was the strict position. Certainly, the conventional legal position before the *Newtons of Wembley* case was that s. 9 and s. 25(1) were considered to validate a sale *as if* the buyer in possession were a mercantile agent, but did not include that he should act in such a way. To clarify the position, the Law Reform Committee, 12th Report, 1966, recommended at para. 23 that the law be amended to restore this position, although nothing has come of this proposal to date.

Despite the fact that the buyer's possession in s. 9 is 'fed' into s. 2(1) of the Factors Act 1889 making it in fact wider than s. 8 of that Act, it is doubtful whether the draftsman intended it to extend to theft. Indeed, the public policy issue of discouraging thieves may very well be the reason for the failure to implement the recommendation found in para. 11 of the 12th Report of the Law Reform Committee. Here it was proposed that the market overt doctrine be abolished and replaced by a provision enabling a person buying in good faith at retail or trade premises, or at a public auction to acquire good title. No attempt was made in the report to consider the frequency of such an occurrence, as well as the degree to which the purchaser's right of action against the retailer under the right to sell provisions is insufficient to protect him.

It may be that a literal construction of s. 9 is contrary to a fundamental rule in the common law. Theft can hardly be considered a contractual defect because it constitutes a real vice which attaches to the movables themselves. This approach was evident in both the Court of Appeal and House of Lords decisions in *National Employers' Mutual General Insurance Association Ltd* v *Jones* [1990] 1 AC 24. In this case, the defendant had purchased a car from a motor dealer, neither party being aware that the vehicle had been stolen from a woman whose interest had subsequently been subrogated to her insurers. In the Court of Appeal, the majority held (Sir Denys Buckley dissenting) that the essence of 'sale' was the transference of the ownership or general property in goods from a seller to a buyer for a price. It was argued that the opening words of s. 25(1) of the 1979 Act and s. 9 of the Factors Act 1889 lay down the condition precedent for the consequences provided by the later words of the section which only contemplate a transaction in which the general property in goods has been acquired, or where it has been agreed that it should be acquired. This approach was summarised in *The Times* law report heading (6 April 1987) as follows: 'Innocent buyer has no title to stolen goods'.

The main objection to the Court of Appeal's approach is that it would seem to involve the consequence that a purported sale of stolen property is outside the provisions of the 1979 Act altogether. Furthermore, it undermines the relativity of title concept which permeates the structure of the Act. This is confirmed by the House of Lords decision in that case where *The Times* law report heading (25 April 1987) summarised the majority judgment as follows: 'Innocent buyer of stolen goods does not obtain *good title as against the owner*'. Consequently, s. 9 does not, as a matter of construction, confer a good title on a purchaser if the mercantile agent from whom the goods had been purchased has come into possession of the goods from a thief. In this situation, the goods would not have been entrusted to the thief by the owner. As Lord Goff held in the House of Lords at p. 33:

> In my opinion, section 9 of the Factors Act 1889 must be read as providing that the delivery or transfer given by the intermediate transferor (B) shall have the same effect as if he was a mercantile agent in possession of the goods or documents of title with the consent of the owner who entrusted them to him (A). . . . The same construction must, of course, be placed upon section 25(1) of the Sale of Goods Act 1979.

In preferring the innocent owner, the thief rule distributes the loss on to the first purchaser from the thief. The second purchaser, if he has to yield the goods to the original owner, has an action against the first buyer for breach of the implied obligations under s. 12 of the Sale of Goods Act 1979 or related provisions in other supply contracts. As such, the chain of actions end with the original purchaser from the thief because the latter will usually be judgment proof. Despite this, the arguments for preferring the innocent owner where there has been theft over and above the good-faith purchaser are finely balanced. It could be maintained, for example, that the bona fide purchaser should be protected not because of his praiseworthy character but rather because such a rule makes buying more attractive. Indeed, this rule will not require an elaborate investigation of property rights. This approach should be contrasted with the fault doctrine encapsulated in *Lickbarrow* v *Mason* (1787) 2 TR 63 which was applied recently by Simon Brown J in *Debs* v *Sibec Developments Ltd* [1990] RTR 91 discussed earlier (see pp. 142–4). The application of the fault formula is difficult since it is a Janus-faced formula, i.e., where the original owner gives up possession to another, without his act of delivery to the possessor, the wrong could not have been perpetrated, but equally indispensable is the act of the innocent purchaser who also trusts the possessor not to sell goods he is not authorised to sell. In the case of theft, these considerations cannot apply because they do not constitute a contractual defect. As such, a non-negotiability rule can be a constraint on theft in that it may increase the incentive for owners to attempt to recover stolen goods. It is wrong to underestimate the recovery of stolen goods by owners since, although the amount of stolen property that is recovered by the police is small, some stolen goods are easier to recover than others. If the non-negotiability rule were overturned, this would have a knock-on effect with regard to the exposure of sellers of stolen goods to actions based on implied-title warranties. Furthermore, the non-negotiability rule will give an extra incentive for the purchaser to take precautions in order to reduce the risk of surrender as he may have become familiar with the goods, and the cost of replacement could be high. This is anticipated in ss. 24 and 25 of the Sale of Goods Act 1979 in that the sale must be in the ordinary course of business, thereby introducing an objective standard in distinguishing between shady and non-shady circumstances.

One way out of the impasse suggested by these finely balanced arguments is to consider whether it may be more economically efficient for the owner of the goods to assume the risk of theft through, for example, insurance cover. Owners are generally in a better position to assess risk in view of the fact that they will normally have information pertaining to the value of the goods, their location, and the frequency of theft. Additionally, market insurance is more available for owners against the theft risk than for purchasers against the risk of the goods bought being stolen. In resolving this dilemma the statistics available are not helpful. Nothing is said of what is recovered from the thief or wrongdoer, and how much is recovered from innocent third parties. This will have significance with regard to insurance because, if the bulk is recovered from the thief, shifting the risk on to the owners might well only have a marginal effect on insurance premiums. Furthermore, there is no information in the statistics about the likelihood of the property being insured.

The law must direct the outcome of a dispute between the original owners and innocent purchasers from thieves since it is rare for them to be aware of each other. Normally, they will not have bargained with respect to each other the risk of debtor misbehaviour. In some extreme circumstances, for example, after a war, the protection of the original owner of the goods may take on additional policy significance for the victorious regime. Thus, in Malaya, household goods were returned to the owner who, on discharge from a Japanese concentration camp found them in the shop of a bona fide purchaser.

The court refused to inquire whether the chattels had been requisitioned by the Japanese or by the returning Allied Forces since it was held that neither could have transferred ownership rights to a bona fide purchaser (see *Martin v World Piano Co.* [1947] MULR 61).

SUPPLIES OF MOTOR VEHICLES

Undoubtedly, any legal system which sanctions the least notice of a division of ownership rights increases the costs to third parties in determining the true legal position. Sometimes these costs can be diminished through self-help mechanisms, i.e., dealers involved in a particular commercial activity setting up their own register of encumbered assets. Perhaps the most celebrated example of this phenomenon in England can be seen in the activities of Hire Purchase Information plc (HPI), of which nearly all finance companies and motor dealers are members. This is a private body which keeps a register of vehicles subject to a hire-purchase agreement. In this respect, if a member of HPI is correctly told that a vehicle is not registered as being subject to a hire-purchase agreement, it is probable that the member will acquire title to the vehicle on the basis of the argument that there has been an estoppel by actual representation through treating HPI as an agent of the member failing to register. Despite being an unofficial record, HPI helps ensure priority for dealers. As such, this mechanism should be distinguished from credit scoring which is essentially a statistical technique assessing the likelihood of payment from the characteristics supplied of the customer.

Problems of sale by non-owners frequently arise with motor vehicles because they are valuable and relatively easy to sell, and also because of the sheer number of vehicles on the road. The private buyer of a second-hand car would have great difficulty in checking whether or not his seller had a right to sell, whereas motor dealers and finance companies can check with HPI. It is for this reason that part III of the Hire-Purchase Act 1964 (substituted by the Consumer Credit Act 1974, s. 192(3)(a) and sch. 4, para. 22) introduced special protection for private buyers of motor vehicles. However, it should be noted that not all business concerns are excluded from part III because the relevant criterion is the status of the buyer as not being a car dealer or a finance company. Thus, a trade or finance purchaser is defined under s. 29(2) of part III to mean a person who carries on a business which consists wholly or partly:

(a) of purchasing motor vehicles for the purpose of offering or exposing them for sale, or

(b) of providing finance by purchasing motor vehicles for the purpose of bailing or (in Scotland) hiring them under hire-purchase agreements or agreeing to sell them under conditional sale agreements.

It was held in *Stevenson v Beverley Bentinck Ltd* [1976] 1 WLR 483 that because s. 29(2) does not contain such a qualification as 'in the course of his business', a motor trader fell within the scope of this provision even though he was buying the vehicle for his own private use.

The special protection for buyers of motor vehicles under part III is encapsulated in s. 27 of the Act which states:

> (1) This section applies where a motor vehicle has been bailed or (in Scotland) hired under a hire-purchase agreement, or has been agreed to be sold under a conditional sale agreement, and, before the property in the vehicle has become vested in the debtor, he disposes of the vehicle to another person.
> (2) Where the disposition referred to in subsection (1) above is to a private purchaser, and he is a purchaser of the motor vehicle in good faith without notice of the hire-purchase or conditional sale agreement (the 'relevant agreement') that disposition shall have effect as if the creditor's title to the vehicle has been vested in the debtor immediately before that disposition

This provision applies irrespective of the qualifying criteria for a consumer credit transaction, such as whether the buyer or hirer is a body corporate, or that the value of the goods is in excess of £15,000. The emphasis upon agreement means that s. 27 does not apply if the proposal form put forward by the hirer or buyer is not accepted, as in the case of *Central Newbury Car Auctions Ltd* v *Unity Finance Ltd* [1957] 1 QB 371. Moreover, if the agreement is void for mistake of identity, or it is avoided before the disposition to the third party, there seems to be little doubt that the operation of part III will be excluded simply because the person in possession is not a 'debtor'. The first requirement of s. 27 is that the vehicle must have been let under a hire-purchase agreement, or been agreed to be sold under a conditional sale agreement. It does not apply to a simple hiring arrangement, for example, an operating lease and neither does it apply to a finance lease (see chapter 13).

By virtue of s. 27(2), where the disposition is to a private purchaser of a motor vehicle in good faith and without notice of the hire-purchase agreement or conditional sale agreement, that disposition has effect as if the creditor's title to the vehicle had been vested in the debtor immediately before that disposition. This approach is consistent with relativity of title so that it does not necessarily defeat the person with the best title, for example, had there been a theft before the creditor let the vehicle out on hire-purchase. It should be noted that part III carefully defines the term 'disposition' which is wider than s. 25(1) of the Sale of Goods Act 1979 in that it does not require delivery, but narrower in the sense that it does not cover pledges and hire, although these are only likely to occur in a motor dealer context and would, in any case, be excluded. Thus s. 29(1) of part III defines 'disposition' to include:

> ... any sale or contract of sale (including a conditional sale agreement), any bailment ... under a hire-purchase agreement and any transfer of the property in goods in pursuance of a provision in that behalf contained in a hire-purchase agreement, and includes any transaction purporting to be a disposition (as so defined).

It is clear from this definition that exchange transactions are excluded. A material issue which arises from this concerns the categorisation of part-exchange transactions as being either sale or barter (see pp. 55–60).

Only a private purchaser in good faith and without notice is protected. 'Notice' is defined by s. 29(3) as actual notice at the time of disposition to him and constructive notice does not, therefore, appear to be relevant. The burden of proving good faith and absence of notice appears to rest upon the purchaser (*Mercantile Credit Co. Ltd* v *Waugh* (1978) 32 Hire Trading (No. 2) 16). Sometimes the first private person to take the vehicle may have acquired it on hire-purchase himself, for example, the original hirer may wrongfully sell to a garage which then disposes of it to a new hire-purchaser. The problem here is that the new hire-purchaser may take in good faith when he enters the hire-purchase transaction but by the time he acquires the option to buy, he may know of the old or unexpired hire-purchase agreement and will not be able to take without notice. Section 27(4) expressly provides for this contingency so that, in these circumstances, the time for determining whether the new hirer is in good faith is when he enters into the agreement and not when he exercises his option to purchase. Even so, a trade or finance purchaser will not be better off as a result of the subsequent disposition because such a purchaser will remain liable in conversion to the original owner by virtue of s. 27(6).

The 1964 Act contains a number of important presumptions laid out in s. 28 which are of considerable importance if the chain of title is a lengthy one. The effect of these presumptions is that the defendant having proved himself to be a purchaser in good faith will prevail. There are two significant exceptions to this. Under s. 27(3) and (4) only the *first* private purchaser after the disposition by the debtor to a trade or finance purchaser is protected, but only if he is in good faith and without notice. If the *first* private purchaser is *established* as not being a purchaser in good faith, *no* subsequent purchaser can acquire a good title under s. 27. The second exception to the presumption that the present holder has good title is where the original owner, usually the original finance company, can prove that the vehicle had been stolen from the hirer as was indeed the case in *National Employers' Mutual General Insurance Association Ltd* v *Jones* [1990] 1 AC 24 discussed above (see pp. 155–7).

SALE UNDER COMMON LAW OR STATUTORY POWERS

The Sale of Goods Act 1979 preserves other exceptions to the general rule of security of property. By virtue of s. 21(2)(b), nothing in the Act shall affect 'the validity of any contract of sale under any special common law or statutory power of sale or under the order of a court of competent jurisdiction'. Many of the statutory powers of sale developed from the common law, for example, the right of a pawnee under ss. 120 and 121 of the Consumer Credit Act 1974, those of a bailee of uncollected goods under ss. 12 and 13 of the Torts (Interference with Goods) Act 1977, and hoteliers' powers to sell guests' goods to meet unpaid hotel fees under s. 1(1) of the Hotel Proprietors Act 1956. Other important statutory powers relate to insolvency and bankruptcy and are consolidated under the Insolvency Act 1986.

The High Court has significant statutory power to order sale if the goods are perishing or depreciating rapidly in value while litigation over them is proceeding (Rules of the Supreme Court 1965, Ord. 29, r. 4; County Courts Act 1984, s. 38). In addition, rules of court allow for the sale of goods seized in execution where a claimant alleges that he is entitled to the goods by way of a security for a debt (Rules of the Supreme Court 1965, Ord. 17, r. 6; County Courts Act 1984, s. 100).

EIGHT
The obligations and remedies of the transferee

DUTY TO ACCEPT DELIVERY

It is anticipated under s. 27 of the Sale of Goods Act 1979 that the buyer is under a duty to accept goods tendered in conformity with the contract. However, where the goods tendered are not in conformity with the contract, the buyer is prima facie entitled to reject them. The contract will still remain alive if the time allowed for delivery has not expired, and the seller is entitled to make a fresh tender. In this respect, the Sale of Goods Act 1979 recognises a limited right to cure which is necessarily confined to unascertained goods and not to specific goods identified to the contract because fresh tender, in this latter circumstance, would be equivalent to the seller changing the contract goods by unilateral action (compare *Borrowman Phillips and Co.* v *Free and Hollis* (1878) 4 QBD 500). If the buyer is contemplating suing for damages, the duty to mitigate may require him to accept a second tender. A right to cure would have substantial implications in the context of consumer sales and, as the law presently stands, allowing a cure might amount to acceptance of the goods whereby the right of rejection is lost. It is for this reason that the Law Commission report, *Sale and Supply of Goods* (Law Com. No. 160, London, 1987) at para. 4.14 rejected the introduction of a statutory right of cure in consumer sales. As a matter of principle this argument is difficult to follow. It could equally be argued that provided the retailer knows of the transferee's efforts to obtain satisfaction, the actions of the transferee should not prejudice the latter's right to reject.

In the case where the non-conforming goods have been delivered to the buyer s. 36 of the Sale of Goods Act 1979 provides that, in the absence of any contrary agreement, the buyer is not bound to return the goods to the seller. It is sufficient if he intimates to the seller that he refuses to accept them. Even though he is not obliged to return them, the buyer must make the goods available to the seller. Meanwhile, as an involuntary bailee of the goods, he must exercise reasonable care in respect of them, otherwise, any risk of damage is on the seller. Where the buyer has had to keep the goods for some length of time before the seller recovers them, although the buyer has no lien on the rejected goods for repayment of the price, he may nevertheless recover in restitution a reasonable charge for the care and custody of the goods.

DUTY TO PAY

It is the duty of the buyer not only to accept the goods but to pay for them in accordance with the terms of the contract of sale (s. 27 of the Sale of Goods Act 1979). A similar undertaking is usually found in contracts of hire and hire-purchase transactions. The payment of the price obligation should be distinguished from a claim for breach of contract. In the case of the former, the creditor must show the occurrence of an event such as property passing, but with regard to the latter, the rules of remoteness, mitigation and penalty apply.

The basic rule laid down in s. 28 of the Sale of Goods Act 1979 is that delivery and payment of the price or rent are concurrent conditions. This is a natural concomitant of the right envisaged in s. 34 to examine the goods. It is curious that s. 10(1) provides that, in the absence of a different intention, stipulations as to time of payment are not deemed to be of the essence of a contract of sale. Everything depends upon the circumstances of the contract including the importance to the parties of timely payment, and the seriousness of the consequences of payment that is untimely. If time is of the essence of delivery then, since under the Sale of Goods Act 1979 payment and delivery are presumed to be contemporaneous, time will also be of the essence of payment. The Sale of Goods Act 1979 provides specifically for this in s. 48(3). It follows from this that in the case of perishable goods, time of payment is of the essence. As regards non-perishable goods, the presumption of s. 10(1) can be overturned by the simple expediency of the seller giving notice to the buyer of his intention to resell. Even where time is not of the essence of the original contract, the delay in payment may be so great as to show an intention to repudiate (*Pearl Mill Co. Ltd* v *Ivy Tannery Co. Ltd* [1919] 1 KB 78).

Part payment and termination
There is no provision in the Sale of Goods Act 1979 as to payment by instalments, but it may be implied from s. 31(1) that payment is prima facie to be made by lump sum. Of course, the parties themselves in the contract may anticipate payment by instalments. The effect of any part payment made will depend upon whether it is a genuine advance instalment of the purchase price, or whether it is a deposit intended to operate as security for the due performance of his obligations. In the case of the former, if the supply contract is not concluded, part payment may be recovered on the basis of total failure of consideration. Under the common law the deposit in this circumstance is forfeited. Nevertheless, in the case of prospective regulated consumer credit agreements, s. 59 of the Consumer Credit Act 1974 provides that the intended deposit becomes recoverable on the grounds of total failure of consideration.

In *Dies* v *British and International Mining and Finance Corpn Ltd* [1939] 1 KB 724, the buyers paid a large part (37 per cent) of the price of the goods in advance and then defaulted in the payment of the balance so the sellers refused to deliver the goods. The buyers admitted their liability for damages but recovered the advance payment on the basis of total failure of consideration. The distinction between a part payment, which is recoverable, and a forfeitable deposit, which is not, is a matter of construction of the contract. In this respect, the *Dies* case may be construed as the buyers' obligation to pay the whole price being replaced by their liability to pay damages. Significant problems arise where a buyer is required by the contract to pay a deposit in advance which has not been paid, and where this would have been forfeited on breach. In principle, the time of payment should not be relevant. This is confirmed in *Damon Cia Naviera SA* v *Hapag-Lloyd International SA* [1985] 1 WLR 435, where a buyer contracted to pay a ship for $2.36 million and to pay a deposit of 10 per cent of the price. The contract expressly provided that if the buyer failed to complete, the deposit would be irrecoverable. It was held that this deposit was forfeitable even though the seller had resold the ship at a small loss which was far less than the amount of the deposit. The plaintiff, as seller, who was suing for the recovery of the deposit succeeded in upholding what was in essence a penal claim. As such, the case demonstrates the court's disinclination to extend equitable relief to forfeiture in commercial contracts.

The House of Lords in *Johnson* v *Agnew* [1980] AC 367 drew a distinction between rescission of the contract *ab initio* which has retrospective effect, and a mere subsequent termination of the contract. This has repercussions if a buyer is under an obligation to pay in advance, but does not do so, and the contract is subsequently terminated. Thus in *Hyundai Heavy Industries Co. Ltd* v *Papadopoulos* [1980] 1 WLR 1129, a shipbuilding case in which the price was payable by instalments as the work proceeded, the House of Lords held that the buyer could be sued for an instalment which fell due on 15 July despite the fact that the seller exercised a cancellation right on 6 September. This approach is over-formalistic and overlooks that the buyer's duty to pay is surely *conditional* on subsequent performance by the other party. Even if the contract involves an element of manufacture and sale, it cannot be appropriate that the seller can sue for the recovery of an advance substantial payment where he has incurred only minimal advance expenditure prior to cancellation.

The method of payment
The method of payment traditionally anticipated in contracts of supply is cash. However, a buyer may pay by negotiable instrument, credit card, charge card, gift voucher or trading stamps dependent upon which of these methods of payment have been agreed in advance or accepted by the seller as payment of the price. The seller in a sale transaction can agree to any form of payment he wishes, and this includes the acceptance of other goods as a trade-in for part of the price so long as this does not turn the contract into one of exchange rather than sale.

Where the seller accepts payment by negotiable instrument it is normally deemed to be a conditional payment. It is possible for such a negotiable instrument to be accepted as absolute payment but an intention must be strictly shown (*Maillard* v *Duke of Argyle* (1843) 6 Mac & G 40). In the case of a credit card transaction, following *Re Charge Card Services Ltd* [1989] Ch 497, it is clear that there is no general principle of law that whenever a method of payment is adopted which involves a risk of non-payment by a third party, there is a presumption that the acceptance of payment through a third party is conditional on the third party making the payment. The Court of Appeal in this case analysed the credit card transaction in terms of quasi-novation, namely, by the underlying credit card scheme, the credit card company had bound the supplier to accept the card and had authorised the cardholder to pledge the company's credit.

GENERAL PRINCIPLE OF RISK

The concept of risk is not defined in any of the statutes dealing with contracts of supply. To a large extent the treatment of risk under the Sale of Goods Act 1979 is to focus upon its parasitical qualities, i.e., feeding off the primary obligations of delivery and payment of the price under s. 27 of the Act. Risk has a narrowly defined ambit otherwise the maxim of *caveat emptor* has little or no content. The buyer takes upon himself all risks as to the quality and the fitness of the goods subject to the statutory implied terms discussed in chapter 5. At the same time it is well-established that any gains made will prima facie accrue to the buyer. This is also the position with bailment and hire-purchase contracts where it is justified on the basis that the bailor should not be allowed the double benefit of rent and gains (see *Tucker* v *Farm and General Investment Trust Ltd* [1966] 2 QB 421).

The passing of risk with regard to loss or damage occurring after the contract is made is governed by s. 20 of the Sale of Goods Act 1979. The basic presumption in s. 20(1) is *res perit domino*, i.e., the passing of risk is linked with the passing of property. In modern retailing, linking risk to property passage does appear to be anomalous. The buyer must bear the risk of loss or accidental destruction where property has passed, in the absence of a contrary agreement, even though payment and delivery under s. 28 of the Sale of Goods Act 1979 are concurrent conditions. A simpler rule would focus upon *who* should bear the insurance cost. Certainly, where goods form part of the seller's stock in trade, the party in possession should insure and should therefore bear the loss. In practice, if the seller is insured and has recovered the loss under the insurance contract, the insurance company may be subrogated to the seller's right to collect the price from the buyer to whom the risk had passed with the property.

The operation of the risk doctrine goes hand in hand with the s. 18 rules discussed earlier. Thus in *Underwood Ltd* v *Burgh Castle Brick and Cement Syndicate* [1922] 1 KB 343, which involved the sale of a bulky condensing machine, it was held that the goods were not in a deliverable state at the time of damage inflicted to them so that neither property nor risk had passed to the buyers. Similarly in contracts of sale or return under s. 18, r. 4, the seller prima facie retains the property and the risk in the goods (see pp. 273–4). Moreover, it may be that until the buyer accepts the goods, the risk will remain with the seller and it would seem that there is nothing to prevent the buyer rejecting the goods merely because they have been accidentally damaged. This seems to be borne out by the decision in *Head* v *Tattersall* (1871) LR 7 Ex 7, the facts of which concerned the sale of a horse warranted to have been hunted by the Bicester hounds, and the plaintiff was given a week in which to return the horse if it did not answer the description. The horse was accidentally injured before the week was up. On close analysis of this case, what seems to be at issue was the buyer's title, i.e., the property in the horse passed to the buyer immediately but defeasibly so that when he rejected the horse, he divested himself of the title and revested it in the seller. If a risk analysis had been adopted, the conclusion would be that the horse was at the seller's risk during the period allowed for its return. Nonetheless, what would have happened if the horse had died? Rescission would not have been possible because the goods could not be returned. In *Chapman* v *Withers* (1888) 20 QBD 824, it was held, with little discussion, that the buyer who had presumably paid the price might maintain an action for breach of a warranty that the horse was 'quiet to ride'. Damages for breach of this warranty were assessed at £42, but it is not clear whether or not this represented the price paid by the buyer.

As noted above, the s. 20(1) rule is only a presumption which is subject to a contrary intention. This may be implied from the circumstances of the case and is intimately connected with the obligation to insure. It is for this reason that in f.o.b. and c.i.f. contracts, risk normally passes on shipment, irrespective of when property passes, because the buyer will be able to rely on a marine insurance policy with respect to the goods.

Risk and unascertained goods
In certain circumstances it is possible for the parties to contract for the passage of risk before appropriation of goods to a supply contract. This can be seen in *Sterns Ltd* v *Vickers Ltd* [1923] 1 KB 78, which concerned a contract for a quantity of white spirit out of a larger bulk held by a storage company. The seller gave the buyer a delivery order for the contract quantity and when this was presented to the storage company, they attorned to the buyer. The buyer decided to leave the spirit in the tank for its own convenience. In the meantime, the spirit deteriorated and the Court of Appeal held that the risk had passed. The exceptional nature of this decision has been emphasised in subsequent cases, the material factor here being the acceptance of the delivery warrant which gave the buyer an immediate right to possession and therefore an insurance interest. This serves to distinguish the case from *Healey* v *Howlett and Sons* [1917] 1 KB 337, where it was held that the risk in 20 boxes of fish dispatched to the buyer (as part of a general consignment of 190 boxes) had not passed to the buyer because there had been no appropriation to the contract of sale.

Risk and the relevance of fault
Deterioration due to the inherent make-up of the goods is something which the buyer must accept. It is otherwise where deterioration has resulted from delay

due to the fault of one party (s. 20(2)). This is particularly significant where there has been a wrongful failure to take delivery of the contract goods on time (see *Demby Hamilton and Co. Ltd* v *Barden* [1949] 1 All ER 435).

The fact that the buyer is late in taking delivery does not mean that the seller is not bound to take all reasonable care of the goods. Section 29(3) of the Sale of Goods Act 1979 provides that allocation of risk does not relieve the seller of his duty as bailee. Where property passes before delivery and the buyer fails to take delivery, the seller becomes either an involuntary or a gratuitous bailee. Even so, he is under a duty to take reasonable care of the goods and will be entitled to claim a reasonable charge for the care and custody of the goods (s. 37(1)). The seller cannot be accused of non-delivery and his obligations relating to merchantability under s. 14 do not extend beyond the appointed time of delivery so that any subsequent harm to the goods can only entitle the buyer to damages. On the other hand, where risk has passed to the buyer and delivery is delayed due to the seller's fault who, when acting as bailee, carelessly allows the goods to be damaged, this will go to the definition of unmerchantability and the buyer may be able to reject on this basis. It cannot be the case that the innocent party has agreed to bear the consequences of the other's fault.

The party at fault only bears the risk of loss or damage *caused* by the fault. It is for the party at fault to show that the harm would have happened anyway, whereas under s. 20(2) of the Sale of Goods Act 1979, the innocent party's burden is only to show that the harm '*might* not have occurred but for such fault'. More difficult problems arise where *both* parties are at fault to which there are two possible solutions: the first approach is to apportion the damage between the parties by the application of the Law Reform (Contributory Negligence) Act 1945; the second approach is to focus upon the chain of causation, i.e., the opportunity for the goods to be damaged would not have arisen but for the delay, but the seller's negligence may be treated as breaking the chain of causation so that he will bear the risk.

Risk and goods in transit
If the seller, without authority, makes an unreasonable contract with the carrier, s. 32(2) entitles the buyer to refuse to treat the delivery to the carrier as delivery to him so that neither property nor risk will pass. Similarly, the goods may be carried at the seller's risk if he fails to give the buyer sufficient insurance cover. Under s. 32(3) of the Sale of Goods Act 1979, if the goods are being sent by sea (as distinct from land or air) under circumstances where it is usual to insure, it is presumed that the seller is to give the buyer sufficient notice of the shipment, so if he fails to do so, the goods are carried at his risk. This rule has been applied to f.o.b. contracts where the normal position is, following *Inglis* v *Stock* (1885) 10 App Cas 263, that risk passes on shipment since the buyer is responsible for arranging shipping space even where property has not passed, for example, where an unascertained part of a specific whole is sold or there is a right of disposal (see *Wimble, Sons and Co.* v *Rosenberg and Sons* [1913] 3 KB 743). It should be noted that the goods will only be at the seller's risk if his failure to give notice disabled the buyer from insuring (compare *Produce Brokers Co. Ltd* v *Olympia Oil and Coke Co. Ltd* [1917] 1 KB 320).

As regards the period of transit, the seller's risk is modified by s. 33 which states:

> Where the seller of goods agrees to deliver them at his own risk at a place other than that where they are when sold, the buyer must nevertheless (unless otherwise agreed) take any risk of deterioration in the goods necessarily incident to the course of transit.

The issue of 'any risk of deterioration in the goods necessarily incident to the course of transit' is qualified by s. 14 which requires not merely that the goods shall be sound when delivered to the carrier, but that they shall be capable of withstanding the conditions of normal transit. Of course, the buyer is not at risk as regards abnormal incidents such as delay in transit as in *Healey* v *Howlett & Sons* [1917] 1 KB 337 discussed above. Sometimes the issues involve very fine questions of interpretation so that in *Mash and Murrell Ltd* v *Joseph I. Emanuel Ltd* [1962] 1 WLR 16, potatoes which became rotten during the course of a sea voyage were held at first instance by Diplock J to constitute a breach of s. 14, but the Court of Appeal reversed the decision on the basis that the conditions met on the voyage had been unusual. Obviously the more hazardous the method of transportation, the greater the scope there is for the category of risks 'necessarily incident to the course of transit'.

TRANSFEREE'S RIGHT TO REJECT

A buyer or a hirer has a series of remedies available to him if the supplier is guilty of a breach of contract or misrepresentation. Indeed, in large measure, the complexity of the law is due to the multiplicity of the remedies available to him. Of particular significance is the right of the transferee to reject the goods tendered and rescind on the grounds of defective performance. However, this right may be lost where the buyer or hirer has accepted the goods as this will be treated as an election to affirm the contract. Often this will revolve around the examination of the goods by the transferee.

Examination of the goods

Unless otherwise agreed, when the seller tenders delivery of goods to the buyer he is bound, on request, to afford the buyer a reasonable opportunity of examining the goods for the purpose of ascertaining whether they are in conformity with the contract. Section 34 of the Sale of Goods Act 1979 provides:

> (1) Where goods are delivered to the buyer, and he has not previously examined them, he is not deemed to have accepted them until he has had a reasonable opportunity of examining them for the purpose of ascertaining whether they are in conformity with the contract.
> (2) Unless otherwise agreed, when the seller tenders delivery of goods to the buyer, he is bound on request to afford the buyer a reasonable opportunity of examining the goods for the purpose of ascertaining whether they are in conformity with the contract.

In a similar fashion it would seem that before accepting delivery and rendering himself liable to pay instalments of rent, the hirer has a right of examination equivalent to that of the buyer (*Farnworth Finance Facilities Ltd* v *Attryde* [1970] 1 WLR 1053).

The importance of this obligation is that where goods are delivered which the transferee has not previously examined, he is not deemed to have accepted them unless he has had a reasonable opportunity of examining them for the purpose of ascertaining whether they are in conformity with the contract. The question of what constitutes a reasonable opportunity for examination is often linked with the place of examination. In *Perkins* v *Bell* [1893] 1 QB 193, it was held that there was a presumption that the place of delivery was the place of inspection, although this presumption may be rebutted if it is impracticable to inspect goods at the delivery point. Thus, inspection at a subbuyer's premises may be considered reasonable if the goods are packed in such a way that they can only be examined when they reach the place where they are to be used, and where the original vendor knows, or it is a necessary inference of the contract of supply, that the goods are going further (*Molling and Co.* v *Dean and Son Ltd* (1901) 18 TLR 217).

A problem that could arise concerns the nature of the buyer's duty, if any, to recollect the goods from the subbuyer. It would seem following s. 37 of the Sale of Goods Act 1979 that the buyer is under no such duty and, in this situation, it would appear to be the seller's responsibility to recover the goods. This can be an onerous task where there has been a subsale to an overseas buyer. In *Molling and Co.* v *Dean and Son Ltd* the subsale of a consignment of books was anticipated by the original seller and because of the method of package, it was considered by the court reasonable to examine the goods at the subbuyer's premises. It was held that the responsibility for retransporting the goods fell on the original seller, notwithstanding that they had been subsold to an American buyer.

Difficulties arise where the goods are suffering from a latent defect. However, it is clear that the issue is whether the buyer has had an opportunity for reasonable examination and *not* whether he has had the time to discover the defect. Of course, the nature of the goods will be relevant in determining a reasonable time for the examination of goods. Indeed, this point was specifically recognised in *Bernstein* v *Pamsons Motors (Golders Green) Ltd* [1987] 2 All ER 220, where Rougier J held that the more complicated the nature of the goods, the longer the time that is allowed. Unless the contract provides otherwise, the buyer is not allowed the time to make an exhaustive evaluation of the goods. This issue goes hand in hand with the criteria for acceptance of goods in contracts of supply and is discussed below.

LOSS OF THE RIGHT TO REJECT

Even though the seller has been guilty of a breach of condition which will prima facie give the buyer the right to reject the goods, he may, in certain circumstances, lose this right and be relegated to a claim for damages. Section 11(4) of the Sale of Goods Act 1979 provides:

Where a contract of sale is not severable and the buyer has accepted the goods or part of them, the breach of a condition to be fulfilled by the seller can only be treated as a breach of warranty, and not as a ground for rejecting the goods and treating the contract as repudiated, unless there is an express or implied term of the contract to that effect.

Acceptance in contracts of sale
The issue of acceptance is crucial to the loss of the right to reject. Section 34 of the Sale of Goods Act 1979 provides that the seller must afford the buyer a reasonable opportunity to examine the goods. Acceptance is an interrelating rule to this right of examination and is defined in s. 35(1) as follows:

The buyer is deemed to have accepted the goods when he intimates to the seller that he has accepted them, or (except where section 34 above otherwise provides) when the goods have been delivered to him and he does any act in relation to them which is inconsistent with the ownership of the seller, or when after the lapse of a reasonable time he retains the goods without intimating to the seller that he has rejected them.

From this it appears that the buyer will lose his right to reject in the following circumstances.

Express acceptance As the buyer has a statutory right to examine the goods, in order to bar his right to reject, it must be shown that the buyer has elected to accept the goods delivered as conforming with the contract. This could amount to a complete waiver of all claims arising under the sale or supply contract. Particularly problematic, in this context, is the acceptance note signed by a buyer before he has had an opportunity to examine the goods. The buyer will lose his right to reject unless he qualifies his signature in some way or other, for example, by writing 'Goods not seen'. In order to prevent consumer buyers being taken advantage of, the Law Commission report, *Sale and Supply of Goods* (Law Com. No. 160, London, 1987), recommended that s. 35 be amended in such a way that a consumer would not be deemed to have accepted the goods without reasonable examination even if he were to intimate acceptance to the seller.

Inconsistent act It is difficult to understand what is meant by an act 'inconsistent with the ownership of the seller'. If the property has passed to the buyer, this can only mean an act which is inconsistent with the reversionary interest of the seller (*Kwei Tek Chao* v *British Traders and Shippers Ltd* [1954] 2 QB 459). The commonest example here would be subsale by the buyer. However, it is important not to be dogmatic as it is difficult to see how the original seller's reversionary interest would be prejudiced, even on subsale, where the subbuyer rejected the goods. Essentially, it is a question of fact to be decided in each case as to what sort of use the buyer has made of the goods and then relating this to the seller's continuing reversionary interest, for example, by pledging or mortgaging the goods.

In *E. Hardy and Co. (London) Ltd* v *Hillerns and Fowler* [1923] 2 KB 490, it was held in the Court of Appeal that there was an act inconsistent with the seller's ownership when the buyers took delivery of part of a cargo and sent it to the subbuyers. As a matter of principle, it is questionable whether the buyer should have lost his right to reject in this situation if he can restore the goods to the seller. This is confirmed by the fact that s. 35 is expressly made subject to s. 34 which provides the statutory right of reasonable examination. The issue is whether the buyer had a reasonable opportunity of examination at the place of delivery. The Law Commission in their report No. 160 have accepted the criticisms of the law and recommended at para. 5.38 that an express provision should be inserted in s. 35 to make it clear that merely because goods are delivered to a subbuyer under a subsale or other disposition, this should not be treated as an act inconsistent with the ownership of the seller. Such an amendment was included in the Consumer Guarantees Bill 1990.

If the buyer is unable to restore the goods in substantially the same condition as when they were delivered, this can be considered inconsistent with the interest of the seller. Moreover, if the goods are damaged, albeit accidentally by the buyer, he will be precluded from rejecting the goods on the basis that *restitutio in integrum* is not possible which as a common law bar to rejection is specifically preserved by s. 62(2) of the Sale of Goods Act 1979. On the other hand, where the goods are damaged without the fault of either the seller or buyer, the latter does have a prima facie right to reject. The issue is one of risk, and it would seem following *Head* v *Tattersall* (1871) LR 7 Ex 7 that the risk of loss in this circumstance falls on the seller.

Lapse of time If the buyer has not rejected the goods, s. 35 provides that he is deemed to have accepted them if he retains them beyond a reasonable time. The issue is one of fact and the court must balance the interests of the parties. Clearly, if the market is a fluctuating one or is seasonal, protection of the seller's interest requires a speedier notification of rejection than when the market remains constant.

The issue of lapse of time has taken on considerable significance in consumer sales. Thus in *Bernstein* v *Pamsons Motors (Golders Green) Ltd* [1987] 2 All ER 220 (see p. 96), although the car was held to be unmerchantable, the plaintiff lost his right to reject because he had used the car for three weeks. This was so even though there was no means of discovering the defect (a piece of sealant in the lubrication system) through a reasonable examination. The only way the buyer could have discovered the sealant would have been to dismantle the engine, but, given the nature of the problem, the engine could have seized up at any time. However, the loss of the right to reject was linked by Rougier J with a sufficient time to give the car a *general* trial. The right to reject is, therefore, not lost on account of any dereliction on the part of the buyer. The question then arises as to the nature of the interest of the seller that is being protected. It can only be that as a result of the passage of time, the seller would have been adversely affected, for example, the seller could have found it difficult to raise the money which he had paid for the goods. This is unlikely in the case of a new car dealer where there exist sophisticated floor plan financing techniques. The general point here is that the buyer's loss of the right to reject is not necessarily tied to any prejudice on the part of the seller, and this suggests that ss. 34 and 35 provide a crude mechanism for the balancing of the respective interests of the parties. It may have made sense in the 19th century for business people whose main interest in the goods was a financial one as articles of commerce, and where the defects in the goods were perhaps more readily discoverable as with agricultural products or simple machinery. However, it makes little sense in the case of a complex product in which faults take time to emerge, and where the buyer is a consumer who is interested in the goods as articles to be used, not as items of commerce to be bought and sold.

Bernstein v *Pamsons Motors (Golders Green) Ltd* shows that the remedies of rejection and rescission are quickly lost in contracts of sale. Only defects likely to be discovered quickly will permit rescission. There is a greater chance of a minor defect such as a cosmetic blemish being spotted quickly than a latent defect that may take a few hundred miles to emerge. Indeed this was specifically recognised in the definition of 'satisfactory quality' under the Consumer Guarantee Bill 1990. The consequence is that the strong remedies are likely to be available in the case of a minor defect, but may well be lost before major mechanical or structural problems surface. Of course, the buyer has a remedy in damages, if necessary, to cover the cost of selling and replacing the vehicle. Nonetheless, such action would not always be justified and, anyway, why should the buyer bear the burden and inconvenience rather than the seller? Damages may be appropriate where the buyer's interest in the goods is a purely financial one, but it is less appropriate when the buyer is interested in using the goods. Moreover the buyer is confronted with a dilemma under the present law: the duty to mitigate his loss will require the buyer to give up the goods for repair to the supplier, but if he does so this could be treated as amounting to acceptance.

In order to assist parties to effect a compromise by the buyer allowing the seller to try to repair the goods, the Law Commission in their report, No. 160 proposed at para. 5.20 that, by itself, this should not amount to an acceptance of the goods. However, for a commercial buyer damages would in almost all cases be an adequate remedy. This explains the Law Commission's proposal at para. 4.21 that links rejection of goods in this context to reasonableness. Thus, in a commercial sale, where the seller is offering to cure the defect this will go to the issue of the *commercial buyer's* reasonableness.

Interestingly, under s. 53(2) of the Sale and Supply of Goods Act 1980 (Republic of Ireland) the matter is taken further, as a statutory right to cure is expressly provided. Here the right to reject may be revived if the buyer, having discovered the breach, promptly requests the seller to cure it and the latter refuses to do so within a reasonable time. In contrast, the DTI consultation paper, *Consumer Guarantees* (London, 1992), treats this as an aspect of the manufacturer's obligation (see pp. 112–13).

Part acceptance Section 11(4) of the Sale of Goods Act 1979 provides that the right to reject is lost if the buyer accepts any part of the goods, unless the contract is severable. The only qualification to this can be seen in s. 30(4) which provides that if the seller delivers 'the goods he contracted to sell mixed with goods of a different description', the buyer may accept the conforming goods and reject the rest. This is an unduly restrictive approach because where the contract is not severable, if all the goods are non-contract goods it is not possible to rely on s. 30(4), but if part of the goods delivered comply with the contract description, the buyer may accept that part and reject the rest *H. M. H. Esmail* v *J. Rosenthal and Sons Ltd* [1964] 2 Lloyd's Rep 447, a decision which was affirmed by the House of Lords). This can lead to some absurd results because a seller who is in breach by delivering non-conforming goods can be in a better position where the contract is not severable than the seller who is in partial breach. Essentially, s. 30(4) is more favourable to the buyer than s. 11(4) though it has the severe limitation of being confined to the case of mixed goods, and will not apply where *all* the goods correspond to contract description even though some of the goods are unmerchantable.

In the light of the above discussion it is little wonder that the Law Commission in their report, No. 160 recommended at para. 6.6 that the buyer should have a right of partial rejection and this has already been accepted by the government (see DTI consultation paper, *Consumer Guarantees* (1992) at para. 13). A right of partial rejection would be provided which, subject to the buyer's right of rejection, would be lost only in relation to goods accepted which formed part of a 'commercial unit'. This is defined under the proposed s. 35(6) as 'a unit division of which would materially impair the value of the goods or the character of the unit'. As a matter of principle, this approach must be correct because when a buyer exercises a right of partial rejection, there is no reason why he should be compelled to reject all non-conforming goods. Even at common law, it is possible to argue that the concept of severability is sufficiently flexible to allow the buyer to accept part and reject part of the goods delivered, so long as the accepted goods can be considered a part of a commercial unit. Nonetheless, there is a theoretical objection here: since the right to reject is an aspect of rescission, it does seem inconsistent for the buyer to rescind the contract and at the same time retain part of the goods.

Acceptance in contracts of supply

The Supply of Goods and Services Act 1982 does not purport to regulate the exercise of the transferee's remedies. The issue concerning the loss of the right to reject is determined by the common law, although there is no substantial divergence from the position under the Sale of Goods Act 1979. There is no doubt that the right to reject lapses after a reasonable time in contracts of hire-purchase (*Jackson* v *Chrysler Acceptances Ltd* [1978] RTR 474). It has been argued that in the case of a contract of hire-purchase, the supplier must supply goods which remain fit to be used throughout the period of hire on the basis of the theory of continuous breach. This approach was firmly scotched by the Court of Appeal in *UCB Leasing Ltd* v *Holtom* [1987] RTR 362.

The question of acceptance in contracts of hire-purchase is construed widely, the courts taking into account factors such as the conduct of the hirer and seller, attempts at repairs, negotiations for a settlement and the discovery of latent defects. Thus in *Porter* v *General Guarantee Corpn Ltd* [1982] RTR

384, the plaintiff acquired a second-hand car from the defendants, a finance company, under a hire-purchase agreement dated 26 January 1980. The agreement was negotiated by third-party dealers who had been informed by the plaintiff that he wished to use the car as a taxi. They informed him that it would be suitable for such use. On delivery, the car was found to be defective in many respects. Repairs, negotiations and inspections continued over a period of two months with the plaintiff continuing to use the vehicle. Finally, the contract was repudiated on 20 March. On the question of whether the plaintiff had lost his right to repudiate by continuing to use the car when he was aware of the defects, Kilner Brown J, stated at p. 394:

> I think it was reasonable to continue negotiation to see whether or not the third party would pay for the work done at the plaintiff's behest and on his own terms. If he was unreasonable in his demands this does not go to affirmation

The plaintiff was allowed to reject the car, the judge indicating that he would be liable for an outstanding instalment under the agreement representing his use of the car over a month during which he was in a position to repudiate. Undoubtedly, following this case, the relevant fact determining the affirmation issue is that of knowledge of the defect and lack of satisfaction with the product. This can be summarised by Lord Denning's approach in *Farnworth Finance Facilities* v *Attryde* [1970] 1 WLR 1053 where, despite the concession that the hirer had used the motor cycle (the object of the hire-purchase contract) for four months and had ridden it for 4,000 miles, it was held at p. 1059:

> A man only affirms a contract when he knows of the defects and by his conduct elects to go on with the contract despite them. In this case [the hirer] complained from the beginning of the defects and sent the machine back for them to be remedied. . . . But the defects were never satisfactorily remedied. . . . [The hirer] was entitled to say then: 'I am not going on with this machine any longer. I have tried it long enough.' After all, it was a contract of hiring. The machine was not his until the three years had been completed.

Rejection and total failure of consideration
In *Rowland* v *Divall* [1923] 2 KB 500, the Court of Appeal held that the buyer of a car was entitled to reject it for breach of s. 12(1) of the Sale of Goods Act 1979 despite the fact that he had resold the car and the sub-buyer had had four months use of it. We have already discussed in chapter 7 that there is nothing wrong in legal logic with recognising a limited notion of 'curing' a title defect. Indeed, this is illustrated by *Butterworth* v *Kingsway Motors* [1954] 1 WLR 1286, where the hirer of a car under a hire-purchase agreement sold it but continued to pay the instalments as they fell due. After almost a year's use, the plaintiff was notified by the finance company that the car was on hire-purchase and he promptly terminated his contract with the defendant. Within a very short time, the hirer paid her final instalment, and it was held that this 'fed' the titles of the intermediate buyers. Thus, although the plaintiff could recover the

full price, all the intermediate buyers who had not terminated before their titles were 'fed' could only recover damages for breach of contract.

It is not surprising that the reasoning of Atkin LJ in *Rowland v Divall* has been restricted in other contexts. For example, it could be applied for breach of s. 13 where what is tendered is something different from what was agreed on. One explanation for the reluctance to extend the reasoning in *Rowland v Divall* to other contexts is the recognition that title is so important that any act on the part of the buyer must be without prejudice to his right to reject for breach of s. 12(1). It is noteworthy that in *Rowland v Divall* the seller never acquired the right to sell the car and could not, therefore, be regarded as having accepted the goods.

It would seem from the above that the crucial question is not whether the party to a contract has received any benefit, but whether he has received that benefit which he was entitled to expect under the contract. So in hire-purchase agreements, the issue is whether the hirer has enjoyed both possession and a valid option to purchase. In *Karflex Ltd v Poole* [1933] 2 KB 251, it was held that despite the fact that the hirer had defaulted on his instalments under a hire-purchase agreement, he was, nevertheless, entitled to repudiate the contract and recover his deposit because the finance company was not the owner of the car at the date of delivery. Nonetheless, in the case of a general supply of goods, it may be that where the contract is divisible, the court can treat each part individually so that one or more parts may be set aside for total failure of consideration notwithstanding that the other parts have been performed.

ACTION FOR DAMAGES

A buyer or hirer may have at his disposal an action for damages against his supplier or third party for breach of the supply contract, or for some collateral contract otherwise concluded. In the alternative, there is no reason why the buyer or hirer should not be able to treat the collateral warranty as a misrepresentation and rescind the contract. Where there has been a fraudulent misrepresentation, the supplier will be liable in tort for deceit. For negligent misrepresentation, damages are available at common law when the misrepresentation results in physical injury, or where there was a breach of a fiduciary duty, or a duty created by a special relationship (*Hedley Byrne and Co. Ltd v Heller and Partners Ltd* [1964] AC 465). A right to damages is now expressly provided by s. 2(1) of the Misrepresentation Act 1967 (see *Royscot Trust Ltd v Rogerson* [1991] 2 QB 297).

It is proposed to concentrate here on the right of the buyer or hirer to damages for breach of the contract of supply. In this respect, the action for damages for breach may take one of two forms: first, it may be an action for damages for non-delivery; secondly, it may be an action with regard to a breach of a term(s) in the contract of supply.

Damages for non-delivery: sale
In the case of non-delivery constituting a repudiation of the contract, the buyer can treat it as being at an end and recover payments made on the basis of total

failure of consideration. As an alternative, the buyer can sue for damages for non-delivery. If the failure does not constitute repudiation, or the buyer chooses not to accept it, the contract continues in force for the benefit of both parties. In this circumstance, the buyer will be able to claim damages for non-delivery.

The measure of damages for non-delivery The counterpart to the seller's action for non-acceptance (s. 50 Sale of Goods Act 1979) is the buyer's action for non-delivery under s. 51 of the Sale of Goods Act 1979. The so-called first rule in *Hadley* v *Baxendale* (1854) 9 Exch 341 is set out in s. 51(2). The second rule is referred to in s. 54 which denotes damages for loss not as a result of some natural consequence of the defendant's breach, but from some special circumstance which the plaintiff must demonstrate ought reasonably to have been within the defendant's contemplation at the time of the loss. Section 51(3) sets out the normal measure of damages available by reference to whether there is an available market.

Where there is an available market The onus of proving the buying price in the available market is upon the buyer. The prima facie measure of damages is the amount by which the market price exceeds the contract price at the stipulated date and place of delivery of the goods or documents of title. If delivery is to be by instalments, the market price is fixed separately for each instalment at the time when it is due (*Roper* v *Johnson* (1873) LR 8 CP 167). Where a contract expressly provides for a period during which delivery is to be made, the seller is not in breach until the last day of the permitted period. Similarly, if the time of delivery has been extended at the request of the seller, the market price is taken at the postponed delivery date (*Ogle* v *Earl Vane* (1868) LR 3 QB 272). Although the buyer has a duty to mitigate his loss, it is unrealistic to maintain that the buyer would be able to buy goods in the market on the very day on which the seller fails to deliver. The buyer is therefore entitled to a reasonable time within which to ascertain the seller's intentions after a failure to deliver, for example, to examine the possibility of a postponed delivery date.

The market rule is of overriding significance and is not easily displaced. It does not matter that the buyer does without the goods, or that having gone into the market he has bought goods of the same description at a lower price. The reasoning here is that the buyer has lost the benefit of two bargains. A distinction should be drawn here with the facts in *R. Pagnan and Fratelli* v *Corbisa Industrial Agropacuaria Limitada* [1970] 1 WLR 1306. In this case, the buyers lawfully rejected the goods, and following negotiations between the parties, the buyers agreed to buy from the sellers at a reduced price the *same* goods which were then resold by the buyers for a profit. It was held that there was a connection with the original contract which could not be ignored, otherwise it would be tantamount to giving the buyers damages for a fictitious loss when they had in fact made a profit. Nevertheless, the general rule is not easily displaced even if the buyer has already contracted to resell the goods to a third party at a price higher (*Williams Bros Ltd* v *Ed. T. Agius Ltd* [1914] AC

510) or lower (*Rodocanachi, Sons and Co.* v *Milburn Brothers* (1886) 18 QBD 67) than the market price at the date when delivery should have been made. The reasoning here is that the buyer will always have the option of obtaining the goods from the market-place in order to fulfil the subcontract.

The question of the determination of the date of the market price is highly relevant in the case of anticipatory breach. The difficulty is that where no fixed time for delivery has been set, following the principle of the House of Lords in *White and Carter (Councils) Ltd* v *McGregor* [1962] AC 413, and the Privy Council decision in *Tai Hing Cotton Mill Ltd* v *Kamsing Knitting Factory* [1979] AC 91, the buyer can keep the seller's obligations alive by refusing to accept the repudiation. If the buyer elects to hold the contract open, the duty to mitigate is deferred. The criticism is that this rule encourages economic waste because the mitigation-of-damages principle will only apply upon termination. However, the courts may view the matter differently if the innocent party has no legitimate interest in the continuing performance of the contract, as can be illustrated in *Clea Shipping Corpn* v *Bulk Oil International Ltd (No. 2)* [1984] 1 All ER 129. In this case, charterers in breach of contract refused to take the ship back after repairs. The owners kept the vessel at anchor, fully crewed, and ready to sail for the rest of charter. It was held that the owners had no legitimate interest in so behaving and could not, therefore, recover the entire rent due under the charter because this would be tantamount to the court enforcing gross economic waste.

Where the buyer elects to accept the repudiation, he comes under an immediate duty to mitigate. Provided the buyer acts reasonably, he is entitled to damages assessed by reference to the price at which he purchases, irrespective of the market value at the due delivery date (*Melachrino* v *Nickoll and Knight* [1920] 1 KB 693).

Where there is no available market This may be the case where demand exceeds supply, or no reasonable substitute for the goods was available. In such cases, the measure of damages payable is by way of compensation for loss of bargain, the object being to put the buyer as nearly as possible in the position he would have been had the contract been performed. The rule in *Hadley* v *Baxendale* (1854) 9 Exch 341 requires consideration of whether the loss could reasonably have been contemplated by the seller as flowing from his breach, a question which is bound up with the extent to which the buyer's intended application of the goods should reasonably have been present in the seller's mind.

The cases are not easy to reconcile and much depends upon the non-remote purpose for which the goods were required. Thus, in the case of a wholesale supply, the buyer's loss will be determined as the normal trade mark-up on subsale (*C. Czarnikow Ltd* v *Koufos* [1969] 1 AC 350). In other circumstances where there has been a subsale, the loss to the buyer will prima facie be the amount by which the value at the date of breach exceeds the contract price, i.e., the buyer is able to recover for his lost profit (*Household Machines Ltd* v *Cosmos Exporters Ltd* [1947] KB 217). The subsale price is not necessarily conclusive evidence of the value of the goods which will primarily depend upon the circumstances of the case. For example, where the subsale contract had been concluded a long time before the due date of delivery, it would be anomalous to visit upon the seller the risk of a falling market (*The Arpad* [1934] P 189).

Particular difficulties are confronted with defining the circumstances in which a buyer is entitled to claim damages in respect of lost subsales. In order for the buyer to recover for this consequential loss, he must show that he purchased the goods for resale and that he had committed himself, or intended to do so, with respect to delivering the same goods (not merely an equivalent amount) to a subpurchaser. Furthermore, the seller should be aware of these facts, or they ought reasonably to have been within his contemplation at the time of entering into the main contract. The main decision is that of *Re R. and H. Hall Ltd and W.H. Pim Junior and Co.'s Arbitration* (1928) 139 LT 50. In this case, there was a standard-term trade-association contract with respect to the supply of wheat which expressly contemplated resale along a string of contracts, these being supplemented by subsidiary agreements. The case involved the sale of a cargo of wheat at 51*s* 9*d* per quarter which the buyer resold at 56*s* 9*d* per quarter. When the sellers refused to deliver, the market price was 53*s* 9*d* per quarter and the sellers argued that they should only be liable for the difference between the contract and market price, i.e., 2*s* per quarter. The House of Lords held the sellers liable for the difference between the contract and resale prices (5*s* per quarter), a decision influenced the original sellers' sharp practice of trying to defer their breach of contract so as reduce their damages in a falling market.

The crucial factors in the above case were that there was a sale of specific cargo, on an identified ship, which had been resold, and this was specifically anticipated in the original contract of sale. As a string contract, there was no available market simply because the resale contract would not allow the buyer to buy a substitute. Everything turns on what the seller could have foreseen under the rules of remoteness, the loss being confined to ordinary loss of profit on subsale unless the seller was aware of a specially lucrative contract lost because of his failure to perform (see *Victoria Laundry (Windsor) Ltd* v *Newman Industries Ltd* [1949] 2 KB 528). It also follows in a non-remote subsale that the seller should be liable for any compensation which the buyer has to pay his sub-buyer by way of damages or indemnity (see *Household Machines Ltd* v *Cosmos Exporters Ltd* [1947] KB 217).

The buyer may not in every case seek to recover damages. As an alternative, he may elect the recovery of expenditure incurred in connection with the transaction. The aim here is the restoration of the position the buyer occupied before entry into the contract. This must be distinguished from special damage which is recoverable in any case for breach, for example, where the buyer has to pay for freight despite the non-delivery of the goods (*E. Braude (London) Ltd* v *Porter* [1959] 2 Lloyd's Rep 161). Expenditure which would not have been incurred but for the breach, including consequential loss, is recoverable in addition to damages for loss of bargain, such as extra freight or insurance charges in connection with the acquisition of substitute goods.

Damages for non-delivery: contracts of supply

In the case of a simple contract of hire or hire-purchase, the measure of damages for failure to deliver should be the difference between the contract hire or hire-purchase rate and the market rate for such transactions. As a matter of consistency in logic, this should also be the case where a hirer lawfully terminates the contract and rescinds. This situation should be distinguished from the case where the hirer has accepted delivery but has subsequently rejected on the basis of continuous breach. In such circumstances, it has been held in *Yeoman Credit Ltd* v *Apps* [1962] 2 QB 508 that the hirer can recover by way of damages the reasonable sum necessary to repair the object bailed. Of course, this is open to the objection that the measure of damages relates to breach of warranty rather than rescission. The theoretical incongruity here in no small measure contributed to the demise of the continuous-breach doctrine (see *UCB Leasing Ltd* v *Holtom* [1987] RTR 362), so the measure of damages is confined where the hirer affirms the contract following a reasonable opportunity to discover the defect.

Damages for breach of condition or warranty

Where there has been a breach of warranty in a contract of sale, it is clearly envisaged in s. 53(1) of the Sale of Goods Act 1979 that the buyer in an action by the seller for the price may counterclaim the seller's breach by way of defence. In addition, s. 53(1) anticipates that the buyer can maintain an action in contract or tort for breach. Where the buyer's loss exceeds the price, s. 53(4) states:

> The fact that the buyer has set up the breach of warranty in diminution or extinction of the price does not prevent him from maintaining an action for the same breach of warranty if he has suffered further damage.

As far as remoteness of damage is concerned, s. 53(2) sets out the first rule in *Hadley* v *Baxendale* (1854) 9 Exch 341 whilst the second rule is referred to in s. 54.

We shall now proceed to consider the various claims of the transferee in respect of the supplier's breach.

Defects in title   As we have seen, the implied term as to title is a condition, the breach of which entitles the buyer or transferee to treat the contract as being repudiated. In addition, the buyer will be able to recover for loss of bargain or, in the alternative, recover any payment made on the basis of total failure of consideration (*Rowland* v *Divall* [1923] 2 KB 500). The transferee may also recover any consequential loss which the supplier ought reasonably to have contemplated would flow as a result of the breach. If the transferee affirms the contract, this is similar to when the transferor's repudiation is accepted and the prima facie level of damages is the purchase (or hire-purchase) price including expenses, since the transferee has not enjoyed the essential benefit contracted for (*Warman* v *Southern Counties Car Finance Corporation Ltd* [1949] 2 KB 576).

Delay in delivery Where time is of the essence, late delivery is treated as a breach of condition. The effect of this is that where a late tender is made, the buyer's lawful rejection makes the case one of non-delivery. In the case of a delay in delivery which the transferee cannot rescind (in the case where time is not of the essence), or he elects not to rescind, the action for damages is akin to a breach of warranty. As such, the contract continues and this has an impact on the transferee's duty to mitigate his loss. Thus, in the situation where goods are bought for resale, where there is an available market, the prima facie measure of damages is the amount by which the market value at the contractual time for delivery exceeds the market value at the actual time of delivery. In this respect, resales by the buyer should be ignored because there is no reason why the original seller should gain from a providential sale by his buyer.

Where there is no available market, the measure of damages is the amount by which the contract price exceeds the actual value at the contractual time for delivery. In the case where goods are bought for resale, since the seller has intimated that he is willing to perform, there is no reason for the buyer to mitigate his loss by buying replacement goods on the due delivery date. This explains why damages are measured not by reference to the price at which the buyer could have bought substitute goods on the due delivery date, but by reference to the price at which he could reasonably be expected to sell them on the actual delivery date (*Kwei Tek Chao* v *British Traders and Shippers Ltd* [1954] 2 QB 459).

Contracts of hire or hire-purchase contain a prohibition of sale by the hirer so there is, by definition, no available market. This will also be the case where goods are bought for use, and the measure of damages here relates to the deprivation of the use of the asset for the period of delay. It follows that where the asset is of an income-producing kind, the transferee should be able to recover for the loss of profit that the transferor could reasonably have contemplated as flowing from the breach.

Defects in quality: sale Where non-conforming goods are tendered by the seller, the buyer may reject the goods, and if the seller cannot or is unwilling to re-tender the goods in due time, the buyer can treat the contract as repudiated. There are two other possible courses of action available to him: first, he can seek to recover the price paid on the basis of total failure of consideration; secondly, he may accept the goods and sue for breach of warranty. The prima facie measure of damages under s. 53(3) is the amount by which the warranted value of the goods exceeds the actual value of the goods delivered and accepted.

It would seem following s. 53(3) that the market price is irrelevant, except insofar as it may be taken to be the value which the goods should have had. Where the buyer has lost the opportunity of rejecting the goods before he has become fully aware of a defect, in cases involving shipping documentation, the courts have awarded the buyer the contract price less the fallen market price (*James Finlay and Co. Ltd* v *NV Kwik Hoo Tong Handel Maatschappij* [1929] 1 KB 400; *Kwei Tek Chao* v *British Traders and Shippers Ltd* [1954] 2 QB 459; compare *Procter and Gamble Philippine Manufacturing Corporation* v *Kurt A.*

Becher GmbH & Co. KG [1988] 2 Lloyd's Rep 21). In principle, there is no reason to apply these cases in ordinary contracts of sale. It would be anomalous to allow a buyer who accepts goods which he is entitled to reject the right to be placed in the same financial position as he would have been in if he had rejected the goods.

Defects in quality: contracts of supply In the case of contracts of hire, the measure of damages should be the difference between the warranted hire rate and the amount which the hired goods could command in their actual state. With contracts of hire-purchase, an allowance should be made for the option to purchase, and account should be taken of the possibility that the hiring may be determined. No general rule can be laid down, but in *Charterhouse Credit Co. Ltd v Tolly* [1963] 2 QB 683, Upjohn LJ suggested that in the absence of the owner terminating the hire-purchase contract, the hirer would have been entitled to the amount required to put the vehicle in a proper state of repair as well as damages for loss of use.

The same principles were applied in *UCB Leasing Ltd v Holtom* [1987] RTR 362 where the sum awarded to the debtor included an amount for inconvenience and distress. These were caused by the fact that during the time the debtor had the car, the object of the hire-purchase contract, it had persistent electrical problems, sometimes suffering a complete electrical failure which could have led to a serious accident. An interesting analogy can be drawn here with *Gibbons v Trapp Motors Ltd* (1970) 9 DLR (3d) 742, a Canadian case on sale of goods. In allowing the purchaser to reject the goods and recover his purchase price, Gould J took into account the fact that he had use of the car for 10 months prior to rejection. The determination of the overall loss to the purchaser was based upon an independent assessment of the monthly rental value for such a car. Once this figure had been arrived at, it was a simple case of multiplying this by 10 in order to determine the valuation of use and enjoyment.

Consequential loss
Consequential loss claims may well arise upon the acceptance of goods which prove to be defective. The rules in *Hadley v Baxendale* (1854) 9 Exch 341 provide a sound and rational basis for paying due regard to the normal and foreseeable results which flow as a result of breach of contract. Nonetheless, there are difficulties with constructing a single formula which expresses the degree of foreseeability necessary. In *C. Czarnikow Ltd v Koufos* [1969] 1 AC 350, the House of Lords seems to have settled on 'not unlikely' as expressing the degree of foreseeability. The problem here is that it may not always be just to impose liability for foreseeable consequences, especially as other factors may be relevant. Thus, in the case of sale of goods, the price of the goods will normally reflect their scarcity value.

A dramatic illustration of the difficulties posed by the foreseeability test can be seen in *H. Parsons (Livestock) Ltd v Uttley Ingham and Co. Ltd* [1978] QB 791. In this case, the defendants supplied and installed a large hopper for holding animal foodstuffs for the plaintiff, a pig farmer. A ventilator at the top of the hopper which could not be seen from the ground was left closed with the result that some of the food became mouldy. The pigs became ill and, subsequently, a more serious condition was triggered off by the first illness with the result that many of the pigs died. The farmer recovered for all his lost and diseased pigs on the basis that this was foreseeable. There does seem to be an air of unreality about the foreseeability test here. It would seem that the only events which can be regarded as unforeseeable following this case are those in which the train of events has been interrupted by conscious human intervention. This seems to go too far.

If the buyer or hirer does not take the normal precautions with a view to discovering any patent or latent defect concerning goods delivered, this may be a *novus actus interveniens* preventing the supplier being liable for the consequences of his breach. Thus, in *Lambert* v *Lewis* [1982] AC 225, a farmer who continued to use a coupling which he knew, or ought to have known, was defective could not claim an indemnity from the seller in respect of the farmer's liability to the plaintiff who was injured when the coupling gave way. However, where the goods have been put to their contemplated use and the defect amounts to a breach of the contract of supply, it has been held that the buyer may recover for personal injury as well as injury to other property (*Bostock and Co. Ltd* v *Nicholson and Sons Ltd* [1904] 1 KB 725). Damages are also available, in appropriate cases, for inconvenience and disappointment (see *Jackson* v *Chrysler Acceptances Ltd* [1978] RTR 474; compare *Kemp* v *Intasun Holidays Ltd* (1987) 7 TrLr 161).

Particular dilemmas have arisen where defective goods are of an income-producing kind. It is clear that the hirer or buyer cannot claim both the diminution in the warranted value at the contract delivery date and the full loss of profit resulting from the nonconformity of the goods as this would allow him to duplicate his compensation. The problem is that there are several ways of calculating loss of profit. In the troublesome case of *Cullinane* v *British 'Rema' Manufacturing Co. Ltd* [1954] 1 QB 292, the Court of Appeal held that the buyer could not split his claim as between capital loss and income loss. This was an indefensible position, although this does not mean that the plaintiff should be free to split his claim in an arbitrary fashion. Reference must surely be made to what a reasonable buyer would do to mitigate his loss, for example, by hiring substitute goods in appropriate cases.

Where the goods are bought for resale, the seller will be liable for loss if it can be shown that the resale was not too remote. The buyer's burden of proof is lighter here than where he claims damages for non delivery; he need only show that the subsales were a reasonable probability in order to recover under s. 54 of the Sale of Goods Act 1979. Nevertheless, to claim damages it has to be demonstrated that the subsale was on substantially similar terms, as it would be anomalous to visit upon the seller liability for a more onerous subcontract. If the subsale is not on the same terms, the buyer can still claim damages paid to the sub-buyer in respect of defects for which the seller would have been liable (per Devlin J in *Biggin and Co. Ltd* v *Permanite Ltd* [1951] 1 KB 422 at p. 434, reversed on other grounds). Where there has been a settlement of a claim, it is open to the seller to contest the amount and demonstrate that the sum paid was excessive in relation to the breach of contract. The legal costs incurred in reasonably defending the sub-buyer's claim will also be recoverable (*Hammond and Co.* v *Bussey* (1887) 20 QBD 79) as will the loss of repeat orders from the sub-buyer where this is within the contemplation of the parties (*GKN Centrax Gears Ltd* v *Matbro Ltd* [1976] 2 Lloyd's Rep 555). Nonetheless, the courts have rejected a claim in respect of loss of a business connection (*Bostock and Co. Ltd* v *Nicholson and Sons Ltd* [1904] 1 KB 725).

Damages in tort
Where the transferor has property and an immediate right to possession, he may sue for wrongful interference with goods. Certainly, if a seller under a conditional sale agreement refuses to deliver the goods to the buyer, the latter will have a cause of action in conversion. Where the buyer is suing a third party, the measure of damages is prima facie the value of the goods at the date of conversion. As between the parties to the contract, suing in tort has no advantages and is rarely used (*The Arpad* [1934] P 189). Moreover, by suing in tort the transferor cannot obtain an order of specific restitution where he could not have obtained a decree of specific performance of the contract (*Cohen* v *Roche* [1927] 1 KB 169).

EQUITABLE REMEDIES

A solution in equity may be found for the invidious position of the pre-paying buyer under the Sale of Goods Act 1979 where property has not passed in law. The main stumbling-block in this context is *Re Wait* [1927] 1 Ch 606. Wait agreed under a c.i.f. contract to purchase 1,000 tons of wheat ex *Challenger*. He subsold 500 tons of this to the respondents and was paid by them except for the proportion of the freight. Subsequently, Wait pledged the bill of lading representing the wheat to the bank in order to secure his overdraft and was later adjudicated bankrupt, no appropriation of the 500 tons having been made. The facts themselves are problematic, especially the issue of whether the seller promised the buyer wheat weighing 500 tons out of the expected cargo to be appropriated by the seller on arrival, or was he rather promising to grant the buyer an undivided share (on a pro rata basis) in the cargo? Two of the judges in the Court of Appeal, Lord Hanworth MR and Atkin LJ considered the first view of the facts to be correct, whereas Sargant LJ took the second or tenant-in-common viewpoint.

The real difficulties with *Re Wait* are not confined to the facts. One of the arguments put forward by counsel was based upon 'equitable assignment', i.e., that a fully paid vendor became a trustee of the property in the whole cargo to give effect to a proprietary interest of the purchaser in part. The majority judgments provided by Lord Hanworth MR and Atkin LJ found against an equitable assignment whilst Sargant LJ, dissenting, came to a different conclusion and held that an equitable interest did arise where a particular portion out of a definite consignment of goods was sold. The decision of the majority can be criticised as being inconsistent with *dicta* in *Hoare* v *Dresser* (1859) 7 HL Cas 290 and *Holroyd* v *Marshall* (1862) 10 HL Cas 191. Certainly,

Lord Cranworth in *Hoare* v *Dresser* gave directions at p. 317 to let a merchant have 100 quarters of wheat out of a cargo of 500 quarters on the basis that 'equity will give the merchant a lien on the larger cargo'. Lord Cranworth's insistence that equity *will* interfere is illuminating, viz., this is a legitimate domain for equitable interference. Although Atkin LJ in *Re Wait* conceded that in Lord Cranworth's illustration a direction to a third person like a consignee to hold 100 quarters out of a cargo of 500 might amount to an equitable assignment, his lordship distinguished *Re Wait* on the basis that the equitable assignment there would arise out of the contract of purchase and not through a direction to a third person. As it is presented, this distinction is difficult to grasp because the creation of an equitable assignment is not limited merely to a direction, and if a lien can arise in this case notwithstanding that there is no precise identification of the actual part of the bulk assigned, why should this factor prove a bar in any other case? Moreover, Lord Westbury in *Holroyd* v *Marshall* confirmed the approach of Lord Cranworth through his famous example of a contract to sell 500 chests of the particular kind of tea 'which is now in my warehouse in Gloucester'. His lordship used this as an illustration of a transaction which would pass the beneficial interest in the purchaser since the subject-matter was of a specific nature which equity would specifically perform. The correctness of this approach was doubted by the majority in *Re Wait* on the basis that there was some scepticism as to whether the reporting of the case was accurate. Such an objection is odd because as Pollock pointed out: 'If these were Lord Westbury's words he uttered a truism too familiar even to novices to call for repetition' (see (1927) 43 LQR 293). A second argument employed by the majority in *Re Wait* involved confining Lord Westbury's approach to the status of mere *dicta*. Unfortunately, this overlooks the fact that specific performance is not normally available in a contract for the sale of ordinary goods. We shall now examine this criticism more fully.

Specific performance
The Divisional Court in *Re Wait* [1926] Ch 962 concluded that the court ought to grant a decree of specific performance and not leave the subpurchasers as Lawrence J put it at p. 974 'to the doubtful remedy of proof for damages in bankruptcy'. The reference to specific performance is interesting since this distinguishes the juridical basis of the equitable treatment accorded to executory and executed contracts. Thus, where consideration has been executed, which is always necessary for an assignment to be valid in equity (*Re Lind* [1915] 2 Ch 345), this does not presuppose the necessity for specific performance because the right of such an assignee is founded on 'a higher right'. In *Re Wait* counsel argued that there should be specific performance of the contract for the sale of 500 tons of wheat by virtue of s. 52 of the Sale of Goods Act 1893. This section replaced s. 2 of the Mercantile Law Amendment Act 1856 which itself was an enabling provision for the decree of specific performance to be awarded by the common law courts. Indeed, the tenor of the 1856 Act reflected the majority view of the Second Report of the Mercantile Law Commissioners published in 1855 which was that the civilian approach to

specific relief be adopted. The generous treatment to the availability of this remedy under civil law may be seen in Scotland where there is a presumption in favour of granting specific performance unless there is a good ground in equity for refusing it.

As we have seen, s. 52 of the Sale of Goods Act 1893 was intended to enlarge the jurisdiction of the courts. Significantly, whereas s. 2 of the 1856 Act referred only to 'specific goods', s. 52 of the 1893 Act gives the court a discretion to order a decree of specific performance in any action for breach of contract to deliver 'specific or ascertained goods'. Nevertheless, the majority in the Court of Appeal in *Re Wait* [1927] 1 CH 606 adopted a restrictive approach to s. 52 which does seem odd, as a matter of statutory interpretation, because why should Chalmers, the draftsman of the Sale of Goods Act 1893, bother to use two synonymous concepts where one would do unless a different treatment was intended?

In the Divisional Court it was held that the property in the 500 tons of wheat had not passed to the subpurchasers, but that the goods were specific goods within the meaning of s. 52 as 'being identified and agreed upon at the time of the contract'. Despite this, in the Court of Appeal, Atkin LJ interpreted 'ascertained' to mean at p. 630:

> identified in accordance with the agreement after the time a contract of sale is made. It seems to be beyond dispute that at the date of this contract there were no goods identified and agreed upon; and I think it equally clear that at no time were there any goods ascertained.

The reasoning evident in the Court of Appeal is one of determining policy. It would seem that the court, as a matter of *policy*, relegated a purchaser who pays merely on the strength of an invoice in favour of the *seller's* creditors. Yet it must be admitted that the seller's interest would not be prejudiced by a decree of specific performance in the case of an unappropriated part of a large stock, at least *outside* the bankruptcy/liquidation context. Even if specific performance is not available under s. 52, there seems to be no reason in principle why specific performance should not be decreed *outside* of s. 52, for example in the case of a long-term supply contract as in *Sky Petroleum Ltd* v *VIP Petroleum Ltd* [1974] 1 WLR 576.

The difficulty with the above approach is that it contradicts the judgment of Atkin LJ in *Re Wait* (which was not cited in *Sky Petroleum Ltd* v *VIP Petroleum Ltd*) where the argument employed was that, as a matter of commercial convenience, the code was meant to be exhaustive. However, this objection is not fatal because the judgment itself undermines s. 62(2) of the Sale of Goods Act 1979 (the common law saving provision), thereby, making the Act appear internally inconsistent. In fact, it is anticipated under the Act that the rules of common law apply save insofar as they are inconsistent with the express provisions of the Act. The code does not carefully set out the circumstances in which specific performance is available, for example, there is no reference to injunctive relief and it is in any case restricted to suits brought by the buyer, the seller only being given an action for the price under s. 49 of the Sale of Goods Act 1979. As such, the narrow issue still remains; should a prepaying or financing buyer be preferred to the seller's creditors? In theory, third-party hardship should not prevent the granting of a decree of specific performance to a plaintiff who is prima facie entitled to it, although it will be a factor in the exercise by the court of its discretion. The policy issue confronted here goes to the heart of the distribution problem among creditors on insolvency (see part 5). It can hardly be said that the objection to applying specific performance is to avoid private abuse of a powerful and intrusive remedy since the 'servitude' which is imposed is no greater than that confronted by secured credit generally. Essentially, the basis of the creditor's case for ordering specific performance is that he had bargained to be preferred and is, therefore, in a different class from the ordinary creditors who had advanced either money or goods without bargaining for such protection.

The decision in *Re Wait* rests on two bases: first, the contract did not sufficiently earmark the property to act as an equitable assignment; secondly, the impossibility of specific performance by reason of the Sale of Goods Act 1979. As we have seen, both approaches are subject to severe criticism on the basis of authority and principle. Even if the case is not overruled, it is important to recognise the narrowness of the *ratio* in the case. Significantly, it was only Atkin LJ who ruled out the possibility of a purchaser's lien for the recovery of the purchase money paid over because, he maintained, the code in defining the remedies of the buyer provides a complete and exhaustive statement. Nevertheless, the buyers' remedies listed in the Act are only concerned with the *seller's contractual obligations*, for example, damages and specific performance. The Act does not deal with recission for innocent misrepresentation, i.e., the restoration of the *status quo ante*. This is exactly what the purchaser is seeking to do in asserting his purchaser's lien. It follows that the issue becomes whether there is any inconsistency in holding that no lien exists over a mass of personalty by virtue of an equitable assignment and, at the same time, allowing a purchaser a lien over the mass for the recovery of money paid for the relevant part? In fact, no conflict need arise. Whereas the first proposition rests on sufficiency of identity of the relevant property so that equity can acknowledge the purchaser's ownership, the latter depends upon whether there is sufficient identity of property such that the vendor would be acting unconscientiously if he were to dispose of the property without either accounting to the purchaser, such as through discharge of indebtedness, or seeking his consent. We shall now proceed to consider this possibility in greater detail.

The equitable lien
The basis of the remedy of equitable lien is the prevention of unjust enrichment. The point here is that the equitable lien presents not the specific equitable right that is related to trust or specific performance, rather, it expresses an equitable *idea* which is that of unjust enrichment. As such, the equitable lien being a right against property is different from a common law lien (see chapter 14) in that the latter is founded on possession and gives, except as modified by statute, a right to detain the property until payment, whereas an equitable lien exists quite irrespective of possession. Such liens are

well-known in the context of realty. A vendor of land who has parted with the legal title before payment has an equitable lien over the land to the extent of the purchase money unpaid subject to a bona fide purchaser of the legal estate without notice. In addition, a purchaser of land who has paid his purchase money before conveyance has a lien in equity to the extent of the purchase money paid. Significantly, the Australian High Court decision in *Hewett* v *Court* (1983) 149 CLR 639 suggests that the list of equitable liens may not be a closed one.

There is no doubt that to the extent that an equitable lien arises by express written agreement in respect of goods, it will constitute a charge which will require registration. Despite this, a failure to register the charge may not be fatal since the property will be impressed by the lien antecedent to its acquisition. In the case of a company, the charge will be registrable under s. 400 of the Companies Act 1985 (as amended) and non-registration will not invalidate the security against the liquidator (*Re Connolly Bros Ltd (No. 2)* [1912] 2 Ch 25). To the extent that the lien operates by law, it will not need registration as a charge under the Companies Act 1985 (*Capital Finance Co. Ltd* v *Stokes* [1969] 1 Ch 261). In addition, since the policy of the Bills of Sale Acts is to strike at documents rather than transactions (see chapter 15), it is probable that an equitable lien arising by operation of law will not be struck down since the essence of an equitable lien is a restitutionary remedy imposed to prevent another's unjust enrichment. The concomitant of this approach is that if other arrangements for security have been made, for example, the insertion of a retention of title clause in the supply contract, an equitable lien will be excluded as being contrary to the parties' intention. As Slade J held in *Re Bond Worth Ltd* [1980] Ch 228 at p. 251:

> On the present facts there is in my judgment no room for implying any vendor's lien arising by operation of law, after completion of the purchase, bearing in mind the express agreement of the parties in the terms embodied in the retention of title clause, which was designed to secure payment of the full purchase price.

Specific restitution
Where property has passed the buyer has the option of claiming a decree of specific restitution under s. 3 of the Torts (Interference with Goods) Act 1977.

Injunctive relief
This will be important to restrain a supplier from delivering the goods in breach of contract to another client. In *Redler Grain Silos Ltd* v *BICC Ltd* [1982] 1 Lloyd's Rep 435, it was held in these circumstances that it was no defence for the sellers to show that damages would be an adequate remedy, an approach which appears to be wider than that seen with specific performance.

PART 3   CREDIT AND PAYMENT

NINE
The bill of exchange

HISTORICAL DEVELOPMENT

The bill of exchange constitutes one of the oldest instruments of credit. Indeed, its antecedents can be traced to classical history which can be illustrated by a story told by Herodotus in the 4th century before Christ. Writing three generations after the failure of one Glaucus to honour a bill in defiance of oracular advice from Delphi, Herodotus describes his whole household as being utterly extirpated from Sparta. This illustration helps to demonstrate the fact that the widespread use of bills of exchange rests on *confidence*, that is, the ability to pay. The reasoning here reflects the legal position, namely, bills of exchange confer only contractual rights so the holder must be reasonably sure that at least one person who is party to the promise can meet the liability.

Historically, the development of the bill of exchange took place in the great City States of Europe during the 14th century. Medieval merchants from different countries engaged in international trade would attend the great merchant fairs to do business. As commerce developed, merchants needed a system whereby they could avoid transporting great sums of money. The practice developed of a merchant-debtor creating a written authority to the effect that the creditor was to be paid in cash at a specified place, normally one of the merchant fairs carried on throughout Europe. The authority was then sent to the creditor who presented it at the specified place and collected cash. This authority to pay came to be called a bill, and the individuals who were authorised to pay or collect cash on behalf of traders can be justifiably regarded as the founders of modern banking practice. Closely allied to this was the medieval bond which constituted an unconditional acknowledgement of indebtedness under seal. The issue of the bond sounded in liability because the court was not concerned with the underlying transaction(s) which gave rise to the bond. The insulation of the medieval bond from the underlying transaction finds its modern equivalent in the performance bond (see pp. 387–9).

The English development of bills of exchange stems from 1697 when bills were first legalised. At the same time, promissory notes developed and became enforceable at common law in a similar fashion. Whereas a bill of exchange is an order by one person to another to pay money, a promissory note constitutes a simple promise by one person to pay money to another. A bank note is a promissory note payable to the bearer on demand and its negotiable status was confirmed in the Bills of Exchange Act 1704. It should be emphasised, the development of the bill of exchange took place independently of the common law through the application of the law merchant, the *lex mercatoria*, which was eventually incorporated into the common law during the 18th century by the great common law judges Holt and Mansfield CJJ.

The long history of bills of exchange and the recognition of negotiability meant that the courts developed comprehensive rules applicable to them before the enactment of the Bills of Exchange Act 1882. Indeed, Disraeli addressing the House of Commons on this matter could say in 1866: 'You [merchant men] have devised and sustained a most marvellous system of credit'. The Bills of Exchange Act 1882 continues to provide a code for the creation and enforcement of bills as well as cheques, and is often portrayed as a model of clear drafting (see chapter 23). The review committee chaired by Professor Robert Jack, *Review of Banking Services Law and Practice* (Cm. 622, 1989), at recommendation 8(2), endorsed the view that the language and style of the 1882 Act should be retained since it was clear, concise and well-understood.

The development of joint-stock banking with its system of cash transfers between branches, and the growing custom of granting overdraft facilities led to a reduction in the use of bills for domestic finance during the 19th century. Even so, the concept of negotiability developed through the bill of exchange and the cheque played a vital part in the development of the modern banking system. It should be noted that cheques are bills and are governed by the 1882 Act which, therefore, governs the most common commercial documents in daily use. Although there have been statutory amendments to the Bills of Exchange Act 1882, these relate largely to cheques (see chapter 10). It is regrettable that the government White Paper setting out its response to the Jack Committee report, *Banking Law and Services* (Cm 1026, 1990), did not accept that there was a need for a new Cheques and Bank Payments Orders Act which would have assisted both the exposition and understanding of the appropriate law.

THE FUNCTION OF BILLS OF EXCHANGE

The documentary bill
The establishment in London of branches of foreign banks and the rise of London accepting houses resulted in the great development of the international bill on London. The intervention of an intermediary finance institution of high standing provides the mechanism enabling the seller or exporter of goods to obtain cash as soon as possible after the dispatch of the goods and yet enables the buyer or importer to defer payment until the goods have reached him or even later. This is the main function of the documentary bill, that is,

The bill of exchange

where the bill is drawn to cover an actual movement of goods from the seller to the buyer and the relevant documents are attached to the bill, for example, bills of lading and insurance documentation. The bill is immediately negotiable so that the seller can receive the cash whilst the buyer does not have to pay until maturity. In this respect, the perfect bill is one just enough to span the interval between shipment by the exporter and receipt of cash from the resale by the importer.

The trade bill

This can provide essential short-term finance for industry, that is, bills can be drawn to finance the holding or processing of stocks of raw materials. It should be noted that City institutions do not look on such finance bills as being quite such attractive investments as bills covering the movement of goods, and the amount of finance paper that can be discounted on the London market is limited.

The cost of bill finance

If the borrower is a merchant and wants short-term finance, the cost will be made up of the following components:

(a) the accepting commission charged by the bank or accepting house which the borrower will individually negotiate; *and*

(b) the rate of discount at which the bill is sold which will, of course, vary according to present and prospective rates for money. The basic formula is:

$$\frac{\text{Discount} \times 365 \times 100}{\text{Face value} \times \text{number of days}}$$

Thus in the case of a 91-day bill with a face value of £425,000 which was discounted on the London market for £415,993.49, the calculation would be as follows:

$$\frac{£9,006.51 \times 365 \times 100}{£425,000 \times 91} = 8.540 \text{ per cent}$$

If the borrower is an importer who arranges for a seller abroad to draw on a London bank or accepting house, the importer will have to pay the accepting commission, but the cost of selling a bill locally and/or discounting it in London will usually fall on the seller who may or may not include part or all of the cost in his invoice.

CHARACTERISTICS OF NEGOTIABLE INSTRUMENTS

These may be stated as follows:

(a) Any 'holder', that is, payee or endorsee in possession or bearer can bring an action to enforce it.

(b) A bill may be transferred from person to person notwithstanding the contractual doctrine of privity.

(c) A good-faith transferee who takes for value an instrument that is complete and regular on its face becomes a 'holder in due course' (see pp. 199–201) and is entitled to enforce payment of the instrument irrespective of the underlying equities. This rule reflects the unconditional nature of the payment obligation created by a bill of exchange, and anything which undermines the separate status of the obligation created by the bill creates uncertainty, thereby undermining the marketability of bills generally. Essentially, bills of exchange are taken as deferred instalments of cash (see *Nova (Jersey) Knit Ltd* v *Kammgarn Spinnerei GmbH* [1977] 1 WLR 713). In general, the payee's liability in the underlying contract cannot be relied upon by way of set-off or counterclaim. The independence of the bill from the underlying transaction ensures that it is equivalent to cash. However, if the breach brings about a total or partial failure of consideration, that is, a liquidated claim, this may be relied upon as between the *immediate* parties to the transaction (see *Cebora SNC* v *SIP (Industrial Products) Ltd* [1976] 1 Lloyd's Rep 271).

The approach of the common law to negotiable instruments contrasts starkly with that adopted with regard to assignment of choses in action. At common law, choses in action could not be transferred or assigned prior to the procedural reform occasioned by the Judicature Acts 1873 to 1875 which later found expression in s. 136 of the Law of Property Act 1925. Strict compliance with the statutory rules is required if the transfer or assignment is not to sound in equity. In chapter 11 we shall discuss the general problems relating to assignment of book debts in the context of credit factoring, especially the thorny issues as to what constitutes 'notice', defects of pre-existing equities, the rule in *Dearle* v *Hall* (1828) 2 Russ 1, and the need to join the original owner as a party to an action on the chose. At common law, negotiable instruments overcome these restrictions because of the practical need of merchants for documents which could represent cash in circumstances where it could be inconvenient, or even dangerous, to pay for goods in cash.

Negotiability
A negotiable instrument operates as a striking exception to the doctrines of both privity of contract and security of property (*nemo dat quod non habet*). Only certain instruments have been recognised as being negotiable in this sense, although the courts continue to give effect to well-established commercial practice, so there is no closed list of negotiable instruments. The negotiability or otherwise of an instrument whose status is not determined by statute is not conclusively established until it is resolved by the courts. The Bills of Exchange Act 1882 has played a large part in this context, not least because s. 97(2) of the Act provides:

> The rules of common law, including the law merchant, save insofar as they are inconsistent with the express provisions of this Act, shall continue to apply to bills of exchange, promissory notes, and cheques.

However, it is significant that while the government recently agreed with the Jack Committee report (1989) that the structure and language of the 1882 Act should be retained, it did not accept the need to extend the 1882 Act to other instruments. Specifically, amendments will have to be introduced to facilitate the denomination of instruments in units of account like the ECU.

At present there are two main classes of negotiable instrument recognised by law, namely, promises to pay (bank notes and promissory notes) and orders to pay (cheques and bills of exchange). Other commercial documents recognised as negotiable are bearer bonds, dividend warrants and share warrants to bearer. Whilst both postal orders and share certificates are 'instruments', they are not negotiable, whereas travellers' cheques, for example, resemble negotiable instruments since they are freely transferable. Sometimes bills of lading are described as negotiable but this is an inaccurate description for the following reasons: first, a bill of lading is not a contract to pay money because it is a document of title; secondly, commercial practice has decided that the title to goods cannot, in normal circumstances, pass free from any equities that affected the title of a previous owner (*Kum* v *Wah Tat Bank Ltd* [1971] 1 Lloyd's Rep 439). Where an instrument is otherwise negotiable, this can be overcome by the simple expedient of crossing the instrument and including the words 'not negotiable', whereupon the transferee will take subject to any defects in the title of the transferor. Herein lies the crucial distinction between the application of the *nemo dat* rule to negotiable instruments and to goods (see chapter 7).

REQUIREMENTS FOR A VALID BILL OF EXCHANGE

Section 3(1) of the Bills of Exchange Act 1882 provides the seminal definition of a valid bill of exchange and is worth setting out in full:

> A bill of exchange is an unconditional order in writing, addressed by one person to another, signed by the person giving it, requiring the person to whom it is addressed to pay on demand or at a fixed or determinable future time a sum certain in money to or to the order of a specified person, or to bearer.

A cheque is defined in s. 73 as 'a bill of exchange drawn on a banker payable on demand'. A document which does not satisfy the requirements set out in s. 3(1) cannot be a valid bill of exchange but this does not necessarily render the instrument inefficacious, for example, it may constitute a contractual obligation which is capable of assignment. Before proceeding to examine the definition in greater detail, it is necessary to describe the parties involved with a bill.

The parties The person who draws the bill and gives the order to pay is called the 'drawer', whilst the 'drawee' is the person whom the bill is ultimately to be drawn against, that is, ordered to pay. When the drawee signifies his assent to the order (acceptance) he is then called the acceptor. Acceptance must be accompanied by the signature of the drawee (s. 17(2)). This is one reason why cheques are not accepted as this procedure would involve the relevant bank in an extremely onerous and time-consuming task. The person specified in the bill as 'payee' is the one to whose order the money is to be paid, whilst if the bill is drawn payable to 'bearer', the person in possession of the bill can order the money to be paid.

The most important function of a bill of exchange is that it can be negotiated, that is, transferred to a third party. A bill payable to order is negotiated by the endorsement of the payee or subsequent transferee which is completed by delivery (s. 31(3)). An endorsement must be written on the bill and consist of the signature of the endorser (s. 32) whilst a bearer bill is negotiated simply by delivery (s. 31(2)). The payee or the endorsee of a bill who is in possession of it, or the bearer of a bill payable to bearer is called the 'holder'.

Whilst the content of a bill of exchange will vary the form can be set out and illustrated as in figure 9.1.

```
                                                    Colum Drive, Cardiff
                                                    27 October 1991

£250

(On demand              )  pay to Paul Todd            )  the
(At sight               )    ,,   Paul Todd or order   )  sum
(Three months after sight)   ,,   the order of Paul Todd)  of
(Six months after date  )  bearer                      )

two hundred and fifty pounds, value received.

To Michael Jones                    Norman Doe
Cambridge Steet
Porth
```

Figure 9.1

The words 'value received' are not essential to the validity of the bill, although the form of the bill must satisfy the following factors which we shall now consider.

Unconditional order There must be a requirement for the drawee to pay expressed in imperative, albeit courteous terms. Thus in *Bavins Jnr and Sims* v *London and South Western Bank Ltd* [1900] 1 QB 270, an order addressed to the drawee requiring him to pay provided that the payee signed a receipt form written on the back of the bill was held to be conditional. In contrast, where the instruction is directed at the payee, this does not render the bill conditional (*Nathan* v *Ogdens Ltd* (1905) 93 LT 533, affirmed (1905) 94 LT 126). An order to pay out of a particular fund is not unconditional (*Fisher* v *Calvert* (1879) 27

WR 301). It is otherwise where there is an *unqualified* order to pay in conjunction with an indication of a particular fund out of which the drawee is to seek reimbursement (*Guaranty Trust Co. of New York* v *Hannay and Co.* [1918] 2 KB 623).

An order to pay must not be dependent on a contingency so that s. 11 of the 1882 Act states: 'An instrument expressed to be payable on a contingency is not a bill, and the happening of the event does not cure the defect'. In *Palmer* v *Pratt* (1824) 2 Bing 185, an instrument ordering payment 30 days after the arrival of the ship *Paragon* at Calcutta was held not to be a valid bill of exchange since this constituted a contingency. It is otherwise where the event is certain, for example, in *Colehan* v *Cooke* (1742) Willes 393, a promissory note payable a certain time after the death of the promisor's father was held to be valid.

In writing The order must be in 'writing' and this, as s. 2 states, includes print. Indeed the Interpretation Act 1978 defines 'writing' to include printing, lithography, photographing and other modes of representing or reproducing words in a visible form. The medium of writing is only limited by the scope of human imagination and there have been celebrated instances of cheques being drawn in favour of the Inland Revenue written on underwear. However, there is a statutory exception in relation to metal (Coinage Act 1870). The requirement of writing does pose an important obstacle to the development of electronic data interchange systems and the White Paper (1990) which followed the Jack report (1989), concluded that there would be efficiency gains if negotiable instruments could be 'dematerialised', that is, issued and traded in purely electronic forms in a depositary system.

Addressed by one person to another The drawee must be named or somehow indicated on the bill with reasonable certainty (s. 6(1)). Whereas a bill addressed to two or more drawees is valid, an order addressed to two or more drawees either in the alternative or in succession is not a bill of exchange (s. 6(2)). There is no reason why the drawer cannot draw a bill in favour of himself a payee. However, the drawer and drawee may not be the same person as in the case of a banker's draft. In this last situation, the holder may treat the instrument at his option either as a bill of exchange or as a promissory note (s. 5(2)).

Signed by the person giving it In order for a bill or cheque to be valid it must be signed by the drawer. Following s. 91(1) of the Act, it is not necessary for the drawer to sign it with his own hand so that the seal or stamp of a company (s. 36A of the Companies Act 1985 as amended), a facsimile signature of an individual, or the 'mark' of an illiterate person would normally be sufficient (*Goodman* v *J. Eban Ltd* [1954] 1 QB 550). All that is necessary is that the signature is impressed with the authority of the drawer. Consequently, if an agent signs a bill of exchange in his own name, the principal will not be liable on it even if the payee is aware that the signer is an agent, but the principal may be liable for misrepresentation or for breach of warrranty of authority (*Starkey* v *Bank of England* [1903] AC 114).

A signature which has been forged, or which has been made without authority is not a valid signature for the purposes of s. 3, although certain estoppels may arise as against the drawer and against the acceptor and any endorser of the bill (see below).

Payable on demand or at a fixed or determinable future time Under s. 10 of the 1882 Act, a bill may be expressed to be payable on demand, 'at sight', or 'on presentation' because in each case the drawee is required to pay as soon as the bill is presented. It is important that the date should be discoverable by the holder so that he can present the bill for payment and, if necessary, give notice of dishonour within the times allowed by s. 49(12) (see pp. 208–9). Extraordinarily, a bill expressed to be payable on *or before* a specified date is not a valid bill because there is no *determinable* future time even though liability is bound to accrue, at the latest, on the date expressed to be payable and the promissor can be considered to have an option to pay before that date (*Williamson* v *Rider* [1963] 1 QB 89; *Claydon* v *Bradley* [1987] 1 WLR 521).

Section 3(4)(a) of the 1882 Act provides that a bill is not invalid simply because it has not been dated, but where a bill is payable so many days after sight, the absence of a date means that the bill is uncertain. However, s. 12 allows any holder to insert the true date so that if the wrong date is inserted and the bill is subsequently negotiated and comes into the hands of a good-faith transferee for value, the inserted date will be treated as the correct date.

A sum certain in money The amount to be paid must be determinable on the face of the bill. 'Money' is not defined in the Act but will obviously include legal tender and a bill may be drawn payable in a foreign currency. Section 9(1)(d) provides for 'exchange as per endorsement' and the rate of exchange will be written on the front or back of the bill with the amount in currency stated against the sterling figure in the front. If the bill does not specify the rate of exchange, the amount of sterling required to pay the bill is calculated by reference to the rate of exchange prevailing on the date the bill is due for payment (s. 72(4)). An order to pay in a unit of account such as European currency units (ECUs) would not be a bill within the existing definition. In the White Paper (1990) which constitutes the government response to the Jack Committee report (1989), it was proposed at paragraph 6.4 to amend the existing law to include a monetary unit of account established by an intergovernmental institution or by agreement between two or more States.

The issue of certainty is not compromised if the bill is expressed as payable by stated instalments so long as at the time of issue the sum can be determined. On the other hand, an order to pay money or, as an alternative, to do some other act is not a valid bill. A dramatic illustration of this latter phenomenon can be seen in the facts of *Smith* v *Boheme*, cited in *Jenmey* v *Herle* (1724) 2 Ld Raym 1361 at p. 1362, where the drawer promised to pay £72 or render the body of X to the Fleet before a certain date.

To the order of a specified person or to bearer It is important for a bill of exchange to specify to whom the bill is payable simply in order for the drawee

The bill of exchange

to know to whom he may properly pay it. Where the name of the payee is left blank, the instrument is incomplete but the person in possession of it may insert the name of the payee in accordance with s. 20 of the 1882 Act (see below). This should be distinguished from the case where the bill is made payable 'to bearer' as the bill may be transferred simply by delivery. However, an instrument made payable 'to cash' is not a bill and falls outside the 1882 Act although, obviously, such an instrument will sound in contract.

The fictitious or non-existing payee   Section 7(3) states that where the payee is a fictitious or non-existing person the bill or cheque may be treated as payable to bearer. This has considerable significance because any signature by way of endorsement on the bill will be non-essential since, as a bearer bill, it is negotiated by simple delivery. In this way, the payee's forged signature which would normally be defeated by the operation of s. 24 of the Act can be disregarded (see below).

The major difficulty with s. 7(3) is that the framers of the Act failed to state what they meant by a fictitious or non-existent payee and it was left to the courts to decide. Perhaps the most celebrated decision in this context is that of the House of Lords in *Bank of England* v *Vagliano Brothers* [1891] AC 107 and it is worth dwelling on the facts. The bills (43 of them in total) were drawn payable to a named payee who was in existence (Petridi and Co). The signature of the drawer on the bills (Vucina) was forged. This was a very clever fraud because the bills were accompanied by a considerable number of other genuine bills of exchange, many of them drawn by Vucina. The drawee accepted the bills in ignorance of the forgery so, in effect, the forger obtained a genuine acceptance on the forged bills. Obviously, the forger did not intend the named payee to receive payment and obtained the money (£71,000) himself through endorsement and presentation to the Bank of England where the merchant banker drawee (Vagliano) had an account. The question was whether the Bank of England was entitled to debit the account of its customer, the acceptor, in respect of the amounts paid out. The House of Lords by a majority held that it was entitled to do so.

The basis of the majority decision is odd since 'fictitious' was equated with feigned or counterfeit, and it was held that what mattered was the intention of the drawer. Whilst this approach is consistent with principle, for example, where the identity of the payee is ambiguous, or where there are two persons (mother and daughter) of the same name (see s. 7(1) of the Bills of Exchange Act 1882), it is otherwise where there has been a forgery. Indeed, Lord Halsbury LC adopted a metaphysical approach in his analysis at p. 121:

> In truth, if strictly construed, the words 'fictitious person' are a contradiction. One may pretend there is a person when there is not. One may assume a character which does not belong to one, but to satisfy the word 'fictitious' as applicable to a person is assuming in one part of the proposition what is denied in the other. Some of the characters in Sir Walter Scott's novels may be fictitious in the sense that no person so named ever lived; but if real names are taken, and events and conduct and character attributed by the writer to

those real names, are the characters less 'fictitious' because persons of those names identified with a totally different history and different qualities did in point of fact exist at one time?.

In a strong dissenting opinion with regard to the above approach, Lord Bramwell held at pp. 137-139 (emphasis added):

> Then, were Petridi and Co. fictitious or non-existing persons? There was a firm of that name, a firm as identifiable . . . as the Bank of England itself would be identifiable if their names appeared as payees of a bill of exchange; and to my mind that shows they were not fictitious or non-existing persons. . . . *in the intention of the makers of the bill, Petridi was a sham, and so fictitious or non-existent; that Petridi and Co. are not fictitious nor non-existent, that they exist in the flesh, yet they are fictitious* qua *payees, constructively fictitious.* . . . *This beats me.* . . .
>
> A bill payable to the Bank of England is payable to a fictitious person if the drawer intends to forge their name and give it to another person. A payee is real or fictitious, at the option of the holder, within the Act.

The majority view, however, was that even if the drawer's name had not been forged but the drawer had inserted the name of the payee as a pretence, the bill would still have been categorised as a bill payable to a fictitious person.

In subsequent cases an attempt has been made to distinguish *Bank of England* v *Vagliano Brothers* and confine it to its particular facts, namely, where both the drawer and payee signature have been forged. Thus in *Vinden* v *Hughes* [1905] 1 KB 795 (see also *North and South Wales Bank Ltd* v *Macbeth* [1908] AC 137), an employee prepared cheques for signature by his employer drawn in favour of known customers. He then forged endorsements and negotiated them with the defendant who gave full value for them in good faith, and obtained payment of them from the plaintiff's bankers. In an action to recover from the defendant the amount received, Warrington J distinguished *Bank of England* v *Vagliano Brothers* on the following basis: there was no drawer in fact and the use of the name of the payee was a mere fiction even though the payee actually existed. Despite this, it could be argued, as a matter of policy, that the loss should fall upon the employer as a business risk rather than upon a subsequent endorsee or drawee (see, for example, the dissenting opinion in *Royal Bank of Canada* v *Concrete Column Clamps (1961) Ltd* (1976) 74 DLR (3d) 26).

NEGOTIATION OF A BILL OF EXCHANGE

The essential characteristic of a bill is that it is negotiable. Of course, it may be that the drawer may wish not to allow the bill to be transferred or negotiated as a way of protection against forgery (see pp. 202-7). Similarly, an endorsee may wish by his endorsement to prohibit further transfers. In this respect, the drawer or endorsee may insert restrictive wording on the face of the bill, for example, 'Not transferable' or 'Pay X only' (see ss. 8(1) and 35(1) to (3) of the Bills of Exchange Act 1882).

Endorsement in blank and special endorsement

Where the bill consists of the signature of the endorser in blank, that is, not specifying an endorsee, the bill becomes payable to bearer (s. 34(1)). In contrast a special endorsement specifies the person to whom, or to whose order, the bill is payable. Where a bill was originally drawn payable to bearer, it cannot be converted into one payable to order by a special endorsement since the original nature of the bill was that the drawer exposed himself to all the risks associated with a bearer bill (see *Miller Associates (Australia) Pty Ltd* v *Bennington Pty Ltd* [1975] 2 NSWLR 506). It is otherwise in the case of a blank endorsement which may be converted into a special endorsement simply by the insertion of an order to pay above the endorsee's signature (s. 34(4)). A person who indorses a bill becomes liable on it and may have to pay the holder if it is dishonoured by the acceptor. Nonetheless, it is possible for an endorser to limit his liability by indorsing the bill 'without recourse' (s. 55(1)).

TRANSFERABILITY OF A BILL

The person who can seek payment on a bill is its holder. Section 2 of the Bills of Exchange Act 1882 provides that a holder is the 'payee or endorsee of a bill or note who is in possession of it, or the bearer thereof'. The *nemo dat* principle has a limited application here because where there has been a forgery of an essential endorsement, that endorsement has no effect (s. 24), so a person whose title derives from a forged endorsement is not a holder (but see ss. 54 to 55 below). It is otherwise in the case of a bearer bill where, even after theft, the holder may validly negotiate the bill and pass good title to a bona fide transferee for value. Whilst it is the case, therefore, that the holder is normally the owner (security of property), in the context of a bearer bill which is the archetypal negotiable instrument there may be both an owner and a holder. This phenomenon may be illustrated as follows:

Drawer	— Acceptor —	Bearer	— Theft —	Good faith
Owner		Bill	Holder	Purchaser

In the above scenario, whilst the true owner can sue the thief holder for its return, following negotiation, the good-faith purchaser becomes the owner/holder leaving the original owner with a personal claim against the thief.

There are three categories of holder recognised under the 1882 Act.

The holder

The mere holder has very limited rights namely, transfer; insertion of the date of the bill, if omitted (s. 12); presentation for payment. Every holder is rebuttably presumed to be a holder in due course, that is, a good-faith purchaser, although s. 30(2) or the 1882 Act provides that if the bill is tainted with fraud, duress, force and fear, or illegality, the burden of proof is shifted unless and until the holder can show that the bill was subsequently transferred for value and in good faith.

The holder for value

Section 2 of the Bills of Exchange Act 1882 defines 'value' to mean valuable consideration in the sense that it must move from the promisee. As between the immediate parties on a bill, value must have been given by the holder who seeks to enforce the obligation (s. 27(1)(b)). However, as between remote parties to the transaction against which the bill relates, value need not be given by the holder so long as value has been given at some time (s. 27(2)). Thus in *Diamond* v *Graham* [1968] 1 WLR 1061, D (the plaintiff) drew a cheque in favour of H, payment of which was stopped until G (the defendant) drew a cheque for a similar amount in D's favour. The whole purpose of this scheme was to provide short-term loan facilities for H. D's cheque in favour of H was presented for payment and was paid, but G's cheque was not met thereby prejudicing D. The Court of Appeal held that value was given for the defendant's cheque when H who was not the holder of the defendant's cheque gave to the defendant his own cheque in return (compare *Pollway Ltd* v *Abdullah* [1974] 1 WLR 493).

An important provision for banks is s. 27(3) of the Act which provides that a person holding a lien over a bill is a holder for value to the extent of his lien. Thus, a bank will have a lien on its customer's cheques where the customer is indebted to the bank, and can retain the customer's cheques which come into its possession in its capacity as a holder for value.

Rights of the holder for value The holder for value has the right, in common with any other holder, to sue on the bill in his own name (s. 38(1)). In enforcing his right, the holder for value will take subject to any 'real' or 'absolute' defences, that is, defences which arise from the invalidity of the instrument including incapacity, forgery, material alteration, the plea of *non est factum*. In addition, a holder for value will be defeated by the defects of title of prior parties and by the personal defences available to prior parties among themselves (see *Arab Bank Ltd* v *Ross* [1952] 2 QB 216). A holder for value will, nevertheless, be entitled to the 'shelter' rule in s. 29(3) of the Act where he derives his title to the bill through a holder in due course (see below).

The requirement of consideration Since the rights and obligations created by a bill are contractual, the acceptor or other payer can refuse payment on the grounds that he received no consideration. The holder can enforce the obligation if he can show consideration, but the Act takes an expansive approach here to include antecedent debt or liability (past consideration) as being adequate which is at variance with the common law position (s. 27(1)(b)). It should be noted that this does not extend to a debt or liability of a third party, and there must be a connection between the bill and the antecedent debt or liability (see *Oliver* v *Davis* [1949] 2 KB 727). As Robert Goff J put it in *Hasan* v *Willson* [1977] 1 Lloyd's Rep 431 at pp. 440–1: 'the antecedent debt or liability referred to in s. 27(1)(b) must be an antecedent debt or liability of the relevant promisor or drawer of the bill of exchange and not of a stranger to the bill' (see also *MK International Development Co. Ltd* v *Housing Bank* (1990) *Financial Times*, 22 January 1991).

The bill of exchange 199

The Jack committee (1989) argued that the formal nature of the bill of exchange means that consideration is not necessary to prove the seriousness of the intention of the drawer and acceptor to accept legal liability to pay. If the committee's recommendation that the requirement of consideration be abolished were implemented, the holder-for-value status would disappear.

The holder in due course
Section 29 of the Bills of Exchange Act 1882 provides that a holder who satisfies certain conditions is a 'holder in due course'. This is a more elegant phrase than the cumbersome common law equivalent of a good-faith purchaser for value without notice. The holder in due course will take free from any defect of title, and in order to qualify the following conditions have to be met which we shall now proceed to discuss.

There must be a holder Although the definition of 'holder' in s. 1 of the Act includes the original payee of an order bill, it was decided by the House of Lords in *R.E. Jones Ltd v Waring and Gillow Ltd* [1926] AC 670 that the original payee of a bill, cheque or note who remains in possession of the instrument cannot be a holder in due course. The Act itself contemplates that a holder in due course must be a holder to whom the instrument is negotiated (ss. 20(2), 21(2) and 29(1)(b)). It also appears that the presumption in s. 27(2) that 'where value has at any time been given for a bill, the holder is deemed to be a holder for value' only applies where the instrument has been negotiated and does not operate in favour of the original payee (see *MK International Development Co. Ltd v Housing Bank* (1990) *Financial Times*, 22 January 1991).

In *Jade International Steel Stahl und Eisen GmbH & Co. KG v Robert Nicholas (Steels) Ltd* [1978] QB 917, it was held by the Court of Appeal that a drawer (and by analogy also the payee) can be a holder in due course by derivation under s. 29(3) of the Act. In that case, a bill having come into the possession of a holder in due course was dishonoured (see below). It ultimately came back into the hands of the drawer when he became liable on it, and it was held that the drawer had the rights of a holder in due course as against the acceptor.

The bill must be complete and regular on its face Where the bill is not complete, no one who takes it can be a holder in due course. This is particularly pertinent in respect of an inchoate instrument, that is, a bill which is incomplete in form, such as where no amount is stated or the payee's name is omitted. An undated bill would appear to be incomplete or at least irregular. By virtue of s. 20(1) of the Act, any person in possession of a bill has prima facie authority to complete the missing item. However, in order to bind the prior parties, an inchoate bill must be completed within a reasonable time and in accordance with the authority given. Of course, it is difficult to determine objectively what the extent of this authority may be, thereby, prejudicing third-party interests. However, if the bill comes into the hands of a holder in due course, it is conclusively presumed that the bill was completed within a reasonable time and in accordance with the signer's instructions (s. 20(2)). It follows from this that the holder in due course can enforce the bill according to its apparent tenor regardless of the authority actually given by the original signer.

Any alteration on the face of a bill will prima facie make it irregular (*Banco di Roma SpA* v *Orru* [1973] 2 Lloyd's Rep 505). Thus in *Arab Bank Ltd* v *Ross* [1952] 2 QB 216, a note which was payable to a Palestinian firm 'Fathi and Faysal Nabulsy Company' and which had been endorsed 'Fathi and Faysal Nabulsy' was held to be irregular because part of the payee's name was omitted in the endorsement. The degree of correspondence is a matter of commercial practice and as Denning LJ held in *Arab Bank Ltd* v *Ross* at p. 227: '. . . that is a practical question which is, as a rule, better answered by a banker than a lawyer'.

The bill must not be overdue A bill will be overdue when the time for payment has passed. If the bill is payable on demand, it is deemed to be overdue when it appears on the face of it to have been in circulation for an unreasonable length of time (s. 36(3)) which is a question of fact. In the case of cheques, banks will regard as 'stale' and require confirmation from the drawer before paying a cheque presented more than six months from the date of issue. It is important to distinguish between an overdue cheque and a stale cheque. A stale cheque is one, as we have noted, where the gap is a long one requiring additional confirmation. It is possible for a court to treat a cheque as being not overdue despite a gap exceeding six months according to the particular facts of the case.

Without notice of dishonour Section 90 of the Bills of Exchange Act 1882 defines good faith in terms of whether a thing 'is in fact done honestly, whether it is done negligently or not'. This is a question of fact and a distinction can be drawn between mere negligence and wilful disregard, or, as Lord Blackburn put it in *Jones* v *Gordon* (1877) 2 App Cas 616, between a man who was 'honestly blundering and careless' and one who 'must have had a suspicion that there was something wrong'. It follows from this that where the circumstances are such as would lead a reasonable man towards suspicion, for example, gross undervalue, this will raise an evidential burden requiring the person asserting good faith to prove that he was not suspicious.

The holder himself must take the bill for value. It is insufficient that by virtue of s. 27(2), a holder in due course is deemed to be a holder for value simply by virtue of the fact that value has at some time been given for the bill (see above).

Without notice of defect in title The transferor's title may be defective where the circumstances in which he acquired the bill or those in which he transferred it can be considered, for the purposes of the Act, defective. A person whose title is defective must be carefully distinguished from a person with no title at all, for example, due to the forgery of an essential signature (see below). Section 29(2) provides that 'the title of a person who negotiates a bill is defective within the meaning of this Act when he obtained the bill, or the acceptance thereof, by fraud, duress, or force and fear, or other unlawful means, or an illegal consideration, or when he negotiates it in breach of faith, or under such circumstances as amount to fraud'. The list is not exhaustive and has indeed

The bill of exchange 201

been added to by statute. Thus, the Consumer Credit Act 1974 restricts the taking and negotiation of negotiable instruments in connection with a regulated agreement (see ss. 8(3), 15(2) and 189(1) of the Consumer Credit Act 1974). This is achieved in three ways: first, the creditor or owner shall not take a negotiable instrument, other than a banknote or cheque, in discharge of any sum payable by the debtor or hirer under a regulated agremeent, or by any person as surety in relation to the agreement (s. 123(1) of the Consumer Credit Act 1974); second, the Act precludes a creditor who has taken a cheque as payment from negotiating this except to a bank; third, the creditor or owner cannot take a negotiable instrument as security, but only as conditional payment (s. 123(3) of the Consumer Credit Act 1974).

The constructive notice doctrine does not apply to commercial transactions (*Manchester Trust* v *Furness* [1895] 2 QB 539) and notice in s. 29(1)(b) means 'actual' notice which includes implied notice, that is, wilfully shutting one's eyes. In this respect, the notice must refer to the specific defect in title or give rise to a suspicion that further enquiry was necessary with regard to a possible defect. The relevant time for notice is when the bill was negotiated to the holder, so after-acquired knowledge is irrelevant in this regard.

Presumption of value and good faith Every holder of a bill is prima facie deemed to be a holder in due course (s. 30(2)). However, where it is admitted or proved that either the acceptance or the issue or negotiation of the bill is affected by fraud, duress or illegality, the holder is presumed not to be a holder in due course. In this instance, it is necessary for the holder to prove that subsequent to the fraud, duress or illegality a person, not necessarily the current holder, provided value for the bill in good faith which will then reinstate the presumption that the holder is a holder in due course.

The liability on the bill

Delivery Liability arises only when a bill or cheque has been issued or delivered, that is, without delivery, the liability that a person would otherwise incur (see below) is not established (s. 21 of the Bills of Exchange Act 1882). This liability arises in relation to every contract on a bill which relates to the drawer, endorser or acceptor. However, where a bill has been negotiated to a holder in due course, a complete and valid delivery by all prior parties is *conclusively* presumed (s. 21(2)) which coheres with the general policy of promoting the transferability of bills.

Capacity The Bills of Exchange Act 1882 envisages that liability is essentially contractual so that no person can be made liable on a bill unless he has capacity to incur contractual liability. Thus with regard to the Minors' Contracts Act 1987, a minor cannot be held liable on a bill which he has signed unless he ratifies his signature on attaining the age of majority. It also appears following s. 35 of the Companies Act 1985 (as amended) that a company, other than a charitable company, which otherwise lacks capacity in respect of a bill (typically because it has no power in its memorandum) may be held liable on it.

It should be noted that if a party to a bill lacks capacity, the bill nevertheless remains fully valid and enforceable against other parties. Signature is essential to liability (s. 23), so it follows that the more signatories there are to an instrument, the more likelihood there is that the holder of the instrument will be able to obtain what is due to him evidenced on the face of the bill. Herein lies an important justification for the restriction of the plea of *non est factum* in this context (see *Saunders* v *Anglia Building Society* [1971] AC 1004). For this defence to succeed, the document must be essentially different from the document it was believed to be and furthermore, the signer must prove that he acted carefully. In *Crédit Lyonnais* v *P.T. Barnard and Associates Ltd* [1976] 1 Lloyd's Rep 557, the defendant's managing director accepted two bills on behalf of the company written in French which he had difficulty in understanding and which were folded over when he signed them. In this case the defence of *non est factum* failed because the defendant company had not discharged the burden of proving that the managing director had acted carefully.

A person who signs on behalf of a partnership is treated as though he had signed in the name of all the partners in the partnership (s. 23(2)). On the other hand, a person who signs in his own name on behalf of a firm or partnership will incur personal liability, whilst a person who signs a bill but adds words to the effect that he is signing only in a representative capacity is not personally liable (s. 26). At the same time, a person may sign a bill so as to incur liability on it through an agent. With this in mind, it is important to distinguish carefully between forged signatures and unauthorised signatures. The reasoning here is that in line with general agency principles, an unauthorised signature (as distinct from a forgery) can be ratified and following this, it is wholly effective. The crucial distinction between a forgery and an unauthorised signature is that a forger does not purport to act on behalf of the person whose name he forges so that, as a matter of logic, there is nothing to be ratified (see ss. 1 and 9 of the Forgery and Counterfeiting Act 1981). On the other hand, there is nothing to stop the adoption of the forger's signature through, for example, an estoppel by express representation (see *Greenwood* v *Martins Bank Ltd* [1933] AC 51).

FORGED SIGNATURES

The general rule is that a forged signature or a signature placed on a bill without authority is 'wholly inoperative' (s. 24 of the Bills of Exchange Act 1882). There are exceptions to this rule recognised under s. 24 itself and these are set out as follows:

> Subject to the provisions of this Act, where a signature on a bill is forged or placed thereon without the authority of the person whose signature it purports to be, the forged or unauthorised signature is wholly inoperative, and no right to retain the bill or to give a discharge therefor or to enforce payment thereof against any party thereto can be acquired through or under that signature, unless the party against whom it is sought to retain or enforce payment of the bill is precluded from setting up the forgery or want of authority.

Provided that nothing in this section shall affect the ratification of an unauthorised signature not amounting to forgery.

The relevant forgery or unauthorised signature on a bill may be that of any of the parties liable on the bill, namely, the drawer, the endorser, or the acceptor. If the drawer's signature is forged, the bill is wholly ineffective and no one can have any right to retain the 'bill' or enforce payment on it. This is because there has been no 'unconditional order in writing signed by the person giving it' as laid down in s. 3(1) of the Bills of Exchange Act 1882. Forgery of the acceptor's signature merely means that the bill is unaccepted. Where an endorsement is forged, the bill is valid but the person whose signature is forged is not liable and the effect of the forgery is to break the chain of title so that, in the absence of estoppel, no one who takes after the forgery can enforce it against parties liable on the bill before the forgery.

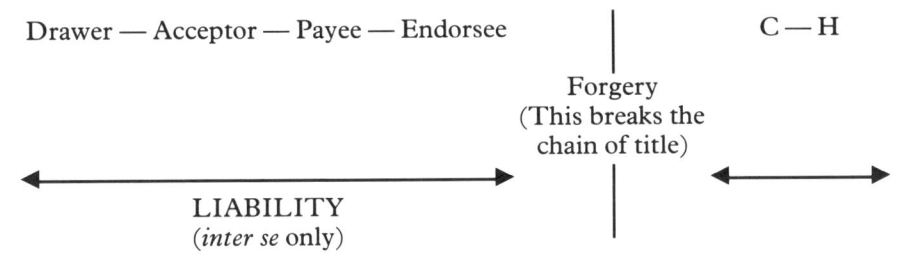

Drawer — Acceptor — Payee — Endorsee | C — H

Forgery
(This breaks the chain of title)

◄─────────────────────► ◄─────────►
LIABILITY
(*inter se* only)

The chain of title may be salvaged in the above illustration where the endorsee is estopped from denying his signature.

Estoppel and forgery or want of authority

Section 24 of the Bills of Exchange Act 1882 expressly provides for an exception to the effects of a forged or unauthorised signature where the party against whom it is sought to enforce payment is precluded from setting up the forgery or want of authority. In addition to the statutory estoppels (see below), other estoppels may arise by representation or by negligence.

Estoppel by representation

There are few cases of estoppel by an express representation other than where a drawee on a bill, or his authorised representative has acknowledged a forged acceptance as his own. This was indeed the case in *Bank of England* v *Vagliano Brothers* [1891] AC 107 where the bank clerk of the Bank of England before paying on the bills sought advice from Vagliano's confidential adviser, Mr Ziffo, who replied: 'I suppose, if they [the bills] are properly advised you must pay them'. In most cases either the representation is implied or it is constituted by silence. Perhaps the most celebrated decision, in this context, is *Greenwood* v *Martins Bank* [1933] AC 51, where it was held that a bank customer who discovers that forged cheques have been drawn on his account owes a duty to the bank to disclose the forgery (see also *Brown* v *Westminster Bank Ltd* [1964] 2 Lloyd's Rep 187).

Estoppel by negligence

In *London Joint Stock Bank Ltd* v *Macmillan and Arthur* [1918] AC 777, a confidential clerk was entrusted by his employers, Macmillan and Arthur, with filling in cheques for their signature. He filled in a cheque payable to a firm or to bearer showing the sum as £2 in figures only. One of the partners signed as drawer. The clerk then altered the figures to £120, filled in the words to match, and cashed the cheque at the London Joint Stock Bank where his employers had their account. The House of Lords held that a duty of care is owed by the customer to his bank in the operation of a current account to avoid drawing a cheque in such a manner as would facilitate fraud or forgery (compare *Scholfield* v *Earl of Londesborough* [1896] AC 514 where no such duty was said to arise in the case of a simple drawer and acceptor relationship). The extent of the duty of care in a banker-customer relationship was considered more recently by the Judicial Committee of the Privy Council in *Tai Hing Cotton Mill Ltd* v *Liu Chong Hing Bank Ltd* [1986] AC 80. In this case it was held that, in the absence of a *clear express* contractual stipulation to the contrary, there was no duty for a customer to check bank statements. The facts centred around the failure of the customer to operate an adequate checking system on its accounts where a clerk employed by the customer was able, over a long period of time, to forge the customer's signature and draw cheques against the drawee bank.

Unauthorised signatures

Where an agent has acted in excess of his actual authority, this act will not be binding on the principal as regards persons having notice that the agent is exceeding his authority. Where there is no notice, the principal will be liable if the agent has apparent authority. The 1882 Act, however, provides that in the case of a 'procuration signature' this operates as notice that the agent's authority is limited, for example, where the procuration is signed 'per pro' (see s. 25). As a matter of principle, though, there is no compelling reason why signatures by procuration should be treated any differently from other representative signatures, and it is for this reason that the Jack Committee (1989) considered that it should be repealed (see app. A, pp. 228–9).

An agent who signs a bill in his own name will incur *personal* liability on the bill even though it is known that he is signing as agent. This is significant where a bill has been addressed to and accepted by a company which is then endorsed by a director on behalf of the company. Such an endorsement may be treated as the personal endorsement of the director (*Elliott* v *Bax-Ironside* [1925] 2 KB 301). It is, in any case, a statutory requirement under s. 349 of the Companies Act 1985 that every bill or cheque must include the name of the company in legible print or writing, otherwise, a person who signs the bill for the company will be personally liable. In order for the agent to avoid personal liability, the bill must make it clear that the agent is not accepting personal liability (s. 26(2) of the Bills of Exchange Act 1882). An objective test is adopted by the court in determining whether the agent has undertaken personal liability and s. 26(2) of the Act provides that in deciding whether a signature is that of the agent or the principal, the court should adopt the interpretation most favourable to the validity of the bill. An endorsement of a bill addressed to and accepted by a company adds no greater validity to the bill than is already conferred by its acceptance so, where a director signs, personal liability is also assumed irrespective of whether or not he adds words to his signature indicating that he is only signing in a representative capacity (*Rolfe Lubell and Co.* v *Keith* [1979] 1 All ER 860; compare the situation of a non-negotiated cheque in *Bondina Ltd* v *Rollaway Shower Blinds Ltd* [1986] 1 WLR 517).

Statutory protection of the paying bank
It would be virtually impossible for a bank to discover whether an endorsement has been forged or is indeed unauthorised. Herein lies the explanation of s. 60 of the Bills of Exchange Act 1882 which states:

> When a bill payable to order on demand is drawn on a banker, and the banker on whom it is drawn pays the bill in good faith and in the ordinary course of business, it is not incumbent on the banker to show that the endorsement of the payee or any subsequent endorsement was made by or under the authority of the person whose endorsement it purports to be, and the banker is deemed to have paid the bill in due course, although such endorsement has been forged or made without authority.

It appears from the above that the paying bank will normally be entitled to debit its customer's account and escape liability to the true owner of the cheque where a cheque payable to order is stolen, and the thief forges the necessary endorsement to himself so as to obtain payment (*Capital and Counties Bank Ltd* v *Gordon* [1903] AC 240). The bank need only act in good faith and in the ordinary course of business: it is not necessary to show that payment was not negligent (see chapter 10).

Statutory estoppel: the acceptor's liability
It is the acceptor who is primarily liable on the bill and to whom the holder looks initially for payment (s. 54(1) of the Bills of Exchange Act 1882) unless the bill is an accommodation bill (see below). Certain statutory estoppels ('preclusions') are raised against the acceptor by virtue of his acceptance. These defences are available only to a holder in due course, that is, a person who would be a holder in due course but for the defence which the acceptor (or endorser under s. 55) is precluded from advancing. The underlying principle here is that the acceptor must be regarded as validating all signatures prior to his own. Thus under s. 54(2)(a), the acceptor is precluded from denying to a holder in due course 'the existence of the drawer, the genuineness of his signature, and his capacity and authority to draw the bill'. A distinction should be carefully drawn between the capacity of the drawer or payee to endorse, and the genuineness of his endorsement. In this respect, the acceptor can contest the validity of any endorsement by the drawer or payee (s. 54(2)(b) and (c)) but, of course, this may be undermined by the operation of s. 7(3) (see pp. 195–6).

Statutory estoppel: the drawer's liability
If the bill is dishonoured by the acceptor (or drawee), secondary liability rests with the drawer (s. 55 of the Bills of Exchange Act 1882). It should be noted

that prior to acceptance, the drawer is primarily liable which is always the case with cheques since they are not accepted. Defences on which the drawer can rely are essentially the same as those open to an acceptor (s. 55(1)). Where there has been dishonour, the drawer's liability is not to pay the bill but rather to provide compensation for its dishonour, that is, the value of the bill plus interest and the costs of enforcement (s. 57).

Statutory estoppel: the endorser's liability
An act of endorsement constitutes a guarantee that all signatures prior to the endorsement are regular and valid. By endorsing a bill, the endorsee agrees to pay the bill should the acceptor dishonour it (s. 55(1)(b)). Liability may be in the form of a demand for compensation by the holder, or a demand for a reimbursement by a subsequent endorser who has had to pay the holder (s. 57(1)).

It must be emphasised that the effect of ss. 54 and 55 is *not* to grant a good title but rather to grant the rights of a quasi holder in due course against certain parties, that is, parties who signed *after* the forgery. As such, parties who signed after the forgery are not affected except where, as sometimes happens, the acceptor signed *before* the drawer.

Drawer — Acceptor — $\dfrac{\text{Payee}}{\text{Forgery}}$ | E — F — G — H

s. 55 deals with liability after forgery

Both drawer and acceptor are severed from the 'holder' and he has no rights against them.

$\dfrac{\text{Drawer}}{\text{Forgery}}$ | Acceptor — E — F — G — H

s. 54 deals with the liability of the acceptor

Although there is no drawer and therefore no valid bill, the acceptor remains tied to the 'holder' and is liable for payment.

Liability of the accommodation party
The position of an accommodation party is like that of a guarantor of the bill, that is, where a person becomes a party to the bill without receiving value simply in order to increase the marketability of the bill (s. 28(2)). An accommodation party is one who has signed 'for the purpose of lending his name to some other person' (s. 28(1)) and so it follows that not all signatories of a bill who have not received value are accommodation parties. Whilst an accommodation party can raise defences such as fraud or duress, these are not available where the bill is held by a holder in due course (s. 56).

Liability of the transferor of a bearer bill
A bearer bill does not require an endorsement to transfer it. If there is no endorsement, the transferor is not liable on the instrument as he is not a party

to the bill. Nonetheless, the transferor may be liable if the bill is dishonoured for whatever reason to the transferee where the bill is a forgery, or if the transferor knew that the bill would not be paid, or if the transferor had a defective title. The transferor will be liable to his immediate transferee for value in the three cases discussed above notwithstanding that he tried to limit liability (s. 16(2)).

The material alteration defence

Any alteration to the date of the bill, the sum payable, or the time or place of payment, or the alteration of the name of the payee is a material alteration (s. 64). In such a case, the bill is avoided as regards all persons who became party to it prior to the alteration unless they consent to the alteration. A distinction is drawn between an apparent and a non-apparent alteration. A holder in due course has the right to 'avail himself of the bill as if it had not been altered' and to 'enforce payment of it according to its original tenor' (s. 64(1)) where there is a non-apparent alteration and, in so doing, protects the negotiability of a bill. However, if the alteration is apparent, the holder cannot complain that prior parties to the alteration are released because he should have been aware of the alteration: this would unfairly prejudice prior parties by effectively making them liable on a contract they never made. The test for material alteration was stated by Starke J in the High Court of Australia in *Automobile Finance Co. of Australia Ltd* v *Law* (1933) 49 CLR 1 at p. 12: 'The alteration may be by addition, interlineation, or otherwise, but it must be visible as an alteration, upon inspection'. This approach echoes the position of Salter J in *Woollatt* v *Stanley* (1928) 138 LT 620, where the relevant test was whether the alteration was such that with reasonable care the intending holder should have observed it.

The general position, as we have already noted above is that the drawer or acceptor of a bill does not owe a duty of care to subsequent holders when drawing or accepting to prevent material alteration (*Scholfield* v *Earl of Londesborough* [1896] AC 514). It is otherwise in the close contractual relationship of banker and customer where the latter owes a duty not to draw cheques so as to facilitate fraud (see *London Joint Stock Bank Ltd* v *Macmillan and Arthur* [1918] AC 777).

ENFORCEMENT OF A BILL

Liability arises on a bill where it has been dishonoured either by non-acceptance or by non-payment. However, without due presentment of the bill there can be no dishonour, and it is necessary to consider briefly the rules dealing with presentment for acceptance and presentment for payment in this regard.

Presentment for acceptance

The bill must be presented by or on behalf of the holder (s. 48(1)(a) of the Bills of Exchange Act 1882) and it must be made to the acceptor or his authorised agent (s. 41(1)(a)), to his personal representative if he is dead (s. 41(1)(c)), or to him or his trustee if he is bankrupt (s. 41(1)(d)). Presentment must be made at a reasonable hour on a business day and before the bill is overdue (s. 41(1)(a)). However, presentment is excused where presentment is impossible despite the exercise of reasonable diligence (s. 41(2)). The mere fact that the holder has reasons to believe that acceptance will be refused does not excuse presentment (s. 41(3)).

Presentment for payment
Similar rules apply here as to presentment for acceptance (see s. 45). Presentment must be made on the specified day if there is one, or, if the bill is payable on demand, within a reasonable time (s. 45(2)). Failure to present for payment is excused where this is impossible after the exercise of reasonable diligence (s. 46(2)), but failure to present for payment at the proper time and place will normally release prior parties (see *Yeoman Credit Ltd v Gregory* [1963] 1 WLR 343). Generally, the proper place for presentment will be the place for payment indicated in the bill, or the drawee's address as stated in the bill (s. 45(4)).

Notice of dishonour
Where a bill is dishonoured by non-acceptance or non-payment (which includes underpayment), notice of dishonour must be served on the drawer and all endorsers if their liability to the immediate holder (but not necessarily subsequent holders in due course) is not to be discharged. Failure to notify any party within a reasonable time (s. 49(12)) has the consequence that he escapes liability (s. 48). The Bills of Exchange Act 1882 contains detailed rules specifying the timing and content of a notice of dishonour (ss. 48 to 50). However, these rules only apply to persons liable on the bill as no notice needs to be given to the transferor of a bearer bill.

We have already noted above that the person primarily liable for payment is the acceptor. If he fails to honour the bill which is then paid by an endorser or by the drawer, the party making payment and all *subsequent* parties are discharged from liability. If the bill is paid by an endorser, he may either enforce the bill against prior parties or renegotiate the bill for value by cancelling all later endorsements (s. 59(2)(b)). A drawer, on the other hand, may not reissue the bill but may enforce it against the acceptor (s. 49(2)(a)).

Acceptance for honour
Anyone not already liable on a bill may accept it for honour (an acceptance 'supra protest'), for example, where the drawee or acceptor fails to pay it on its due date (ss. 65 to 68). Normally where a bill is accepted or paid for honour it must be 'protested' (see below).

Noting and protesting of a bill
The Bills of Exchange Act 1882 distinguishes between 'inland' and 'foreign' bills. Whilst noting and protesting are optional duties in respect of inland bills, a foreign bill must be noted and protested following dishonour in order to retain the liability of the drawer and any endorsers. What is meant by

'protesting' the bill is that the holder presents the bill for acceptance or payment so as to obtain proof of dishonour. The notary then notes this fact on the bill and draws up a formal protest. It has been argued that where a foreign bill is enforced in the UK, the fact that the bill has not been protested in the foreign jurisdiction is generally irrelevant as far as it is sought to enforce it within the UK (*Irvani* v *G. und H. Montage GmbH* [1989] FLR 390).

DISCHARGE OF A BILL

A bill ceases to be an effective instrument and all parties are released from their obligations if it is paid in due course, if the payee renounces his rights, or if the payee cancels the bill (s. 59 of the Bills of Exchange Act 1882). Payment in due course occurs when payment is made by or on behalf of the drawee and acceptor. However, if the payer pays someone other than a holder, albeit innocently after a forgery, the bill is not discharged. As we have seen, there is some statutory protection for a paying bank in this situation (s. 60) but there is no similar protection for drawees of other bills. In this circumstance, recovery of the money paid may be possible on the basis of mistake of fact (compare the Law Commission consultation paper, *Restitution of Payments Made under a Mistake of Law* (Law Com. No. 120, 1991)). Although this is a difficult area of law and the case law is often irreconcilable, certain principles do emerge: first, there must be a mistake of fact; second, payment must result from a *material* mistake which is common to both parties.

The payer may be estopped from recovering on the basis of mistake of fact, for example, by an unequivocal representation which was relied upon by the holder (see *United Overseas Bank* v *Jiwani* [1976] 1 WLR 964). In the case of accounting errors resulting in overpayment, such a representation will be easy to discern because as between the payer and recipient, the payer is under a duty to ensure that the payment is accurate (*Holt* v *Markham* [1923] 1 KB 504).

If the acceptor pays the payee, this will release the drawer from his obligations. Of course, it is open to the payee to renounce in writing payment or the liability of a party (s. 63). Cancellation must be intentioned and apparent on the face of the bill (s. 63(1)). Lastly, it is worth noting that an apparent material alteration to a bill operates to discharge all *prior* parties (s. 64).

SCREEN-BASED TRANSFERS?

The Jack committee (1989) recommended at paras 8.33 to 8.38 that a new Bills of Exchange Act should contain provisions relating to transactions taking place in a screen-based or book-entry depository system, and these should be operated by an approved depository. The reference here is to an electronic bill of exchange, that is, a mechanism capable of instantaneous transmission between computer terminals removing the need to transfer a piece of paper. The function of the approved depository would be to record the transfer, the transferee, thereby, having the same rights as an endorsee of a traditional bill of exchange whilst the transferor would incur liabilities like those of an endorser.

TEN
Cheques and analogous instruments on a banker

CHEQUES AND BILLS

The Bills of Exchange Act 1882 treats the cheque as a mere adjunct to bills of exchange, that is, as a bill of exchange drawn on a banker. The major difficulty with this approach is that it undermines the function of a cheque: first, it allows a customer, in conjunction with other mechanisms such as plastic cards which operate automatic teller machines (ATMs), to effectuate withdrawals from his account with the bank; second, it enables a customer to take advantage of any overdraft facilities accorded to him by the bank with respect to his current account. In this regard the modern cheque is not negotiated in the same sense as a bill of exchange, rather, a cheque is more often than not simply used as a money payment order. Of course, it should be appreciated that there are other mechanisms by which such payments may be made, for example, standing orders, direct debits and other mandates to pay. As a matter of principle, therefore, a distinction may be drawn between a negotiable cheque which is analogous to a bill of exchange, and a non-negotiable cheque which simply authorises the designated payee to cash it or pay it into a bank account.

Section 73 of the Bills of Exchange Act 1882 defines a cheque as 'a bill of exchange drawn on a banker payable on demand'. As a consequence, the rules for the formation of a valid bill are relevant. The major difference is that the bill is a credit instrument, that is, it is drawn payable at a future date and is often discounted. Cheques do not operate in this way; they are not 'accepted' in the same sense that a bill is, so the bank in a cheque scenario incurs no liability to the payee if it fails to pay although, of course, the bank will be liable to its customers if it wrongfully dishonours the cheque. Under the Bills of Exchange Act 1882, therefore, a cheque is treated as an unaccepted bill of exchange and the primary liability rests with the drawer. As we shall see below (see pp. 213–15), provided there are sufficient funds credited to the account, the bank has a legal duty to its customer to honour cheques drawn on the account unless the order to pay is countermanded, or the bank is prevented from making payment by a judgment creditor obtaining a garnishee order to attach a debt, or alternatively a *Mareva* injunction (see pp. 463–5).

The essence of a cheque is that it constitutes a bill of exchange drawn on a banker so that any treatment of cheques necessarily involves some discussion of banks.

THE ROLES OF THE BANK AND CUSTOMER

There are considerable problems of definition associated with the term 'bank'. Indeed, the main regulatory statute, the Banking Act 1987 avoids any such definition and refers instead to an 'authorised institution', namely, an institution authorised by the Bank of England under the Act. Section 2 of the Bills of Exchange Act 1882 defines a bank as 'any body of persons, whether incorporated or not, who carry on the business of banking'. Of course, this begs the question as to what constitutes 'the business of banking'? This is incapable of precise definition for the following reasons: first, banking activity is not of a uniform kind; second, in recent times, institutions including savings banks, building societies, finance houses and the Post Office have moved into areas which were previously the province of the clearing banks; third, the nature of banking activity has changed through greater introduction of computerisation and electronic processes including ATMs (automated teller machines) and EFTPOS systems (electronic funds transfer at point of sale), 'cheque truncation' whereby cheques are cleared electronically, and banking conducted by telephone. All of these developments indicate the foolishness of determining the nature and scope of the business of banking by reference to banking practices in existence at a particular time.

In *United Dominions Trust Ltd* v *Kirkwood* [1966] 2 QB 431, it was held that a finance house which provided funds for hire-purchase transactions was a bank. The Court of Appeal unanimously held that the payment and collection of customers' cheques was an essential constituent of the business of banking. Another factor here was that the *banking community* recognised that the finance house was carrying on the business of banking. Since the business of banking is not static, it is quite possible to envisage a scenario where the business of banking could be engaged in without any need for cheques or any other paper-based orders to pay. It is little wonder that Lawton LJ in *Re Roe's Legal Charge* [1982] 2 Lloyd's Rep 370 at p. 382 was reluctant to define the word 'bank' saying: 'I have no intention whatsoever of attempting to define that which Parliament for so many years has decided not to define'.

The definition of 'banker' is used in the Bills of Exchange Act 1882 and the Cheques Act 1957. The significance of this status is that unless an institution is recognised as a bank, it will not enjoy the statutory protection afforded to banks which pay or collect payment for a person who is not the true owner of the cheque. This is especially important in the light of the increasing banking role of building societies anticipated under the Building Societies Act 1986 so that building societies have assumed corporate status, and provide a wide range of financial services to customers including current accounts operated by cheque-books. It is noteworthy that the statutory defences available to a banker under the Bills of Exchange Act 1882 and the Cheques Act 1957 are extended to building societies by sch. 8, part 4, para. 3 of the Building Societies Act 1986. The increasing liberalisation of financial services within the EEC will ensure greater competition for banking services within the UK in 1993 to which the definition of bank will be most pertinent.

The banker-customer relationship
The question of who is the bank's customer will be essential in order to determine if a bank can rely on the statutory defences available to banks paying and collecting cheques under the Bills of Exchange Act 1882 and the Cheques Act 1957. Unfortunately, neither Act defines 'customer' and so we must turn to the common law, where it has been held that a customer is someone who has an account at a bank in his own name even if the account was opened for the sole purpose of collecting one cheque (see *Ladbroke and Co. v Todd* (1914) 30 TLR 433; *Woods v Martins Bank Ltd* [1959] 1 QB 55). However, there must be a formal arrangement so that where a bank carries out a casual service such as changing notes into coins or cashing a cheque for a stranger, this does not make that person a customer.

The basis of the banker-customer relationship is essentially contractual. The general contract between the bank and the customer may, of course, have an impact on a number of subsidiary contracts, for example, a cheque guarantee card with respect to a particular retail transaction. There is little statutory regulation of the banker-customer relationship despite the recent widespread criticisms lodged against banks in their dealings with (especially) small businesses during the recession of 1989–92 which provoked a report from the Office of Fair Trading. The review committee, the Jack committee, in its report, *Banking Services Law and Practice* (Cm 622, 1989), rejected the idea of imposing a model contract on banks since the fear was expressed that it would stultify competition. Instead, there exists a system of self-regulation with the banks adopting and complying with a code of best practice monitored by the banking ombudsman (see pp. 226–7).

The relationship of banker and customer imposes duties on both parties. It is proposed to focus upon only those duties which pertain to cheques in this chapter but before doing so, it should be noted that the basis of the relationship is that of debtor and creditor although a bank, in carrying out its customer's instructions, may be acting as an agent. The relationship of banker and customer is not a fiduciary one, so in the event that the bank becomes insolvent, the customer's only right to repayment is as an ordinary unsecured creditor unless the bank holds a fund as property on trust for the customer (see *Space Investments Ltd v Canadian Imperial Bank of Commerce Trust Co. (Bahamas) Ltd* [1986] 1 WLR 1072).

The bank's duties

Repayment The duty of a banker to pay his customer's cheque where there are sufficient funds in the account is an aspect of contract. Thus, a failure by the bank to honour the customer's mandate either by cheque or by some other written order, or ATM, or EFTPOS, constitutes a breach of contract for which the bank may be liable in damages which may be substantial in the case of a business. In the absence of actual loss, in other cases, a customer is entitled only to nominal damages, for example, £20 in *Rae* v *Yorkshire Bank plc*, *The Times*, 12 October 1987. However, where a cheque is returned unpaid, the wording on the cheque, such as 'refer to drawer' may be defamatory thereby allowing the customer to claim damages for libel (see below).

The position of the banker is analogous to that of an agent acting on behalf of a principal, so his duty and authority to pay may be determined by the customer giving him notice of revocation at any time before the mandate is carried out. This countermand may be made in any effective form but the banker is not bound to accept an unauthenticated message. What is essential is that the countermand must be brought to the actual knowledge of the banker. In *Curtice* v *London City and Midland Bank Ltd* [1908] 1 KB 293, a telegram stopping payment of a cheque was placed in the letter-box of the bank, but due to the bank's error was not removed from the letter-box until after the cheque had been paid. It was held that payment had not effectively been countermanded, although this does not affect the liability of the bank in negligence in such a situation. The issue then is one of *effective* countermand, and it has been held that notice of countermand given to one branch of a bank is not an effective notice vis-à-vis a cheque drawn on another branch of the same bank (*Burnett* v *Westminster Bank Ltd* [1966] 1 QB 742). The demand must be made within business hours and the bank is entitled to refuse payment if the cheque is 'stale', that is, if it is presented more than six months after the date when it was drawn.

The duty of a banker to pay his customer's cheque may be affected by statute, for example, under s. 127 of the Insolvency Act 1986 in a winding up by the court (see chapter 19), any disposition of the company's property made after the commencement of the winding up is, unless the court orders otherwise, void (for the position in personal bankruptcy see s. 284 of the Insolvency Act 1986). The right of the bank to combine accounts will obviously have significance in the context of the insolvency regime (see part 5). Similarly under the Drug Trafficking Offences Act 1986 or the Prevention of Terrorism (Temporary Provisions) Act 1989, a restraint order may be made on public policy grounds. Furthermore, a banker is bound to refuse to pay a demand of his customer where to do so would render him liable as a constructive trustee, that is, where the bank has knowledge of the breach of trust and/or fraud of the customer's agent. The degree of knowledge of the dishonest design must be such that the bank had acted negligently in that it had failed to make such inquiries as a reasonable man would make so as to make the bank a constructive trustee of the consequences of that design (see *Baden, Delvaux and Lecuit* v *Société Général pour Favoriser le Développement du Commerce et de l'Industrie en France SA* [1983] BCLC 325; *Re Montagu's Settlement Trusts* [1987] Ch 264; *Agip (Africa) Ltd* v *Jackson* [1990] Ch 265; *Lipkin Gorman* v *Karpnale Ltd* [1989] 1 WLR 1340).

It is clearly important to be somewhat circumspect with regard to the position of the bank as constructive trustee because the funds deposited with the bank are its own property and not that of the customer. Nevertheless, the bank does owe a duty of care in the performance of its functions (*Barclays Bank plc* v *Quincecare Ltd* [1988] FLR 166), although recent case law appears to be more realistic about the modern banking context by recognising that banks deal with a high volume of cheques. Moreover, if a risk analysis is adopted, it could be argued that it is the principal (the customer) who has placed trust in the agent, placing him in a position to commit the fraud so that he must primarily bear the loss unless the circumstances are quite exceptional.

The cheque guarantee card This consists of a contractual undertaking given by the bank through the agency of its customer to the payee not to dishonour the cheque for want of funds (*Re Charge Card Services Ltd* [1987] Ch 150, affirmed [1989] Ch 497). The effect of the presentation of the cheque card is that the customer has lost his right of countermand, that is, by doing so he has authorised the bank to incur a personal liability and he cannot revoke the bank's authority to discharge it. Of course, it is otherwise where the customer's signature is forged unless the terms and conditions governing the use of the card clearly state that the bank is entitled to debit its customer's account in this instance.

The duty of confidentiality The bank's duty of confidentiality was comprehensively discussed by the Court of Appeal in *Tournier* v *National Provincial and Union Bank of England* [1924] 1 KB 461, and it was held that the duty arose from the nature of the contract between bank and customer. The breach of this duty will sound in damages which may be substantial where the information can, perhaps, be exploited by potential competitors to the banker's customer. However, the duty is subject to a number of exceptions, and Bankes LJ in the *Tournier* case recognised four broad categories of exception justifying disclosure of information which would otherwise be covered by the duty:

(a) Where disclosure is compelled by law. This is a significant inroad into the duty as there are now at least 20 statutes which require banks to reveal information about their customers ranging from Inland Revenue requests, for example, under s. 20 of the Taxes Management Act 1970, through to drug trafficking proceeds under the Drug Trafficking Offences Act 1986. Furthermore, there is no implied term in the contract between the customer and the bank requiring the latter to tell the client that it has provided such information to the relevant authority (*Barclays Bank plc* v *Taylor* [1989] 1 WLR 1066).

(b) Where there is a public duty to disclose the information. There is here a substantial overlap with (a) but there is one fundamental distinction, namely, whereas the first exception covers cases where disclosure is compulsory, the second applies to permit disclosure at the bank's discretion.

(c) Where the interests of the bank require disclosure. The typical situation is where a bank sues its customer for repayment of an overdraft where the bank may state the amount of the overdraft on the writ. There are difficulties with the scope of this exception because modern banking commercial practice will sometimes involve a bank disclosing financial information to subsidiaries as a marketing opportunity for other services, for example, insurance, unit trusts, shares, estate agency. At first sight, disclosure to such a subsidiary, albeit wholly owned by the bank, constitutes a breach of this exception because of the separate corporate identity of the company. Of course, it may be argued that disclosure can be justified on the basis that it is in the bank's interest. It is for this reason that the White Paper on *Banking Law and Services* (Cm 1026, 1990) recommended that the banks issue a voluntary code of practice, which they have now done, explaining the duty of confidentiality in respect of financial information disclosed to subsidiaries or to credit reference agencies. The use of personal data held in computers is, in any case, regulated by the Data Protection Act 1984.

(d) Where the disclosure is made with the express or implied consent of the customer. Banks often justify financial disclosure about customers to subsidiaries on the basis of implied consent. This is also the underlying rationale for references given by banks about the financial standing of customers where the request comes from another bank on behalf of one of its customers. In giving such information, the bank must use reasonable care and can be liable for negligent misstatements causing financial loss (*Hedley Byrne and Co. Ltd* v *Heller and Partners Ltd* [1964] AC 465). If the bank gives an unsatisfactory reference without justification, it may be liable to its customer in defamation and insofar as an attempt is made to disclaim liability, this is only effective to the extent that it is reasonable under s. 2 of the Unfair Contract Terms Act 1977 (*Smith* v *Eric S. Bush* [1990] 1 AC 831).

The duty of the customer: drawing cheques with due care
The customer is bound by all express and implied terms in his contract with the bank. In addition, the customer owes a duty of care to the bank which is of limited application as we shall now consider.

The duty to inform the bank of forgeries The most celebrated case in this context is *Greenwood* v *Martins Bank Ltd* [1933] AC 51 where a husband discovered that his wife had forged his signature as drawer on several occasions but refrained from informing the bank. Later he decided to tell the bank, whereupon she committed suicide. He still brought an action against the bank for wrongfully debiting his account, but the House of Lords held that he was under a duty to inform the bank of the forgeries and his failure to do so constituted an estoppel by representation by him that the cheques were genuine. The detriment suffered by the bank here was the opportunity to sue both the wife and husband who, at that time, was liable for his wife's torts.

The duty to avoid negligence There is an implied obligation on the customer to take reasonable precautions to avoid forgery or fraud. This can be illustrated in the facts of *London Joint Stock Bank Ltd* v *Macmillan and Arthur* [1918] AC 777 which were considered on p. 204. The extent of the duty in *London Joint Stock Bank Ltd* v *Macmillan and Arthur* is a limited one and does not apply to others concerned with the cheque, for example, the payee. This can be illustrated by the facts in *Lumsden and Co.* v *London Trustee Savings Bank*

[1971] 1 Lloyd's Rep 114, where the payees of a cheque were designated in an abbreviated form, 'Brown', which enabled the rogue to insert the initials 'J.A.G.' in the gap and obtain payment. It was held that the collecting bank was liable to the plaintiffs in conversion, but the plaintiff's damages were reduced by 10% on account of their contributory negligence. This is now specifically provided for under s. 47 of the Banking Act 1979 (see also *Slingsby v District Bank Ltd* [1932] 1 KB 544).

The question whether a customer owes to his bank a duty to take reasonable precautions in the conduct of his business so as to prevent cheques being presented to the bank for payment was considered by the Judicial Committee of the Privy Council in *Tai Hing Cotton Mill Ltd* v *Liu Chong Hing Bank Ltd* [1986] AC 80. In this case, a dishonest clerk forged, over a period of six years, the signatures of his employer and in total obtained a sum of $HK5.5 million from his employer's account. The company did not check its monthly bank statements, and the first-instance judge described the company's system of internal financial control as inadequate. Nevertheless, the Privy Council held that the company was not required to check its bank statements nor to operate a system of internal control to prevent fraud, that is, the customer was not, in the absence of any knowledge of the forgeries, estopped from asserting that the account was wrongfully debited. It follows from this case that, in the absence of a clear and unambiguous contractual provision, there is no duty on the customer to examine with reasonable care periodic statements received from his bank. Such a new term would require clear notice to be given to the customer and would obviously have to be supported by consideration moving from the bank to the customer.

The *Tai Hing* case represents judicial recognition of the legal position of the banks with regard to monthly bank statements. The other side of the coin is where the monthly statement is inaccurate. Obviously, the bank is under a duty to maintain a proper account, so if the customer has relied upon a misleading statement as to the state of his account and has materially changed his position on the strength of this statement, the bank will be prevented from reclaiming the money wrongly credited to the customer. Mere alteration of position by, for example, spending the money is not sufficient to establish the estoppel; rather, it must be shown that the circumstances are such as to make it inequitable for him to be compelled to repay the amount credited. Thus in *United Overseas Bank* v *Jiwani* [1976] 1 WLR 964, the bank was able to recover money wrongly credited to the customer's account even though part of it had been spent in the purchase of a hotel because, it was established, he did not rely upon the representation of the bank and would have bought the hotel in any case.

Termination of the customer-banker relationship The relationship will automatically be terminated in accordance with the terms of the contract. In the case of an ordinary current account where the sum is repayable on demand, the customer can terminate the relationship when he chooses simply by demanding repayment and closing the account. On the other hand, a bank is not entitled to close a customer's account without giving reasonable notice so as to allow him to rearrange his affairs (*Prosperity Ltd* v *Lloyds Bank Ltd* (1923) 39 TLR 372). The question of what constitutes reasonable notice is one of fact and must at least be a sufficient time to allow payments made by or to the order of the customer in the collection process to be honoured (see *Joachimson* v *Swiss Bank Corpn* [1921] 3 KB 110). Lastly, since the banker-customer relationship is a personal one, it will be terminated by the death or bankruptcy of the customer, or by the liquidation of a corporate customer, or, as has been graphically illustrated in the BCCI débâcle, by the liquidation of the bank.

A closely allied issue to the termination of the banker-customer relationship is that of resolution of disputes. Besides litigation, an alternative has been provided through the banking ombudsman scheme which has become of increasing importance in dispute resolution during recent years where high interest rates and the charging policy of banks have provoked considerable consternation among commercial and private customers of banks. The ombudsman has wide powers to investigate complaints and he can seek ways to promote a settlement, including the payment of an award. To date, the greatest level of complaint is associated with ATM disputes and allegations of wrongful debiting of accounts. Between 1985 and 1990 there have been 2,000 ATM complaints which constitute an average of 12% of all complaints made. However, this figure should be seen within the context of 3 million undisputed ATM transactions carried out *each day*. The main criticism of the banking ombudsman scheme is that it is wholly voluntary and claims over £100,000 are excluded entirely from the scheme. Furthermore, the banking ombudsman has different functions from the building society ombudsman despite the similarity of the services provided. The building society ombudsman scheme was created under part IX of the Building Societies Act 1986, the major difference in function being that the building society ombudsman has no power to make binding awards.

LEGAL REGULATION OF CHEQUES

The cheque represents a conflict of form and fiction; despite the fact that it is a bill of exchange, in practice, it is rarely negotiated except in the rare case where a cheque is drawn in favour of a person with no bank account. The convenience of a cheque is that it is treated as being equivalent to cash (see *D and C Builders Ltd* v *Rees* [1966] 2 QB 617). Indeed, recommendation 7(7) made by the Jack committee, 1989, was that the cheque should be recognised as a non-transferable instrument, but this was rejected in the White Paper on *Banking Law and Services* (1990), para. 5.3, on the basis that it could cause more uncertainty, and what was called for in the alternative was greater clarification of the law relating to cheques.

One of the major uncertainties pertaining to the law of cheques generally relates to the effect of crossings on cheques. Section 76 of the Bills of Exchange Act 1882 provides that a cheque may be 'crossed generally' if it bears two transverse parallel lines between which may be added 'and Co' or 'not negotiable'. Section 76 also permits a cheque to be 'crossed specially' which means that it bears the name of a bank; that is, the cheque may only be presented for payment through the bank named in the crossing. The crossing 'Not negotiable' is used more widely than 'and company' which serves no purpose today. The effect of 'Not negotiable' does not prevent transfer of the cheque; rather, if the cheque is transferred, the transferee can acquire no better title than the transferor had (s. 81 of the Bills of Exchange Act 1882).

Banks which ignore a crossing do so at their peril. Section 79(2) provides that if such payment is made in a non-specified way, and it transpires that the money was not paid to the true owner of the cheque, this constitutes conversion and the bank will have to pay the true owner the money due on the cheque. Nevertheless, a defence is provided for the bank under s. 79(2) where it pays in good faith and without negligence, other than to a bank (or specified bank) and the cheque presented for payment appears to be an uncrossed cheque. Thus, where there is a non-apparent alteration to the crossing, the bank may pay in accordance with the apparent tenor of the cheque. On the other hand, the general rule is that an unauthorised alteration of a crossing is a material alteration which renders the cheque unenforceable against prior parties who have not consented to the alteration. It is otherwise where the alteration cannot prejudice prior parties, such as the holder crossing an uncrossed cheque.

Under the Cheques Act 1992 which inserts s. 81A into the Bills of Exchange Act 1882, a crossing containing the words 'account payee' or 'account payee only' has the effect of rendering the cheque non-transferable. Under this new system a collecting bank must, presumably, refuse to collect a cheque rendered non-negotiable by the addition of these words. This is unfortunate because under the old law, a cheque so crossed could be collected for a person other than the named payee, for instance, for the account of his spouse, if an explanation was forthcoming. In effect, the negotiability of the cheque has been compromised by the Cheques Act 1992. This has been achieved without conferring on the customer defences significantly more effective than those under the old law. The previous legal position was that the words were held to constitute a warning to the collecting bank that the instrument should not be collected for an account other than the named payee, so if it did collect it, the bank did so at its own risk (see *Universal Guarantee Pty Ltd* v *National Bank of Australasia Ltd* [1965] 1 WLR 691).

The clearing system is at the heart of the cheque as a payment mechanism. Most cheques are presented through the general clearing system which handles bulk paper-based payment orders. A separate clearing system operates for high-value orders so that the Clearing House Automated Payment System (CHAPS), as an electronic system, allows same-day settlement of individual orders to pay sums in excess of £10,000. The process of clearing consists of the payee paying in the cheque to any bank for collection since the banks, via the Bank Giro system, have agreed to act as each other's agents for collection. The customer's account is then credited and the cheque is sent to the bank's clearing department for collection. It is then sent to the clearing department of the drawee bank where it is processed by computer using the magnetic ink on each cheque. Settlement or otherwise is made between the drawer and payee's bank and is effected by a transfer, as part of a global transaction, between the accounts of the two banks at the Bank of England.

The actual presentation of the cheque is when it is sent to the drawer's bank where the account is held. It is at this stage that the decision is taken whether or not to honour the cheque (*Barclays Bank plc* v *Bank of England* [1985] 1 All ER 385). All in all, the clearing process takes at least three days because the requirement in s. 43 of the Bills of Exchange Act 1882 that the cheque be presented for payment at the place where it is drawn prevents electronic presentation of cheques. This is unduly archaic which led the White Paper on *Banking Law and Services* (1990), to propose introduction of amending legislation in this regard so as to remove the need for physical presentation. The effect of truncation (electronic presentation) is that the paying bank will not be able to examine the signature and determine whether or not it is a forgery.

The Jack committee, 1989, noted that the cheque remains, after cash, the most commonly used mechanism for making payment to third parties. The sheer volume of the clearing process has progressively risen during the 20th century. This has tended to highlight the dilemmas which exist, namely, a bank which exceeds its customer's mandate has no general right to debit the account, but it may incur liability for wrongful dishonour if it dishonours a cheque drawn on it. Furthermore, a bank which pays or collects a cheque for someone other than a true owner may incur liability on it, that is, a holder in due course, or a payee, or endorsee of it with title (see chapter 9). However, a number of defences are available to paying and collecting banks which, in large measure, protect the banks from liability.

The paying bank and true owners
It is sometimes maintained that a bank can be exposed to double liability, that is, by being liable to the true owner in conversion and at the same time being unable to debit the customer's account. This approach is fallacious because where a bill is payable to bearer, although liability may be outstanding as regards the true owner, the bank's payment will be a payment in due course so discharging the drawer, thereby enabling the bank to debit his account. Where the cheque is payable to order and there has been a forgery of an essential endorsement, the bank may not debit the customer's account but, at the same time, will incur liability to the true owner because there has been no payment in due course, so the cheque will remain enforceable.

Even though liability for breach of the customer's mandate or for conversion is strict, a number of defences are available to the paying bank.

Common law defences We have already examined (see pp. 203–4) the scope of the estoppel doctrine. The customer's duty of care, in the absence of an express contractual provision to the contrary, is an extremely limited one (*Tai Hing Cotton Mill Ltd* v *Liu Chong Hing Bank Ltd* [1986] AC 80 above). Such an approach has recently been confirmed in the context of travellers' cheques (see below) where it was held in *El Awadi* v *Bank of Credit and Commerce International SA Ltd* [1990] 1 QB 606 that there is no implied contractual or tortious duty of care which requires a customer who buys travellers' cheques to take care of them.

Restitutionary principles apply where a bank makes a payment which discharges its customer of liability notwithstanding absence of mandate. In this situation, the bank can be subrogated to the rights of the holder of the cheque whose claim its payment extinguishes, otherwise the customer would be unjustly enriched. A closely allied issue is the recovery by the bank of money paid by mistake into its customer's account. On the other hand, where a bank pays on a cheque after receiving instructions not to pay, it was held in *Barclays Bank Ltd v W.J. Simms Son and Cooke (Southern) Ltd* [1980] QB 677 that a restitutionary claim may fail if payment is made for good consideration and does discharge a debt owed to the payee by the payer. Paying in breach of mandate, in the absence of notification to the payee, operates as payment to extinguish liability for the simple reason that the bank has apparent authority to pay and the payee may have relied upon this. In this situation, the bank will be subrogated to the rights of the payee against the drawer so entitling the bank to debit its customer's account (compare a mistaken payment in a credit factoring context see pp. 246–7).

Statutory defences These have developed in a somewhat piecemeal fashion and there is considerable overlap between the statutory provisions protecting the paying banker. The first provision is s. 60 of the Bills of Exchange Act 1882 which was framed to relieve the paying banker who had paid a *cheque* (as distinct from any other kind of bill) from further liability to the true owner of a cheque where, on the cheque, there has been a forgery of an essential endorsement, or one has been made without authority. The protection afforded to the banker requires the commercial reality of the banking context to be addressed, namely, a bank will pay upon presentation of millions of cheques each year and it is physically impossible to make enquiries as to the validity of prior endorsements. Section 60 applies only if the cheque is still a valid negotiable instrument so it will not apply if the cheque is materially altered, and neither are irregular endorsements covered. Furthermore, although payment is presumed to have been made in good faith, more difficulty is posed by the requirement that payment must be made in the ordinary course of business. There is some controversy as to whether s. 60 applies where the paying banker has been negligent (see *Carpenters' Co. v British Mutual Banking Co. Ltd* [1938] 1 KB 511), although there is no doubt that payment of a large sum in cash over the counter will not be in the ordinary course of business if there are circumstances giving rise to suspicion, for example, relating to the demeanour and appearance of the claimant (see *Bank of England v Vagliano Brothers* [1891] AC 107). It is probable that s. 60 will not apply where payment is made following truncation, that is, data electronically transmitted to allow payment of a cheque to the payee's account with simultaneous debit of the drawer's account (see above p. 205). Where the requirements of the section are fulfilled, the paying banker is deemed to have paid the bill in due course.

As an alternative to s. 60, the bank may rely upon the defence provided by s. 80 of the 1882 Act which only applies to crossed cheques. The problem faced by the paying bank is that it cannot be certain that the money it is paying to the collecting bank is being collected for the true owner. In an attempt to address this problem, s. 80 provides that where a bank pays a crossed cheque in accordance with the crossing, provided it acts in good faith and without negligence it cannot be liable to the true owner if the payment was in fact made to someone else. It follows that if a bank is absolved from liability to the true owner by virtue of s. 80, the drawer also ceases to be liable to the true owner provided that the cheque had, at some point of time, come into the hands of the payee.

There is some uncertainty as to whether there is a difference between the requirement in s. 60 that the paying bank should act in the ordinary course of business and that in s. 80 that it should act without negligence. A distinction is sometimes made between 'negligence' and 'ordinary course of business'. In *Carpenters' Co.* v *British Mutual Banking Co. Ltd* [1938] 1 KB 511, Greer LJ held that payment would not be made in the ordinary course of business if the banker acted negligently, but a contrary view was taken by Slesser and Mackinnon LJJ in that case. Given the large measure of overlap between s. 60 and s. 80, it is surprising that they depend upon different criteria. It is for this reason that the government in its White Paper (1990) accepted recommendation 7(5) of the Jack committee 1989 and proposed to introduce legislation removing the requirement that the bank act in the 'ordinary course of business' and that *all* the statutory defences, including s. 1 of the Cheques Act 1957 (below), be available where the banker had acted 'in good faith and without negligence', which is the language employed by s. 80 of the Bills of Exchange Act 1882.

A further protection is provided for the bank in s. 1 of the Cheques Act 1957, the principal purpose of which was to remove the need for endorsement. Protection is extended to certain instruments analogous to cheques, for example, interest and dividend warrants, bankers' drafts and also 'cheques' made payable to cash. The section provides that where a paying bank has acted in good faith and in the ordinary course of business in paying an order cheque, the cheque is validly discharged by payment, even though there is an absence of or irregularity of an endorsement. Section 1 does not apply if a bank pays a cheque to a person who is not the original payee and it is the case that the endorsement of the original payee or any other prior endorser is missing or irregular. In this situation, the bank can only rely on ss. 60 and 80 of the Bills of Exchange Act 1882. Despite the fact that the Cheques Act 1957 was intended to remove the need for endorsements, a circular issued by the Committee of London Clearing Bankers in 1957 lays down principles of good banking practice and this requires endorsement where a cheque is presented for cash payment, or where the cheque has a receipt form attached. Non-compliance with this circular of good practice would, in all probability, be regarded as not acting in the ordinary course of business and so would be unprotected by s. 1.

Liability of the collecting bank
A bank which collects payment of a valid cheque for anyone other than its true owner can be sued in conversion or for money had and received by the true owner. Liability in both actions is strict, and the measure of damages payable

to the true owner is the face value of the cheque in conversion, or the proceeds of the cheque in an action for money had and received. In certain respects, liability based upon the face of the cheque is somewhat anomalous because it fails to address the possibility that the cheque might not have been honoured on presentation as an aspect of commercial risk.

The Bills of Exchange Act 1882 recognised in s. 82 the impracticability of a bank being required to verify its customer's title to a cheque before collecting it. In this respect, the common law strict position was modified by a statutory defence which has been repealed and replaced by s. 4(1) of the Cheques Act 1957. This provides that:

Where a banker in good faith and without negligence—
    (a) receives payment for a customer of an instrument to which this section applies; or
    (b) having credited a customer's account with the amount of such an instrument, receives payment thereof for himself;
and the customer has no title, or a defective title to the instrument, the banker does not incur any liability to the true owner of the instrument by reason only of having received payment thereof.

This section affords protection to a collecting bank in relation to cheques, bankers' drafts and also 'cheques' made payable to cash which are not bills because no payee is named.

Section 4 of the Cheques Act 1957 only applies where the collecting bank is both an agent for collection and a holder for value it receives for itself. There are three typical scenarios: first, where the bank exchanges an uncleared cheque for cash; second, where the customer with the consent of the bank draws against the cheque before clearance; third, where the bank has a lien on the uncleared cheque, for example, to secure an existing overdraft. Where the bank does not collect the cheque for itself, it is only protected if it collects for a customer. The word 'customer' is not defined in either the 1957 or the 1882 Act but it must include a person who has opened an account with the bank, for example, a deposit account (*Great Western Railway Co. v London and County Banking Co. Ltd* [1901] AC 414). The mere performance for a person of some casual service by a banker, even if it is on a regular basis, is not sufficient to make that person a customer although it is rare, nowadays, for banks to collect cheques other than for customers. If the word 'customer' in s. 4 means only a customer of the banker who receives payment or who credits the account, this will threaten mutual arrangements between banks, that is, where banks collect cheques for each other unless the collecting bank could be treated as agent for the crediting bank and, therefore, entitled to the protection afforded to its principal.

The protection afforded to the collecting bank under s. 4 presupposes that it acted in good faith and without negligence. The question of negligence is one of fact and is determined by whether there has been a breach of duty owed to the true owner. In general, negligence is judged by the standards of ordinary reasonable banking practice so that in *Lloyds Bank Ltd v E.B. Savory and Co.* [1933] AC 201, Lord Warrington held at p. 221:

The standard by which the absence, or otherwise, of negligence is to be determined must in my opinion be ascertained by reference to the practice of reasonable men carrying on the business of bankers, and endeavouring to do so in such a manner as may be calculated to protect themselves and others against fraud.

See also *Commissioners of Taxation* v *English, Scottish and Australian Bank Ltd* [1920] AC 683. It is unlikely that the court will hold an established banking practice to be negligent and, more recently, in *Marfani and Co. Ltd* v *Midland Bank Ltd* [1968] 1 WLR 956, Diplock LJ focused upon foreseeability based upon the facts which ought to have been known to the banker, that is, depending upon *current* banking practice what inquiries should the bank have made, and which facts should cause the bank to reasonably suspect that the customer was not the true owner. It is clear from this that bankers are not required to adopt a microscopic examination of each customer's account, not least because this would render current banking impracticable. For the sake of convenience, the case law may be subdivided as follows: the circumstances surrounding the manner in which the cheque is drawn or paid in; the manner in which the customer's account is opened. It should be noted that where a bank is unable to rely on the statutory defence provided by s. 4, it may raise the contributory negligence of the true owner as a partial defence to a claim (see s. 47 of the Banking Act 1987).

The circumstances surrounding the manner in which the cheque is paid in The typical scenario concerns misappropriation by employees, agents or other fiduciaries. It is important to note that the bank's negligence in these circumstances is not an absolute one but consists, rather, of the bank's failure to enquire where the circumstances should have put the bank on enquiry. Thus, it has been held that a bank is negligent if it collects cheques, without enquiry, where a salesman of a firm has endorsed by per pro endorsements a number of cheques payable to the firm and arranged for them to be credited to his private account (*Bissell and Co.* v *Fox Bros and Co.* (1884) 53 LT 193); or where the owner of a company endorsed on behalf of the company a number of cheques payable to the company and paid them into his own private account (*A.L. Underwood Ltd* v *Bank of Liverpool and Martins* [1924] 1 KB 775).

The conduct of the account may also be relevant to the question of the bank's negligence. The typical situation referred to is where a number of cheques drawn payable to a third party purporting to be endorsed are paid in, which is followed by quick withdrawal of the proceeds (see *Baker* v *Barclays Bank Ltd* [1955] 1 WLR 822). This situation should certainly put the bank on enquiry. In this regard, the past banking history of the customer may be relevant, but this must be combined with other suspicious circumstances in order to render the bank liable (see *Motor Traders' Guarantee Corpn Ltd* v *Midland Bank Ltd* [1937] 4 All ER 90).

Opening the account A failure to make proper enquiries concerning a new customer who opens an account may mean that the banker will be negligent in collecting the cheque for that customer because the purpose of opening the new account may be to facilitate fraud (see *Marfani and Co. Ltd* v *Midland Bank Ltd* [1968] 1 WLR 956). Current banking practice will be relevant here. Thus in *Lloyds Bank Ltd* v *E.B. Savory and Co.* [1933] AC 201, a bank was held to be liable in negligence since it failed to enquire as to the name of the new customer's husband's employer. It is unlikely that such an approach coheres with modern-day banking practice and it would, in any case, probably constitute unlawful discrimination merely to require women to state their husband's/partner's employment. It is impracticable to require such information because people move jobs more frequently today and besides, as Harman LJ put it in *Orbit Mining and Trading Co. Ltd* v *Westminster Bank Ltd* [1963] 1 QB 794 at p. 825: 'It cannot at any rate be the duty of the bank continually to keep itself up to date as to the identity of the customer's employer'.

There is no doubt that the bank must exercise reasonable care to establish the good faith of a customer when opening a new account. The taking up of references would appear to constitute an obvious precaution but, again, these can be subject to manipulation (see, for example, *Lumsden and Co.* v *London Trustee Savings Bank* [1971] 1 Lloyd's Rep 114). The Jack committee (1989) in its report recommended at para. 6.26 that a code of best banking practice should require banks to follow satisfactory procedures on opening accounts to enable them to determine the identity of new customers, including obtaining references. The banks' code of practice recommends that, wherever possible, the bank should require solid evidence of identity, for example, a passport or a full driving licence.

OTHER PAPER INSTRUMENTS

Promissory notes

A promissory note is an unconditional promise made in writing by one person to another signed by the maker engaging to pay, on demand, or at a fixed or determinable future time, a sum certain in money to, or to the order of a specified person or to bearer (s. 83(1) of the Bills of Exchange Act 1882). A mere acknowledgement of a debt such as an IOU is not a promissory note and does not constitute an instrument at all. Whilst a promissory note is not a bill of exchange, it does, nevertheless, share many of the characteristics of a bill of exchange and the provisions of the Bills of Exchange Act 1882 apply (ss. 83 to 89) with the necessary modifications. These modifications relate to the fact that there is no acceptor, so the provisions as to presentment for acceptance and also acceptance itself do not apply. The rules as to liabilities and estoppel of the maker mirror the law on bills (s. 88), whilst by virtue of s. 89(1) and (2) the endorser of a promissory note accepts the same duties and liabilities as an endorser of a bill under s. 55(2).

Promissory notes, other than bank notes, are not now widely used but they do exist, especially in the context of export credits.

Travellers' cheques

It is unlikely that a traveller's cheque can be categorised as a bill of exchange because the order or promise to pay is conditional upon the signatures on the face of the traveller's cheque (two in all) corresponding with each other (s. 3(1) of the Bills of Exchange Act 1882). However, as a matter of commercial usage, travellers' cheques are treated as being negotiable even though they are not technically bills of exchange; travellers' cheques are transferred by endorsement or delivery depending upon the manner in which they are drawn, and a transferee who qualifies as a holder in due course can take free of the underlying equities (see pp. 199–201). This approach must be correct, as a matter of principle, because a person to whom the traveller's cheque is transferred can only safeguard himself against fraud by checking the two signatures' correspondence, that is, the traveller is required to sign the cheques once when collecting them from the bank and then to countersign them when issuing them to the payee. This loss will, in the absence of an express contractual provision to the contrary with the traveller, normally fall on the bank which coheres with the commercial purpose of such travellers' cheques to secure the traveller against loss. The bank charges for this in its commission and can spread the risk of loss.

The rights of the traveller against the issuing bank are determined as an aspect of contract. Thus, in *Braithwaite* v *Thomas Cook Travellers' Cheques Ltd* [1989] QB 553, the contract provided that the right of refund on the occurrence of theft was conditional upon the traveller having properly safeguarded against theft or loss. In this case, the traveller lost the cheques or they were stolen when he was drunk and, at that time, he was carrying them in an unsigned state in a plastic bag. In contrast, there was no such contractual provision in *El Awadi* v *Bank of Credit and Commerce International SA Ltd* [1990] 1 QB 606, and it was held that the traveller was entitled to a refund even though the cheques were stolen as a result of his negligence. A material factor which influenced the decision in this case was that the (now) notorious bank had, in its advertising material, emphasised the security advantages of travellers' cheques over cash and the fact that as the travellers' cheques had not been countersigned, the bank could protect itself against loss by checking that the signatures and countersignatures matched.

PAPERLESS PAYMENT ORDERS

The Bank Giro System

Most giro payments are made through the Clearing House Automated Payment System (CHAPS). This is an electronic system where the payer's bank prepares a computer tape containing details of payments to be made on a particular day. The practical significance is in the case of standing orders initiated by the drawer to make payments to a number of different payees, or direct debits which are initiated by the payee, in that he obtains an authority from the payer to order the payer's bank to pay such sums as the payee may demand from time to time. It is not necessary in the giro system for the payee bank to present any instrument, thereby cutting down the possibility of fraud or theft, except in the case of direct debits where the payee may demand an unauthorised amount. Nevertheless, the general rule still applies: the paying and collecting banks act as agents for their respective customers, and the payer's bank can only debit his account if it acts in accordance with the mandate laid down in the giro order which is revocable until payment is complete. There are uncertainties as to what constitutes completion in this context, and the Jack committee (1989) recommended at para. 12(2) that new legislation should define the time of completion of payment.

Electronic fund transfers
Electronic funds transfer (EFT) systems is the generic term to describe the technological advances which enable the banking process (payment and collecting function) to be effectuated by electronic means. The customer may provide his mandate to pay electronically, principally through automated teller machines (ATMs) and also through electronic funds transfer at point of sale (EFTPOS) systems which are used for payment for goods and services. The legal problems raised by these systems were considered by the Jack committee (1989). It is worth noting that, in contrast to credit cards, there is little statutory regulation of such systems, and the legal regime is based almost entirely upon contract. Most of the complaints between customers and their banks or building societies which are dealt with by the ombudsmen have been concerned with ATMs. It is significant that in their various reports the ombudsmen have not, in the main, struck down the contractual provisions relating to ATMs on the basis that they breach the reasonableness test encapsulated in ss. 3 and 11 of and sch. 2 to the Unfair Contract Terms Act 1977. Between 1985 and 1990 ATMs have consistently topped the complaints to the banking ombudsman. In 1991, for the first time, complaints about ATMs slipped down to third place, outdone by complaints about charges and interest and about lending policies. However, in 1991 also cheque volumes fell for the first time since 1945 and the Association for Payment Clearing Systems estimate that by 1996 debit card use will overtake cheque volumes.

One of the main fears of statutory regulation of electronic banking is that the law may tend towards technological Ludditism. It is for this reason that the Jack committee (1989) recommended at para. 9:30 for minimum statutory regulation supplemented by a code of best practice. Furthermore, it was recognised that the use of ATM and EFT cards differs from that of credit cards, and it was recommended at para. 10:10 where either the bank or customer can be shown to have been guilty of gross negligence, that party should be liable for the full amount of loss. The typical scenario envisaged is where the customer writes his personal identification number (PIN) on the back of his card. The real issue with EFTs is the way in which the law can regulate prospectively new technology. In this respect, the Jack committee recommended that the banks themselves should constantly monitor new technology which could improve security and privacy of especially PIN numbers.

The new code of banking practice which was produced in the wake of the Jack committee report took effect in March 1992. In large measure, the code incorporates a wide range of safeguards for consumers. The main features of the code are as follows:

(a) The onus is transferred from the customer to banks and building societies to prove their case in a dispute about withdrawals from ATMs.

(b) Strict confidentiality with banks and building societies regarding the release of account details unless legally required to do so.

(c) Charges for basic account services to be published.

(d) Interest rates to be clearly notified to customers, including the way interest is calculated and when it will be charged.

(e) Banks and building societies bear all the losses when a card is not received by a customer and is misused.

(f) A limit of £50 to customer liability for losses incurred on a missing card.

It is important to emphasise that these provisions represent minimum standards for the financial institutions, and some banks have agreed even tougher codes of practice.

ELEVEN
Credit factoring and the securitisation of receivables

LATE PAYMENT OF DEBTS

A simple source of short-term funding for companies is the old-fashioned trade credit, that is, delaying payment on liquidated debts. This is a widespread and established phenomenon so that, for example, in 1986, the Forum of Private Businesses announced that an amount of £57 billion was owed to their 11,000 members by slow payers and that it was leading a campaign for legislation to give the right to interest. It is significant that the Law Commission working paper, *Interest* (No. 66, 1976), pointed out that the general rule in Europe is that withholding a debt entitled the creditor to interest. The European Commission in the proposed Terms of Payment Directive, which is based upon German legislation, makes late-paying companies liable for the extra costs that delayed payments cause their suppliers. Under the German system, creditor firms have the right to charge interest on overdue payments and the extra expenses immediately after the first formal reminder is sent out. In England, the Law Commission report, *Interest* (Cmnd 7229, 1978), concluded that the existing law does not provide adequate means of redress for the creditor who is kept out of his money by his debtor and, accordingly, recommended the introduction of statutory interest.

The business dilemma posed by late payment was illustrated in the CBI survey of small and medium-sized businesses, *Late Payment of Trade Debts* (London, 1991). The conclusions derived from this survey are as follows:

(a) Late payment of bills is causing major or significant problems for a majority of businesses, endangering the survival of nearly 20 per cent of the survey group of over 400 small and medium-sized companies.

(b) Many small and medium-sized firms acknowledge that *they* pay their own bills late which, in turn, reflects the knock-on effect of repayment through the customer-supplier chain.

(c) The effect on cash flow is the most significant factor for smaller businesses, although the loss of management time chasing unpaid bills was also a major concern.

(d) Few small businesses include an interest clause in their contracts mainly because of the ill feeling attendant with enforcement.

(e) A majority of companies feel inhibited about taking a strong line with overdue bills on the basis that it would affect continued commercial intercourse.

An important finding from the above CBI report was that a large majority of small and medium-sized businesses believe that a statutory right to interest on outstanding debts would make a real difference to the speed with which bills are paid.

The late payments issue was transformed in the 1992 Budget from being a concern of the small business lobby to a mainstream political issue. Chancellor Lamont in his 1992 Budget announced measures aimed at speeding up the settlement of invoices, but stopped short of legislation providing for a statutory right to interest. Legislation has been introduced with threefold objectives: first, requiring large companies to state in their annual report and accounts how quickly they pay their bills; second, simplifying procedures dealing with small claims and debt recovery cases in the courts, for example, dispensing with preliminary hearings in small claims cases; third, by making prime contractors to government departments include a clause in their agreements with subcontractors to pay them promptly within 30 days. It is worth noting that both the main opposition political parties during the general election campaign of 1992 in the UK promised, in their respective manifestos, to give businesses the automatic right to interest on overdue debts through the introduction of legislation.

In the absence of legislative initiative in this area, the basic common law rule confirmed in *President of India* v *Lips Maritime Corporation* [1988] AC 395 is that a creditor cannot, without the benefit of an express or implied interest payment clause in the contract, recover damages for late payment of a debt. However, in this respect it is important to identify different categories of debt: first, a debt paid late but before proceedings are commenced; secondly, a debt paid late but after proceedings are commenced; thirdly, a debt paid late after proceedings are commenced but at the time of judgment (see *President of India* v *La Pintada Compania Navigacion SA* [1985] AC 104). Statutory relief under the Administration of Justice Act 1982 is available at the discretion of the court with respect to the last two categories. This is not the case with regard to the first category following the decision in *London, Chatham and Dover Railway Co.* v *South Eastern Railway Co.* [1893] AC 429, which has meant that a creditor has been unable to recover interest on late payments as general damages from the defaulting payer. Clearly, Lord Herschell LC came to his conclusion reluctantly in view of the merits, which he identified as follows at p. 437:

> ... when money is owing from one party to another and that other is driven to have recourse to legal proceedings in order to recover the amount due to

him, the party who is wrongfully withholding the money from the other ought not in justice to benefit by having that money in his possession and enjoying the use of it, when the money ought to be in the possession of the other party who is entitled to its use.

It is odd that no reference was made in the House of Lords to *Hadley* v *Baxendale* (1854) 9 Exch 341, and the problem was not generally seen in the light of the law relating to breach of contract. Despite this, significant judicial inroads have been made into *London, Chatham and Dover Railway Co.* v *South Eastern Railway Co.* so that in *Trans Trust SPRL* v *Danubian Trading Co. Ltd* [1952] 2 QB 297, Denning LJ stated at p. 306:

> ... when the circumstances are such that there is a special loss foreseeable at the time of the contract as the consequence of non payment, then I think such loss may well be recoverable.

It would seem, therefore, that interest payment may not be too remote. This approach was confirmed in *Wadsworth* v *Lydall* [1981] 1 WLR 598 where Brightman LJ held at p. 603:

> In my view the court is not so constrained by the decision of the House of Lords [in *London, Chatham and Dover Railway Co.* v *South Eastern Railway Co.*].... The House was concerned only with a claim for interest by way of general damages. If a plaintiff ... can prove that he has suffered special damage ... and such damage is not too remote on the principle of *Hadley* v *Baxendale* (1854) 9 Exch 341, I can see no logical reason why such special damage should be irrecoverable.

As a matter of consistency, one could argue that, if interest can be claimed under the second limb of damages under the *Hadley* v *Baxendale* rule then it should also be recoverable under the first limb, namely, where damages are such 'as may fairly and reasonable be considered as arising naturally' from the breach.

There is no doubt that long delays in payment can be an inhibiting element for the business prospects of a firm. If one were to take a simple example of a company with an annual sales turnover of £1 million and with an average debt turnover of five times per year (an average payment time of 73 days); if the outstanding debt at any one time involved £200,000 then this would at 10 per cent interest cost the company £20,000 in interest alone per annum, whereas, if these debts were collected just one week earlier, a saving of £2,000 per annum in interest charges would be achieved and the £200,000 previously tied up would be released. There are often liquidity concerns attendant with the slower capital turnover rate caused by the supply of credit and this has been explained by Gilbert, T.H., 'Financing and Factoring Accounts Receivable', (1952) 33 *Harvard Business Review*, at p. 39:

> Our worried businessman's balance sheet may show quite a favourable ratio of current assets to current liabilities. His dificulty is that his current assets

consist almost entirely of ever-increasing accounts receivable and inventories and ever-decreasing liquid working capital. Thus his assets may be 'quick' in accounting parlance, but for the purpose of building up his business they are as frozen as the polar icecap. As fast as current receivables are paid, new ones take their place; and the more the business expands the deeper they freeze.

The velocity of cash flow is likely to become sluggish unless payment is speeded up, and this is often achieved through the intervention of a third party who specialises in debt collection and the financing of receivables. Credit factoring and invoice discounting are the mechanisms employed in this context.

Invoice discounting
This is where the financing institution is concerned solely with the provision of finance, that is, an agreed percentage (typically 80 per cent) of the current sales invoices value so as to provide instant working capital. Essentially, this is a cash-flow service and is, more often than not, confidential in the sense that the financing institution never normally contacts its client's customers. This can be a risky business for the invoice discounter because he is not closely involved in his client's affairs. Thus, clients may be tempted to send in invoices before the goods are shipped, create completely bogus 'fresh air' invoices, or hang on to customer payments which should have been passed on to the invoice discounter.

Credit factoring
This type of agreement provides for a continuing relationship between a financier and its client, whereby the factoring company undertakes to purchase the entire book debts of the client at the end of the agreed period. Factoring is almost invariably carried out by way of outright sale of receivables, which avoids the need to register an assignment of receivables as a charge on book debts under s. 396 of the Companies Act 1985 (as amended). Factoring may be without recourse or with recourse to the client if its customer defaults. In the case of the latter, the sale versus form issue encountered in other contexts discussed in the course of this book is highly relevant (see pp. 346–54). The mere fact that there is a right of recourse should not affect the categorisation of the transaction as a sale because the assignor's liability is not to repay an advance but rather to pay a sum in discharge of a recourse obligation.

In addition to the financing aspect of the relationship, factoring is concerned with the provision of a number of other services. Undoubtedly, the service element will help to ensure that the factoring industry will still have an important role to play even if the payment performance of British business improves in the light of the new initiatives introduced in the 1992 Budget.

An accounting function Once a client has entered into an agreement with the factoring company, the latter may undertake to take over all the bookkeeping for the client. In this way, the client enjoys the economies of scale associated with a financing institution. It is significant that a condition of the factoring agreement for clients with a turnover of less than £300,000 per annum is often that the sales ledger administration is taken over by the factoring company. In large measure, this practice will ensure the continuity of this particular service element as, essentially, a policing function for the credit factoring company. However, the development of microcomputers and accountancy programs to run the sales ledger operation of companies may threaten this service element in the factoring arrangement, but the certainty of cash flow will continue to be attractive.

A credit control function Often the factoring company undertakes to advise the client whether existing or potential customers are bad debts risks. This will be accompanied with a viewdata facility showing details of funds available, payments received, and customer information. In addition, the factoring company will take on board a debt-collecting function and simply by being more efficient in handling invoices and reminder notices, this can increase velocity of cash flow in a company typically by up to 20 per cent. The factoring company bears no relation to the old debt-collectors who used to buy debts at a fraction of the price and exert strong-arm pressure on debtors. In contrast, the factoring company will not enforce a debt by legal action without consulting its client first so as to ensure that the *business* logic of this legal action is also fully considered.

Profile of clients suitable for credit factoring functions It is unlikely that very big companies, in terms of turnover, will benefit from credit factoring simply because such a company will be able to provide for its own service functions. Few companies with an annual turnover of over £5 million per annum factor their book debts. The typical factoring scenario involves concerns with a turnover of over £100,000 where the customers (representing the invoices generated) are well spread with ideally no single customer representing more than 30 per cent of the book debts. An insufficient profit is made on smaller turnovers to justify the cost of factoring, although an exception may be made in respect of smaller turnovers where the client shows good growth potential, and a factor may be prepared to give support for a relatively low immediate return in anticipation of improved profitability through later growth. Encouraged by incentives and technological developments, an increasing number of cash-hungry firms are starting up which factors cannot afford to ignore, so the idea of an 'ideal' client may die.

The sectoral breakdown provided by the Association of British Factors and Distributors in 1990 shows that manufacturing remains the greatest user of factoring, whilst distributing services also having a significant (over 33 per cent) share. Factoring and invoice discounting have enjoyed an average of over 20 per cent growth in total sales volume for each year during the 1980s which can, therefore, be described as the decade of factoring. Thus, starting from a low base of £2 billion in 1980, the total business for factoring and discounting rose to £14 billion by 1990 which demonstrates the continued stability and underlying strength of the industry. It is not surprising to note that one recent trend from, especially, 1989 onwards has been the increase in value of bad debts absorbed by factoring companies on behalf of their clients reflecting, of course, the general adverse economic circumstances.

The principal varieties of factoring

There are different types of factoring ranging from a whole-turnover basis to block discounting where the factoring company, from time to time, merely purchases a block of existing debts. The sale of debts may be with recourse, or without recourse as in the case of 'approved' accounts. Some debts will initially be ineligible for discounting, that is, those debts which before factoring began were in excess of reasonable limits of credit. The process of investigation involves the factoring company assessing the credit standing of a potential client's trade debts, and a 'perfect client' would be one with few unfactorable debts such as conditional sales or debts subject to a charge.

The raw mechanism of the factoring arrangement involves the factoring company purchasing a specific account for the net amount of the invoice, minus a discount or factoring commission of between 1 and 2 per cent. The 'net amount of the invoice' means the face value less the trade discount, freight allowance, or other items which the account debtor is entitled to deduct. The factor may advance the full purchase price of the accounts immediately upon assignment but often it will hold back 10 and 15 per cent to cover merchandise disputes, although it is not unknown for factors to advance 100 per cent minus a service charge. As the factor's calculations are based upon shortest selling terms, trade discounts not taken by the account debtor usually belong to the factor in compensation for the time the account remains unpaid beyond the shortest selling terms. General assignments are almost always 'with recourse'. During the currency of the general assignment agreement, the assignor/borrower is normally required to submit a monthly statement of his receivables which are invariably held on a trust basis for the benefit of the factor so that, in this way, the factor can police the account. A variation in the established pattern of advances and payments will usually alert the factor to a potential problem and the financier may then claim payment for moneys outstanding.

To draw distinctions between the principal varieties of factoring is somewhat misleading because one category will often merge into another. Nevertheless, the following represent the broad categories of credit factoring:

(a) *Old-line factoring* where there is a global agreement insofar as the client assigns his entire book debts to the factoring company, the latter providing all the normal attendant services.

(b) *Recourse factoring* where there is no element of credit insurance.

(c) *Maturity factoring* which does not involve an immediate advance to the client but rather the factoring company and the client mutually agree the date when the book debts assigned are deemed to have been paid and, if they are not, the factoring company forwards the agreed invoice value.

(d) *Advance factoring* which involves an immediate advance to the client.

(e) *Bank participation factoring schemes*, whereby factoring companies have close links with banks in the sense that the factoring company will handle the service elements of the agreement whilst the bank handles the financial aspect.

(f) *Back-to-back arrangements* which are essentially concerned with the international trade context. They involve the export factor entering into a full factoring agreement with the client exporter and then making arrangements with the import factor to act as his correspondent factor. Subsequently, the import factor enters into a factoring agreement with the distributor for his domestic sales. As we can see, the back-to-back arrangement deals with the problem of middlemen in trade. Outside an export context it can operate as follows: the domestic factoring agreement is with the distributor who agrees to accept instructions to pay a percentage of the purchase price of each invoice to the supplier, the purpose of such an arrangement being to give the supplier confidence in the granting of credit to the distributor.

(g) *Bulk factoring* which is suitable in the case of a client who has a huge number of very small customers. This is analogous to invoice discounting as the service element is virtually eliminated.

As we can see, factoring is a multifarious activity and is assuming an increasingly important role in the British economy. Even so, there is much ignorance concerning what precisely the factor sets out to do when he undertakes to purchase a company's book debts. Thus in a survey of businesses from *The Times* top 100 companies conducted by the *Accountancy* periodical in January 1987, only 3 out of the 60 companies which replied said that they used a factor; only 5 companies associated factoring with debt collecting, although 27 saw it as a means of improving cash flow, whilst 21 saw it as a means of obtaining additional finance. Many of the 14 'non replies' explained that they had not the time to examine the details of a possible factoring service. Given this level of uncertainty of function, it is beneficial to consider briefly the role of the modern-day factor within an historical context.

The renaissance of the commercial factor The Blackwell Hall factor in the 17th and 18th centuries presents a good example of an agent whose dominant position within his own branch of commerce led him to adopt the role of financier. When acting for foreign purchasers, it became customary for the factor to allow the foreign merchant six months' credit. In turn, the factor's payment to the home clothier tended to be dilatory and, as a result, the clothier was obliged to purchase his own raw materials on credit. It eventually became the practice for the factors to offer a guarantee to the clothiers that payment would be made to them in 12 months, and for this form of credit insurance they made a charge of $2\frac{1}{2}$ per cent. It seems that the Blackwell Hall factor portrays in embryo several credit devices — the allowance of business credit, the making of advances, and the provision of credit insurance. Here we see the vital link between the traditional buying and selling agent and the modern financial factor.

It was not until the 19th century that the factor came to assume more overt financial functions so that, if a factor was unable to effect an immediate advantageous sale of the goods, it was not uncommon for the principal to draw bills on his factor which the latter would accept (see chapter 9). The factor would thus be often pressed for funds to meet the bills when they fell due, particularly if market conditions did not favour the selling of the merchandise. The prohibition on pledging the principal's goods made it extremely difficult for a factor since he could pass no better title than his. This caused hardship for pledgees. Relief came with the Factors Acts 1823–1889 (see chapter 7), though they created an entirely new class of agent who could not be described as factors in spite of the title of the Act, viz. the mercantile agent. The passage of the Factors Act 1889 coincided with the period which witnesses the decline of the factor. A number of reasons may account for this, notably improved means of communication, the institution of bankers' commercial credits and other forms of credit insurance. It is on account of the factor's apparent decline in importance as a buying and selling agent and financier of trade from the end of the 19th century that his reappearance, in an apparently new role, in the UK in the early 1970s is of especial interest and significance.

The factoring process

1. *Application for credit by factoring company's client*

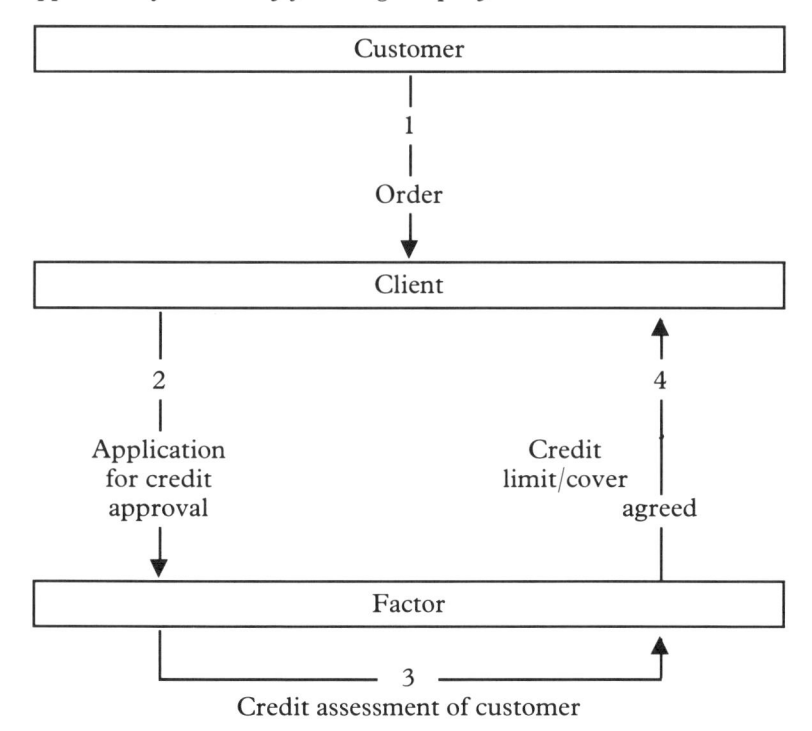

```
┌─────────────────────────────────────────┐
│               Customer                  │
└─────────────────────────────────────────┘
                    │
                    1
                    │
                  Order
                    ↓
┌─────────────────────────────────────────┐
│                Client                   │
└─────────────────────────────────────────┘
       │                          ↑
       2                          4
       │                          │
   Application               Credit
   for credit                limit/cover
   approval                  agreed
       ↓                          │
┌─────────────────────────────────────────┐
│                Factor                   │
└─────────────────────────────────────────┘
       └─────────────3──────────────┘
           Credit assessment of customer
```

2. *Delivery of goods and invoice raised*

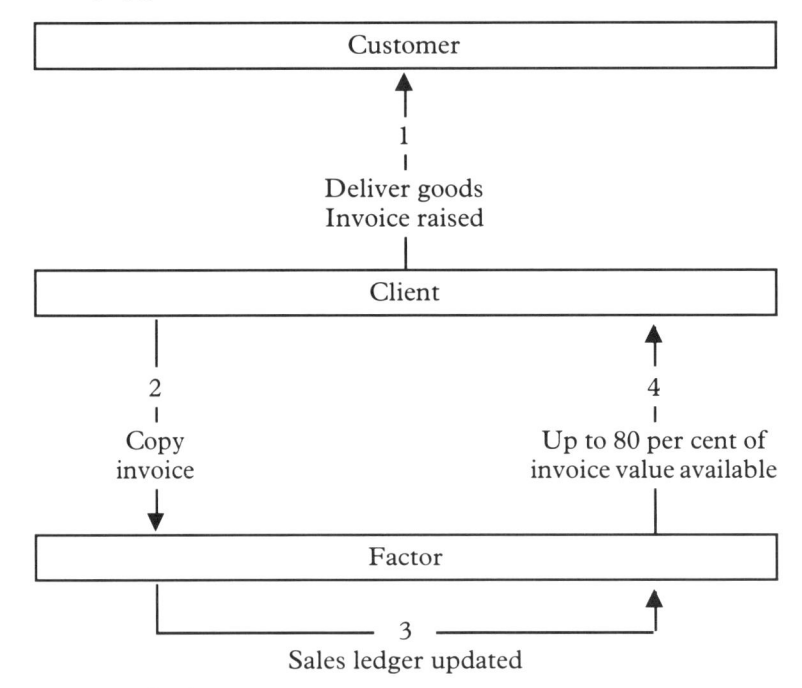

```
                    Customer
                       ↑
                       1
                 Deliver goods
                 Invoice raised
                     Client
          2                        4
        Copy              Up to 80 per cent of
       invoice            invoice value available
          ↓                        ↑
                     Factor
                  ─── 3 ───
                Sales ledger updated
```

3. *Payment collection*

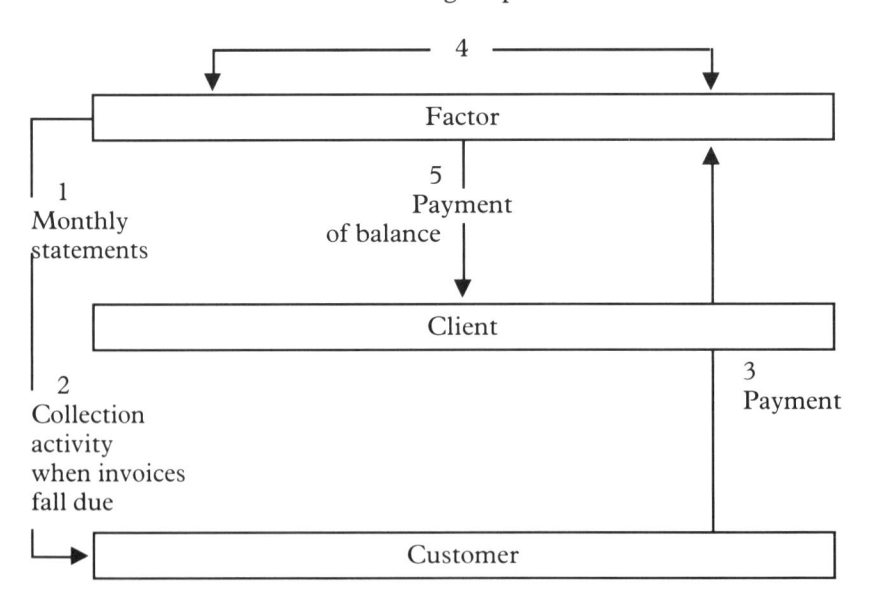

```
              Sales ledger updated
                  ─── 4 ───
                     Factor
                       5
                    Payment
                   of balance
     1                 ↓
  Monthly            Client              ↑
  statements                             3
                                      Payment
     2
  Collection
  activity
  when invoices
  fall due
     └──→        Customer
```

In addition to the obvious cash-flow advantages of credit factoring from the client's perspective, banks will often take an assignment of receivables precisely because the device will require the assignor/borrower to review the state of his business. For the purposes of a going concern, most of the assets of a business, other than accounts receivable, must either be retained or replaced by others of similar kind. The conversion of receivables into cash cannot, by itself, hurt the capacity of the business to proceed. In this respect, it is logical that accounts receivable financing should be an important prop in the structure of commercial and industrial credit. It is, therefore, important to consider the major legal difficulties associated with factoring which fall into two main broad categories: first, those associated with the factoring arrangement; second, significant priority issues arise. These will now be discussed in turn.

LEGAL PROBLEMS ASSOCIATED WITH CREDIT FACTORING

The factoring arrangement

Modern commercial law views the right to money due under a contract as a property right. This represents the developed legal position because, as Cozens-Hardy LJ pointed out in *Fitzroy* v *Cave* [1905] 2 KB 364 at p. 372 (emphasis added):

> At common law, a debt was looked upon as a *strictly personal obligation*, and an assignment of it was regarded as a mere assignment of a right to bring an action at law against the debtor.

This was not the view of equity. Chancery imposed a duty on the assignor of allowing his name to be used by the assignee in an action for the enforcement of the chose in action in a court of common law. If the assignor would not voluntarily lend his name, the assignee would have to bring a suit in equity against the assignor, and equity would invoke the maxim that it acted *in personam* and would, thereby, compel the assignor to be a party to the action. This action was treated under the common law as the assignor's action, and the defences available to the debtor against the assignor could be employed and equity would not interfere where the equities were equal (see *Wilson* v *Gabriel* (1863) 4 B & S 243). Where the action was purely equitable and was absolutely assigned, the assignee could sue in his own name in a court of equity. However, a non-absolute assignment of an equitable chose in action, or any legal chose in action required both the assignor and the assignee as necessary parties.

The Judicature Acts 1873 to 1875 introduced a statutory form of assignment which enables an assignee to sue in his own name. These Acts have given statutory recognition to such assignments provided that the assignment is absolute and not by way of charge, that it is evidenced in writing, and written notice is given to the debtor. This approach was substantially replicated in s. 136(1) of the Law of Property Act 1925 which states:

> Any absolute assignment by writing under the hand of the assignor (not purporting to be by way of charge only) of any debt or other legal thing in

action, of which express notice in writing has been given to the debtor . . . is effectual in law (subject to equities having priority over the right of the assignee) to pass and transfer from the date of such notice—
(a) the legal right to such debt or thing in action;
(b) all legal and other remedies for the same; and
(c) the power to give a good discharge for the same without the concurrence of the assignor.

There are major problems which emerge from this formalistic approach. Indeed, it is worth examining the underlying English legal environment to credit factoring as this appears to be hostile to its development.

Ad valorem duty An assignment of a debt is a conveyance or transfer of property and any instrument evidencing such a conveyance or transfer is liable under s. 1 of the Stamp Act 1891 to *ad valorem* duty. The rate of duty is 1 per cent subject to an exemption which relates to any independent transaction whereof the consideration does not exceed £30,000. A sale of receivables is ordinarily liable to stamp duty if carried out through a *document* but not otherwise. It is a tax on instruments and not on transactions, so if the transaction can be carried out without an instrument then no duty is payable (*Oughtred* v *Inland Revenue Commissioners* [1960] AC 206). Furthermore, whilst a *sale* of receivables attracts *ad valorem* duty, a mortgage does not (ss. 63 and 69 of the Finance Act 1971).

In the case of an equitable assignment which does not have to be evidenced in writing, the agreement will not be stampable. From this it may follow that written notification *after* the creation of a valid equitable instrument is not stampable, but the majority of the House of Lords held in *Oughtred* v *Inland Revenue Commissioners* that a subsequent conveyance of a prior oral contract of sale was liable to *ad valorem* duty: it did not matter that it constituted a formal act confirming that which, in equity, already belonged to the transferee. However, the better view here is that such reasoning does not apply in the assignment-of-receivables context for two main reasons: first, in the case of land, full title can only be transferred by instrument which is not true of receivables; second, written notification of a sale of receivables is *not* the instrument whereby receivables are sold as it constitutes merely evidence of the sale and this document is not thereby stampable (*Inland Revenue Commissioners* v *G. Angus and Co.* (1889) 23 QBD 579).

One further method of avoiding stamp duty, which is often regarded as distorting the economics of credit factoring, is through a device of keeping the schedules of receivables below £30,000. It is unlikely that this approach will succeed if it can be shown that, in reality, there is only one transaction. This is so, despite the logic of stamp duty which is a tax on instruments rather than transactions (*Ingram* v *Inland Revenue Commissioners* [1986] Ch 585). Furthermore, s. 34(4) of the Finance Act 1958 provides that a certificate of value for the purposes of stamping is required to contain a statement certifying that the transaction effected by the instrument does not form part of a larger transaction, or a series of transactions, where the aggregate value of the consideration exceeds £30,000. In *Attorney-General* v *Cohen* [1937] 1 KB 478, Greene LJ held that the phrase 'series of transactions' relates to the situation where the relationship between the transactions is not fortuitous but is an integral one. This must be the case with a factoring agreement on a facility or whole-turnover basis since these will be governed by a single master agreement (compare *Lloyds and Scottish Finance Ltd* v *Prentice* (1977) 121 SJ 847).

The question of notice   Section 136(1) of the Law of Property Act 1925 constitutes a procedural device which permits an assignor to pass legal title to the assignee so that the latter can sue the debtor in his own name. Even after the Judicature Acts 1873 to 1875, an assignee of a legal chose in action who could not bring himself within the statute is required to bring the assignor into the fray as either a co-plaintiff or co-defendant (*Performing Rights Society Ltd* v *London Theatre of Varieties Ltd* [1924] AC 1. Compare liquidation where joinder is not necessary as in *Tolhurst* v *Associated Portland Cement Manufacturers (1900) Ltd* [1903] AC 414). Non-joinder of the assignor is not a ground for dismissing the action, but the plaintiff will usually have to pay the costs involved in amending the pleadings so as to join the assignor (Rules of the Supreme Court 1965, Ord. 15, r. 6(1)).

The formal requirements under s. 136(1) are very strict: first the assignment has to be evidenced in a document; second, the assignment must be an absolute one, although this requirement does not preclude security assignments; third, notice in writing must be given to the debtor. It is this last requirement which has posed the most difficulty. The courts have restrictively interpreted the express notice requirement as referring to the notice in the document itself rather than notice of assignment generally. Consequently, if the date of the assignment is wrongly stated on the notice it is ineffectual as notice under the Section (*Stanley* v *English Fibres Industries Ltd* (1899) 68 LJ QB 839). In *W.F. Harrison and Co. Ltd* v *Burke* [1956] 1 WLR 419, a gloss was introduced to the effect that, if the wrong date was post the assignment, this was valid on the basis that at least an assignment was in existence at this time. Such an approach is anomalous because the *purpose* of notice is to bring to the debtor's attention with reasonable certainty that the debt has been assigned (*Denney, Gasquet and Metcalfe* v *Conklin* [1913] 3 KB 177). Furthermore, as Widgery LJ pointed out in *Van Lynn Developments Ltd* v *Pelias Construction Co. Ltd* [1969] 1 QB 607, what is important is the date of notice to the *debtor* and not the date when the assignment took place because the former is the relevant date pertaining to priority issues, and also in ensuring that the debtor pays the factor directly.

As far as an equitable assignment is concerned, the question is whether the assignor has given plain and unambiguous notice to the debtor. Even here, the courts have been restrictive in their construction of assignment clauses. Thus, in *James Talcott Ltd* v *John Lewis and Co. Ltd* [1940] 3 All ER 592, the words: 'To facilitate our accountancy and banking arrangements it has been agreed that this invoice be transferred to . . . [James Talcott]' were not deemed to be sufficiently plain to give the creditor notice that the debt had been assigned to a third party (compare Lord Goddard's strong dissenting judgment at p. 603).

One explanation for the approach adopted in this case is that the defendants did not expect a 'notice' of this kind from its suppliers, a North American firm, in favour of James Talcott Ltd who were, at that time, the third largest factoring company in the USA. It is significant that following this case, factoring companies advise clients to inform their customers in writing that debts are now being assigned and, insofar as invoices are being stamped to this effect, the colour of the stamp is bright and the print is large so as to effectuate actual notice.

The assignee takes subject to 'equities' One of the major policy dilemmas associated with receivables financing is the need to balance the use of receivables as the basis of security and, at the same time, protect the debtor by preserving his cross-claims and defences against the assignor. Of course, if the law were to permit a wide scope of cross-claims, this will punish the receivables financier who has no control over relations between assignor and debtor. This explains why clauses are often inserted into factoring agreements whereby a client is required to provide an express warranty that he has performed what the invoice relates to, and he will fulfil his obligations to the customer (see figure 11.1). Sometimes, the client will even warrant that the customer will not reject the goods delivered! It is doubtful whether this latter warranty can be enforced and it is for this reason that the factoring company will reserve the right to convert an 'approved' invoice to a 'disapproved' invoice.

The outer fringes of the rule that the assignee of receivables takes subject to equities having priority over his right are reasonably clear. First, the assignee takes no better right than the assignor had, so the assignment will be tainted by any defect in the underlying contract and also any proper defences against the assignor available to the debtor at the date of notice of the assignment (*Christie v Taunton, Delmard, Lane and Co.* [1893] 2 Ch 175). Interestingly, the debtor's right to rescind the contract is not barred by the assignee's intervention unlike the case of a bona fide purchaser for value of goods without notice. The exception to the *nemo dat* rule whilst protecting transferees of the *goods* from the buyer does not extend to transferees of the seller's right to receive payment, the basis of the distinction being the continuing allure of possession as the basic indicium of title to goods (see chapter 2). Second, the assignee takes subject to the state of the account between the debtor and the assignor at the date of notice of the assignment. Thus, a debtor who has a liquidated cross-claim against the assignor at the date he receives notice of the assignment can set it off against the assignee, even though the cross-claim has no connection with the debt assigned (*Roxburghe* v *Cox* (1881) 17 ChD 520; *Young* v *Kitchin* (1878) 3 ExD 127). Of course, it is otherwise where the cross-claim arises *after* notice of the assignment (*N.W. Robbie and Co. Ltd* v *Witney Warehouse Co. Ltd* [1963] 1 WLR 1324). A closely connected concept here is the debtor's right of abatement at common law for defective performance of sale of goods with a warranty (s. 53(1)(a) of the Sale of Goods Act 1979), so the assignee will take subject to this right. The doctrine of abatement (see *Street* v *Blay* (1831) 2 B & Ad 456; *Mondel* v *Steel* (1841) 8 M & W 868) is confined to a strictly limited group of contracts including sale of goods, supply by way of lease, hire-purchase, and contracts of work and materials (*Gilbert-Ash (Northern) Ltd* v *Modern Engineering (Bristol) Ltd* [1974] AC 689 at p. 717).

Undoubtedly, the debtor's rights of set-off constitute the most important arm of his enforceable equities, not least because monetary cross-claims dominate the debtor's equities. In the case of an equitable set-off, the claim and cross-claim whilst not necessarily arising out of the same contract must, nevertheless, be closely connected so much so that it would be inequitable not to allow credit for it (see *Dole Dried Fruit and Nut Co.* v *Trustin Kerwood Ltd* [1990] 2 Lloyd's Rep 309). Thus, it is reasonably clear that unliquidated damages unconnected with the contract from which the debt arose cannot, in the absence of a contrary agreement, be set off against the debt (see *Axel Johnson Petroleum AB* v *MG Mineral Group AG* [1992] 1 WLR 270). The classical exposition of this approach can be seen in the House of Lords decision in *Rawson* v *Samuel* (1841) Cr & Ph 161, a case involving a single agreement which gave rise both to the plaintiff's claim and to the counterclaim which, it was argued, constituted a set-off. It was held by Lord Cottenham in this case at p. 179 that in order to be effective as a set-off, the counterclaim had to be of such a kind that it 'impeached the title to the legal demand'. On the other hand, where the contract between the assignor and debtor provides that the debtor may deduct from the debt sums due to him from the assignor, this will apply to post-notice cross-claims for the simple reason that the debt and the contract of set-off arise from the *same* transaction, and the assignee cannot take this debt independent of this obligation since this was included in the original contract to which the debt relates (see above).

It has been suggested that in cases concerning an inseparable connection, the assignee may take subject not only to a right of equitable set-off available to the debtor as a defence to an action brought against him by the assignor, but also, in some cases, subject to an unliquidated demand that could only have been brought forward as a counterclaim in the assignor's action, that is, not susceptible of equitable set-off. Indeed the Privy Council in its judgment in *Government of Newfoundland* v *Newfoundland Railway Co.* (1888) 13 App Cas 199, specifically referred to counterclaims, though it is by no means clear that the Privy Council was using the term in its technical sense because the nature of the cross-claim here was one of a true equitable set-off. As a matter of principle, it would be anomalous to allow the debtor to enforce a true counterclaim, especially where the latter has no set-off against the assignor, perhaps, because of the absence of a relevant connection. When it is said that an assignee takes subject to equities, the epithet 'equities' is intended to connote rights in the nature of defences available to the debtor against the assignor. Before the Judicature Acts 1873 to 1875, a cross-claim possessed by the defendant in an action had to be prosecuted in a totally separate action at law against the plaintiff unless it could be employed in a set-off. It did not constitute a defence; nor did it give rise to an equity analogous to a defence available to the defendant in the plaintiff's action. The Judicature Acts 1873 to 1875, in introducing a right of counterclaim, only affected matters of procedure: it was not intended to alter the rights of the parties (*Stumore* v *Campbell and Co.* [1892] 1 QB 314). Consequently, it should still be the law that an assignee does not take subject to a cross-demand that could not have formed the basis of a set-off in an action brought by the assignor.

The scope of the factoring arrangement In equity, it is possible to have an assignment of future receivables so long as they can be identified as falling within the scope of the agreement without the need for appropriation. No problems should arise in respect of identification, especially with regard to the assignment of a special category of receivables (*Tailby* v *Official Receiver* (1888) 13 App Cas 523). Receivables arising within the scope of the factoring agreement will vest in the factor, even after liquidation, unless they came into existence as a result of post-liquidation activity by the liquidator or the company (compare *Re Lind* [1915] 2 Ch 345; *Re Collins* [1925] Ch 556).

A factoring agreement which provides that the client sells an agreed percentage of his book debts is vague since it would not be possible from the terms of the agreement to determine which receivables were within the agreement. Significantly, under the UNIDROIT Convention on International Factoring (UNIDROIT Bulletin 1988 N75/76), art. 5(1) provides that future receivables are covered by the Convention so long as they can reasonably be identified at the time of the conclusion of the contract. This rule operates *inter partes* the factor and supplier and, by virtue of art. 8, will not bind the debtor unless he has written notice relating to the receivables arising under a contract of sale of goods made at or before the time when notice is given (art. 8). The written-notice requirement means that non-notification factoring is excluded from the scope of the Convention which appears at variance with the acknowledged purpose of the Convention, namely, to facilitate factoring in international transactions.

Prohibition of assignment The contract between the customer and the factoring company's client may expressly prohibit or restrict assignment of rights under it. Although the Judicature Acts 1873 to 1875 facilitate assignments, they do not deal with the case of prohibition which is particularly troublesome in view of the fact that some standard-form contracts incorporate such a provision (see below). An assignment may be valid as between the assignee and assignor even though the obligor is not affected by it (*Gorringe* v *Irwell India Rubber and Gutta Percha Works* (1886) 34 ChD 128). As between the parties themselves, it would be anomalous if a third party could restrict their contractual undertaking. It may be that the assignor warranted that he could give good title to the debt, so if there was a non-assignment clause, the breach of warranty will enable the assignee to recover the consideration paid for the assignment and also possibly damages for loss of expectation. The obligor may, despite the non-assignment clause, be willing to assign the contract and this being a valuable right in itself means that the assignor will be in no position to prevent him from assigning the debt. It was in this context that Darling J uttered his famous *dictum* in *Tom Shaw and Co.* v *Moss Empires Ltd* (1908) 25 TLR 190 at p. 191:

> [A prohibition] could no more operate to invalidate the assignment than it could to interfere with the laws of gravitation.

Insofar as such a clause aimed to extinguish the rights of the obligee under the contract, such a prohibition clause could be struck down in equity as an unconscionable forfeiture, at least with regard to moneys already earned under the contract.

Some of the English cases have been concerned with the debtor exposing himself to double liability by ignoring a notice of assignment. This is particularly pertinent in the context of *Brice v Bannister* (1878) 3 QBD 569, which is the only English authority for the proposition that notification after assignment is ineffective against the assignee. The facts of this case revolved around the assignment of proceeds of a shipbuilding contract and following notification, payment was to be made by the obligor directly to the assignee. The shipbuilder fell into difficulties and requested that the obligor pay him directly, and indeed the money so advanced to the assignor enabled him to complete the contract. A majority of the Court of Appeal held that an amount equal to sums so paid could be recovered from the obligor by the assignee. The majority acknowledged that the assignor's failure to perform would have excused the obligor from paying these sums to the assignee. While acknowledging that the obligor's direct payment to the assignor had avoided the latter's failure, the majority reasoned at p. 578 that the obligor could neither 'defeat nor prejudice the [assignee's] right'. It is little wonder, therefore, that Bramwell LJ observed *obiter* at p. 581:

> [It] may be, if in the contract with A it was expressly stipulated that an assignment to B should give no rights to him, such a stipulation would be binding. I hope it would be.

In contrast, a vigorous dissent was delivered by Brett LJ who could not agree (at p. 579) that the theory underlying the assignee's rights:

> ... should be extended so as to prevent the parties to an unfulfilled contract from either cancelling or modifying, or dealing with regard to it in the ordinary course of business [and in good faith] ... If they cannot modify it, it seems ... to denote a state of slavery in business that ought not to be suffered.

This dissenting approach has been adopted in many jurisdictions in North America (s. 9-318(2) of the Uniform Commercial Code).

The legal treatment of prohibition-of-assignment clauses must be seen within the context of the fact that, historically, choses in action were unassignable at common law. The major objections from the common law perspective were the following: first, there was a deeply entrenched notion that property, whatever its nature, could not be transferred without delivery; second, it constituted maintenance; third, a debt was too personal to be assigned; fourth, a debt was too uncertain to be assigned. It was generally taken as settled that a non-assignment clause could prevent an assignee from acquiring rights against the obligor. In some cases, the law categorises certain assets as being incapable of alienation. Thus, under Roman law, the holder of the *usufruct* interest, the *usufructory*, could not alienate to a third party but could release his interest back to the *dominus*, the owner of the property (Gaius,

Institutes II, 30). In England, the general rule is that easements in gross are inalienable, so any effort to create one results only in a licence between the parties. The fear here is that the free transfer of the easement to a third party will impose a surcharge against the owner of the burdened land. Restraint on alienation is also important where the parties stand in a personal relationship, for example, a partnership, where neither party relishes the thought of suddenly being in business with a stranger.

Prohibition against assignment as a distinctive legal feature was confirmed in the case of *Helstan Securities Ltd* v *Hertfordshire County Council* [1978] 3 All ER 262. The facts of the case were relatively simple. A local authority employed a firm of contractors, Renholds, to carry out road works and incorporated into their contract a standard Institute of Civil Engineers condition (clause 15) that:

> ... the contractor shall not assign the contract or any part thereof or any benefit or interest therein or thereunder without the written consent of the employer.

The contractors were owed by the authority £46,000 and as a means of raising finance, they sold the debts to the plaintiffs without first obtaining the consent of the council. The plaintiffs gave notice in writing of the assignment and, in due course, unsuccessfully sued the council as legal assignee of the debts owed to Renholds. The counter-argument employed by the local authority was that Renholds had defrauded it of the sum of £85,000. The general effect of previous authorities which had considered such a prohibition was held by Croom-Johnson J to bind the assignor, so the assignee could not purport to acquire any rights under the contract against the debtor (see *United Dominions Trust (Commercial) Ltd* v *Parkway Motors Ltd* [1955] 1 WLR 719; *Spellman* v *Spellman* [1961] 1 WLR 921).

Although the payment to one party rather than another may not seem a great hardship, the debtor may have perfectly good commercial reasons for stipulating that he will not accept the assignment: first, a debtor who overlooks receipt of a notice of assignment and pays the assignor does not get a good discharge and can be compelled to pay a second time to the assignee; second, an assignment to some extent restricts the efficacy of mutual dealings between the debtor and the assignor in that the debtor cannot set up against the assignee equities arising after receipt by him of notice of assignment. The problem in *Helstan Securities Ltd* v *Hertfordshire County Council* was the defendant's assertion that the effect of the prohibition against assignment not only rendered the purported assignment ineffective against the debtor and creditor but also rendered it ineffective as between the assignor and assignee. Even though such a contention was not necessary for the defendants' success, regrettably, Croom-Johnson J appears to have considered it well-founded and held the assignment as being totally void. This approach fails to distinguish the transfer of the *benefit* of the contract from the delegation of the duty to perform, for example, a personal obligation. Moreover, there is a failure to distinguish between ineffectiveness of the assignment with regard to the debtor and as between the assignor/assignee.

The policy arguments espoused by Croom-Johnson J in championing the prohibition clause focused upon the double liability problem and the fact that an assignee may be less willing to settle disputes. Additionally, the obligor could find himself liable to perform the contract in favour of someone with whom he would have refused to contract directly and, on assignment, the obligee might in any case lose interest in the performance. These factors concentrate upon a duty to perform a contract of personal services and they have little relevance to credit factoring which is concerned with a contractual right to a sum of money. This obligation is not of such a personal nature that the identity of the payee is of any real significance to the debtor. As a matter of consistency, the effect of this approach should sound where there has been a mistaken payment by the obligor, as where payments have been made in ignorance of the defences which could be asserted against the assigned claim. In a submission by the representatives of the professional factoring association to the 1986 UNIDROIT discussions on international factoring (UNIDROIT Study 58, Doc. 25), it was argued that while the debtor ought not to find himself in a worse position as a result of the assignment neither should it be ignored. From this it followed that in the event of the supplier's bankruptcy, the debtor should not be able to recover from the factor when he would not have been able to do so had there been no factoring contract. This argument is fallacious because if the factor can enjoy the rights of the supplier against the debtor as in the case of subrogation then *mutatis mutandis*, he should take the obligations as well. Subrogation is particularly important with regard to stoppage in transit (see chapter 6) where receivables have been sold without recourse. Under art. 7 of the UNIDROIT Convention on International Factoring 1988, it is envisaged that the factor can enjoy all of the supplier's rights deriving from the sale of goods including a reservation of title clause (see chapter 12).

The argument adopted in *Helstan Securities Ltd* v *Hertfordshire County Council*, that an assignee can protect himself by making proper inquiry as to prohibitory conditions before buying the debt, ignores commercial realities as far as factoring is concerned. The very extent of absolute receivables financing makes investigation of individual contracts quite impracticable and the effect of *Helstan Securities Ltd* v *Hertfordshire County Council*, if literally interpreted, would mean that banks are unable to lend safely on the security of a fixed or floating charge over book debts (see chapter 15). The *Helstan* case has serious commercial implications because it threatens to turn off this source of finance for small and medium-sized companies. It is for this reason that art. 5 of the UNIDROIT Convention on International Factoring 1988 outlaws prohibition of assignments between supplier and debtor. Of course, it is still possible to restrict the effect of prohibition clauses by strictly construing them, for example, the clause could be construed as preventing the substitution of performance of the contract and not the assignment of rights arising under it. Furthermore, if the debtor has overlooked his own contractual prohibition term by paying the factor then, if this constitutes an established pattern of behaviour, the debtor would appear to have waived the prohibition.

The dilemma of mistaken payment by the obligor As a matter of policy, in the case of mistaken payment the issue can be described as that of allocation of risk between the mistaken payer/obligor and the assignee. On the conceptual level, such allocation can be achieved either by providing a narrow definition of the type of mistake that justifies restitution, so mistakes of law are not recoverable (but see now the recommendations of the Law Commission consultation paper, *Restitution of Payments Made under a Mistake of Law* (No. 20, 1991)) or by recognising a defence for the assignee. An example of the former approach can be seen in Bramwell B's dictum in *Aiken* v *Short* (1856) 1 H & N 210 at p. 215:

> In order to entitle a person to recover back money paid under a mistake of fact, the mistake must be as to a fact which, if true, would make the person paying liable to pay the money, not where, if true, it would merely make it desirable that he should pay the money.

Other cases have required the mistake of fact to be 'as between' the plaintiff and the defendant. Turning to the question of granting a creditor a defence against the mistaken payer, it was stated in *Barclays Bank Ltd* v *W.J. Simms Son and Cooke (Southern) Ltd* [1980] QB 677 that a restitutionary claim may fail if:

> ... a payment is made for good consideration, in particular if the money is paid to discharge and does discharge, a debt owed to the payee ... by the payor.

This approach would prove to be anomalous if it applied against the payer in a credit factoring setting since the payment was made without a full knowledge of the facts.

A distinction should be drawn between a bank's recovery of payment under a stopped cheque and the position of a financing assignee. It could be argued that there is a strong interest in the finality of the payment of a genuine cheque to a bona fide creditor and as soon as the creditor receives, in good faith, payment in discharge of a genuine cheque, he should not once again be subject to the risk of his debtor's insolvency. This is not true in the credit factoring context since the assignee receives the money in any case with full knowledge that he is taking the receivables subject to the equities. Indeed, assignment in this context improves the position of the obligor since he will always be an unsecured creditor *vis-à-vis* defects in the goods supplied. This risk will be minimised by the financial standing of the assignee. Such an approach has been recognised in the USA in *Firestone Tire and Rubber Co.* v *Central National Bank of Cleveland* (1953) 112 NE 2d 636. As a matter of principle this approach must be correct because the financing assignee does take the credit risk of both client and customer but will seek a guarantee by way of indemnity against the assignor for any misrepresentations made by him. Where the factor pays the customer and the goods prove to be defective, the factor can then reduce his payment to his client. If the latter is insolvent, such a reduction cannot be viewed as a preference since the factor is legally obliged to repay where there has been a mistake of fact and cannot be considered as acting voluntarily or officiously (see chapter 21).

Priority questions
Significant problems arise in distinguishing between the purchase of receivables and the lending of money on the security of book debts. This distinction is particularly fine where the assignor gives recourse as the effect is the same as borrowing on the security of receivables. The Crowther committee report, *Consumer Credit* (Cmnd 4596, 1971) noted at app. 3, para. 5:

> ... those buying receivables, whether with or without recourse, are careful to exact a set of warranties from the assignor designed to ensure as far as possible that the receivables assigned are not only legally enforceable but likely to be paid. Since a breach of any of these warranties may entitle the assignee to recover his loss from the assignor the difference between sales with recourse and sales without recourse is not as clear as it might appear.

The mere fact that there is a right of recourse should not necessarily affect the categorisation of the transaction as a sale. The assignor's liability is not to repay an advance, i.e., an exchange of money for money as in the case of a mortgage, rather, it is to pay a sum in discharge of a recourse obligation. This approach is confirmed by the accounting treatment where the relevant criterion is not that of recourse but whether the transferor has surrendered the *control* of future economic benefits embodied in the receivables.

The difficulty which surrounds both the question of assignment and security over book debts arises because of the common law's traditional outlawing of secret liens (see chapter 16). Interests reflected by neither possession nor notice amount to fraud at common law. The policy justification for this is that it is far less costly for a creditor out of possession to make his lien public than it is for third parties to discover surreptitious conveyances. Opponents of the secret lien in the context of receivables found a willing champion in Justice Brandeis in the notable US case of *Benedict* v *Ratner* (1925) 268 US 353. Here it was held that even though possession of accounts cannot be transferred physically — there being nothing to transfer — and even though the transferor cannot maintain possession, permitting a debtor to use proceeds from the sale of collateral is so antithetical to the concept of conveyance that the practice amounted to fraud. Instead of looking to the New York assignment cases, Justice Brandeis drew the analogy with chattel mortgages. Under the chattel mortgage cases, a mortgagee who allowed the mortgagor to sell his inventory and keep the proceeds without accounting for them had a fraudulent conveyance.

Benedict v *Ratner* did not initially arouse much interest because it was not until the 1930s that non-notification financing of receivables in the USA burgeoned. Although it was possible under New York chattel mortgage law for the mortgagee to file a supplemental mortgage covering after-acquired property and thereby protect his interest, this was not practical in the context of receivables financing where hundreds of new accounts arose every day. The development of non-notification financing of receivables in the USA was initially impeded and then transformed by the Supreme Court's decision in *Benedict* v *Ratner*. The result of that case was that receivables financing became professionalised so that commercial banks devised a procedure known as 'revolving' the collateral, i.e., gearing the credit as a means of complying with the requirement of 'policing' the collateral imposed by the Supreme Court. However, the *Benedict* rule was severely criticised on the basis that it seriously hampered working capital loans. Indeed, it could be argued that the rule prevented the development of the floating charge in the USA. Since one of the purposes of the Americal Uniform Commercial Code was to facilitate the creation of security devices (see chapter 16), it is not surprising that the *Benedict* rule has been overturned.

An important adjunct to the *Benedict* rule was the competing approach to priority in the USA before the adoption of the Uniform Commercial Code. Under the New York rule, the first assignee was accorded unqualified protection against all subsequent claimants, 'first in time first in right'. After non-notification financing came to predominate, the English rule of *Dearle* v *Hall* (1828) 3 Russ 1 found in many States was clearly prejudicial to this form of financing. Under this rule, notification to the account debtor is required and the order of priority between successive assignees is determined by the order in which the assignees give notice to the account debtor. In *Corn Exchange National Bank and Trust Co.* v *Klauder* (1943) 318 US 434, a Philadelphia bank had entered into a non-notification accounts receivable financing arrangement where the *Dearle* v *Hall* rule applied. The Supreme Court held that the rule under which a non-notifying asssignee could be relegated to a subsequent assignee applied in the context of US bankruptcy legislation, so non-notification was construed as being a voidable preference. One immediate effect of this decision was that most States which had the *Dearle* v *Hall* rule passed accounts receivable statutes which protected the priority of the non-notifying assignees.

In England, the conceptual development of the rule in *Dearle* v *Hall* is still pertinent in the factoring context. The rule only determines priority between competing *assignees* (see *Compaq Computer Ltd* v *Abercorn Group Ltd* [1991] BCC 484); it is necessary in the case of a competition between the assignee and third parties to apply a different analysis which raises difficult problems. In particular, the quagmire of English personal property security law is demonstrated by its failure to deal satisfactorily with the competition between a factoring company, as a purchaser of receivables, and a supplier of goods with a proceeds retention of title clause (see chapter 12). It is anticipated here that the supplier of goods with a retention of title clause claims the proceeds of the goods either because the sale was unauthorised resulting in a constructive trust of the proceeds, or, if the dispositions were authorised, there was an agreement to account *in specie* for the proceeds of the goods. If the efficacy of such a clause were established, its widespread use could compromise factoring as an efficient commercial instrument since it would require very close scrutiny of the debts bought in order to ensure that they really belong to the business concerned and not to a supplier of goods with a retention of title clause. We will consider in chapter 12 the validity of such a proceeds clause and in this chapter it is only necessary to focus more directly upon the priority issues.

The rule in Dearle v Hall (1828) There is no doubt that factoring companies justifiably fear for their priority because the seller's equitable interest will be first in time, *qui prior est in tempore potior est in iure*. The question then arises whether the factor may, by giving value and without notice, gain priority by subsequently taking a statutory assignment even if by then he knows of the seller's interest, that is, *tabula in naufragio*. It could be maintained that because retention of title clauses are common, the factor will have imputed notice of the seller's equitable interest. Nevertheless, the courts have been reluctant to apply the doctrine of notice to commercial transactions and indeed, in *E. Pfeiffer Weinkellerei-Weineinkauf GmbH & Co.* v *Arbuthnot Factors Ltd* [1988] 1 WLR 150, it was accepted that it could not be suggested that the defendant factoring company had constructive notice of the proceeds clause. Furthermore, s. 410 of the Companies Act 1985 (as amended) provides that a person shall not be taken to have notice of any matter merely because it has been disclosed in any register. It is considered that this new provision will protect purchasers of charged movable personalty in the ordinary course of business and, presumably also, factoring companies buying book debts.

A serious difficulty for the factor is that s. 136 of the Law of Property Act 1925 makes a statutory assignment of a legal chose in action effective in law 'subject to equities having priority over the right of the assignee'. Essentially, the matter is one of policy depending upon which of two schemes for regulating priority interests is adopted. The first, as already noted, consists of determining priority according to the *time* of creation of the interest and is the equitable equivalent of the common law *nemo dat* doctrine. As an alternative, the rule in *Dearle* v *Hall* (1828) 3 Russ 1 calls for a determination of which of the two innocent parties had contributed most to his unfortunate position. In practice, it appears that the factoring company will give notice of its rights to the debtor, as was the case in *E. Pfeiffer Weinkellerei-Weineinkauf GmbH & Co.* v *Arbuthnot Factors Ltd*, thereby ensuring the factoring company's priority under the *Dearle* v *Hall* rule. It is a matter of controversy whether the rule in *Dearle* v *Hall* should be applied to the competition between a supplier's equitable interest in proceeds by virtue of a retention of title clause, and the interest of the factoring company under its factoring arrangement with the dealer. In the *Arbuthnot Factors Ltd* case the rule was uncritically applied by Phillips J, although technically the observations made by his lordship are *obiter*. This was because of the finding that the retention of title clause was void as an unregistered charge and, as a matter of logic, the rule in *Dearle* v *Hall* presupposes the existence of two *valid* claims. Even so, this approach was mirrored by Mummery J in *Compaq Computer Ltd* v *Abercorn Group Ltd* [1991] BCC 484.

In a perfect commercial world, a rule should be rational, clear and just. Unfortunately, the rule in *Dearle* v *Hall* falls considerably short of these objectives. Although Sir Thomas Plumer MR in his judgment continuously stressed that he was applying old law, in effect a new rule was adopted as the only authority cited dealt with the law of bankruptcy (*Ryall* v *Rowles* (1750) 1 Ves Sen 348). The original substantive rationale of the rule was that an assignee who omitted to give notice was at fault, an omission which Sir Thomas Plumer MR characterised as negligence prejudicing a subsequent assignee who could not discover the existence of the prior assignment by enquiry of the debtor or trustee. Subsequent case law has eroded this rationale. In *Re Lake. ex parte Cavendish* [1903] 1 KB 151, the material facts revolved around a deposit of money by a client with a solicitor for investment purposes. The solicitor misappropriated the money although he executed a mortgage of certain life policies in favour of the client to secure part of the money he had taken, but did not inform the client of the existence of the mortgage. He then took out a second mortgage of the same policies from a clerk in his office without disclosing the first mortgage. Even though the client had no knowledge of the existence of his interest, precluding any charge of negligence, it was held that the second mortgagee was entitled to priority since he had given notice to the insurance company. A further erosion followed in *Ward* v *Duncombe* [1893] AC 369, which called into question whether a debtor is under a duty to inform an assignee of any prior assignment of which he had received notice. The technical nature of the rule was recognised by Lord Macnaghten in that case at p. 394:

> I am inclined to think that the rule in *Dearle* v *Hall* has on the whole produced as much injustice as it has prevented ... it seems to me that when your lordships are asked to extend the rule to a case not already covered by authority, it is proper to enquire into the principles upon which the rule is said to be founded ... I do not think that those principles are so clear or so convincing that the rule ought to be extended to a new case.

This kind of reasoning has led to two limitations on the rule, and the application of these exceptions will prejudice the factor at least *outside* the sphere of competing equitable assignments. The first exception arises from the unanimous decision of the House of Lords in *B.S. Lyle Ltd* v *Rosher* [1959] 1 WLR 8, namely, the rule does not apply where the assignor has no beneficial interest. This approach is questionable, especially as the rule has been applied where the assignor had, at the time of the second assignment, no beneficial interest because of a previous involuntary assignment like bankruptcy. In *Meux* v *Bell* (1841) 1 Hare 73, the rule was applied to a case where the assignor had never possessed the beneficial interest which he purported to assign to the second assignee. From this, it seems unlikely that *B.S. Lyle Ltd* v *Rosher* will be applied to the contest between seller and factor for the book debts. Furthermore, even if the case was good authority, it may be distinguished on the grounds that in *B.S. Lyle Ltd* v *Rosher*, the assignor had neither legal nor beneficial ownership of the property whereas the assignor, the buyer in a retention of title situation, will usually have the legal title to the debt.

The second objection to the factor's priority, and the most fundamental, rests on the *dictum* of Eve J in *Hill* v *Peters* [1918] 2 Ch 273 at p. 279:

> The principle on which the rule in *Dearle* v *Hall* is founded, which regards the giving of notice by the assignee as the nearest approach to the taking of

possession, has no application, in my opinion, to the beneficiary who has no right to possession himself, and who can only assert his claim to receive through his trustee.

It follows from this that a cestui que trust has priority over a subsequent assignee even if he has given notice of his interest to the fund-holder. In *B.S. Lyle Ltd* v *Rosher*, Lord Reid expressly approved and applied *Hill* v *Peters*, although the other Law Lords left open the question whether, for the purposes of the rule in *Dearle* v *Hall*, there was a difference between an equitable assignment and a declaration of trust. As a matter of consistency, it could be argued that the object of a trust by way of security is the same as the object of an assignment by way of security and this should have no bearing on priorities. In addition, a trust is often regarded as a snare for unsecured creditors because, if no requirement of notice is imposed on a cestui que trust, there is no way that third parties can discover the existence of the trust.

The above argument has been developed by Professor Goode on the basis that it is inequitable for the seller to rely upon being first in time as it offends against the doctrine of conscience in equity, that is, the equities are unequal (see (1977) 93 LQR 487). Essentially, the main issue being addressed here is the absence of a comprehensive filing system of personal property security interests in England (see chapter 16). There is no reason in principle why a supplier of goods should be prejudiced simply because there is no efficient registration mechanism.

It is unfortunate that the courts in *E. Pfeiffer Weinkellerei-Weineinkauf* v *Arbuthnot Factors Ltd* [1988] 1 WLR 150 and *Compaq Computer Ltd* v *Abercorn Group Ltd* [1991] BCC 484 accepted the proposition that the rule in *Dearle* v *Hall* must apply in all cases of equitable assignments. Such a conclusion leads to substantial injustice where a first assignee does not give notice to the debtor-obligor, perhaps because he is aware of a prohibition of assignment clause in the latter's contract with the assignor. If it is the case that the obligor can prevent the assignee from acquiring rights against him, the whole point of giving notice evaporates. The rationale here for such notice is, as Buckley J pointed out in *Re Dallas* [1904] 2 Ch 385 at p. 396, to enable the assignee to acquire a right *in rem* against the fund as distinct from 'a right against the conscience of the assignor of the fund'. Furthermore, if *Dearle* v *Hall* is the nearest approach to taking possession, it should have no relevance where the obligor can prevent this. At least by applying a first-in-time rule, provided the equities are equal, the courts could take into account the effect of a non-assignment clause.

The position is unsatisfactory. In any case, as the Crowther committee report, *Consumer Credit* (Cmnd 4596, 1971) showed, the rule in *Dearle* v *Hall* does not offer factoring firms a practical solution. The rule assumes that notice given to the debtor is equivalent to notice given to the second assignee. However, as the debtor has no duty to inform the assignee, this is not necessarily the case. Moreover, if a factor were to take an assignment of future choses in action, he has the problem of *dicta* in *Performing Rights Society Ltd* v *London Theatre of Varieties Ltd* [1924] AC 1 falling in on him through being 'trumped' by a bona fide purchaser of the legal estate for value without notice. In essence, what a factor requires is effective security in a transaction which will encompass future receivables. The rule in *Dearle* v *Hall* does not provide this.

The effect of notice This fixes the date for determining the debtor's equities subject to which the debtor takes, although this does not deny post-notice equities so long as there is an inseparable connection with the underlying contract to which the assignment relates (see above). Nevertheless, the general rule is that notice of assignment crystallises the debtor's equities enforceable against the assignee. Thus, where the cross-claim is a contingent liability this must be due before the notice date and also payable before the assigned debt becomes payable. An illustration of this can be seen in the facts of *Jeffryes* v *Agra and Masterman's Bank* (1866) LR 2 Eq 674, where a bank indebted to a customer tried to set off against an assignee of the debt the customer's contingent liability of certain bills of exchange of which the bank was the holder for value (see chapter 9). The liability here was contingent simply because if the acceptor paid on maturity there would be nothing due from the customer. The justification for not recognising contingent cross-claims in this context is the unfairness of requiring the assignee, who may have given present value, to wait until the cross-claim has matured into an actual payable debt (see also *Christie* v *Taunton, Delmard, Lane and Co.* [1893] 2 Ch 175). The legal position was summarised by Templeman J in *Business Computers Ltd* v *Anglo-African Leasing Ltd* [1977] 1 WLR 578 as follows at p. 585:

> The result of the relevant authorities is that a debt which accrues due before notice of an assignment is received, whether or not it is payable before that date, or a debt which arises out of the same contract as that which gives rise to the assigned debt, or is closely connected with that contract, may be set off against the assignee. But a debt which is neither accrued nor connected may not be set off even though it arises from a contract made before the assignment.

Further interesting problems arise in respect of future choses in action where an assignee gives notice of his assignment before the debt arises, and the debtor subsequently raises cross-claims based on subsequent events but before the assigned debt arises. As a matter of principle, the cross-claim will be enforceable against the assignee because the debt generated by the executory contract was always subject to the debtor's cross-claim. This is particularly pertinent in the context of a 'whole turnover' factoring agreement where what is involved is an assignment of expectant receivables (see *Rother Iron Works Ltd* v *Canterbury Precision Engineers Ltd* [1974] QB 1). An illustration of this phenomenon can be seen in the facts of *Canadian Admiral Corporation Ltd* v *L.F. Dommerich and Co. Inc.* (1964) 43 DLR (2d) 1 (Supreme Court of Canada). Here there was an agreement to factor receivables but the notice of assignment was stamped on each invoice sent. It was held that the customer of the client could not set off a subsequent debt since, it was argued, only the *specific* assignment in respect of which invoices were sent to the debtor were operative for the purpose of the notice element, irrespective of the date of notice of the master factoring agreement.

Other chargee conflicts The Companies Act 1989 introduced a new s. 410 into the Companies Act 1985 by which a person shall not be deemed to have notice of any matter solely because of its being disclosed in any document kept by the company for inspection. However, there is an important caveat here as a factor will be deemed to have knowledge of a duly registered charge where he ought reasonably to have made enquiry of the companies register of charges (s. 711A(2) of the Companies Act 1985 as amended). It could be argued that as the question of charges over debts of a prospective client is of material importance to a factor, the enquiries which he ought to make for the purposes of s. 711A(2) before entering into a factoring agreement should include enquiries as to charges created by a prospective client. Even though the constructive notice doctrine may have been abolished by the Companies Act 1985 this does not affect issues of *inferred* knowledge, that is, a failure to make such enquiries as ought reasonably to be expected to be made. It is plausible, therefore, that restrictive covenants in prior floating charges could impeach the factor's proprietary rights to the debts (compare the approach adopted by the Scottish Second Division court in *Tay Valley Joinery Ltd* v *CF Financial Services Ltd* 1987 SLT 207). Certainly, this will be the position in the case of a fixed charge over book debts because this postulates in terms of its very nature such a restriction.

Lastly, it should be noted that in the case of subsequent registered charges to the factoring agreement, the rule in *Dearle* v *Hall* (1828) 3 Russ 1 may very well work against the factoring company. If the chargee is unaware of the factoring agreement, for example, because this is arranged on a confidential basis, the subsequent chargee in point of time could get a notice sent to the debtor(s) first and obtain priority.

SECURITISATION OF RECEIVABLES

In a sense, the process involved in securitisation is the reverse side of credit factoring in that the raising of finance on receivables is geared towards financial institutions rather than manufacturing industry. The essential framework of securitisation involves a sale of a stream of receivables, or a sale coupled with a subcharge by the purchaser. Pools of receivables are 'packaged' together and are then transferred to a special-purpose company. The purchase price is raised by this special-purpose company through the transfer of the original debt obligation into a new instrument that can be negotiated.

It is worth emphasising that the term 'securitisation' refers to the transfer of financial assets from the original lender to the market and, as such, it does not denote security for payment. An alternative method of securitisation is through the issue of loan notes secured on the receivables. Under this arrangement, the transferor has the benefit of any profit margin constituting the difference between the interest rate paid to the shareholders and that paid on the original loans by the borrowers.

Economic advantages of securitisation for issuers

Cheaper source of funds Securitisation lowers the cost of funding because it isolates risk, that is, investors can buy a specific package of receivables generated from a particular retail sector (or in the case of land, house mortgages) with a knowable level of risk, for example, receivables generated from the financing of a particular make and model of a car, caravan or boat. It has to be admitted that asset-backed securitisation in the UK is dwarfed by the mortgage market. Up to 1989 there existed an important regulatory barrier to asset-based securitisation which restricted securitisation to long-term debt receivables (five years and beyond). Following the 1989 Budget, short and intermediate maturities are allowed so the opportunities exist for asset-backed securitisation.

It is clear from the above that companies, through this method, can borrow more cheaply and obtain a better return than by more conventional means of obtaining finance. Securitisation of receivables is linked to disintermediation, the process by which banks move out of their traditional lending function (loans etc.) and instead act as intermediaries between borrowers and lenders through brokerage and underwriting activities.

Offbalance sheet financing This can be very important where the issuer is a bank because securitisation takes assets off the balance sheet, thereby allowing banks to meet capital adequacy requirements laid down by the Bank of England. Furthermore, risky assets can be transferred off balance sheet which can help the issuer's overall credit standing. Securitisation assists in the issuer's risk management and this can be extremely beneficial to finance companies that are highly sensitive to interest-rate fluctuations. Moreover, it provides a means of overcoming any mismatch there may occur in the issuer's portfolio of assets, for example, between fixed interest rates and market rates.

Legal impediments to securitisation

Stamp duty We have already considered this in the context of credit factoring and the same considerations apply to the securitisation of receivables.

The impact of consumer protection laws These may have a significant impact on the ability of the seller and buyer to enforce an obligation against the borrower. The ambit of the Consumer Credit Act 1974 relates to sales on credit under £15,000 and provides for licensing and other control of traders concerned with the provision of credit for the supply of goods on hire or hire-purchase. If the licensing requirement has not been met, the debt may be unenforceable. Furthermore, the cancellation provisions of the Consumer Credit Act 1974 are significant.

The legal nature of the transfer of the original debt
The major difficulty here is the English rule that obligations cannot be transferred (*Tolhurst* v *Associated Portland Cement Manufacturers (1900) Ltd*

[1902] 2 KB 660). Nevertheless, it is possible for financial assets to be transferred in one of three ways. The cleanest transfer of risk is achieved by *novation* which is essentially the process of substitution. A properly structured legal or equitable *assignment* can be an effective method of transferring the seller's rights and remedies. The third and probably most common technique is *sub-participation* which does not, strictly speaking, involve any transfer of rights, remedies, or obligations from seller to buyer as it constitutes a separate non-recourse funding arrangement in that the buyer places funds with the seller in exchange for a beneficial interest only in the underlying loan. We shall now consider in greater detail the implications of the different methods under English law.

Novation This is the only way of effectively transferring both rights and obligations because it effectively involves substituting the original rights and obligations for new ones. In effect, the only substantive difference is the identity of the lender, otherwise, the novation can be overturned for lack of consideration. The major difficulty with this technique is that it requires the consent of all the parties to the original loan which will obviously be cumbersome especially where there has been syndication.

In order to cover the practical difficulties in obtaining consent, many loans are now structured to facilitate transfer. Essentially all the parties to the loan agree in advance that all or part of it can be transferred, so subsequent buyers can take advantage of the transferable loan facility (TLF). In the case of novation, the transferable loan certificate (TLC) is used which obviously assists in increasing the liquidity of the underlying asset. Such a TLC will expressly provide that it is subject to the terms and conditions of the credit instrument under which it is issued and will not, thereby, be considered as a negotiable instrument under s. 3(1) of the Bills of Exchange Act 1882 because it does not contain an *unconditional* promise to pay a specified amount. Nevertheless, as we have seen (see pp. 192–3), the Bills of Exchange Act 1882 does not deal with all forms of negotiable instrument and it must be the case that an English court will confer the legal character of negotiability where the instrument is expressed to be payable to bearer, and where business people treat the instrument as being negotiable. There is no doubt that the efficacy of the TLC is assured under English law because it can be considered to be a unilateral contract, that is, an offer made to the world at large (*Carlill* v *Carbolic Smoke Ball Co.* [1893] 1 QB 256) which is enforceable where the requisite reliance can be shown.

The Bank of England treats a novation as a 'clean' transfer and will be excluded from the seller's (in the case of a bank) risk-asset ratio as it is included in the buyer's instead (see Loan Transfers and Securitisation BSD/1989/1 February 1989). The major legal difficulties associated with novation centre around priorities and questions as to the value given by the buyer to avoid preferences and invalidation of floating charges under the Insolvency Act 1986 (see chapter 21).

Assignment We have already considered the legal problems relating to assignment of choses in action in relation to our discussion of receivables financing. It is sufficient here to note that the seller will retain an outstanding obligation(s), while the buyer's rights may be impaired by any rights of set-off that exist between the borrower and the seller. Moreover, where there has been no notice of the assignment to the borrower, there will be additional risks for the buyer, not least that the seller will continue as the lender of record and will remain subject to the underlying equities of the contract between the seller and borrower.

Whilst the Bank of England regards an assignment with or without notification as a 'clean' transfer, in the case of a silent assignment the additional risks identified above may, in an appropriate case, lead the Bank to disregard a transfer of a loan in calculating the risk-asset ratio of the seller (see BSD/1989/1). In order to assist in transferring loan facilities, it is common for all of the participants involved in the original lending to issue a transferable loan instrument (TLI) which is based on a legal assignment and can only be used when the loan is fully drawn. The TLI can relate to a proportion of the outstanding obligation which obviously makes a substantial asset more easily tradable, that is, certificates may be issued to represent one or more identified portion(s) of a right to payment of principal, interest or income.

Sub-participation In the case of sub-participation, the buyer does not have any recourse to the borrower and is not able to exercise any of the seller's rights against the borrower. The sub-participation is a separate legal agreement from the underlying loan creating a debtor-creditor relationship between buyer and seller. What is involved here is a sale of a loan by way of a back-to-back non-recourse funding arrangement. The buyer (the sub-participant) deposits with the original lender (the seller or lead bank) a sum of money which represents a proportion of the amount advanced by the lead bank, the buyer receiving in exchange the right to acquire from the lead bank a sum equal to the same proportion (plus interest) of the amount repaid by the borrower. An important feature of sub-participation is the double jeopardy of the buyer in the sense that he assumes a credit exposure of both the seller and the underlying borrower. There are two ways to avoid this credit exposure:

(a) By way of mortgage or charge. Usually the buyer's sub-loan is secured by way of mortgage or charge over the seller's loan to the borrower. This will obviously entail registration under s. 396 of the Companies Act 1985 (as amended).

(b) Declaration of trust. The lead bank could declare itself a trustee of the loan as security for performance of its obligations to the sub-participant. In the absence of a declaration of trust, the court would require evidence of the intention to create a trust; for example, if it could be shown that the lead bank was under a duty to keep the proceeds as a fund separately from its own moneys.

There can be no question of a security interest being 'created' in the normal sub-participation arrangement. The lead bank retains the loan documentation and also full control over the loan; as such, the lead bank does not receive from

… the buyer a sub-loan which it can call in, rather, the lead bank pays a sum equal to the agreed proportion of what it receives. In order to make sub-participation arrangements marketable, the transferable participation certificate ('TPC') has been devised. This avoids multi-tiered sub-participations which enables a new buyer to step clearly into the shoes of the old buyer and thus have a direct contractual relationship with the original seller.

PART 4   SECURED FINANCING

TWELVE
The retention of title clause

One consequence of the passing of property on credit in transactions involving sale is that the relationship of buyer and seller becomes simply one of debtor and creditor. Other than certain proprietary remedies available under parts V and VI of the Sale of Goods Act 1979 which usually cease on delivery, the seller's only remedy following the insolvency of the buyer is to prove in competition with other unsecured creditors. We have already considered in chapter 2 that the passing of property under English law, is an aspect of contract rather than conveyance (see ss. 17 to 19 of the Sale of Goods Act 1979). By reserving title to the goods, the seller may adversely affect third-party interests especially those of the buyer's creditors. Moreover, through this simple mechanism, the seller will enjoy a status equivalent to a secured creditor, notwithstanding that there is an apparent conflict here with the principle that a person in possession of an article is presumed owner (see chapter 16).

The common law does evince a certain inconsistency with regard to the consequences of delivery. In relation to sales subject to a condition precedent, property in the goods remains with the seller until (usually) the payment of the price, whereas the effect of a sale subject to a condition subsequent is said to impose only a personal obligation upon the buyer. Thus, in the situation where property in the goods passes to the buyer on or before delivery subject to the obligation of the buyer to return the goods, the effect of which is to revest the property in the seller (or at a reasonable time thereafter), it was held by Sumner LJ in *The Vesta* [1921] 1 AC 774 at p. 783:

> Even if the seller had such a right [an absolute right to require the buyer to return unsuitable goods] . . . this would be a personal right, the breach of which would sound in damages only.

Consequently, different results are seen: on the one hand, the delivery of movable property under a retention of title clause is said to give the seller a right analogous to other real rights, such as his lien under the Sale of Goods Act 1979, whilst on the other hand, delivery subject to a first option clause gives the seller only a personal right against the buyer. This reveals a lack of consistency in logic in the law's present policy regarding the effects of delivery. Nevertheless, the distinction is vital for a trade creditor since the reservation of a proprietary interest (*ius in re aliena*) bestows upon the creditor a real proprietary right which goes to the core of a successful pursuit for security. Indeed, the proliferation of such clauses could be said to indicate the law's present inability to protect trade creditors.

The form by which commerce adopts the reservation of title clause depends very much on the reception accorded to it by the judiciary and, as such, is an example of the impact of law on practice. Since each case turned on the construction of its individual reservation of title clause, the discovery of a valid form is elusive. It will be instructive, therefore, to consider the principal cases in greater detail.

THE PRINCIPAL CASES

Aluminium Industrie Vaassen BV v Romalpa Aluminium Ltd [1976] 1 WLR 676

Given the reception accorded to this decision by the legal community, it is curious that it was not officially reported in the *Law Reports*. One counsel referred to it as the most important case for 25 years and doubted whether any case decided this century has created a greater impact on the commercial world. In this vein, the decision was welcomed by business people engaged in the international sale of goods whilst others considered that the decision took us to a commercial precipice. The cynical explanation regarding the absence of the case from the *Law Reports* is that it was thought to be unreportable, although Roskill LJ in the Court of Appeal did say that the decision turned on the construction of the particular contract: 'a rather simple contract not altogether happily expressed in the English language but [which] could not govern any other case'.

The facts are relatively simple. The defendants owed the plaintiffs (a Dutch firm) £122,000 and they possessed £35,000 in a separate account which represented the proceeds of sale of the foil supplied by the plaintiffs (AIV). In addition, the defendants had in their possession unsold foil valued at £50,000. The plaintiffs relied on their reservation of title clause (number 13 in their contract of supply) in order to recover these assets which provided: 'The ownership of the material to be delivered by AIV will only be transferred to purchaser when he has met all that is owing to AIV, no matter on what grounds'. Additionally, Romalpa was required to store the material in such a way that it could be identified as the property of AIV. Secondly, an assignment of future unascertained property was provided (i.e., the manufactured goods processed from the foil) as surety for AIV until full payment had been made. Lastly, a right was provided to sell the finished product with a transfer of all claims against the sub-buyers.

In *Romalpa* at first instance, Mocatta J reasoned by analogy that as the goods themselves were not owned by the buyer until payment, this must also apply to cash proceeds in the separate account opened by the receiver which represented the proceeds of the sale of the foil. The approach taken by Mocatta J which was confirmed in the Court of Appeal is difficult to sustain. To recognise a clause reserving ownership to secure payment of sums due on *other* transactions, some of which might be totally unrelated to the sale of specific goods (inherent in clause 13), seems to go far beyond the confines of the law on sale of goods. Moreover, in view of the fact that Romalpa was allowed to mix money with its own, this would prima facie appear incompatible with a presently subsisting fiduciary relationship (*Re Nevill, ex parte White* (1871) LR 6 Ch App 397; *Foley* v *Hill* (1848) 2 HL Cas 28; *South Australian Insurance Co.* v *Randell* (1869) LR 3 PC 101; *Henry* v *Hammond* [1913] 2 KB 515).

The Court of Appeal construed Romalpa's relationship with AIV as being a fiduciary one with the result that proprietary tracing rights were available. The problem of identifying the proceeds did not arise because the receiver had opened a separate bank account. Nonetheless, the question regarding the capacity of Romalpa in disposing of the goods reveals the difficulties inherent in the approach taken by the Court of Appeal since the nature of the fiduciary relationship was never established. Indeed, the confusion was reflected in *Borden (UK) Ltd* v *Scottish Timber Products Ltd* [1981] Ch 25, where Bridge LJ, having conceded that the defendants in *Romalpa* were bailees, then proceeded to describe them as agents. This issue goes to the heart of the legal recognition of the more extended type of clause and will be considered later.

Re Bond Worth Ltd [1980] Ch 228

This case was decided three years after the *Romalpa* decision. The conditions of sale under which Monsanto, the plaintiffs, had supplied Acrilan to Bond Worth for use in making carpets provided that:

> Equitable and beneficial ownership shall remain with [Monsanto] until full payment has been received . . . or until prior resale, in which case [Monsanto's] beneficial entitlement shall attach to the proceeds of resale or to the claim for such proceeds. Should the goods become constituents of or be converted into other products while subject to [Monsanto's] equitable and beneficial ownership [Monsanto] shall have the equitable and beneficial ownership in such other products as if they were simply and solely the goods.

The reference to Monsanto's 'equitable and beneficial ownership' cannot be regarded as importing its usual meaning. Equity has never recognised that where total ownership is vested in one person he has a 'dual' ownership in the sense that he may transmit his equitable interest free of his legal dominion.

It is doubtful whether an equitable title in goods can subsist after the Sale of Goods Act 1893, especially in the light of Atkin LJ's judgment in *Re Wait* [1927] 1 Ch 606 at pp. 635-6:

> It would have been futile in a code intended for commercial men to have created an elaborate structure of rules dealing with rights at law, if at the same time it was intended to leave, subsisting with the legal rights, equitable

The retention of title clause

rights inconsistent with, more extensive, and coming into existence earlier than the rights so carefully set out in various sections of the code.

As a matter of principle, it could be argued, if the conduct of the parties can produce a situation where the burdens of beneficial ownership pass to the buyer (*Sterns Ltd* v *Vickers Ltd* [1923] 1 KB 78), it is surely illogical that they should not also pass all of the corresponding benefits, for example, equitable ownership of the goods. Nevertheless, Atkin LJ in *Re Wait* only referred to legal rights and duties *dehors* the contract of sale which is the equitable charge or mortgage, and this was the approach taken by Slade J in *Bond Worth*.

The buyers in *Bond Worth* enjoyed rights under the contract in the Acrilan which were equivalent to those normally enjoyed by a *sui iuris* person. Despite this, the fact that Bond Worth had legal title whilst Monsanto claimed a beneficial title should have strengthened the argument that there was a fiduciary relationship. Furthermore, it can be argued following the approach of the House of Lords in *Abbey National Building Society* v *Cann* [1991] 1 AC 56, that no security was ever 'created' by Bond Worth requiring registration under s. 396 of the Companies Act 1985 (as amended) because at no stage was Bond Worth's interest as against Monsanto unencumbered, that is, it was always 'informed' by the seller's equity in the goods (see pp. 354–7).

Borden (UK) Ltd v Scottish Timber Products Ltd [1981] Ch 25

Borden supplied Scottish Timber Products with urea formaldehyde resin which was used in the manufacture of chipboard. In the ordinary course, the chipboard resin was mixed by the buyers with certain hardeners and wax emulsion to form 'glue mix'. This was an irreversible chemical reaction, and the buyers generally did this mixing of the resin within two days of receiving it, the suppliers being well aware of this fact. The glue mix was then mixed with wood chippings and pressed to make chipboard.

The buyers went into liquidation with an outstanding debt to the sellers amounting to £318,332. The retention of title clause on which they sought to rely provided:

> Goods supplied by the company shall be at the purchaser's risk immediately on delivery to the purchaser or into custody on the purchaser's behalf (whichever is the sooner) and the purchaser should therefore be insured accordingly. Property in goods supplied hereunder will pass to the customer when: (a) the goods the subject of this contract; and (b) all other goods the subject of any other contract between the company and the customer which, at the time of payment of the full price of the goods sold under this contract, have been delivered to the customer but not paid for in full, have been paid for in full.

No stipulation was made in respect of a charge over the goods into which the chipboard resin had been consumed. Inevitably, the clause was a poor means of protection for Borden in view of the fact that the chipboard resin was never intended to remain for long in its original state.

At first instance ([1979] 2 Lloyd's Rep 168), Judge Rubin held that a fiduciary relationship existed giving rise to an equitable right to trace into the finished product and proceeds. This reasoning appears inconsistent because, although STP received the resin as bailees, to make commercial sense of the arrangement a term had to be implied giving STP a licence to use the resin in their manufacturing process. The Court of Appeal reversed this conclusion recognising, as Slade J did in *Re Bond Worth Ltd* [1980] Ch 228, that what was involved here after the 'tearing away of the mask' was a sale since it was never intended that the resin be recovered either in its original or altered form. In particular, this attitude can be seen in the judgment of Templeman LJ who was wary of manipulating principles of equity in order to produce a new equitable tracing right having the same effect as a charge but being immune from the requirements of registration.

In *Borden*, the plaintiffs had no right to call for the return of the resin once incorporated, and it was never intended that the resin be recovered either in its original or altered form. The Court of Appeal was not asked to rule on the right to claim back the unprocessed resin which was not really a valuable right given the fact that there was only two days' supply on the premises at any given time.

The combined effect of the decisions of *Re Bond Worth Ltd* and *Borden (UK) Ltd v Scottish Timber Products Ltd* was to limit the retention of title clause in *Romalpa* to its special facts. These two cases also appeared to limit the intrusion of equitable principles of trusts, fiduciary relationships and equitable tracing into contracts for the sale of goods. In subsequent cases, even the simple *in specie* clause was restrictively construed. One technique employed by the courts included construing the clause in the light of the doctrine of sham, as in the next case discussed below.

Re Peachdart Ltd [1984] Ch 131

Freudenberg Leather Co. Ltd supplied leather to Peachdart Ltd for use in the manufacture of high-quality leather handbags. On the latter's insolvency, Freudenberg sought to rely upon its retention of title clause incorporated into its standard conditions of sale to recover the outstanding debt of £16,200. The clause provided as follows:

> ... ownership of the Products shall remain with the Seller which reserves the right to dispose of the products until payment in full for all the Products has been received. ... If any of the products are incorporated in or used as materials for other goods before such payment the property in the whole of such other goods shall be and remain with the Seller until such payment has been made. ...
>
> Until the Seller is paid in full for all the Products the relationship of the Buyer to the Seller shall be fiduciary in respect of the Products.

Counsel for the (administrative) receiver conceded that the property in the unused stocks of leather which came into the hands of the (administrative) receiver when he was appointed remained with Freudenberg. As such, the case is similar to *Romalpa*. However, as far as the proceeds of sale of partly

The retention of title clause

manufactured and completely manufactured handbags were concerned, Vinelott J came to the conclusion, at p. 142, despite the clear wording of the retention of title clause, that:

> ... it is impossible to suppose that ... the parties intended that until a parcel of leather had been fully paid for the company would remain a bailee of each piece of leather comprised in the parcel throughout the whole process of manufacture ... and that on the sale of a completed handbag the company would be under an obligation to pay the proceeds of sale into a separate interest-bearing account and to keep them apart from their other moneys and not employ them in the trade.

Although this approach is consistent with *Borden (UK) Ltd* v *Scottish Timber Products Ltd* [1981] Ch 23, and is also mirrored in the subsequent case of *Re Andrabell Ltd* [1984] 3 All ER 407, it may nevertheless be criticised on the basis that it is difficult to reconcile with *Romalpa*. In *Re Peachdart Ltd*, Vinelott J not only felt unable to imply terms, as in *Borden*, he actually chose to disregard express contractual provisions. A better way, one would have thought, to reach this conclusion would have been by looking at the business operation in practice and demonstrating that this was totally at variance with the objectives of the clause.

Any hopes of claiming the manufactured and partly manufactured goods by virtue of the common law doctrine of *accessio*, whereby the owner of a principal chattel (i.e., the leather) may claim ownership of it and the accession (for example, thread, buckles etc.) in the absence of a contrary intention (see chapter 2), were dashed by Vinelott J's finding that the parties had intended that once Peachdart had appropriated a piece of leather to the manufacture of a handbag, the leather ceased to be the exclusive property of Freudenberg. It was also held that such a contrary intention could be implied since, in the absence of records, it would be impossible to ascertain whether those handbags made from the supplier's leather were sold before or after receivership. Obviously, this would be important in determining whether the (administrative) receiver may have wrongfully disposed of the property after his appointment. This conclusion is difficult to understand given the previous concession in the case that it was possible to say for any given handbag whether or not it comprised the supplier's leather.

Hendy Lennox (Industrial Engines) Ltd v *Grahame Puttick Ltd* [1984] 1 WLR 485

This case revolved around the sale of engines which both parties envisaged would eventually be incorporated into diesel generating sets for subsale. Each engine remained identifiable by virtue of its serial number. Following the defendant's insolvency, the outstanding debt owed to the plaintiff seller amounted to over £46,000 which was of little or no value since the buyer owed the debenture holders over £700,000, and the latter held a charge over the buyer's assets. The seller sought to rely upon the retention of title clause incorporated in its standard conditions of sale which provided: '... all goods

... shall be and remain the property of the Company [Hendy Lennox] until the full purchase price thereof shall be paid'.

The above clause contradicted the period of credit provided for under the conditions of sale, and the seller conceded that the right to retake possession of and retain permanently any unpaid-for goods was only exercisable when the buyer was in default of payment, i.e., when the period of credit had expired (up to two months) and the price had not been paid. In addition, the seller conceded an implied term in its contracts with the buyer that he was entitled to sell the goods in advance of paying the price thereof to the seller.

The case finally revolved around conflicting claims in respect of three engines still on the buyer's premises when the (administrative) receiver was appointed. The supplier claimed a proprietary right to these engines which became a direct claim to the proceeds of subsale by virtue of an interlocutory injunction (see chapter 22). Only with respect to one engine did Staughton J find that the seller had a proprietary claim based on its retention of title clause. On the facts, it was held that this engine was not appropriated to any contract of subsale at the time when the credit period conceded by the seller in its conditions of sale expired, thereby giving the seller the right to reclaim the engine. Furthermore, by virtue of the interlocutory proceedings, the seller had a derivative claim against the proceeds of subsale (£1,237) in substitution for the direct claim to retake the engine. With respect to the proceeds of subsale of the other generator sets, a debtor-creditor relationship was held to have intervened.

Undoubtedly, the purpose of the arrangement in *Hendy Lennox*, read as a whole, was a security device because the seller was only concerned with recovering the amount outstanding on the engines. Essentially, the point is that a *Romalpa* clause has a double function, i.e., it contains the elements of both sale and security which is a necessary consequence of the Sale of Goods Act 1979 approach whereby property passing is an aspect of contract rather than conveyance.

Re Andrabell Ltd [1984] 3 All ER 407

The plaintiff supplied travel bags worth nearly £29,000 to Andrabell Ltd, a firm which carried on business as retailers and exporters of travel bags and which went into liquidation before paying any of the money owed to Airborne Accessories Ltd. The contract of sale reserved title until payment but allowed the buyer company 45 days credit. The company resold the bags and paid the proceeds into its general bank account so commingling them with its other moneys. Shortly afterwards, the company went into liquidation.

The approach taken by Peter Gibson J in this case was similar to that adopted by Staughton J in *Hendy Lennox (Industrial Engines) Ltd* v *Grahame Puttick Ltd* [1984] 1 WLR 485, namely, there was no express acknowledgement of a fiduciary situation. The following indicia were considered crucial in the determination of this question:

(a) There was no provision obliging the company to store the bags in a manner which manifested the plaintiff's ownership of the bags.

The retention of title clause

(b) The company was not selling as agent or on the plaintiff's account.
(c) There was no obligation on the company to keep the proceeds from the sale of bags supplied by the plaintiff separate from its own moneys.
(d) There was no duty to account for proceeds.
(e) During the 45-day credit period it was inferred that the company was free to use the proceeds received from the sale of the bags as it liked which was not compatible with the plaintiff having an interest in the proceeds of sale.

It is significant that in both *Hendy Lennox (Industrial Engines) Ltd* v *Grahame Puttick Ltd* and *Re Andrabell Ltd* the provision of credit was considered inconsistent with the equitable duty to account. Nevertheless, this is not an inevitable consequence of a credit period because this could be construed as being subject to a duty to account for proceeds of sale on receipt, thereby reducing the buyer's price indebtedness. It follows that the existence of a credit period does not deprive the duty to account of its effect as it merely postpones this to the end of the credit period except in relation to proceeds of sale received during that period.

Clough Mill Ltd v *Martin* [1985] 1 WLR 111

The facts involved four contracts relating to the sale of yarn by Clough Mill Ltd to Heatherdale Fabrics Ltd between December 1979 and March 1980. On the appointment of the (administrative) receiver, part of the purchase price on each of the four yarn contracts remained outstanding, although 375 kg of unused yarn valued at £1,190 remained on the buyer's premises. Clough Mill sought to rely upon its retention of title clause (condition 12) incorporated into its standard conditions of sale which provided:

> However, the ownership of the material shall remain with the seller, which reserves the right to dispose of the material until payment in full for all the material has been received by it in accordance with the terms of this contract or until such time as the buyer sells the material to its customers by way of bona fide sale at full market value.
> If such payment is overdue in whole or in part the seller may (without prejudice to any of its other rights) recover or resell the material or any of it and may enter upon the buyer's premises by its servants or agents for that purpose.
> Such payment shall become due immediately upon the commencement of any act or proceeding in which the buyer's solvency is involved.
> If any of the material is incorporated in or used as material for other goods before such payment the property in the whole of such goods shall be and remain with the seller until such payment has been made, or the other goods have been sold as aforesaid, and all the seller's rights hereunder in the material shall extend to those other goods.

The (administrative) receiver refused to give up the yarn and instead allowed it to be used in a manufacturing process. An action was brought in conversion for damages against the receiver who, it was argued, remained personally accountable. The present legal position is encapsulated in s. 234(4)(a) of the Insolvency Act 1986 which removes liability if the administrative receiver, or liquidator, *reasonably* believes that the goods belong to the insolvent company and is not negligent. The modern position requires proof of fault which is a higher standard of proof than conversion. As a consequence, the supplier is in an invidious position because he will have to prove that his goods were on the premises at the time of the receivership. Moreover, even if the administrative receiver disposes of the goods negligently, s. 234(4)(b) of the Insolvency Act 1986 anticipates that he can retain a lien on the proceeds of disposal for his own expenses.

Clough Mill Ltd v *Martin* illustrates the dilemma posed by retention of title clauses to the administrative receiver. One of the latter's functions is to generate sufficient cash flow to enable a company to meet its necessary outgoings. This is important since a business sold as a 'going concern' produces a better realisation figure as well as maintaining employment. In contrast, a retention of title clause will prohibit the sale of stock-in-trade or retention of its proceeds. Nonetheless, the approach taken at first instance in *Clough Mill Ltd* v *Martin* ([1984] 1 WLR 1067) would appear to resolve the administrative receiver's dilemma. Judge O'Donoghue came to the conclusion that the prime purpose of the retention of title clause was a security device and, in reaching this conclusion, a subjective test was applied. This involved construing the relevant clause as manifesting an intention to pass property immediately in the goods subject to a grant back by the buyer by way of a charge.

The decision given by Judge O'Donoghue at first instance appeared to have left few of the *Romalpa* principles subsisting. The learned judge held that condition 12 of the supply contract (the retention of title clause) should be read as a whole, and that even the first part of the clause retaining title to goods *in specie* constituted a charge which was void for lack of registration under the Companies Act. This approach was in stark contrast to the previous cases where it had consistently been held that unsold goods supplied under a retention of title clause which were identifiable and still in the possession of the '*Romalpa*-type' buyer on the date of the appointment of the receiver belonged to the supplier. The reasoning here was that crystallisation of a floating charge only operated as an equitable assignment of the goods *owned* by the company at the date of the appointment (see pp. 336–8).

The position adopted by the Court of Appeal which found in favour of Clough Mill can be seen as a mere restatement of the conventional legal position regarding retention of title clauses. The concomitant of this was that there could be no question of a registrable charge being created by the buyer as this presupposes the grant of a security interest. Thus, Oliver LJ in distinguishing *Re Bond Worth* (1980) held at p. 123:

> The operative word here, however, is 'confers' and the whole of Slade J's judgment in that case [*Re Bond Worth Ltd*] was based upon the fact, as he found, that the legal title to the goods had passed to the buyer. That was in the context of a clause which, in terms, sought to reserve only to the seller the 'beneficial' interest and to seek to apply it to the clause now under

consideration is to assume the very thing that is sought to be proved. Of course, where the legal title has passed, security can be provided by a charge created by the new legal owner. But it is not a necessary incident of the seller's securing his position that he should pass the legal title. The whole question is, how has his position been secured? If in fact he has retained the legal title to the goods, then by definition the buyer cannot have charged them in his favour.

This approach would suggest that the reservation of the legal title by the seller is *necessarily* inconsistent with the creation of a charge. However, this analysis is problematical with respect to an extended 'all-liabilities' type of clause. The buyer must be treated as the 'owner' of the goods when he has fully paid for them, otherwise the clause will be void for total failure of consideration (see below).

The treatment of an all-liabilities clause as a charge is going to prove more beneficial to the seller in *any case*. For example, if the supplier delivers goods under separate contracts and is paid in full under one contract but not for the other, it follows that if the supplier repossesses the goods and sells them, he will have to account to the buyer for the sums the seller received under the first contract. This is pertinent when the price achieved in reselling the goods is less than the combined value of the two contracts. The reason for this is that whereas a seller can treat non-payment of part of the purchase price under a single contract as a breach of the entire contract, a seller who has entered into several contracts cannot treat a failure to make payments under one contract as a breach of the other contracts. Nonetheless, there is intuitive attraction in the logic applied in *Clough Mill Ltd v Martin* with respect to an all-liabilities proceeds clause. As an aspect of freedom of contract, the seller can impose any conditions he wants to for the transfer of ownership to his buyer and there is nothing wrong in principle, therefore, with the seller insisting that his buyer should have discharged his indebtedness to him. It could be argued that the seller's giving up possession to the buyer of the goods subject to an all-liabilities clause will not amount to a charge because the buyer is not conferring rights over his *own* goods. This appears to have been the analysis adopted, at least inferentially, in the Court of Appeal approach in *Clough Mill Ltd v Martin*.

Armour v *Thyssen Edelstahlwerke AG* [1991] 2 AC 339
The facts in this case relate to the supply of steel strip by Thyssen (a German company) to a Scottish manufacturer (Carron) of metal, plastic and general engineering products. The conditions of supply included a retention of title clause which, when translated from the German, read as follows:

> All goods delivered by us remain our property (goods remaining in our ownership) until all debts owed to us including any balances existing at relevant times — due to us on any legal grounds — are settled. This also holds good if payments are made for the purpose of settlement of specially designated claims. Debts owed to companies, being members of our combine, are deemed to be such debts.

In August 1982, Carron went into receivership. At this time, there was lying in Carron's works some 67,423 kg of steel strip most of it being in the state in which it had been delivered. The invoice value of the steel was £71,769 and no part of this had been paid.

Following the appointment of receivers, a dispute arose concerning the ownership of the steel strip. The receivers agreed that if Thyssen could establish an effective reservation of title clause, the steel strip would be returned or paid for if used. Litigation ensued in the Scottish courts which raged for eight years and matters were not finally resolved until the recent House of Lords decision. The lower Scottish court decisions focused upon the law to be applied in the case as well as the validity of an all-sums retention of title clause under Scottish law. In a sense, the House of Lords restated the conventional legal position, namely, the reservation of title clause in a contract of *sale* does not constitute a security interest which may require registration under the Companies Act 1985 since it arises by way of reservation of title rather than the grant by the debtor of a charge or mortgage.

An interesting problem that arises out of an all-liabilities retention of title clause, in relation to goods which have been repossessed by the seller, is whether a buyer has the right to reclaim money paid over to the seller because of the latter's total failure of consideration. In order to succeed in this submission, the buyer will have to show that he received no benefit from the contract. The mere fact that the buyer has enjoyed possession of the goods does not constitute a benefit in the sense that it precludes the buyer from recovering money paid over. This is because the essence of a sale contract involves the passage of general property in the goods (s. 2(1) of the Sale of Goods Act 1979).

In *Armour*, the House of Lords endorsed the policy that where there is security with recourse to property which can be effected by means other than a transaction of loan or charge, this is not treated as registrable under s. 395 of the Companies Act 1985 (as amended). This is so even though the exact economic effect might be carried out through a transaction which in form was registrable as a security interest in goods (chapter 15). Nonetheless, the question still remains whether property passing by agreement under the Sale of Goods Act 1979 can by itself adequately deal with the problems posed in the *Romalpa* case context.

IDENTIFICATION OF RETENTION OF TITLE CLAUSES

There is no doubt that the approach taken by the Court of Appeal in *Clough Mill Ltd* v *Martin* [1985] 1 WLR 111 and the House of Lords in *Armour* v *Thyssen Edelstahlwerke AG* [1991] 2 AC 339 restores the lustre in retention of title clauses to suppliers of goods. One reason for this is that great emphasis was placed upon the *agreement* between the two parties as being determinative of the issues. In this vein concerning the proceeds of sale of goods held in a fiduciary capacity, Robert Goff LJ said in *Clough Mill Ltd* v *Martin* at p. 116:

> I do not see why the relationship between A and B, pending sale or consumption, should not be the relationship of bailor and bailee, even though A has no right to trace the property in his goods into the proceeds of

sale. If that is what the parties have agreed should happen, I can see no reason why the law should not give effect to that intention.

Although it was not really at issue in *Clough Mill Ltd* v *Martin*, both Robert Goff and Oliver LJJ held that at common law property in new goods made by material supplied could vest in the supplier so long as there was an agreement to this effect. Despite the seemingly unequivocal approach taken by some of the judges in the Court of Appeal, it is trite law that parties cannot by their contractual stipulations alone alter the application of the principles and the rules of the law of property.

In the light of the above, it is appropriate to consider the different contractual formulations of retention of title clauses and determine their validity on the basis of legal principle and authority. Broadly speaking, there is the primary clause reserving title to goods *in specie* followed by horizontal extensions into debts; there are also vertical extensions which seek to follow the goods supplied into a finished product or its proceeds. For the sake of convenience, the different types of clauses may be set out as follows:

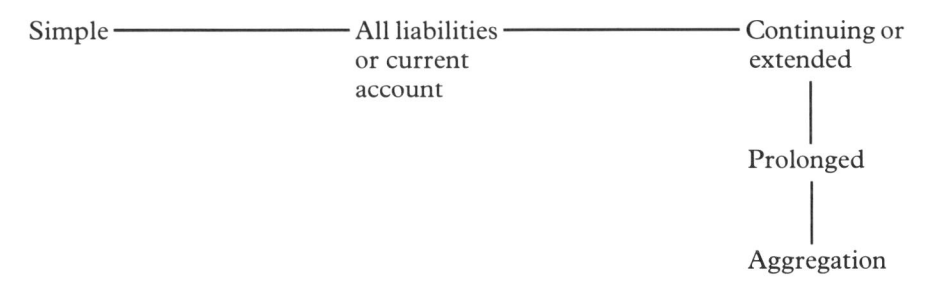

Simple ———————————— All liabilities ———————————— Continuing or
                                      or current   extended
                                        account
                                                                                                            Prolonged
                                                                                                            Aggregation

Description

    (a) *Simple clause*: where the seller retains ownership until the full purchase price for those goods has been paid

    (b) *All liabilities or current account*: this links property passage with the satisfaction of all debts outstanding between the buyer and seller

    (c) *Continuing or extended*: the seller retains ownership on the basis of (a) and/or (b) as against the buyer and any sub-buyer

    (d) *Prolonged*: this includes elements of (a) to (c) above but on subsale seeks to retain title to the proceeds of sale or of the right to sue the sub-buyer for the proceeds.

    (e) *Aggregation*: where elements (a) to (d) may be included but claims ownership of manufactured property from the goods supplied, or of a proportionate part of it equal to the contribution made to the manufacturing process by the original goods.

We have seen from the case law that the English courts have championed the first two horizontal types of clauses. With regard to the further horizontal extension, and especially the vertical applications of the clause, there are significant conceptual and practical difficulties which we shall now discuss.

The question regarding the *capacity* of Romalpa when disposing of the aluminium foil reflects the difficulties inherent in the Court of Appeal analysis. Indeed, the nature of the fiduciary relationship was never established. The relationship between the supplier and possessor-debtor pending payment, subsale or incorporation of the material delivered into a finished product is important as it will govern the supplier's ability to recover the goods. Nonetheless, the case law demonstrates confusion which is reflected in *Borden (UK) Ltd* v *Scottish Timber Products* [1981] Ch 25 where Bridge LJ having conceded that the defendants in *Romalpa* were bailees then proceeded to describe them as agents. We shall now consider the ramifications of each of these legal categorisations in the context of retention of title clauses.

BAILMENT AND VERTICAL EXTENSION

The issue of what constitutes a bailment is a question of law, and the *nature* of bailment is particularly important where the supply contract is silent as to the rights and duties of the possessor. In this respect, it would be unlikely that the nature of the bailment in the *Romalpa* context is gratuitous. Such a conclusion would reduce the position of the bailee to that of a mere tenant at will and, as a matter of principle, this cannot be correct for the whole system of credit selling would then lose its attraction. The best approach is to consider the bailment element as being incidental to the contract of sale which will state the circumstances under which the seller should be entitled to repossession. The necessary implication follows that until the events isolated in the contract of sale occur, the buyer is entitled to retain possession.

It would seem odd, bearing in mind the subject-matter of many supply contracts including a retention of title clause (i.e. raw materials or semi-manufactured goods) to categorise the nature of the bailment as being one of hire. The main objections include: first, there is no point in superimposing an agreement for hire on top of an agreement for sale; second, it would lead to the necessary conclusion that the hirer/buyer was undertaking to purchase a second-hand chattel at the end of the period of hire which is incorrect; third, it can be demonstrated that no part of the purchase price is allocable on account of the bailment, for example, if delivery was delayed until the purchase price was paid this would not affect the purchase price. The approach appears to lead us to the conclusion that the bailment can only be categorised as one 'for valuable consideration'. At the same time, it is important not to suppose that the categories of bailment are closed, or that Lord Holt's enumeration of them in *Coggs* v *Bernard* (1703) 2 Ld Raym 909 was exhaustive. As Peter Gibson J pointed out in *Re Andrabell Ltd* [1984] 3 All ER 407 at p. 414:

> The present case seems to me to differ from that of a mere bailee with whom goods are deposited for safe-keeping or any other ordinary form of bailment an essential element of which would appear to be an undertaking to return the bailed chattels in their original or altered form or otherwise deal with them in accordance with the directions of the bailor.

The consideration for the buyer's right to possession should be analysed not as a notional aspect of the purchase price but rather as his agreeing to enter into the contract of sale and purchase. If this is the case, repossession by the seller, in the absence of an express prohibition in the contract, does not *ipso facto* terminate the contract because the seller may repossess only to increase his own security without necessarily forfeiting the buyer's right to pay any unsatisfied part of the price and so perfecting his ownership.

Field warehousing

A sophisticated trade creditor in the *Romalpa* context may not place the burden of separation of the goods supplied so that they can be identified upon the debtor. The trade creditor himself may undertake the supervision of the bailment mechanism. What is envisaged here is the classic field warehousing arrangement. This is intimately connected with the idea of possessory control and, as such, has an aura of esoterica surrounding it. The mechanism developed in the depression-ridden 1930s in the USA. It provided an important way of financing manufacturing processes at a time of general capital starvation when conventional security devices were not available, mainly because of over-collateralisation in previous loans. Field warehousing came into its own as it predominantly dealt with raw materials awaiting manufacture. The manufacturer creates a field warehouse through leasing a portion of his premises containing the materials to a warehouse company. Essentially, it is a device designed to enable a borrower to pledge his inventory as security for advances without moving the inventory from its usual place of storage. In effect, the field warehouseman brings the warehouse to the goods, reversing the usual procedure of 'terminal' warehousing.

An area where the goods are stored is leased and sealed off; the employees of the borrower who normally control the stock-in-trade are hired and bonded by the warehouse company pursuant to formal written agreements. Signs are posted throughout the leased area giving notice of the field warehouseman's possession. Keys to the warehouse area are maintained by the bonded employees, and warehouse receipts, usually non-negotiable in form, are issued for commodities deposited by the borrower. The crucial element for a valid field warehousing arrangement is that 'dominion and control' is held by the supplier.

Field warehousing in the USA is usually undertaken by a professional warehousing company which is insured for loss or dissipation of the collateral and thereby the lender achieves excellent security. Furthermore, since the goods are under the pledgee's control, he can release them to the debtor in accordance with a prearranged collateral-to-loan ratio. With the right combination of creditor risk-aversion, debtor suspiciousness, asset volatility, a limited need for direct access as in stockpiles of out-of-season goods with relatively high unit value, the field warehouse is an excellent monitoring mechanism. Thus, when the manufacturer desires to process the materials, he can obtain temporary possession for that purpose and is policed by the warehouseman. Of course, if the goods or warehouse receipts are released there is always the danger of an unscrupulous borrower repledging them as security for another loan (see *Lloyds Bank Ltd* v *Bank of America National Trust and Savings Association* [1938] 2 KB 147). If the goods are released and sold on credit, the lender will often have an account receivable assigned to it as substitute security for the warehouse receipt covering the goods. Alternatively, the manufacturer could obtain a warehouse receipt from the lender on a trust receipt and, after processing, either the finished product could be turned over to the warehouse, or it could be sold and the proceeds used to pay off the outstanding indebtedness.

It is self-evident that a borrower who makes use of field warehousing will not be a strong enterprise. The latter should obviously prefer to borrow on an unsecured basis or on the strength of its receivables rather than have its inventory (stock-in-trade) tied up in a warehouse. Moreover, a major limiting effect of the field warehousing arrangement is that, by definition, it can only apply to goods *in specie*. Nevertheless, the bailment mechanism is sufficiently flexible to accommodate a more extensive clause, most notably, the bailment *locatio operis faciendi* or commodity processing.

Commodity processing bailments
This occurs in many different areas, typically, where a party performs the processing, converting or finishing material supplied by shippers and then 'returns' the finished or semi-finished material or an agreed quantity of equivalent material in exchange for a fee. The phenomenon was evident before the New Zealand Court of Appeal in *Coleman* v *Harvey* [1989] 1 NZLR 723 and the facts are set out and discussed on pp. 38–9.

The bailment analysis is not without difficulty especially if bailment is defined in terms of obliging the bailee to return the chattel to the bailor at the end of the period. The issue goes to the heart of the definition of bailment itself. On the basis of authority and principle, it is not fatal to the characterisation of bailment that the bailee is under no duty to return the bailed goods to the bailor. It is only necessary for the former to deal with the goods in accordance with the latter's instructions, so persons fraudulently converting to their own use goods held by them on a 'sale or return' basis have been convicted of larceny by a bailee (see *R* v *Henderson* (1870) 11 Cox CC 593; *R* v *Richmond* (1873) 12 Cox CC 495). The material question in this context is, which party does the contract leave that level of control of the goods which is consistent with (complete) ownership? Such an approach is sensible since a bailment does not contemplate a transfer of (complete) ownership to the bailee.

It could be argued that from an economic and functional perspective, the best way of analysing commodity processing is not in terms of bailment but rather as an exchange. What is envisaged here is a series of back-to-back transactions in which the shipper supplies raw material to the possessor, the latter agrees to 'exchange' the finished product, and the difference in value between the two is reflected in a 'fee' paid in money by the shipper to approximate the processor's variable costs of upgrading plus a margin to reflect the return on investment required to keep him in business. The concomitant of this approach is that property passes immediately, so prejudicing the secured position of the supplier. Nonetheless, such an argument is unlikely to prevail in England in the light of the formalistic approach adopted by the Sale of Goods Act 1979. This phenomenon can be further illustrated with 'consignments' or 'sale or return' transactions.

Consignment sales and retention of title

From the functional perspective there are obvious similarities between commodity processing and 'consignments' or 'sale or return'. Both transactions involve delivery of goods to a second party; with consignments, the delivery is for redistribution to third parties while in the processing case, the model calls for the delivery of raw material by the shipper and the delivery by the processor of upgraded and hence related material to the shipper. The essence of both models calls for retention of title — by the consignor until his agent consignee sells the goods for the consigner, and by the shipper throughout performance of the entire transaction. Moreover, both transactions fulfil as part of their essential purpose a financing function.

In a sense, the idea of a 'consignment sale' is self-contradictory because one part of the phrase is assuming what the other contradicts. The position becomes clear if one keeps in mind the distinction between wholesale and retail financing since the consignment is a transaction in which the consignee/bailee carries out the sale on the basis of principal and agent. As an agency arrangement, the consignment is outside the scope of the Sale of Goods Act 1979.

Section 18, r. 4 of the Sale of Goods Act 1979 provides that:

When goods are delivered to the buyer on approval or on sale or return or other similar terms the property in the goods passes to the buyer:—
    (a) when he signifies his approval or acceptance to the seller or does any other act adopting the transaction;
    (b) if he does not signify his approval or acceptance to the seller but retains the goods without giving notice of rejection, then, if a time has been fixed for the return of the goods, on the expiration of that time, and, if no time has been fixed, on the expiration of a reasonable time.

It is interesting that this does not refer to goods being 'sold' but rather refers to delivery. It is clear that through this method, Chalmers, the draftsman of the Sale of Goods Act 1893, accommodated both 'a contract of sale' and an 'agreement to sell'. The latter analysis does not entirely fit conceptually the 'sale or return' transaction, that is, here there is an agreement to sell subject to the buyer adopting the transaction. Moreover, in the case of 'sales on approval', many of these are 'sales' (in the sense of property passing) subject to a right of rescission. The crucial question here is whether the buyer has engaged in an 'act adopting the transaction'. This was considered by the Court of Appeal in *Kirkham* v *Attenborough* [1897] 1 QB 201, the facts of which concerned the plaintiff, a manufacturer of jewellery, entrusting the jewellery to a rogue on a sale or return basis. The rogue pledged the goods with the defendant, but the Court of Appeal refused the plaintiff's claim for the return of the goods on the basis that the rogue by pledging the goods had adopted the transaction (see also *Genn* v *Winkel* (1912) 107 LT 434).

The question of what constitutes a 'true' consignment sale is highly pertinent in the *Romalpa* context. The reason for this is that there is a natural judicial hostility to security consignments which can be considered to constitute secret liens. This factor may explain the restrictive interpretation of proceeds clauses in the post *Romalpa* case law (see below).

AGENCY AND VERTICAL EXTENSION

The failure of the Court of Appeal in *Aluminium Industrie Vaassen BV* v *Romalpa Aluminium Ltd* [1976] 1 WLR 676 to define the precise nature of the fiduciary relationship is fundamental because a bailment differs functionally as well as conceptually from agency. In this respect, whereas a bailment may be for the benefit of the bailee or bailor or both, an agency relationship is either for the benefit of the principal alone where the agency is gratuitous, or for both parties where it is for consideration. A bailment is concerned with the physical possession of chattels whilst agency is also concerned with the making of contracts in relation to the property.

The legal incidents of agency are very important in the *Romalpa* context and go to the issue of the relationship between the supplier (as undisclosed principal) and the subpurchasers, together with raising questions of ownership with regard to sale proceeds. It is anticipated here that the supplier of goods with a retention of title clause claims the proceeds of the goods either because the sale was unauthorised resulting in a constructive trust of the proceeds, or, if the dispositions were authorised, there was an agreement to account *in specie* for the proceeds of the goods. If the efficacy of such a clause were established, its widespread use could compromise factoring as an efficient commercial instrument since it would require very close scrutiny of the debts bought in order to ensure that they really belong to the business concerned and not to a '*Romalpa*-type' seller. It is for this reason that Phillips J was anxious to dismiss the fiduciary argument in *E. Pfeiffer Weinkellerei-Weineinkauf GmbH & Co.* v *Arbuthnot Factors Ltd* [1988] 1 WLR 150 (see also the approach of Mummery J in *Compaq Computer Ltd* v *Abercorn Group Ltd* [1991] BCC 484). We shall now consider this question in greater detail.

The validity of proceeds clauses

One important effect of a valid proceeds clause is that it makes the purchaser a bare trustee of the sale proceeds for the supplier of goods and the relationship can be categorised as principal and agent. The logic here is that since the agent's relation to the principal's assets is that of bailee and the principal does not agree that the agent should stand in relation to those assets as owner, then, as was pointed out in *Foley* v *Hill* (1848) 2 HL Cas 28 at p. 35:

> The goods remain the goods of the owner or principal until the sale takes place, and the moment the money is received the money remains the property of the principal.

Of course, the principal and agent are able to limit and exclude some of their fiduciary obligations. However, if the parties wish the agency to continue *vis à vis* those assets, they cannot stipulate that they are owned by the agent. The whole purpose of agency is to govern the relationships that arise when one person is vested with the power mainly to affect the liabilities of another. To protect against abuse of this power the law imposes fiduciary duties on the agent which cannot be excluded, i.e., the agent cannot pass to himself the ownership of those assets unless a debtor–creditor relationship arises (compare *Len Vidgen Ski and Leisure Ltd* v *Timaru Marine Supplies (1982) Ltd* [1986] 1 NZLR 349).

The establishment of the agency relationship Even though agency relationships may exist for a particular purpose at one stage of the parties' dealings, the rest of their dealings may show that the parties intended to create a relationship of creditor and debtor by way of dealing with each other *as principals* and not as principal and agent (see *Re Stenning* [1895] 2 Ch 433; *Wilsons and Furness-Leyland Line Ltd* v *British and Continental Shipping Co. Ltd* (1907) 23 TLR 397; *King* v *Hutton* (1900) 83 LT 68). Significantly, in *E. Pfeiffer Weinkellerei-Weineninkauf GmbH & Co.* v *Arbuthnot Factors Ltd* [1988] 1 WLR 150, it is clear that Phillips J considered at p. 159 it inappropriate to describe the relationship of a seller and a buyer in possession (to whom title had not yet passed) as that of bailor and bailee:

Where the seller retains title by way of security prior to subsale, but the contract expressly or impliedly authorises the buyer to effect subsales, I do not consider that any prima facie implication arises that sub-sales are to be effected by the buyer as agent for and for the account of the seller. On the contrary, I consider that the normal implication that arises from the relationship of buyer and seller is that if the buyer is permitted to subsell in the normal course of his business, he will do so for his own account.

The main objection against an agency relation is that the dealer is permitted to keep the profits on subsale. In *Re Bond Worth Ltd* [1980] Ch 228, Slade J cited *Re Nevill, ex parte White* (1871) LR 6 Ch App 397 as authority for this proposition. However, it is important to recognise that the court in that case was concerned with the *substance* of the relationship between supplier and dealer. The court considered that, on the facts, the two month credit period together with the fact that the dealer was under no duty to account and could sell the goods for whatever price he wished, pointed to a debtor-creditor relationship. This was confirmed in the later case of *Re Smith, ex parte Bright* (1879) 10 ChD 566 where Jessel MR held at p. 570:

There is nothing to prevent the principal from remunerating the agent by a commission varying according to the amount of the profit obtained by the sale. *A fortiori* there is nothing to prevent his paying a commission depending upon the surplus which the agent can obtain over and above the price which will satisfy the principal.

Neither should a credit period count against beneficial ownership of the proceeds; the credit allows the dealer to extend a similar period of credit to a subsequent purchaser even if the dealer had to account as soon as the proceeds were in fact received.

The main characteristic of an agency relationship is that the agent is invested with a 'legal power' to alter his principal's legal relations with third parties. The ability or the power which the agent has to affect his principal's legal position is a question of law, i.e., once a person is recognised by the law as having such power to affect his principal's legal relations by the making of contracts or the disposition of property, the latter is liable even though he has not authorised the former to act on his behalf (*Summers* v *Solomon* (1857) 7 E & B 879). It is for this reason that the supplier must seek an indemnity against the dealer for any potential liability to sub-buyers in contract or tort.

The lack of a contractual nexus between the supplier and sub-buyer may not be a decisive factor in showing that no agency exists between the supplier and dealer because the latter may be a commission agent. Historically, the commission agent charges his correspondent with the price of the goods and a commission for his services. It was the fact that the commission agent did not establish privity between his principal and third party that distinguished him from the factor and the broker. This explains Roskill LJ's allusion in *Aluminium Industrie Vaassen BV* v *Romalpa Aluminium Ltd* [1976] 1 WLR 676 at p. 690:

> I see no difficulty in the contractual concept that, as between the defendants and their subpurchasers, the defendants sold as principals, but that, as between themselves and the plaintiffs, those goods which they were selling as principals within their implied authority from the plaintiffs were the plaintiffs' goods which they were selling as agents for the plaintiffs to whom they remained fully accountable.

In principle, there should be no conceptual obstacle in viewing the agent as being both principal under the contract and at the same time as agent of the (undisclosed) principal in conveying the latter's title to the sub-buyer. Such an approach is consistent with relativity of title seen under sales law, whereby the agent confers his *own* title to the buyer (possessory title) and also contracts to pass the principal's property to the third party. This does not necessarily give rise to any contractual nexus and therefore liability between them. The basis of the undisclosed principal's action against the buyer is that the debt is owed to him by virtue of the former's ownership of the *res* and its delivery to the buyer.

It was argued in *Re Andrabell Ltd* [1984] 3 All ER 407 that, since the dealer was under an obligation to pay irrespective of whether the subpurchasers had paid, an agency relationship could not then be established. This is not an inevitable conclusion so that in *Churchill and Sim* v *Goddard* [1937] 1 KB 92, Lord Roche indicated at p. 101:

> Several cases were cited to the judge [Branson J at first instance] as showing the history of similar dealings over a number of years as showing how well

The retention of title clause

known to the trade was the course of business by which brokers acted *del credere* and paid the sellers before the buyers paid them.

It may be also that the agents themselves can have the option to buy if they wish so to do. An option should be distinguished from a duty to buy since the latter is tantamount to a seller–buyer relationship.

The fiduciary incidents of an agency relationship In the cases dealing with retention of title clauses, much emphasis has been placed upon the lack of a duty to separate proceeds. It does seem odd that the 'business efficacy' test has been used to exclude such an implication, for example, in *Re Andrabell Ltd* [1984] 3 All ER 407, because the issue is whether, *as a matter of law*, such a duty to account arises by virtue of the categorisation of the relationship as that of principal and agent. The wider question here is whether the categorisation of the relationship as being fiduciary necessarily in all cases carries the incidents of a normal fiduciary relation. Both Staughton J in *Hendy Lennox (Industrial Engines) Ltd v Grahame Puttick Ltd* [1984] 1 WLR 485 and Peter Gibson J in *Re Andrabell Ltd* rejected the idea that the bailor–bailee relationship was necessarily a fiduciary one. Nonetheless, it has to be admitted that there is some disagreement between Staughton J and Peter Gibson J about the probability that bailees occupy a fiduciary position. Thus, Staughton J considered at one point in his judgment that there is a presumption that bailees are fiduciaries although, at a later stage, he opined that each case should be examined to see whether it was of a fiduciary nature. It is clear that Peter Gibson J in *Re Andrabell Ltd* preferred the latter view. Undoubtedly, there is confusion here.

Some academic writers have expressed the view that the relationship of principal and agent especially does not always carry the incidents of a normal fiduciary relationship. It is essential here to examine this view in the light of the authorities which are relied upon for support (see Sealy, 'Fiduciary Relationships' [1962] CLJ 69; Brunyate, *Limitation of Actions in Equity* (London, 1932), at pp. 86–7; Langdell, *A Brief Survey of Equity Jurisdiction*, 2nd ed. (London, 1908)). Thus, Dr Sealy concluded that if I send my car to a dealer to sell it on my behalf, he is, like any other agent, in a fiduciary position towards me. Up to the time of sale, he holds the car on my behalf, i.e., I can recover the car as my property. As from the time of sale, the agent is my debtor only as regards the proceeds. The reason, as Dr Sealy puts it at p. 81 is:

> As in almost all commercial transactions, it is understood that he will owe me the amount of the sale price, but not that he will keep intact the actual moneys which he has received and hold them for my benefit. He is my debtor, not my trustee.

In support of this result, Dr Sealy referred to *Henry v Hammond* [1913] 2 KB 515, *New Zealand and Australian Land Co. v Ruston* (1880) 5 QBD 474 and to Brunyate, on *Limitation of Actions*, who in turn said at p. 86 that:

In the 18th and early 19th century a factor was regarded as a trustee of the money of his principal, but at the present day [1932] he will probably not be so regarded . . . a selling agent may be a trustee of the property which he is to sell until it is sold and yet not be a trustee of the proceeds of sale.

In support of his conclusion, Brunyate cited *Friend* v *Young* [1897] 2 Ch 421 and *Henry* v *Hammond*. Moreover, Langdell referred to some types of agents, such as stockbrokers and auctioneers, saying that they receive the proceeds of their principal's property as debtors and not trustees and referred to some cases (citing *Scott* v *Surman* (1742) Willes 400; *Ex parte Dumas* (1754) 1 Atk 232). These cases were decided at the time when equity had not yet developed the metaphysical approach of identifying money (see below). Furthermore, the judges who decided those cases based their decisions on the fact that money has no earmark and cannot therefore be identified.

If the conclusion which the learned writers above arrived at is to deprive the principal of a commercial agent priority over the general creditors to recover money or the proceeds of property which the agent is employed to sell, the cases which they referred to cannot support that result. Thus, in *New Zealand and Australian Land Co.* v *Ruston*, the Court of Appeal found on the facts that there was no relationship of principal and agent but had there been such a relationship, the Lord Justices had no doubt of the principal's right to follow. In this respect, Baggallay LJ said at pp. 483–4:

> There is no question as regards the doctrine well known in equity . . . with respect to property disposed of by persons standing in a fiduciary position, namely, that such property, or the proceeds of it can be followed if it can be identified, and it is also equally well known that there is no distinction as regards this doctrine between an express trustee or an agent or bailee standing in a similar fiduciary position.

The other two cases which were cited to support the different conclusion were *Friend* v *Young* and *Henry* v *Hammond*. In both of those cases, the agents, who were commission and shipping agents respectively, pleaded the Statute of Limitations and the court allowed the defence. They are not insolvency cases. At any rate, if the commercial character of the agency is to affect the principal's right with regard to the Statute of Limitations, it does not affect the principal's priority to trace money in the hands of his bankrupt agent as if the latter were an express trustee. There are many cases of insolvent agents whose commercial character is not in dispute which confirm the principal's right to trace (see for example, *Re Strachan, ex parte Cooke* (1876) 4 ChD 123; *Harris* v *Truman* (1882) 9 QBD 264; *Hancock* v *Smith* (1889) 41 ChD 456; *Re Wreford* (1897) 13 TLR 153; *Re Arthur Wheeler and Co.* (1933) 102 LJ Ch 341). The present law appears to be that the insolvent agent should be treated as a trustee for his principal, the latter can recover assets as if he were a *cestui que trust* without any distinction being drawn between commercial and non-commercial agents. In accordance with general principles, this tracing right only fails when the proceeds cease to be identifiable, or when the property has passed to a purchaser for value of the legal estate without notice as in the case where proceeds are used to pay off debts of the purchaser (*Taylor* v *Blakelock* (1886) 32 ChD 560).

By virtue of the supplier's beneficial interest in the (identifiable) proceeds, it could be argued that there can be no possible application of the rule in *Dearle* v *Hall* (1828) 3 Russ 1 in a priority dispute with a factoring company since there is no competition between successive assignees of the *same* debt. The supplier is the equitable owner of the debt. The essential issue is whether a fiduciary obligation has been established. A mere contractual obligation to account for the proceeds of sale to the extent of the debts owing to the supplier does not amount to a fiduciary relationship (see *Compaq Computer Ltd* v *Abercorn Group Ltd* [1991] BCC 484).

EQUITABLE INFILTRATION INTO COMMERCIAL LAW

There is no doubt that the vertical application of a retention of title clause represents an attempt to introduce equitable doctrine into the law of sale mainly through the trust instrument. The trust is sometimes considered a 'snare' for secured and unsecured creditors since reasonable investigation may not reveal that a company holds assets on trust for another. An inevitable accompaniment to the trust instrument is the tracing remedy.

Tracing involves essentially an *in specie* claim to property in which the claimant has no property interest other than that which the right provides but which is identifiably linked to misappropriated property. The concept is restitutionary in the sense that it is premised on the principle of unjust enrichment, the 'unjust' element often being satisfied by the defendant's violation of his fiduciary duties. In the late 19th century, Anglo-American courts declared that tracing claims reach all fiduciaries (see *Re Hallett's Estate* (1879) 13 ChD 696) who violate their duties, although the types of misappropriation that may give rise to tracing are varied including conversion, fraud, mistake, and where specific performance is available against breaches of contract. Tracing is most useful to a claimant when it provides him with a larger recovery than he would have received through a simple money judgment, for example, against an insolvent wrongdoer or by allowing him to sue solvent third parties who have traceable property. Moreover, a claimant may trace an asset into the hands of an insolvent defendant when the asset is worth more than the claimant's actual loss.

Attempts have been made to restrict the reaches of the tracing doctrine as in the case of 'innocent' converters through the Torts (Interference with Goods) Act 1977, and by reference to considerations of 'fairness' evident in the dissenting judgments of Viscount Dilhorne and Lord Upjohn in *Boardman* v *Phipps* [1967] 2 AC 46. The arguments are often predicated upon the thesis that the defrauded person's recovery of the increased value of the trust property is a windfall. Interestingly, tracing analysis is still applied, but this is restricted to the *loss* incurred. Difficulties arise in measuring the loss and the courts in applying tracing rules do not generally effect a sophisticated analysis concerning the question of 'benefit' to the wrongdoer. In the context of a

Romalpa setting, the problem can be conceptually illustrated as follows: the bailee wrongfully converts the goods of the bailor/trade creditor by incorporating them in an industrial process (manufacturing) contrary to the supply agreement. By concentrating on *physical* events, tracing conclusively presumes that the wrongdoer would not have acquired the 'product' but for the conversion.

If an inquiry were made into the *causal* events, this might illuminate the problem of quantifying the wrongdoer's benefit which under tracing rules has to be disgorged. For example, why should it be assumed that the wrongdoer could *only* have obtained the 'product' by conversion? The wrongdoer may very well have a line of credit available to him from a creditor which would have enabled him to pay for the material supplied. Indeed, a credit period is often incorporated in a retention of title clause which will be relevant for conversion purposes as was illustrated in *Hendy Lennox (Industrial Engines) Ltd* v *Grahame Puttick Ltd* [1984] 1 WLR 485. If this is the case, benefit should instead be caculated as the value of the misappropriation of the asset at the time of its occurrence plus the interest on that value based on the rate available for the wrongdoer if he had borrowed a sum equivalent to that value.

More difficult considerations are brought into focus where the wrongdoer lacks the wealth or borrowing capacity to purchase the asset. If the wrongdoer augments the value of the asset, for example, through manufacturing, there are two aspects to the causal approach: first, the wrongdoer would not have had the asset 'but for' the misappropriation; secondly, the traceable product that the owner claims may not have been so valuable 'but for' the wrongdoer's efforts. It would seem that in identifying the benefit, the wrongdoer should receive credit for the actual value of any expenditures of time and money to the extent that such expenditures augment the value of the traceable item. The real issue, however, surrounds the question whether to apportion any profits gained as a consequence of sale. In this situation, a balance has to be struck between the policies of encouraging productive use of property and deterring wrongful conduct. With regard to conscious wrongdoing, no profit should be apportioned and the latter policy should prevail whereas in the case of the ignorant wrongdoer, the former policy is stronger. These divergent approaches may pose significant problems of application in the *Romalpa* scenario because of the great difficulty in identifying goods which have exceeded the credit period of supply for the conscious wrongdoing purpose. Besides, as is seen in *Borden (UK) Ltd* v *Scottish Timber Products Ltd* [1981] Ch 25, lack of warehousing facilities may frustrate the imposition of such a requirement in any case.

Tracing is essentially a rough doctrine of causation. The assumption is that the defendant has benefited at the claimant's expense and that the amount of the benefit is the value of the traceable product. In contrast if tracing is not available, the court assumes that a wrongdoer has not benefited beyond receiving the value of the misappropriation. The dilemma, of course, is that essentially the inequity occasioned to victim one and victim two is the same, but the remedy depends upon the whim of the wrongdoer, i.e., whether he decided to use the proceeds to 'consume' or to 'invest'. It may be possible to argue that the victim who cannot trace could maintain that the misappropriation enabled the wrongdoer to free up and use other funds or assets to purchase a product. At least this approach goes some way to addressing the arbitrariness involved in tracing which overcompensates one victim but creates distinctions between claimants on, for example, the basis of 'identifiability'. Thus, in *Borden (UK) Ltd* v *Scottish Timber Products Ltd*, Templeman LJ at p. 32 referred to the task before the court as one of: '. . . unearthing the unearthable, tracing the untraceable and calculating the incalculable.' Similarly, Bridge LJ in that case posed the question whether the manufacturer of cattle cake who sells it to a farmer, who in turn feeds it to his cattle, can claim that the cow is a 'mixed fund'? His lordship maintained that although the doctrine of tracing might apply where a bailee/trustee mixed goods of his bailor/beneficiary with goods of his own, this could not be the case where the mixing was of dissimilar items.

The tracing rules are not consistent which can easily be demonstrated in the case of commingled funds. Money is an abstract means of dissolving all kinds of property into mere quantities and can serve as a medium of exchange as well as a store of value. The law of tracing assets may have some interest in these aspects which give money its economic functions, and in a sense, money might be equated with any fungible thing for neither of them can be distinguished and earmarked so as to be recovered. Whether money is viewed as an actual object which serves as a medium of exchange or a unit of account by reference to which means of payment are denominated, the problem of fact with regard to identifiability arises. Although banknotes are identifiable in that their serial numbers can be recorded, this will entail that the person who receives a banknote should inquire into the title of the person who passes it. Since bank notes are *currency*, such an approach is inconsistent with their economic function.

There is also an historical explanation for the restrictive attitude towards the tracing of money. In 1537, it was laid down in *Core's Case* (1537) Dyer 20 at p. 22b:

> . . . if I bail twenty pounds to one to keep for my use, if the twenty pounds were not contained in a bag, coffer, or box, an action of detinue doth not lie, because the twenty pounds could not be discovered or known to be mine, but debt and account lie at my pleasure.

Up to the beginning of the 18th century, money meant coins only. When the banknotes which goldsmiths and bankers used began to appear as promises to pay a named person, they developed into bearer notes. They were considered as documentary instruments and treated as chattels capable of being followed because they were distinguishable and identifiable by marks and numbers on them. By the middle of the 18th century when the circulation of banknotes became more common, a chattel view of banknotes was impossible to sustain and they were treated as cash just as coins were (see *Miller* v *Race* (1758) 1 Burr 452). Their economic function dictated that they could not be followed *in specie*.

The inability of the Judicature Acts 1873 to 1875 to fuse law and equity completely makes it necessary to examine the scope of both common law and equitable tracing procedures. However, there are clear indications from the judgments of the Law Lords in *Lipkin Gorman* v *Karpnale Ltd* [1991] 2 AC 548 of the desirability that the relevant equitable and common law rules be made uniform.

The common law approach to tracing proceeds

The orthodox approach to common law tracing stresses its materialism which rests on an interpretation of various *dicta* in *Taylor* v *Plumer* (1815) 3 M & S 562. In this case, Lord Ellenborough CJ held at p. 575:

> It makes no difference in reason or law into what other form, different from the original, the change may have been made . . . for the product of or substitute for the original thing still follows the nature of the thing itself, as long as it can be ascertained to be such, and the right only ceases when the means of ascertainment fail.

This is commonly referred to as the 'exchange-product' theory. At issue here was whether Sir Thomas Plumer, who had seized from his fraudulent stockbroker securities and bullion which the stockbroker had acquired by misapplying Sir Thomas's money, could retain these securities and bullion as against the assignees in bankruptcy of the stockbroker. It was held that Sir Thomas retained a beneficial interest in the property and the plaintiffs were unable to show a better right of possession to maintain their action in trover. Seemingly, the words of Lord Ellenborough far from showing the limitations of the common law rather exposed the limitations of equity. It would appear that the common law has never suffered from such a materialist approach which was confirmed by the House of Lords in *Lipkin Gorman* v *Karpnale Ltd* [1991] 2 AC 548.

The true limits on the common law right to trace into proceeds depend on whether the proceeds are identifiable. The existence of a mixed fund does not necessarily thwart this, but the success of equity's intervention in this sphere has meant that the courts have had only recently the opportunity of developing common law rules for tracing money into mixed funds. This was exactly one of the issues before the House of Lords in the celebrated case of *Lipkin Gorman* v *Karpnale Ltd*. The plaintiff firm of solicitors had a partner with a gambling addiction. This was Cass, who funded his gambling at the defendant's club by misappropriating money. Three techniques were used to extract money which amounted to over £300,000 over a nine-month period: first, Cass would draw a cheque on the firm's client account payable to cash, which was immediately cashed; secondly, he drew cheques payable to a building society, the proceeds of which were credited to an account with the building society, opened by Cass in the firm's name; thirdly, he drew a cheque which he exchanged with the bank for a banker's draft. The cash obtained was used to purchase plastic chips at the club. A substantial issue before the House of Lords was whether the defendant could rely for its defence on a claim based on change of position. However, for our purposes, the significance of the case lies in the judgment of Lord Goff of Chieveley who held that the plaintiffs had title to the moneys at the time they were given to the club on the ground that they had been *sourced* from the plaintiffs' bank account. It would appear, therefore, to be the modern position at common law that the plaintiff claims *not* specific coins or their product; rather that he claims an equivalent amount so long as they are identifiable (see *Banque Belge* v *Hambrouck* [1921] 1 KB 321). This approach appears to overrule the position adopted recently in *Agip (Africa) Ltd* v *Jackson* [1990] Ch 265, where the facts involved an elaborate money-laundering scheme. It was held by Millett J that the plaintiff would have had a cause of action at common law if it had been tracing a physical asset, but in this case there was no cheque or equivalent since the money, which was the subject of the claim, had been transmitted by telegraphic transfer, thereby becoming mixed with other money when it passed through the bank clearing system in New York.

Tracing at common law will not provide a supplier with priority on the insolvency of a *Romalpa*-type purchaser. This is because the seller's right to account at common law is a personal one and is, thereby, an unsecured interest. Furthermore, when money is paid into a bank account, the bank's relationship with its customer is simply that of debtor and creditor (see *Foley* v *Hill* (1848) 2 HL Cas 28). This debt being a chose in action is intangible and is susceptible only to an equitable proprietary claim. The position is different where the bank has not given value for money, for example, by not promising to repay on demand. In this case, the owner would have a direct claim for the money against the bank by reason of the latter's receipt of it as a tangible asset and not a chose in action or debt.

The common law duty of account will be important in a *Romalpa* situation where a *Romalpa*-type purchaser disposes of goods without the authority of the supplier, the payment of the goods being set off against a previous loan owed by the *Romalpa*-type buyer to a subpurchaser. In this situation, no equitable proprietary remedy is possible since this presumes the existence of a fund and it is difficult to see how a set-off can constitute this. As a matter of policy, the supplier in this instance should prevail (subject to the *nemo dat* exception in s. 25(1) of the Sale of Goods Act 1979) over the subpurchaser. The latter should have no greater standing than a general creditor on the insolvency of the *Romalpa*-type buyer since he has received property which did not belong to his debtor.

The approach of equity to tracing proceeds
In order for a plaintiff to trace in equity, it must be established that the defendant or a third party is in a fiduciary relationship to the plaintiff (compare *Elders Pastoral Ltd* v *Bank of New Zealand* [1989] 2 NZLR 180). Of course, it is anomalous that equity allows the tracing remedy where a fiduciary agent steals goods from his principal but not where a total stranger steals from the owner. Despite objections to this fiduciary requirement, it still appears to be settled law (see for example *Chase Manhattan Bank NA* v *Israel-British Bank (London) Ltd* [1981] Ch 105), although the anomaly is ameliorated by the fact that the class of fiduciaries is very wide.

An additional requirement to trace in equity is that the property must be identified. A fund so identified can in equity be regarded as a fund belonging to the claimant (*Polly Peck International plc* v *Nadir* (1992) *The Times*, 24 March 1992). During the course of the 18th and 19th centuries, equity developed a metaphysical approach to the identification of money. The argument for such a development happened in this way: no principal or beneficiary is interested to recover the very notes or coins which his fiduciary received on his behalf; the beneficiary is only interested in recovering an equivalent amount; if anybody is to be required to identify mixed money, it should be the agent or fiduciary who caused the whole difficulty to begin with. As such, this *general* approach does not contradict the *economic function* of money, but equity has employed technical and often irrational rules which retention of title clauses highlight. The situations in which these rules are applied will now be considered, with particular attention being given to the scenario where money or proceeds are deliberately mixed with other moneys belonging to the fiduciary.

Where the fund has appreciated in value   The fact that money has no earmark is a good reason why the claimant cannot insist that any particular part of the mixed fund is his own. Nevertheless, it is no reason why he should be denied an interest in the fund since the wrongdoer is to blame for failing to identify his own contribution. This situation is squarely covered in the *Re Hallett's Estate* (1879) 13 ChD 696, where Jessell MR held at p. 709:

> ... where a trustee has mixed the money with his own . . .. the cestui que trust, or beneficial owner can no longer elect to take the property, because it is no longer bought with the trust money simply and purely, but with a mixed fund. He is still entitled to a charge on the property purchased, for the amount of the trust money laid out in the purchase; and that charge is quite independent of the fact of the amount laid out by the trustee.

It is arguable by analogy with *Boardman* v *Phipps* [1967] 2 AC 46 that where the trustee has acted fraudulently, he should disgorge all the profits made. In this case, a solicitor who acted for a family trust and one of its beneficiaries who acted with him were held accountable to the trust for the profits that they had made through the use of confidential information relating to a company which the solicitor had acquired through representing the trust. The case has been criticised on the basis that the stresses of equity may impose upon a fiduciary an unfair burden, especially where the exploitation of the information is beyond the capabilities of the trust or principal. Moreover, if the trustee is required to disgorge all profits made, as *Boardman* v *Phipps* suggests, a proceeds clause will ensure, on this occasion, a windfall for the suppliers whilst at the same time it might lead to the insolvency of the *Romalpa*-type purchaser. As a result, the position of a debenture holder will be prejudiced since the clause will reduce the value of a floating charge by taking any of the profits made from the transaction.

Where the fund has been dissipated   The courts have frequently dealt with the rights of the claimant as though they depended on the determination of the question whether the part withdrawn or the part remaining was the claimant's money. This is the classic formulation in *Clayton's case* (*Devaynes* v *Noble* (1817) 1 Mer 572). In this case, money was deposited by Clayton with a firm of private bankers. On the death of one member of the firm, Devaynes, the remaining partners decided to to carry on. At this time, a balance was due to Clayton. When the firm became insolvent, Clayton sought to recover this balance from the estate of the deceased partner even though the withdrawals from his account with the partners subsequent to Devayne's death largely exceeded the balance due. The rule 'first in first out' was applied. In its application, this rule seems fair as between depositor and banker, but this is not the case as between trustee and beneficiary. It has created an arbitrary hazard to tracing actions by making such an action dependent for its success on the accident of how the trustee kept his accounts with the banker.

An attempt was made to avoid the inconvenient result identified above when the court in *Re Hallett's Estate* (1879) 13 ChD 696 invented the fiction of the trustee's presumed honest intention. It was quickly realised, though, that it was equally arbitrary and unjust to apply this presumption where the wrongdoer withdraws his own money first and subsequently proceeds to dissipate the rest of the fund. Thus in *Re Oatway* [1903] 2 Ch 356 at p. 359, Joyce J held that the person who had brought about the mixing was:

> ... entitled to claim his proper quantity, but subject to the quantity of the other proprietor being first made good out of the whole mass.

Consequently, the investments resulting from the first withdrawal were treated as belonging to the beneficiaries of the trust.

Where subsequent additions are made to the dissipating fund Where the account of the fund never falls below the amount of the supplier's money, the supplier will be entitled to a lien equal to the whole amount of his contribution. Problems arise where the balance falls below this amount, and in *James Roscoe (Bolton) Ltd* v *Winder* [1915] 1 Ch 62 at p. 69, it was held by Sargant J to be:

> ... impossible to attribute to [the trustee] that by the mere payment into the account of further moneys, which to a large extent he subsequently used for purposes of his own, he intended to clothe those moneys with a trust.

Here the question is one of balancing interests between the duty of the wrongdoer in making restitution to the claimant and also the duty he owes to all his creditors. As a matter of principle, it could be argued that there is no logical reason to apply mechanically the artificial presumption formulated in *Re Hallett's Estate* (1879) 13 ChD 696 to totally different facts.

Where the wrongdoing fiduciary mixes money belonging to several trust funds but not with his own money This scenario is quite conceivable where the *Romalpa*-type buyer opens up a proceeds account for his several suppliers each supplying under similar retention clauses. The uncomplicated view is that the claimants have an interest in the mixed fund in proportion to their contributions, an approach which was adopted by Lord Hatherley in *Lord Provost of Edinburgh* v *Lord Advocate* (1879) 4 App Cas 823, and also by the House of Lords in *Sinclair* v *Brougham* [1914] AC 398. As a matter of consistency, where the property depreciates in value the loss should be borne pro rata.

Problems arise where several funds impressed with a fiduciary relationship are mixed together and this is followed by a withdrawal. It is clear that as between trustees and beneficiaries, *Re Hallett's Estate* (1879) 13 ChD 696 establishes that there is no room for the application of *Clayton's* rule, that is first in first out (see *Re Stenning* [1895] 2 Ch 433). Nevertheless, this rule has been applied between competing beneficiaries and *Re Diplock* [1948] Ch 465 endorses this approach. *Clayton's case* was applied in *Re Diplock* ostensibly because otherwise the 'greatest difficulty and complication would result.' An inconsistency is evident because later on in the Court of Appeal's judgment in that case, no difficulty was found in applying the *pari passu* principle to a claim against a mixture of stock having no distinguishing mark but which had been subject to similar dealings and depletions. Essentially, the court failed to recognise a bank account as comprising of two different things to which different rules apply: when a bank account is seen as a debt, rules as to appropriation of debts including *Clayton's* case are appropriate; conversely, when a bank account is considered a piece of property, rules as to confusion of identical property should apply since it is impossible to say which notes or coins have been taken out of the mixed fund.

The application of *Clayton's* case will often lead to inconvenient results. This may account for the court's reluctance to follow it as well as its confinement to current unbroken bank accounts and not deposit accounts. Seemingly the tracing procedure, insofar as it rests on *Clayton's* case, is far from rational and the authorities conflict. As such, the rule does not guarantee a *Romalpa*-type supplier priority. Indeed, where the trust fund is mixed, it may actually favour certain suppliers at the expense of others depending on the accident of how a banker keeps his books. There is force, therefore, in the argument that because tracing depends upon select transactional links rather than concentrating on causal links, the tracing remedy is not an acceptable means of determining whether the wrongdoer's creditors are in fact benefiting from the victim's loss. In the light of this, it is odd that the Crowther report, *Consumer Credit* (Cmnd 4596, 1971), at para. 5.7.63 merely called for a declaration of the established principles of tracing proceeds, whilst the Cork committee report, *Insolvency* (Cmnd 8558, 1982), at para. 1643 did not wish there to be any reform of the law of tracing. More recently, Professor Diamond's DTI report, *Security Interests in Personal Property* (1989), does not even specifically deal with the problems involved in tracing.

The doctrine of tracing is in danger of creeping into inexorable disorderliness if the courts, moved by the plight of some victims, were to recognise a 'swollen asset' or 'augmentation' theory of tracing. Such a perspective was evidenced in the judgment of Lord Templeman on behalf of the Privy Council in *Space Investments Ltd* v *Canadian Imperial Bank of Commerce Trust Co. (Bahamas) Ltd* [1986] 1 WLR 1072 at pp. 1076–7:

Whether a bank trustee lawfully receives deposits or wrongly treats trust money as on deposit from trusts, all the moneys are in fact dealt with and expended by the bank for the general purposes of the bank. In these circumstances it is impossible for the beneficiaries in trust money misappropriated from their trust to trace their money to any particular asset belonging to the trustee bank. But equity allows the beneficiaries, or a new trustee appointed in place of an insolvent bank trustee to protect the interests of the beneficiaries, to trace the trust money to all the assets of the bank and to recover the trust money by the exercise of an equitable charge over all the assets of the bank. Where an insolvent bank goes into liquidation that equitable charge secures for the beneficiaries and the trust priority over the claims of the customers in respect of their deposits and over the claims of all other unsecured creditors. This priority is conferred because the customers and other unsecured creditors voluntarily accept the risk that the trustee bank might become insolvent and unable to discharge its obligations in full. On the other hand, the settlor of the trust and the beneficiaries interested under the trust never accept any risks involved in the possible insolvency of the trustee bank.

The effect of this approach is that it completely rids tracing of its property heritage by eliminating equitable ownership of identifiable property as the basis of relief. This will inevitably prejudice other creditors and highlights the need to balance the competing interests of injured creditors. In many ways this issue goes to the heart of the *Romalpa* clause debate. A close analogy may be drawn here with the infiltration of equitable doctrine in the form of the trust as a device, in commercial cases, for protecting the interests of lenders, bankers and customers against trustees in bankruptcy of a business which has become insolvent.

The trust device
The existence of the trust may not even require the establishment of an agreement between the parties. Thus in *Re Kayford Ltd* [1975] 1 WLR 279, a mail order company, acting on the advice of an accountant, unilaterally placed all money received from customers after a certain date into a separate customers' trust deposit account. It was held that this was an effective method of creating a trust for the benefit of the customers, despite the fact that a unilateral declaration of trust by Kayford Ltd, one would have thought, would seem to constitute a fraudulent preference invalidated by s. 239 of the Insolvency Act 1986 (this replaced s. 320(1) of the Companies Act 1948). The absence of agreement was not fatal, and Megarry J reasoned as follows at p. 282:

> [I]t is well settled that a trust can be created without using the words 'trust' or 'confidence' or the like; the question is whether, in substance, a sufficient intention to create a trust has been manifested.

This rule was applied in the case of *Re Multi Guarantee Co. Ltd* [1987] BCLC 257. In this case, money was deposited in a joint account which represented proceeds handed over by a retail chain to an extended warranty insurance company for domestic appliances. On these facts it was held that there was no intention to create a trust: the account into which the insurance warranty proceeds had been placed was a mere holding device (but compare *Re EVTR Ltd* [1987] BCLC 646).

The principle applied in *Barclays Bank Ltd* v *Quistclose Investments Ltd* [1970] AC 567 is directly analogous to the *Romalpa* scenario in the context of moneylending, or payment in advance contracts. In this case, the House of Lords held that money having been paid into a bank account for a specific purpose communicated to the bank would be fixed with a trust when the purpose failed, so the money could not be applied as intended. The bank could not claim a right to set off a debt owed to it by the account holder in respect of another account, as it held the credit balance on trust in favour of the respondents (see *Re Nanwa Gold Mines Ltd* [1955] 1 WLR 1080). Lord Wilberforce rejected the argument that the lender only had contractual rights in a loan transaction on the basis at p. 581 that:

> There is surely no difficulty in recognising the coexistence in one transaction of legal and equitable rights and remedies: when the money is advanced, the lender acquires an equitable right to see that it is applied for the primary designated purpose.

It would appear from this that if the primary function for which money is advanced fails, the recipient cannot then keep the property (compare *Carreras Rothmans Ltd* v *Freeman Mathews Treasure Ltd* [1985] Ch 207).

The primary purpose of a retention of title clause is payment. Where this is not achieved, the issues centre around whether redelivery to the seller can be effectuated, and the extent to which the remedies of equity may be invoked to ensure this goal. Essentially, the question reduces itself to which *policy* should be applied when distributing the (usually) limited assets of a company being wound up; should the suppliers of goods, or the payers of money enjoy a super-privileged position over the debtor's assets?

THIRTEEN
The finance lease

The essence of a lease, whether of goods or land, is to allow the lessee to acquire possession and use without paying the full capital cost. At the same time, it enables the lessor to receive a return on its (in the case of a company) investment while retaining the title and security in the goods or land. The lease is by no means a new phenomenon and, indeed, it is possible to trace its antecedents to Hammurabi, whilst the extent of Roman involvement in this area is seen in bk 3 of Justinian's *Institutes*. In England, leases appear frequently only from the 13th century onwards; the Statute of Wales 1284 declared that the action of covenant was available for leases of movable property as well as land. Nevertheless, it was only in the wake of the industrial revolution that the leasing of movable property became particularly prevalent.

In the 19th century, entrepreneurs would lease coal wagons to collieries. The idea of using the contract of hire as a disguised contract of sale was common among the costermongers in the East End of London who would hire their barrows on a weekly basis extending over many years. Similarly, in this century, the equipment lease has been used to enforce 'tying agreements' in the case of highly specialised capital equipment which the original manufacturer is reluctant to sell either because of service or maintenance problems, a long life and limited replacement market, or the desire to control the sale of raw materials or components processed by leased equipment. Thus, some computer manufacturing companies' leasing policies restrict the free movement of used computers, thereby preventing the reconfiguration of mainframe systems. However, there is little doubt that such practices today sound in the anti-competition provisions of arts 85 and 86 of the Treaty of Rome 1957.

PROBLEMS OF DEFINITION

There are two basic types of lease which, although somewhat similar, differ in respect of the leasing company's ability to recover fully the cost of the equipment through the contracted lease rentals.

The operating lease
This is the standard contract of hire of plant and machinery, i.e., where the hirer rents the equipment for a period which is less than its useful life and for hire payments totalling less than the purchase cost of the item. Reliance is placed on the realisation of a residual value on disposal or re-leasing of the equipment. The owner-lessor will be intimately concerned with the maintenance, insurance and taxing of the equipment but these costs will figure in the rental rate. Such an arrangement enables a hirer to operate on a small capital base where equipment involving high capital cost is required temporarily or for a fluctuating time, thereby achieving an efficient utilisation of investment capital. In addition, it enables a hirer, where the equipment is new and unproven, great flexibility without incurring the risks of obsolescence whilst giving a manufacturer-lessor the opportunity, through servicing the equipment on the customer's premises, of customer-orientated research and product development which may facilitate future sales or leases. Servicing and maintaining such equipment by the lessor may be more economically efficient for the hirer since the lessor will build up vast experience in maintenance as well as enjoying economies of sale. Where the lessor carries out the functions of handling, licensing and registration of, for example, vehicles on a volume basis, administrative costs may be dramatically cut. This will be an important consideration for a fleet-lorry operator who can then reduce the number of his administrative staff. Such savings would not be available where the fleet-lorry operator had bought his lorries on hire-purchase as he would be responsible for attending to these matters.

The finance or net lease
The finance agreement is one where the primary period rentals are sufficient for the lessor to recover the cost of the equipment, financing costs, overhead expenses and also to earn a return on the investment in the lease. The primary period usually approximates to between 50 and 75 per cent of the estimated useful life of the equipment and at the end of this period, the lessee may continue to use the equipment in return for a nominal rent. Potential obsolescence before the end of the equipment's useful life is taken into account by the lessor where the terms are so arranged that the lessee is indirectly paying for this.

Even though the distinction between a finance lease and an operating lease is relatively easy to draw in abstract, sometimes the distinction will become blurred, for example, in the case of a leased computer for a five-year primary period which can be returned or traded in at any time (subject to a minimum payment clause) and which will probably be re-leased to another lessee on termination. The resolution of this problem may well depend on the attitude of the lessee. If he sees leasing as an alternative to buying the property, this will tend towards the finance lease, whereas an operating lease will arise when the lessee does not consider buying the property as a viable alternative. The distinction between the two types of lease will be important as it goes to the root of the question of the lessor's liability for defective equipment (see pp. 299–302).

The distinction between the two different types of lease is often characterised as one of a conflict between a 'true' or operating lease, and a 'security' or finance lease. This reference to a finance lease is concerned with the ostensible ownership problem where there is a separation of ownership and possession. The argument here is that a person wishing to take a non-possessory property interest should bear the burden of 'curing' the ostensible ownership problem through a notice mechanism (see chapter 16). In a dynamic commercial setting, it may not be sensible to try to distinguish between a sale and a finance lease. However, insofar as a distinction is made, much will depend upon the attitude of the lessee. If he sees leasing as an alternative to buying the property, this will tend towards the finance lease, whereas an operating lease will arise when the lessee does not consider buying the property as a viable alternative.

It is important to adopt a balanced approach. A distinction can be drawn between leases and conditional sales which represent a security interest, in particular, where the leases are of short duration which do not look to the ultimate acquisition of the goods by the lessee. In this context, application to the true lease of the remedies traditionally associated with the conditional sale would do violence to the contract rights of the parties. Nonetheless, the question of public notice still remains. In this respect, Professor Diamond in the Department of Trade and Industry paper, *A Review of Security Interests In Property* (1989), recommended at para. 9.7.15 that a notice filing mechanism similar to the American model should be adopted in England and there should be a requirement to file, subject to a *de minimis* period of 3 years, all finance lease transactions. However, it would still be necessary, as a matter of substance, to determine the 'true' or 'security' lease distinction which will depend upon such factors as the intention of the parties and the size of the rental payments including any option to purchase.

The growth of finance leasing The leasing of business and industrial equipment has become a popular and viable alternative to other methods of financing capital acquisition. In this respect, the volume of finance leasing business (that is where there is no purchase option) has increased from £2,175,000 in 1980, to £9,569,000 in 1990, showing a fourfold increase in 10 years. Leasing by members of the Equipment Leasing Association, the national association for UK equipment lessors, now finances 20 per cent of all UK fixed investment in equipment in all economic sectors.

Undoubtedly, fiscal stimulus to leasing in the UK has accounted for much of the growth in this area during the early years of the 1980s. The fiscal stimulus was due to investment incentives, although they have in large measure by now been withdrawn. It would appear that taxation has taken on a diminishing role in the context of finance leasing, but financial management has now become more important. One of the greatest advantages of the equipment lease is flexible financing. The timing of payments can be finely coordinated with the lessee's expected cash flows so that his disbursements occur at those times when he is best able to meet them, and when he has the least attractive alternative uses for his money. Thus, payments to the lessor can be level or 'bullet' payments, declining or 'step' payments, increasing in amount or 'balloon' payments. To a company experiencing a cash shortage, leasing can be useful because, unlike a purchase, it does not require a down-payment and therefore no immediate capital drain. It appears that most companies lease for cash-flow-related reasons rather than tax-related reasons.

LEGAL PROBLEMS ASSOCIATED WITH FINANCE LEASING

In recent years the finance lease has been recognised as constituting a unique and asset-based financing device. Indeed, even at the private international law level, UNIDROIT, which has worked on the subject since 1974, recognises the *sui generis* characteristic of the finance leasing transaction. The Leasing Rules attempt to reflect the economic reality of the transaction as evidenced by the parties in their respective contracts so as to facilitate the removal of certain legal impediments to the international financial leasing of equipment (see the Convention adopted on 28 May 1988, UNIDROIT *News Bulletin*, Nos. 75/76 October 1988). In a similar vein, art. 2A to the American Uniform Commercial Code (UCC) recognises a finance lease as a unique kind of lease which is defined in s. 2A–103(1) as follows:

> 'Finance lease' means a lease in which (i) the lessor does not select, manufacture or supply the goods, (ii) the lessor acquires the goods or the right to possession and use of the goods in connection with the lease, and (iii) either the lessee receives a copy of the contract evidencing the lessor's purchase of the goods on or before signing the lease contract, or the lessee's approval of the contract evidencing the lessor's purchase of the goods is a condition to effectiveness of the lease contract.

A finance lease is unique because of the *control* that the lessee exercises in the selection, acquisition by the lessor, and approval of the equipment subject to the lease. This can be illustrated by reference to the standard terms and conditions of a typical finance lease where the onus is firmly placed on the supplier and the lessee.

We shall now consider the legal problems associated with the asset delivered to the lessee and then examine the remedies available to the lessor following the lessee's default. The legal dilemmas emerge from the following transaction which may be represented diagrammatically as follows:

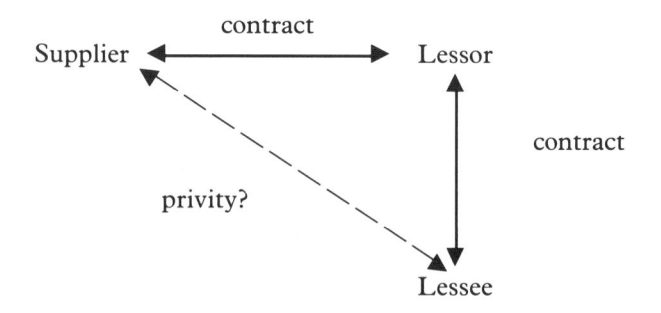

```
              contract
  Supplier  ◄──────────►  Lessor
         ╲                   ▲
          ╲                  │
           ╲                 │ contract
            ╲                │
    privity? ╲               │
              ╲              ▼
               ╲────────► Lessee
```

The supplier-lessor relationship: novation

Essentially, the ideal leasing arrangement involves the passing of property in machinery or plant to the lessor who, after taking delivery of the equipment, delivers it to the lessee pursuant to the terms of the lease. Of course, this presupposes that the lessee contemplated from the very beginning that he intended to arrange for equipment to be acquired by a particular lessor according to terms and conditions mutually satisfactory for them. Inevitably, there will be instances where an order for equipment has been placed with a supplier by a potential lessee before entering into the lease arrangement.

In order to circumvent this problem, the finance lessor, by arranging a novation, will acquire title to the new and unused equipment, which is important for tax reasons. Novation is the only method by which the original obligor can be effectively replaced by another: A, B and C must make a new contract by which in consideration of A (the supplier) releasing B (the potential lessee) from his obligation, C (the lessor) agrees that he will assume responsibility for its performance. It would appear that it will be necessary for the lessor and supplier to contract on the same terms with the lessor paying the cost of the equipment. Thus, any similar sums already paid by the lessee will have to be returned, and this will clearly show that the debt between the lessee and supplier has been extinguished so providing consideration for the arrangement. Seemingly, therefore, any exclusion clause governing the first agreement, for example, relating to ss. 13 to 15 of the Sale of Goods Act 1979 would have to be included in the novation as well. This may prove fatal for the novation since the enforceability of an exclusion clause is subject to the requirement of reasonableness which is, of course, a question of law and not mere contractual intention (see s. 11 of and sch. 2 to the Unfair Contract Terms Act 1977).

The lessor-lessee relationship: statutory implied terms

Due to the interrelated nature of the finance leasing transaction, it is clear that any breach of the supply agreement between the supplier and the lessor will ultimately affect the lessee who has chosen the equipment and has contracted for its use and possession. In many cases, it may be that a breach of the supply agreement by the supplier will, in turn, result in a breach of the leasing agreement as well. Inevitably the question arises whether the lessor, as primarily a financier, should be responsible for any defects? Significantly under art. 2A of the UCC, the lessee in a finance lease, as distinguished from other leases, does not benefit from warranties against 'infringement' (s. 2A–211), or implied warranties of merchantability, or fitness for purpose (ss. 2A–212, 2A–213). The finance lessee must shoulder the risk of loss (s. 2A–219) and has irrevocable independent obligations upon acceptance of the equipment (s. 2A–407) entailing that he may not revoke acceptance of the equipment under the same circumstances as other leases (s. 2A–517). Undoubtedly, the justification for this approach is the recognition of the economic reality underlying the transaction which is, in large measure, echoed in the UNIDROIT Convention on International Financial Leasing done at Ottawa on 28 May 1988.

The English position with regard to contracts of hire has been clarified in the Supply of Goods and Services Act 1982. In particular, s. 8 of the Act provides that goods under hire should correspond with description or sample and is analogous with the Sale of Goods Act 1979 in this respect. More difficult problems arise in relation to fitness for purpose and merchantability. As a matter of logic, it is difficult to see what the term 'merchantable quality' can mean in a contract of hire since there is no question of the hirer acquiring ownership. Nevertheless, the common law did refer to the owner being under an obligation to hire out goods of a reasonable fitness, and 'merchantability' was included as part of this obligation. The appropriateness of this analysis is open to question in the context of finance leasing, as distinct from consumer hire or operating leases where the element of reliance can be great, and it may be necessary to highlight the distinction between merchantable quality and fitness for a particular purpose (see pp. 93–105). It will not be unjust to expect the finance lessor to accept *some* responsibility for the quality of the goods supplied since the lessor has chosen the particular lease form as a *financing* venture. However, the fact that the hirer has inspected the chattel beforehand may be relevant in indicating that the agreement was to hire the chattel subject to all the defects and characteristics that were evident upon an inspection of the kind that had been made. No liability is envisaged against the finance lessor as far as the obligation to supply goods for a particular purpose is concerned where it is clear that the hirer had not relied, or that it was unreasonable for him to rely, on the owner's skill or judgment. This is seen in ss. 9(3) and 9(6) of the Supply of Goods and Services Act 1982.

In one important respect, the Supply of Goods and Services Act 1982 goes very far in the sense that s. 9(4)(b) provides that: if a bailee expressly or by implication, makes known to a credit-broker in the course of negotiations conducted by that broker in relation to goods sold by him to the bailor before forming the subject matter of the contract, any particular purpose for which the goods are being bailed the bailor is deemed to have knowledge of the purpose for which the goods are sought by the lessee. Such a liability seems inappropriate between commercial concerns bargaining at arm's length since it distorts the leasing transaction, and the finance lessor would be forced to shift its cost of insurance on to the lessee thereby increasing the cost of leasing to him. This is recognised under s. 9(6) of the Supply of Goods and Services Act 1982.

Even if an extreme approach is taken in regard to freedom of contract analysis with finance leasing, there is no doubt that the essential aspect of the finance leasing transaction is quiet possession. This is reflected in s. 7 of the Supply of Goods and Services Act 1982 where the lessor impliedly warrants that the hirer will enjoy uninterrupted use and enjoyment of the goods for the period of the hire. This may prove problematical for a sublessee where the intermediary lessor (the finance lessee) had no right to sublease the goods: use of the goods by the sublessee might amount to conversion. If the action is brought by the finance lessor after the subsidiary hiring term expired, it will be difficult to establish that such action creates an incursion upon the subsidiary hirer's quiet possession (see chapter 2).

Of course, the lessee too will have responsibilities relating to the care and use of the equipment. In the unlikely event of the lessee's duty of care not being elaborated in the lease document, the common law position has to be examined. The seminal decision here is that of Lord Holt in *Coggs v Bernard* (1704) 2 Ld Raym 909. In this case, Lord Holt declared that the respective duties owed by the bailee to the bailor depended upon the nature of the bailment. Relying upon the writings of Roman jurists, Lord Holt identified six types of bailment: (a) *depositum*, (b) *commodatum*, (c) *locatio et conductio*, (d) *pignori acceptum*, (e) delivery of chattels to be transported by the bailee, and (f) *mandatum*.

Depositum or deposit is a bailment of personal property to be kept for the bailor without recompense and to be returned when the bailor shall require them. In ordinary deposits, the bailee, in the absence of a special undertaking to keep the goods as he would his own, is liable only for gross neglect.

Commodatum is a bailment of goods to be used gratuitously by the bailee temporarily or for a certain time. In the case of *commodatum*, the borrower, because he derived a benefit from the transaction, is held to the 'strictest care and diligence' and is answerable for the least neglect.

Locatio et conductio or lending for hire. Here Lord Holt declared at p. 112: 'the hirer is bound to utmost diligence, such as the most diligent father of the family uses; and if he used that, he shall be discharged'.

Pignori acceptum or pledge is a bailment of goods to a creditor as security for a debt or engagement. According to Lord Holt at p.112, the bailee is absolved of liability for the loss of the pledged property if he has exercised 'true diligence' because 'the law requires nothing extraordinary of the pawnee, but only that he shall use ordinary care in restoring the goods'.

Delivery of chattels to be transported by the bailee. Lord Holt divided the fifth class of bailment, delivery to carry or otherwise manage for a reward, into two categories. The first involves delivery to a common carrier: the bailee in such a case is liable for any injury to the property except those arising from either acts of God or public enemies. A more relaxed standard of care is applied to the second category: cases involving private persons who agree to transport goods for compensation. These bailees are merely required to exercise reasonable care.

Mandatum or mandate is a bailment of something for some service to be performed upon it gratuitously to the bailee. According to Lord Holt at pp. 113-14, the bailee in such cases must exercise 'diligent management' and is liable if he acts negligently.

Subsequent commentators have revised this classification. In this regard, the approach of Sir William Jones should be noted who, in his treatise, *Essay on the Law of Bailments*, 3rd ed. (London, 1828), divided bailments into five categories instead of six: (1) *depositum*, (2) *mandatum*, (3) *commodatum*, (4) *pignori acceptum* and (5) *locatum*. The fifth category, *locatum* or lending for reward, was further divided into three subcategories: (a) *locatio rei* or hire for temporary use, (b) *locatio operis faciendi*, where work or labour were to be bestowed on the property, and (c) *locatio operis mercium vehendarum* or the bailment of goods to either a common carrier or a private person for transportation.

Supplier-lessor-lessee: contractual privity and finance leasing

The tripartite nature of the finance lease transaction introduces complex legal problems. The financing lessor is the intermediary who concludes a contract with the client and another contract with the supplier; it would seem that no contract is directly created between the client and the supplier. It cannot be that the supplier and client are total strangers since the object of the contract is for the use of the client and, in any case, it may be that the supplier was chosen by the client who laid down detailed specifications for the object sold. The interrelated nature of the contracts makes it impossible to treat each contract separately or to view the contracts as one transaction between the supplier and the lessee. By treating the transaction as two independent contracts, this permits the supplier and the lessor to modify the supply agreement without notifying the lessee. Since the finance lessee will have negotiated the technical aspects of the supply agreement and will ultimately use the goods and be directly affected by their specifications, no changes should be made without the lessee's consent. This consent requirement flows from the principle that neither the lessee nor the lessor should act to jeopardise the rights of the other.

Most domestic lease transactions are structured to minimise the privity problem posed in a finance leasing context. Typically, the lease agreement may assign to the lessee those warranties created in the supply agreement. However, this will not give the lessee adequate protection since it does not address those warranties given to the lessee in the supplier-lessee negotiations. Nonetheless, any such guarantee made by the supplier to the lessee during negotiations could be construed as an express warranty which will bind the supplier under a collateral contract, the consideration for which being the lessee entering into the main agreement (see *Shanklin Pier Ltd* v *Detel Products Ltd* [1951] 2 KB 854). The lessee, as the assignee of the warranties, may be limited to damages suffered by the lessor due to the supplier's breach rather than recovering for its own damages. The difficulty here is that the interests of the lessor and the lessee are not the same, nor are the damages suffered by each. In the case of a delay in delivery when payment is conditional upon delivery, the loss or damage to the lessor may be minimal. On the other hand, the lessee may have suffered huge consequential losses. The question is not of transferring rights from the lessor to the lessee but of giving the lessee an independent cause of action against the supplier. Significantly, in the absence of agreement, some US courts have allowed a direct action against the supplier on the basis of the latter's strict liability, the lessor being regarded as merely performing a financing function (see *Citicorp Leasing Inc.* v *Allied Institutional Distributors Inc.* (1977) 454 F Supp 511; *Atlas Industries Inc.* v *National Cash Register Co.* (1975) 531 P 2d 41).

In England, it is unlikely that the identity of object and the connection in fact between the lessee and the supplier will triumph over the principle of contractual privity. The privity doctrine is still entrenched and is applied, albeit reluctantly by the courts, as seen in Lord Scarman's approach in *Woodar Investment Development Ltd* v *Wimpey Construction UK Ltd* [1980] 1 WLR 277 at p. 300:

I respectfully agree with Lord Reid that the denial by English Law of a *ius quaesitum tertio* calls for reconsideration.... If the opportunity arises, I hope the House will reconsider *Tweddle* v *Atkinson* (1861) 1 B & S 393 and the other cases which stand guard over the unjust rule.

Many of the arguments used to justify privity are especially spurious in the finance leasing context. In this respect, privity is sometimes justified on the basis that the promisor would otherwise be subject to a double performance liability. This is not problematic in finance leasing because there is only *one* promise and, once it is enforced by the promisee or the third party, the promisor will have realised his liability. It is sometimes argued that third-party intervention would inhibit or disallow the original parties from varying or rescinding their contract, but what is objectionable in this if this is indeed what the original parties bargained for? Furthermore, there is nothing gratuitous about the position of the third party since the lessor in the finance lease will have paid for the promise, and the lessee will have relied upon this by entering into the lease contract.

The general rule remains in English law that a third party cannot enforce a contract made for his benefit. It is for this reason that the Law Commission's consultation paper, *Privity of Contracts: Contracts for the Benefit of Third Parties* (Law Com. No. 121, 1991) at para. 6.3 provisionally recommended a legislative initiative enabling a third party to sue on a contract made for his benefit where it is the intention of the contracting parties that he be given enforceable rights. This would appear to apply directly to the finance leasing scenario. However, the problem of remoteness and the lessee's consequential losses as a result of the supplier's breach will still remain. These issues were not addressed by the Law Commission where the focus of the discussion was confined to the *nature* of the rights created in favour of a third party. The Law Commission provisionally recommended that these rights extend: (a) to the right to receive the promised performance from the promisor where this is an appropriate remedy, and also the right to pursue remedies; (b) to the right to rely on any provisions in the contract restricting or excluding the third party's liability to a contracting party as if the third party were a party to the contract (para. 5.17).

The damages recoverable by the lessee may be wholly inadequate even if the Law Commission's proposals are implemented. Thus, in *Victoria Laundry (Windsor) Ltd* v *Newman Industries Ltd* [1949] 2 KB 528, the defendants had contracted to sell a large boiler to the plaintiff laundry company and the defendants were well aware of the fact that there was, at the time, an acute shortage of laundries and the plaintiff was proposing to put the boiler into use at the earliest possible time in order to expand its business. When the defendants damaged the boiler in delivering it to the plaintiff company with consequent delay in bringing it into use, it was held that they were liable for the estimated loss of profits which the plaintiff had incurred, that is, the reasonably foreseeable damage coming within the rules set out in *Hadley* v *Baxendale* (1854) 9 Exch 341. However, the plaintiff company was not entitled to damages for loss of certain highly lucrative dyeing contracts of which the defendants had no knowledge. The issue is whether the event is foreseeable as a substantial possibility (*C. Czarnikow Ltd* v *Koufos* [1969] 1 AC 350). It would appear following *H. Parsons (Livestock) Ltd* v *Uttley, Ingham and Co. Ltd* [1978] QB 791, that the measure of damages is the same in both contract and tort, so the lessee in the finance leasing scenario should be able to recover for consequential losses if they fall within the reasonable anticipation of the defendant in the light of circumstances known to him. Thus, the lessee will have to prove that the supplier had knowledge of any special contract entered into by the lessee, that it was reasonably foreseeable and that such a contract would be lost as a result of the breach. In practice, this will be a difficult burden to displace. Of course, where the finance lessor is suing under the supply contract, the loss will be limited to the rentals withheld under the leasing agreement as a result of the supplier's breach.

The position in tort The doctrine of privity of contract only means that a non-contracting party cannot bring an action on the contract and it does not exclude a successful action being brought in tort. In *Junior Books Ltd* v *Veitchi Co. Ltd* [1983] 1 AC 520, the House of Lords awarded damages for the misperformance of a construction subcontract to a pursuer company which was not party to the contract, by allowing it an action in negligence against the defaulting subcontractor. Lord Roskill's speech in that case represents the recent high-water mark of the development of the tort of negligence in relation to recovery for economic loss. His lordship considered the pursuer's claim as one based on pure economic loss and not physical damage. Through the application of Lord Wilberforce's two-stage test in *Anns* v *Merton London Borough Council* [1978] AC 728, it was held that there was sufficient 'proximity' between the parties to give rise to a duty of care which, on breach, allowed the non-contracting party to sue for losses, including economic loss caused to him by a failure to provide the expected contractual benefit. Undoubtedly, the implications of the case for the law of contracts and product liability are staggering.

Subsequent case law has restricted *Junior Books Ltd* v *Veitchi Co. Ltd* either as being a case confined to its own facts or, on the basis that the pursuer had suffered damage to its property (see *Governors of the Peabody Donation Fund* v *Sir Lindsay Parkinson and Co. Ltd* [1985] AC 210; *Candlewood Navigation Corpn Ltd* v *Mitsui OSK Lines Ltd* [1986] AC 1; *Leigh & Sillavan Ltd* v *Aliakmon Shipping Co. Ltd* [1986] AC 785; *D and F Estates Ltd* v *Church Commissioners for England* [1989] AC 177; *Simaan General Contracting Co.* v *Pilkington Glass Ltd (No. 2)* [1988] QB 758; *Greater Nottingham Cooperative Society Ltd* v *Cementation Piling and Foundations Ltd* [1989] QB 71; *Pacific Associates Inc.* v *Baxter* [1990] 1 QB 993). In the meantime, *Anns* v *Merton London Borough Council* case has been expressly overruled (see *Murphy* v *Brentwood District Council* [1991] 1 AC 398).

The settled position would now appear to be that whereas a manufacturer may be liable in tort for injury to persons or damage to property caused by a defective chattel, in the absence of a contract, no liability arises in tort to purchasers of a chattel who suffer economic loss because it is defective in *quality*. The damage to property versus defective quality issue is a thorny one as can be illustrated in the case of *Simaan General Contracting Co.* v *Pilkington Glass Ltd (No. 2)*. The plaintiffs were the main contractors of a building erected in Abu Dhabi for which the plans and specifications required double glazed units of green glass to be incorporated into curtain walling. The supply and erection of this was subcontracted to an Italian company Feal which, as required by the terms of the subcontract, ordered the glass panels from the defendant. The glass supplied was not of a uniform colour and the building owner withheld payment from Simaan until the panels were replaced. In the Court of Appeal, it was held that in the absence of a contract between the main contractor and the glass supplier, the main contractor could not sue the glass supplier directly for economic loss. Reference was made to the way *Junior Books Ltd* v *Veitchi Co. Ltd* had been interpreted in subsequent decisions as involving damage to property. Even though there had been in *Simaan* a failure to comply with the description, merchantability and fitness for purpose conditions under the Sale of Goods Act 1979, this was not considered to constitute damage to *property*. As Bingham LJ held at pp. 781–2:

> There is in my view no physical damage in this case. The units are as good as ever they were and will not deteriorate. . . . What we have here are not in my view, defects but failures to comply with Sale of Goods Act conditions. . . . It would, I think, be an abuse of language to describe these units as damaged.

The significance of this analysis in the context of finance leasing goes to the question of acceptance of the goods by the lessee, as well as the lessor's duty to supply goods of the correct specification.

The reform of the third-party rule anticipated by the Law Commission in their consultation paper No. 121 would allow the finance lessee to sue upon the supply contract. Such a contractual solution has the following advantages in the context of finance leasing: first, the choice-orientated approach adopted in contract seems more appropriate than the locus of the 'accident' tort approach; secondly, the measure of damages in contract ensures full expectation loss; thirdly, great problems would arise if one relationship is subject to one limitation period rule and the other relationship subject to another. Furthermore, the privity rule can be criticised on the grounds of economic efficiency. If the finance lessor wishes to provide the lessee with an enforceable benefit from a contract with the supplier, the lessor must first contract with the supplier and then the latter must contract with the lessee who must provide some nominal consideration. The supplier will be required to perform in the same way in any case, but extra transactional costs are incurred.

Finance lessor and third parties: a supplier of goods or finance?
An outstanding policy question which arises is whether liability as against the finance lessor could be envisaged, in the absence of proof of negligence, through the application of strict liability. Part I of the Consumer Protection Act 1987 in seeking to implement the EC Directive 85/374 on Product

Liability, 1985, aims to make producers and certain others involved in the chain of distribution liable for death, personal injury or specified property damage resulting from unsafe products (see chapter 5). The Act is primarily aimed at 'producers', which means manufacturers, persons who win or abstract substances as well as persons who carry out an industrial or other process on products not manufactured. There are two other categories of persons similarly civilly liable; first, anyone who has held himself out to be the producer of the product; secondly, anyone who, in the course of business, has imported the product into any State in the European Community from any place outside the Community. In addition to the 'primary defendants', the Act makes *certain* suppliers liable to the plaintiff. Any person who supplied a defective product, not necessarily to the plaintiff, may be liable to the plaintiff if he fails to identify one or more of the primary defendants or his own supplier after receiving a request from the plaintiff. Supply, for both primary and substitute defendants embraces selling, hiring out, lending, hire-purchase, prizes and gifts, contracts for work and materials. Where a finance company acquired goods from a dealer and finances their provision to a customer by means of a hire-purchase or leasing agreement, the person supplying under the Act will be the dealer so that the finance lessor would appear to be exempt. However, the European Commission has more recently issued proposals for a Directive on liability for defective services which could affect lessors who supply services in conjunction with the supply of goods. This EC draft Directive would reverse the normal burden of proof so that the provider of the service would have to show that no negligence had taken place.

It is important to consider the acknowledged policy factors influencing the application of strict liability so as to examine the position of the finance lessor in this regard.

Reliance on representations made that the products are safe By placing their products in the stream of commerce, sellers impliedly represent to the public that they are safe. Product advertising reinforces this expectation. However, the finance lessor will not represent that the equipment leased is safe since the latter will often have no specialist knowledge of the quality of the equipment. Whatever reliance there is will be on the representations made by the manufacturers or the lessees who operate the equipment.

The enterprise held strictly liable can spread the losses more readily than can an injured plaintiff The finance lessor could shift its costs either directly on to the lessee (e.g., through indemnity) or by spreading the loss over all the leasing activities. This second approach is objectionable because it may foster distorted allocation of costs, i.e., the cost of providing insurance for every person involved in the 'producing and marketing enterprise' is likely to be greater than the cost of insuring one person alone, even though the various insurance policies would only cover the one risk. There would be an increase in premium in aggregate to take account of the extra administration costs, and the extra litigation costs that would be incurred if the injured person were able to bring claims against four or five persons in the chain of distribution and production instead of one. From this, it would seem logical for the finance lessor to adopt the first course, and so increase the cost of finance leasing to the lessee. This amounts to the same allocation that would have been produced had the liability been imposed directly on the finance lessee in the first place.

The enterprise has a 'deep pocket' which can be tapped Since banks frequently assume the role of finance lessors, it is reasonable to assume that they have 'deep pockets'. By itself this is not an adequate justification for the imposition of strict liability for at least two reasons: first, finance lessees also have deep pockets since major airlines, for example, find finance leasing a favourable method of acquiring multimillion-dollar aircraft; secondly, and more compellingly, if the 'deep pocket' approach justifies liability in finance leasing, why should it not also apply to more traditional forms of financing methods, such as where the dealer sells direct to a buyer with third-party finance?

The deterrent effect of being held strictly liable thereby promoting safety In most cases, the ultimate safety of a product depends upon the design and production of the product; it is the manufacturer who exerts the greatest control over these products. A conventional lessor may also have a great effect on the safety of the product, especially where the lessor puts the same product into public use many times. Under a finance lease, on the other hand, the lessor can have no direct effect on the safety of the equipment since it will possess no expertise in its maintenance and, furthermore, it is the lessee who undertakes the burden of maintaining the equipment. Many US courts have justified their refusal to hold finance lessors strictly liable on the ground that these lessors are not part of the physical process by which products are distributed to the public. Even so it is simplistic to argue that finance lessors are not in the distribution process. Finance lessors not only assist businesses in acquiring products but often have a continuing business relationship with their lessees. The imposition of liability will certainly have an indirect effect on safety through market deterrence, i.e., a finance lessor will take into account its liability potential on a specific chattel which will reflect itself through higher leasing charges. This may lead some potential lessees to seek cheaper and, presumably, safer substitutes for the high-priced liability-causing goods. The finance lessor has chosen this type of financing; instead of financing the purchase directly and taking a chattel mortgage (see chapter 15), the finance lessor obtains title to the property and does have some ability, thereby, to control risk.

There is no doubt that the finance lessor considers itself to be a supplier of *money* rather than a product. The essence of the transaction to the lessor is that its investment will be 'paid out' in full by the end of the lease term. This financial role is recognised both in art. 2A of the UCC and the UNIDROIT rules which tolerate even 'hell or high water' clauses under which the lessee agrees to pay rentals to the lessor whatever happens, and regardless of whether the goods prove to be defective. The crucial point is the time at which the promise to pay becomes enforceable which, in the case of the finance lease, is upon the lessee's acceptance of the goods. Interestingly under the 1985 UNIDROIT draft rules, a limited 'right to cure' was recognised in the sense that, by virtue of art. 10(2), the lessor and supplier were given an additional period of time to substitute a conforming tender. This has been replaced under the Convention, and the lessor's right to cure a failure in performance is now expressed to be exercisable on the same conditions, and in the same manner, as if the lessee had agreed to buy the equipment from the lessor under the terms of the supply agreement (art. 12(1) and (2)). The balance is still firmly tilted in favour of the lessor as the supplier of the finance because, after acceptance of the goods, the lessee has no right to withhold rentals for nonconforming delivery.

Given that the primary role of the finance lessor is as a provider of money rather than equipment, it is necessary to consider the remedies available to the lessor for protecting its investment. In this context, a crucial distinction should be drawn between 'ordinary' contracts of hire or hire-purchase and the finance lease.

REMEDIES UNDER LEASE AND HIRE CONTRACTS

The law may not be satisfactory from the finance lessor's point of view since the case law turns on two unrelated principles of law: first, a lease of chattels is analogous to the lease of real property and therefore attracts some of the principles of landlord and tenant; secondly, the rule against penalties developed in contract law applies.

Remedies available to the lessor while keeping the lease on foot

There is no doubt that the lessor may upon default leave the equipment in the possession of the lessee and recover the rental payment as it falls due. In addition, damages will be available for a specific breach of the contract such as a failure to insure the equipment or maintain it. At least two other approaches are available to the finance lessor under this heading.

Acceleration clauses The lease contract may provide for rental payments being called up in full upon the lessee's default. Sometimes, the agreement will provide for automatic acceleration of liability on the occurrence of stated events. Such an approach is likely to prove inflexible, so creditors will often take powers to accelerate indebtedness on default only after notice has been given to the lessee. Where there is a 'true' lease, such a clause can be considered foreign to the lessor–lessee relationship because, unlike a defaulting buyer or borrower, a lessee is generally not obligated under the rules of damages to pay a specific predetermined sum to the lessor. Although the lessor will be entitled to damages for breach of contract, there is no certainty that those damages will be assessed to be the equivalent of all rental payments owing under the lease discounted for early payment and also realisation of the chattel.

Under a finance lease, where the lessor has no interest in the return of the asset, an acceleration clause is not foreign to the lease transaction. Indeed, an acceleration clause can be considered a natural and necessary part of the *financing* aspect of the transaction. It is obvious, in this circumstance, that the lessee is contractually obligated to make rental payments equivalent to the instalment purchase price of the chattel. The term of the lease dealing with default will provide for acceleration of all unpaid lease payments since it is the only way to guarantee the lessor recovery of capital and a return on its investment. No question of penalty can arise in a contract where there is a stipulation that the entire rent be immediately due but the lessor agrees to accept payment of it by instalments, i.e., *debitum in praesenti solvendum in futuro*. Nevertheless, two Australian cases have demonstrated the difficulty of drafting such a clause (see *O'Dea* v *Allstates Leasing System (WA) Pty Ltd* (1983) 152 CLR 359; *AMEV-UDC Finance Ltd* v *Austin* (1986) 162 CLR 170). It has been held that an entitlement to this rent is fundamentally inconsistent with an early right to repossession on the basis that entitlement to the entire rent is consistent only with an affirmation of the contract of hire, whereas entitlement to repossession is consistent only with its termination. Following on from this, there is no doubt that where the acceleration clause is combined with a right of repossession, this will invite scrutiny on the basis of the court's jurisdiction to grant a hirer equitable relief from forfeiture.

Before a court will grant relief from forfeiture there would have to be a concession that rentals made were, in the case of hire-purchase, on account of the purchase price and that, therefore, there had been a partial failure of consideration. In *Stockloser* v *Johnson* [1954] 1 QB 476, Denning LJ pointed out that there were two main criteria for the application of equitable relief: first, the forfeiture clause had to be penal in nature; secondly, that it was unconscionable for the seller to retain the money. There has been statutory interference in relation to regulated consumer credit agreements so that s. 132(1) of the Consumer Credit Act 1974 provides:

(1) Where the owner under a regulated consumer hire agreement recovers possession of goods to which the agreement relates otherwise than by action, the hirer may apply to the court for an order that—
   (a) the whole or part of any sum paid by the hirer to the owner in respect of the goods shall be repaid, and
   (b) the obligation to pay the whole or part of any sum owed by the hirer to the owner in respect of the goods shall cease,
and if it appears to the court just to do so, having regard to the extent of the enjoyment of the goods by the hirer, the court shall grant the application in full or in part.

Similar powers are also conferred on the court in the case of where an owner brings an action for repossession as distinct from recaption of the goods (s. 132(2) of the Consumer Credit Act 1974).

An acceleration clause in the case of a regulated consumer credit agreement is not considered void as being a restriction on the statutory right of the debtor to terminate the contract (see *Wadham Stringer Finance Ltd* v *Meaney* [1981] 1 WLR 39). This is because the sum payable under such a clause may be considered a 'final payment' for the purposes of s. 99(1) of the Consumer Credit Act 1974 which states:

At any time before the final payment by the debtor under a regulated hire-purchase or regulated conditional sale agreement falls due, the debtor shall be entitled to terminate the agreement by giving notice to any person entitled or authorised to receive the sums payable under the agreement.

It should be noted that under a regulated consumer credit agreement, s. 93 of the Consumer Credit Act 1974 protects the debtor against default interest, i.e., an increase in the rate of interest on default, and he is also granted the benefit of a seven-day notice period (ss. 76(1)(a) and 87(1)(b) of the Consumer Credit Act 1974).

Subleasing Where the lessee has defaulted in his agreement with the lessor, in an attempt to sustain the lease and also to fulfil the duty imposed by the law of contract to mitigate the loss, the lessor may act as agent of the lessee and assign or sublease the equipment. Such an act by the finance lessor may be regarded as inconsistent with the continued existence of the lease, thereby releasing the lessee from his obligations under it and leaving the finance lessor with recovery only for breaches occurring before the date of release (see *Total Oil Great Britain Ltd* v *Thompson Garages (Biggin Hill) Ltd* [1972] 1 QB 318). However in *Highway Properties Ltd* v *Kelly Douglas and Co. Ltd* (1971) 17 DLR (3d) 710, the Supreme Court of Canada showed that as dealings in commercial property developed, maintaining a theoretically pure approach to leases as executed contracts conflicts with practical reality because once the tenant abandons the premises, the landlord can very easily resume possession and mitigate the losses. As Laskin CJ held at p. 721:

> It is no longer sensible to pretend that a commercial lease, such as the one before this court, is simply a conveyance and not also a contract. It is equally untenable to persist in denying resort to the full armoury of remedies ordinarily available to redress repudiation of covenants, merely because the covenants may be associated with an estate in land. Finally, there is merit here as in other situations in avoiding multiplicity of actions that may otherwise be a concomitant of insistence that a landlord engage in instalment litigation against a repudiating tenant.

This judgment represents Laskin CJ's attempt to bring property concepts into line with contract principles. Such a reconciliation is both fairer and more efficient for society, in the sense that a productive use will be made of the property, promoting activity, and minimising waste. If this approach were adopted in the context of finance leasing, the lessor's contractual rights under the lease would be protected. Consequently, a claim for any loss resulting from the subletting such as the difference in the rent received could be recovered.

Remedies available where the lease is not kept on foot

Self-help The possibility of repossession of the equipment by the lessor is predicated upon the idea that the equipment is worth more than the costs involved with repossession. In this regard, it may be possible for the finance lessor to insure against depreciation in the residual value of the equipment at the end of the lease term. Often the equipment will be unique and not easily marketable so that as a matter of prudence, the lessor should institute a thorough credit check on every prospective lessee. In this respect, sophisticated computer programs have been devised which assess such factors as the financial soundness of the lessee, the type of equipment to be leased, and the conditions of the leasing contract. Additionally, the lessor should monitor the lessee's creditworthiness throughout the term of the lease so that problems can be identified and acted upon as soon as possible.

Following a failure by the hirer or lessee to return to goods after a request by the owner, the latter is entitled to use reasonable force to recapt the goods. Of course, the question of what constitutes reasonable force is a matter of degree, so if unreasonable force is used, this will amount to an assault (*Dyer* v *Munday* [1895] 1 QB 742). Moreover, there is the criminal offence of unlawful harassment of debtors encapsulated in s. 40(1) of the Administration of Justice Act 1970. The Act is notoriously imprecise in scope. It provides a defence for anything done by a person which is reasonable for the following purposes under s. 40(3): '(a) of securing the discharge of an obligation due, or believed by him to be due, to himself or to persons for whom he acts, or protecting himself or them from future loss' or '(b) of the enforcement of any liability by legal process'. The difficulty here is the precise determination of reasonableness within the meaning of s. 40(3).

One alternative to recaption is repossession through court action on the basis of the hirer or lessee's neglect or refusal to return the goods, which is adverse to the owner's right to immediate possession. The forms of judgment available where goods are wrongfully detained can be found in s. 3 of the Torts (Interference with Goods) Act 1977. The relief is as follows:

(a) an order for delivery of the goods, and for payment of any consequential damages' (s. 3(2)(a)). This is a discretionary remedy (s. 3(3)(b)), and similar criteria applicable to the remedy of specific performance will apply;

(b) an order for delivery of the goods, but giving the defendant the alternative of paying damages by reference to the value of the goods, together in either alternative with payment of any consequential damages (s. 3(2)(b)). Here delivery of the goods is anticipated within a period of time unless payment is made plus damages for their detention. The court does have the power under both s. 3(2)(a) and (b) to impose conditions requiring an additional allowance to be made to the owner where damages 'by reference to the value of the goods would not be the whole of the value of the goods' (s. 3(5));

(c) 'damages' (s. 3(2)(c)). In this situation, the owner cannot insist on the return of the goods but can seize the goods which still belong to him until the judgment is satisfied. In this last situation, the owner would be deemed to have waived his right under the judgment to their value.

Self-help and third-party interests The liquidation value of the equipment may be well in excess of the lessor's loss on the default of the lessee. However, if the equipment retains its value only if it is not removed from the premises, or if the equipment is 'attached' to the real estate or to other equipment in which others have an interest, the lessor may not be able to realise fully the equipment collateral. In this respect, it will be necessary for a lessor to determine in advance of funding what impact the various third-party positions may have upon the collateral. Thus, there is a presumption that a chattel fixed to realty is a fixture, though this may be displaced in the case of an equipment lease where the transaction would indicate that the chattel was only intended to be used for the period of the lease. The position may be otherwise in the case of hire-purchase which might result in the presumption of permanent annexation on the basis of the hirer's option to purchase (*Vaudeville Electric Cinema Ltd* v *Muriset* [1923] 2 Ch 74).

The leasing arrangement may contain an express provision entitling the lessor to enter the lessee's land on his default and recover physical possession of the equipment. Such a vested right in the lessor will constitute an irrevocable licence to enter which provides immunity from an action for trespass so long as there has been no breach of the peace (*Hurst* v *Picture Theatres Ltd* [1915] 1 KB 1). The issue of what constitutes a fixture does not depend solely on the intention of the parties but involves questions of law to which the degree of physical affixation will be highly relevant.

The primary rule governing fixtures is that they become the property of the owner of the land. The rigours of this rule have been ameliorated through the distinction drawn between chattels fixed by the tenant which he is not entitled to remove, and those which he may remove, for example, trade fixtures. The right of the owner of a chattel to enter and seize the chattel on default by a lessee will also bind the lessee's landlord. This interest arises from the fact that the chattel owner stands in the same position as the tenant. On the expiration of the tenant's term, the owner's right to removal will, therefore, normally be exhausted. The interest is basically *sui generis* and is incapable of registration under the Land Registration Act 1925. It follows that the interest of a legal mortgagee who takes without notice of the chattel owner's prior equitable right will prevail (see *Hobson* v *Gorringe* [1897] 1 Ch 182).

The legal position described above may be different where the legal mortgage was granted prior to affixation. This is because the legal mortgagee, by leaving the legal mortgagor in possession, may have impliedly authorised the mortgagor to carry on his business in the usual way. Often this will include the right to affix hired goods to the property and granting the owner of the goods a right to remove them on termination of the hiring contract (see *Gough* v *Wood and Co.* [1894] 1 QB 713). Nonetheless, the mortgage deed may negative the mortgagor's implied authority. From this it appears that the finance lessor's position is precarious. The situation is just as awkward where the hirer has sold the land on which the equipment is leased since a purchaser of a legal estate is entitled to all fixtures attached to the land at the time of the contract purchase.

Third-party interests, especially the repairer's lien, may prevail against the finance lessor on repossession. Since this lien arises by operation of law, it may be immaterial to the creation of a valid lien that the equipment owner is a stranger to the contract, or that the lessor without the repairer's knowledge has specifically prohibited the creation of the lien. The principles of agency apply here so that even where there is no express obligation to repair, this may be implied when the object of the bailment, as in a finance lease, is to enable the bailee to use the equipment where incidental to this use would be the need to repair it (see *Tappenden* v *Artus* [1964] 2 QB 185).

Even if the rights of the repairer are successfully excluded by an express clause in the leasing contract prohibiting repairs without the prior consultation and approval of the finance lessor, the repairer, in the absence of estoppel on the part of the finance lessor, may be able to take advantage of the innocent improver provisions under the common law. Thus in *Greenwood* v *Bennett* [1973] QB 195, a person who mistakenly improved another's chattel was allowed a restitutionary claim against the owner. Since then, the Torts (Interference with Goods) Act 1977 provides, in proceedings for 'wrongful interference with goods', an allowance to an innocent improver to the extent to which 'the value of the goods is attributable to the improvement'. The Act is unhappily worded. No direct guidance is given as to what is the relevant time for assessing the value of the goods. If the conversion value is assessed as at the date of the conversion which is the common law position, unless the improver commits a fresh act of conversion by selling the goods so improved, the improvement would normally be excluded from the award of damages. However, in *IBL Ltd* v *Coussens* [1991] 2 All ER 133, the Court of Appeal held that in appropriate circumstances, the owner might be entitled to be compensated for the value of converted goods at the date of judgment and not at the date of the conversion. Factors that will influence the court include whether the goods would have been kept by the owner, or whether he should have been obliged to replace them. If the goods would have been kept and it was decided that the plaintiff was not obliged to replace them, or would have been unable to do so, the damages will be assessed in the light of those findings probably by reference to their value at the date of judgment.

Undoubtedly, the wording of the 1977 Act is obscure. If it has reversed the common law rule, so a repairer's lien not only now arises where the repairer is in possession of the goods with the consent of the owner, the Act will have the effect of cutting across contractual boundaries, unjustifiably redistributing to the owner the burden of risks, for example, the creditworthiness of a contracting party which the artificer assumed in his contract with the hirer. This was not the case in *Greenwood* v *Bennett* because the contract between the innocent improver and the rogue was one of *sale*. It follows from this that the innocent improver's restitutionary claim against the owner for the value of the repairs was independent of and did not spring from the contract of sale. If this approach were adopted in the context of finance leasing, the finance lessor would be able to avoid the repairer's lien.

Repudiation and termination Where the lessee acts in such a way as to renounce his future obligations under the lease, and the lessor accepts this repudiation, the agreement will be terminated. The classic statement of principle is that provided by Pollock and Wright, *Possession in the Common Law* (London, 1888), at p. 132:

> Any act or disposition which is wholly repugnant to or as it were an absolute disclaimer of the holding as bailee revests the bailor's right to possession, and therefore also his immediate right to maintain trover or detinue even where the bailment is for a term or is otherwise not revocable at will.

A failure to pay the agreed rental is a breach of contract which entitles the owner to sue for damages. Normally, a single lapse will not amount to repudiation, but where there is a persistent refusal, or where the agreement specifically provides for termination in this event, it will amount to repudiation of the contract. Here the lessor can claim damages in respect of loss of profit on further rentals to which it would have been entitled had the leasing run its full course (see *Yeoman Credit Ltd* v *Waragowski* [1961] 1 WLR 1124; *Yeoman Credit Ltd* v *McLean* [1962] 1 WLR 131; *Overstone Ltd* v *Shipway* [1962] 1 WLR 117). Mitigation of damages will be a difficult factor where the leased chattel is unique. The rentals are discounted in order to allow for acceleration of payments. In the case of hire-purchase, no account is taken of the hirer's right to terminate which would militate against recovery of the whole hire-purchase price (see *Union Transport Finance Ltd* v *British Car Auctions Ltd* [1978] 2 All ER 385). As against the hirer, or his assignee, the courts have restricted the supplier to the outstanding balance of the hire-purchase price. Of course, in principle, where the agreement has been terminated the supplier should be entitled to the full value of the goods. The explanation here is that the hire-purchase rule is *sui generis* (see *Belsize Motor Supply Co.* v *Cox* [1914] 1 KB 244; *Belvoir Finance Co. Ltd* v *Stapleton* [1971] 1 QB 210).

The effects of a repudiatory breach   One of the only English cases dealing with the effect of repudiation in a finance lease is *Lombard North Central plc* v *Butterworth* [1987] QB 527. It is worth dwelling upon the facts. The plaintiffs, a finance company, leased a computer to the defendant for a period of five years on payment of an initial sum of £584.05 and 19 subsequent quarterly instalments of the same amount. Clause 2(a) of the agreement made punctual payment of each instalment the essence of the agreement, and failure to make such payments entitled the plaintiffs to terminate the agreement. Clause 6 of the agreement provided that following termination, the plaintiffs were entitled to all arrears of instalments and all future instalments which would have fallen due had the agreement not been terminated. When the sixth instalment was six weeks overdue, the plaintiffs terminated the agreement and having recovered possession of the computer sold it for only £172.88. The plaintiffs brought an action against the defendant claiming the sixth unpaid instalment and the 13 future instalments or, alternatively, damages for breach of contract. Before the Court of Appeal, the defendant contended that he ought not to be held liable for more than the amount due and unpaid at the date of termination. The argument employed was that clause 6 of the agreement created a penalty and that the defendant's conduct had not amounted to a repudiation. The plaintiffs argued that clause 2(a) of the agreement entitled them to treat default in one payment as a repudiation of the agreement, thereby enabling them to recover their loss in respect of the whole transaction.

The lessor succeeded in the Court of Appeal and recovered for the loss of bargain under the general law of damages irrespective of the fact that the liquidated damages provision could be struck down as a penalty. This conclusion was arrived at by the Court of Appeal somewhat reluctantly because, as Nicholls LJ pointed out at p. 543, there was 'no practical difference' between the terms of the contract in this case and the previous decision of the Court of Appeal in *Financings Ltd v Baldock* [1963] 2 QB 104. In the latter case, an owner had terminated a hire-purchase agreement under an express provision entitling him to terminate for non-payment of hire. It was held that he was, in the absence of repudiation, entitled to no more than the amount of the hire unpaid at the time of termination. As Nicholls LJ said in *Lombard North Central plc v Butterworth* at p. 546 (emphasis added):

> There is no practical difference between (1) an agreement containing such a power [for termination] and (2) an agreement containing a provision to the effect that time for payment of each instalment is of the essence so that any breach will go to the root of the contract. The difference between these two agreements is one of drafting form and wholly without substance. *Yet under an agreement drafted in the first form, the owner's damages claim arising on his exercise of the power of termination is confined to damages for breaches up to the date of termination, whereas under an agreement drafted in the second form the owner's damages claim, arising on his acceptance of an identical breach as a repudiation of the agreement will extend to damages for loss of the whole transaction.*

The above comment fails to take into account the following matters: first, merely because the parties refer to a term (time in this case) as a condition, this is not necessarily determinative of the question insofar as it describes the legal *nature* of the breach; secondly, a finance lease is a financing venture where payment schedules go to the root of the contract because the lessor looks primarily towards the rental stream rather than repossession of the asset. Thus, on the facts of this case, there was a considerable risk of obsolescence which is not so prevalent in the normal hire-purchase transaction involving consumer durables.

Where the breach is not deemed repudiatory, the courts have, in the context of hire-purchase transactions, taken into account the existence of the right to terminate as in *Financings Ltd v Baldock* [1963] 2 QB 104. In this case, Lord Denning enunciated a new general principle of law at pp. 110–11:

> I see no difference in this respect between the letting of a vehicle on hire and the letting of land on a lease. If a lessor under a proviso for re-entry, re-enters on the ground of non-payment of rent or of disrepair, he gets the arrears of rent up to the date of re-entry and damages for want of repair at that date, but he does not get damages for loss of rent thereafter or for breaches of repair thereafter.

What was awarded to the owner in *Financings Ltd* v *Baldock* having 'unreasonably terminated the agreement' was the two instalments of rent in arrears plus interest. The major objection to this is the failure to recognise that a lease of real property is both a conveyance and a contract and, usually, a minimum payment clause (indemnity) will govern termination of an agreement.

More recently in *UCB Leasing Ltd* v *Holtom* [1987] RTR 362, the Court of Appeal refused to follow the approach of Holroyd Pearce LJ in *Yeoman Credit Ltd* v *Apps* [1962] 2 QB 508. In the latter case, his lordship held that if the hirer affirms the contract but the goods subsequently remain unfit, the continuing breach entitles the hirer to reject the goods. In *UCB Leasing Ltd* v *Holtom*, the hirer did not reject the car until he had had it for seven months, and the court held that he had affirmed the contract by virtue of a lapse of a reasonable period of time. The owners were held entitled to all instalments due until rejection. The Court of Appeal applied *Financings Ltd* v *Baldock*, namely, the hirer by returning the car had not repudiated the agreement and the owners were not entitled to payment in respect of the future instalments that had not fallen due before the owner's termination of the agreement. Interestingly, Balcombe LJ in *UCB Leasing Ltd* v *Holtom* pointed out that since the owner had made payment on time the essence of the contract, the owners were entitled to treat the contract as repudiated and, following *Lombard North Central plc* v *Butterworth* were entitled to compensation for loss of future instalments subject to the hirer's counterclaim for damages (see *Charterhouse Credit Co. Ltd* v *Tolly* [1963] 2 QB 683).

In *AMEV-UDC Finance Ltd* v *Austin* (1986) 162 CLR 170, the Australian High Court pointed out that there was nothing objectionable about an indemnity clause which anticipated the recovery of actual loss on early termination. Nevertheless, the majority held that where the indemnity clause was penal, it was not for the courts to rewrite the stipulation so as to limit it to what could be recovered as an indemnity. The court held that the lessor's claim should be limited to loss flowing from the breach which did not include loss of bargain where there was no repudiation. Such an approach is unduly restrictive in a finance leasing context. Significantly, in *Robophone Facilities Ltd* v *Blank* [1966] 1 WLR 1428, Diplock LJ suggested that a liquidated damages clause could properly include compensation for a loss which would normally be too remote. Such an argument is attractive in a non-consumer case, for example *Lombard North Central plc* v *Butterworth* [1987] QB 527, since business people should be expected to understand the terms offered in their contracts of supply.

Lawful termination In order to protect itself against loss in value through depreciation, the finance lessor will provide for payment of specific sums by the lessee on default. The difficulty here concerns the question of what actually constitutes a genuine pre-estimate of loss? In addition, to what extent is it possible to accommodate the doctrine of penalties in the context of finance leasing bearing in mind the theoretical underpinnings of contract law? Occasionally, the agreement will represent neither, especially since both English and Australian courts have affirmed that a term will not be characterised as a penalty clause if it is expressed to take effect upon an event other than a breach of contract by the hirer. In *Bridge* v *Campbell Discount Co. Ltd* [1962] AC 600, the House of Lords was divided on this question, and Lord Denning pointed out at p. 629 that equity, by this method, commits itself to an 'absurd paradox' appearing to grant relief only on breach of contract. Nevertheless, this reluctance has been overturned by the House of Lords in *Export Credits Guarantee Department* v *Universal Oil Products Co.* [1983] 1 WLR 399. The reasoning here is that it has never been the function of the courts to relieve a party from a contract on the mere ground that it proves to be onerous or imprudent.

One important effect of the above approach is that it allows a skilled legal draftsperson to avoid the rule against penalties. Ironically, a lessee who honours his obligations by terminating the agreement in a manner prescribed by the contract will be in a worse position than an irresponsible lessee who breaks the contract, and whose liability will be avoided because of the rule relating to penalties. Be that as it may, any attempt by a finance lessor to circumscribe the rule against penalties through mechanistically invoking an acceleration clause and then proceeding to terminate the lease for default in payment of the accelerated rentals is unlikely to succeed before the courts. Such conduct is similar to sharp practice making it inequitable to allow the finance lessor to retain the benefit of its full legal rights without allowing the lessee a *locus poenitentiae* under the rules against forfeiture (see *Barton Thompson and Co. Ltd* v *Stapling Machines Co.* [1966] Ch 499). On the other hand, the exercise by the lessor of a contractual power of termination for breach is enforceable.

Penalty clauses In an attempt to protect its investment on the lessee's default, the finance lessor may invoke a 'minimum payment' clause. One of the main difficulties here concerns the genuineness of the pre-estimate of loss. Care has to be taken in drafting a deemed repudiation clause so as realistically to limit the acts of default that would be considered to constitute a repudiation to such matters as go to the root of the contract. Since finance leases will often contain a long list of events of default, for example, failure to insure or to repair, these very contractual provisions may run foul of the rule against penalties. The court may not consider all of these breaches of contract as being sufficiently serious to amount to repudiation by the lessee.

All the relevant English cases to date have concerned minimum payment clauses with no realistic provision being made for the value of the repossessed equipment or for the acceleration of rentals. In *Bridge* v *Campbell Discount Co. Ltd* [1962] AC 600, a clause which provided that a sum should be paid equalling two-thirds of the hire-purchase price, and that expenses incurred by the owner should be payable was considered not to be a genuine pre-estimate of liquidated damages. In spite of this, it is clear from the judgments given in the House of Lords that had the default clause been properly drawn as a genuine pre-estimate of damages it would have been enforceable. Even so, such an ideal has proved elusive in subsequent cases. Thus in *Anglo Auto Finance Co. Ltd* v *James* [1963] 1 WLR 1042, the Court of Appeal considered a minimum payment clause which required payment of all moneys in arrears, and a sum equal to the amount by which the hire-purchase price (less the deposit and monthly instalments already paid) exceeded the net amount realised by the sale of the vehicle to be penal. The judgments seem to indicate that, since in *Bridge* v *Campbell Discount Co. Ltd* two thirds of the hire-purchase price recoverable under the minimum payment clause was held to be penal, a clause providing for 100 per cent of the purchase price had to be penal. Unfortunately, the judgments fail to take account of one essential difference; the clause in *Anglo Auto Finance Co. Ltd* v *James* provided for the resale price of the car being deducted from the hire-purchase price in computing the damages, but admittedly it did fail to take into account a discount for acceleration of payment resulting from the disposal of the repossessed goods. Only in this latter sense could the clause be considered penal. As a matter of principle, there is nothing oppressive in a clause enabling the owner to place upon the lessee the risk of any deficiency resulting from repossession and resale from the discounted hire-purchase price, except where the deficiency is increased as a result of the owner's negligence.

In order to draft a remedy clause successfully, an allowance will have to be given to the lessee both for the value of the equipment repossessed and also for the accelerated payments given to the lessor. The difference between computing the owner's loss under a hire-purchase agreement and that incurred under a finance lease is that in the case of the former, the full net proceeds of sale must be brought into account, whereas in the case of the finance lease, the owner would, in any event, have regained the goods at the end of the period. The finance lessor's potential gain, for which it will have to give allowance if the clause is not to be struck down as penal, will not equal the full proceeds of sale, but the amount by which this exceeds what would have been the value of the goods at the end of the hiring period. A useful summary of the damages formula is any past-due rentals plus interest, or delay damages; plus the present value of the future rent stream; plus the value of any insurance, maintenance and tax liabilities assumed by the lessee; plus the present value of the end-of-term residual value, adjusted for any loss due to abusive use; and plus the additional costs and expenses of realisation.

There may be problems in determining the appropriate discount rate applicable. To the extent that the above formulation makes prior estimation of the loss by the lessor very difficult to assess, the court might favour a 'broad brush' approach. In *Robophone Facilities Ltd* v *Blank* [1966] 1 WLR 1428, it was held that a clause providing for the pre-estimate of damages involving the repudiation of an operating lease of telephone-answering equipment was not a penalty, even though it was not precise, because it was 'reasonably close' to the actual loss likely to be occasioned to the plaintiffs so far as it was capable of prediction. The clause required payment, as liquidated damages, of 50 per cent of the gross rents which would have been payable, and this was accepted by the court as a *via media* of the actual loss of the plaintiff which was estimated to lie within a range of 47 to 58 per cent of the gross rents for the unexpired term of the contract. Such a provision was commended by the court for its sound business sense in that it attempted to avoid the uncertainty of proving in a court the actual loss sustained.

The finance lease 313

In applying the discount rate, credit should be given to the finance lessor for initial expenses incurred in setting up the transaction in the first instance. Of course, these initial expenses will figure prominently in the first few payments of the lease. In this respect, it would seem that a rebate on a straight apportionment may not do justice to the lessor, i.e., to treat the finance charge as incurred evenly over the period of the lease. This is particularly the case in the 'balloon' type of lease (see p. 291–2).

Subletting of the goods The difficulties involved in quantifying damages often lead to the inclusion in a finance lease of a right to sublease. This right to sublease will be limited to the duration of the main leasing agreement unless the subhirer can establish that the finance lessor held out the lessee as being the owner, or as being authorised to sublet for a period not limited to the main hiring agreement. Such a conclusion is unlikely in the light of the fact that the courts, at least in hire-purchase cases, have consistently held that the owner is not estopped from denying the hirer's authority to sell by mere delivery of possession unless there is some representation which can be spelled out from the owner's conduct (see *Lloyds and Scottish Finance Ltd* v *Williamson* [1965] 1 WLR 404). It normally follows that the termination of the main leasing agreement will automatically terminate the sublease. Indeed, if the subhirer refuses to deliver up possession, he may be sued for 'wrongful interference' by virtue of s. 3 of the Torts (Interference with Goods) Act 1977 (see p. 305).

Clearly, the finance lessor will be interested in continuing the sublease on the insolvency of the lessee. The alternative of repossession will be costly, and full recovery of damages under a minimum payment clause or otherwise may be impossible where there are insufficient funds. The lessor will often re-lease the goods on different terms than the original lease in order to satisfy the needs of the new lessee. Determining the fair market-value of the lease in order to award market-price damages will be extremely difficult when the only evidence of the secondary market is the re-lease itself. Some leases set forth the anticipated value of the goods following the termination of the lease providing that, upon breach, the lessee is liable for all future rentals plus the termination value minus the proceeds of any re-lease. As an alternative, it is possible to set forth the depreciated value of the goods at given periods during the lease and provide that the lessee should have a credit against future rentals for the depreciation saved by early cancellation. If the figures in these schedules represent good-faith approximations of the actual values, such clauses should be upheld.

The assignment of the benefit of the lease, for example, the rights of the lessee under the sublease including the right to terminate or to accept termination by the sublessee, will only bind the lessee's liquidator if it was made before the commencement of the compulsory winding up of the company. Such an assignment to the finance lessor of the subrentals due could be categorised as a charge of the lessee's book debts which will be void as against the liquidator unless registered (s. 396(c)(iii) of the Companies Act 1985 as amended).

An interesting problem in the case of a sub-bailment is whether the sub-bailee can rely upon an exemption clause in the contract of sub-bailment against the original bailor. In *Morris* v *C.W. Martin and Sons Ltd* [1966] 1 QB 716, Lord Denning held that the original bailor would be bound by the conditions of the contract of sub-bailment if he had expressly or impliedly consented to the bailee making a sub-bailment containing those conditions. However, in the more recent case of *Johnson Matthey and Co. Ltd* v *Constantine Terminals Ltd* [1976] 2 Lloyd's Rep 215, Donaldson J went further than Lord Denning since he held that a bailor is bound by any terms which constitute the consideration upon which the sub-bailee accepted the goods, irrespective of the bailor's consent. Whichever approach is adopted, it would appear that the finance lessor would be bound in circumstances where the finance lease includes a subletting provision (see also *Singer Co. (UK) Ltd* v *Tees and Hartlepool Port Authority* [1988] 2 Lloyd's Rep 164). These cases represent a desire on the part of the courts to avoid uncommercial results which would follow from a rigid application of the privity rule.

LEASING AND THE CONSUMER CREDIT ACT 1974

Turning to the effect of the Consumer Credit Act 1974 on finance leasing it will be obvious, on any analysis, that the provisions of the Act will rarely extend to this form of commercial activity. The 1974 Act is concerned with consumer hire agreements which consist of agreements made by a person with an individual for a bailment of goods which is not a hire-purchase agreement, and is capable of subsisting for more than three months. The definition of 'individual' is defined in s. 189(1) as including: 'a partnership or other unincorporated body of persons not consisting entirely of bodies corporate'. It follows that the Consumer Credit Act 1974 applies wherever the debtor is not a body corporate and would presumably apply to an unincorporated club, or charity, or trade union or small business. Significantly, the government has decided to amend the Act to take small businesses outside its ambit ((1987) 42 CC5/24). In any case, very many commercial leasing arrangements will usually involve sums over £15,000 which is outside the current credit limit for the application of the Consumer Credit Act 1974 (s. 8(2) of the Consumer Credit Act 1974; Consumer Credit (Increase of Monetary Limits) Order 1983, SI 1983 No. 1878).

The Act may apply in relation to the exercise by the lessor of any remedies under the lease contract. The exercise of the creditor's remedies are covered by the Act irrespective of the different forms of hiring agreement, for example, leasing, hire, contract hire or rental, and any distinctions between them are regarded as purely functional and having little legal significance. Thus, a provision in the lease that the full balance shall immediately become payable is covered by s. 76 of the Act which requires seven days' notice in prescribed form to be given by the owner to the hirer. By virtue of s. 87(1), service of a default notice in accordance with s. 88 is necessary before the owner can become entitled, following a breach by the debtor or hirer, to terminate the agreement, demand earlier payment of any sum, and recover the goods.

One of the most worrying aspects of the Consumer Credit Act 1974 from the finance lessor's point of view could have been the provision under s. 101(1) enabling the hirer under a regulated consumer hire agreement to terminate the agreement by giving notice after 18 months. As we have seen, rental terms for equipment leases usually involve a time period of five years so the foregoing provision would have made small equipment leases to sole traders and partnerships uneconomic. It is for this reason that Parliament provided the s. 101(7) exemption to three categories of lease:

(a) where the minimum rental exceeds £900 per year (problematic in the case of balloon rentals);
(b) where the goods are bailed to the hirer for the purposes of his business under a directly financed transaction;
(c) where the hirer requires the goods for a subleasing business.

The underlying rationale is that this part of the leasing business has not been found to generate abuse, that is, it did not lock hirers into burdensome contracts for long periods of time where the total rental amounted to many times the value of the goods.

It is worth noting the powerful effect of s. 132 of the Consumer Credit Act 1974. This enables the court to order a total or partial repayment of rentals to the hirer and release the hirer from all or part of any future liability under the agreement in any case where the hirer repossesses the goods, or obtains an order for their return, whether this results from termination by the owner for the hirer's default or termination by the hirer himself. In addition, the court has a wide discretion as to time orders under ss. 129 and 130 of the Consumer Credit Act 1974 where no limitation is imposed on the court in allowing time for repayment by the hirer, so long as the time does not go beyond the contract period of hire.

Termination of a regulated consumer credit agreement

The debtor under a regulated consumer credit agreement has a right to repay early (s. 94 of the Consumer Credit Act 1974). There is also a further right to a rebate (s. 95), the amount of which is determined by the Consumer Credit (Rebate on Early Settlement) Regulations 1983 (SI 1983/1562). The debtor, as distinct from a consumer hirer, has a statutory right on his written request to a written statement of the sum outstanding (s. 97). He may then elect to make early payment of that sum (s. 172), upon which he is is entitled to a statutory rebate in respect of future instalments.

In the all too common case where the debtor cannot repay, considerable protection is afforded by the Consumer Credit Act 1974. Thus the debtor is given a statutory right under s. 99 to terminate a regulated conditional sale or hire-purchase agreement, except where he has subsold the goods (s. 99(4)). The general effect here is to assimilate hire-purchase and conditional sale transactions. To meet the unusual case where the property has already passed to the conditional buyer before termination, for example, by operation of law in the case of *accessio* (see chapter 2), s. 99(5) provides that: 'the property in the goods shall thereupon vest in the person (the "previous owner") in whom it was vested immediately before it became vested in the debtor'. Special provision is also made under s. 99(5) for the situation where the 'previous owner' has died or become bankrupt in the meantime. The liability of the debtor outside of this is limited to a maximum of 50 per cent of the total price of the goods (s. 100(1)), but if the agreement lays down a lower figure than this, the debtor can rely upon that (s. 100(1)). The court is also empowered to lay down a lower figure if this more accurately reflects the creditor's loss (s. 100(3)).

There are important procedural safeguards which protect the defaulting debtor, so effectively providing him with another opportunity to honour his agreement. Under s. 87 of the Consumer Credit Act 1974, the debtor must be supplied with a written default notice before the creditor can take any form of action. As expanded by regulations, the notice must specify the nature of the alleged breach which must not have been waived by the owner, and the action required of the debtor or hirer. Such action will depend upon whether it is a remediable breach under s. 88(1)(b), or an irremediable breach under s. 88(1)(c). Moreover, s. 88(5) makes it clear that a default notice may activate a provision in a regulated agreement that the agreement or hiring is terminable for arrears.

On receipt of the default notice in its prescribed form, the debtor or hirer is allowed at least seven days' grace (ss. 76(1), 88(2) and 98(1)). During this period, the debtor may seek relief from the courts where a time order may be granted in situations considered by the court to be just. In the case of hire-purchase and conditional sale agreements, a time order can reschedule all remaining instalments so that it will not be confined to those instalments which have fallen due (s. 130(2)). Additionally, the court may make a transfer order dividing the goods between the debtor and the creditor. Section 133 contains special rules to compensate the creditor for having to accept the return of used goods.

The consumer credit agreement may contain provisions relating to termination on death or insolvency. In these situations, the general rule still pertains so that no action can be taken without the giving of seven days' notice (s. 76). The position on death is that the creditor must obtain a court order before taking action, but no action may be taken if the agreement is fully secured. Unfortunately, the distinction between fully secured and partly secured or unsecured is not defined under the Act. Section 189(1) provides that:

> 'security', in relation to an actual or prospective consumer credit agreement or consumer hire agreement, or any linked transaction, means a mortgage, charge, pledge, bond, debenture, indemnity, guarantee, bill, note or other right provided by the debtor or hirer, or at his request (express or implied), to secure the carrying out of the obligations of the debtor or hirer under the agreement.

It is difficult to determine from this whether a hire-purchase contract constitutes a 'fully secured' agreement. Although the creditor in this circumstance has the right to the return of his goods, has this right been 'provided by the debtor'? It would appear that an agreement is 'fully secured' if the debtor gives the creditor the right to take possession of the goods upon the termination of the agreement. Of course, the real problem here is the categorisation of security as the *granting* of an interest as distinct from the *retention* of title (see chapter 15).

Repossession Repossession, as the most dramatic illustration of self-help exercised by the creditor, is rigorously controlled by the Consumer Credit Act 1974 with regard to regulated hire or hire-purchase or conditional sale agreements. Thus, s. 92(1) of the Consumer Credit Act 1974 provides:

> Except under an order of the court, the creditor or owner shall not be entitled to enter any premises to take possession of goods subject to a regulated hire-purchase agreement, regulated conditional sale agreement or regulated consumer hire agreement.

Further protection is afforded under such an agreement where the debtor has paid one third or more of the total price of the goods. Following this circumstance, the goods are considered to be 'protected goods', and can only be repossessed by an order of court. In determining what proportion the debtor has paid, special provision is made under s. 90(2) for compulsory installation charges, so one third of the total price is construed, for this purpose, as the aggregate of the installation charge and one third of the remainder of the total price. Special provision is also seen in the case of successive linked agreements so that where the first agreement falls within s. 90, both the old and new goods will fall within this section regardless of any amount paid.

A severe sanction attaches to wrongful repossession; the agreement is terminated under s. 91 of the Consumer Credit Act 1974 and the debtor can recover all the money he has paid out under it. However, 'protected goods' status is lost if the debtor has exercised his right of termination under s. 90(5), or has consented to repossession *at the time* of recaption. To be an effective consent, the debtor should be informed what his rights would be if he refused consent (*Chartered Trust plc* v *Pitcher* [1987] RTR 72). If the debtor has abandoned the goods, the creditor can seize them without contravening s. 90 because he will not have seized them 'from the debtor'.

It should be noted that the protection of possession anticipated under s. 90 is limited to the debtor, or his assignee or authorised bailee, since the goods will be deemed to be in the debtor's possession. It follows that such protection does not extend to a sub-buyer (see *Bentinck Ltd* v *Cromwell Engineering Co.* [1971] 1 QB 324).

FOURTEEN
Possessory security

PLEDGE

There is an intuitive attraction to possession as being the greatest indicia of ownership. Indeed, it is the ostensible ownership problem whereby property is separated from possession which is at the root of many modern personal property registration systems (see chapter 16). On the one hand, the pledge 'cures' the ostensible ownership problem in the sense that the holder of the security interest has possession of the goods, but on the other hand, it is clear the pledgee is not the owner of the goods. This can be demonstrated in Roman law where the pledge was known as the contract of *pignus*. In classical Roman terminology what was envisaged here was interdictal possession of the thing passing to the creditor while *dominium* remained with the debtor. The *interdicta* was the procedure by which the *praetor* (a Roman magistrate) ordered something to be done chiefly in disputes about possession.

The common law attached great significance to possession (see pp. 20–24), so even the mortgage of land was originally in the nature of a pledge, that is, the mortgagee took possession until payment. It was not until the 16th century that the non-possessory mortgage of land became established, whilst the non-possessory chattel mortgage was not established until the Bills of Sale Act 1854. The two overriding characteristics of the pledge are: first, possession of the items deposited; secondly, ownership of the item(s) pledged remains with the pledgor. These characteristics are emphasised in Willes J's *dictum* in *Halliday* v *Holgate* (1868) LR 3 Ex 299 at p. 302:

> There are three kinds of security: the first, a simple lien; the second, a mortgage, passing the property out and out; the third, a security intermediate between a lien and a mortgage — viz. a pledge — where by contract a deposit of goods is made a security for a debt, and the right to the property vests in the pledgee so far as is necessary to secure the debt. It is true the

pledgor has such a property in the article pledged as he can convey to a third person, but he has no right to the goods without paying off the debt, and until the debt is paid off the pledgee has the whole present interest.

Pledge and chattel mortgages

The possessory nature of the pledge which involves the physical transfer of possession of property in the goods is the main distinguishing feature of the modern mortgage and pledge. Insofar as the mortgagee takes possession of the item mortgaged, this is done by virtue of the mortgagee's title in the item as his security whilst the pledgee is given possession as his security. This has important consequences as to registration of bills of sale under the Bills of Sale Acts 1854 to 1891. The policy of this legislation is to strike at the ostensible ownership problem by requiring public registration of other persons' interests in the things of which the borrower is in possession. If possession is given to the lender there is no need for registration under these Acts (*Re Hardwick, ex parte Hubbard* (1886) 18 QBD 690). However, the legislation deals only with documents (bills of sale) and *not* transactions. As a consequence, the parties to an agreement may escape altogether the effects of bills of sale legislation provided the agreement is informal.

Pledge and liens

Whereas a pledge refers to the *nature* of the *transaction* by which the pledgee retains possession of the goods, the lien consists of a right, as distinct from a transaction, given to the lienee covering goods in his possession belonging to the lienor. Both the pledgee and lienee are bailees of the goods and are liable as such. The major difference between the lien and the pledge is that the pledgee forbears to sue for the credit period, whilst the lien, as a right, is given in addition to the lienee's right to recover the debt by legal action. The nature of the lien is that it is a personal right in the sense that the lienee cannot deal with his interest and, more significantly, execution cannot be levied against the goods for the lienee's debts (*Legg* v *Evans* (1840) 6 M & W 36). In contrast, the pledgee can dispose of *his* interest in the goods which constitute assets against which execution can be made (*Re Rollason, Rollason* v *Rollason, Halse's Claim* (1887) 34 ChD 495).

Whilst the basic distinction between pledge and lien is clear, there has been a tendency in recent years to obscure the distinction. In part, this is due to statutory intervention where a right to sell may be provided, for example, s. 12 of the Torts (Interference with Goods) Act 1977 which gives the bailee a power of sale in the case of uncollected goods. In addition, it is common for a lienee in his contract to expressly stipulate for a right to sell. Nonetheless, the distinction remains: a lienee cannot by contract create a disponible interest similar to that of a pledgee nor has the lienee an implied right to sell the goods.

Pledge and equitable mortgages

Any type of corporeal movable may be pledged. Of course, the commonest pledges are of goods, but documents including insurance policies and share certificates may be pledged. It is difficult to see how the deposit of a dispensable piece of paper like an insurance policy can afford any security to the creditor since the contract will remain valid and enforceable even if the policy document is lost or destroyed. Clearly, this form of security can only operate on the footing that the debtor is not dishonest.

Where the deposit of the document was supported by an agreement that it was in fact made for the purpose of creating security, this would constitute an equitable mortgage which is binding upon any subsequent purchaser or mortgagee who knows or ought to have known of its existence. Thus, in *Harrold* v *Plenty* [1901] 2 Ch 314 at p. 316, Cozens-Hardy J held that the deposit of a share certificate could not constitute a pledge: 'A share is a chose in action. The certificate is merely evidence of title, and whatever may be the result of the deposit of a bearer bond . . . [the] deposit of a certificate by way of security for the debt . . . [amounts] to an equitable mortgage.' The effect of an equitable mortgage is that, unlike a pledge, there can be foreclosure (see *Stubbs* v *Slater* [1910] 1 Ch 632). In summary, an equitable mortgagee can apply to the court for sale or foreclosure while the pledgee of a share certificate can do neither: he can sell only the piece of paper which gives no right to the shares.

The form of the pledge transaction

Pledges made by individuals have long been subject to consumer protection measures (Pawnbrokers Acts 1872 to 1960) and the modern controls can be found in the Consumer Credit Act 1974. This Act contains important provisions which affect the validity of the transaction. Thus, a pawnbroker who takes pawns by way of business is required to have a licence (s. 39) where the credit is less than £15,000, and insofar as he does not have such a licence, a curing order from the Director General of Fair Trading is required for the agreement to be enforced against the consumer (s. 40). There are also certain formalities which have to be observed, for example, informing the pawnor of his rights (s. 114(1)) and failure to do so will render the pawnee criminally liable (s. 115).

No particular form is prescribed by statute for pledges outside the scope of the Consumer Credit Act 1974. It should be noted that pledges are commonly used in commerce, for example, pledges of documents of title to banks are often used to secure an advance made.

LIEN

A lien is a right normally given by operation of law to one person over the goods of another person to secure payment of a sum of money owed by that other person to the lienee. A careful distinction should be drawn between possessory and non-possessory or equitable liens.

Possessory (common law) liens

A possessory lien confers no proprietary interest in the lienee and is not assignable: it is purely a personal right and cannot be taken in execution by the lienee's creditors. The possessory lien may be subclassified as follows:

General liens

A general lien entitles the lienee to retain possession of *any* of his debtor's chattels to secure payment of all sums due on a general balance of account between them. Thus, a general lien is exercisable in respect of a debt or account which has no relation to the chattel subject to the lien. A general lien is usually created by usage and is confined to a small number of trades and professions. This is because they are not viewed with favour by the courts since their comprehensive nature tends to prejudice other creditors in the event of the debtor's insolvency. On the other hand, where the parties deal with each other on a regular basis, the general lien is, in fact, mutually beneficial since it allows the lienee to release individual goods without immediate payment because he will have recourse to other goods as security for the debt if this proves necessary.

A trader seeking to establish a general lien bears a heavy burden of proof (see *Rushforth* v *Hadfield* (1805) 6 East 519 and (1806) 7 East 224). In practice, therefore, general liens are the creatures of contract. However, long usage has established general liens in the following circumstances.

Solicitors' liens   A solicitor will have a general lien on the deeds and other documents in his possession belonging to the client so as to secure payment of all costs due from the client (*Ex parte Sterling* (1809) 16 Ves Jr 258). Even so, the lien cannot be exerted so as to interfere with the process of litigation (*Re Galland* (1885) 31 ChD 296). The public interest in justice demands that all documents needed in court be produced. When this purpose has been satisfied, the documents will then be returned to the solicitor who will not, thereby, be prejudiced.

Bankers' liens   This is a lien enjoyed in relation to papers or documents of title representing money, for example, share certificates (*National Westminster Bank Ltd* v *Halesowen Presswork and Assemblies Ltd* [1972] AC 785). However, the lien may be excluded by the circumstances of the bank's possession such as where securities are deposited for a special purpose only, typically, for safe custody.

It is important to distinguish the banker's lien from the banker's right of set-off. The limitations of contractual set-off have forced banks to examine the legal possibility of charging their own accounts.

Other agents' liens   The following agents have also been held to have general liens as a matter of usage: factors (*Kruger* v *Wilcocks* (1755) Amb 252); stockbrokers (*Re London and Globe Finance Corpn* [1902] 2 Ch 416); insurance brokers (*Hewison* v *Guthrie* (1836) 2 Bing NC 755). It should be noted that the transferee of an interest in goods held under a general lien takes it subject to the extent of the balance of account owing to the lienee when he receives notice of the transfer.

Particular liens

A particular lien entitles the lienee to retain possession only of those of his debtor's chattels in respect of which the debt arose, that is, it entitles the lienee to hold the debtor's goods pending payment of charges incurred in relation to the goods detained, there being no right to retain the goods for the purpose of securing payment of some other debt due from the owner unconnected with the goods in question.

Particular liens are favoured by the courts because they are not seriously prejudicial to general creditors on the debtor's insolvency and are analogous to the purchase-money security interest (see chapter 15). Of course, the terms of the transaction may prevent the lien from coming into existence in the first place as in the case of a credit period (*Wilson* v *Lombank Ltd* [1963] 1 WLR 1294).

Particular liens created by contract   These may arise expressly or impliedly from a prior course of dealing between the parties. Custom is important here as many classes of traders have established usages in their favour.

Particular liens created by statute   The most important of these is the unpaid vendor's lien which arises under ss. 41 to 43 of the Sale of Goods Act 1979 (see chapter 6).

Particular liens created by judicially recognised usage   Where the lienee is obliged by law to receive other persons' goods as in the case of innkeepers and common carriers, the courts have ameliorated this burden by the recognition of liens over guests' belongings and goods carried. The lien is enforceable against persons generally and not merely against the person for whom the charges are due. Thus, in the case of an innkeeper's lien, that is, the lien of a hotel proprietor by virtue of s. 1(1) of the Hotel Proprietors Act 1963, it has been held that even if the goods have been stolen by the person depositing them with the innkeeper, this does not deprive him of his lien. The innkeeper's knowledge of the fact that the guest is not the owner of the goods does not, in itself, deprive him of his lien, but the position is otherwise if the innkeeper knows that the guest is wrongfully in possession of them (*Gordon* v *Silber* (1890) 25 QBD 991; *Marsh* v *Commissioner of Police* [1944] 2 All ER 392).

Common carrier's lien   A common carrier as distinct from a private carrier has a lien for his charges (*Skinner* v *Upshaw* (1701) 2 Ld Raym 752). This lien only arises when the charges *become due*, normally, when the goods arrive at their destination. Difficulties arise where there has been a fundamental breach of the carriage contract, for example, deviation, and it is doubtful whether a lien could be maintained in these circumstances as it would constitute the enforcement of a lien earned by unlawful means (*Bernal* v *Pim* (1835) 1 Gale 17).

Innkeeper's lien   This lien is restricted to the belongings the *guest* brings with him for the amount of the bill. There are restrictions to the scope of the lien both at common law and by statute: first, guests are not to be made prisoners in the inn so that the lien will not apply to the clothes in which the guest is standing (*Sunbolf* v *Alford* (1838) 3 M & W 248); secondly, s. 2(2) of the Hotel Proprietors Act 1956 provides that the innkeeper's lien shall not embrace any vehicle or any horse or other live animal or its harness or other equipment.

Artificer's lien This arises where the lienee has by his labour and/or skill improved another's chattel. The courts have taken a restrictive view of what constitutes an improvement so that in *Re Southern Livestock Producers Ltd* [1964] 1 WLR 24, it was held that a farmer housing, feeding and caring for pigs had no lien on them for sums spent, one of the reasons being that routine care was not improvement (see also *Hatton v Car Maintenance Co. Ltd* [1915] 1 Ch 621). In contrast, there would be a common law lien on charges for veterinary attention and, in a similar way, professionals would have a lien on documents they work on such as architects (*Hughes v Lenny* (1839) 5 M & W 183), and accountants (*Woodworth v Conroy* [1976] QB 884). The lien only arises for work already *completed* or work done before the owner prevents completion (*Lilley v Barnsley* (1844) 1 Car and Kir 344).

The antithesis of the improver's lien is the salvor's lien for his services recognised in maritime law (*The Goring* [1987] QB 687). The essence of the salvor's lien is that he helps to prevent injury to another's goods which would, of course, not constitute an improvement for the purposes of the artificer's lien.

Non-possessory liens

These are rights conferred by equity in various circumstances which entitle creditors to have particular property in the possession of their debtors to be realised by legal process in order to satisfy their debts. Examples include the vendor's lien on land conveyed in respect of any unpaid portion of the price, and the purchaser's lien on land sold but not yet conveyed regarding any part of the price already paid (compare *Re Wait* [1927] 1 Ch 606).

An unpaid seller of goods has only got a possessory lien (ss. 41 to 43 of the Sale of Goods Act 1979). Nevertheless, an equitable lien may arise in respect of personal property other than 'goods' which are the subject of a contract of sale, for example, patents and shares. Such liens bind all those acquiring interests in the property concerned except bona fide purchasers of legal interests without notice of the lien.

POSSESSION AS THE BASE CONCEPT

As we have discussed earlier (see pp. 23–4), possession is a highly fluid concept as it may be either factual or constructive. Moreover constructive possession might take many forms including attornment (see pp. 33–6) and symbolic delivery, for example, the handing over of keys to the store where the pledged goods are housed so as to ensure exclusivity of possession (*Hilton v Tucker* (1888) 39 ChD 669). The endorsement and delivery of a bill of lading or some other document of title operates as delivery of the goods which it represents and may, therefore, be pledged. In *Official Assignee of Madras v Mercantile Bank of India Ltd* [1935] AC 53, Lord Wright summarised the position at p. 58 as follows:

> At the common law a pledge could not be created except by a delivery of possession of the thing pledged, either actual or constructive. It involved a bailment. If the pledgor had the actual goods in his physical possession, he

could effect the pledge by actual delivery; in other cases he could give possession by some symbolic act, such as handing over the key of the store in which they were. If, however, the goods were in the custody of a third person, who held for the bailor so that in law his possession was that of the bailor, the pledge could be effected by a change of the possession of the third party, that is by an order to him from the pledgor to hold for the pledgee, the change being perfected by the third party attorning to the pledgee, that is acknowledging that he thereupon held for him. . . . But where goods were represented by documents the transfer of the documents did not change the possession of the goods, save for one exception, unless the custodier (carrier, warehouseman or such) was notified of the transfer and agreed to hold in future as bailee for the pledgee. The one exception was the case of bills of lading, the transfer of which by the law merchant operated as a transfer of the possession of, as well as the property in, the goods. . . . a pledge of the documents (always excepting a bill of lading) is merely a pledge of the *ipsa corpora* of them; the common law continued to regard them as merely tokens of an authority to receive possession.

The issue of exclusivity of possession is essential. In this respect, the lienee must have obtained actual or constructive possession *lawfully* and must have the right to uninterrupted possession with no express or implied provision incompatible with this. Thus, in *Forth* v *Simpson* (1843) 13 QB 680, it was held that a trainer had no lien over a racehorse because he had no right of *continuing* possession since the owner could take him away for any race he chose and also select any jockey he chose. A related question concerns the legality of the creditor's possession which demonstrates the consensual basis of liens and pledges. Where true consent is not forthcoming the debtor will not be bound, for example, where there has been fraud or misrepresentation (*Madden* v *Kempster* (1807) 1 Camp 12), or where the goods have been obtained by force or any other tortious method (*Bernal* v *Pim* (1835) 1 Gale 17).

Where the creditor parts with the possession of the goods, this cannot normally be re-established by recaption (*Pennington* v *Reliance Motor Works Ltd* [1923] 1 KB 127). It is otherwise in the case of sale of goods where the right of stoppage *in transitu* arises by operation of law (see chapter 6).

Effect of giving up possession
The natural presumption is that the effect of redelivery of the goods is that possession has been surrendered. There are some difficult authorities which uphold the creditor's rights where the capacity of the debtor's possession is that of a bailee. The typical context here is where the object is needed as a tool of trade for the debtor, for example, a chronometer where the debtor was the master of a ship (*Reeves* v *Capper* (1838) 5 Bing NC 136), or a taxi in the case where the debtor was a taxi-cab operator (*Albemarle Supply Co. Ltd* v *Hind and Co.* [1928] 1 KB 307). Clearly, ostensible ownership problems are presented here and it is little wonder that in jurisdictions which have sophisticated personal property security registers, such interests have to be registered in order to be perfected (see for example, in Canada, the Repair and Storage Liens Act 1989, s. 7).

Trust receipt

Although at common law, a parting of the goods is destructive of the pledge, a redelivery of the goods for a limited purpose has been permitted. Given that possession is normally vital for the efficacy of the pledge, the trust receipt instrument has evolved to deal with the frequent situation, especially in international trade, where lenders release the goods to the borrower so that they can be sold or incorporated in some manufacturing process. The basis of the trust receipt is that the pledgor acknowledges that the goods and the proceeds of sale thereof are held on trust for the pledgee. The leading authority here is *Re David Allester Ltd* [1922] 2 Ch 211 where the lender was held to have priority over the liquidator representing the borrower's creditors in relation to proceeds realised by the sale under a letter of trust, primarily because the hypothecation was disregarded as the bank had by reason of *the pledge* a title to the proceeds of sale. Since the title could be shown without recourse to the document, the bills of sale legislation did not apply since the policy of this legislation is to strike at documents rather than transactions (see chapters 15 and 16).

The trust receipt should be carefully distinguished from the case where the creditor is given as an aspect of contract the right to seize the goods so as to enforce his security right. Such an arrangement is a security bill of sale and must comply with the rules relating to registration and other formalities. Similarly, where the contract provides for the creditor having a present lien over goods not in his possession, this will amount to a security bill of sale. It should be noted that s. 396(1)(c) of the Companies Act 1985 as originally enacted provided for registration of 'a charge created or evidenced by an instrument which, if executed by an individual, would require registration as a bill of sale'. Now s. 396(1)(b) (as amended) requires registration of 'a charge on goods or any interest in goods'. This may prove problematic because the bills of sale legislation contained important exemptions in s. 4 of the Bills of Sale Act 1878. Most notably, 'documents used in the ordinary course of business' were exempt which will not survive the new amendments made to the Companies Act 1985. However, it is unlikely that this will prejudice trust receipts since they are not bills of sale at all because they may be rationalised as *continuing* pledges. Of course, this explanation will not be available for letters of hypothecation, delivery orders and warehouse receipts.

Delivery to a third party Since the interest of the lienee is a personal one, the lienee's interest will terminate where he loses his immediate right to possess because by so doing he will have given up his ability to redeliver the goods (*Mulliner* v *Florence* (1878) 3 QBD 484). There are special policy considerations regarding the unpaid seller's lien, so where the disposition is by way of resale, s. 48(2) of the Sale of Goods Act 1979 ensures that the original buyer cannot claim the goods even if he tenders the agreed price. The effect of this statutory rule is that it facilitates resale as a self-help remedy for unpaid sellers of goods (see chapter 6).

In the case of a pledge, the pledgee has a special property interest in the goods and can dispose of *this* interest (*Donald* v *Suckling* (1866) LR 1 QB 585).

Insofar as the pledgee acts wrongfully either by selling the goods prematurely, or by subpledging the goods for an excessive amount in relation to his interest, the disposition is ineffective and the debtor cannot sue in conversion but must still tender the amount due. In this way, the special property interest of the pledgee is respected and protected (*Halliday* v *Holgate* (1868) LR 3 Ex 299). Once tender of the amount owed has been made, the pledgee can be sued in conversion if he refuses to deliver up the goods (compare *Franklin* v *Neate* (1844) 13 M & W 481).

POWERS OF SALE

Lien

The common law lien, being a possessory lien, is enforced by retaining possession of the goods until the debt is paid. A lienee has no automatic right to sell the goods, and if he does so wrongfully then this would terminate the lien and amount to conversion. A power of sale may, however, be conferred by contract, trade usage or statute, for example, s. 12 of the Torts (Interference with Goods) Act 1977. The sale must be conducted providently and the surplus proceeds must be disgorged to the lienor. Where there is a shortfall, the lienee can sue the lienor in debt for the balance due.

Pledge

The pledgee at common law can sell the whole interest in the chattel after the due date for repayment, or, if no date had been fixed, after proper demand. Such a sale must be provident and the surplus held on account for the pledgor. If the amount of the debt is not realised, the pledgee is free to sue the pledgor for any outstanding balance (*Jones* v *Marshall* (1889) 24 QBD 269).

In the case of pledges or pawns regulated by the Consumer Credit Act 1974, no sale can be made within six months of the pawning of the goods (s. 116(1)). Before a sale does take place, s. 121(1) stipulates that the pawnee must give notice of his intention to sell and must inform the pawnor of the asking price.

Termination of the interest

Where factual possession is lost, we have already seen that the interest of the lienee or pledgee will be prejudiced. In addition, the interest of the lienee or pledgee will be terminated in the following circumstances:

(a) Tender of amount due.

(b) Waiver, for example, the taking of some other security for the debt where it is clear that this is to *replace* the pledge or lien (*Bank of Africa* v *Salisbury Gold Mining Co.* [1892] AC 281).

(c) Breach. It is difficult to establish a breach of the terms on which the pledgee holds the goods so as to terminate his interest short of intentionally destroying the goods or consuming them (*Cooke* v *Haddon* (1862) 3 F & F 229). In the case of a lien, the lienee's interest will be divested for breach where the goods are used (*Rust* v *McNaught and Co. Ltd* (1918) 144 LT Jo 440), or where the lienee claims for an unjustifiable amount (*Jones* v *Tarleton* (1842) 9 M & W 675; compare *Scarfe* v *Morgan* (1838) 4 M & W 270).

FIFTEEN
Non-possessory security interests

The growth of non-possessory security interests in chattels was dealt a severe blow in *Twyne's Case* (1601) 3 Co Rep 80b. In the case it was held that because the transfer to Twyne was secret it was fraudulent and therefore void. This principle has, to a large extent, shaped the entire law dealing with security interests in personal property.

In *Twyne's Case*, the justices detected an inherent dishonesty in conveying all ownership rights in goods while retaining the possession and use of them. However, it has to be stressed that this was not a case of a creditor relying to his *detriment* on the debtor's possesion of goods which were not his own. In fact, the creditor had extended credit to Pierce (the debtor) before Pierce conveyed to Twyne and it follows from this that the case cannot be explained as an example of judicial concern over the deceptive potential of ostensible ownership. Essentially, the decision illustrates the difficulties surrounding the effect of delivery and property passing in English law discussed in chapters 12 and 13.

The legal principle associated with *Twyne's Case* is very simple and can be stated as follows: in order to obtain priority in an asset which prevails against third parties, it is not only necessary to receive the consent of the prior owner but also to secure the possession of the chattel. The difficulty with this possession-based rule is that it makes tracing claims very difficult and hence increases the risk of theft since the chain of title is very short. In addition, the possession rule militates against the temporal division of ownership of property. Nevertheless, towards the latter part of the 18th century the presumption of fraud was abrogated. Thus, in *Edwards* v *Harben* (1788) 2 TR 587, great emphasis was placed on the fact that the mortgage instrument had not provided for retention of possession which was otherwise deemed fraudulent. By 1832, it was held in *Martindale* v *Booth* (1832) 3 B & Ad 498 that retention of possession was no longer even prima facie evidence of fraud when the possession was consistent with the mortgage contract.

THE AFTER-ACQUIRED PROPERTY INTEREST

The response of equity

In England, it was the intervention of equity which provided the legal framework to utilise future property for present credit, most notably with the decision of the House of Lords in *Holroyd* v *Marshall* (1862) 10 HL Cas 191. Twenty years before this decision, Justice Joseph Story in the US case of *Mitchell* v *Winslow* (1843) 17 F Cas 527 (No. 9673) (CD Me) employed the civilian concept of a 'mortgage on an estate to come'. It is not surprising that the law generally took a more lenient attitude in its approach to mortgaging as distinct from selling future property since the assumption of risk is fundamentally different. In the case of a sale, the risk of loss is transferred to the buyer, whereas with a mortgage, it remains with the mortgagor. Although equity follows the law in that there cannot be a valid assignment of future property, nevertheless, where consideration has been given, equity will treat an assignment of future property as a contract to assign the property. By this method equity will compel performance of the contract, so the beneficial interest passes to the assignee immediately upon the acquisition of the property by the assignor. The significance of this can be illustrated in *Re Lind* [1915] 2 Ch 345 because the attachment being retroactive greatly increases the value of a security interest, in particular, as a method of circumventing the time preference period in insolvency (see part 5). Thus, the after-acquired property clause will bind the debtor's trustee in bankruptcy himself (*Re Collins* [1925] Ch 556).

A major difficulty is presented with the question of *how* equity will compel performance. In this respect, there is a conflict of authorities: first, Lord Westbury LC in *Holroyd* v *Marshall* appears to assert that the assignment can only be effective if specific performance of the contract to assign could have been decreed at the date on which property came into the hands of the assignor; secondly, Lord Macnaghten in *Tailby* v *Official Receiver* (1888) 13 App Cas 523 maintains that the doctrine of equitable assignment is entirely distinct from that of specific performance. These divergent approaches will now be discussed in greater detail.

Holroyd v *Marshall (1862) 10 HL Cas 191* The facts of this case are as follows. The appellants had purchased the machinery and implements in a mill belonging to Taylor who was in financial difficulty, but agreed to resell them to him for £500. Taylor did not have this amount of money, so the property was transferred to a third party as trustee for Taylor who had instructions that, if Taylor defaulted, the trustee was to sell the property and use the proceeds of the sale to pay the appellants holding any surplus for Taylor. In addition, there was an after-acquired property clause, the purchase price was secured on both presently existing machinery and machinery to be acquired in the future. Taylor bought more machinery but did not convey this machinery to the appellants who performed no act amounting to a formal taking of possession of the machinery. When Taylor fell into further financial difficulties, agents of the respondent, the High Sheriff of York, levied execution against the new machinery on behalf of two judgment creditors although they had *notice of the bill of sale*. Holroyd brought an action against Marshall claiming that there had been a valid equitable assignment to the trustee which was good against the judgment creditors. At first instance, Stuart V-C ((1860) 2 Giff 382) decided both points in favour of Holroyd, but on appeal his decision was reversed by Lord Campbell LC ((1860) 2 De G F & J 596) who held that, in order for Holroyd to prevail over the judgment creditors, he would have to perfect his title to the new machinery by taking possession and that until this was done, Holroyd had merely an equitable right (*ius ad rem*) which could not prevail against the judgment creditors.

In the House of Lords, the approach taken by Lord Campbell was supported by counsel for the respondents. Additionally, counsel cited the dictum of Parke B in *Mogg* v *Baker* (1838) 3 M & W 195, a common law case, where it was said at p. 198:

> If the agreement was to mortgage certain specific furniture of which the corpus was ascertained, that would constitute an equitable title in the defendant, so as to prevent it passing to the assignees of the insolvent, and then the assignment would make that equitable title a legal one; but if it was only an agreement to mortgage furniture to be subsequently acquired — to give a bill of sale on a future day of the furniture and other goods of the insolvent — then it would cover no specific furniture, and would confer no right in equity.

Lord Westbury LC was concerned with the proposition of counsel for the respondents that the right to specific performance of an agreement to transfer property is a 'mere personal equity' as this struck at the very core of equitable titles. What his lordship set out to do was dispel the confusion that existed between equitable assignment and the common law with its 'new act' doctrine (see below). Lord Westbury dismissed Parke B's *dictum* on the basis that in a case where the agreement did not define any specific property, the equitable principles he envisaged would not apply. Moreover, Lord Westbury at p. 211 ignored the implication of Parke B that an agreement relating to future property could not relate to specific property:

> . . . if a vendor or mortgagor agrees to sell or mortgage property, real or personal, of which he is not possessed at the time, and he receives the consideration for the contract, and afterwards becomes possessed of property answering the description in the contract, there is no doubt that a court of equity would compel him to perform the contract, and that the contract would, in equity, transfer the beneficial interest to the mortgagee or purchaser immediately on the property being acquired. This, of course, assumes that the supposed contract is one of that class of which a court of equity would decree the specific performance.

It has proved difficult to determine whether the reference in Lord Westbury's judgment to specific performance is a prerequisite for equitable intervention.

To a large extent since it had been conceded that the case was one for which specific performance could have been decreed, the reference to specific performance may, as Lord Macnaghten in *Tailby* v *Official Receiver* (1888) 13 App Cas 547 said, have been purely illustrative. Nevertheless, this approach does seem to contradict the plain meaning the Lord Westbury's words, although it may be possible in Lord Westbury's treatment to distinguish between existing property and future property. With regard to the former, the Lord Chancellor referred to the necessity of the contract as being 'one of which a court of equity *will* declare specific performance' (p. 209), but with regard to the latter, reference was made to 'one of *that class* of which a Court of Equity *would* decree the specific performance' (p. 211). The use of 'would' and 'class' terminology may indicate that a different emphasis is placed as to the availability of the remedy where the contract is wholly executory from the case where consideration has been executed. It would follow, therefore, that the principles of specific performance will have relevance in executory contracts not involving equitable assignments. This will take on considerable significance, as we have seen (see pp. 182–6), with regard to the diverse treatment given in English law to the holder of an after-acquired property interest and a prepaying buyer such as in *Re Wait* [1927] 1 Ch 606.

Tailby v *Official Receiver (1888) 13 App Cas 523* The requirement of specific performance was questioned by Lords Watson and Macnaghten in *Tailby* v *Official Receiver*. The facts of this case involved an assignment by way of mortgage of 'all the book debts due and owing or which may during the continuance of this security become due and owing to the said mortgagor' in the course of his business. A conflict arose between an assignee of the mortgagee and the official receiver in relation to a debt which had become due prior to the bankruptcy. In the Court of Appeal ((1886) 18 QBD 25) it was held that the assignment was too vague. This was reversed in the House of Lords where the majority held it sufficient that property which had come into the hands of the assignor could be identified as falling within the description in the instrument of assignment of the property subject to it. Furthermore, Lords Watson and Macnaghten adopted the approach that once consideration had been given for the assignment, it ceased to depend on the availability of specific performance at all.

The substantial argument adopted by Lord Macnaghten involved scrutiny of the scope of the parties' agreement, and so long as the property was sufficiently defined then he said at pp. 547–8:

> ... you have only to apply the principle that equity considers that done which ought to be done if the principle is applicable under the circumstances of the case.

Lord Macnaghten argued principally on the basis of *Metcalfe* v *Archbishop of York* (1836) 1 My & Cr 547 that, as a matter of authority, the doctrines of equitable assignment and specific performance are independent. In this case, a clergyman covenanted in 1811 for value to charge any future benefice to which he might be preferred with the payment of an annuity to C. By 1813, C assigned all his rights to the plaintiff, but, although in 1814 the incumbent was preferred to another benefice, he failed to execute a charge. Three years later, legislation was passed making it illegal to charge any benefice in this way. In 1818, the incumbent attempted to create the legal charge he had covenanted to make and it was held the charge was valid in equity since, when the incumbent was preferred to the second benefice in 1814, specific performance might have been obtained. However, this case does not conclusively establish that equitable assignment and specific relief are independent because although it is true that at the time the action was brought specific performance could not be granted, the effectiveness of the assignment is determined rather at the date the property came into the hands of the assignor and at that time (the relevant time), specific relief might have been granted. It would appear therefore that Lord Macnaghten went too far in *Tailby* and that the principles of specific performance may still be relevant.

The creditor cannot enforce his security against the debtor or any third party until he has actually advanced the money, that is, the consideration is executed. A commitment to advance the money will not suffice as equity will not decree specific performance of a contract to borrow or lend money (*Rogers* v *Challis* (1859) 27 Beav 175).

The legislative response

The demands for credit in the wake of the industrial revolution often meant that the only asset a trade debtor had at his disposal was stock-in-trade. In some Commonwealth jurisdictions, the practice of leasing land holdings from the Crown often including clauses prohibiting the use of land as security for loans meant that it was *only* stock-in-trade that farmers could use as security. Significantly, in New South Wales, the Liens on Wool Act was passed in 1843 thus preempting English bills of sale legislation by a full 10 years. The Australian Act set up a system of registration of liens which, if duly registered under s. 1, provided that:

> . . . the possession of the [wool] by the said proprietor [grantor] shall be to all intents and purposes in law the possession of the person or persons making such purchase or advances.

Several Acts relating to produce security including growing crops were passed in New Zealand and Australia from the mid-19th century onwards.

It was not until 1928 that the broadly equivalent English legislation was passed. Under the provisions of the English Agricultural Credits Act 1928, a farmer, notwithstanding any clause in his contract of tenancy to the contrary, may, by an instrument in writing, create in favour of a bank an agricultural charge on all or part of his agricultural assets including stock for a short-term loan. This charge can be a fixed one (see below pp. 335–6) even in respect of after-acquired property like progeny and crops. Furthermore, there is an obligation on the farmer to account for any proceeds of sale to the extent of the charge. This includes any moneys paid under a contract of insurance where compensation has been paid (s. 6(2) of the Agricultural Credits Act 1928). There are sound policy reasons for this extensive approach. If the market value of the farm as a going concern is higher than its liquidation value, a farmer may be able to borrow on better terms from one creditor who is given a security interest over a group of assets or all the farmer's assets rather than from several creditors who are each given a security interest in individual assets. Moreover, the use of individualistic remedies may lead to a piecemeal dismantling of a debtor's business by the untimely removal of necessary operating assets (compare the office of administrator under the Insolvency Act 1986 discussed in chapter 19).

In a sense, the Agricultural Credits Act 1928 is a successor to the interest in progeny recognised in the more developed common law. Yet, an early attempt to create an interest in future property was held void on the basis that 'a man cannot grant or charge that which he hath no' (Perkins, *Profitable Book* 15th ed. (London, 1827), p. 15). The 17th-century case of *Grantham* v *Hawley* (1616) Hob 132 departed from this logic by introducing the concept of potential existence so that if the process of creation had already begun, it was possible to own something which in the normal course would lead to fruition. Thus, the court said at p. 132a:

> A parson may grant all the tithewool that he shall have in . . . a year; yet perhaps he shall have none; but a man cannot grant all the wool, that shall grow upon his sheep that he shall buy hereafter; for there he hath it neither actually nor potentially.

This doctrine was never applied to the fruits of manufacture where the courts relied instead on the notoriously uncertain 'new act' doctrine (*Lunn* v *Thornton* (1845) 1 CB 379). The major difficulty with this doctrine concerns the extent to which the parties should be free to select their 'new act'. It would seem reasonable to presume that no act could be selected which was not one of the ordinary steps involved in the process of passing title.

It was inevitable that in a rapidly industrialising country like England was during the 19th century, the need for new sources of security would lead to the development of legal devices that embraced future property. The after-acquired property clause is a response to the quest for security of current assets which by nature are transient, that is, they are sold, transformed into accounts receivable which are subsequently paid and the proceeds used to purchase fresh goods. The volatility here should not mask the true significance of this form of capital provision.

The Bills of Sale Acts 1854 to 1891 It would be wrong to suppose that the circumstances which led to the growth of the chattel mortgage and its regulation by statute were unique to the 19th century. Perhaps an early example of a chattel mortgage can be seen during the War of the Roses in England. On 15 December 1452, Richard Duke of York, executed a 'letter of saal' (sale) wherein he 'bargained, aliened, sold, granted and confirmed unto John Fastolf, Knight, the jewels underwritten, *habendum* to the grantee, his executors and assignees forever'. A second document, three days later in date (18 December 1452), recites the bill of sale and provides that if the Duke shall pay Fastolf 'or his attorney, his heirs or to his executors', 437 pounds on St John Baptist's Day next ensuing (Midsummer Day), the previous bill of sale shall be held for nought, and the lender shall surrender the jewels; but in the event of default, then the bill of sale shall 'stand in full strength and virtue, this indenture notwithstanding'. Still another document, nine years later in date (the Duke of York having meanwhile been killed at the Battle of Wakefield, and his son, Edward IV, being now King of England) recites that the jewellery which the King's father had 'let to pledge' in the earlier transaction, had lately been redeemed, for the King's account, by Sir John Paston and Thomas Howes, priest. Their liege lord, therefore, promises, 'on the word of a King', to reimburse his faithful friends, by means of instalment payments, and assigns as security the revenues to accrue from 'the fee farm of our city of Norwich' and of all other royal properties. (See *Paston Letters*, ed. Gardner (London, 1910), vol. 1, p. 249, vol. 2, p. 33.)

The modern history of the recognition and regulation of non-possessory security interests in the common law countries is often said to have commenced with the English Bills of Sale Act 1854. In fact, it is doubtful whether the 1854 Act was concerned with future property, coming as it did eight years before *Holroyd* v *Marshall* (1862) 10 HL Cas 191; rather, the rationale of the Act was to combat the difficulties posed by apparent ownership. The reputed ownership provisions of the Bankruptcy Acts 1603 to 1914 were confined to bankruptcy and did nothing to protect creditors from lending excessive credit as a result of their failure to assess the true risks involved. It was because of this that the 1854 Act introduced a system of publicity through registration. Indeed, this was strengthened by the subsequent 1878 Act as this not only shortened the registration period from 21 to 7 days (ss. 8 and 14), but also inserted a special prescription against the practice of repeated execution of non-registered instruments to circumvent the limitation on registrability (s. 9). A further example of the strengthening of the publicity requirement is provided by s. 20 of the 1878 Act as this excluded chattels comprised in a registered bill of sale from reputed ownership. An immediate effect of these provisions was to make bills of sale more attractive to creditors since security was preserved even on the grantor's bankruptcy. The only requirement that had to be satisfied was registration. No restrictions were imposed on the type of property which might be the subject of the bill, and also on the terms incorporated in the bill.

During the period 1877 to 1880 the number of bills registered increased dramatically. Often the interest rates charged were oppressive and the nature of the security taken covered present and future chattels. Nevertheless, it would be simplistic to argue that within the short space of four years the *concept* of the after-acquired property clause after being initially favoured was now considered fraudulent. This conclusion is unlikely as it is clear from the Select Committee Report on the Bills of Sale Act (1878) Amendment Bill that the 1882 Act was aimed at the unscrupulous practice of moneylenders in *enforcing* their security. The 1882 Act is an early example of Parliament interfering with unconscionable behaviour and, as such, constituted an important policy change on the part of the legislature. All the previous legislation had been concerned with protecting creditors against non-possessory interests in chattels being created by debtors in possession. The 1882 Act laid down a prescribed form to which all security bills had to conform and outlawed powers of repossession by the grantee except for specified causes (s. 8). The term 'bill of sale' only applies to documents relating to personal chattels which excludes intangible property and general assignments of book debts (*Tailby* v *Official Receiver* (1883) 13 App Cas 523). Significantly, 'transfers of goods in the ordinary course of business of any trade or calling' are not within the statutory definition of bill of sale. Indeed, the Bills of Sale Act 1878 includes a catalogue of instruments which are specifically excluded from the definition of bill of sale (see ss. 4, 5 and 7 of the Bills of Sale Act 1878).

Although s. 9 of the Bills of Sale Act (1878) Amendment Act 1882 rendered after-acquired property clauses void against third-party creditors, on the other hand, s. 5 of the Act contemplates only a partial prohibition not including the grantor of the bill. This ambivalence has caused dilemmas as to whether the 1882 Act extends to future goods. In *Thomas* v *Kelly* (1888) 13 App Cas 506, the House of Lords held that a bill of sale covering after-acquired chattels was incapable of being specifically defined and, therefore, violated s. 1. The effect of this approach was to transform a qualified avoidance into an absolute one. It may be that the 1882 Act does not cover security in future goods, at least, as far as the equitable doctrine of *Holroyd* v *Marshall* (1862) 10 HL Cas 191 is concerned. This seems to be the approach adopted by Lord Macnaghten in *Thomas* v *Kelly* where the argument revolved around the expression 'personal chattels' used in the 1882 Act. The same expression is found in s. 7 of the 1854 Act which also included the phrase 'capable of complete transfer by delivery'. It is arguable from this that the time of capability of delivery is at the time the bill was executed and, since the 1878 Act substantially reproduced this definition, the legislation may be taken not to prohibit securities over future goods.

The major difficulty with Lord Macnaghten's approach in *Thomas* v *Kelly* is that it failed to take account of the *extended* definition of bill of sale found in the 1878 Act to include:

> ... any agreement, whether intended or not to be followed by the execution of any other instrument, by which a right of equity to any personal chattels, or to any charge or security thereon shall be conferred.

These words were inserted in the light of authorities, especially the case of *Brown* v *Bateman* (1867) LR 2 CP 272. Here it was held under the 1854 Act that an agreement on the part of the builder to the effect that all building material brought on site would belong to the owner, creating an equitable interest in the materials to be brought on the owner's land, did not constitute a bill of sale. The 1878 definition took account of this, the significance here being that the building materials would be future goods which might suggest that the extended definition of bills of sale was to include future goods. A further difficulty with Lord Macnaghten's approach concerns his lordship's treatment of the words 'specifically described' in s. 4 of the 1882 Act when he argued that these words were more easily applicable to actually existing chattels at the time of the transaction. This was the basis used for reconciling ss. 5 and 9 so that after-acquired property which was in existence at the time of the execution of the bill of sale and, therefore, capable of being specifically described was caught by s. 5 whereas s. 9 covered property which was not in existence and which it was not possible to describe specifically. However, this argument is open to the objection that it is equally possible for goods not in existence to be specifically described, for example, goods which are going to be manufactured as part of a mass production programme. It is significant that at first instance in *Welsh Development Agency* v *Export Finance Co. Ltd* [1990] BCC 393 (reversed by the Court of Appeal on another ground [1992] BCC 270) the decision of Lord Macnaghten in *Thomas* v *Kelly* in this respect was treated as being *obiter* and it was held that future goods could not comply with the writing requirement contained in the 1882 Act. For practical purposes, this makes it impossible to register a security bill of sale in respect of future personal chattels.

A major effect of the 1882 Act was to inhibit creditors taking security in future goods from individual borrowers. At the same time, the reluctance of creditors to take security in future goods from individual borrowers following the 1882 Act was matched by the development of such a security in the corporate sphere. This development was facilitated by the fact that s. 17 of the 1882 Act excludes its application to debentures issued by companies (*Re Standard Manufacturing Co.* [1891] 1 Ch 627), and the reputed ownership clause of bankruptcy legislation was never applied to companies. Furthermore, the requirement of identification of after-acquired property is not an onerous one, so all these factors have combined to allow the full potential of the equitable doctrine in *Holroyd* v *Marshall* to be realised in the corporate sphere through the advent of the floating charge.

It is somewhat surprising that the 19th century which is characterised as the great age of English commercial codes (see chapter 23) also produced the Bills of Sale legislation. The main problem is that the Bills of Sale Act (1878) Amendment Act 1882 has two, almost contradictory purposes: first, protecting third-party creditors from being deceived by a secret transaction between the parties to a bill of sale; second, protecting the grantor from the excesses of the grantee. These divergent objectives were incapable as a matter of legal logic of producing integrated legislation.

FIXED AND FLOATING CHARGES

Fixed charges
In general a charge can only be created by contract, that is, supported by valuable consideration. In the case where property is transferred to the chargor on condition that he holds it subject to the charge, the law will give effect to the charge without the need to establish the existence of a bargain, otherwise, the law would occasion an inequity.

Unlike a mortgage, the creation of a fixed charge does not involve a transfer of assets; rather, the chargee obtains rights in relation to the secured assets which may be pursued following the default of the chargor. The legal significance of a fixed charge is that even *before* default, the chargee enjoys an equitable proprietary interest in the secured assets, so the property cannot be disposed of free of the charge to anyone other than a good-faith purchaser. This has the effect of immobilising the asset and is a restrictive form of financing from the chargor's perspective.

Fixed charges may be conferred by any person. Where the debtor is a private individual, the bills of sale legislation restricts security being taken over after-acquired property in a significant manner. Thus, in relation to 'personal chattels', security over future assets (that is, where the individual is not the owner at the time the instrument is executed) is ineffective against everyone except the individual himself (s. 5 of the Bills of Sale Act (1878) Amendment Act 1882). It is only in the corporate sphere that this has found fruition in the genesis of the floating charge.

The floating charge

The floating charge is often referred to as an example of the ingenuity of English lawyers in that it secures present and future assets whilst leaving the company free to deal with its assets in the ordinary course of business. The device was first ruled effective by the Court of Appeal in *Re Panama, New Zealand and Australian Royal Mail Co.* (1870) LR 5 Ch App 318, a decision upheld and applied in *Re Yorkshire Woolcombers Association Ltd* [1903] 2 Ch 284.

The after-acquired property security interest received generally unfavourable treatment in the USA before the adoption of the Uniform Commercial Code (the UCC). This is expressed in the official comment to s. 9-204 as follows:

> The widespread 19th-century prejudice against the floating charge was based on a feeling, often inarticulate in the opinions, that a commercial borrower should not be allowed to encumber all his assets present and future, and that for the protection not only of the borrower but of his other creditors a cushion of free assets should be preserved.

Although the US courts adopted the presumption of fraud argument seen in *Twyne's Case* (1601), this did not mean that pre-UCC law was impotent to ensure security over future stock-in-trade. Significantly, the factor's lien legislation modelled closely on the New York Personal Property Law 1911 actually did envisage after-acquired property interests. Some US courts recognised security devices such as field warehousing (see pp. 271–2) and consignment sale (see pp. 273–4) but, as Professor Gilmore pointed out in his seminal work, *Security Interests in Personal Property*, vol. 1, (New York, 1965) at p. 24:

> The state of almost intolerable complexity which our security law reached by the end of the century [the 19th] was not matched in England [referring

to the floating charge]. The specialised devices which grew up in this country [the USA] — the trust receipt, the factor's lien, the equipment trust, the bailment lease and so on — were American exclusives. English law and American law in this area, split apart in the courts of the century.

As we have discussed in chapters 12 and 13, it is probable that Professor Gilmore has over-exaggerated the extent to which English and American law have split apart, especially bearing in mind the 20th-century developments in English commercial law.

The juridical nature of the floating charge A floating charge is a *present* security, and is not an agreement to create security in the future. This was clearly expressed by Buckley LJ in *Evans* v *Rival Granite Quarries Ltd* [1910] 2 KB 979 at p. 999:

> A floating charge is not a future security; it is a present security, which presently affects all the assets of the company expressed to be included in it. ... A floating security is not a specific mortgage of the assets, plus a licence to the mortgagor to dispose of them in the course of his business, but is a floating mortgage applying to every item comprised in the security, but not specifically affecting any item until some event occurs or some act on the part of the mortgagee is done which causes it to crystallise into a fixed security.

The ambulatory nature of the floating charge derives from two particular aspects: first, the company can dispose of the assets freely; second, the floating charge will generally attach to the after-acquired property of the *type* specified in the charging instrument, normally, the debenture. Guidance in this respect can be found in Romer LJ's often-quoted dictum in *Re Yorkshire Woolcombers Association Ltd* [1903] 2 Ch 284 at p. 295:

> I certainly do not intend to attempt to give an exact definition of the term 'floating charge', nor am I prepared to say that there will not be a floating charge within the meaning of the Act, which does not contain all the three characteristics that I am about to mention, but I certainly think that if a charge has the three characteristics that I am about to mention it is a floating charge. (1) If it is a charge on a class of assets of a company present and future; (2) if that class is one which, in the ordinary course of the business of the company, would be changing from time to time; and (3) if you find that by the charge it is contemplated that, until some future step is taken by or on behalf of those interested in the charge, the company may carry on its business in the ordinary way as far as concerns the particular class of assets I am dealing with.

The uniqueness of the floating charge is that it has an immediate existence even prior to attachment.

The present nature of the security and the freedom of the chargor to deal with the assets until some supervening event occurs which causes it to attach specifically appear to be contradictory. This has fuelled considerable academic debate with one school of thought maintaining that until crystallisation, that is attachment, the chargee can obtain no proprietary interest. On the other hand, it has been argued that a floating charge does give rise to an interest amounting to an equitable interest even before crystallisation. A variation of this present-interest theory is that a debenture holder has a present interest in a fund which, following crystallisation, becomes a present interest in specific assets.

The cases are not very helpful in resolving this dilemma, the judgments often resorting to a descriptive approach as to the ambulatory and shifting nature of a floating charge. An example of this phenomenon can be seen in the judgment of Wickham J in *Landall Holdings Ltd* v *Caratti* [1979] WAR 97 at p. 108:

> The 'floating' metaphor needs to be carried right through. Movement is relative and if the charge is said to be floating then it follows that the equitable proprietary interest created by the charge is also relatively floating. It may spring up when the thing comes within the ambit of the charge, e.g. is acquired by the chargor, and it may float away from under the charge, e.g. when an equitable interest in another is conferred by the chargor.

(For the classical exposition here see the approach of Fitzgibbon LJ in the Irish case of *Re Old Bushmills Distillery, ex parte Brett* [1897] 1 IR 488.) The better view, it is submitted, is that a floating charge does constitute a present equitable interest which indeed can be enforced against *some* third parties, for example, the holder of a second floating charge over the same property (*Re Benjamin Cope and Sons Ltd* [1914] 1 Ch 800) or negative pledge clauses (see p. 364). Essentially, the floating charge represents an agreement made between the parties as to which assets are subject to the charge, but with the proviso that the company may deal with these assets freely (as the case may be). Even so, the practical consequences of categorising a floating charge as involving a present interest are minimal; a company remains free to deal with its assets in the ordinary course of business and third parties who acquire rights resulting from dealings with the company are not postponed to the debenture holder's interest. However, the proprietary interest of a floating-charge debenture holder is not entirely irrelevant: first, restrictions in the floating charge on dealings in the assets by the company bind a subsequent party taking with notice of these restrictions; second, the floating-charge debenture holder can obtain an injunction to restrain the company from dealing outside the ordinary course of business; third, the debenture holder has the right to apply to the court for the appointment of an administrative receiver where his security is jeopardised (see part 5).

The floating charge versus the fixed charge

The advantages of a fixed charge have become increasingly obvious for creditors, especially where the economic circumstances are adverse. The major advantages of a fixed charge over and above a floating charge are as follows: first, the fixed chargee has an immediate proprietary right which can only be cut off by 'equity's darling', namely, a good-faith purchaser of the legal estate. Since most of the fixed charges are registrable, most categories of third parties will have notice of the fixed charge; second, a fixed charge has priority over all unsecured claims, preferential or otherwise; third, not all fixed charges need to be registered under s. 396 of the Companies Act 1985 (as amended), whereas all floating charges need to be registered.

Following the seminal decision of *Siebe Gorman and Co. Ltd v Barclays Bank Ltd* [1979] 2 Lloyd's Rep 142, a security hybrid in *economic* terms was recognised by the courts, that is, a fixed charge which incorporated all the advantages of a floating charge but with none of the *statutory* limitations which are: first, preferential debts are paid first (ss. 40 and 174 of the Insolvency Act 1986); second, floating charges are invalid if created within 12 months of the onset of insolvent liquidation except as to new value (s. 245 of the Insolvency Act 1986). In *Siebe Gorman and Co. Ltd v Barclays Bank Ltd*, the terms of the debenture charged 'by way of first fixed charge all book debts and other debts now and from time to time due or owing to the company'. In addition, the company undertook to pay all moneys received in respect of such debts into the company's account with the bank, and not to charge or assign the same to any other person without the written consent of the bank. Slade J held that there was a sufficient restriction here on the debtor's freedom to manage its assets in the ordinary course of business to constitute a fixed charge on the book debts of the debtor. He explained his decision thus at p. 159:

> In my judgment, however, it is perfectly possible in law for a mortgagor, by way of continuing security for future advances, to grant to a mortgagee a charge on future book debts in a form which creates in equity a specific charge on the proceeds of such debts as soon as they are received and consequently prevents the mortgagor from disposing of an unencumbered title to the subject-matter of such charge without the mortgagee's consent, even before the mortgagee has taken steps to enforce its security.... This in my judgment was the effect of the debenture in the present case. I see no reason why the court should not give effect to the intention of the parties, as stated in [the terms of the debenture], that the charge should be a first fixed charge on book debts....
>
> This conclusion that the charge is a specific charge involves the further conclusion that, during the continuance of the security, the bank would have the right, if it chose, to assert its lien under the charge on the proceeds of the book debts, even at a time when the particular account into which they were paid was temporarily in credit. However, I see nothing surprising in this conclusion, bearing in mind that the charge afforded continuing security to the bank not only in respect of any other indebtedness on that particular account but also in respect of any other indebtedness of [the borrower] to the bank. The bank's lien would, after all, continue only during the subsistence of the debenture, which the debtor would at all times have the right to redeem.

In *Re Keenan Bros Ltd* [1986] BCLC 242, the restriction was even more tightly drawn. In this case, the company was obliged to pay the proceeds of all debts into a designated account with the bank and 'not without the prior consent of the bank in writing to make any withdrawals or direct any payment from the said account.' This was held to be a fixed charge as it was a sufficient restriction on the management autonomy of the chargor (see also *Barclays Bank plc* v *Willowbrook International Ltd* [1987] 1 FTLR 386). It would appear, therefore, whether a purported specific charge will be recognised and given effect to, as such, depends upon whether the debtor has management autonomy which must exist in law and fact. Thus in the Northern Irish case of *Re Armagh Shoes Ltd* [1984] BCLC 405, *Siebe Gorman and Co. Ltd* v *Barclays Bank Ltd* was distinguished on the ground that the terms of the debenture under consideration contained no comparable covenant. In *Re Brightlife Ltd* [1987] Ch 200, the debtor company, though prohibited from selling, factoring, or discounting the charged debts without the consent of the debenture holder, was nevertheless left free to collect in the debts, pay the proceeds into the bank account and use them. It was held by Hoffmann J in that case at p. 209:

> In this debenture, the significant feature is that Brightlife was free to collect its debts and pay the proceeds into its bank account. Once in the account they would be outside the charge over debts and at the free disposal of the company. In my judgment a right to deal in this way with the charged assets for its own account is a badge of a floating charge and is inconsistent with a fixed charge.

Re Brightlife Ltd shows the difficulty for non-bank creditors taking a specific security over present and future receivables. It is important to emphasise that the case is *not* authority for the proposition that such a charge must always be a floating security; management autonomy by the creditor must be shown, for example, through the creditor retaining *effective control* over a fund representing the proceeds of the receivables. It is probable that the validity of the fixed charge concept will be relevant only in the context of receivables; a restriction on the management autonomy of the debtor in respect of stock-in-trade or raw materials and goods in the process of manufacture will prove to be counter-productive and probably unacceptable from a commercial perspective. This is because stock and raw materials are held for the purpose of sale, and a company simply will not be able to operate unless it can dispose of stock in such a way as to give purchasers unencumbered title.

Crystallisation of a floating charge This is the event which converts a floating security into a specific charge. What events have this effect, it seems, depends upon the express or implied terms of the charging instrument. Where the ability of the company to deal with its assets ceases the charge will crystallise, for example, on winding up (*Re Crompton and Co. Ltd* [1914] 1 Ch 954); the appointment of a receiver (*George Barker (Transport) Ltd* v *Eynon* [1974] 1 WLR 462); on the cessation of business (*Re Woodroffes (Musical Instruments) Ltd* [1986] Ch 366). It is probable that a floating charge will crystallise automatically on the crystallisation of another charge over the same assets but, perhaps, not *different* assets. The reasoning here is that the management autonomy of the company will be severely impaired after the appointment of the administrative receiver with respect to the same assets covered by the charge because the powers of the directors are inversely related to the scope of the administrative receivership (see chapter 19).

It is possible for the parties to expressly provide for a crystallising event, for example, where the contract stipulates for crystallisation by notice (*Re Brightlife Ltd*). Indeed in *Re Permanent Houses (Holdings) Ltd* [1988] BCLC 563, Hoffmann J explicitly stated at p. 567 that 'provided the language of the debentures was sufficiently clear, there was no conceptual reason why the parties should not agree that any specified event should cause the charge to crystallise'. Thus, the contract may state that the appointment of an administrator crystallises the floating charge. It is doubtful whether the appointment of an administrator can, in the absence of contract, crystallise the floating charge unless the purpose of the administration order is to lead to a more advantageous realisation of the company's assets than is possible in liquidation, or for sanctioning an arrangement or a compromise with creditors under s. 425 of the Companies Act 1985. The reason for this is that the administration order has been made with a view to winding up which provides essentially a disinvestment of a company's assets (see part 5).

Automatic crystallisation of a floating charge Creditors have adopted the springing security mechanism of the automatic crystallisation clause in the context of a floating charge. The theory here is that the security, until sprung, leaves the company free to deal with its assets for normal trading purposes. As we have already noted, in *Re Brightlife Ltd* [1987] Ch 200, Hoffmann J held that it is possible for a floating charge to crystallise by a notice issued pursuant to an express provision in a charge form. From this it would appear that the question of the validity of a properly drawn-up automatic crystallisation clause is now settled (see, for example *Re Permanent Houses (Holdings) Ltd* [1988] BCLC 563; *Fire Nymph Products Ltd* v *The Heating Centre Pty Ltd* (1988) 14 NSWLR 460). However, there are undoubted public policy considerations which may lead a court to construe such a clause restrictively: a third party who deals with a company may be unable to discover whether or not a floating charge has automatically crystallised. The Cork committee report, *Insolvency Law and Practice* (Cmnd 8558, 1982) noted at para. 1575:

> The possibility of automatic crystallisation puts at risk anyone who dealt with a company which has given a floating charge. There is no provision for registration of any notice of crystallisation.

In large measure, the sting has been removed from the tail of automatic crystallisation clauses by the amended definition of a floating charge to mean a charge which, *as created*, was a floating charge (Insolvency Act 1986, ss. 40(1) and 251; Companies Act 1985, s. 196(1) as amended by Insolvency Act 1986, s. 439(1) and sch. 13). The practical effect of this is that preferential debts will be paid in priority to the debenture holder, notwithstanding the issue of automatic crystallisation and, in the same manner, the powers of an administrator to deal with the assets covered by the floating charge will not be affected by this question. Nevertheless, in other contexts the issue of whether the security has been sprung will be relevant, for example, execution creditors and subsequent holders of an *equitable* interest. One possible way of ameliorating the position is by reference to the doctrine of estoppel, so where the debenture holder has 'slept' on his rights, equity will intervene to the relief of an innocent transferee in these circumstances, that is, the debenture holder is estopped from denying the apparent position which is that the charge has not crystallised.

A careful note of warning should be sounded here. An analogy is sometimes drawn in this context with agency principles, so Bell has argued in *Modern Law of Personal Property in England and Ireland* (London, 1989), at p. 179:

> Early termination of the company's authority to deal with its assets could be treated in the same way as breach of a restriction on the kind of dealing permitted, just as, in the law of agency, a principal who terminates his agent's mandate will be bound by his continuing appearance of authority.

Such an approach cannot be sustained, as a matter of legal principle, for the following reasons: first, the priority of charges does not depend upon a concept of actual authority and, in any case, management autonomy does not terminate following crystallisation as it merely converts a floating charge into a specific charge; second, the determination of priority is a matter of registration and notice rather than apparent authority; third, the argument smacks of the reputed ownership doctrine which never applied to companies and has, in any case, been now firmly scotched in the context of personal bankruptcy (s. 283(3) of the Insolvency Act 1986). A more satisfying and elegant approach would be to include an obligation to register an automatic crystallisation clause as a prioritising event. Unfortunately, the Insolvency Act 1986 is silent as to this point, despite the Cork committee's conclusion at para. 1579 that 'there is no place for it [automatic crystallisation] in a modern insolvency law'. Interestingly, s. 410 of the Companies Act 1985 (as amended) gives the Secretary of State delegated power to make regulations concerning the giving of notice to bodies as being affected by the crystallisation of a floating charge.

Partial crystallisation of the floating charge There is no reason in principle which militates against the parties stipulating, *as a matter of contract*, to provide for the partial crystallisation of the charge. The main advantage of this is that it protects the security of the chargee whilst, at the same time, cutting down the overkill danger associated with automatic crystallisation clauses by paralysing the business unnecessarily. A closely related phenomenon is that of decrystallisation and subsequent reflotating of the charge. Interesting priority problems arise where the reflotation is categorised as creating a security interest requiring (re-)registration under the Companies Act 1985.

Charges and mortgages

A mortgage is conceptually different from a charge by virtue of the fact that a mortgage vests legal or equitable ownership in the creditor (mortgagee). Thus, unless the debenture, for example, entitled the chargee to reinforce his charge by calling for a mortgage, there is no right of foreclosure because this is a remedy limited to mortgagees as a consequence of their *security* ownership. In contrast, a charge merely involves the conferment of a special security interest rather than the vesting of ownership.

The great contribution of equity to the law of mortgages is the equity of redemption which gives the mortgagor the right to redeem the property even though the stipulated time for redemption is past. The practical reality therefore is, because the mortgagee's rights are so qualified by the mortgagor's equity of redemption, that the difference between a charge and a mortgage is not significant. Moreover foreclosure of personalty mortgages is uncommon in England as other methods of enforcement are often applied, notably through a power of sale in the mortgage deed (compare *Re Morritt* (1886) 18 QBD 222). Whether such a power of sale can be implied is a more difficult question and it is unlikely that any analogy can be drawn here with pledges (see chapter 14). However, in the case of intangible property, an implied power of sale is well-established (see, for example, in relation to stocks and shares *Stubbs* v *Slater* [1910] 1 Ch 632).

The accommodation of the floating charge in a functional reform of English personal property security law

There is no doubt that art. 9 of the US Uniform Commercial Code (the UCC) has influenced the debate over reform of personal property security interests in England. The proposed Lending and Security Act suggested by the Crowther committee, *Report on Consumer Credit* (Cmnd 4596, 1971) leaned very heavily on art. 9, whilst the Cork committee, *Report on Insolvency Law and Practice* (Cmnd 8558, 1982), suggested at para. 1638 that an art. 9 type of notice-filing system 'could be adopted and tailored for use in this country and forms a helpful precedent'. Continued impetus to the question of art. 9 as a model for law reform was provided by the Scottish Law Commission (Halliday Committee) working paper, *Security over Moveable Property* (1986) and also by Professor Diamond's DTI report, *A Review of Security Interests In Property* (1989).

One of the most notable features of art. 9, which has no parallel in prior law, is the conceptual unity inherent in the adoption of 'the security interest' as the essential factor identifying the transaction to which the legislation applies. A distinction is then drawn under art. 9 between the enforceability of the security interest as between the parties and as against third parties. As between the parties, an agreement which creates or provides for a security interest together with 'attachment' of the security interest are all that is required. Normally, three conditions have to be fulfilled for attachment to occur, namely, the parties must *intend* attachment; value must be given; the debtor must have rights in the collateral. In order to obtain priority as against *third parties*, on the other hand, it is necessary to 'perfect' the security interest. This occurs when the security interest has attached and all the steps required for perfection have been completed which means either possession or registration of a financing statement.

Whilst it is clear that the concept of security interest is rooted in common law and equitable principles, the drafters of art. 9 adopted this term precisely because it did not signal a well-established concept or set of concepts. Moreover, one of the major policy objectives underlying art. 9 was to jettison the conceptual and administration structure that had come to characterise the legal regulation of the legislation. Nonetheless, art. 9 does create a system of law under which the secured party by agreement may obtain real rights in the debtor's property. These rights are *relative* depending upon the debtor's rights in the property and come into existence when the security interest attaches. As the official comment to s. 9-204 of the UCC points out:

> ... a security interest arising by virtue of an after-acquired property clause has equal status with a security interest in collateral in which the debtor has rights at the time value is given under the security agreement. That is to say: the security interest in after-acquired property is not merely an 'equitable' interest.

This would suggest that an art. 9 type of regime creates a statutory legal interest. Inevitably, such an analysis has repercussions for the accommodation into such a scheme of the floating charge which dominates present English corporate security law.

The floating charge as a security interest The problems associated with the interrelationship of a non-specific equitable mortgage into a scheme which recognises only *fixed* security interests cannot be ignored. Although the floating lien of art. 9 has direct parallels conceptually and functionally with the doctrine of equitable mortgages of future property as in *Holroyd* v *Marshall* (1862) 10 HL Cas 191, the development of equitable floating charges was arrested in the US by widespread judicial hostility, and it was unnecessary for the drafters of art. 9 to make provision for it. Indeed, the principal draftsman of art. 9, Professor Gilmore, pointed out that if floating charges had become common in the USA some of the pressure for change which brought about art. 9 would have been lacking.

The conceptual framework of an art. 9 type of regime sits uneasily with a floating charge since it only recognises two legal states for security interests: attached but unperfected and perfected. No intermediate state of perfected but non-specific or floating charge is recognised. If the parties, by agreement, postpone attachment the secured party's interest is unperfected until attachment — it is not a non-specific present interest with a quasi-perfected status. Crystallisation has no priority significance since this is determined on the basis of statutory rules that make no mention of crystallisation or other similar concepts. Moreover, since the floating-charge aspect of the security interest no longer exists, there is no need to include the standard clauses restricting the debtor's right to create other charges ranking in priority to or *pari passu* with the security interest. In fact, if the use of terminology like 'floating charge' was adopted under the new structure, it would mean that the secured interest involved would be severely prejudiced. If its use meant that the debtor is free to carry on business as before and deal with the floating collateral without hindrance until crystallisation, he will also be able to create security interests and there is no method like a negative pledge clause to restrict his ability to do so (see p. 364). This does seem incongruous in the light of the stated object in art. 9 to promote security and ensure priority through the filing of a finance statement (see chapter 16).

In the DTI paper prepared by Professor Diamond in 1989, the view was expressed that in order for a new scheme to be comprehensive it would have to encompass floating charges. Certainly, an attempt has been made in Ontario to accommodate the floating charge which was, indeed, inserted in the 1970 Canadian Model Uniform Personal Property Security Act although it has by now been withdrawn. This is not surprising given the Ontario experience before the 1989 Ontario revision, where the Personal Property Security Act 1970 (Ontario) did not apply at all to 'a mortgage, charge or assignment whose registration is provided for in the Corporation Securities Registration Act'. As a consequence, two distinct systems of personal property security law came into force. Inevitably, the question of delineation between the Acts caused considerable problems.

There are overwhelming difficulties with a system of double legislation and registration. In this respect, the Halliday committee (1986) recommendation at paragraph 60, that somehow the floating charge should continue to exist outside the new proposed scheme is difficult to sustain. Even if the floating charge is accommodated within the new structure it would threaten the conceptual elegance of the scheme as is demonstrated, for example, in cases where there is provision for an automatic crystallisation clause. This is so because the registration of a financing statement under an art. 9 type of regime relates to notice of the *existence* of a security interest and does not provide notice of the security agreement (with the accompanying automatic crystallisation clause) to which it relates. Thus, the constructive notice question so prevalent under existing companies legislation will still persist (see chapter 16). Moreover, reconciling the attachment and perfection requirements of a security interest with the floating charge concept is no easy task due to the ambiguities surrounding established jurisprudence concerning floating charges.

The essence of the floating charge can still be preserved even under an art. 9 type of regime, by regarding it as an implied subordination of the creditor's perfected security interest to such subsequent assignments and encumbrances as the debtor is permitted to create under his floating charge. This approach transforms the nature of the floating charge from being ambulatory and unfixed whilst floating into a fixed charge with a licence or consent in favour of the debtor to deal with the charged property. This allows the giving of good title free of the floating charge, as well as the creation of a security interest ranking prior to the floating charge. Essentially, the floating charge has been metamorphosed into the art. 9 concept of a floating lien, that is, a fixed charge with a provision for subordination.

UNCONVENTIONAL SECURITY DEVICES

The characterisation and systematisation of the legal relations at different points in the sales process is particularly pertinent in the context of retention of title clauses. This is especially so if the seller's right is categorised as 'reserved' ownership since this would indicate that both parties have some kind of ownership. In this respect, the analysis would be consistent with the doctrine of relativity of title discussed in chapter 2. The emphasis on property reservation is that it allows the owner to seize the property should the debtor fail in one of his primary obligations. In a sense, virtually all extensions of credit give the creditor a contingent right to take property of the debtor in order to limit the extent of the indebtedness, i.e., after a court judgment the creditor can 'execute' or 'levy' some of the debtor's property in order to satisfy the judgment. While the secured creditor has the right not enjoyed by the unsecured creditor to take property without the post-default consent of the debtor and without going to court, this may not be so valuable outside liquidation, and even sometimes at liquidation, because a debtor's active objection will require the secured creditor to go to court as well.

Since the purpose of the property retention is only to ensure *priority*, the supplier is not essentially retaining the asset himself, but rather the right to *use* the asset to gain repayment of the debtor's debt to him. Thus, art. 9 of the UCC does not allow the secured creditor to keep the collateral without the consent of the debtor since the ultimate remedy is to sell the asset in the market-place and use the cash in order to diminish the indebtedness. The secured creditor is not entitled to any value derived from its continued use so that, for example, in the Court of Appeal in *Clough Mill Ltd* v *Martin* [1985] 1 WLR 111, Robert Goff LJ said *obiter* that the seller should retain the title to the material as trustee upon trust for sale accounting to the buyer for any surplus achieved. This approach is anomalous in the light of s. 48(4) of the Sale of Goods Act 1979 which would appear to insist that a sale contract will be rescinded in this circumstance (see pp. 125–6). The effect of this is that the seller in reselling is acting in his *own* capacity and should, therefore, be entitled to any profits which accrue on resale. This approach was confirmed by the House of Lords in *Armour* v *Thyssen Edelstahlwerke AG* [1991] 2 AC 339. Of course, where the transaction is categorised as creating a security interest for the seller, it is perfectly proper for the buyer to be entitled to any surplus gained on resale on the basis that property will have passed to him.

Undoubtedly, a tension exists between the *creation* of a security interest and retention of title which does not, strictly speaking, constitute a security interest since it does not arise by virtue of an assignment of a proprietary interest by way of mortgage or charge.

Retention of title: a triumph for legal form?

Scottish law with its emphasis upon a unitary concept of ownership in which possession is central (*possession vaut titre*) is reluctant to recognise non-possessory security rights. Nonetheless, the Sale of Goods Act 1979 does make some attempt to deal with the Scottish dilemma *vis-à-vis* non-possessory security interests through s. 61(4) of the 1893 Act (now s. 62(4) of the 1979 Act), which was a provision specifically drafted for Scotland though it also applies to England. Section 62(4) states:

> The provisions of this Act about contracts of sale do not apply to a transaction in the form of a contract of sale which is intended to operate by way of mortgage, pledge, charge, or other security.

The difficulties involved in determining the 'true intentions' of the parties anticipated in s. 62(4) of the Sale of Goods Act 1979 were demonstrated in *Welsh Development Agency* v *Export Finance Co. Ltd* [1992] BCC 270. The facts revolved around a company, Parrott Ltd, in which the Welsh Development Agency (WDA) was a principal shareholder. The company, by a debenture dated in October 1985, charged its book debts and other property and assets in favour of the WDA. By May 1989, the company was insolvent and the WDA appointed receivers under the debenture. The WDA claimed that, by virtue of its charge, it was entitled to receive payment of all debts owed by overseas buyers in relation to goods exported to them by Parrot. However, the defendant (EXFINCO) claimed that it was entitled to the debts on the basis of its agreement with Parrot, namely, that Parrot sold goods on the basis of an agency relationship for EXFINCO. The merits of the scheme for EXFINCO were as follows: first, debts due under the contracts to sell goods to overseas buyers would never have been the property of Parrot but belonged to EXFINCO as undisclosed principal, so they would not be subject to any prior floating charge over Parrot's debt or property; second, such a transaction would be a sale and not a secured borrowing and, as a result, the transaction would involve 'off balance sheet' accounting.

At first instance ([1990] BCC 393) it was held that the transaction amounted in substance to a charge and was void for non-registration. This judgment was reversed by the Court of Appeal which upheld the arrangement as a genuine agency agreement. This was so despite the fact that the parties had constructed the agreement in such a way as to avoid all contact between the financier and the overseas buyer. Furthermore, the manufacturer's mandate to sell on behalf of the financier was limited to goods that complied with the sale contract, including the statutory implied terms of merchantable quality and fitness for purpose. This ensured that there would be no recourse against the financier for breach of contract. Nevertheless, the Court of Appeal held that an agent's authority to bind an undisclosed principal must have existed when the agent made the contract ostensibly as principal (compare *Keighley Maxsted and Co.* v *Durant* [1901] AC 240).

It is the policy of the courts, in England, where there is security with recourse to property which can be effected by means other than a transaction of loan or charge not to treat it as registrable under s. 396 of the Companies Act 1985 (as amended). This is so, even though the exact economic effect might be carried out through a transaction which in form was registrable as a security interest in the goods. In this respect, a document purporting to be a sale of hire-purchase agreements was construed by Eve J at first instance in *Re George*

Inglefield Ltd [1933] Ch 1 as a charge on book debts, whereas in the Court of Appeal, it was held to be a sale (see also *Lloyds and Scottish Finance Ltd* v *Cyril Lord Carpets Sales Ltd* (1979) 129 NLJ 366). The approach adopted by Romer LJ in the Court of Appeal is instructive. His lordship said at p. 27:

> The only question that we have to determine is whether, looking at the matter as one of substance, and not of form, the discount company has financed the dealers in this case by means of a transaction of mortgage and charge, or by means of a transaction of sale; because, of course, financing can be done in either the one way or the other, and to point out that it is a transaction of financing throws no light upon the question that we have to determine.

He then went on, in a very well-known passage, to analyse the differences between a transaction of sale and a transaction of mortgage or charge at p. 27:

> It appears to me that the matter admits of a very short answer, if one bears in mind the essential differences that exist between a transaction of sale and a transaction of mortgage or charge. In a transaction of sale the vendor is not entitled to get back the subject-matter of the sale by returning to the purchaser the money that has passed between them. In the case of a mortgage or charge, the mortgagor is entitled, until he has been foreclosed, to get back the subject-matter of the mortgage or charge by returning to the mortgagee the money that has passed between them. The second essential difference is that if the mortgagee realises the subject-matter of the mortgage for a sum more than sufficient to repay him, with interest and the costs, the money that has passed between him and the mortgagor he has to account to the mortgagor for the surplus. If the purchaser sells the subject-matter of the purchase, and realises a profit, of course he has not got to account to the vendor for the profit. Thirdly, if the mortgagee realises the mortgage property for a sum that is insufficient to repay him the money that he has paid to the mortgagor, together with interest and costs, then the mortgagee is entitled to recover from the mortgagor the balance of the money, either because there is a covenant by the mortgagor to repay the money advanced by the mortgagee, or because of the existence of the simple contract debt which is created by the mere fact of the advance having been made. If the purchaser were to resell the purchased property at a price which was insufficient to recoup him the money that he had paid to the vendor, of course he would not be entitled to recover the balance from the vendor.

In that particular case, it was found that there was a transaction of sale and not one of mortgage or charge. This contrasts with the decision in *Re Curtain Dream plc* [1990] BCLC 925 where an agreement for the sale of stock by a company to a finance company, and for resale of the stock to the company on terms reserving title in the stock to the finance company, created a charge on the stock which was void as against creditors in the receivership of the company for want of registration. The critical indication of charge that impressed

Knox J was the company's *entitlement* to redeem by repurchasing the stock which was confirmed by the facility letter containing references to 'interest' and a 'credit line'.

The main distinction between a chattel mortgage and an executory agreement to sell is that the first assumes an immutable debt or obligation for the performance of which the debtor's goods serve as security. In this sense, ownership is divided with legal title vested in the mortgagee, and the beneficial ownership in the mortgagor who carries the burden of loss or damage, taxation and other costs. In the case of an executory contract of sale, there is no absolute debt — only a *promise* to pay. It is simplistic to argue that the buyer obtains no interest in the goods because, how is it possible to maintain that the seller has full title in the goods where another has the right to acquire them by acts within his own control?

We have already identified relativity of title as the key concept for understanding the property-passing provision of the Sale of Goods Act 1979 (see chapter 2). With this in mind, ownership may be described as being analogous with a bundle of sticks, so algebraically, a chattel mortgage can be expressed as follows:

$$O - SC = SD$$

This is where O = full ownership, and SC = the secured creditor's interest, whereas SD = the security interest of the debtor. What we are doing here is dealing with a division into two of the bundle of rights making up ownership. It must be remembered that O and SC and SD are variables, so the debtor will start out with a bundle of varying size depending on the extent of his interest in the property to be used as security. In contrast to the chattel mortgage, the object of the debtor in a conditional sale is to acquire the *res*/property in question, i.e., 'sale' credit as distinct from 'loan' credit. The transaction may be translated as follows:

$$O - SD = SC$$

When one compares the chattel mortgage we have the same result:

$$O - SC = SD \quad \text{(chattel mortgage)}$$
$$O - SD = SC \quad \text{(conditional sale)}$$

Each transaction involves a process of subtraction. In the chattel mortgage, the debtor initially had the whole bundle of sticks and passed over some sticks to the creditor and kept some for himself, whereas in the conditional sale, the creditor had the bundle and passed over some sticks to the debtor and kept some for himself.

It may be that, as a matter of consistency, the unifying elements in the transactions identified above should be recognised and a similar legal response to each should ensue. We shall now consider this matter further in relation to the contractual mechanisms discussed below which provide for retention of title.

The finance lease In a dynamic commercial setting it may not be sensible to try to distinguish sale from lease because what is involved in both is an allocation of *risks* and benefits *vis-à-vis* economic assets. Nevertheless, the traditional way in which the Sale of Goods Act 1979 deals with the question of risk is to associate it with property (*res perit domino*), a position which was replicated under the US Uniform Sales Act. Interestingly the UCC, at least in theory, has expunged the 'property' solution concentrating in art. 9 upon whether a security interest has been created. The main distinguishing factor is that if the creditor has a right to a surplus and is liable to a deficiency, this is a sale agreement, i.e., the 'benefits' and 'burdens' of ownership. The major difficulty with this analysis is that under the finance lease *both* the lessor and the lessee enjoy the 'benefits' and 'burdens' of ownership. Here the lessee will enjoy 95 to 99 per cent of the residual value of the *res* at the end of the lease term, but will not enjoy an option to purchase (at least in the UK) since the lessee is still essentially selling its own tax depreciation to the lessor.

At the same time, the lessor is exposed to both benefits and burdens because the *term itself* involves a risk, for example, if rental terms diminish or increase. This is particularly pertinent in the case of long-term leases (over five years) where the residual value at the end is small. If a finance lessor wants to be sure that an asset will have an accountable, specified minimum value at a predetermined date in the future, an important method of minimising risk exposure is through a residual value insurance policy. Even if the lessor can retain the surplus realised by resale of the asset at the end of the lease term, it is obvious that because the opportunity and risk associated with the *res* can be separated from those associated with the 'use of thing', this would suggest that there is no tenable distinction between a lease and a security interest (see pp. 290–91).

In many periodic payment transactions, it is difficult to determine which part, if any, of the total payments is 'principal' and which is interest. This demonstrates the difficulty of distinguishing between a lease/conditional sale/hire-purchase transaction and sale. It has been argued that market conditions and other factors may prompt the transferee to agree to pay an amount equivalent to the value of the goods without the expectation of becoming owner. This approach is exceptional and it must be that the rental price will constitute a strong indication of the *nature* of the financing arrangement. In this respect, it will be instructive to look at the English position as it developed with regard to hire-purchase transactions.

Hire-purchase It is elementary learning that in *Helby* v *Matthews* [1895] AC 471 (compare *Lee* v *Butler* [1893] 2 QB 269), the House of Lords decided that a hirer under a hire-purchase agreement, who was entitled to terminate the hiring agreement at any time, was not a person who had agreed to buy the goods within the meaning of s. 9 of the Factors Act 1889 (see chapter 7). An important question arising out of the case was whether a hire-purchase agreement where the rentals payable by the hirer were equivalent or substantially equivalent to the purchase price, but where an option had to be exercised by the hirer before title to the goods vested in him, could be treated as an agreement for sale. Since

Lord Herschell affirmed in *Helby* v *Matthews* that the substance and not the mere form of the agreement had to be looked at, one would have thought that the answer admitted of little doubt. However, the English courts showed little hesitation in applying the terms of a hire-purchase type of agreement literally. Thus, a deposit paid ostensibly on account of the option to purchase was treated as just that, and not for what it is in economic reality, a part of the purchase price (*Kelly* v *Lombard Banking Co. Ltd* [1959] 1 WLR 41). The option to purchase was treated as a separate and severable part of the agreement (*Whiteley Ltd* v *Hilt* [1918] 2 KB 808; *Belsize Motor Supply Co.* v *Cox* [1914] 1 KB 244), and therefore, unless the agreement otherwise provided (*United Dominions Trust (Commercial) Ltd* v *Parkway Motors Ltd* [1955] WLR 719), survived any termination of the contract of bailment. It took legislation, the Hire-Purchase Act 1964, the Supply of Goods (Implied Terms) Act 1973, and the Consumer Credit Act 1974 to assimilate hire-purchase generally and formally to sale on credit.

Recourse credit factoring Significant problems arise in distinguishing between the purchase of receivables and the lending of money on the security of book debts. This distinction is particularly fine where the assignor gives recourse, as the effect is the same as borrowing on the security of receivables. The Crowther committee report, *Consumer Credit* (Cmnd 4596, 1971), noted in app. 3, para. 5:

> ... those buying receivables, whether with or without recourse, are careful to exact a set of warranties from the assignor designed to ensure as far as possible that the receivables assigned are not only legally enforceable but likely to be paid. Since a breach of any of these warranties may entitle the assignee to recover his loss from the assignor, the difference between sales with recourse and sales without recourse is not as clear as it might appear.

The mere fact that there is a right of recourse should not necessarily affect the categorisation of the transaction as a sale. The assignor's liability is not to repay an advance, i.e., an exchange of money for money as in the case of a mortgage, but rather to pay a sum in discharge of a recourse obligation (*Lloyds and Scottish Finance Ltd* v *Cyril Lord Carpets Sales Ltd* (1979) 129 NLJ 366). This approach is confirmed by the accounting treatment where the relevant criterion is not that of recourse but whether the transferor has surrendered the *control* of future economic benefits embodied in the receivables.

Consignment sales Under the UCC, a 'sale on approval' is a special form of contract for sale in that the buyer may return the goods after trial even if they fully conform to the contract description. The most significant aspect of sale on approval, for our purposes, is that the buyer's creditors have no claims to the goods until acceptance, and the seller bears the risk and expense of the return of the goods. In the case of a sale or return, the UCC treats this as functionally similar to consignment. The buyer takes the goods primarily for resale and, in most cases, is a merchant. Unless otherwise agreed, the buyer will bear the risk of loss and expense when exercising his option to return the goods, and while the goods are in his possession they are subject to the claims of his creditors in accordance with s. 2-326(2).

If despite the delivery to the buyer the supplier retains title, this is treated as a reservation of a security interest which attaches and is perfected pursuant to art. 9. No such distinction is drawn under the Sale of Goods Act 1979, although s. 18, r. 4, does not refer to goods as being 'sold' but rather refers to delivery. It is clear that through this method Chalmers accommodated both 'a contract of sale' and an 'agreement to sell'. The latter analysis does not entirely fit conceptually the 'sale or return' transaction, i.e., here there is an agreement to sell subject to the buyer adopting the transaction. Moreover in the case of 'sale on approval', many of these are 'sales' (in the sense of property passing) subject to a right of rescission.

The question of what constitutes a 'true' consignment sale and not a disguised security interest is highly pertinent in the retention of title clause context. The reason for this is that there is a natural judicial hostility to security consignments which are considered to be secret liens. This factor may explain the restrictive interpretation of proceeds clauses in the post-*Romalpa* case law. In the USA, the 'true' consignment sale is linked with a price-fixing mechanism which brings into focus important antitrust questions especially following the celebrated decision in *Simpson* v *Union Oil Co. of California* (1964) 377 US 13. It may be that the purpose of a 'true' consignment sale is to ensure quality of marketing and after-sales service. On the other hand, it could be argued that the most significant factor is the determination of the relationship as being one of principal and agent. Certainly in Canada, one of the common law tests for a 'true' consignment was that the commission to be earned by the retailer was to be equal to the difference between the retail price of the goods charged and a net fixed price established by the supplier. This would suggest that if a consignee is not obligated to pay the price of the goods until sale and can return unsold goods before subsale, this is a true agency relationship. The determining feature of a 'false' consignment is whether the consignee is absolutely liable for the price of the 'consigned' goods with no right to return the goods unsold.

The importance of consignment as a financing mechanism has waned in the USA. One major reason for this is that the 'true' consignment gives the consignee a right to return goods not sold. Naturally, this is not attractive to sellers as they are required to assume the risk of market failure. Furthermore, the use of consignments for security purposes is minimal due to the ease by which security interests in inventory can be created under the UCC. It may be that the absence of a similar UCC type of regime in England accounts for the importance of the consignment/agency question in the wake of the *Romalpa* line of case law (see chapter 12).

'Romalpa' clauses The process of reasoning described above is of importance insofar as it offers a guide to how far English courts may be prepared to go in ignoring form for substance in other situations. The court views the use by the parties of non-registrable forms of secured borrowing transactions as the

exercise of a legitimate option conferred by the legislation, notwithstanding that the transaction may be within the mischief of s. 396 of the Companies Act 1985 (as amended). Donaldson MR, described the situation perfectly in *Clough Mill Ltd v Martin* [1985] 1 WLR 111 at p. 125:

> The argument that the object of the exercise was to give the plaintiff security for the price of the yarn does not of itself advance the matter. Just as it is possible to increase the amount of cash available to a business by borrowing, buying on hire-purchase or credit sale terms, factoring book debts or raising additional share capital, all with different legal incidents, so it is possible to achieve security for an unpaid purchase price in different ways, with different legal consequences. The parties have chosen not to use the charging method in relation to unused yarn.

As a matter of legal form, a distinction is drawn between the granting of a security interest (i.e., of a *ius in re aliena*) and the reservation of property which is not considered an orthodox security device requiring registration. The conventional position was restated by the judgments in the House of Lords in *Armour v Thyssen Edelstahlwerke AG* [1991] 2 AC 339.

One of the major criticisms of the retention of title mechanism is that debenture holders face the reduction of their traditional priority position. Nevertheless, an extravagantly drawn floating charge accompanied by a long catalogue of crystallising events is as much open to criticism as the retention of title clause, mainly because of the lending monopoly danger associated with an after-acquired property clause. What is assumed here is that a creditor with an after-acquired property provision enjoys a special competitive advantage over other lenders in all his subsequent dealings with the debtor in that the clause could, if unchecked, effectively tie the debtor's hands to an existing and often exhausted line of credit, thereby making it impossible to obtain fresh capital. It is possible to argue that it could lead to a refined sort of peonage by locking a borrower into a closed system of credit.

Undoubtedly, the after-acquired property clause does create a 'situational monopoly' in the sense that assets which come under the purview of the clause cannot, without the first creditor's consent, give another creditor a prior claim to those assets. Following on from this it is no surprise to discover a link between the law's recognition of an after-acquired property clause and the priority rule for purchase-money security. Insofar as the latter is based on the idea of 'new money', it can be argued that if there was perfect competition in the lending market, the purchase-money priority interest would figure in a contract containing an after-acquired property clause in any case. These reasoning here is that it is impossible to determine how much the interest rate of the holder of an after-acquired property clause should compensate the debtor for the adverse effects of the creditor's situational monopoly. This would require an assessment of future contingencies as well as taking into account the relative bargaining strengths of the parties. In this sense, a retention of title clause, as an example of a purchase-money provision, is a consistent accompaniment to an after-acquired property clause precisely in order to reduce these transaction costs. We shall now proceed to consider this concept in greater detail.

The purchase-money security interest

The statutorification of personal property security law in the US evident in art. 9 of the Uniform Commercial Code is predicated upon two major theses: first, the idea of security as a bargained-for right which justifiably, in the absence of fraud, supersedes the *pari passu* principle of distribution; Second, security is conceived as being desirable *per se* as it stimulates economic growth and the modernisation of business. In this respect, the architects of the UCC were concerned with expanding the pool of assets available through the recognition of the floating lien accompanied by a simple first-to-file priority rule. It is doubtful whether any previous security statute has so warmly embraced the after-acquired property interest.

In the course of the drafting of art. 9, the validation of the floating lien met significant opposition. To combat the perceived dangers of the after-acquired property clause, the draftsman of art. 9 included the purchase-money security interest (the PMSI). This is defined in s. 9-107 as follows:

> A security interest is a 'purchase-money security interest' to the extent that it is
> (a) taken or retained by the seller of the collateral to secure all or part of its price; or
> (b) taken by a person who by making advances or incurring an obligation gives value to enable the debtor to acquire rights in or the use of collateral if such value is in fact so used.

From this it would appear that s. 9-107(a) requires a specific correlation between the collateral in which priority is claimed and the specific price (obligation) relating to that particular item of collateral. Third-party financiers under s. 9-107(b) need not show an express tie, so long as the purchase-money financier can prove that the outstanding indebtedness to be secured was in fact used by the debtor to acquire new assets. The point here is that purchase-money loans contemplate a strict foreclosure, i.e., the debtor's payments are designed to correspond to the new asset's economic depreciation, so repossession of the asset will normally satisfy the purchase-money creditor. There is, therefore, no question of the PMSI undermining the interest of other creditors, for example, by shrinking the cushion of free assets that protects the earlier lender against default.

It is odd that although the UCC recognises a PMSI, the creditor with the after-acquired property clause still enjoys some situational monopoly. Thus, there are important procedural requirements necessary for obtaining a perfected PMSI in inventory which are set out in s. 9-312(3). The most important requirements involve notification in writing to the holder of a conflicting security interest, the tracing requirement and the necessity that the 'seller of the collateral' be able to identify the collateral sold. Seemingly, the obtaining of a PMSI will involve transaction costs that a creditor with an after-acquired property clause need not incur in order to get priority. These costs can be substantial, for example, the tracing requirement *vis-à-vis* shifting stocks which can be so onerous as to prove virtually unacceptable. In particular with regard to raw materials, if the after-acquired property clause extends to a certain category and the debtor borrows funds from another creditor to buy raw materials of the same sort, the debtor will have to segregate physically the new materials from the older in order to give the second creditor a purchase-money security interest. It would appear that even though the UCC is a sophisticated security statute, it does not avoid many of the policy dilemmas presented by a *Romalpa* clause in England.

When the draftsmen of the UCC encapsulated the after-acquired property provision, it was natural that they should read the PMSI as widely as possible. Indeed, in the 1949 and 1952 drafts of the UCC, provision was made for the financing buyer which recognised the latter as being engaged in another form of financing acquisition of goods by equating the financing buyer with the purchase-money lender. This approach would have necessitated a liberal tracing requirement and s. 9-107(c) of the 1952 draft envisaged a security interest where 'the debtor receives possession of the collateral even though value given is not in fact used to pay the price'. Subsequently, this provision was dropped from the final draft because it was considered to extend the PMSI to an unacceptable degree in that it took the concept beyond its common law heritage, i.e., identification of the asset. By abolishing s. 9-107(c), the draftsmen were merely confirming a tracing rule. Indeed, it is the strict tracing requirement under art. 9 which has proved a significant handicap to the holder of a PMSI, especially if the materials supplied are commingled with other materials. In a similar way, the *Romalpa* line of case law reflects this dilemma.

The scintilla temporis doctrine Where an asset is purchased with the assistance of moneys provided on loan, as in the case with the retention of title clause, a crucial question is whether the security interest was *created* before the beneficial interest of those entitled in equity to the purchased property. As a matter of principle, priority should be enjoyed by the purchase-money supplier (see above). Thus, in *Capital Finance Co. Ltd* v *Stokes* [1969] 1 Ch 261, an equitable security took the form that a purchaser of land (a company) agreed to execute a legal mortgage in favour of the vendor upon completion. An equitable mortgage was, therefore, created immediately and this equitable security later merged into the legal interest. Where there is no such provision it might be argued, as did counsel for Monsanto in *Re Bond Worth Ltd* [1980] Ch 228, that no security was ever 'created' by the company as a purchaser under s. 396 of the Companies Act 1985 (as amended). This indeed was the position in *Re Connolly Bros Ltd (No. 2)* [1912] 2 Ch 25), where a company sought to buy land and, for this purpose, entered into an agreement with a lender who paid money and received a charge as security for the advance. Previously, the company had entered into agreements with the debenture holders not to 'create' a 'prior' mortgage. It was held that at no stage was the company, as against the lender, that is, the unencumbered or the absolute owner of the legal fee simple so as to be free separately to charge the fee simple, that is, the purchaser never acquired more than an equity of redemption. The House of Lords in *Abbey National Building Society* v *Cann* [1991] 1 AC 56 upheld the principle expounded in *Re Connolly Bros Ltd (No. 2)* and the significance of this is, the buyer company in a *Romalpa* scenario could be deemed to acquire no more than an equity of redemption in future goods, so it does not 'create' a charge registrable under s. 396 of the Companies Act 1985 (as amended).

The approach of the House of Lords in *Abbey National Building Society* v *Cann* has great significance for retention of title clauses. In *Re Bond Worth Ltd*, the judgment of Slade J proceeded on the basis that there existed a *scintilla temporis* in which the buyer became the owner of both the legal and equitable interests in the goods. However, this is difficult to reconcile with the practical realities of the case since the seller (Monsanto) would not have agreed to supply the goods but for the retention of title clause. It appears, following *Abbey National Building Society* v *Cann* that the issue of priority depends upon whether or not the purchase-money security interest precedes the exchange of contracts, so there is nothing upon which the prior debenture with its after-acquired property clause may bite.

Title retention devices are no more registrable charges under the new legislation than they were under the old. Under s. 395(2) of the Companies Act 1985 (as amended), a 'charge' is defined as:

> ... any form of security interest (fixed or floating) over property, other than an interest arising by operation of law; and 'property', in the context of what is the subject of a charge, includes future property.

It is unlikely that this amendment alters the conventional legal position. Insofar as Professor Diamond suggested in the DTI report, *A Review of Security Law* (1989), a wide definition of security to encompass rights of retention, this was envisaged within a much wider context of the reform of English personal property security law. A wide definition of security would catch *inter alia* consignment sales and finance leasing mechanisms. This is at variance with the common law position where a bailee has no *general* proprietary interest in the goods bailed to him. Without a clear direction that this was indeed the intention of the legislature, the conclusion must be that only conventional security devices need to be registered.

Super purchase-money security interests In England, there has been a natural judicial reluctance to recognise retention of title clauses which have the effect of being super purchase-money security interests. The real dilemma here, as we have seen, is that English law focuses upon *form* as distinct from *economic function*. The emphasis on property reservation is that it allows the owner to seize the property should the debtor fail in one of his primary obligations, most notably, the payment of the price. Essentially, the commercial purpose of property retention is only to ensure priority; the supplier is not retaining the asset itself but rather the right to *use* the asset to gain repayment of the debtor's debt. On the basis of this approach, if the supplier recovers the goods for failure of the contract, the supplier should not be able to claim any surplus profit made on resale. However, the Sale of Goods Act 1979 does not allow for this conclusion as a natural consequence of a *sale* transaction (see pp. 125–6). Even so, the Court of Appeal in *Clough Mill Ltd* v *Martin* [1985] 1 WLR 111 suggested that it was possible for such a resale to take place without rescission. It is probable that a sale contract would be rescinded in this circumstance which was the conclusion of the House of Lords in *Armour* v *Thyssen Edelstahlwerke AG* [1991] 2 AC 339.

A closely related problem to the above issue arises out of 'all-liabilities' retention of title clauses (see pp. 268–70). It is significant that the seller in *Armour* v *Thyssen Edelstahlwerke AG* would *not* have a special purchase-money security interest under the UCC. As a matter of principle, the buyer must be treated as the 'owner' of the goods when he has fully paid for them, otherwise the clause will be void for total failure of consideration.

SIXTEEN
Ostensible ownership and registration of security interests

The common law rule outlawing ostensible ownership (see chapter 15) is mirrored in the 17th-century decision of Coke CJ in the Star Chamber in *Twyne's Case* (1601) 3 Co Rep 80b. In that case, the vice in the conveyance was not limited to its secrecy, as the court was concerned that the conveyance was being used to shield the debtor (Pierce) from his creditor, Chamberlin. The 'immorality' lay in Pierce continuing to enjoy the assets after purporting to place them beyond the reach of Chamberlin. In this respect, the timing and generality of the conveyance were relevant; retained possession was objectionable because it showed that Twyne had agreed to treat his apparently insolvent debtor favourably. It is precisely to avoid the charge that a conveyance is being used as a shield that Coke CJ advised at p. 80b that 'the goods and chattels be appraised by good people to the very value'. Following this case, the English treatment of the ostensible ownership problem, where a person had acquired possession of the chattel but the ownership had been retained, was to equate this behaviour with reputed ownership. Indeed, this principle was incorporated in bankruptcy legislation which was only finally overturned under the Insolvency Act 1986.

The legal system, illustrated in *Twyne's Case* and elaborated in English bankruptcy legislation, demonstrated a simple rule, namely, in order to obtain priority in an asset over third parties, it was not only necessary to receive the consent of the prior owner but also possession of the chattel. Thus, Coke CJ said in *Twyne's Case* at p. 80b:

> 1st, Let it [the transfer] be made in a public manner, and before the neighbours, and not in private, for secrecy is a mark of fraud.

Although a 'possession only' rule has the virtue of simplicity, this is bought at considerable indirect cost as can be illustrated with stock-in-trade financing where a possession-based rule presents serious difficulties. The reason for this is that the creditor only wants a *contingent* right to take collateral at a specified time, usually on default. In a sense, both parties are simultaneously asserting some of the elements of ownership. A possession-based system cannot accommodate the split of rights between two parties. Even if the ostensible-ownership problem is 'cured' by the lender taking possession, this in itself creates ostensible-ownership problems since the focus shifts away from the creditors of the debtor to the creditors of the lender. It may be that, like a pawnbroker or a bank which are 'known' to engage in possessing the assets of others, the ostensible ownership problem is cured through public notoriety. Where this notoriety is absent, the only other ways to resolve the dilemma are for the debtor and lender either to merge their operation, thereby removing the division, of ownership or, alternatively, through a field warehousing arrangement (see pp. 271–2). These mechanisms are costly.

THE ENGLISH LEGAL RESPONSE TO OSTENSIBLE OWNERSHIP

The traditional method adopted by the common law in curing the ostensible ownership problem posed by a creditor being out of possession is through public filing. The filing of a security interest is seen as an alternative to the taking of possession of the secured property by the secured party. It is clear that land is an obvious candidate for recordation because it is permanent and in one location. In this respect, the locus of the filing of the security interest in land should not pose significant cross-border problems. Moreover, there are strong pressures to divide land into multiple interests and as questions of title become more elaborate, recordation becomes more necessary. In pre-recordation days in English law, the buyer could protect himself by requiring a physical transfer of title deeds. This was only effective with total conveyances of land and could not cope with life estates or second mortgages over land. In addition, proof of title depended on showing previous dealings with land, and because there was no obvious point at which the proof would commence, the rule eventually established, in the absence of a contractual provision to the contrary, required the vendor to show a chain of title going back at least 60 years. The basic difficulty, of course, was that this did not determine the quality of the title to which the purchaser was entitled. Furthermore, the title proof period did not affect third parties who would prevail against the purchaser if they had a legal interest.

Insofar as the law imposes a recordation requirement, this brings into focus the tension between private volition and social control, i.e., when should the law defer to the intentions of the various parties, and to what extent should the law limit individual freedom of action? At the same time, it is important to appreciate the range of possibilities presented through filing systems which can range from title-based systems to a security system, leaving title claims to be based on possessory rules or a combination of both. There are significant cost factors involved in the different types of filing systems. In the case of land which is valuable, permanent, and definable, this is the paradigm for which a filing system of title claims is superior. Even so, it is important not to overemphasise the claims for title recordation in the case of land, especially if the recording system establishes only *evidence* of ownership and nothing more because, for example, adverse possession which is not recorded may be significant in this context. If the title-recording system is badly indexed or it is unwieldy in the sense that several files must be checked, it will in any case not be all-encompassing. Nevertheless, the alternative, a possessory-based title system will convey no information about the predecessors of the person who now claims to be the owner.

Filing systems are generally better than possessory systems when the property involved is valuable, when the property is not transferred often, and when it is important to share ownership among several individuals. In particular, filing is very advantageous when the property in question is needed for use, or if the property right is an abstract one as in the case of patents, copyrights and trade marks which appears to be the English solution (see, for example, the Copyright, Designs and Patents Act 1988). Here, in order to provide information concerning property rights, a legal system faces a choice of either assimilating rights to a possession-based regime through reification of the abstract right by representing it with a piece of paper or, in the alternative, to rely on a title-recording system. It could be argued that reifying intellectual property interests is more advantageous, especially in the case of outright transfers, since the cost of administering such a system would be very low. Reification, on the other hand, would not be able to accommodate partial ownership interests such as security interests which a file is uniquely able to do. Of course, one way to avoid recordation is to cut down the number of interests in a *res* which is the position with regard to chattels where, as a general rule, the creation of life estates and similar limited interests is prohibited. Nevertheless, the need for financing stock-in-trade (inventory) during the 19th century led to the creation of future interests and the enactment of filing mechanisms (see below). At the same time the issue of possession as raising ostensible ownership problems was questioned predominantly on the basis that the doctrine developed in an atmosphere of a simpler and more rural economy. The reputed ownership doctrine in bankruptcy became increasingly discredited and the report of the Blagden committee, *Bankruptcy Law and Deeds of Arrangement Law Amendment* (Cmnd 222, 1957), unanimously recommended at para. 110 that the reputed ownership clause be omitted from any future Bankruptcy Act. The basis of the argument is that no creditor today assumes that goods in a debtor's possession are his own property, nor do creditors extend credit on the strength of such possession. It is for this reason that reputed ownership no longer applies under the Insolvency Act 1986. The modern position appears to be that the general credit rating of the customer rather than the extent of his *visible* possessions is the main criterion for the granting or withholding of credit.

Recordation of personal property security interests
It is necessary to distinguish between lodgement of particulars relating to the security and lodging the security instrument itself, or a copy of it. The

distinction is important because the filing of a security instrument or copy is public notice of its *contents*, whereas registration of particulars of the security interest constitutes notice only of the *existence* of the security and the particulars that have to be registered. This approach suggests at least four methods of giving public notice. First, recording, which entails copying the original instrument in full in a permanent book preserved in the record office. This is undoubtedly the most satisfactory device for giving notice of real estate transactions where permanent title records are needed. Although the setting up of the system may be costly, for example, surveying and describing the land, this is a once-and-for-all cost since land lasts for ever.

There are also significant costs in maintaining such a recording system, but these are small compared to the relative value of the property involved in which the owner may want to give a security interest. A second system involves registration of a security interest which is the method used, for example, where the Torrens system is in effect. The state of the title to a tract of land appears on a certificate in a public record and on a duplicate held by the owners. What is involved here is filing by reference to an asset, which is only possible for substantial assets that are uniquely identifiable like ships and aircraft. No current English register relating to movables is indexed by asset although, with respect to registered land, an index map and parcels index enables a person making a search to discover whether a particular property has been registered. It is otherwise in some states in the USA where Certificate of Title Acts require the notation of a lien on the certificate of title in order for it to be good against subsequent purchasers or encumbrancers. It can be seen, therefore, that these first two methods of giving public notice involve reference to asset rather than to debtor. Contrastingly, the third and fourth methods involve reference only to the debtor. Thus in the case of instrument filing, the original document is lodged or copied and then left permanently in the record office, whereas, notice filing involves a statement being filed that the debtor has given a security interest in his property or intends to do so.

Instrument filing is prevalent as a mechanism for providing public notice of a personal property security interest under English law. The method of registration can be highly cumbersome as demonstrated in the mechanism anticipated in the Bills of Sale Act 1878.

Registration under the Bills of Sale Act 1878
The bill of sale with every schedule or inventory referred to or annexed, and a true copy of the bill, and every schedule or inventory, and every attestation of the execution of such a bill in addition to an affidavit containing certain required particulars, must be presented to the registrar (s. 49). The copy of the bill of sale and the original affidavit must be filed with the registrar (s. 10(2)), the original bill being handed back after inspection. Significantly, the filing of the bills of sale must be effected *in person* as no bills of sale are accepted for filing by post. Furthermore, there is a local registration requirement regarding people described in the affidavit of due execution living outside the London bankruptcy district, or if the chattels described in the bill are outside this. The registrar, the Queen's Bench masters, must within three clear days, exclusive

of the day of registration in the principal registry, transmit a copy of such a bill of sale to the county court registrar in whose district the relevant places are situated. In order to facilitate this, there must in addition to the copy of the bill of sale and other schedules and inventories be sufficient number of copies of the bill and every schedule and inventory annexed thereto, as the registrar deems necessary for the purpose of local registration.

The time allowed for registration of a security bill of sale is within seven clear days after its execution or, if executed out of England, within seven clear days after the time at which it would, in the ordinary course of post, arrive in England if posted immediately after execution (s. 8 of the Bills of Sale Act (1878) Amendment Act 1882). During the time allowed for registration, the bill of sale is valid irrespective of the fact that the registration proved to be insufficient rendering the seizing execution creditor liable in conversion. However, once the period allowed for registration has expired, the bill becomes void as to the chattels comprised in it, so the execution creditor would prevail. It would seem that the scheme of compliance makes it difficult and unrewarding to register bills of sale which ensures that they are little used in the granting of credit.

Other registers

There are other registers known in English law which are set out below, including their jurisdictional application within the constitutional arrangement of the UK:

Merchant Shipping Act 1894, s. 31	Great Britain
Agricultural Credits Act 1928, ss. 8 and 14, and Agricultural Marketing Act 1958, s. 15	England and Wales
Agricultural Credits (Scotland) Act 1929, s. 8, and Agricultural Marketing Act 1958, s. 15	Scotland
Trade Marks Act 1938, s. 25	Great Britain
Registered Designs Act 1949, s. 19	Great Britain
Industrial and Provident Societies Act 1967, s. 1	England and Wales
Industrial and Provident Societies Act 1967, ss. 3 to 6	Scotland
Patents Act 1977, s. 33	Great Britain
Civil Aviation Act 1985 (as amended), s. 86 and Mortgaging of Aircraft Order 1972, SI 1972 No. 1268, as amended	Great Britain
Companies Act 1985 (as amended), s. 396	England and Wales and Scotland
Merchant Shipping Act 1988, sch. 3	United Kingdom

No consistent policy is evident under English chattel security law with respect to registration. Since the object of registration is to give notice of the security interest to third parties, it is consistent to argue that failure to register ought not to affect the enforceability of the security against the debtor himself. However, under s. 8 of the Bills of Sale Act (1878) Amendment Act 1882, non-registration invalidates the security even against the debtor himself. Additionally, there is a failure to distinguish between the 'public notice' function of filing, that is, for the information of the general public, and the 'notice filing' aspect, which is the ranking of priorities. Thus, in the case of ships and aircraft, in order to preserve the validity of the security as against third parties, the mortgage must be registered as a company charge under part XII of the Companies Act 1985 (where the mortgagor is a company) despite the fact that it is properly registered under the Merchant Shipping Acts or the Civil Aviation Act 1982.

Under the Bills of Sale Act (1878) Amendment Act 1882, the effect of valid registration is *itself* anomalous because it does not *per se* constitute notice to third parties (s. 8). In the case of a grantee with a legal title, this rule is unlikely to prejudice him unduly since, subject to the *nemo dat* exceptions, he will be able to assert his interest against the whole world. Only the market overt exception applies, and this is illustrated in the case of a successive grant of an *absolute* bill of sale because priority is accorded to the first person to file even though that bill may not be first as regards point of time (see Bills of Sale Act 1878, s. 19). This is an exception to the *nemo dat* rule because the requirement that the grantor of a bill must be the true owner appears only in s. 3 of the 1882 Act which is limited to security bills (compare *Edwards* v *Edwards* (1876) 2 ChD 291). A purchaser who does not search the bills of sale register will not be considered to have notice of the bill merely by reason of registration. The seminal decision in this context is *Joseph* v *Lyons* (1884) 15 QBD 280, where the Court of Appeal held that the equitable doctrine of constructive notice should not be extended to commercial transactions and it did not, in any case, apply to documents registered in fulfilment of the Bills of Sale Acts 1854 to 1891. Furthermore, the *effects* of the *failure* to register vary: in the case of a security bill it will be void as against the holder of the other interest if it is a security bill; a general bill is only void as against the grantor's execution creditors and his trustee in bankruptcy or an assignee under an assignment for the benefit of creditors.

Registration under the Companies Act 1985 (as amended)
Registration under the Companies Act 1985 is merely a perfection requirement. Provided that the interest is registered within 21 days, it has priority according to the date of its creation. Registration is notice of the existence of registered *prescribed* particulars to all other *chargees* (s. 416(1)). In this respect, other chargees are charge holders whose securities require registration so this would not include, for example, a fixed charge over debts other than book debts (s. 396(1)(c)(iii); see *Northern Bank Ltd* v *Ross* [1991] BCLC 504). Such chargees and other persons are not taken to have notice 'of any matter by reason of its being disclosed on the register or by reason of his having failed to search the register in the course of making such inquiries as ought reasonably to be made' (s. 416(2)). It follows that the distinction between a 'sale' as a triumph of legal form and a security interest will be crucial in this regard (see pp. 346–57). To this extent constructive notice arising from registration of corporate charges is abolished so that s. 711A(1) of the Companies Act 1985 (as amended) states:

A person shall not be taken to have notice of any matter merely because of its being disclosed in any document kept by the registrar of companies (and thus available for inspection) or made available by the company for inspection.

However, this is without prejudice to any other enactment imposing such a notice (s. 416(3)).

It would seem that registration merely gives notice of matters that have to be registered: information voluntarily filed at the registry will not constitute notice to a subsequent chargee, although a person who inspects and finds such extras cannot take free from them. In the case of a negative pledge, that is, where the instrument creating a floating charge limits the powers of the company to deal with the relevant assets, registration does not affect a subsequent chargee since this constitutes notice only of the charge's existence and *not* its terms (*Siebe Gorman and Co. Ltd* v *Barclays Bank Ltd* [1979] 2 Lloyd's Rep 142). However, the position will be altered by s. 415(2)(a) of the Companies Act 1985 (as amended) where registrable prescribed particulars include whether the company has undertaken not to create other charges ranking in priority to or *pari passu* with the registered charge.

Where the registered particulars of a charge are not accurate, the charge is void to the extent that rights are not disclosed by the registered particulars which would be disclosed if they were complete and accurate (s. 402(1)). A person who has registered incomplete or inaccurate particulars may apply to the court for a declaration of priority over certain rights acquired whilst the registered charge remained incomplete or inaccurate. To found jurisdiction, s. 402(2) of the Companies Act 1985 (as amended) provides that it must be proved to the satisfaction of the court that the omission or error was unlikely to have misled *any unsecured creditor materially to his prejudice*, or that *no person became an unsecured creditor at a time when the registered particulars remained incomplete or inaccurate*. To a large extent the issue is one of *reliance* on the integrity of the register.

The amendments made to the Companies Act 1985 still fail to address some fundamental issues in English personal property security law notably, the treatment of a purchase-money security interest (see pp. 354-7). In addition, the difficulties associated with reconciling the effect of registration on different registers such as shipping, aircraft and patents with the companies register still persist. There are also problems concerning the scope of registrable charges; should there be registration of a charge over unascertained chattels and, if so, what description of the property should suffice? To the extent that any security is exempted from registration in the companies register, the intending creditor's search will be incomplete, and multiple searching is required if there are other registers which may contain relevant information in order for the intending creditor to get the full picture concerning the debtor's position. This position contrasts starkly with the conceptual unity seen in art. 9 of the American Uniform Commercial Code (the UCC).

There is no doubt that art. 9 of the UCC has influenced the debate over reform of personal property security interests in England. In 1971, the proposed Lending and Security Act suggested by the Crowther Committee, *Report on Consumer Credit* (Cmnd 4596, 1971) leaned very heavily on art. 9. The adoption of the Crowther scheme would involve a register of security interests of all types, in property corporeal and incorporeal of all kinds except land, whether granted by a corporation, a partnership or an individual. An essential accompaniment to this is the notice filing mechanism and the first-to-file rule. In the light of the Crowther and Diamond reports that such a registration system be adopted in England, Wales and Scotland, it is instructive to survey briefly the US experience. Subsequently, we shall consider the Canadian approach. This is pertinent because the question whether or not art. 9 is exportable has in large measure been answered affirmatively in Canada. Indeed Ontario adopted a similar scheme which fully came into force in April 1976 which provided the catalyst for other schemes in the rest of Canada, especially the western provinces. The Ontario Personal Property Security Act was fully revised in 1989 by taking into account the experiences of the other provinces, in particular, that of Saskatchewan.

NOTICE FILING: THE US EXPERIENCE

Notice filing and ostensible ownership problems under art. 9 of the Uniform Commercial Code

Although based on real-estate recording systems, personal-property filing mechanisms are fundamentally different. A real-estate recording system uniquely identifies a particular piece of property. By contrast art. 9, although it provides a filing system similar to that used for real estate, is more limited in its scope. The difficulties in this context have revolved around the nature of the particulars that have to be filed as the UCC has adopted a simple and uncomplicated procedure, namely, the financing statement needs to indicate the name and address of the debtor and the secured party, and the type(s) of collateral encumbered in the past, or which might be encumbered in the future. These requirements are not to be construed in a technical manner which provides a striking contrast to the strict requirements of the old 'English-type' registers. The onus is placed upon creditors to seek further information from the debtor which is by no means an easy task given that time is not static. Therefore, although potential creditors may ask the debtor to verify a list of collateral over which a security interest is subsisting (s. 9-208), by definition such a list would not include all potential future transactions involving the same category of collateral. Furthermore, the extent of the possibility of such future security is handicapped by the inconsistency in art. 9 which, on the one hand, requires the secured party's address in the financing statement (s. 9-402(1)) but, on the other, does not compel the secured party to respond to enquiries from a prospective creditor.

Any filing system will inevitably be of some limited assistance for the unsecured creditor since it will at least put him on notice to enquire further of the debtor. Of course, it does not guarantee that the debtor will not misinform him. If the object of notice filing is to prevent debtor misbehaviour, it does not achieve this as this can be done only through a system of civil and criminal penalties, or requiring more information in the filing system. A notice filing system will, however, cut down the *potential* for making misrepresentations, so a trade creditor by checking the file may decide not to send goods on open account but rather insist either on a purchase-money security interest (see pp. 354–7), or a subordination agreement (see pp. 437–40). This approach still does not *justify* the amount of information required on the present notice file under art. 9. Indeed, this is a particularly troublesome question since the person who checks the file is in no substantially better position than a potential creditor who simply asks the debtor for details at the start. The dilemma is easily resolved if one recognises that the art. 9 filing system is principally to serve the interests of *secured* creditors because the date of filing determines the priority of competing claims. As such, its function is not to give the world at large notice of security interests.

Defects in art. 9 as a model Article 9 appears to grant to an initial creditor an opportunity, by filing an appropriate notice, to gain control over the entire financing venture of a particular debtor. The present and future line of credit can be secured not only with the debtor's present assets but with any of the debtor's after-acquired property as well (s. 9-204). Moreover, the initial creditor's priority for the entire venture will date generally from the time of filing even though the filing predates the decision to commit funds to the enterprise. It may be argued that a notice filing system increases the debtor's costs of borrowing from later creditors and makes it more difficult for these creditors to lend. On the other hand, when the collateral is rapidly and constantly changing such as inventory and receivables financing, the notice filing system is justified. Thus, Jackson and Kronman have contended (see (1979) 88 Yale LJ 1143) that the UCC goes too far in limiting compulsory disclosures as to the secured obligation, i.e., with respect to 'equipment or other large and relatively stable items of property', they would return to a form of transaction filing where each filing would secure only a specified amount of debt. This proposal, which attempts to cut down the secured party's situational monopoly, presupposes that it is possible to determine exactly the types of financing which do not involve repeated extensions of value by the financer. This is unlikely.

A major weakness in the Jackson and Kronman approach discussed above is that it fails to accommodate fully the delicate balancing of the conflicting interests involved in a notice filing system. In the first place, there is the debtor's privacy interest which may be severely disadvantaged if the public record discloses the amount he has borrowed, the interest rate, and a specific description of the new inventory he is planning to market. A secured financer might also want to keep private the fact that he has identified a financing opportunity and should therefore be allowed to exploit this to his advantage. However, at the same time, these interests have to be balanced with the need for disclosure as a way of protecting interested parties from mistake or fraud on the part of the debtor. This approach has further to be reconciled with the art. 9 policy of promoting the facilitation of security; a goal that can only be maximised through a mechanism that increases the certainty for the secured party that his interest will prevail. What is clear is that if the facilitation and privacy interests are not safeguarded, secured lending will be discouraged. The most notorious example of this is the English bills of sale legislation 1854 to 1891 which has made the bill of sale a last-resort type of financing, contributing in no small measure to the rise of the unconventional security devices already discussed (see chapter 15). Nevertheless, the balancing of these interests involves difficult questions of degree so that, for example, the Canadian treatment, especially that seen in Saskatchewan, differs significantly from that adopted under the UCC (see below).

Article 9 of the UCC makes filing easy with little information necessary. In order to understand the first-in-time priority rule with the system of notice filing, some reference must be made to the legislative background of the Code. Originally, the drafters of art. 9 considered abandoning filing systems altogether and replacing them with rules to protect potential creditors from debtor misrepresentations. The proposal was for a 'due diligence' provision, i.e., the secured creditor would have been under an obligation to ensure that his debtor's financial statements disclosed fully his security interest, and debtors misled by improper statements could recover to the extent of their loss caused by good-faith reliance. This proposal was an attempted statutorification of a policing function by secured creditors. Given the context of previous legislation where filing was exceedingly cumbersome, it is odd that the greatest opposition to this proposal emanated from secured creditors. Undoubtedly, this reflected the fact that a once-and-for-all filing was *less* onerous than a general duty of diligence. Such a duty would invite court scrutiny and involve a fact-laden enquiry as to whether financial statements had been fraudulently substituted when presented to other potential lenders. This approach was never translated into statutory language, and the notice filing mechanism was established which fits well with a first-to-file rule.

The first-to-file priority rule provides a clear and precise legal consequence and the secured party must weigh the cost associated with filing against the loss of priority attendant with failure to file. Insofar as there are exceptions to this perfection and priority rule, they constitute real risks for secured creditors, but such exceptions are inevitable in order to balance the interests involved between competing sets of secured creditors. Thus, secured parties must accept both a risk that the filing system may be incomplete or inaccurate *vis-à-vis* earlier secured claims, as well as the duty of updating information about their interests for the benefit of subsequent secured parties. Special policy factors apply to consumer goods, so s. 9-302(1)(d) provides for automatic perfection of purchase-money interests in consumer goods irrespective of filing. The idea here is that financers lend money not on the security of goods but rather on the debtor's ability to repay. Of course, it is always possible to quarrel with the particular balance struck by art. 9, for example, why restrict automatic perfection in the context of consumer goods to purchase-money security interests? However, it is inevitable that some sort of compromise must be reached. Even so, there are some internal weaknesses under the UCC which are wholly unacceptable, for example, the lack of a central registry, and the inability of the filing system to cope with conferring information concerning collateral crossing borders.

Inherent UCC weaknesses When the Canadian Catzman committee in 1965 considered the art. 9 framework as a starting-point for updating the law of security and personal property, attention was given by the Ontario drafters to the possibility of substituting for the antiquated manual public notice provisions of art. 9 a computer system which would give a quicker and more accurate response to filing questions (see Report of the Ontario Law Reform Commission, *Personal Property Security Legislation* (No. 3 1965)). Article 9 was originally promulgated and adopted by the USA in a world when the computer had not come of age and, to a great extent the US filing system has outlived its usefulness. In the absence of a computer system, no great thought was given to the possiblity of a national filing regime when art. 9 was first drafted.

The influence of possession on the filing requirement in the Code is a result of the idea that filing is a functional substitute for possession. In this respect, the art. 9 drafters oriented the time and place of filing to the geographical and temporal states of possession. It is odd, given the fact that the filing mechanism is pre-eminent to possession as a method of perfection under the UCC, that possessory notions permeate the filing mechanism. The underpinning of possession to filing suffered a severe blow by the 1972 revision of the UCC. This is because the revision consolidated chattel paper (see below) and mobile equipment with accounts receivable in the sense that registration is required in the place where the debtor is located. An extension of this approach may be to question whether possession should be a significant factor in determining priority. Despite this, both the English Crowther committee, 1971, and the Halliday report, 1986, accept *uncritically* the general proposition of perfection by possession. Thus, the Crowther scheme suggested at para. 5.6.2:

> If a security interest is created by deposit of the security or documents representing it — as where life assurance policies or hire-purchase agreements are deposited with a bank by way of security — no written instrument is necessary, since possession is given to the secured party.

The Halliday committee rejected this approach at para. 39:

> This reference to the deposit of documents is of course a reference to the equitable mortgage, which (as the Crowther committee recognise) does not extend to Scotland. Under English law the deposit must be supported by an agreement that it was in fact made for the purpose of creating security, but this agreement may be oral or simply inferred from the circumstances. The equitable mortgage is binding upon any subsequent purchaser or mortgagee who knows or ought to know of its existence. Our view is that to introduce this concept into Scots law would be to create uncertainty.

This might explain why the Halliday report envisaged at para. 25(2) that existing Scottish law should apply to creating security over corporeal movables by their delivery to the secured creditor. However, the reference to equitable mortgage is odd given the fact that art. 9 does not depend on any distinction between legal and equitable interests. The Crowther view was rather that no one is likely to buy or take security over documents of title or goods or the reversion of a hire-purchase agreement or an insurance policy (i.e. chattel paper) without taking possession of the document. Even so, the growth of paperless transactions over the last few years threatens the art. 9 rules on possession.

We shall now proceed to consider the registry systems set up under Canadian personal property security legislation, as they all provide examples of computer registries. The extent and diversity of the information which can be achieved is the major difference between the older system, typified by the UCC, which consists of index books lodged in different registry offices. Particular emphasis will be placed upon the Saskatchewan Personal Property Security Act (SPPSA) which can be viewed as a second generation of Canadian personal property security legislation, i.e., although it adopts the basic structure and conceptual framework of the unamended Ontario Act (OPPSA) and, therefore, the UCC, it eliminates many of the identified deficiencies and uncertainties of the earlier legislation.

THE CANADIAN APPROACH TO FILING PERSONAL PROPERTY SECURITY INTERESTS

Although the SPPSA draws upon the experience of art. 9 of the UCC, there are significant differences. The main divergence is that, under the SPPSA, registration is permitted to perfect a security interest in any type of collateral (SPPSA s. 25). In contrast, while the UCC permits registration as a method of perfecting security interests in certain types of tangible property and documentary intangible property (s. 9-304), the UCC permits perfection *only by possession* where the security interest is in securities, negotiable documents of title, or letters of credit. The fear expressed was that if registration of security interests in the collateral were allowed, negotiability or free transferability would be destroyed.

The possession-based rule has proved highly problematic especially if the only way a debtor can pay his debt on a negotiable instrument is by realising it. Under the SPPSA, transferees of money and good-faith purchasers of security instruments and negotiable documents of title are given a special priority position superior to that of the secured party if they have acquired the money, security instrument or document of title under the circumstances prescribed in the Act which are equivalent to negotiation (SPPSA s. 25). Furthermore, a secured party is permitted to register a single financing statement covering a wide range of collateral including negotiable property, and to have protection against attacks from a trustee in bankruptcy or the execution creditor of the debtor. At the same time, the free transferability of negotiable and quasi-negotiable property is preserved.

Methods of indexing
It is impossible to discuss registration without referring to the method of indexing. A registration system involves *both* the recording of information and

search for recorded information. This will depend upon the manner of indexing, which can either be against the name of the person who created the interest, or against the chattels themselves. In fact, computer technology has made it possible to accommodate both sorts of indexing, thereby increasing the amount of information available and reducing the difficulties of wholesale reliance on each individual approach. Thus, for example, a major difficulty with indexing against the name of the person who created the interest is the problem of the 'alias', i.e., where X creates a security interest over an object and then creates another security interest in the same object but this time describing himself as Y. A variant on this theme is the so-called A-B-C-D problem as in the case where A takes a security interest in property owned by B and perfects his security interest by registration. It follows that A's interest is recorded against B's name. But if B sells the property to C who then sells it to D, the latter acquiring it in good faith and for value without notice, a priority problem emerges since, before buying, D will have searched a registry using C's name as the search criterion. If D were to prevail, this would undermine the entire system of registration which is to effect priority for the first to file. At the same time, the system presupposes the *notice* function of filing. One method of protecting D is through additional serial number registration, i.e., filing with reference to asset, although this will depend upon whether the chattel carries a serial number and that this is regular.

Categorisation of chattels Whatever notice filing system is devised, a delicate balance has to be struck between flexibility (allowing for after-acquired property financing) and the demand for information. The Saskatchewan approach, in this respect, requires detailed descriptions of particular items of collateral when a motor vehicle or aircraft held by the debtor as equipment or consumer goods is involved (SPPSA s. 9), but with regard to other collateral only a general description is required. In the development of the SPPSA the drafters of the legislation had available to them several models. The first model was that outlined in art. 9 of the UCC, which anticipates under s. 9-402 the registration of 'a statement indicating the types, or describing the items of collateral'. The Code does not define 'type', but it cannot be that a detailed description is entailed because notice filing seeks to accommodate the possibility that the parties will not know at the outset of their relationship what property will be subject to the security interest. The whole purpose of the financing statement is only to alert a reasonable enquirer to the need for further investigation to determine the identity of the collateral.

Nevertheless, designating a type can serve to reduce the number of investigations which a searcher must make. An alternative approach was that adopted in Ontario before the 1989 reform which required the classification of collateral as 'consumer goods', 'inventory', 'equipment', 'book debts' or 'other'. The main difficulty here was that the *nature* of the collateral was not described only the *use* to which the goods were being put. This approach was not necessarily helpful because, for example, the use could change, as in the case of a car held as 'inventory' which can be converted into 'equipment' by the decision of the debtor to use it as part of his business operations, and finally, into 'consumer goods' where the debtor uses the same car for leisure.

In drafting the SPPSA none of these models were selected. The Saskatchewan Act requires the same collateral description for the purposes of the security agreement and the financing statement. The emphasis is upon a 'type or kind' description which requires a generic classification of each of the registration categories, namely, consumer goods, equipment and inventory. It is important to remind ourselves of the purpose of registration. It is both a means of perfecting security interests and a means by which prospective purchasers and lenders can verify the liabilities of their sellers and debtors. There must be a balancing between secured parties whose interests must not be invalidated by too stringent requirements, and prospective buyers, and creditors who must be able to determine if further enquiries are necessary before buying property or lending money.

Errors in documents or registration It may take as long as five working days under the SPPSA from receipt and preliminary screening of a financing statement to its final check and coding so as to enable it to be searchable. The procedure inevitably creates ostensible ownership problems. A registry employee must read the financing statement and reproduce it on a keyboard, and errors in transposition are inevitable. Although there are computer programs under the Saskatchewan system designed to identify these errors, nonetheless, each time an entry is made in data storage, the computer automatically prints out a verification statement containing the information entered. Errors identified can be corrected through the use of a verification statement containing the correction. In addition, in order to curb the danger of over-collateralisation, a discharge form is sent, so the secured party is saved the clerical costs and the possibility of error in the preparation of a financing change statement which would otherwise be required to discharge his registration.

Unless a program is specifically designed to provide flexibility, the search criterion used by a person seeking information from data storage must correspond exactly to the criterion to which the computer is programmed to respond. The SPPSA has been designed to reduce the need for total accuracy, and the coding system used is a modified form of code system developed by the New York State Information and Intelligence Service (NYSIIS). By breaking down the digits in the search request, the code ensures matches, although it is the registry clerk who chooses what the exact matches and similar matches are to the search request. This can be criticised on the basis that it is the registry clerk, and not the searching party, who makes a legal judgment that essentially belongs to the searching party. However, the effect of error is not necessarily fatal to the efficacy of the registration. One of the major characteristics of the Canadian personal property security legislation has been the shift away from the tendency to require fanatical precision in complying with registration requirements under previous chattel security legislation.

The UCC and the SPPSA focus upon the materiality of the error. Under s. 9-402(8) of the UCC, the test is whether the error is seriously misleading. The *ad hoc* approach of the UCC concentrates not on whether the filing was made in the debtor's 'true' name (the method of indexation), but rather on whether the inaccurate name as measured against the real name was such that a reasonable search would not uncover the filing. Unlike the UCC, the SPPSA (s. 66(1)) does not concentrate on the nature or magnitude of a defect, irregularity or omission but instead focuses upon the issue whether or not *non-compliance* has the effect of being seriously misleading. This cannot be stated in abstract, although the computerised nature of the SPPSA filing system, together with its various fail-safe formulae will help to determine the seriousness or otherwise of the defect or omission. The test is an objective one, and requires the courts to focus attention on all hypothetical users and not as to whether an error is misleading qua a particular party. This approach has also been adopted in s. 43(8) of the Alberta Personal Property Security Act 1988. There are important reasons why an objective test is employed: First, a subjective test raises questions as to what *kind* of defect, irregularity, error or omission amounts to non-compliance. Second, a subjective test reintroduces into the registry system difficult issues of proof. Third, a subjective test carries the danger of circular priority problems.

The question of knowledge It is important to distinguish between reliance and knowledge. In this respect, it is beneficial to consider the different types of recording systems, namely, 'notice', 'race notice', and 'race' statutes. Under a 'notice' statute, the question is whether a party has notice either record or actual, or constructive knowledge at the time of entering the transaction. It is anticipated that a party without knowledge or notice of an earlier party's interest will prevail regardless of whether either party has ever filed. In contrast, under a 'race' statute, not only must the party have neither actual nor constructive knowledge at the time of entering the transaction, there is an obligation in the post-transaction period to record the interest first before priority is ultimately determined.

The pure race system established under the UCC and the Canadian Personal Property Security Acts is a deviation from pre-Code chattel mortgage systems since the first party to file and hence the first to give record notice prevails. Any enquiry into knowledge is likely to be expensive, and time-consuming, and seems to be at variance with the policy of encouraging simplicity of creation and certainty of security interests. It may be that there are good reasons for denying the power to a thief to convey good title and also for discouraging fraud; it is unlikely that these reasons extend to penalising a person merely because he has knowledge. Such a rule is likely to discourage people from gathering information about property in the first instance and favours one who is at fault in not recording, thereby tending to weaken the incentive to record. This is particularly pertinent when the requirement to file is not costly and, as a matter of convenience for the administration of the legal system, any inquiry into subjective knowledge is going to be costly in the sense of the attendant litigation it generates. The issue is simply one of perfection through filing first.

The present English law suffers from a number of difficulties such as the obvious lack of systematisation of the law concerning the effect of registration. In striking contrast, the two key features of an art. 9 type scheme are a functional classification of security interests, and a priority system based on the order of registration of those interests. However, art. 9 is not consistent in this respect since the role of possession as a perfecting mechanism poses significant definitional problems, as well as undermining the integrity of a first-to-file rule. Furthermore, it may be that art. 9's championing of the facilitation of secured credit has been achieved at the cost of *sufficient* disclosure of the security interest. In this regard, more recent Canadian personal property security legislation using modern computer registries has, in large measure, redressed the balance.

SEVENTEEN
Guarantees

Guarantees have considerable commercial significance. Each year a great deal of money is lent on the security of a guarantee furnished by a third party. Indeed, much of the export trade of the UK is based upon guarantees furnished by institutional lenders whilst in domestic commercial transactions, finance institutions will sometimes insist upon a guarantee.

In this chapter we shall consider the substantive legal principles involved in contracts of guarantee. Often the commercial sense of the guarantee will not cohere with its legal meaning and we shall discuss this phenomenon particularly in the context of bank guarantees, and the performance bond.

THE SUBSTANTIVE LAW

Before proceeding to examine the principles of suretyship, it is important, first of all, to deal with the definitional problem.

The definition of guarantee and indemnity
The guarantee is an accessory contract in the sense that the surety's obligations spring out of those of the principal debtor, and the liability of the surety is coterminous with that of the principal debtor. The guarantee is simply a mechanism which provides for a (usually) deeper second pocket to pay if the first pocket is empty. What we have here is a unilateral contract whose effect is contingent upon the creditor making an advance to the debtor. It follows that the offer of guarantee may be terminated at any time before the advance.

Since the guarantee is an accessory contract to the main obligation, where this is vitiated on the basis of common mistake, the guarantee agreement will be avoided as well. This was illustrated in *Associated Japanese Bank (International) Ltd* v *Crédit du Nord SA* [1989] 1 WLR 255, where the facts involved the sale to the plaintiffs and leaseback of non-existent machines. The defendants separately agreed with the plaintiffs to guarantee the seller's obligations under the leaseback agreement and, following the default of the, now, lessee it was discovered that the machines did not exist. It was held that the machines constituted the principal security of the defendants as guarantors and, since these did not exist, the guarantee contract was void *ab initio* for common mistake at common law (see *Couturier* v *Hastie* (1856) 5 HL Cas 673. Compare *McRae* v *Commonwealth Disposals Commission* (1951) 84 CLR 377). As a consequence, the plaintiffs' claim under the guarantee agreement failed. Here we are confronted once again with the Janus-faced fault doctrine which was discussed earlier (see pp. 156–7).

In contrast to the guarantee contract, the indemnity is a primary obligation in its own right, that is, the indemnifier contracts as principal to pay in the event of a stipulated loss occurring.

A question of construction The courts have shown a willingness to adopt a sympathetic approach to the question of construction as to whether a document is a guarantee or indemnity. This is evident in the approach of Lord Reid, for example, in the House of Lords in *Moschi* v *Lep Air Services Ltd* [1973] AC 331, where he said at p. 344:

> I would not proceed by saying this is a contract of guarantee and there is a general rule applicable to all guarantees. Parties are free to make any agreement they like and we must I think determine just what this agreement means.
>
> With regard to making good to the creditor payments of instalments by the principal debtor there are at least two possible forms of agreement. A person might undertake no more than that if the principal debtor fails to pay any instalment he will pay it. That would be a conditional agreement. . . . If for any reason the debtor ceased to have any obligation to pay the instalment on the due date then he could not fail to pay it on that date. The condition attached to the undertaking would never be purified and the subsidiary obligation would never arise.
>
> On the other hand, the guarantor's obligation might be of a different kind. He might undertake that the principal debtor will carry out his contract. Then if at any time and for any reason the principal debtor acts or fails to act as required by his contract, he not only breaks his own contract but he also puts the guarantor in breach of his contract of guarantee.

It should be noted, however, that the mere inclusion of the word 'guarantee' is not conclusive of the matter. Thus in *Heald* v *O'Connor* [1971] 1 WLR 497, the provision in the guarantee that 'the liability of the guarantor shall be as a primary obligor and not merely as surety' was dismissed by Fisher J as indemnity on the basis, at p. 503, that it was 'merely part of the common-form provision'. The significance of this finding as a matter of construction of the guarantee contract was that it thereby failed since the primary contract was unenforceable because a company was financing the purchase of its own shares which at the time was contrary to the provisions of the Companies Act 1948. In contrast, in the earlier case of *Garrard* v *James* [1925] Ch 616 involving similar issues, Lawrence J construed the covenant, at p. 622, as being essentially an indemnity so that 'if the company does not perform its obligations under the agreement, the defendants will themselves perform those obligations'.

SURETYSHIP CONTRACTS

The contractual principles developed in English law will apply to all suretyship contracts. Thus, the objective of the agreement achieved is one of construction of the suretyship contract. Of course, the normal rules as to revocation of the offer prior to acceptance will apply to suretyship contracts. This point was eloquently made by Erle CJ in the Court of Common Pleas in the mid-19th century case of *Offord* v *Davies* (1862) 12 CB (NS) 748:

> The promise [of guarantee] by itself creates no obligation. It is in effect conditioned to be binding if the plaintiff acts on it, either to the benefit of the defendants or to the detriment of himself. But until the condition has been at least in part fulfilled, the defendant has the power of revoking it.

In a commercial context, the presumption must be that the parties intended their agreement to give rise to binding obligations, that is, to sound in law (see *Ford Motor Co. Ltd* v *Amalgamated Union of Engineering and Foundry Workers* [1969] 2 QB 303).

Suretyship contracts must either be made by deed or otherwise supported by consideration. This is normally furnished by the creditor agreeing to provide a new or extend an existing credit facility to the borrower. A guarantee taken to cover a past advance is unenforceable for want of consideration, unless there has been consideration in the form of a forbearance by the creditor in suing the borrower for the debt (compare *Provincial Bank of Ireland Ltd* v *Donnell* [1934] NI 33).

The letter of comfort

In recent times, the phenomenon of the comfort letter has emerged which sometimes takes the form of a non-legally-binding obligation. Typically, this consists of a simple acknowledgement that a parent company, for example, is aware of credit facilities supplied by the creditor(s) and that the parent company does not have any *present* intention of withdrawing its support from the subsidiary, or materially changing the nature of its business. This is the legal equivalent of a placebo in the sense that it does not give rise to an enforceable legal obligation (in the absence of fraud) by the parent company, that is, it is the archetypal 'gentleman's agreement'. A 'gentleman's agreement' has been defined in an observation ascribed to Vaisey J by Sir Robert Megarry, *A Second Miscellany-at-Law* (1973) at p. 326 as one 'which is not an agreement, made between two persons, neither of whom is a gentleman, whereby each expects the other to be strictly bound without himself being bound at all'. With this observation in mind, it is fitting that the burden of proof is upon the author of the comfort letter to show that there was no intention to create legal relations (see *Kleinwort Benson Ltd* v *Malaysia Mining Corporation Bhd* [1988] 1 WLR 799).

A comfort letter which states that the parent company will ensure that its subsidiary will be in a position to satisfy its financial obligations is enforceable so long as it is supported by good consideration, for example, the granting of a *new* facility. It is not easy to distinguish between enforceable and non-enforceable letters of comfort as very often the distinction will centre around the nature of the representation made, and the context in which the letters were drawn. This point arose out of the litigation surrounding the collapse of the London-based International Tin Council. In *Kleinwort Benson Ltd* v *Malaysia Mining Corporation Bhd*, the plaintiff bank agreed with the defendants to make a loan facility of up to £10 million available to the defendant's wholly owned subsidiary X which traded on the London Metal Exchange. In consideration for this facility, the defendants provided two letters of comfort to the plaintiffs stating that: 'It is our policy to ensure that the business of [X] is at all times in a position to meet its liabilities to you under the [loan facility agreement]'. Following the collapse of the tin market, X went into liquidation and the plaintiff sought payment of the amount owing to it. At first instance, Hirst J held that in the circumstances in which the letters of comfort had been written, there was a presumption that they had been intended to have legal effect. In the Court of Appeal, a different construction was put on the letters, and it was considered that their terms represented a statement of present fact which related to the intention of the parent company rather than a contractual promise as to future conduct. It is not surprising, therefore, given the legal ambiguity of such letters of comfort, that they have constituted a source of considerable confusion for bankers and auditors alike. There is no doubt that the Court of Appeal in *Kleinwort Benson Ltd* v *Malaysia Mining Corporation Bhd* engaged in minute textual analysis of the comfort letter, perhaps, at the expense of recognising that it was a commercial document. In effect, the construction given rendered the document scrap paper. In these circumstances, it is unwise for such instruments to be regarded as security instruments.

The form of suretyship contracts
Statutory regulation of suretyship contracts is provided for under the Consumer Credit Act 1974 and the Statute of Frauds 1677 with its amendment of 1828.

The Consumer Credit Act 1974 Security instruments which relate to agreements regulated under the Act must comply with formal requirements. It is noteworthy that the definition of security instruments includes 'sureties' (s. 189 of the Consumer Credit Act 1974) so that it applies to obligors under both contracts of guarantee and indemnity. The formalities require that the agreement be in legible writing, that a copy should be presented to the surety, and other specific information should be brought to his attention (s. 105(1), (3), and (7)).

The Statute of Frauds 1677 and amendment Apart from transactions under the Consumer Credit Act 1974, all guarantees must comply with the Statute of

Frauds 1677. Section 4 states that a guarantee must be in writing and specifically provides as follows:

> No action shall be brought whereby to charge the defendant upon any special promise to answer for the debt, default, or miscarriage of another person ... unless the agreement upon which such action shall be brought, or some memorandum, or note thereof, shall be in writing and signed by the party to be charged therewith or some other person thereunto by him lawfully authorised.

It is obviously desirable that there should be some record in writing of the guarantee. Inevitably, the writing requirement can prove to be problematical where the parties have attempted an oral variation of the guarantee. However in this respect, it was held in *Perrylease Ltd* v *Imecar AG* [1988] 1 WLR 463, that objective extrinsic evidence was admissible to explain the terms of a written guarantee governed by s. 4 of the Statute of Frauds 1677. Since s. 4 applies only to secondary obligations, the formal requirements do not apply to indemnities.

It is clear that s. 4 prescribes two separate ways in which a contract of guarantee may be made enforceable. The first way, as has been noted above, is by having a written agreement signed by the party to be charged or his agent. The second way is by having a note or memorandum of the (oral) agreement similarly signed. It was held by the House of Lords in *Elpis Maritime Co. Ltd* v *Martin Chartering Co. Inc.* [1992] 1 AC 21, that the intention or capacity of the person signing the memorandum was irrelevant since all that was necessary under s. 4 was the existence of a note or memorandum of a promise to answer for the debt, default or miscarriages of another person signed by the party to be charged.

Construction of suretyship contracts
Most suretyship contracts issued by institutional lenders will be on standard form prepared by the institution concerned reflecting its assumption-of-risk policy. Since these contracts are drafted by skilled legal drafters, the courts will construe them *contra proferentem*. As Browne-Wilkinson V-C put it at first instance in *Welsh Development Agency* v *Export Finance Co. Ltd* [1990] BCC 393 at p. 403: 'Those who live by the sword [referring to the contract drafter] may also die by the sword'.

Limitations may be placed upon the guarantee both as to time and amount.

Continuing guarantees It is obviously necessary for the guarantee to state clearly what the specified time-limit means, for example, insofar as it relates to obligations maturing before or incurred before the expiry of the period. Of course, there may be a continuing guarantee which is not limited to a specific transaction or period of time, for example, by guaranteeing 'the balance outstanding' on a specific account.

Limitation as to amount It is important to distinguish between the guarantee of a fixed sum and the guarantee of the entire indebtedness with a limit of liability. In the former case, the guaranteed part of the debt is treated as a separate part of the debt, thereby entitling the surety to share rateably in securities held by the creditor for the full indebtedness. Furthermore, the payment by the guarantor does not discharge the principal debt *pro tanto* so that the principal debtor can be sued for the entire debt (*Ulster Bank Ltd* v *Lambe* [1966] NI 161). On the other hand, where the surety guarantees the whole indebtedness but with a limit of liability, the guaranteed indebtedness remains indivisible, so the surety cannot take over securities or prove in the insolvency of the debtor unless the surety discharges the entire indebtedness (*Re Sass* [1896] 2 QB 12).

The application of *Clayton's Case* (1817) 1 Mer 527 (see p. 285) to the balance of the accounts of the debtor can be highly relevant as regards the liability of the surety. Thus, where the guarantee provides for its termination on the occurrence of a specific event, this will fix the moment at which the debit balance to which the guarantee relates is determined. So if further sums are placed into the account, the rule in *Clayton's Case*, unless it is excluded, states that such sums will go to the reduction of the earliest indebtedness first, namely, the indebtedness covered by the guarantee. Of course, this will be avoided if the creditor freezes the account of the debtor and ensures that all future receipts credit a separate account (*Re Sherry* (1884) 25 ChD 692).

LEGAL PRESUMPTIONS

The legal position of the surety in relation to the creditor

It is simplistic to argue that the guarantor enjoys certain 'rights' against the creditor or, conversely, that the creditor owes certain 'duties' to the guarantor, as this would suggest that a guarantor has an independent cause of action irrespective of the terms and conditions of the contract of suretyship. Of course, it is possible for the creditor expressly or by implication to assume positive obligations to the surety. However, in the absence of these positive obligations, the surety's interest in proper performance by the creditor is limited to the amount of his own liability under the guarantee and there is no positive right of action. Expressed in Hohfeldian terms, the surety's 'rights' are immunities in the sense that the creditor's (mis)behaviour discharges the surety from liability, so he has effectively received the protection to which he is entitled.

The above analysis has considerable significance regarding the applicability of the Unfair Contract Terms Act 1977 to any clause seeking to restrict or exclude the creditor's duty of care *vis-à-vis* the surety's interests. Since the breach of such an undertaking is not a positive duty but merely a defence to the creditor's claim, it is not governed by the provisions for reasonableness under the Act, that is, such a clause does not seek to exclude liability but rather seeks to define the extent of the liability in the first place by negating the immunity the surety would otherwise enjoy. At the same time, it should be noted that the courts have been generous in releasing the surety from his obligations where the creditor has acted in such a way as to injuriously affect the position of the surety. Indeed, it is possible to identify various presumptions, in this respect, which can be said to apply in the absence of an express provision to the contrary in the suretyship contract. We shall now consider these in greater detail.

Variation of the contract The suretyship contract is predicated upon the principle of substitution, that is, the surety undertakes to meet stipulated liabilities in the event of the principal debtor's failure to do so. If, therefore, the creditor and principal debtor agree to a variation of the terms of their agreement, this will alter the basis of the surety's undertaking to guarantee the debtor's obligations. In this circumstance, he will be discharged of his liability unless he has agreed to the change, or it is trivial, or clearly beneficial to him. As Chitty J held in *Bolton* v *Salmon* [1891] 2 Ch 48 at p. 54:

> The true rule ... is that if there is any agreement between the principals with reference to the contract guaranteed, the surety ought to be consulted, and that if there is any alteration, which is not obviously either unsubstantial or for the benefit of the surety, he is to be the sole judge whether he will remain liable. This reasoning applies with the same force to a security given by the surety as it does to a personal obligation entered into by him.

What is trivial and what is substantial will depend on the circumstances of each case. This is especially so with an 'all-moneys' guarantee which appears to guarantee all advances. If no limit is specified, the problem may arise as to whether a guarantee given in respect of a small overdraft extends to a subsequent substantial loan provided. In this circumstance, much will depend upon the construction of the guarantee agreement. Here the court may construe the guarantee strictly as seen, for example, by the approach of the Privy Council in *Burnes* v *Trade Credits Ltd* [1981] 1 WLR 805. In this case it was held that an agreement to extend a facility, at an increased rate of interest, was a material variation of the loan agreement and went beyond anything contemplated by the guarantee clause which purported to give the borrower 'time or any other indulgence or consideration'.

The granting of time or indulgence normally amounts to a material variation since it is unlikely to be beneficial to a surety as the financial position of the principal debtor may deteriorate. On the other hand, the granting of time may be implied into a suretyship contract where this is within the normal usages of a particular trade.

Release of the principal debtor A surety is released if the debt he has guaranteed is paid or satisfied. This is also the case where the obligation due is neutralised, for example, as in the case where the principal debtor acquires a right of set-off or counterclaim. This was explained in the following terms by Willes J in *Bechervaise* v *Lewis* (1872) LR 7 CP 372 at p. 377:

> A surety has a right, as against the creditor, when he has paid the debt, to have for reimbursement the benefit of all securities which the creditor holds against the principal. ... The surety, however, has another right, viz. that,

as soon as his obligation to pay is become absolute, he has a right in equity to be exonerated by his principal. Thus we have a creditor who is equally liable to the principal as the principal to him, and against whom the principal has a good defence in law and equity, and a surety who is entitled in equity to call upon the principal to exonerate him. In this state of things, we are bound to conclude that the surety has a defence in equity against the creditor.

It is, of course, otherwise in indemnity contracts which assume primary obligations and are not parasitic upon the underlying loan contract, so if the principal debtor has a defence against the creditor, this defence will be of no avail to the liability of the indemnifier.

Where a surety has paid more than his proportionate share of the indebtedness, he is entitled to a contribution, normally, the excess from his co-surety. It follows that where a co-surety is released this will, in the absence of agreement, discharge a surety because this action prejudices his right to a contribution. Such is the case even where a surety has signed a several guarantee not making it part of the contract that a like guarantee would be given by others. This was explained by the Privy Council in *Ward* v *National Bank of New Zealand Ltd* (1883) 8 App Cas 755 where it was held at p. 766:

> The claim of a several surety to be released upon the creditor releasing another surety, arises not from the creditor having broken his contract, but from his having deprived the surety of his remedy for contribution in equity [based upon the equitable maxim that equality is equity]. The surety, therefore, in order to support his claim, must show that he had a right to contribution, and that that right had been taken away or injuriously affected.

A distinction should be drawn between a release of a surety and a covenant not to sue, or *pactum de non petendo*. This was explained by Lord Porter in *Mahant Singh* v *U Ba Yi* [1939] AC 601 in the following terms at p. 607:

> Where an absolute release is given, there is no room for any reservation of remedies against the surety. . . . Where, however, the debt has not been actually released, the creditor may reserve his rights by notifying the debtor that he does so, and this reservation is effective not only where the time of payment is postponed but even where the creditor has entered into an agreement not to sue the debtor. In neither case is there any deception of the debtor, since he knows that he is still exposed to a suit at the will of the surety.

Release of security The presumption is that a surety will be discharged from his obligation on the release of security by the creditor because, otherwise, his right to subrogation will be prejudiced. However, this presupposes that, on the true construction of the agreement for the guarantee, the validity of the security or the perfection of a security interest like a debenture was a precondition for the validity of the guarantee (see *TCB Ltd* v *Gray* [1988] 1 All ER 108). If this is not the case, the guarantee continues to be enforceable. It should be noted that the release of security does not discharge the surety's liability *in toto* and is limited to the value of the assets released. This can be considered, in the absence of a promissory condition in the guarantee contract, merely as a breach of the equitable obligation to respect the surety's interests so far as this is consistent with the protection of the creditor's own interests.

Suretyship contracts are not immune from being set aside because of fraud, illegality or misrepresentation.

Undue influence The exercise of undue influence to procure a guarantee or indemnity will provide a defence to an action against a surety (see *Lloyds Bank Ltd* v *Bundy* [1975] QB 326). The House of Lords in *National Westminster Bank plc* v *Morgan* [1985] AC 686 restricted the ambit of the undue influence doctrine, so the relationship of the party *by itself* is insufficient to establish undue influence: the test was whether the transaction was wrongful in the sense that the party was sufficiently disadvantaged which, failing proof to the contrary, could only be explained on the basis of undue influence. There may be actual undue influence or a breach of a confidential relationship. This was defined by Nourse LJ in *Goldsworthy* v *Brickell* [1987] Ch 378 at p. 400 as: 'a relationship wherein one party has ceded such a degree of trust and confidence as to require the other, on grounds of public policy, to show that it has not been betrayed or abused'. Typically, the circumstances envisaged here would be where a child guarantees its parent (*Lancashire Loans Ltd* v *Black* [1934] 1 KB 380), or elderly parents guarantee their child (*Avon Finance Co. Ltd* v *Bridger* [1985] 2 All ER 281).

It appears from the cases that where the surety is one step removed from the debtor, there is a duty imposed upon the creditor to point out the desirability of seeking independent advice. The matter was summed up by Dillon LJ in *Kings North Trust Ltd* v *Bell* [1986] 1 WLR 119 at p. 123:

> ... if a creditor, or potential creditor, of a husband desires to obtain, by way of security for the husband's indebtedness, a guarantee from his wife or a charge on property of his wife and if the creditor entrusts to the husband himself the task of obtaining the execution of the relevant document by the wife, then the creditor can be in no better position than the husband himself, and the creditor cannot enforce the guarantee or the security against the wife if it is established that the execution of the document by the wife was procured by undue influence by the husband and the wife had no independent advice. This is clear law.

Where the activities of the principal debtor in procuring the participation of the secondary debtor was not authorised by the lenders and the latter have no knowledge, or reason to suspect, that undue influence was brought to bear, they are not tainted by that influence (*Coldunell Ltd* v *Gallon* [1986] QB 1184).

Misrepresentation In practice it would appear that innocent misrepresentation is the defence most often employed to avoid a suretyship obligation. The general principle is that there is no duty to disclose so long as there is no misrepresentation. Nonetheless, where the creditor, typically a bank, purports to explain the extent of the guarantee, it must not do so negligently, otherwise liability will sound in damages (*Cornish* v *Midland Bank plc* [1985] 3 All ER 513).

Non est factum The presumption is that the guarantor will be bound by the terms of the written guarantee upon the appending of his signature. However he will be able to escape liability by pleading *non est factum*, 'not my deed'. Here a heavy evidentiary burden must be displaced because it will be necessary for the defendant to show both that he had acted carefully, and that he was not aware of the nature of the document that he had signed (*Saunders* v *Anglia Building Society* [1971] AC 1004).

Illegality Guarantees for the performance of illegal contracts are unenforceable, which provides a striking contrast to the primary liability of an indemnifier in this same circumstance. Nevertheless, if the illegality does not go to the root of the contract and there are no public policy objections, the guarantee may be enforceable following the severance of the illegal part. Thus in *Carney* v *Herbert* [1985] AC 301, Lord Brightman said in the Privy Council at p. 311:

> There are . . . two matters to be considered where a contract contains an illegal term, first, whether as a matter of construction the lawful part of the contract can be severed from the unlawful part, thus enabling the plaintiff to sue on a promise unaffected by any illegality; secondly, whether, despite severability, there is a bar to enforceability arising out of the nature of the illegality.

In that case, it was held that the illegal mortgage under New South Wales legislation did not go to the basis of the transaction, so the primary obligations of the vendors and the purchaser still remained.

A guarantee of the liabilities of a minor incurred after 9 June 1987 will now be enforceable against the guarantor under s. 2 of the Minors' Contracts Act 1987.

It is worth emphasising at the end of this section that the legal presumptions identified above can be excluded under the terms of the guarantee contract. Typically, standard-form guarantees make such exclusions, for example, that the creditor's rights against the surety shall not be prejudiced or affected by the grant of any time or indulgence to the debtor or a co-surety, or by the creditor's failure to take, perfect or hold unimpaired any security taken from the debtor or a co-surety.

The legal position of the surety in relation to the debtor
The surety's liability extends not merely to the primary undischarged indebtedness, but also to any secondary liability for damages incurred by the debtor as a result of repudiating the principal contract. Indeed, the creditor's election to accept the debtor's repudiation can be viewed as the enforcement of the guarantee. This can be illustrated by the decision of the House of Lords

in *Moschi* v *Lep Air Services Ltd* [1973] AC 331. In this case, the appellant guaranteed the obligations of a company under an agreement by which the company undertook to discharge its existing indebtedness to the respondents by instalments. The company failed to pay the instalments on several occasions and the respondents treated the default as constituting a repudiation of the contract. The appellant (guarantor) maintained that this discharged him from liability as the actions of the respondents constituted an unauthorised variation of the contract. Had this contention been maintained by the House of Lords, the whole basis of the guarantee would have been eroded. However, the House of Lords held that the appellant's true liability was not for payment of the instalments but for the performance of the company's obligations (see also *Hyundai Heavy Industries Co. Ltd* v *Papadopoulos* [1980] 1 WLR 1129).

Rights of the surety: indemnity and contribution Where the guarantee was given at the request of the debtor, the surety has a right to be indemnified by the debtor for liability properly incurred. Where the guarantee is provided at the request of the creditor only, typically where a finance house insists that a car dealer guarantees the liability of the consumer under a hire-purchase contract, the guarantor will have no right of indemnity, as such, although the right of subrogation is unaffected in this circumstance (see below).

Where there are co-sureties, in the absence of a contrary agreement, if one surety has paid more than his *pro rata* share under the guarantee, he is entitled to a contribution against all other sureties for the same liabilities on the basis of the equitable maxim 'equality is equity'. In practice, where there are co-sureties the agreement will normally provide for the liabilities of the co-sureties to be joint and several. In this situation, s. 3 of the Civil Liability (Contribution) Act 1987 provides as follows:

> Judgment recovered against any person liable in respect of any debt or damage shall not be a bar to an action, or to the continuance of an action, against any other person who is (apart from any such bar) jointly liable with him in respect of the same damage.

Guarantors must contribute in proportion to the shares of the debt for which they have agreed to make themselves responsible (*Steel* v *Dixon* (1881) 17 ChD 825). Of course, there is nothing to stop an arrangement whereby one guarantor may be himself backed by secondary guarantees. In this circumstance, contribution cannot be claimed from such a subsurety as he undertakes no liability except on the surety's default, and he is entitled, in any case, to be indemnified by the surety for whom he gives his subguarantee (*Scholefield Goodman and Sons Ltd* v *Zyngier* [1986] AC 562).

Right of the surety: recourse to security By virtue of s. 5 of the Mercantile Law Amendment Act 1856, where the creditor has taken security for the debt, a surety who is required to make payment under the guarantee is entitled to have recourse to that security. Indeed, a guarantor in this situation can stand in the place of the creditor and rank as a preferential creditor (*Re Lamplugh Iron Ore*

Co. Ltd [1927] 1 Ch 308). The surety's right to the security, in the absence of an express term to the contrary, has priority over any rights of the creditor even in relation to other debts owed to the creditor in relation to which the security was also taken (*Leicestershire Banking Co. Ltd* v *Hawkins* (1900) TLR 317). It is common practice for bank guarantees to contain express agreement to the contrary.

Rights of the surety: subrogation This doctrine allows the guarantor to stand in the shoes of the creditor in respect of the latter's rights against the debtor regarding any securities held by the creditor. There can be no right of subrogation until the guarantor has extinguished his liability; partial fulfilment of liability gives no right of *pro rata* subrogation. A creditor has a duty of care to ensure that he does not prejudice the rights of the surety with respect to the security. As Pollock CB put it in *Watts* v *Shuttleworth* (1860) 5 H & N 235 at p. 247:

> The substantial question in the case is, whether the omission to insure [the secured property] discharges the defendant, the surety. The rule upon the subject seem to be that if the person guaranteed does any act injurious to the surety, or inconsistent with his rights, or if he omits to do any act which his duty enjoins him to do, and the omission proves injurious to the surety, the latter will be discharged.

(See also *China and South Sea Bank Ltd* v *Tan Soon Gin* [1990] 1 AC 536.)

Subrogation is a right given by law to prevent the unjust enrichment of the debtor. It should be noted that the right is limited to what is necessary for the guarantor to recoup the money actually paid by him to discharge the liability; any surplus is disgorged to the principal debtor.

THE IMPACT OF INSOLVENCY

In part 5 the legal regulation of corporate insolvency is discussed. For the purposes of the discussion below, it is assumed that the guarantee contract is not vulnerable to attack under the new insolvency legal regime.

The insolvency of the debtor

The general principle of equity is that until the creditor has received payment *in full* of the guaranteed debt, the surety cannot prove in the insolvent's estate for a sum paid by him to the creditor (*Ellis* v *Emmanuel* (1876) 1 ExD 157; *Re Sass* [1896] 2 QB 12). The reasoning behind this rule is that if the creditor were required to give credit in this situation, neither the creditor nor the surety could prove in the insolvency for the amount of the part payment, thereby unjustly enriching the general body of creditors who are adequately protected by a separate rule against double proof of the same debt. It is otherwise where the surety has guaranteed only part of the debt and paid that part. In this situation, the surety becomes entitled to prove in respect of the part debt so paid unless this is excluded by the terms of the original guarantee.

In the case of a negotiable instrument, the creditor who receives part payment from the endorser/acceptor whose position is analogous to that of a surety must reduce his proof by the amount of that payment (*Re Blackburne* (1892) 9 Morr 249; *Re Houlder* [1929] 1 Ch 205). The reasons for the exception to the general rule are unclear and the position appears anomalous in the light of the fact that where payment is received *after* the creditor has lodged his proof, he need not give credit for any sum(s) received. This would appear to offend the principle of double proof because the debt owed to the surety is not independent of that which he has guaranteed. Of course, the general rule is that the creditor may lodge a proof for the full balance outstanding and, simultaneously, sue the surety for the debt; the discharge of the debtor does not affect the surety's liability (s. 281(7) of the Insolvency Act 1986).

The insolvency of the surety
The general rule is that the creditor must deduct from the amount of his proof against the surety's assets sums received before but not after proof. The relevant date for taking account of these payments made by the principal debtor is the date the proof against the surety is submitted and not the date it is admitted (*Re Amalgamated Investment and Property Co. Ltd* [1985] Ch 349). In the case where the surety has only guaranteed part of the debt, it is a matter of appropriation as between the debtor and creditor whether the payment is to be attributed to the guaranteed part of the indebtedness (*Re Sherry* (1884) 25 ChD 692).

In the case of a negotiable instrument, the creditor must credit sums received before proof from *any* party liable on the bill, but sums received after proof need not be deducted (*Re London, Bombay and Mediterranean Bank* (1874) LR 9 Ch App 686).

The co-surety Payments received from a co-surety do not have to be deducted by the creditor even if received before submission of the proof against the surety's assets (*Re Blakeley* (1892) 9 Morr 173). The rule against double proof prevents the co-surety from proof unless he has paid to the creditor in full, whereupon he becomes subrogated to the rights of the creditor (s. 5 of the Mercantile Law Amendment Act 1856).

The insolvency of both the debtor and surety
Such a scenario is not an unlikely one in the light of the so-called 'ripple effect' phenomenon, that is, the insolvency of one firm which affects other firms who are major creditors, or where there is a failure of both a subsidiary and a parent company. The general rule is that the creditor is entitled to maintain a proof in both estates for the full amount of the debt, subject to him not receiving more than the full amount of the total indebtedness. Again, it is otherwise in the case of negotiable instruments where credit must be given for both sums received and dividends declared if he has *already* lodged his proof in one estate. Once proof has been submitted, he is not obliged to revise this in the light of any receipts or declarations of dividend from the other estate (*Re London, Bombay and Mediterranean Bank* (1874) LR 9 Ch App 686).

QUASI-GUARANTEES

The commercial *sense* of a guarantee as simply an undertaking by a contracting party is often championed by English courts, notwithstanding that this does not cohere with the strict legal sense of the word. Where a financial institution issues a 'guarantee' which matures on virtually any evidence of default, this cannot be characterised as a guarantee in the strict legal sense as it is essentially an independent primary obligation. Various types of bank 'guarantees' exist but there are two major categories: a bank guarantee will either be a conditional or demand guarantee. In the case of a demand guarantee, the bank must pay the beneficiary on first demand. This is by far the most frequently used type of guarantee in international transactions. Under a conditional guarantee the bank will not pay unless certain conditions, as the name suggests, are met. These may include the production of a document showing that a judgment or award in favour of the beneficiary has been made; a certificate issued by an independent third party showing that the beneficiary has become entitled to the guarantee, or a written statement of the beneficiary in proper form, if any, stating that the other party has defaulted. The types of bank guarantees or bonds that the seller may be asked to provide include performance, bid or tender, repayment/advance payment, retention money and maintenance guarantees or bonds. In addition, there are counter-guarantees, superguarantees and syndicated bond facilities, all of which may either be first-demand or conditional guarantees.

Performance-based guarantees
Bank guarantees in export trade are based on the principle that parties to a contract of sale must honour their obligations or else lose money for non-performance or mal-performance. Such guarantees may be arranged by either the seller or the buyer. A seller may insist on a bank guarantee to be arranged by the buyer in order to ensure that a certain agreed and guaranteed payment will be received from the bank if the buyer fails to take up the goods. On the other hand, a buyer may insist that the seller secures a bank guarantee in order to ensure that the buyer gets a payment immediately the seller fails to deliver the goods, or delivers non-contractual goods. These types of guarantees are known as performance guarantees or performance bonds.

There are very difficult definitional problems encountered in this context. Sometimes, a performance bond is equated with an undertaking by an insurance company or financial institution to provide recompense for the principal debtor's failure to perform. In contrast, a first-demand guarantee is an undertaking to make a payment (usually between 5 and 10 per cent of the contract price) at the request of the beneficiary. The characteristic of the first-demand bond is its irrevocable nature and its independence from the underlying contract. The bank must pay even where the seller raises objections, no matter how genuine those objections might be, excepting, of course, established fraud. (See especially *United Trading Corpn SA* v *Allied Arab Bank Ltd* [1985] 2 Lloyd's Rep 554. Compare *IE Contractors Ltd* v *Lloyds Bank plc* [1990] 2 Lloyd's Rep 496.) The classical explanation for such a bond is that it overcomes the 'gap of distrust' that exists in (especially) international trade because the buyer and seller are separated from each other not only by distance but also by differences in culture, society and economics. Since the buyer must commit resources in advance to the performance of the seller, it is natural for the buyer to look to a third party of high repute, for example, to guarantee the performance of the seller by undertaking to pay certain sums of money on the occurrence of stated conditions. The bond is seen as an important mechanism to reduce commercial risk factors from the buyer's perspective as it will not be affected by frustrating events such as the outbreak of war between the exporter's and importer's countries. This provides a striking contrast with the liability of a surety which is coextensive with that of the principal debtor (see above). Moreover, the fact that the third-party obligation is a bond and, therefore, under seal is significant because it avoids the jurisprudential puzzle of finding consideration as seen in the context of irrevocable letters of credit in international trade.

Performance bonds which envisage the guarantor taking over the principal's obligation, or which are contingent upon the non-performance of the underlying contract are not usually issued by banks. Such conditional bonds are uncontentious as English law will only allow recovery to the extent of the loss actually incurred or suffered. Indeed, Lord Atkin said in *Trade Indemnity Co. Ltd* v *Workington Harbour and Dock Board* [1937] AC 1 at p. 21 that a particularly wide-ranging clause preserving the liability of a surety for an alteration or variation of a contract would be restrictively construed 'so as not to include such changes as have been suggested as substituting a cathedral for a dock, or the construction of a dock elsewhere, or possibly such an enlargement of the works as would double the financial liability'. Such bonds are issued by specialist English insurance or bonding companies who, when assessing a contractor's status regarding the possibility of issuing a bond, not only consider the general financial standing of the contractor but crucially take into account its *technical capacity* to perform the work in the light of all the circumstances including present commitments.

As we have noted above, in the case of the conditional type of bond, the normal rules of surety-creditor-debtor apply. Thus, the surety's liability will only arise upon the principal debtor's default and will generally be circumscribed by any act of misconduct on the part of the creditor. Significantly, where there is a material variation in the terms of the principal contract, the surety will be discharged from liability (*Browne* v *Carr* (1831) 7 Bing 508). This rule could prove extremely onerous especially in construction contracts where extension of time for completion is quite common. In order to cover this problem, the matter is anticipated in the original performance bond by expressly retaining the surety's liability where the contract is so varied (see, for example, the Institute of Civil Engineers' standard-form performance bond). Clearly, where the variation is so extensive that it destroys the character of the contract then a new surety contract would have to be negotiated.

Advance payment or repayment guarantees
This type of guarantee is secured by a seller under a contract that requires the

Guarantees

buyer to make advance payment of a percentage of the sale price. The purpose of the guarantee by the seller is to provide a refund-source of money for the buyer in the event that the seller fails to deliver the goods. Under these circumstances, the buyer can call the advance payment guarantee to recoup the advance payment.

Retention money guarantee or bond
These are used mainly in contracts which call for a percentage of each payment made by the buyer to be withheld until the project is completed and accepted by the buyer or employer (in construction contracts). The Joint Contracts Tribunal's (JCT) standard-form contracts include such a retention clause (clause 30.2 JCT 80 as amended). The clause provides that out of the amount due and payable under an architect's interim certificate, the employer can retain a proportion for a set period. If within this period defects appear in the contractor's work, the employer can use the retention moneys to cover the cost of setting the defects right. Such a clause benefits the employer in two ways: first, it provides a virtually costless means of recovery against the contractor; secondly, it avoids the risk of the insolvency of the contractor.

The juridical basis of such a retention clause is interesting as it essentially treats the employer as being a trustee of a debt *which he owes*. Although the employer's duty as a fiduciary has recently been confirmed by the Court of Appeal in *Wates Construction (London) Ltd* v *Franthom Property Ltd* (1991) 53 BLR 23, difficulties will inevitably arise where an insolvent employer has failed to set aside the retention moneys in a separate fund. On this eventuality, there is no separate (identifiable) trust property so the contractor is left to prove his claim as an unsecured creditor (see *Re Jartay Developments Ltd* (1982) 22 BLR 134). In the case of a solvent employer, the contractor will usually succeed in an application for specific performance of the obligation to set aside and constitute a separate trust fund of the retention moneys on the basis of the equitable maxim that equity looks on that as done which ought to be done (*Re Arthur Sanders Ltd* (1981) 17 BLR 125). Where there is a contractual provision to open a separate account for the retention moneys withheld, the court will normally grant a mandatory injunction to require such a fund to be established in order to protect the contractor against the employer's insolvency (*Concorde Construction Co. Ltd* v *Colgan Co. Ltd* (1984) 29 BLR 120).

Counter-guarantees or bonds
Counter-guarantees arise where the buyer or employer in sales and construction contracts asks the (usually foreign) seller or contractor to provide a performance guarantee. In the case of a foreign seller, the latter will arrange for the performance guarantee to be issued by a local bank in his own country. That bank in the seller's country, in turn, gives a guarantee to a bank in the country of the buyer (employer) but not directly to the buyer. It is then the local bank in the country of the buyer that issues the performance guarantee to the buyer. This may be illustrated diagrammatically as follows:

```
Country of Seller                    Country of Buyer
Seller ────────▶ Bank ────────▶ Bank ────────▶ Buyer
       ╲                   ╲
        ▶ Counter-          ╲
          indemnity           ▶ Indemnity
           ╲                       ╲
            ▶ Counter-performance   ▶ Performance
              guarantee               guarantee
```

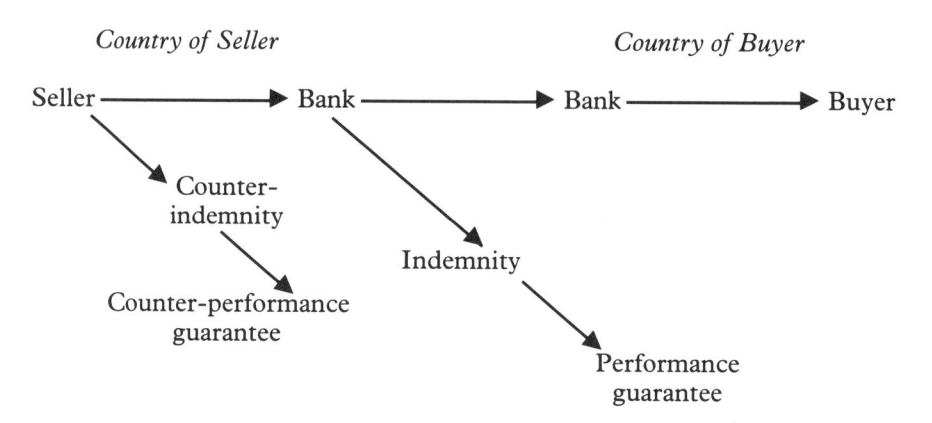

The counter-indemnity provided by the seller to his local bank is a security for the bank's issuance of the performance guarantee on his behalf. Likewise the bank, in turn, gives an indemnity to the bank in the country of the buyer as security for that bank's issuance of the performance guarantee to the buyer. The buyer is happy as he only has to look to the local bank for the satisfaction of the performance guarantee arranged by the seller. As such, the arrangement is similar to that of a back-to-back credit.

Superguarantees

A superguarantee, though not very common, arises where the beneficiary of the performance guarantee insists on another bank providing an additional guarantee in support of the first. He does this where the performance guarantee is issued by a bank which is not well-known in banking and business circles. The little-known bank guarantees to reimburse by counter-indemnity all payments made by the superguarantor, i.e., the well-known bank. Again the superguarantee must correspond to the terms and conditions of the first performance guarantee. In effect, the first bank's guarantee is replaced by that of the second guarantor bank and it is this second guarantee that is known as a superguarantee.

Syndicated bond facilities

In major international construction contracts, contract guarantees can be very large indeed. In order to spread the risk assumed by guarantors, the guarantees are issued as syndicated bond facilities. Several banks get together and provide an indemnity to the bank that issues the performance bond. In this way, no one bank takes on the huge risks attendant on unconditional demand bonds. In the event that the employer calls in the bond, the issuing bank pays the guarantee and falls back on the indemnity agreement between itself and the participating banks for any loss suffered.

PART 5 CORPORATE INSOLVENCY

EIGHTEEN
The framework of corporate insolvency law

INTRODUCTION

Insolvency is concerned with the situation where upon the balance of liabilities and assets, the debtor has insufficient assets to discharge, in full, all the liabilities at the time of falling due. Inability to pay should be carefully distinguished from reluctance to pay, for example, to keep the debtor out of the assets, or because of some dispute relating to those assets. This last issue focuses upon the relationship of the parties *inter se* as an aspect of freedom of contract, where the creditor is not concerned with the rights or interests of other creditors of the same debtor. It is otherwise with insolvency because the collectivisation of the procedure avoids the deleterious consequence of creditors seeking individual remedies. Insolvency proceedings form an important exception to the general hostility of English law to class actions, so s. 130(4) of the Insolvency Act 1986 provides that an order for winding up operates in favour of all creditors and contributories of the company as if made on a joint petition of a creditor and of a contributory.

Insolvency proceedings form a consistent legal accompaniment to the institution of credit-borrowing against future income. In a society where the medium of exchange was simultaneous, as in the case of barter or cash sales, there would never be a situation where an individual's financial status was that liabilities exceeded assets. Of course, this does not mean that even in this type of society financial ruin was impossible, for example, where there had been a breach of contract or tortious injury sounding in damages.

A distinction should be drawn between the fact of insolvency and the *status* of bankruptcy (in the case of an individual) or wound up (in the case of a company). In the case of insolvency, it is possible for insolvency proceedings to take place in response to a cash-flow crisis, that is, where assets are not *sufficiently* liquid to satisfy present liabilities or, alternatively, insolvency proceedings may be initiated in the case of absolute or balance sheet insolvency where the total debts, present, future, contingent, exceed the assets even if they were realised at their most favourable value. Bankruptcy is a status conferred by the law, namely, a creditor to whom full and timely payment has been made can initiate insolvency proceedings on the basis that the debtor's insolvency can be inferred from the circumstances. The effect of this is that a company may be wound up merely because it has refused to pay one debt which it could afford to discharge. We shall consider this matter more fully at the end of this chapter.

HISTORICAL DEVELOPMENT OF THE LAW

It is important to consider briefly the historical background of the law because herein lies the explanation for perhaps the most unique characteristic of English law which is the distinction drawn between the insolvency of individuals and corporate insolvency. Despite the fact that the Cork committee report, *Insolvency Law and Practice* (Cmnd 8558, London, 1982), was concerned with developing a coherent and unified insolvency law, nevertheless, the distinction still persists.

At first, the common law did not concern itself with bankruptcy; it was an institution of the law merchant. It was from the 14th century onwards that the common law courts, over a period of time, superseded the local courts merchant and courts maritime on the basis that the law administered here was a part of the common law of England. Bankruptcy emerged in England in 1542 when Parliament enacted 'An Act Against Such Persons As Do Make Bankrupt' (34 and 35 Hen 8 c 4), which was concerned with dealing with absconding debtors through crimininalising them and also providing for rateable distribution among creditors. Interestingly, the name 'bankruptcy' derives from statutes of Italian city States where it was referred to as *banca rupta* after a mediaeval custom of breaking the bench of a banker or tradesman who absconded with the property of his creditors.

The original English bankruptcy Act referred to above was further supplemented by a statute outlawing fraudulent conveyances (the Fraudulent Conveyances Act 1572, 13 Eliz 1 c 5; the Bankrupts Act 1572, 13 Eliz 1 c 7). The application of these early statutes was confined to 'insolvent traders' which demonstrated the law merchant roots. It was not until the Bankruptcy Act 1861 that the provisions of bankruptcy applied to all debtors, irrespective of whether they were traders or not. Before that time, individuals were subjected to the rigours of individual creditor remedies and especially debtors' prison.

Distinction between personal and corporate insolvency

The rise of corporate insolvency as a separate branch of law in England came about with the development of the limited liability concept during the first half of the 19th century. Under the Companies Winding Up Act 1844, the legislature treated insolvent companies as a species of individual bankruptcy. Parliament enacted the Joint Stock Companies Act 1844 which provided for the incorporation of a company as a distinct legal entity, although members were still liable for the debts since incorporation could be revoked, so proceedings took place in the Bankruptcy Court. An element of confusion emerged with the Joint Stock Companies Winding-up Act 1848, whereby shareholders of a company could bring about its dissolution via a winding up petition presented to the Chancery Court. This overlapping jurisdiction caused confusion and this was not finally resolved until the Joint Stock Companies Act 1856 and the Joint Stock Companies Winding-up Amendment Act 1857 left winding up exclusively in the province of the Court of Chancery. Herein lay the foundation for the distinctive development of corporate insolvency law unknown to most other systems of law other than those systems which have closely followed England including New Zealand, Australia and Ireland.

It was not until the Limited Liability Act 1855 which confirmed the status of limited liability for members that corporate insolvency took on a distinctive status. From 1862 with the passing of the first modern company law statute, insolvency evolved into specialised branches whose provisions were contained in two separate sets of statutes — the Bankruptcy Acts and the Companies Acts — administered in different courts under different sets of procedural rules. This is not to say that they did not share common doctrines, for example, the doctrine of fraudulent preference was made directly applicable to the winding up of companies by the Joint Stock Companies Act 1856, and provable debts were shared in common. Even after the consolidation of the whole law of insolvency following the Cork Committee report in 1982, and the changes made to the Companies Act 1985 by the Insolvency Act 1985 consolidated by the Insolvency Act 1986 which repealed and re-enacted the Insolvency Act 1985 and most of the provisions of the Companies Act 1985, fundamental differences in treatment still exist between the two branches of insolvency law. A small group of provisions of the Insolvency Act 1985 concerned with the disqualification of company directors were separately consolidated together with similar provisions drawn from the Companies Act 1985, and enacted as the Company Directors Disqualification Act 1986 which came into force at the same time as the Insolvency Act 1986.

The agitation for reform
English law has been conspicuous for its lack of an overall systematic treatment of the law relating to credit, security and insolvency. Thus, only certain aspects of the debtor-creditor relationship were examined by the Payne committee, *Report of the Committee on Judgment Debts* (Cmnd 3909, London, 1969) and the Crowther committee, *Report of the Committee on Consumer Credit* (Cmnd 4596, London, 1971). Moreover, no comprehensive review of insolvency law was undertaken before the setting up of the Cork committee in 1977. In part, the stimulus for setting up this committee was twofold: first, the worsening economic position and the ravages of inflation highlighted the inadequacies of existing insolvency law; second, the accession of the UK to the EEC necessitated an examination of the implication of the adoption of the Draft EEC Bankruptcy Convention by the UK. Indeed, the Cork advisory committee which was set up to consider this question concluded that a review of insolvency law was urgently required as a matter of practical necessity, so to allow the UK to participate effectively on the EEC stage. A committee was

appointed to consider insolvency law and practice under the aegis of Sir Kenneth Cork in January 1977. This was a review committee set up by the Secretary of State for Trade; it is regrettable that the Law Commission in England and Wales has never had any formal involvement in the reform of the law in this area despite its obvious significance to the law in general. In contrast, the Scottish Law Commission has not been so sanguine in this respect and Scottish bankruptcy law has appeared as part of their programme of law reform.

It is unfortunate that the Cork committee's terms of reference did not include a general review of the law of credit and security nor the issue of the remedies available for debt enforcement. Furthermore, the lack of resources made available to the committee precluded sustained empirical work. This contrasts starkly with the US Bankruptcy Reform Act 1978 which had the benefit of well-funded research. The final report published in 1982 recommended a fundamental reform of insolvency which found expression in the Insolvency Act 1986. Before focusing upon the reverberations of this Act in the context of corporate insolvency, a preliminary issue which needs to be examined concerns the identification of the objectives and principles of insolvency law.

OBJECTIVES AND PRINCIPLES OF INSOLVENCY LAW

The objectives and principles of insolvency law are set out in ch. 4 of the Cork committee report (1982).

The objectives of insolvency law

The objectives of insolvency law may be stated as follows including the matters identified below.

To recognise the social and financial implications of insolvency One of the aims of insolvency law is to ensure the rescue of companies in financial difficulty which recognises the need to preserve employment. The Insolvency Act 1986 envisages the appointment of an administrator as the official corporate rescuer whilst, at the same time, the continued existence of the company is facilitated by suspending the rights and remedies of individual creditors. However, it is simplistic to argue that the exclusive role of insolvency law is to keep firms in operation. Not all businesses are worth more as a going concern than as a gone concern. The real issue is one of identifying *which* companies insolvency law should assist and why.

The *effect* of insolvency proceedings is that directors are in practice divested of their management powers and unless specifically retained to assist an insolvency practitioner, it is the latter who performs the management functions of the company. In this respect, the Cork committee considered at para. 198(g) that one of the aims of a modern insolvency law was 'to ensure that the processes of realisation and distribution are administered in an honest and competent manner'. This is ensured under ss. 230(2) and 390 to 392 of the Insolvency Act 1986 by requiring insolvency practitioners to be qualified by authorisation from a recognised professional body, the Secretary of State, or a competent authority designated by the Secretary of State (see Insolvency Practitioners (Recognised Professional Bodies) Order 1986, SI 1986, No. 1764).

To provide for the orderly distribution of assets and ranking of claims This involves identifying both assets and liabilities. Valuation of entitlements is at the moment before collective proceedings started, so rights are frozen as of that time. One of the issues is the determination of what the rights are worth in the abstract, that is, the nominal value which disregards insolvency. The fact is that the debtor is insolvent, so the issue then translates itself into one of relative value, namely, who gets what and in what order.

Determining issues of culpability for insolvency and protection of the public One major function of insolvency litigation is the imposition of criminal and/or civil liability on a manager of the company who has been guilty of culpable acts or omissions causing loss to creditors, and his reporting to the Secretary of State on the basis of his apparent unfitness as a director concerned with the management of a company. In order to protect the public against future delinquent or improper trading, a disqualification process is included.

The principles of insolvency law

The basis of insolvency law is debt-collection, that is, where debts are more than assets. The role of insolvency law is to determine two main questions: do we place limits on what creditors take from their creditors? How do we decide competing claims as between creditors? The number and type of creditors are multifarious, for example, bank or trade creditors, a worker who works a month in hand, the government as a tax collector, involuntary creditors such as tort claimants.

The fundamental principles which underlie the Insolvency Act 1986 are not easily extracted from it so that, in effect, this Act is not the best place to start any investigation of the principles of the law. Nevertheless, the principles which emerge can be simply stated.

Corporate insolvency law recognises pre-insolvency entitlements Insolvency collectivises what have been, hitherto, individual remedies. It should not change the issue of pre-insolvency entitlements because this will prejudice the goal of insolvency law which includes collective interest, by introducing self-interest through providing an incentive for a creditor to liquidate the debtor company. In this respect, the liquidator stands in no better position than the company itself and will take subject to the same rights and defences accorded under the general law to the debtor. However, the liquidator may enjoy the benefit of asserting defences which the company could not have raised prior to the liquidation, for example, transactions at an undervalue or preference (ss. 238 to 243 of the Insolvency Act 1986).

For shareholders, liquidation fixes their status which cannot be altered by post-liquidation divestment of their shares (s. 88 of the Insolvency Act 1986).

Even so, members of a company are not, as such, liable for its debts which is a concomitant of corporate personality, that is, the separation of the company from its members. Perhaps the most celebrated decision in this context is *Salomon v A. Salomon and Co. Ltd* [1897] AC 22, where a shareholder of a company, by virtue of holding a debenture over the company's assets to secure payment over value provided by him, enjoyed priority over unsecured creditors when the company became insolvent. The courts are reluctant to pierce the corporate veil and visit liability on its members, and will only do so when the establishment of a company was a creature designed for fraud. Of course, members of a company may incur personal liability by way of guarantee, or where the company acts as their agent.

Creditors rank pari passu Insolvency is concerned with solving a common pool problem which, in turn, invites scrutiny of the issue of *relative* values. Collective action is prejudiced if a secured creditor can remove collateral from the debtor's estate and remain outside the collective proceedings. Herein lies the rationale for the *pro rata* treatment of general unsecured creditors on the basis of equality in equity. It is one of the most fundamental principles of corporate insolvency law.

The *pari passu* principle does not mean that the value of the secured creditor's entitlement cannot be respected, even in a collective proceeding. Thus, a creditor has an immediate right of proof of debts, including those payable in the future or on a contingency, so the debts are effectively accelerated. Future debts not due are discounted (r. 11.13 of the Insolvency Rules 1986) whilst contingent debts are valued (r. 4.86(1) of the Insolvency Rules 1986). Since there are no bargained-for rights in the case of unsecured creditors, it is consistent with principle that a similarly situated group (unsecured creditors) should split their assets on a *pro rata* basis. Of course, distributive justice issues may arise in the context of insolvency, for example, a worker has not got a diversified portfolio of investments as maybe a general creditor enjoys and, therefore, a worker should be preferred because he has more to lose. However, reallocating values is not an insolvency issue, rather, it is a matter of public policy which is perhaps informed by issues of distributive justice.

Insolvency is a collective proceeding and involves a statutory trust Insolvent liquidation is no more than a forum, a collective and mandatory one, for the translation of the assets and liabilities of the debtor. Because it is a collective procedure, the court will not allow a creditor to obtain a collateral personal advantage, for example, a petition presented ostensibly for winding up but in reality to obtain a forfeiture of the company's lease is an abuse of process (*Re a Company* [1983] BCLC 492). The collective nature of insolvency proceedings is emphasised by s. 130(4) of the Insolvency Act 1986, which provides that an order for winding up operates in favour of all creditors and contributories of the company as if made on a joint petition of a creditor and of a contributory.

The collectivisation of insolvency proceedings is mandatory, so it binds all unsecured creditors. An important adjunct to this is s. 153 of the Insolvency

Act 1986 which allows the court to fix a time within which creditors must prove their claims or otherwise be excluded. The basic problem that insolvency law is designed to handle is the system of *individual* remedies which are bad for creditors, as a group, where there are insufficient assets to satisfy all the demands. The defects with individual creditor remedies can be identified as follows:

(a) Individual creditor remedies may lead to a piecemeal dismantling of a debtor's business by the untimely removal of necessary operating assets.

(b) If there were no collective system there would only be a grab system. This would have serious repercussions for risk-averse creditors who derive an advantage in their risk assessment from having a collective proceeding.

(c) There are costs involved in the individualised approach. A theoretical justification for the collectivisation of actions in insolvency proceedings is that it reflects the kind of contract that creditors would agree to if they were able to negotiate with each other before extending credit. The allusion here is to John Rawl's notion in *A Theory of Justice* (New York, 1972) of bargaining in the 'original position' behind a 'veil of ignorance'.

(d) Since insolvency is a collective action, it has its own costs which may lead creditors to act consensually as between themselves to avoid these costs, for example, through subordination agreements (see below pp. 437–40).

The collective assets and realisations are held on statutory trust. The creditors have no proprietary interest of any kind in the assets or realisations (*Ayerst* v *C & K (Construction) Ltd* [1976] AC 167). During the process of winding up, the company holds the asset not on behalf of persons but rather for statutory purposes. The effect of this is that creditors' rights are confined to involving the protection of the court to ensure that the liquidator fulfils his statutory duties. The liquidator's duties are owed to the creditors as a whole.

Insolvency proceedings involve scrutiny of the question of identification both of the assets and the pool of owners. How the rights of secured creditors, unsecured creditors and shareholders are identified as between themselves is a question of non-bankruptcy entitlements. We shall return to this theme in succeeding chapters.

NINETEEN
The state of insolvency and its legal regime

THE TESTS FOR INSOLVENCY

The onset of insolvency proceedings is a signal to the world at large that the firm is experiencing financial difficulties. Such proceedings have information connotations which can be harmful to the firm, for example, it might find it difficult to get buyers for its products because of the fear that it will not be able to honour its warranties. In addition, the firm may find it difficult to collect debts because of the 'lame duck' syndrome, that is, the firm no longer matters since there is little prospect of continuing commercial intercourse, so business occupational morality no longer operates in the sense that debtors often settle their debts out of fear of losing their commercial reputation. These factors may lead to the creation of strategic initiatives to avoid using insolvency proceedings, for example, late filing of accounts as this makes public a business's profitability and liquidity.

Undoubtedly, the financial decline of a firm is likely to be recognised first of all by the firm's managers and principal shareholders. They have no incentive to liquidate and will often play an 'end-game'; since they will get nothing, or very little, following insolvency proceedings, their incentive is to delay this day as long as possible and instead 'gamble' with the remaining assets of the firm. This has led some commentators in the US to argue in favour of providing shareholders with a counterbalancing incentive — a 'bounty' to encourage them to initiate insolvency proceedings at the appropriate time, for example, based upon a rough calculation of the net increased value of the assets owing to the use of the insolvency process and giving the shareholders a portion of the difference in value (see especially Landes and Posner, 'Private Enforcement of Law' (1975) 4 J Legal Stud 1).

When referring to the state of insolvency, the Insolvency Act 1986 equates this with the inability to pay debts. This financial condition can best be described as insolvency in the cash-flow sense where there is a genuine liquidity crisis which can objectively be recognised as such. The state of insolvency is relevant for several reasons under the Insolvency Act 1986:

(a) It is a ground for winding up (s. 122(1)(f)). This procedure may be retroactive in the sense that an earlier state of insolvency is recognised.
(b) An administration order can be made (s. 8).
(c) Liability for wrongful trading attaches to this concept (s. 214) as does an order for disqualification of a director (s. 6(1) of the Company Directors Disqualification Act 1986).
(d) Transactions at an undervalue or preferences relate to this if the company subsequently goes into administration or liquidation (ss. 238 to 242 of the Insolvency Act 1986).
(e) A floating charge for past value given by a company unable to pay its debts may be void if the company subsequently goes into administration or liquidation (ss. 238 to 242).

It should be noted that inability to pay debts establishes the statutory ground for an order under the Act. Nevertheless, the court has an inherent discretion as to whether to make the order where, for example, this would in the opinion of the court be unfair or inequitable (*Re Condon, ex parte James* (1874) LR 9 Ch App 609).

Any test devised to determine the insolvency of a firm is going to be crude because there is so much uncertainty at the beginning of a case. Perhaps a simple test would be for those advocating that a state of insolvency exists to show that there is a reasonable likelihood that the debtor is, or might become in the future, unable to pay off its creditors in full. However, this might not be sufficient where, for example, creditors may have agreed not to initiate insolvency proceedings because of start-up costs of a firm, or where technology is under development. In a start-up company, it is unlikely that the creditors will advance their interests by seeking to take over the entire firm simply because the future of the firm will often lie in the skills and knowledge of the workers of the company. As we can see then, the determination of insolvency is a difficult question.

We shall now examine the tests of inability to pay seen under the Insolvency Act 1986.

The cash-flow test
This is easy to understand as it relates to the inability of a company to pay debts as they fall due except in the case of a good-faith dispute relating to indebtedness. Only due debts are considered, namely, liquidated *demands* — debts which are technically due in, such as overdrafts, are ignored unless called in. As such, default in payment is sufficient evidence of inability to pay. Thus, in the celebrated case of *Cornhill Insurance plc* v *Improvement Services Ltd* [1986] 1 WLR 114, it was held, refusing to continue an *ex parte* injunction, that the defendants were entitled to present a petition for winding up against a prosperous insurance company where the latter was tardy in paying out an agreed insurance claim sum (£1,154) relating to damage by fire (see also *Re a Company (No. 003079 of 1990)* [1991] BCLC 235).

The balance sheet test

This involves a scrutiny of the assets of the company and the determination of the question whether these are sufficient to discharge the liabilities of the company. Often this is referred to as 'insolvency in the bankruptcy sense'. Inevitably some element of prophetic ability is necessary here, especially the valuation of the assets *vis-à-vis* liabilities as this will include contingent liabilities. A company which is a going concern is more likely to satisfy the balance sheet test for solvency since its break-up value will be less than its assets in use value. There are significant problems here in determining the relevant date for the valuation of the assets, for example, where the business, despite attempts to do so, cannot be sold as a going concern.

The balance sheet test is the only test applied in relation to 'inability to pay debts' for the purpose of wrongful trading because creditors only suffer a loss on winding up where assets are insufficient in relation to the liabilities (s. 214). Furthermore, it is the only test applied for the purpose of the disqualification of directors under s. 6 of the Company Directors Disqualification Act 1986.

The issue of what a liability is will clearly be wider than the payment of *debts* as they fall due. The term 'contingent liability' is potentially very wide and it would appear that the most prudent approach, to give it some legal meaning, would be to confine it to a liability which may arise out of an *existing* legal commitment, for example, where the company is a defendant or prospective defendant (in the sense that action is already contemplated) in a claim for negligence which may or may not succeed. Prospective liabilities would include an unmatured liability which will, in the passage of time ripen, typically, a liability on a present debt as yet unliquidated such as work in progress.

Problems of valuation can be crucial especially in marginal cases. Here the accounting treatment and the prudence concept of accounting ('true and fair view') will be crucial. To a large extent this is a term of art, and it is perfectly possible for a conflict to occur between accountants as to the issue of the valuation of the assets (see Smith, T., *Accounting for Growth*, London, 1992). The resolution of this problem must be by reference to the balance of proof — it is for the plaintiff or applicant to show that, on the balance of probabilities, the company was insolvent at the relevant time. The issue of *relevant* time is essential, especially with regard to the issue of personal liability for wrongful trading or setting aside transactions on the basis of undervalue or preference. The benefit of hindsight is of limited value here.

It is well worth noting that side by side with liabilities, there are prospective assets attached to those liabilities which should also be taken into account. An example of this can be seen where the company is an endorser of a bill of exchange where recourse may be had against other endorsers if the acceptor, as the party primarily liable, fails to pay (see chapter 9).

Other tests for inability to pay debts

In the case of winding up or administration proceedings, the Insolvency Act 1986 incorporates alternative methods of satisfying the court regarding the proof of the issue of inability to pay debts. One of the commonest methods

The state of insolvency and its legal regime 401

involves the creditor making a statutory demand for payment in a prescribed form, and if the company fails to comply with this within three weeks, a petition can be made (s. 123(1)(a)). There are some restrictions here:

(a) The failure to pay must be indicative of an inability to pay rather than a general unwillingness to pay.
(b) A statutory demand can only be made in respect of a prescribed figure — currently the minimum amount is £750. In the case of a smaller claim, the creditor has two alternatives either (a) to join with another creditor so that the value of the combined claim exceeds this figure, or (b) the creditor may fall back on the general ground that it is just equitable that the company be wound up.

A statutory demand is not the only way of demonstrating inability to pay debts. If judgment has been obtained against the company and the judgment is wholly or partly unsatisfied, this is also an indicator (s. 123(1)(b) to (d)). Like the statutory demand, this is of relevance only where the creditor's claim is for due payment. At the same time, the cash-flow test and the balance sheet test apply here, that is, it is open to the creditor to show that the debtor, having regard to contingent and prospective liabilities, cannot pay debts as they fall due (s. 123(1)(e)), or that the value of the assets is less than the amount of the debtor company's liabilities (s. 123(2)). There is one other criterion applicable in the case of an administration order, namely, the court may grant this if the company, though currently able to do so, is *likely* to become unable to pay its debts where recovery prospects are firm (s. 8(1)).

The issue of insolvency in the case of a members' voluntary winding up is treated differently under the Insolvency Act 1986. The assumption here is that the company is ultimately solvent, which is attested by a formal statutory declaration of solvency under s. 89 of the Insolvency Act 1986. Such a declaration is pursuant to the directors having made a full enquiry into the affairs of the company and that, having done so, a majority (where there are more than two directors) have formed the opinion that the company will be able to pay its debts in full within a stated period, not exceeding 12 months, from the beginning of the winding up. This declaration, if it is to have effect, must be made within five weeks preceding the date of the passing of the resolution for winding up, and it must contain a statement of the company's assets and liabilities. In theory, through this method, it is possible to circumvent the cash-flow and balance sheet tests for solvency although, in practice, if it is the case that a company's immediate future prospects (i.e., within a period of 12 months) are good, the company should in any case be able to obtain financing for debts as they fall due.

English law recognises four types of insolvency proceedings: voluntary arrangement; administration; administrative receivership; and liquidation. The effects of these proceedings vary greatly so that, for example, whilst voluntary arrangement and liquidation are primarily concerned with distribution, administration is not. Also, whilst liquidation is both collective and mandatory, administrative receivership is neither. We shall now consider the four types of insolvency proceedings in greater detail.

VOLUNTARY ARRANGEMENTS

The Cork committee report, *Insolvency Law and Practice* (Cmnd 8558, 1982), at ch. 7, recognised the need for a simple procedure whereby a company unable to pay its debts as they fall due could conclude a legally effective arrangement with its creditors. Whilst s. 425 of the Companies Act 1985 refers to a 'compromise or arrangement' which is a creditors' court-sanctioned scheme irrespective of whether or not the company is in liquidation, nevertheless, the procedure is excessively cumbersome. Indeed the Cork committee remarked at para. 419 (emphasis added):

> ... we believe that the court procedure could be substantially streamlined and greatly improved. We cannot believe that there is the need for quite so many applications to, or attendances on, the court. *We doubt whether painstaking perusal of documents by court officials with little or no experience of commerce or finance provides any real protection for creditors or contributories.*

In response to this, the Cork committee proposed a new form of voluntary arrangement (paras 419–22, 428–30) which has now been implemented in part I of the Insolvency Act 1986. The salient features of this are:

(a) It can be concluded without a court order but it constitutes a binding arrangement between the company and its creditors.

(b) Any voluntary arrangement concluded is required initially to be appraised and endorsed and then administered and implemented by a qualified insolvency practitioner.

The terms of the proposal which are seen as complementing the administration order are encapsulated in s. 1. The proposal must embody the terms of the scheme of arrangement of the company's affairs, for example, subordination agreements which envisage some kind of benefit for the creditors. Alternatively, the arrangement may sanction, more formally, a surrender of rights where creditors collectively agree to accept less than what is due to them. The arrangement is supervised by an insolvency practitioner (s. 1(2)) whose appointment assures minimum standards of competence, integrity and experience (see Insolvency Practitioners Regulations 1986 (SI 1986, No. 1995) (as amended by (SI 1986 No. 2247)) and the Insolvency Practitioners (Recognised Professional Bodies) Order 1986 (SI 1986, No. 1764)). This helps to ensure quality control which was one of the main planks of the Cork committee report.

Despite the cumbersome nature of s. 425 of the Companies Act 1985, it still has some advantages over the voluntary arrangements included in part I of the Insolvency Act 1986. The first is that the court has the power to order the distribution of assets other than in strict accordance with legal rights because s. 425 includes elaborate safeguards to protect dissenting creditors. Second, the only creditors bound by part I are those who had notice of and were entitled to vote at the meeting of the arrangement (s. 5(2)(b) of the Insolvency Act 1986). Thus, s. 6 of the Insolvency Act 1986 provides a right to challenge within a

28-day period either the approved voluntary arrangement itself, or the manner by which this approval was obtained. In contrast, under s. 425 of the Companies Act 1985, once the scheme of arrangement has been approved by the court, all creditors are bound.

THE ADMINISTRATION ORDER

Although insolvency proceedings promote the collective will, it is doubtful whether the repossession of collateral by the secured creditor should interfere with this insolvency goal since if the secured party's collateral is worth more to the firm than the third party, the collateral should end up back in the hands of the firm, notwithstanding its repossession by the secured creditor in the interim. In practice though, there is no doubt that such repossession would hinder efforts to preserve the firm as a 'going concern', and there may be substantial costs involved in repossession and subsequent repurchase. One way of balancing the tensions here is to substitute for a secured party's actual substantive *rights* a requirement that the secured creditor accept the equivalent *value* of those rights (see generally s. 43(1) of the Insolvency Act 1986). There is nothing anomalous in this approach because if the firm is worth more as a going concern than if it is broken up, giving the secured creditor the benefit of his bargain should not prevent a firm from staying together. Indeed, a failure to recognise the secured creditor's rights in full would prejudice the bankruptcy goal of ensuring that the assets are used to advance the interests of everyone.

An overall strategy advocated by the Cork committee (1982) was for the provision of effective alternatives to the winding up of an insolvent, or near-insolvent company, where there exist reasonable prospects of reviving the company. The administration order was one of the main planks to this objective. This procedure envisages the appointment of an administrator whose task is one of creative rehabilitation of the company with a view to leaving it in a better economic condition that when he found it while, at the same time, safeguarding the interests of the secured creditors.

The power to make an administration order is encapsulated in part II of the Insolvency Act 1986 (ss. 8 to 27). An administration order is defined in s. 8(2) as follows:

> An administration order is an order directing that, during the period for which the order is in force, the affairs, business and property of the company shall be managed by a person ('the administrator') appointed for the purpose by the court.

In a sense, the administrator is the official corporate 'rescuer' who attempts to salvage the company before it becomes too damaged by the problems of insolvency. In this respect, he enjoys wide-ranging powers to deal with situations which may hinder the realisation of this aim (see below).

There are three parties who can petition the court for an administration order, namely, the company, the directors or indeed any creditor of the company (s. 9(1) of the Insolvency Act 1986). Neither the Insolvency Act 1986 nor the Insolvency Rules make provision for an obligation to notify creditors generally save that s. 9(2) of the Act provides:

> Where a petition is presented to the court—
> (a) notice of the petition shall be given forthwith to any person who has appointed, or is or may be entitled to appoint, an administrative receiver of the company, and to such other persons as may be prescribed, and
> (b) the petition shall not be withdrawn except with the leave of the court.

The effect of this provision is that a person with power to appoint an administrative receiver will have an adequate opportunity of considering whether to exercise his power, which is tantamount to a veto on the appointment of an administrator (see *Re a Company (No. 00175 of 1987)* [1987] BCLC 467).

The lightweight floating charge
There are good reasons, from a chargee's point of view, why an administration order should be prevented:

(a) The administrator has a potentially unlimited tenure.
(b) The chargee loses the ability to control the timing and conduct of the realisation of his security.
(c) The administrator may not sell the property either at all or only after a long time.

In order to reduce this exposure, a first mortgagee may insist upon a floating charge, even where he has specific security, to ensure against exposure. Such a floating charge is a 'lightweight charge' because it need not contain all the covenants and restrictions found in typical floating charges. Indeed, the only restriction necessary would be a negative pledge clause, that is, restrictions on the creation of other floating charges ranking ahead of or *pari passu* with the existing floating charge.

The importance of the floating charge is demonstrated by the decision in *Re Croftbell Ltd* [1990] BCC 781, which focused upon the arguments as to the nature of the floating charge in the context of the administration order. The facts revolved around an application by a debenture holder, Benchmark Bank plc, to dismiss an administration order petition on the basis that an administrative receiver had been appointed since the petition was presented (s. 9(3) of the Insolvency Act 1986). The debenture in question related to a £1.7 million loan to purchase the company's only substantial asset, namely, the share capital of another company. This debenture appeared to create a floating charge since it stated that in consideration of Benchmark affording or continuing to afford banking facilities, the company charged by way of floating charge, the whole of its undertaking and all its property and assets as continuing security for the company's indebtedness, both present and future. It also gave the power to appoint a receiver when a petition for an administration order was presented.

The problem in this case, however, was that the company also executed a fixed charge of these shares to Benchmark, and had given a second fixed charge over the shares to another lender to secure a £400,000 advance. Therefore, the company argued that the 'floating charge' did not fall within the definition of a floating charge given by Romer J in *Re Yorkshire Woolcombers Association Ltd* [1903] 2 Ch 284 at p. 295, namely, that it had to be a charge on a class of assets of the company, present and future, which, in the ordinary course of business changed from time to time and with which the company could carry on its business in the ordinary way until crystallisation. It was argued that the shares were the only asset, and that the company had no business and did not trade, that is, it only held the shares and entered into intercompany transactions with companies in the same group. It followed from this that the class of assets would not change. In addition, if it was a floating charge, it was a mere device which was tacked on to the fixed charge that the bank had on the shares in order to avoid the possibility of an administration order. The company argued that the device should not prevent the granting of an administration order as this would defeat the purpose of the legislation.

In *Re Croftbell Ltd*, the important provision of the Insolvency Act 1986 for Vinelott J was s. 29(2) giving the definition of an administrative receiver. This meant that it was necessary to see whether the receiver was the receiver of 'the whole or substantially the whole of the company's property'. He adopted a flexible approach to the definition of floating charge and stated that Romer J was not laying down any strict and literal requirements, but was merely indicating features necessary to distinguish a floating charge from a fixed charge. A floating charge, therefore, included a charge which theoretically extended to future assets, even if when the charge was created, the company had no assets or no assets which were not the subject of a fixed charge (and which could not be dealt with without consent of a fixed charge holder). Theoretically, there was nothing to stop more assets being acquired and the company's intentions, and Benchmark's knowledge of those intentions, was irrelevant. In addition, there was no fixed charge on assets other than the shares. If there had been, it would have prevented the company making the payments that it undoubtedly was making to the parent company, and would have prevented the company entering into intergroup transactions without consent.

In a practical sense, Vinelott J did not wish to exclude the common case of floating charges given by companies who have no assets at the time the charge is given, but need the finance thereby secured for the commencement of business. However, there are profound implications for administration orders and for the drafting of debentures. All that is necessary is that a fixed charge is taken over an asset, and the floating charge covers all, or substantially all, of the company's assets which can be limited to the assets covered by the fixed charge, so long as it is theoretically possible for the company to have other assets comprised in the floating charge. Drafters will only have to ensure that they refer to a charge as floating and as covering the whole or substantially the whole of the company's property. Even so, the reference in s. 29(2) to a receiver of 'the whole (or substantially the whole) of a company's property' would suggest that only one administrative receiver can hold office at any one time, except where joint administrative receivers are appointed. If only one administrative receiver can be *in situ* at one point of time, the person with the best right to appoint an administrative receiver is the senior chargee. It would be anomalous if this right were removed by a strategic early appointment by a junior chargee who would not have a right to possession and control of the whole, or substantially the whole of the company's assets.

The decision in *Re Croftbell Ltd* is of particular importance because of the reluctance of Vinelott J to deal with the question of looking behind the form of a document to the parties' intentions in order to achieve the true purpose of the insolvency regime by ruling out of order artificial devices intended to dislodge the administration order. This would, however, be a very difficult task, fraught with difficulties, relating to intention and the scope of charges. The problem is that the Insolvency Act 1986 itself invites such devices by preserving such a crucial role for the floating charge holder to prevent an administration. It is important to recall the policy purpose for the right to veto an administration order: a creditor of substantially the whole of the assets of a company should be given the option of consenting or otherwise to the administration order. It would be anomalous to give this option to a junior creditor merely because he has a floating charge. This does not mean that lightweight charges cannot be utilised; the issue is whether, in conjunction with other fixed charges, the senior creditor has *effective* prior charges over the whole or substantially the whole of the company's assets. In combination with these fixed charges, a lightweight floating charge should enable the lender to appoint an administrative receiver which he could not do without it.

The power to make the administration order
The power of the court to make an administration order can be found in s. 8(1) and (3) of the Insolvency Act 1986, which state:

(1) Subject to this section, if the court—
   (a) is satisfied that a company is or is likely to become unable to pay its debts (within the meaning given to that expression by section 123 of this Act), and
   (b) considers that the making of an order under this section would be likely to achieve one or more of the purposes mentioned below,
the court may make an administration order in relation to the company. . . .
(3) The purposes for whose achievement an administration order may be made are—
   (a) the survival of the company, and the whole or any part of its undertaking, as a going concern;
   (b) the approval of a voluntary arrangement under part I;
   (c) the sanctioning under section 425 of the Companies Act of a compromise or arrangement between the company and any such persons as are mentioned in that section; and
   (d) a more advantageous realisation of the company's assets than would be effected on a winding up;
and the order shall specify the purpose or purposes for which it is made.

It would appear that a higher standard of persuasion is needed in s. 8(1)(a) ('satisfied') than s. 8(1)(b) ('considers'), so it will be necessary to show where the company is not insolvent at the time of the petition that it is more likely than not to become unable to pay its debts (see *Re Harris Simons Construction Ltd* [1989] 1 WLR 368).

There has been some judicial disagreement as to the quantification of the degree of probability necessary that one of the purposes for making an order under s. 8(3) would be achieved. In para. 508 of the Cork report (1982) which recommended the introduction of administratorship, a reference was made to 'a real prospect of returning to profitability or selling as a going concern'. In *Re Consumer and Industrial Press Ltd* (1987) 4 BCC 68, Peter Gibson J referred to the necessity of proving at p. 70 'that the purpose in question will more probably than not be achieved'. More recently, a lesser standard was laid down by Hoffmann J in *Re Harris Simons Construction Ltd* [1989] 1 WLR 368 at p. 371:

> For my part, therefore, I would hold that the requirements of section 8(1)(b) are satisfied if the court considers that there is a real prospect that one or more of the stated purposes may be achieved. It may be said that phrases like 'real prospect' lack precision compared with 0.5 on the scale of probability. But the courts are used to dealing in other contexts with such indications of the degree of persuasion they must feel. 'Prima facie case' and 'good arguable case' are well known examples. Such phrases are like tempo markings in music; although there is inevitably a degree of subjectivity in the way they are interpreted, they are nevertheless meaningful and useful.

This approach was confirmed in *Re Primlaks (UK) Ltd* [1989] BCLC 734, where the criterion applied was whether the purpose(s) of the administration order was 'likely' to be achieved.

Of course, it is open to any creditor, including a retention of title claimant, to oppose the making of an administration order. It may well be that such creditors will have notification of the prospect of an administration order through informal sources: local and national newspapers, drivers and sales representatives making routine calls, and the 'trade' grapevine. Even so, it is unlikely that such creditors will have sufficient detailed knowledge of the company's affairs to oppose such an order.

Notification duties after appointment Once an order is made s. 21 of the Insolvency Act 1986 and r. 2.10 of the Insolvency Rules require the administrator to give notice of the making of the administration order:

(a)   to any person who has appointed, or is or may be entitled to appoint, an administrative receiver of the company;
(b)   if an administrative receiver has been appointed to him;
(c)   if there is pending a petition for the winding up of the company, to the petitioner and also to the provisional liquidator, if any;
(d)   to the registrar of companies;

(e) by advertisement in the *London Gazette* and other newspapers he thinks are appropriate for ensuring that the order comes to the notice of the company's creditors.

Once an order is in force, s. 12(1) provides that 'Every invoice, order for goods or business letter which . . . is issued by or on behalf of the company or the administrator' on which the company's name appears has to state that the company is now subject to such an order. It is likely, for example, that the supplier of goods subject to a retention of title clause will become aware of the order through this and other mechanisms (see above). Nevertheless, he will be prevented under s. 11(3)(c) of the Act from enforcing his rights over the goods although, in general, the administrator is given no superior proprietary rights over the goods than those already enjoyed by the buyer company itself.

The effect of administration
The corollary to the transfer of all managerial power to the administrator is that the powers of the directors are, in practice, suspended for the duration of the administration order (s. 14(2)). Furthermore, the administrator has power to remove any director in order to achieve the purposes for which he was appointed himself (see *Re P & C and R & T (Stockport) Ltd* [1991] BCLC 366).

The presentation of a petition for an administration order marks the beginning of a statutory moratorium over the company's affairs. During this period, no security can be enforced (s. 10(1)(b)), and neither can goods held under retention of title agreements be repossessed without the leave of the court. No resolution for winding up can be made (s. 10(1)(a)). This does not preclude the presentation of a *petition* for the winding up of the company, but the petition will not be disposed of until the administration order is dismissed. Finally, no other proceedings, and no execution or other legal process may be commenced or continued, and no distress may be levied against the company or its property without the leave of the court (s. 10(1)(c)). It is worth noting that the general effect of these provisions is that they do not constitute a freeze on the enforcement of other proprietary rights. Of course, there is a problem of legal form here because, presumably, a purchaser of book debts would not be covered, whilst a mortgagee or chargee of such debts who without consent collects payment from the account debtor would fall within the scope of the prohibition.

When the administration order has been made, the moratorium on enforcement similar to that which applies on presentation of the petition, but with the additional option of enforcement taking place with the consent of the administrator (s. 11(3)(c)). However, no administrative receiver may be appointed and, except with the consent of the administrator or the leave of the court, no winding-up petition may be presented (s. 11(3)(d)). The question of the enforcement of security and the rights of creditors, as well as the particular issue of obtaining the leave of the Courts under s. 11(3)(c) arose in *Re Atlantic Computers Systems plc* [1992] 2 WLR 367. It is worth setting out the facts as they illustrate starkly the issues involved in this context.

An administration order was made in relation to *Atlantic Computers plc* in April 1990. The problem was that, in many cases, the computers being leased

The state of insolvency and its legal regime 409

were not actually owned by the company but by 'funders' who included the Norwich Union and Allied Irish Bank plc. The computers were let to the company under hire-purchase agreements or leases and then sublet to end users (see chapter 13). The administrators requested the end users to continue paying their rental to the company which amounted to over £1.7 million in the period from April to June. However, no payments had been made to the funders under the head leases and hire-purchase agreements. Section 11(3)(c) of the Insolvency Act 1986 provides that during the period of an adminstration order, no steps may be taken to enforce security over the company's property or to repossess goods in the company's possession except with the administrator's consent, which had been refused, or the leave of the court.

The funders applied to the court so as to determine whether they could receive their contractual payments during the administration; whether the goods were in the company's possession for the purposes of seeking leave under s. 11(3)(c) when technically they were in the hands of the end users; and whether that leave would be granted. They finally resorted to the last-ditch protection provision in s. 27 Insolvency Act 1986 which allows a creditor to apply for relief on the basis of unfairly prejudicial conduct in the management of the company by the administrator (which is similarly worded to the provision in s. 459 of the Companies Act 1985).

At first instance ([1990] BCC 439), Ferris J held at p. 454 that where property belonging to another was used in the company's business whilst the administration order was in force, the contractual payments were 'an expense of the administration' and had to be paid to the owner. The question of leave was not relevant because Ferris J held that the equipment was in the physical possession of the end users and was not in the company's possession within s. 11(3)(c).

The Court of Appeal did not agree with any of these points and in particular stated that, although it was clear that there was a concept of liquidation expenses and that the court had an overriding discretion under s. 130(2) of the Insolvency Act 1986 to direct the liquidator to make payments as an expense of the liquidation in a situation such as this, there was no such entitlement in respect of administrative receivership. The essence of an administration was flexibility, and the hard and fast rules of the liquidation were not relevant. Therefore, such expenses would not automatically rank as administration expenses. Thus it would appear that contractual payments were unlikely to gain any priority and the real issue, therefore, was the question of leave actually to enforce the security.

On the question of leave, the Court of Appeal first held that s. 11(3)(c) did apply because the goods were within the company's possession and so could not be repossessed, except with the administrator's consent or the leave of the court; secondly, the court referred to the principles governing the exercise of this leave which will be an important question for many creditors in this situation. Not surprisingly, the Court of Appeal held that leave would not automatically be granted and referred to the decision of Peter Gibson J in *Re Meesan Investments Ltd* (1988) 4 BCC 788, where it had been held that the court had a general discretion, and had to have regard to all the relevant circumstances. It would appear to be very much a balancing exercise between the likely outcome of the administration and the effect on the applicants if leave is refused. The Court of Appeal granted leave (which had been refused in *Re Meesan Investments Ltd*) after looking at the terms of the hire-purchase and lease agreements, the company's financial position, the administrator's proposals, the effect on the administration if it was refused. Other factors were the prospect of a successful outcome to the administration if leave was refused, and the conduct of the parties.

Certainly, there must be some sympathy with the position of the funders because large sums of contractual payments which were due to them were being used to keep the company in business, but the deciding factors seem to have been the realisation that the position was hopeless, in any event, since the administration was only a prelude to liquidation. The Court of Appeal stressed that s. 11(3)(c) was not intended to strengthen the administrator's negotiating position when he sought to modify the funders' proprietary rights under an administration proposal. The balance, therefore, rested with the funders.

This decision is important in laying down some guidelines which assist in assessing when the court will grant leave for a creditor to enforce his security or repossess his property. Nevertheless, it should not be viewed as any relaxation of the moratorium rule. In order for the balance to be weighed in favour of the creditor, it may be that he would have to be seeking repossession of his own property in circumstances where the administration cannot succeed in rescuing the company. Any counterbalancing points will more likely than not result in leave being refused. It was stressed in *Re Meesan Investments Ltd* that the onus of establishing that leave should be granted is firmly on the creditor and that the bank, in that case, was likely to be repaid in full within a reasonable time even though the administration had continued for 10 months.

The onus is upon the secured creditor when seeking leave under s. 11(3) to enforce his security to show that it was a proper case for leave to be given. In this respect, the discretion exercised by the court will take into account all the circumstances, and it is not essential to demonstrate some criticism of the administrator's conduct (see *Royal Trust Bank v Buchler* [1989] BCLC 130). In the Practice Guidelines (Insolvency Administration) issued by the Court of Appeal following its decision in *Re Atlantic Computers*, the following factors were highlighted as being relevant for the granting of leave under s. 11(3):

(a) Where the existence, validity or nature of the security sought to be enforced was in dispute, the court only needed to be satisfied that the applicant had a seriously arguable case.

(b) Each case called for the exercise of judgment, in which the court sought to give effect to the purpose of the statutory provisions having regard to the parties' interests and all the circumstances of the case.

(c) In carrying out the balancing exercise, great weight was to be given to proprietary interests.

(d) It would normally be sufficient ground for the grant of leave if significant loss would be caused to the applicant, but this has to be balanced with loss caused to others by the grant of leave. In assessing these respective

The state of insolvency and its legal regime 411

losses, the court would have regard to such matters as the company's financial position, the administrator's proposals, the period during which the administration order had been in force and was expected to remain in force, the effect on the administration if leave were given, the effect on the applicant if leave were refused, the end result sought to be achieved by the administration and the prospects of it being achieved.

(e) It was necessary to balance the probability of suggested consequences of leave being granted or refused.

(f) The conduct of the parties might be relevant to the issue of granting or refusing leave, to a decision to impose terms if leave was granted, or conditional upon the administrator's particular conduct of the administration (see ss. 14(3) and 17).

Legal form and avoidance of administration order

There are arguments which, if employed successfully could avoid the moratorium altogether. The first argument involves the exhaustive definition of retention of title agreements used in s. 251 of the Insolvency Act 1986 as the basis of restraint under ss. 10 and 11. This provides:

'retention of title agreement' means an agreement for the sale of goods to a company, being an agreement—
(a) which does not constitute a charge on the goods, but
(b) under which, if the seller is not paid and the company is wound up, the seller will have priority over all other creditors of the company as respects the goods or any property representing the goods.

Although para. (a) is accurate in the sense that reference can be made to a 'charge' as being registrable under the Companies Act 1985 (as amended), more difficulty is presented with paragraph (b). This is because the seller is not seeking 'priority over all other creditors' *stricto sensu*, rather, he is seeking recovery of the goods as a proprietor and not as someone with a security interest in the goods. Nonetheless, this argument is unduly legalistic and it is probable that the court will be reluctant to uphold it, especially since it would have the effect of totally undermining the mischief of the Act which was designed to cover all types of retention of title clause. Security is given the widest possible meaning in s. 248(b) where it is defined as 'any mortgage, charge, lien or other security' (see *Exchange Travel Agency* v *Triton Property Trust plc* [1991] BCLC 396).

Powers of the administrator

The general powers conferred upon an administrator are wide-ranging and he is expressly empowered to do 'all such things as may be necessary for the management of the affairs, business and property of the company' (s. 14(1) of and sch. 1 to the Insolvency Act 1986). A principal aspect of the legal status of the administrator is that, in exercising his powers, he is deemed to be acting as agent of the company (s. 14(5)). The effect of this is that the company is bound by and is liable in respect of all acts validly performed by the administrator.

Moreover third parties are protected in their dealings with the administrator because so long as they are dealing in good faith and for value, they need not enquire whether the administrator is acting within his powers (s. 14(6)).

Once in office, the administrator has considerable power to deal with charged property under s. 15 of the Act. Under s. 15(1), where there is property of the company subject to a security which, as created, was a floating charge, the administrator may dispose of or otherwise exercise his powers in relation to that property as though it was not subject to the security. Subsection (4) supplies the necessary protection for the holder of the security in question by providing that where property is disposed of in this manner, the charge holder shall have the same priority in respect of any property directly or indirectly representing the property disposed of as he would have had in respect of the property subject to the security in its original form. The administrator can dispose of goods in the company's possession which are subject to a retention of title clause as if they were unencumbered. This is achieved following an application by the administrator to the court under s. 15(2). However, the court must be satisfied that the disposal would be likely to promote the purpose or one or more of the purposes specified in the administration order (see s. 8 above). In this respect, s. 15(5) and (6) provide:

(5) It shall be a condition of an order under subsection (2) that—
   (a) the net proceeds of the disposal, and
   (b) where those proceeds are less than such amount as may be determined by the court to be the net amount which would be realised on a sale of the property or goods in the open market by a willing vendor, such sums as may be required to make good the deficiency,
shall be applied towards discharging the sums secured by the security or payable under the hire-purchase agreement.

(6) Where a condition imposed in pursuance of subsection (5) relates to two or more securities, that condition requires the net proceeds of the disposal and, where paragraph (b) of that subsection applies, the sums mentioned in that paragraph to be applied towards discharging the sums secured by those securities in the order of their priorities.

Where the administrator applies to the court to dispose of the goods, the court must fix a venue (rr. 13.1 and 13.6 of the Insolvency Rules 1986) for the hearing, and the administrator must give notice of the venue to the owner under the agreement (r. 2.51(1) and (2). Rule 7.4(6) deals with cases of urgency where full notice (at least 14 days under r. 7.4(5)) would frustrate the purposes for which an administration order was made. In this instance the court may:

(a) hear the application immediately, either with or without notice to, or the attendance of, other parties, or
(b) authorise a shorter period of notice.

There are substantial difficulties posed by s. 15 for the unpaid supplier: first, s. 15 does not incorporate a mechanism by which the supplier can object to disposal on the basis that it will either reveal the secrets of a product design or it will flood the market with cut-price goods; second, the concepts of 'open market' will often depend upon the nature of the goods which, in turn, will determine what is adequate publicity for the sale so as to avoid the accusation that it is a private deal made on a confidential basis. Even more difficulty is presented with the phrase 'willing vendor' (who is not an 'anxious vendor': see *Inland Revenue Commissioners* v *Clay* [1914] 3 KB 466) as it relates to the market value of the goods. This is especially the case since the court is under no obligation to view the invoice value at the time of supply as being equivalent to the market value on disposal (see *Re ARV Aviation Ltd* [1989] BCLC 664). An estimate must be made of the price which would be realised in an open market, on a particular date, where there existed reasonable competitive conditions (see *Duke of Buccleuch* v *Inland Revenue Commissioners* [1967] 1 AC 506).

Creditor protection An important mechanism for creditor protection during the administration period is provided under s. 27 of the Insolvency Act 1986. In this respect, s. 27(1) provides:

At any time when an administration order is in force, a creditor or member of the company may apply to the court by petition for an order under this section on the ground—
   (a) that the company's affairs, business and property are being or have been managed by the administrator in a manner which is unfairly prejudicial to the interests of its creditors or members generally, or of some part of its creditors or members (including at least himself), or
   (b) that any actual or proposed act or omission of the administrator is or would be so prejudicial.

The court may grant such relief as it thinks fit and, in particular, may by virtue of s. 27(4):

   (a) regulate the future management by the administrator of the company's affairs, business and property;
   (b) require the administrator to refrain from doing or continuing an act complained of by the petitioner, or to do an act which the petitioner has complained he has omitted to do;
   (c) require the summoning of a meeting of creditors or members for the purpose of considering such matters as the court may direct;
   (d) discharge the administration order and make such consequential provision as the court thinks fit.

There are two principal limitations to this discretionary power: first, no application shall prejudice a voluntary arrangement sanctioned, for example, under s. 425 of the Companies Act 1985 (see s. 27(3)(a) of the Insolvency Act 1986); second, the order cannot prejudice the administrator's proposals or revised proposals if it is applied for more than 28 days after the approval of such proposals, thereby effectively preventing the disruption of the administrator's work (s. 27(3)(b)). Essentially, this forces, for example, a supplier of goods subject to a retention of title clause to consider quickly the implications of the administrator's proposals for any of his goods remaining on the company's premises.

The power of relief under s. 27(4) of the Act is wide. Moreover the criterion of 'Unfairly prejudicial' (s. 27(1)(a)) which is taken from s. 459 of the Companies Act 1985 is an objective test. Here the emphasis is upon the *result* of the conduct complained of and not the motive behind it (see *Re R. A. Noble and Sons (Clothing) Ltd* [1983] BCLC 273). It is clear that under s. 27 there is no need to prove that the petitioner was less fairly treated than other members or creditors, and 'some part of' found in s. 27(1)(a) can apply to one creditor or member.

In *Re Charnley Davies Ltd* [1990] BCC 605, a petition was brought under s. 27. The petition alleged that the administrator had acted in breach of his duty in that he had sold the company's business too quickly and had not taken all reasonable steps to obtain the best price, and that this conduct was 'unfairly prejudicial to the creditors' interests'. The petition failed on the basis that the allegation was a complaint of professional negligence and the administrator, judged by the standards of the ordinary skilled practitioner, had not been negligent. It was held by Millett J that s. 27, like its equivalent provision in the Companies Act 1985 (s. 459), was directed at the manner in which the company's affairs had been managed, not at specific breaches of duty unless those breaches were evidence of the unfairly prejudicial manner in which the company was managed. This meant that the burden of proof based solely on an allegation of professional negligence would be very difficult to discharge. The petitioners would have to establish that this professional negligence was evidence of instances of the administrator's management of the company in a way which was unfairly prejudicial to their interests. There had been no attempt to establish this and it was a hopeless task. Thus, establishing professional negligence on its own would not amount to unfairly prejudicial conduct. It was possible that, this allegation notwithstanding, the administrator might have managed the business endeavouring to do his best for the creditors, in a general sense, and having a proper regard for their interests.

Whilst Millett J was undoubtedly correct in stating that s. 459 of the Companies Act 1985 is directed at the manner in which the company is managed, it is also quite clear that s. 459 unfairly prejudicial conduct does not require a course of conduct, and a single act or omission will suffice in this respect. Although the misfeasance remedy is possible in these circumstances once the company is in liquidation, the interpretation of s. 27 used by Millett J is very restrictive and is not wholly compatible with s. 459 which will, therefore, affect the usefulness of s. 27 as a means of relief.

General duties of the administrator Following the administration order, the administrator is bound to investigate the company's affairs and also prepare a statement of proposals to a meeting of the company's creditors (ss. 23 to 24 of the Insolvency Act 1986). The administrator is required to send a statement of his proposals to the registrar of companies and to all company members, so long as their addressses are known.

It may be that one of the purposes specified in the administration order is for a voluntary arrangement. Such an arrangement will only bind those creditors who are entitled to vote. Other creditors will be free to pursue their claims *in full* after the discharge of the administration order, for example, those creditors who were not known or creditors for unliquidated amounts.

Discharge of the administration order   One important goal of an administration order is to seek the rehabilitation of the company. Where this is successful, the management of the company's affairs will be restored to its directors and shareholders. Thus, the administrator is obliged under s. 18(2) of the Insolvency Act 1986 to make an application to the court if it appears to him that each of the purposes specified in the order has either been achieved, or is incapable of achievement. Section 18 also provides a general enabling power for the administrator to apply to the court for an administration order to be varied so as to specify an additional purpose. Following discharge of an administrator, there is no power to make an immediate winding-up order unless a petition has already been presented (*Re Brooke Marine Ltd* [1988] BCLC 546).

An administrator ceases to hold office on death, on resignation in conformity with the Insolvency Rules, on ceasing to be qualified to act as an insolvency practitioner, or on removal by the court (s. 19(1) and (2) of the Insolvency Act 1986).

ADMINISTRATIVE RECEIVERSHIP

This is not a true collective insolvency proceeding because, in substance, it is the method by which a debenture holder can enforce his security. The Cork committee, 1982, recommended at para. 1538 the creation of a 10 per cent fund for unsecured creditors out of assets subject to a floating charge. Had this proposal been accepted by the government, this would have given administrative receivership a collective proceedings element, but its rejection has left this form of *insolvency* proceeding devoid of any meaningful content.

The effect of the Insolvency Act 1986 is that it treats the administrative receiver as an office holder in collective insolvency proceedings in much the same way as an administrator or liquidator. Thus, an administrative receiver is required to obtain a statement of affairs from the officers of the company and to send a report to the registrar of companies and to creditors (ss. 47 and 48). He can only be removed by the court (s. 45(1)) and he cannot be appointed during the period for which an administration order is in force (s. 11(3)(b)) and must vacate office on the making of an administration order (s. 11(1)(b)).

An administrative receiver is appointed by a debenture holder under a floating charge. There is little advantage in applying to the court for the appointment of a receiver since besides the deleterious effects of time and expense, the court order could be seen as fettering the receiver's powers in the sense that he would have to work within a judicial framework. Because the administrative receiver performs a management function, it is normally the case that the debenture holder's security encompasses substantially the whole of the company's property, otherwise his powers of management will be confined to dealings in the assets which constitute the security. Undoubtedly, it is the floating charge element which is essential (see pp. 404–6 above).

The administrative receiver's functions are somewhat unique: he owes a duty of care to the debenture holder who appointed him and also a separate duty of care to the company as its deemed agent. The agency of the company exists for the protection of the interests of the debenture holder, but at the same time, the latter cannot give directions to the receiver in the conduct of the receivership and, indeed, the administrative receiver cannot be removed from office without a court order (s. 45(1)). Whilst the receiver owes no duty of care to unsecured creditors who are deemed to be adequately protected by virtue of his duty to the company, nonetheless, he does owe a duty of care to a party which has an interest in the equity of redemption, for example, to a surety who enjoys immunities against a negligent creditor or receiver in the disposal of assets which would otherwise reduce the surety's liability.

Undoubtedly, the greatest effect that administrative receivership has is that it blocks an administration order. It is impossible for these two functions to exist concurrently (s. 11). Of course, it is otherwise if the floating charge to which the administrative receivership relates could be avoided, for example, a floating charge given for past value by an insolvent company (s. 245), or it related to a transaction at an undervalue or a preference (s. 9(3)). Assuming that a debenture holder is not vulnerable in this way, he has the power to block an administration order. As we have seen, notice of the petition of an administrative order must be given to him forthwith (s. 9(2)(a)) and the Insolvency Rules provide that a copy of the petition and accompanying documentation must be served on him, normally, five days before the hearing (Insolvency Rules 1986, rr. 2.6, 2.7(1) and 12.9).

Validity of the appointment
Where the company is already being, or is going to be wound up, the appointment is invalid. Furthermore, the preference provisions are also applicable here, for example, if the floating charge can be overturned as being a transaction at an undervalue, subsequent avoidance of the security nullifies the appointment retrospectively. The appointment must relate to a valid claim, i.e., a properly registered charge under s. 396 of the Companies Act 1985 (as amended); the debenture must be a valid contract; and the power to appoint must have become exercisable under the terms of the debenture, as in the case where a valid demand for payment has been made and the company has not satisfied this demand.

The administrative receiver must also be an insolvency practitioner which was the mechanism the Cork committee (1982) advocated as ensuring competence, skill and integrity. The primary requirement here is membership of a recognised professional body to whose disciplinary supervision the insolvency practitioner would be subject. In the alternative, insolvency practitioners not belonging to a recognised professional body are required to obtain a personal licence to practise from the Secretary of State, or a competent authority designated by the Secretary of State (ss. 390 to 392 of the Insolvency Act 1986; Insolvency Practitioners (Recognised Professional Bodies) Order 1986 (SI 1986 No. 1764).

Where the appointment of the administrative receiver is defective or invalid, s. 232 of the Insolvency Act 1986 validates certain acts, for example, where the defects relate merely to form or procedure. It does not validate acts done where appointment came about under an invalid security or when the appointee was disqualified. In these circumstances, in the absence of the company ratifying the appointment, or estoppel, the appointee is liable to the company in damages for trespass or conversion or, in relation to assets coming into his hands as constructive trustee (*Rolled Steel Products (Holdings) Ltd v British Steel Corporation* [1986] Ch 246). By virtue of s. 34 of the Insolvency Act 1986, the appointee can seek a court order requiring the debenture holder to indemnify him against any legal liability incurred by reason of the invalidity of the appointment.

The administrative receiver's powers During the currency of the receivership, the management powers of the directors of the company are effectively divested, at least in relation to the assets which are subject to the debenture. (See *Newhart Developments Ltd v Cooperative Commercial Bank Ltd* [1978] 2 All ER 896. Compare *Tudor Grange Holdings Ltd v Citibank NA* [1991] 4 All ER 1.) Schedule 1 to the Insolvency Act 1986 lists 22 specific powers followed by a general power to do all things incidental to the exercise of the specific powers. It should be noted that these are not separate statutory powers; rather, these are powers deemed by the Act to be included *in the debenture* except so far as inconsistent with its provisions (s. 42(1)). The powers listed cover virtually every aspect of management of the business as well as the assets comprised in the security. One of the receiver's most significant powers is, with the leave of the court, to dispose of property subject to a prior or equal security interest. This can only be exercised where the court is satisfied that the disposal would be likely to promote a more advantageous realisation of the company's assets than would otherwise be effected (s. 43). The priority position of the secured creditor is protected because of the stipulation that an order giving leave to dispose must provide the net proceeds of sale, plus the amount by which those proceeds fall short of the value determined by the court as the net amount which would be realised by sale on the open market, by a willing vendor, are applied to discharge the sums secured by the displaced security (s. 43(3)).

The receiver owes a duty of care to the debenture holder in the conduct of the receivership. The receiver will only become the debenture holder's agent when the lender directs or interferes with the conduct of the receivership. It would appear that ordinary liaison with the lender is insufficient to constitute this. It has been held that where there was constant communication between the lender and the receiver, so the receiver sought the lender's approval for his actions, the lender was liable as principal (*American Express International Bank Corp v Hurley* [1985] 3 All ER 564). It is important not to overgeneralise here because, necessarily, the threshold of unacceptable interference must be a high one simply in order to allow for the flow of information between the receiver and the debenture holder. Insofar as the debenture holder instructs the receiver in the performance of his duties, he will be liable to the company for the receiver's negligent acts or omissions subject to a right of indemnity.

In the ordinary course, the receiver is deemed to be the company's agent (s. 44(1)(a)) and, in this respect, he can enter into fresh contracts committing the company to future liabilities. However, the receiver will be personally liable on such new contracts (s. 44(1)(b)) but is entitled to an indemnity in respect of that liability out of the free assets of the company. With regard to existing contracts, the receiver does not incur personal liability in the absence of a collateral undertaking by him. This is because the receiver is exercising his normal managerial functions. As such, there is only one limit to the receiver's right of disclaimer, namely, the question of duty of care.

It is worth noting that since the power to carry on the business derives from the debenture, and since the receiver's function is to protect the debenture holder's security, the receiver may repudiate existing contracts and not incur personal liability so long as he is acting in good faith and is not needlessly damaging the company's goodwill (*Airlines Airspares Ltd* v *Handley Page Ltd* [1970] Ch 193). The receiver, in exercising his managerial powers, must be free to shut down what he considers to be an unprofitable part of the business which threatens the debenture holder's position. Moreover, the contracting party must be taken to assume the risk when contracting with a company that a receiver would seek to protect the assets of the debenture holder. Of course, it is open for the contracting party to sue the *company* for breach. At the same time, the administrative receiver is bound to respect existing legal or equitable proprietary rights such as liens or specific performance (compare *Schering Pty Ltd* v *Forrest Pharmaceutical Co. Pty Ltd* [1982] 1 NSWLR 286).

It should be noted that the receiver is not a *successor* to the business in right of the company like a liquidator is; rather, the receiver takes beneficial occupation as manager so that he acts in the capacity of the company. The question of whether the receiver will be bound to continue the mortgagor's business must surely be seen in terms of the receiver's duties to the mortgagor and mortgagee. The receiver will be bound to continue the mortgagor's business where this is beneficial to the realisation of the mortgaged assets and where not to do so would be a breach of his duty of care to the mortgagor. There can be no general duty to continue the business of the mortgagor precisely because this could diminish the quality of the lender's security.

In one significant respect the receiver does undertake personal liability where he adopts contracts of employment. It would appear that a receiver is deemed to adopt a contract of employment after a period of 14 days from appointment, or through any act or acquiescence on his part which treats the contract as subsisting (s. 44). There is a statutory right to indemnity for the receiver out of the assets of the company in respect of his personal liability on contracts entered into on behalf of the company or contracts of employment adopted by him (s. 44(1)(c)). The receiver cannot, however, resort to assets of third parties, or to the assets of the company which are subject to a security interest ranking in priority to that of his debenture holder.

In the light of the definition of floating charge proferred under s. 251 Insolvency Act 1986 (see pp. 341–2), preferential creditors in existence at the date of the receiver's appointment will have priority irrespective of the question of crystallisation. The receiver will still have recourse to the free assets of the company. A receiver with notice of a preferential claim who disregards this is liable in damages in tort, as well as for breach of statutory duty to the extent of the preferential creditor's loss. The position is somewhat different in the case of the disposal of third-party goods or equipment which may have been disposed of by an administrative receiver or administrator.

The administrative receiver is required to pay preferential creditors out of assets covered by a charge which started life as a floating security where there are insufficient free assets of the company to pay them (s. 40 of the Insolvency Act 1986). However, where a receiver is appointed under a debenture secured by a fixed and a floating charge, the priority of preferential creditors is limited to assets subject to the floating charge. The reason for this is that, in the order of distribution (see chapter 20), preferential creditors do not prevail over specific mortgagees.

Termination of receiver's agency The administrative receiver's powers fall away once liquidation supervenes since the receiver's status as an agent of the company comes to an end (s. 44(1)(a)). In this circumstance, the powers of the receiver regarding the enforcement of security interests or acts taken to preserve the security still remain. Following liquidation, any duties owed by the receiver to the company as its deemed agent may be enforced by the liquidator in the name of the company, who may also take proceedings against the receiver for misfeasance (s. 212(1)(b)). The receiver has a duty to give accounts to the liquidator. The receiver is entitled to retain assets regarding security ranking in priority to the charge under which he was appointed. He is also entitled to retain assets to ensure his expenses, liabilities and remuneration.

If the receivership comes to an end where the company has not gone into liquidation, an infrequent occurrence, it is the duty of the receiver to hand back control of the company to the directors.

Administrator and administrative receiver: a comparison of function
Both the administrator and administrative receiver exercise similar management functions. However, there are some crucial distinctions:

(a) The administrator enjoys the benefit of the statutory freeze on the enforcement of creditors' rights and remedies.

(b) The administrator represents the general body of creditors rather than a particular secured creditor, for example, a debenture holder.

(c) The administrator is appointed by the court and would appear to be subject to a general and overriding duty to display good faith in his dealings with third parties, just as is required of a liquidator in a winding up by the court. It would follow that the rule in *Re Condon, ex parte James* (1874) LR 9 Ch App 609 should apply to an administrator. This would require the administrator to act in an exemplary manner by forbearing to insist upon his legal entitlement to retain money or property by reference to principles of natural justice and equity in its untechnical sense. (See *Re Wyvern Developments Ltd* [1974] 1 WLR 1097).

(d) The administrator is not personally liable on contracts he enters into or on employment contracts he adopts. In this respect, he is much less vulnerable than an administrative receiver.

(e) An administrator is not in a position analogous to an administrative receiver as regards pre-administration contracts. An administrator's power of disclaimer is exactly equal to the company's power of disclaimer. In contrast, administrative receivers can disregard the company's current contracts and expose the company to damages provided they do not, thereby, cause the company avoidable loss.

The disposal of property: the liability of administrative receivers and administrators Under the Insolvency Act 1986, the administrator and administrative receiver are classified for certain purposes as 'office-holders' and, as such, are given certain responsibilities. Under s. 234, an office-holder is not liable for any loss or damage resulting from the seizure or disposal of goods, notwithstanding that they are not the property of the company. Immunity is given where the office-holder mistakenly but *bona fide* seizes or disposes of the goods in these circumstances (s. 234(3)), although liability does arise in respect of the office-holder's negligence (s. 234(4)). In the latter situation, the owner can still sue for the recovery of property or the proceeds of the sale. The immunity is limited in any case to *tangible* property and does not apply where choses in action are involved because, strictly speaking, these cannot be 'seized' as required by s. 234(3) and (4) of the Insolvency Act 1986 (see *Welsh Development Agency* v *Export Finance Co. Ltd* [1992] BCC 270).

It is unclear what amounts to negligence for the purpose of s. 234. In the case of an administration the moratorium would prevent this. On the other hand, more difficulty surrounds the appointment of an administrative receiver: should he be deemed to have constructive knowledge of disputed ownership where he is appointed to an industry where retention of title clauses form part of the standard conditions of supply? This liability would, if it arises, be an onerous one and must surely be tempered by other factors, for example, whether there has been compliance with creditor notification requirements, and the information provided by officers of the company to which the appointment relates.

There are two particular problems with s. 234 which are worth noting in the context of retention of title clauses. In the first place, although the right to trace property and proceeds subsists where the office-holder is negligent, the problem of identification and being able to link goods with invoices remains. Moreover, the bona fide purchaser rule may prevent tracing especially since ss. 14(6) and 42(3) provide that a person dealing with an administrator or administrative receiver in good faith and for value is not concerned to inquire whether he is acting within his powers, although this provision does not protect a party who, for example, deals with a person acting as an administrative receiver who was never validly appointed. Furthermore, the office-holder enjoys a lien on the property, or the proceeds of its sale, for such expenses as have been incurred in connection with the seizure or disposal regardless of the issue of negligence (s. 234(4)(b)).

LIQUIDATION

This is a collective process which leads to the dissolution of the company. The winding up of a company may be either voluntary or compulsory. Insofar as the distinction suggests that compulsory winding up is imposed upon unwilling creditors, this is misleading because it is often brought about by the creditors and even the shareholders themselves. The distinction is, rather, between liquidation of a company by its own appointee, or liquidation carried out by a court-approved liquidator.

Voluntary winding up

This starts with a resolution of the shareholders. Normally, a special resolution is required (s. 378 of the Companies Act 1985), but if the company in its general meeting resolves that it cannot continue its business in view of its liabilities, an extraordinary resolution is all that is then required (s. 378(1) of the Companies Act 1985). Of course, it may be that the articles of association of the company may provide for dissolution on the happening of a specified event, or after the passage of time and, following either of these, all that is required is an ordinary resolution.

We have already discussed the declaration of solvency in a members' winding up, and this will ensure that the liquidator will be appointed by the shareholders alone. The interests of creditors are protected, however, because under part XIII of the Insolvency Act 1986, all persons who occupy the position of liquidator of a company must fulfil various requirements as to experience, or qualifications, and are subject to administrative and disciplinary control. Where the liquidator is of the opinion that the company will be unable to pay its debts in full within the period stated in the directors' declaration of solvency, the liquidation will be converted into a creditors' winding up (s. 95 of the Insolvency Act 1986). Where no declaration of solvency has been made, the winding up is a creditors' voluntary winding up. A creditors' meeting must be called and they have the right to nominate a person to act as liquidator. If the nominations of the members and the creditors conflict, the creditors prevail unless the court otherwise directs following an application by a director, member, or creditor.

Compulsory winding up

The declaration of solvency in a members' voluntary winding up has no binding consequences for creditors of the company who are entirely free to present a petition for winding up if they can prove that the company is actually insolvent. Even in a creditors' winding up, any creditor may seek to petition the court for a compulsory winding up (s. 116), and no requirement of prejudice need be shown. Of course, in practice, the court will have regard to the wishes of the majority of the creditors on the overall merits of the case, for example, where the appointment of the liquidator is suspicious in the sense that he may have been subject to undue influence by the directors. Nonetheless, the requirement under part XIII of the Insolvency Act 1986 that only a duly qualified insolvency practitioner may act as a liquidator will, in the main, ensure that the prejudicial risks to the creditors' interests on voluntary winding up are diminished. A compulsory winding up is a more formal procedure than the voluntary variety and is more closely controlled by the court. Indeed, the official receiver becomes the liquidator unless and until an outside liquidator is appointed (ss. 136(2), 137, 139 and 140 of the Insolvency Act 1986).

The grounds upon which a petition may be based are encapsulated in s. 122(1) of the Insolvency Act 1986 and may be set out as follows:

(a) A special resolution to wind up has been made by the shareholders.

(b) As a registered public company, it has failed within one year to be issued with the necessary certificate regarding minimum share capital without which it is unable to do business or borrow money.

(c) The company is an old public company within the meaning of s. 1 of the Companies Consolidation (Consequential Provisions) Act 1985, i.e. it has failed to re-register.

(d) The company does not commence its business within a year from its incorporation, or suspends its business for a whole year.

(e) The number of members is less than two.

(f) The company is unable to pay its debts.

(g) The court is of the opinion that it is just and equitable that the company should be wound up.

As can be seen from the list above, most of these grounds are not solvency issues. Indeed, it is part of the statutory scheme that compulsory winding up may take place in respect of a company which is fully solvent.

Although it is usually the creditors who seek a court order that starts the process of winding up, this is not always the case. The following are given *locus standi* to present a petition under the Insolvency Act 1986:

(a) The company (s. 124(1)).

(b) The directors (s. 124(1)).

(c) Any creditor (which includes any contingent or prospective creditor).

(d) A contributory (past or present), although subject to certain safeguards which are designed to prevent a person from buying shares in order to qualify himself to harass the company (s. 124(2)).

(e) The official receiver (s. 124(5)).

(f) The relevant officer (the supervisor, the receiver, the administrator).

(g) The Secretary of State (ss. 124(4) and 124A of the Insolvency Act 1986).

(h) The Bank of England (s. 18 of the Banking Act 1979).

(i) The Attorney-General (s. 30(1) of the Charities Act 1960).
(j) The Chief Registrar of Friendly Societies.

Even though the right to petition is a statutory right, not all the grounds for winding up are available to everyone with *locus standi*, for example, the fact that the company is an old public one can be relied on only by the Secretary of State.

The consequences of winding up The most significant effect of winding up is that as the result of the collectivisation procedure, claims against the company cease to be actionable (the automatic stay) and become, instead, rights to prove in the winding up (s. 130(2)). The role of the liquidator is to secure the optimum realisation of the assets of the company, to ascertain claims and, after covering the expenses of the liquidation, to distribute the proceeds to the creditors according to the priority rules laid down under the Insolvency Act 1986 and the Insolvency Rules. In this respect, to ensure that the company's assets are available to its creditors, dispositions made by it after winding up has commenced are void without the consent of the liquidator.

The liquidator must act in good faith at all times in accordance with the purposes of the liquidation, with complete impartiality, and the absence of any conflict of interest affecting him personally. In contrast to an administrative receiver or administrator, a liquidator has no power to carry on the business except insofar as this may be necessary to ensure a beneficial winding up (s. 87(1) and sch. 4, para. 5). The liquidator cannot exercise his powers with a view to the financial reconstruction of the business. Before exercising his powers, a creditors' meeting is required (s. 98) unless his action is sanctioned by the court (s. 166(2)). Having taken control of the company's assets and ascertained the liabilities and discharged them in the proper order (ss. 175, 386, sch. 6), the company is then dissolved following a final meeting of the company's creditors (s. 146), subject to the power of the court to restore it on application under s. 651 of the Companies Act 1985. The liquidator must also furnish the official receiver with information including the assets, debts and liabilities, the names, addresses and occupations of the company's creditors, their securities and any other relevant information (s. 131(2)). This information is used in order to assist the official receiver in the performance of his official investigative function, for example, s. 132 of the Insolvency Act 1986 imposes a duty upon the official receiver in every case where a winding-up order is made by the court to investigate the promotion, formation, business dealings and affairs of the company (see Insolvency Rules 1986, r. 4.43). This report will have significance in any proceedings for wrongful trading under the Insolvency Act 1986 and the Company Directors Disqualification Act 1986, or questions of voidable preference or transactions at undervalue (see pp. 444–6). In conducting an investigation into the affairs of the company (ss. 235 and 236), officers of the company are under a duty to assist and are not entitled to rely on the privilege against self-incrimination (see *Bishopsgate Investment Ltd (in provisional liquidation)* v *Maxwell and another* [1992] 2 All ER 856).

The raising of standards of behaviour in the conduct of the affairs of companies was identified in the Cork committee report (1982) as being of concern to all those involved in commerce. As a result of the investigative role of the official receiver, criminal proceedings may be brought, for example, in relation to offences under the Companies Act 1985 committed prior to the commencement of the winding up or, indeed, for offences under the Insolvency Act 1986.

In the next chapter we shall consider the distribution of assets available following liquidation and the order in which they are to be distributed. The interplay of these two issues is common to both types of winding up.

Collective proceedings of administration and liquidation

The function of administration is to keep the firm intact rather than to dissolve it. In this respect, assets are frozen in administration and the *pari passu* principle of distribution has no role to play. Furthermore, in administration proceedings, the assets of the company remain its property and do not become subject to a statutory trust as in the case of liquidation. It follows that the administrator has full management powers whilst the liquidator can only carry on the business with a view to winding up and distributing the assets of the company.

TWENTY
Distribution and ordering of claims following corporate insolvency

ASSETS AVAILABLE FOR DISTRIBUTION

The assets of the debtor determine what is available for distribution to claimants. Assets include all the legal or equitable interests of the debtor in property at the beginning of the insolvency. Here it is important to distinguish between individual bankruptcy and corporate insolvency. With regard to the former, there are public policy considerations of 'fresh start', so some assets are not available for distribution, for example, future income stream from labour, and exempt property including tools necessary for the personal use of the bankrupt in the context of earning a livelihood (s. 283(2) of the Insolvency Act 1986). It is almost inconceivable to think that a company, as debtor, could have an asset that is not available to its claimants.

The assets of a company must be determined according to the general principles of property law and contract law. The key point which determines the asset issue is whether or not the company in liquidation has a *beneficial interest* in the property (see *Re Marwalt plc* [1992] BCC 32). Of course, there may be factors which limit this interest under the general law; we have already considered co-ownership, tenancy-in-common principles, the bailee under a hire-purchase or lease contract. In addition to these, there are pure contractual rights, for example, the right of the company as a dealer in options, or futures, or foreign currency to any credit balance in its favour which results from the netting out of the sums payable by and to the company under separate contracts.

There is a closely related almost symbiotic connection between assets and liabilities. Quite simply, the issue is one of determining how much there is from the perspective of the unsecured creditors. In this respect, the company's rights under a contract may be vulnerable to rescission in the case of misrepresentation, or, if there is a failure of a condition precedent the contract will be void *ab initio*. The liquidator stands in the shoes of the company regarding the assets of the company which are determinable or defeasible. Moreover, the assets of the company may be swelled for the benefit of the general group of creditors through post-liquidation receipts and recoveries. The most notable, in this context, are assets recovered by virtue of the preference provisions of the Insolvency Act 1986 (see pp. 446–8). A careful distinction should be drawn here with the case where a charge which would otherwise rank in priority to the debenture is rendered void by reason of non-registration. In this situation, the invalidity of the prior charge promotes the debenture holder's floating charge to senior status permitting recovery of the surplus (if any) gained from the realisation of the charged assets. It is also worth noting that assets can be swelled by the post-liquidation performance of contracts by the liquidator, and no after-acquired property clause can attach to these assets which enure for the benefit of the general body of creditors (*Re Collins* [1925] Ch 556).

It is important to distinguish between assets, properly so-called which may be subject to a countervailing liability or obligation and may be properly set off from the case where there are inherent limitations to the assets themselves. This point is dramatically illustrated by the facts in *Re Charge Card Services Ltd* [1987] Ch 150 (first instance), [1989] Ch 497 (Court of Appeal). The case involved a credit card company obtaining finance by way of recourse factoring (see chapter 11). Although the factoring arrangements were framed to provide for absolute sales by the credit card company to the factoring company, there were recourse provisions if the customer's debt proved irrecoverable. The factoring company held a balance of 15 per cent of the full value of the debt back, and the factoring company had the right, if the credit card company entered insolvent liquidation to terminate the agreement and require the credit card company to repurchase from the factoring company any purchased debt outstanding. Following the liquidation of the credit card company, the liquidator claimed that these provisions were void for non-registration under s. 396 of the Companies Act 1985 or, alternatively, that they constituted an attempt to contract out of the statutory rules of set-off. The factoring company's retention right was upheld by Millett J at first instance and also in the Court of Appeal on the basis that it constituted a running account in that it ensured that the factoring company did not overpay.

In large measure, the question as to the available assets for distribution goes hand in hand with whether the creditors of the debtor company have bargained for security. Thus, in the case of an executed contract, if the solvent party has fully performed, its only remedy is to prove in competition with other creditors for a dividend in the winding up of the insolvent party. This may be justified as an aspect of commercial risk. An interesting problem here is whether the court can order specific performance by the (now insolvent) company of an unperformed obligation, for example, to deliver goods under a contract of sale entered into prior to the liquidation. This issue often translates itself into a plea for the financing buyer (see pp. 182–6). One argument is that the right to specific performance should be considered as a property right which gives the creditor full recovery on the debtor's insolvency (see Schwartz, 'The Case for

Specific Performance' (1979) 89 Yale LJ 271; Kronman, 'Specific Performance' (1978) 45 U Chi L Rev 35). A major difficulty with this approach is that it fails to accommodate the fact that the liquidator is given the option of adopting or rejecting an executory contract. Perhaps a more appropriate approach, in this context, would be to distinguish between property rights and priority rights. The courts will be concerned about the prospect of conferring a priority right on the party seeking specific performance. Thus, if the non-insolvent party has fully performed by, for example, paying over his money, the contract will not be executory and the issue will revolve around a *particular* claim which is essentially a *priority* question.

Disclaimer of onerous property and executory contracts
As well as the liquidator's power to order the company not to perform its contractual obligations, ss. 178 to 182 of the Insolvency Act 1986 regulate the power of the liquidator to disclaim onerous property, thereby extinguishing the rights, interests and liabilities of the company in the property disclaimed. The concept of onerous property in s. 178(3) is broader than that formerly included in s. 618 of the Companies Act 1985, and now means:

(a) any unprofitable contract; or
(b) any other property of the company which is unsaleable, or not readily saleable or which is such that it may give rise to a liability to pay money or perform any other onerous act.

Leave of the court is no longer required to disclaim onerous property, and s. 178(2) allows the liquidator to exercise the power of disclaimer notwithstanding that he has taken possession of the property, endeavoured to sell it, or otherwise exercised rights of ownership in relation to it. There is no specified time-limit within which the liquidator must exercise the power of disclaimer. However, he loses the right to disclaim if he fails to give notice of disclaimer within 28 days, or a longer period as the court may allow, if a person interested in the property has made an application by serving a written notice on him requiring him to decide whether to disclaim or not (s. 178(5)). The effect of failure here is that the liquidator loses his right to terminate the contract unilaterally by notice. It is up to the liquidator to decide whether to allow the company to default on its obligation, thereupon, ordinary contract repudiation principles apply. Where damages are awarded, these can be proved as a debt in the winding up (s. 186(1)).

The power of the liquidator to disclaim onerous contracts encapsulated in s. 178 does not distinguish between executory and executed contracts. Apart from hire and lease contracts, it is hard to envisage other circumstances in which a liquidator would have power to disclaim an executed contract. It would appear that it is in the case of executory contracts where difficult problems will emerge on insolvency. An executory contract involves a contract on which substantial performance remains due by both contracting parties, so the failure of either side gives a right of repudiation. Rejection constitutes a breach of contract and the injured party is a creditor just like any other unsecured creditor unless he has protected himself with a security interest, or he has such an interest arising by operation of law, for example, a lien.

Insolvency will often constitute either renunciation of or incapacity to perform an executory contract. What we have here is an anticipatory breach of contract which, if accepted by the other party, will accelerate performance of the insolvent's secondary obligations, namely, payment of damages. The law takes a very narrow approach to the question of incapacity to perform; insolvency will only be incapacitatory if sufficient assets are not set aside to meet performance at the relevant time. In effect, this allows the liquidator to 'cherry-pick' the company's pre-insolvency contracts (see *Bloomer* v *Bernstein* (1874) LR 9 CP 588; *Re Phoenix Bessemer Steel Co.* (1876) 4 ChD 108). One obvious way of avoiding this dilemma is through the insertion of an *ipso facto* clause, that is, to give the solvent party a right to accelerate liability on insolvency. The effect of such a clause is that it operates as a contractual limitation of the insolvent's interest under the executory contract. A justification for such a clause is that it performs a policing role similar to a restrictive covenant clause — by identifying misbehaviour, it tells the contracting party the consequences of his actions. The idea here is that the clause puts a cost upon the debtor misbehaving in the sense that the debtor avoids engaging in activities which increase the likelihood of insolvency.

Insurance

The normal rule is that a company which chooses to insure against a contingency or liability is entitled to retain these proceeds as an asset which enures for the benefit of the general body of creditors. However, there is a statutory exception to this approach under the Third Parties (Rights against Insurers) Act 1930. By virtue of s. 1 of this Act, if any liability is incurred by the insured company either before or after it became insolvent then, upon the winding up, these rights (so long as they still subsist and have not been paid out) are transferred to and vest in the third party to whom liability was incurred.

Assets belonging to third parties

We have already discussed in part 4 that many creditors are not in a position to exact any formal security, whether of a fixed or floating nature, from the company which becomes indebted to them. Proving as an unsecured creditor does not provide an attractive option for suppliers of money or goods. This factor accounts for the burgeoning of unconventional security devices in recent years, for example, retention of title clauses, trust devices, and finance leasing (pp. 346–54).

The intervention of equitable doctrine is a notable feature here. Thus, in *Chase Manhattan Bank NA* v *Israel-British Bank (London) Ltd* [1981] Ch 105, where there was a mistaken payment, the court held that there was an equitable proprietary right to follow the transfer into the hands of the transferee to the prejudice of other creditors.

THE *PARI PASSU* PRINCIPLE OF DISTRIBUTION

This is the most fundamental principle of insolvency law, namely, that of rateable distribution as between all creditors (s. 107 of the Insolvency Act 1986). In relation to compulsory winding up, r. 4.181(1) of the Insolvency Rules 1986 provides that: 'Debts other than preferential debts rank equally between themselves in the winding up'. Essentially, the *pari passu* principle is an aspect of the collectivisation of the insolvency process where the creditor must have recourse to legal process rather than self-help. The principle is supported by provisions striking down unfair preferences.

The *pari passu* principle of distribution is in practice rarely achieved. There are two main reasons for this: first, there is English law's insistence on protection of property rights (rights *in rem*) which do not form part of the assets available for distribution; secondly, the legislature itself has failed to live up to the rateable-distribution ideal though its recognition of pre-preferential and preferential debts (see pp. 441–2). As the Cork committee report, *Insolvency Law and Practice* (Cmnd 8558, 1982), pointed out at para. 1396:

> It is a fundamental objective of the law of insolvency to achieve a rateable, that is to say *pari passu*, distribution of the uncharged assets of the insolvent among the unsecured creditors. In practice, however, this objective is seldom, if ever, attained. In the overwhelming majority of cases it is substantially frustrated by the existence of preferential debts. These are unsecured debts which, by force of statute, fall to be paid in bankruptcy or winding up in priority to all other unsecured debts.

Despite the fact that the objective of the *pari passu* principle is often frustrated, nonetheless it has important practical repercussions due to its mandatory nature in insolvency proceedings.

The mandatory nature of the *pari passu* principle

In commercial practice, it is often the case where there are a series of contracts involving the same parties, the same subject-matter, and performance on the same date, to resort to some form of settlement netting. The object here is to reduce the amount of bargains which have to be settled and at the same time reduce exposure. A particularly sophisticated example of this phenomenon can be seen with multilateral netting involving clearing houses, that is, a non-mutual set-off of claims. Typically this arrangement takes place in commodities trading swap contracts and credit 'transfers' between banks. The object here is to avoid massive numbers of credit transfers by the simple expedient of accounting for net balances. This may be done in two ways: first, where the function of the clearing house is to act as an agent in calculating the state of accounts through supplying details of net balances to the participants; second, by making the clearing house the beneficial holder of the claims and also personally liable on the claims so that the clearing house bears all the risk of a dealer default.

The leading authority in this context is *British Eagle International Air Lines Ltd* v *Compagnie Nationale Air France* [1975] 1 WLR 758, a case which finally established the inability of parties to 'contract out of' *pari passu* distribution. Here the International Air Transport Association had established a clearing-house system for the monthly settlement of debits and credits arising when members performed services for one another. A balance would be struck between the total sum owing to a particular member in respect of services supplied by it *for* all other members, and the total owing to that member in respect of services supplied *by* all other members. The clearance took effect within five days after the 30th day of each calendar month in relation to the month prior to that calendar month. Members with an overall debit balance would pay into the clearing house the amount of the debit, while the clearing house would pay to members with an overall credit balance the sums due to them. The House of Lords said that any clearance that had taken place before the commencement of a member's liquidation should be binding on the liquidator since there was no question of a fraudulent preference. Despite this, the majority held that the clearing-house system could not operate after the commencement of the liquidation in respect of debits and credits not actually cleared at that date. This was considered to be contrary to the statutory injunction that the property of a company should be applied in its winding up in satisfaction of its liabilities *pari passu*.

It is clear that the *British Eagle* case was concerned with the first kind of netting arrangement. There could not be an objection to the second type of netting arrangement which provides for contracts initially being novated to the clearing house. The reasoning here is that payment and delivery obligations become owed to the clearing house *itself* which, therefore, allows for the netting out of obligations without offending the *British Eagle* principle. In the case of the first kind of netting arrangement, the insolvent company could be deprived of an asset in the form of its claim against one of the members of the clearing house by any cross-claims by the clearing house against the company in liquidation. As one leading author has succinctly put it, Wood, P., *English and International Set-Off* (London, 1989), at para. 5-123:

> To remove this [the insolvent company's claim] by a netting-out is no different from a creditor walking into the insolvent's house and helping himself to the furniture.

One of the most remarkable recent developments in English law has been the recognition of the concept of a market as a distinct entity which for its success depends not only upon sound institutional structures and administrative procedures, but also upon a legal framework. Part VII of the Companies Act 1989 (ss. 154 to 191) does, in large measure, protect certain market dealings through its recognition of the general inviolability of the market, that is, in the sense of a recognised investment exchange or clearing house under the Financial Services Act 1986. In particular, this can be demonstrated with regard to netting agreements on the international swaps and foreign exchange market where the *British Eagle* approach was considered to compromise the market. The argument that this could lead to a loss of business from London prompted the government to introduce a set of provisions, remarkable for their breadth, to *insulate* market contracts from insolvency law. As a consequence, post-liquidation netting is now possible, so s. 159(1) and (2) of the Companies Act 1989 provide:

(1) None of the following shall be regarded as to any extent invalid at law on the ground of inconsistency with the law relating to the distribution of the assets of a person on bankruptcy, winding up or sequestration, or in the administration of an insolvent estate—
  (a) a market contract,
  (b) the default rules of a recognised investment exchange or recognised clearing house,
  (c) the rules of a recognised investment exchange or recognised clearing house as to the settlement of market contracts not dealt with under its default rules.

(2) The powers of a relevant office-holder in his capacity as such, and the powers of the court under the Insolvency Act 1986 or the Bankruptcy (Scotland) Act 1985 shall not be exercised in such a way as to prevent or interfere with—
  (a) the settlement in accordance with the rules of a recognised investment exchange or recognised clearing house of a market contract not dealt with under its default rules, or
  (b) any action taken under the default rules of such an exchange or clearing house.

This does not prevent a relevant office-holder from afterwards seeking to recover any amount under section 163(4) or 164(4) or prevent the court from afterwards making any such order or decree as is mentioned in section 165(1) or (2) (but subject to subsections (3) and (4) of that section).

Market contracts are further championed by curtailing the powers of the liquidator or other office-holders, as well as administrators, from interfering with market rules (ss. 161 and 175(1) of the Companies Act 1989). Even the court is precluded, in the case of market contracts, from setting aside a transaction at an undervalue, a preference or a transaction defrauding creditors (s. 164 of the Companies Act 1989). Furthermore, it is worth noting the powers of the Secretary of State under s. 166 of the 1989 Act to give directions in relation to a recognised UK investment exchange or recognised UK clearing house, as well as the power under s. 158(4) to make further regulations modifying the law of insolvency to market contracts.

EXCEPTIONS TO THE *PARI PASSU* PRINCIPLE

Rights of set-off
Set-offs constitute a procedural device that save parties from the inequity of having to repay debts without simultaneously having the right to claim debts owed by their creditors. A set-off is a countervailing claim available to a

defendant absolving him wholly or partially from liability to the plaintiff. As such, it is to be distinguished from counterclaim which is an entirely independent action brought by the defendant against the plaintiff and can, therefore, be used offensively in the same action (see chapter 11).

The amount of case law on the subject of set-off is so large that a sustained and detailed treatment is hardly feasible within the confines of this book. More specialist texts are available to which the reader is directed. In this chapter, we shall examine only the principles involved in the mutual credit provision in insolvency where a general right of set-off has been statutorily recognised since 1705 (4 Anne c. 17, s. 11). Here it was provided that commissioners in bankruptcy should adjust the accounts when there had been mutual credits between a bankrupt and his debtor-creditor so that, in this situation, the debtor-creditor of the bankrupt would be compelled to pay any balance still owing to the bankrupt. This approach was confirmed in the Statutes of Set-Off (7 Geo 1 c. 31; 2 Geo II c. 25; 5 Geo II c. 30; 8 Geo II c. 24; see now Supreme Court Act 1981, s. 49(2)). Despite the fact that by allowing set-off this would appear to infringe the *pari passu* principle, the basic premise of insolvency statutory set-off has never been questioned. The purpose of insolvency set-off is perceived, not so much in terms of avoiding circuity of action, which is the case with set-off outside insolvency, but rather as an accounting process giving the party asserting a set-off a preference on the basis that it does justice between the parties. Indeed, the purpose of insolvency set-off was explained by Parke B in *Forster* v *Wilson* (1843) 12 M & W 191 as being 'to do substantial justice between the parties where a debt is really due from the bankrupt to the debtor to his estate'.

The modern position is encapsulated in bankruptcy by s. 323 of the Insolvency Act 1986, whereas r. 4.90 of the Insolvency Rules 1986 governs liquidations. The two sets of rules are in substance identical. Rule 4.90 provides as follows:

(1) This Rule applies where, before the company goes into liquidation there have been mutual credits, mutual debts or other mutual dealings between the company and any creditor of the company proving or claiming to prove for a debt in the liquidation.

(2) An account shall be taken of what is due from each party to the other in respect of the mutual dealings, and the sums due from one party shall be set off against the sums due from the other.

(3) Sums due from the company to another party shall not be included in the account taken under paragraph (2) if that other party had notice at the time they became due that a meeting of creditors had been summoned under section 98 or (as the case may be) a petition for the winding up of the company was pending.

(4) Only the balance (if any) of the account is provable in the liquidation. Alternatively (as the case may be) the amount shall be paid to the liquidator as part of the assets.

A number of points arise in connection with the provisions of r. 4.90. Before considering these issues, it should be noted that the statutory set-off provisions apply only on the making of a winding-up order (compare *Re Norman Holding Co. Ltd* [1991] BCLC 1), so it is necessary to consider briefly the position of the administrative receiver and the administrator.

The administrative receiver and set-off The relevant principle here is that applicable to the assignment of debts. This is because the nature of the machinery for administrative receivership is that of enforcement of real security, so the debenture holder must take subject to the equities of the debt which is secured by the floating charge. Thus, a receiver is bound by the equities in existence at the date of crystallisation or notice of receivership (*Biggerstaff* v *Rowatt's Wharf Ltd* [1896] 2 Ch 93). Moreover, post-receivership cross-claims have been upheld where they are inseparably connected with and flow out of the transaction to which the debt subject to the receivership arose (*Rother Iron Works Ltd* v *Canterbury Precision Engineers Ltd* [1974] QB 1).

The administrator and set-off The principles of administrative receivership are not necessarily pertinent here because there is no assignment of property involved in administration, that is, there is no crystallisation. It would appear that set-off rights will apply even though prima facie they would appear potentially to frustrate the rescue attempt of the company which is, of course, the purpose of administration. A security for the purpose of the moratorium on enforcement is defined in s. 248(b) of the Insolvency Act 1986 as 'any mortgage, charge, lien or other security.' A set-off is merely a right to set up one personal claim against another and does not constitute a proprietary right to which a security interest can attach. The reference to 'other security' in s. 248(b) must be read *eiusdem generis* with the other *conventional* security devices (see p. 356). From an economic, functional perspective, we are confronted here with the same policy dilemma as with retention of title clause mechanisms which are specifically provided for in administration. It has to be admitted that the line between set-off and security interest is a fuzzy one. As Murray has argued, 'Banks versus Creditors of their Customers: Set-offs against Customers' Accounts' (1977) 82 Commer Law J 449 at p. 464:

> The set-off principle when confined to two parties who are both creditors and debtors of each other is most logical because it facilitates the quick and economic adjusting of their affairs. . . . When the rights of third parties arise, the answer seems less clear. . . . Reduced to its basic terms: why should any unsecured creditor (banker or non-banker) receive more than his pro rata share merely because he has been lucky enough or astute enough to keep his hands on other property of the debtor? . . .
> If pro rata sharing of loss is the touchstone of creditors' rights, set-off seems to be an aberration.

Insolvency set-off
The courts have consistently interpreted insolvency set-off in terms of it being mandatory in orientation. Outside insolvency, solvent parties can exclude

set-off claims arising out of mutual dealing. There may be very good commercial reasons for this. As Parker LJ explained in *Continental Illinois National Bank and Trust Co. of Chicago* v *Pananicolaou* [1986] 2 Lloyd's Rep 441 at p. 445:

> ... the parties have specifically provided both in the loan agreement and the guarantees that payment should be made free of any set-off or counterclaim. It would defeat the whole commercial purpose of the transaction, would be out of touch with business realities and would keep the bank waiting for payment, which both the borrowers and the guarantors intended that it should have, whilst protracted proceedings on the alleged counterclaims were litigated.

There are significant problems associated with the mandatory nature of insolvency set-off which can be illustrated in the House of Lords' decision in *National Westminster Bank Ltd* v *Halesowen Presswork and Assemblies Ltd* [1972] AC 785.

Before the decision of the House of Lords in *National Westminster Bank* v *Halesowen Presswork and Assemblies Ltd*, it was common for banks to open a new account for a company in financial difficulties with the stipulation that they were not to set off any credit balances on the new account against existing indebtedness. Such an arrangement effectively ensured that the fund could be handed over to the liquidator intact, and that the bank would not automatically be preferred. This was struck down by a majority in the House of Lords which held that the operation of the set-off section may not be excluded by agreement between the parties. The agreement in question was that in the absence of materially changed circumstances, the bank would adhere to the arrangement for a period of four months while an attempt was made to sell the business as a going concern. As a matter of construction, the agreement was only intended to remain in force during the subsistence of the banker-customer relationship so that upon the resolution for a winding up, the accounts could be regarded as combined. While their lordships held that the set-off section also applied, the question of set-off would, in fact, only have become relevant if the agreement to keep the accounts separate was intended to survive the liquidation.

Lord Cross of Chelsea delivered a strong dissenting judgment at p. 813:

> I cannot see why in principle the person in whose interest it would be to invoke the rule of 'set-off' should not be entitled to agree in advance that in the event of the bankruptcy of the other party he will not invoke it. In general '*quilibet potest renunciare iuri pro se introducto*'.... So, apart from authority, I would have thought that the section, though mandatory in its terms, should be read as being subject to any agreement to the contrary.

In the light of this approach, it is odd that Lord Cross delivered the majority judgment of the House of Lords in *British Eagle International Air Lines Ltd* v *Compagnie Nationale Air France* [1975] 1 WLR 758 discussed earlier. In delivering the majority judgment, Lord Cross distinguished *National Westminster Bank Ltd* v *Halesowen Presswork and Assemblies Ltd* in the last sentence of his judgment on the basis that it was irrelevant for the purpose of the *British Eagle* case as it dealt with the set-off provisions and not the *pari passu* provisions. However, this does not accord with the rest of his judgment which reaches the same conclusion as the *Halesowen* case, namely, that it is against public policy to contract out of statutory provisions dealing with liquidation. In this respect, it is possible to argue that Lord Cross was inconsistent in his judicial approach to this question.

Essentially, the issue is whether the creditor should, from the point of view of policy, be permitted, as the Cork committee (1982) recommended at para. 1342, to agree in advance to waive his right to invoke the section, particularly when the creditor is the party who otherwise would have benefited by a set-off. This is a salutary proposal, and it is a pity that it has not translated itself into the Insolvency Act 1986. It can be argued that there is nothing wrong or unfair in a subordination agreement since no one is prejudiced except the intending creditors themselves who have agreed to waive their claims to a division of the assets *pari passu*.

There are several limitations to the statutory right of set-off encapsulated in r. 4.90 which we shall now proceed to examine.

There must be mutual credits, mutual debts and other mutual dealings   Set-off is in principle confined to mutual money obligations. What is implied by mutuality is that the claim and cross-claim be between the *same* parties in the *same* right so that, for example, third-party rights must be respected (see *Barclays Bank Ltd* v *Quistclose Investments Ltd* [1970] AC 567; *Neste Oy* v *Lloyds Bank plc* [1983] 2 Lloyd's Rep 658). It is not necessary to show two enforceable debts at the time of the commencement of the liquidation so long as there are, at that time, mutual dealings which create absolute or contingent rights maturing into obligations sounding in pecuniary demands capable of set-off. There is no mutuality between a liquidating company and a solvent person holding a money claim as a trustee for a special purpose (*Bailey* v *Finch* (1871) LR 7 QB 34). The reason for this is that the designation of the special purpose removes the sum from the accounting *between* both parties, thereby precluding set-off in the absence of the restriction being released (*Re City Equitable Fire Insurance Co. Ltd (No. 2)* [1930] 2 Ch 293).

The principle established in *Rose* v *Hart* (1818) 8 Taunt 499 is sometimes referred to as an exception to the rule that trust funds are not susceptible to set-off. The essence of this rule is that where a debtor delivers property to his creditor with directions to convert it into money, if the direction is not revoked, and the conversion into money is effected after the debtor has become insolvent, there is mutuality for the purpose of insolvency set-off. The true basis of *Rose* v *Hart* however, is not in relation to trust funds but rather that the credit envisaged is in the form of a *debt*. An analogy may be drawn with the retention-of-title line of case law where poorly drafted proceeds clauses were considered by the courts in *Re Andrabell Ltd* [1984] 3 All ER 407, and *Hendy Lennox (Industrial Engines) Ltd* v *Grahame Puttick Ltd* [1984] 1 WLR 485 not to constitute an obligation to account so that a debtor-creditor relationship intervened, that is, the buyer was merely a debtor for the amount of the proceeds (but compare *Rolls Razor Ltd* v *Cox* [1967] 1 QB 552).

The debts must be proved This requirement was recently illustrated in *Re Norman Holding Co. Ltd* [1991] 1 WLR 10. In this case the creditor, Harrowby Street Properties Ltd, was a secured creditor of the insolvent company for £400,000 relating to the purchase price of a property which the company had purchased from Harrowby. Harrowby was also an unsecured creditor and submitted a proof of debt in the company's liquidation. The insolvent company, Norman Holdings, was also an unsecured creditor of Harrowby in respect of sums due under a rental warranty given by Harrowby in the property purchase agreement. The property had been sold in the liquidation and Harrowby wanted to be paid out of the proceeds. It was alleged, however, that Harrowby's secured claim had been discharged by the operation of the set-off.

In giving his decision, Mervyn Davies J read r. 4.90 of the Insolvency Rules 1986 literally so as to apply the set-off to creditors proving in the liquidation. However, he limited the set-off to the unsecured debts proved and would not extend it to secured debts which it was chosen not to prove and Harrowby were proving in the liquidation only for the unsecured debt. Rule 4.90 did not give a clear answer as to whether the set-off operated against the secured debt, but Mervyn Davies J accepted that it was important that a secured creditor did not have to prove in the liquidation for that debt and could instead realise his security to cover his debt. Indeed, Harrowby had elected to do just that with regard to their secured debt. It would lead to a curious result if a secured creditor, who also has an unsecured debt and who proves that unsecured debt should be subject to the set-off for both the secured and unsecured amounts. Therefore, a secured creditor who does not prove that debt is not involved in the litigation in respect of that debt even if he is involved with respect to some other debt that he does prove.

Mutual dealings must have taken place prior to the winding up Although r. 4.90 links set-off to mutual dealings before liquidation, it is not necessary that there should be mutual debts at that time so long as there are obligations on both sides arising from mutual dealings which will mature into mutual debts.

The claims on both sides must relate to sums of money due The wording of the third part of r. 4.90 has posed considerable dilemmas. One of the important distinctions that can be drawn between the Insolvency Act 1986 and the Act it replaced, s. 31 of the Bankruptcy Act 1914, is that the latter referred to notice 'at the time of giving credit' rather than the time when the relevant debts 'became due'. It could be argued, therefore, that contingent debts do not 'become due' until their due date, so contingent debts are not under the new rules provable (compare the first instance approach of Millett J in *Re Charge Card Services Ltd* [1987] Ch 150).

The main object of r. 4.90(3) is to prevent creditors from improving their position where an insolvency is imminent. The object is to prevent the unfair build up of set-offs, so liabilities which remain contingent at the time of the account are not eligible for set-off. However, the Cork committee (1982) considered at para. 1356 that set-off was available for contingent debts so that contingent claims which are provable, in the sense that they are capable of valuation, can be made eligible for set-off. This conclusion is consistent with the mischief of r. 4.90(3) which has nothing to do with the maturity of claims, but rather is concerned with when they are incurred so as to prevent voluntary building up of preferential set-offs.

No notice of petition or the summoning of a creditors' meeting when the sums claimed become due   Unless the court otherwise directs, winding up petitions must be advertised in the *London Gazette* (r. 4.11). A section 98 notice of a creditors' meeting must be advertised in the *London Gazette* and in at least two local newspapers. An advertisement in the *London Gazette* is notice to all the world of the petition but only as from such time as they may reasonably be supposed to have seen it.

Insolvency set-off and preferential debts   In *Re Unit 2 Windows Ltd* [1985] 1 WLR 1383, Walton J in his judgment considered the situation in which a creditor has two claims against a company in liquidation, one of which is preferential, and the creditor is also indebted to the company. If the set-off was operated in reduction of the debt which was not preferred, the creditor would be better off because the preferred debt would still be in existence after the set-off and would have priority. This conclusion was resisted by Walton J who held on the basis of the maxim that equality is equity that the set-off should be marshalled, that is, to operate rateably between the preferential and the non-preferential debts (see also *Smit Tak International Zeesleepen Bergingsbedrijf BV* v *Selco Salvage Ltd* [1988] 2 Lloyd's Rep 398. For an instructive discussion on the application of the marshalling doctrine in set-off cases see Derham, R., 'Set-off against an Assignee: The Relevance of Marshalling Contribution and Subrogation' (1991) 107 LQR 126).

SUBORDINATION

The essence of any subordination agreement is the provision that under certain defined circumstances, normally the bankruptcy of the common debtor, no payments on the subordinating creditor's claim (the junior creditor) will be made until the claim of the senior creditor (or class of creditors) is fully paid by their common debtor. Subordination is different from waiver in that the junior creditor retains its priority against interests other than the senior interest, that is, priorities are reversed. If the security is waived, the waiver will be binding on the secured creditor if consideration was given for it, and the latter may be estopped by his conduct from denying the waiver against a third party who acted to his detriment in reliance upon it. An enforceable waiver will be binding on an assignee of the security unless the assignee is a bona fide purchaser of a legal estate without notice. The practice is to endorse notices of release on the security document so that assignees will have notice.

The purposes of subordination are varied: for example, the debtor may wish to enlarge its capital base by encouraging fresh senior credit, or through increasing its borrowing limits imposed by borrowing restrictions as seen with negative pledge clauses. In some instances, subordination may be used to avoid insolvency as where major suppliers to a debtor company are persuaded to subordinate their claims so as to induce bank creditors from enforcing their loans through an administrative receivership. Since a subordination agreement ranks one creditor prior to another, it increases the money available and demonstrates the importance of security in the sense of priority for institutional lenders.

Subordination falls within that difficult interface between priority and security. There are two basic types: first, *ab initio* subordination as where the junior creditor has always been subordinated in order, typically, to avoid a negative pledge clause; secondly, subsequent subordination as where an existing general creditor of the common debtor agrees to subordinate his claim to the senior's claim. There are several variations to this basic pattern. In the case of a complete subordination, no payments on the subordinate debt can be made until the senior debt has been paid in full, whereas with an inchoate subordination, payments of both interest and principal can be made on the subordinated debt until an event of subordination occurs such as liquidation. There are dangers associated with this latter form of subordination; if the agreement permits the junior creditor to take pre-insolvency payments, it is possible for the junior creditor and the common debtor to repeal the subordination agreement over the protests of the senior creditor.

Subordination and set-off
Considerable problems arise with the enforceability of subordination agreements on insolvency. If a junior creditor can set off the junior debt against a debt owed by the junior creditor to the debtor, this will destroy the purpose of subordination. Whilst English law does champion pre-insolvency contracts against set-off as an aspect of freedom of contract doctrine, more difficulties are posed by insolvency set-off which is mandatory where there is the requisite mutuality. In the case of a debtor-creditor subordination where the junior creditor agrees to pay the senior creditor the amount of the junior debt, there would be mutuality, so set-off is available since the junior creditor is the beneficial owner of the junior debt. It would appear then that contractual subordination, where there is no transfer of property to the senior creditor, has the effect of making the junior creditor senior in the sense of set-off. It is otherwise in the case of a subordination trust of the entire junior claim which will destroy the mutuality necessary for the simple reason that one person's money must not be used to pay another's debt.

Subordination and the *pari passu* principle
As we have seen, the courts in England have persistently interpreted the *pari passu* principle of insolvency law as being mandatory in nature so, no device calculated to defeat its operation will be enforced. The policy of the *pari passu* rule encapsulated in s. 107 of the Insolvency Act 1986 and r. 4.181(1) of the

Insolvency Rules 1986 (as amended) is to ensure that a creditor is not paid ahead of the general body of creditors. No policy of insolvency law would appear to be offended where one creditor agreed to be deferred through a subordination agreement. The reason for this is that the agreement does not operate to withdraw unencumbered assets from the fund available for distribution among all the creditors. Indeed, this was the approach adopted by Southwell J in the Australian case of *Horne v Chester and Fein Property Developments Pty Ltd* [1987] VR 913. It is not the function of insolvency law to overturn existing rights the scope of which must be determined by *common law* and *statutory principles*. Moreover, as a matter of consistency, since a creditor does not have to prove his right if he wishes not to, he should surely be able to agree by contract to renounce his right to prove. In any case, r. 11.11(1) of the Insolvency Rules 1986 recognises that a liquidator can be required to pay dividends to the assignee of those dividends under, for example, a turnover subordinate trust. This would appear to avoid the *pari passu* dilemma as well as having the advantage of avoiding the risk that the junior creditor might divert the proceeds.

It is hard to understand what possible public policy objection exists against post-liquidation subordinations which affect only the creditors concerned and in no way affect the entitlement of creditors not a party to that agreement. This position should be compared with that of *British Eagle International Air Lines Ltd v Compagnie Nationale Air France* [1975] 1 WLR 758 which, had the clearing scheme been enforced, would have withdrawn debts due from Air France from the fund available for other credits. Even this post-liquidation netting arrangement, as we have seen, is now possible following the Companies Act 1989. The effect of removing such market contracts from the ambit of insolvency law is that it provides yet a further example of the legislature itself undermining the *pari passu* principle of distribution.

Subordination and proof

The problem posed by all subordination agreements is that the creditors of the junior do not have notice of the fact that an apparent asset (the junior's claim against the common debtor) has, in effect, been encumbered in favour of the senior. This difficulty becomes particularly acute on the dual insolvency of the common debtor and junior creditor. This is not necessarily an unusual event given that there may be insolvency because of a common cause, for example, where the financial condition of the junior is intertwined with that of the common debtor. In this respect, the juridical rationale for the subordination agreement is important. If it is a property interest, will it be defeasible on satisfaction of the senior creditor's debt? Is it an assignment by a non-recourse guarantor in order to secure the senior claim with all the repercussions pertaining to assignment of choses in action?

The assignment theory is interesting since, as a proprietary right, it bridges the gap between a junior creditor's personal obligation enforceable by damages and a claim against the *res* or property itself. If the junior creditor fails to prove in the liquidation process in the hope of defeating the senior creditor's double dividends then, by treating subordinations as assignments, the senior creditor will be able to prove for the junior creditor. Even the notoriously difficult rule in *Dearle* v *Hall* (1828) 3 Russ 1 should not prove unduly onerous in the context of subordination since the common debtor will usually have notice of the debt. It is otherwise in the case of a subordination trust or a conditional debt since the subordinated debt remains in law and equity an obligation owed to the junior creditor. Consequently, the senior creditor as transferee of the proceeds of the junior debt will not be the 'creditor' for the purpose of proof and voting on the common debtor's insolvency.

Subordination and security
On the insolvency of the junior creditor, in order for the subordination agreement to prevail over third-party claimants of the junior creditor, for example, the junior creditor's liquidator, or administrator, or execution creditor, it will be necessary to show that the agreement gives the senior creditor proprietary rights over the junior debt. A mere personal right will not be sufficient to gain priority (compare *Pritchard* v *Briggs* [1980] Ch 338). Insofar as there is an absolute transfer of the junior debt this should not constitute a charge requiring registration under s. 396 of the Companies Act 1985 (as amended). English law, as we have seen (see chapter 15), is slow to treat a transfer of property as a security interest in the absence of a sham, for example, where the transferor has an equity of redemption. It is unlikely that a subordination *trust*, consisting of a *trust* of receipts by the junior creditor in favour of the senior creditor up to the amount of the senior debt, constitutes a security interest since there is no equity of redemption here, that is, there is no property to give back to the transferor. An analogy here may be drawn with effective proceeds clauses in retention of title (see chapter 12).

It is possible to argue in the case of a subordination *assignment* of the whole junior debt that it constitutes a security interest. This is because the junior creditor has an equity of redemption for any surplus achieved on the junior debt to the extent that it exceeded the unpaid amount of the senior debt. Even if a security interest has been created, this may not necessarily require registration. Thus, where proceeds receivable on the junior debt are assigned, this will not require registration as a charge on book debts because the proceeds of the debt are not the debt itself. In this respect, book debts have been defined by Lord Esher MR in *Official Receiver* v *Tailby* (1886) 18 QBD 25 at p. 29 as debts arising in a business which ought to be entered in the company's books. Moreover, as a matter of principle, it is difficult to argue that there can be a book debt here since the subject-matter (the object of the charge) is the *loan* made by the junior creditor. On the other hand, there will be a requirement of registration in relation to a floating charge where this represents the interest of the junior creditor in the junior debt. Of course, this will depend upon the amount of autonomy enjoyed by the junior debtor in this regard which is a question of fact to be decided in each case.

DISTRIBUTION OF ASSETS

Only provable claims are eligible to be paid out of the company's assets. The list of claims that can be proved is an extensive one, namely, all debts and all claims against the company, present or future, certain or contingent, ascertained or sounding in damages (s. 322 of the Insolvency Act 1986, r. 12.3 of the Insolvency Rules 1986). It would appear now that unliquidated claims in tort are provable. Future debts must be discounted to show present value (rr. 6.114 and 11.13 of the Insolvency Rules 1986) whilst contingent claims must be estimated (r. 4.86).

The order of distribution
The first call on the company's assets is payment of the expenses of the insolvency itself. In this respect, the liquidator may need to continue trading so as to ensure a beneficial winding up of the company and the obligations entered into here, including the liquidator's own remuneration, are referred to as pre-preferential debts (see s. 115 of the Insolvency Act 1986 dealing with voluntary winding up and r. 4.180(1) of the Insolvency Rules 1986 in the case of both forms of winding up). It should be noted that in *Re MC Bacon Ltd* [1991] Ch 127, Millett J held that liquidation expenses (in the sense of being pre-preferential) did not include the cost incurred in proceedings initiated by the liquidator to set aside a floating charge as a transaction at an undervalue or preference.

In many cases, it is difficult to distinguish between a post-liquidation creditor who is entitled to priority from a pre-liquidation creditor who is only entitled to proof. This is especially the case with leases as these may impose a continuing obligation. If the liquidator adopts the lease, liability accruing *after* adoption is an expense of the liquidation and is therefore payable.

It used to be the case that monopoly suppliers, especially public utilities like electricity and gas, would insist on payment of pre-liquidation claims in order to ensure future supply. In large measure, this constituted an exploitation of their monopoly position and attracted much criticism in the Cork committee report (1982). As a result of the Cork committee's recommendation at para. 1462, such suppliers are now prohibited from making payment of outstanding pre-liquidation charges a condition of the continuance of supply (s. 233 of the Insolvency Act 1986). Even so, despite the fact that the Insolvency Act 1986 has cut down the number of preferential claims on insolvency, there are still significant departures from the principle of equal treatment of all creditors which we shall now proceed to examine.

Secured creditors Such creditors enjoy priority over all others. Indeed, only after the secured creditors have been fully satisfied does the property form part of the assets available to the liquidator. We have already considered the general issue of whether, in fact, the taking of security is in the economic interest of either the debtor or creditor (see chapter 1). In addition, we have discussed the ranking as between secured creditors themselves which involves issues of priority to which the *pari passu* principle of distribution does not apply (see part 4).

Preferential creditors The claims that receive preferential treatment fall into two distinct groups which, in contrast to pre-preferential debts, rank *pari passu* among themselves (s. 175(2)(a) of the Insolvency Act 1986). The first group relates to State claims for taxes and other levies such as VAT, PAYE income tax and national insurance contributions. The reasoning here is that in a *non-technical sense*, these are moneys held in trust by the taxpayer on behalf of the Crown. The second group of favoured claims consists of amounts due to employees: salary or wages, holiday pay and, by extension, the claims of third parties who have advanced money to pay these. It would appear that protection is afforded to those who are in a special position of dependence on the company (see sch 6, category 5, of the Insolvency Act 1986).

Preferential debts have priority over the claims of holders of debentures secured by any floating charge created by the company (s. 175(2)(b) of the Insolvency Act 1986). Automatic crystallisation clauses have only a limited effect on insolvency following the amended definition of floating charge contained in s. 251 of the Insolvency Act 1986 to include 'a charge which, as created, was a floating charge'. Of course, the rights of creditors under a floating charge are preconditional upon the validity of the charge itself, and any priority agreements or negative pledge clauses relating to the floating charge. To the extent that a floating charge has, by virtue of a priority agreement, priority over a subsequent fixed charge which, in turn, has priority over preferential debts, the floating chargee is subrogated to the rights of the fixed chargee to the amount of the sum secured by the floating charge.

Ordinary creditors Once all the debts and expenses relating to the categories discussed above have been fully paid out, the liquidator may then distribute dividends to the general body of ordinary creditors. The ordinary creditors rank *pari passu* and generally the remaining assets will prove inadequate as claimants will only receive a proportion of what they are owed (r. 4.181 of the Insolvency Rules 1986). There are certain classes of indebtedness which, by virtue of some statutory provision, are deferred for payment in a liquidation until the company's other debts and liabilities have been paid in full (see ss. 2(3)(d) and 3 of the Partnership Act 1890; s. 178(3) to (6) of the Companies Act 1985; s. 74(2)(f) of the Insolvency Act 1986).

Disposal of any surplus Exceptionally, there may be assets left after all the claims have been met and these are distributed among shareholders.

TWENTY-ONE
Avoiding powers and the liability of directors and others for improper trading

It is important to recall the function of insolvency law which constitutes, primarily, a set of distributional rules by which the assets of the insolvent are distributed to creditors according to their pre-liquidation entitlements. It is not the function of insolvency law to dislocate pre-liquidation transactions in the absence of some superior policy reasons. These policy reasons underlie the rationale for avoidance of certain transactions which amount to preference. Of course, outside insolvency, preferences are permitted as an aspect of freedom of contract but on the onset of the collective proceedings of insolvency, the pursuit of individual interest may leave the group of creditors worse off. Preference law is concerned with post-loan behaviour where one creditor tries to improve his status, for example, from unsecured to becoming a secured creditor.

The championing of the collective process in insolvency requires the cutting down of individual rights including vulnerable floating charges (s. 245 of the Insolvency Act 1986), undue preferences (s. 239), and post-liquidation dispositions (s. 127). A careful distinction can be drawn here with legal powers which are directed at penalising debtor or creditor misbehaviour as these are pertinent whether or not insolvency proceedings are commenced, for example, the avoidance of transactions at an undervalue (ss. 238, 240 and 241), extortionate credit bargains (s. 244), and transactions defrauding creditors (ss. 423 to 425). Even here special policy considerations may apply. Thus, in response to the expression of concern by the City of London that UK insolvency law might threaten market contracts (incidentally, a valuable source of 'invisible' earnings for the British economy), the preference provisions do not apply. Section 165 of the Companies Act 1989 outlaws the application of ss. 238, 239, 339, 340 and 423 of the Insolvency Act 1986 to market contracts which include margin and netting agreements, or settlements provided for in accordance with the rules of a recognised clearing house or commodity exchange.

In general, the onset of insolvent liquidation is the occasion for the reopening of a number of pre-liquidation transactions for scrutiny in the light of the avoiding powers encapsulated in the Insolvency Act 1986. The main purpose of these powers is to prevent the improper disposition of company assets where a company is in a questionable state of liquidity during that twilight period before a petition for winding up is heard. Obviously, there is no need for such protection where the company is solvent (*Re a Company (No. 005685 of 1988) (No. 2)* [1989] BCLC 424) because unsecured creditors can adequately protect their position by instituting proceedings, taking judgment, and subsequently enforcement by one of the available forms of execution including seizure and sale of the company's property.

The mischief behind the avoiding powers is the diminution of the company's assets and the absence or inadequacy of new value supplied. Where an administration order is made, or the company goes into insolvent liquidation, the court has power under the Insolvency Act 1986 to reopen a transaction at an undervalue and to make such order as it thinks fit for restoring the position to what it would have been had the company not entered into the transaction (s. 238). It is the advent of liquidation or administration within a specified time which provides the cause of action since this relates to the attempt to bypass the collective nature of the proceeding and the principle of *pari passu* distribution.

We shall now consider the specific heads under which dispositions made in the period leading up to the making of the winding-up order may be invalidated. Before doing so, it is important to note that the application of the statutory provisions may depend on whether the other party to the transaction was a person connected with the company. A person is 'connected' within the meaning of ss. 249 and 439 of the Insolvency Act 1986 if he is a director or shadow director of the company, or if he is an associate of such an individual or of the company itself. A wide meaning is given to 'associate' for these purposes. In relation to an individual, it includes a person's husband or wife, parent, brother, sister or child, and any relative of the person or of the person's husband or wife. In relation to a company, 'associate' includes another company under the control of the same person, or a company under the control of an associate of the person controlling the first company. In all cases, a partner or an employee are associates.

TRANSACTIONS AT UNDERVALUE

A transfer of company property may be set aside under the Insolvency Act 1986 on the ground that full value was not given for it. The statutory test is contained in s. 238(4) which states that a company enters into such a transaction with a person if:

(a) the company makes a gift to that person or otherwise enters into a transaction with that person on terms that provide for the company to receive no consideration, or

(b) the company enters into a transaction with that person for a consideration the value of which, in money or money's worth, is significantly less than the value, in money or money's worth, of the consideration provided by the company.

A transfer can only be attacked if made within two years before the commencement of the winding up so long as, at the time, the company was unable to pay its debts, or became unable to pay them as a result of the transaction. In the case of a connected person, there is a rebuttable presumption that the company was unable to pay its debts. Clearly, this last approach is correct in principle because connected persons are likely to have inside information as to the company's financial predicament, and can also influence the company's decision to enter into the transaction.

It would appear from s. 238(4) that gifts may be avoided. A payment to charity could, therefore, be avoided as there is no defence of good-faith receipt. More difficulty is posed with bonus payments to employees, for example, a reward for targets met or other gratuities such as a Christmas bonus. It is probable that such 'emoluments' are covered by s. 238(5) of the Insolvency Act 1986. This subsection is designed to enable the company to engage in genuine business transactions carried out in good faith in the reasonable belief that they will benefit the company. Notwithstanding that these transactions are at 'undervalue' under any objective criteria, they will retain their validity by virtue of s. 238(5) so long as there is belief *in fact* on such grounds. If no reasonable grounds for belief exist, mere honest belief in the existence of such grounds is insufficient. The party whose good faith attracts the defence is the company and not the transferee. There is a separate statutory defence in favour of a good-faith recipient for *value* and without notice provided by s. 241(2) of the Insolvency Act 1986.

In addition to gifts, a company enters into a transaction at an undervalue if the consideration provided by the other party is 'significantly less' than that furnished by the company (s. 238(4)(b)). What is 'significantly less' is a question of fact, but in any case, as in general contract law, past consideration does not suffice. Thus, it would appear that the subordination of an existing debt in the suspect period could be set aside if there is an element of undervalue, and there is no defence under s. 238(5). More problems are posed by guarantees, for example, where a company gives a guarantee in respect of advances to be made to its parent company by a third party. In determining whether there is an element of undervalue here, reference must be made *not* to the time when payment was demanded under the guarantee but rather to the time when the surety became bound by the guarantee. In establishing undervalue, the liquidator or other office holder must show that the contingent liability of the surety at the *time of granting the guarantee* was significantly greater than the value of the benefit received by the surety from the advance to the parent company. Because of the difficulties in valuing the contingent benefit and liability, it is unlikely that a guarantee will be held to constitute a transaction at undervalue, for example, where there was a high chance of the parent company's insolvency and the creditor had recourse to no other security to secure the advance made. Where there is other security, for example, a mortgage or charge on the company's property, the surety is given a right of subrogation so as to ensure that all of the burden of payment does not fall upon the surety. It follows from this that in valuing the benefits of the guarantee to the creditor, account must be taken of any real security taken from the principal debtor by the creditor.

General powers of the court
Under s. 238(3) of the Insolvency Act 1986, the court may make such an order as it thinks fit for restoring the position to what it would have been if the company had not entered into the avoided transaction. This is a wide power which can take into account additional profits which the transferor company would have likely earned had the transaction not taken place.

Specific powers of the court
The range of orders, without prejudicing the generality of s. 238(2), which the court might make are listed in s. 241 of the Insolvency Act 1986. The general effect of these powers is to preserve the validity of the original transaction but the adverse effects are reversed, for example, through conveyance or reconveyance of property, or through payment of a sum of money, or the discharge of any security. There is no jurisdiction to make any order which does not have as its aim the restoration of the position immediately before the transaction at an undervalue: The court is bound to make an order for restoring the *status quo ante* the impugned transaction. It is important to note that the transferee is not a trustee of the property which is the subject of the impugned transaction. In this respect, tracing principles and associated rules as in *Clayton's Case* (*Devaynes* v *Noble* (1816) 1 Mer 572) will not apply. The court may simply make an *in personam* order to ensure that the company is no worse off than it would have been if it had never entered into the transaction in the first place. This does not necessarily require the transferee to disgorge profits made from the property acquired.

To prevent windfall profits in transactions at an undervalue, the court will usually require repayment by the company through a court officer, such as a liquidator, of any sum received in exchange for property ordered to be reconveyed to the company unless it was a transfer for value. In the latter instance, there is no injustice to the transferee to prove in competition with other creditors since the transferee had not bargained for this right.

Orders affecting third parties
The court cannot make an order which will prejudice rights acquired in good faith for value and without notice of the relevant circumstances (s. 241(2) of the Insolvency Act 1986). It would appear that reference to relevant circumstances includes both notice of the fact that there was a transaction at an undervalue, and that the company was unable to pay its debts at the time of the transaction or became so in consequence of it.

PREFERENCES

In the case of voidable preferences it was argued in the Cork committee report, 1982, at para. 1270–6, that the burden of repayment should be borne by the party whom it was intended to prefer. The drafting of the statutory test for the giving of a preference under s. 239(4) reflects this recommendation, so it is now possible to proceed directly against the party who has been preferred, for example, a surety or guarantor, independently of any proceedings which may be taken against the creditor. The typical case here is where a company's account in a bank has been guaranteed by the directors of the company who, at a time when the company is insolvent, arrange for it to repay the bank not out of any desire to improve the bank's position but to release themselves from their own liability to the bank — this is the so-called 'end-game'.

In order for the transaction to be impugned it must have been entered into at a time when the company was insolvent in the sense that it was unable to pay its debts, or became unable to pay them as a result of the transaction. The requisite period for preference before the commencement of the winding up is six months (s. 240(1)(b)), or where the third party is a connected person, other than an employee, the period is two years (s. 240(1)(a)).

Undue preference is given where the recipient is a creditor and the company does, or omits to do something, which has the effect of putting the creditor in a better position in any subsequent insolvent liquidation than he would have been in if the preference had not been given (s. 239(4)). There is no requirement to demonstrate an objective intention to prefer; it is necessary to show, however, that there was a *desire* to put the creditor or surety in a better position than he would otherwise have been had the preference not been given, namely, a subjective test. The issue of the creditor's good faith is irrelevant except insofar as payment is made in the normal course of business which will indicate no *desire* to favour the creditor to whom payment has been made. Moreover, where a company yields to the application of genuine commercial pressure by a creditor and makes a payment, this is unlikely to be attacked on the ground of preference since the company did not 'desire' the effect. A man can choose the lesser of two evils without desiring either (see *Re MC Bacon Ltd* [1990] BCC 78). It is only necessary to show that the desire to create an advantageous position was present in the minds of those who cause the company to confer a preference, and this may be proved by direct or circumstantial evidence.

A preference granted to a connected person should not be difficult to establish since the desire to prefer is presumed unless the contrary is shown (s. 239(6)). As a matter of principle, it is better to have clear rules rather than standards. The costs of such rules which constitute an objectivisation of preference law are less than the costs of a fuzzy standard which requires case-by-case inquiry into the bona fides of the creditor's (and debtor's) payment motives. Preference law has never felt comfortable with any balance between a rule and a standard (see Weisberg, 'Commercial Morality, the Merchant Character, and the History of the Voidable Preference' (1986) 39 Stan L Rev 1).

There can be no question of preference where the creditor gives new value because, by doing so, he has not depleted the assets available for general disposition on the insolvency of the company. Difficulties arise where there is a current-account relationship between the parties. Are the deals to be treated as isolated transactions requiring fresh value, or as entries in a continuous account? The latter approach can be commended as it coheres with economic reality and, in any case, where there is a series of mutual dealings with debits and credits on both sides, this will usually be sufficient to negate an intention to prefer. This is especially important for banks because if an insolvent customer whose account is overdrawn pays in cheques, this has the effect of improving the bank's position for it will have a lien on the cheque to secure the overdraft and, thus, a security interest in the proceeds where the cheque is given to the bank simply for collection (see *National Australia Bank Ltd* v *KDS Construction Services Pty Ltd* (1987) 163 CLR 668).

Where a creditor has a valid security interest, a payment not exceeding the value of the security cannot be a preference since there is no diminution of the pool of assets available for the payment of unsecured debts. It is otherwise in the case of a floating security since the payment may enable the debenture holder, for example, to rank above the statutory priority of preferential creditors. However, the relevant time here relates to a *hypothetical* liquidation when the payment was made, so only preferential debts then in existence will be relevant.

General powers of the court

On an application by the office-holder for an order under s. 239 of the Insolvency Act 1986, the court, if satisfied that the conditions have been met, is required to make such order as it thinks fit for restoring the position to what it would have been had the company not given the preference.

Specific powers of the court

These are the same as for transactions at an undervalue. We have already mentioned above the court's power to make an order for payment directly against the surety unless the payment was made solely to prefer the creditor. In this circumstance, the surety may be able to rely on the good-faith defence provided by s. 241(2)(b) if he received the benefit for value (unlikely) and without notice of the relevant circumstances (again unlikely in the case of directors of a company). Finally, it is worth noting that a payment made to prefer the surety can be ordered to be repaid by the creditor for he is also a recipient of a preference and a benefit under s. 241(1)(c).

EXTORTIONATE CREDIT TRANSACTIONS

Section 244 of the Insolvency Act 1986 empowers the court to set aside an extortionate transaction involving the provision of credit to a company entered into within three years of the administration order, or of the commencement of winding up. Section 244(2) is drafted in such a way as to allow a credit bargain to be reopened whether or not the contract is still running and current at the date of the application to the court by the office-holder. A credit transaction is extortionate if, having regard to the risks accepted by the financing creditor, the terms of credit are such as to require grossly exorbitant payments to be made by the company, or the transaction otherwise grossly contravened ordinary principles of fair dealing (s. 244(3)). This provision is modelled on s. 138(1) of the Consumer Credit Act 1974.

Although s. 244(3) of the Insolvency Act 1986 requires it to be presumed that a transaction is extortionate unless the contrary is proved, decisions under s. 138 of the Consumer Credit Act 1974 make it clear that the court will have regard to the risk accepted by the creditor. It is not enough to show that the transaction was burdensome so that in *Davies* v *Directloans Ltd* [1986] 1 WLR 823, it was held, in relation to interest rates in the context of secured consumer loans at p. 837:

> I cannot regard the difference between the 18 per cent which he submitted was proper and the 21.6 per cent which the defendant actually charged as anywhere near large enough to render the latter grossly exorbitant.

It must be shown that the bargain was oppressive, reflecting a severe imbalance in bargaining power between the two parties.

The powers of the court

The court may at its discretion insert any of the orders included in s. 244(4) of the Insolvency Act 1986. These include the setting aside of the whole or part of any obligation created by the transaction; the variation of any of the terms of the transaction, or of the terms on which any related security is held; restitutional orders to be made against persons who have been party to the transaction or who hold property as security for the purposes of the transaction; and provisions directing the taking of accounts between persons.

The powers of the court, by virtue of s. 244(5) are exercisable concurrently with any powers exercisable in relation to the transaction as a transaction at an undervalue (ss. 238, 240 and 241 of the Insolvency Act 1986).

FLOATING CHARGES

Section 245 of the Insolvency Act 1986 applies to a floating charge created within 12 months of a petition for an administration order, or the commencement of winding up if the company was at the time, or in consequence of the transaction became, unable to pay its debts. If the debenture is in favour of a 'connected person', the 12-month period is extended to two years and it is immaterial that the company was solvent at the date of the charge. Such a person is likely to be aware that a state of insolvency is probable and, therefore, act to protect his own interests at the expense of other creditors.

Section 245(2) and (6) of the Insolvency Act 1986 enact:

> (2) Subject as follows, a floating charge on the company's undertaking or property created at a relevant time is invalid except to the extent of the aggregate of—
>
> (a) the value of so much of the consideration for the creation of the charge as consists of money paid, or goods or services supplied, to the company at the same time as, or after, the creation of the charge,

(b) the value of so much of that consideration as consist of the discharge or reduction, at the same time as, or after, the creation of the charge, of any debt of the company, and

(c) the amount of such interest (if any) as is payable on the amount falling within paragraph (a) or (b) in pursuance of any agreement under which the money was so paid, the goods or services were so supplied or the debt was so discharged or reduced.

(6) For the purposes of subsection (2)(a) the value of any goods or services supplied by way of consideration for a floating charge is the amount in money which at the time they were supplied could reasonably have been expected to be obtained for supplying the goods or services in the ordinary course of business and on the same terms (apart from the consideration) as those on which they were supplied to the company.

The section only applies to floating charges and not to fixed charges. Moreover, the charge is valid for new money, goods or services and for the full contractual rate of interest. Other tangible and intangible assets are excluded such as land and buildings, receivables and intellectual property rights. Furthermore, the money must be paid for the *benefit* of the company creating the charge. Thus, it was held in *Re Destone Fabrics Ltd* [1941] Ch 319, where the company was no more than a conduit pipe through which the payment was passed to the directors, the floating charge was not created for any consideration.

It is probable that s. 245 will be dwarfed in practice by the wider provisions of s. 238 which, as we have discussed above, relate to transactions at an undervalue which reach back *in all cases* two years. However, the application of s. 245 will be relevant especially as regards bank creditors. The reason for this is that if some fresh additional capital, or other consideration is furnished at or after the time of the creation of the floating charge, it will be valid to the extent of the actual value of that new consideration (see for example, *Re Matthew Ellis Ltd* [1933] Ch 458). The application of *Clayton's Case* (see p. 285), where there is a presumption that in the case of a current account items credited to the account are applied to the earliest indebtedness first, may turn past indebtedness into a fresh advance. Thus, where a floating charge is taken by a bank to secure a pre-existing overdraft, the rule in *Clayton's Case* will ensure that the turnover of money in the account will convert old value into new. Despite being criticised by the Cork committee report, 1982, at para. 1561-2, there is nothing anomalous about the application of *Clayton's Case* in this context because, by honouring cheques, the bank provides new money which is used to pay other creditors to whom the bank was not liable.

The invalidation of a floating charge under s. 245 does not affect the existence of the debt to which the charge was sought to secure; this debt will remain subject to proof in the liquidation proceedings. If the debt is paid before the charge is attacked, there is nothing for the liquidator to avoid who cannot, therefore, recover the proceeds paid over to the creditor (*Mace Builders (Glasgow) Ltd* v *Lunn* [1987] Ch 191).

TRANSACTIONS DEFRAUDING CREDITORS

Section 172 of the Law of Property Act 1925 which dealt with fraudulent conveyances was repealed by ss. 423 to 425 of the Insolvency Act 1986. There is now no precondition of insolvency for the operation of the new provisions which are applicable to individual or corporate personalities, who enter into a transaction at an undervalue for the purpose of putting assets beyond the reach of a person actually or potentially prejudiced by the transaction. The definition of a transaction at an undervalue in the corporate sphere is the same as under s. 238(4) of the Insolvency Act 1986 which we considered earlier (see pp. 444–6).

It is incumbent upon the party seeking to impeach the transaction to prove that the requisite motive was present on the debtor's side. Section 424 specifies which persons have standing to apply for an order under s. 423: In the first place, where the debtor has been wound up or is in administration, application may be made by the relevant office-holder; second, with the leave of the court, by a 'victim' of the transaction. 'Victim' is defined by s. 423(5) to mean 'a person who is, or is capable of being, prejudiced' by the transaction. In the third instance, where a 'victim' of the transaction is bound by a voluntary arrangement, application may be made by the supervisor of the voluntary arrangement.

The powers of the court

Under s. 423(2) of the Insolvency Act 1986, the court enjoys wide discretionary powers to make any order restoring the position to what it would have been if the transaction had not been entered into, and for generally protecting the interests of persons who are victims of the transaction. Specific orders are set out in s. 425 which, in broad measure, correspond with s. 421 of the Act already discussed. There is, however, the usual protection for bona fide third parties, that is, those who have dealt in good faith for value and without notice of the relevant circumstances (s. 425(2)).

DISPOSITIONS OF PROPERTY MADE AFTER THE COMMENCEMENT OF COMPULSORY WINDING UP

Any disposition made by the company after the commencement of the winding up is void unless validated by the court (s. 127 of the Insolvency Act 1986). Compulsory liquidation relates back to the date of the petition for winding up (s. 129), the purpose being to prevent an improper depletion of the company's assets where it is in severe financial difficulty. The court takes a wide view of disposition which includes any sale, lease, charge, gift or any agreement whereby the company surrenders a contractual right including a contractual set-off. A post-petition non-mutual set-off which divests the assets of an insolvent will be covered as it infringes the *pari passu* principle of distribution. Following the passage of part VII of the Companies Act 1989, it would appear that clearing-house rules providing for such non-mutual set-offs where, for example, market debts are novated to the clearing house are not affected by s. 127 of the Insolvency Act 1986.

It should be noted that only dispositions of the company's property are affected. Thus in the case where the company's account with a bank is in overdraft there cannot, as a matter of logic, be a disposition of the company's asset since all we have here is an increase in *liability* to the bank which, in no sense, can be considered to be an asset (compare *Re Gray's Inn Construction Co. Ltd* [1980] 1 WLR 711). It would appear that an after-acquired property clause in a charge given by a company is effective to catch this property coming into the company's hands after the beginning of the winding up of the company (*Re Lind* [1915] 2 Ch 345). This is because the security interest relates back to the security agreement itself and can be justified as a bargained-for right. The charged property is not property beneficially owned by the company at the commencement of the winding-up. This explains why, if a carrier has goods relating to a post-liquidation disposition, he can retain a lien over the goods with respect to the freight contract (*George Barker (Transport) Ltd v Eynon* [1974] 1 WLR 462). This is also the position in the case of a bank which, in the ordinary course of business, collects a cheque for its customer and credits the proceeds to an overdrawn account; the bank will have a lien over the cheque as a negotiable instrument and a security interest in the proceeds. By crediting the account, the bank is merely realising its security right, otherwise its security would be valueless (see *National Australia Bank Ltd v KDS Construction Services Pty Ltd* (1987) 163 CLR 668). Similarly, the completion of a pre-liquidation contract capable of specific performance after the commencement of winding up is not avoided (*Re French's Wine Bar Ltd* [1987] BCLC 499).

Blanket avoidance of dispositions would, in effect, paralyse the company's business as soon as a petition seeking compulsory liquidation is presented. The courts take a broad view of their discretionary jurisdiction to validate offending dispositions. The court will have regard to all the circumstances including whether the disposition is for the benefit of the company, for example, to ensure continuity of supply of a vital commodity (see *Denney v John Hudson and Co. Ltd, Financial Times*, 8 May 1992), and also whether the disponee had notice of the winding-up proceedings (see *Re Gray's Inn Construction Co. Ltd* [1980] 1 WLR 711). If he did not have notice, a disposition carried out in good faith and in the ordinary course of business will normally be validated because a normal incident of such a transaction is that it will not have diminished the company's net assets. Occasionally, there are special considerations for validating the disposition such as was the case in *Re A.I. Levy (Holdings) Ltd* [1964] Ch 19, where the payment of a pre-liquidation debt was an intrinsic part of a post-liquidation transaction which would benefit all creditors.

NON-REGISTRATION OF A REGISTRABLE CHARGE

The general rule is that where a charge is created and no particulars in the prescribed form are delivered for registration within 21 days of creation, the charge is void against an administrator or liquidator of the company creating the charge, the creditors of the company, and any person who for value acquires an interest over the property (s. 399(1) of the Companies Act 1985 (as amended)). The policy justification here is that the rule champions the priority point of registration; there may be unsecured creditors who were misled by the lack of registration into extending credit to the insolvent company.

It should be noted that the invalidity of an unregistered charge does not avoid the obligation secured. Even so, registration is important because of the provisions of s. 406 of the Companies Act 1985 (as amended) which apply where the chargee has disposed of property subject to an unregistered charge. Where the section applies, the money received by the chargee shall be held on trust by him and applied, first of all, in discharge of any sum effectively secured by prior encumbrances; secondly, in discharge of any sum effectively secured by the charge and encumbrances ranking *pari passu* with the charge; thirdly, in discharge of any sum effectively secured by encumbrances ranking after the charge. The previous legal position was that if the company went into liquidation, the prior avoidance of the unregistered charge had no impact on the chargee because his security had been satisfied leaving nothing for the liquidator to avoid (see *Re Row Dal Constructions Pty Ltd* [1966] VR 249).

It is not necessary to obtain the leave of the court to register a charge out of time. However, where the charge is so registered and the company is at that date unable to pay its debts, or subsequently becomes unable to do so in consequence of the transaction under which the charge is created, and insolvency proceedings begin before the end of the relevant period beginning with the date of delivery of the particulars, the charge is void against the administrator or liquidator (s. 400(2) of the Companies Act 1985 (as amended)). In the case of a floating charge, the relevant period is two years if the chargee is a connected person or one year in any other case, and for any other security, six months (s. 400(3)(b) of the Companies Act 1985 (as amended)).

THE POLICIES BEHIND THE VARIOUS AVOIDING POWERS

There are two principles which exist to inform the exercise of the various avoiding powers: first, the powers represent an attempt to prevent the opting out of the insolvency law regime for the distribution of assets; Second, the powers represent a significant buttress against debtor or creditor misbehaviour. Despite the superficial appeal of the idea that the avoiding powers are concerned to swell the assets of the insolvent in favour of *unsecured* creditors, it is doubtful whether this should be a valid aim of insolvency law because this would provide an incentive for unsecured creditors to use the insolvency process even where this is not in the best interest of the creditors as a whole.

The approach of the new English insolvency law regime is to empower the court to make such an order as it thinks fit for restoring the position to what it would have been if the company had not entered into the avoided transaction. This does not necessarily mean redistribution to unsecured creditors. Indeed, in the case of extortionate credit bargains, the court is bound to make an order restoring the *status quo ante*, and there is a range of orders prescribed by statute in this respect. In the case of a transaction defrauding creditors, the order which the court will make will primarily be for the benefit of those who were the 'victims' of the transaction, so the effect of the order is not generally distributional. Similarly, where there is an invalid floating charge, the benefit of the avoidance goes to junior encumbrancers whose security interest cover property comprised in the invalid charge.

FRAUDULENT TRADING

A series of statutory provisions visit upon directors or managers of a firm criminal or civil liability following insolvency. Not only do these provide a deterrent against improper conduct, they can also swell the assets available for distribution to creditors (see below). However, it should be noted that the liquidator or administrator cannot pursue individual creditor claims but only claims vested in the company itself on the basis that damage to the company had been caused prior to winding up or administration. The liquidator has no such cause of action where the company is solvent and is likely to remain so.

Criminality of conduct

If any business of the company is carried on with intent to defraud creditors of the company, or creditors of any other person, or for any fraudulent purpose, every person who was knowingly a party to the carrying on of the business in that manner is guilty of a criminal offence (s. 458 of the Companies Act 1985). By sch. 24 to the Companies Act 1985, the sanctions available in cases of conviction are up to seven years' imprisonment, or an unlimited fine or both. The court may also, on the application of the liquidator, declare that any persons knowingly party to the fraudulent trading are to be liable to make such contributions (if any) to the company's assets as the court thinks proper (s. 213 of the Insolvency Act 1986). Liability is imposed upon a wider circle of participants than merely the directors and officers of the company. Furthermore, criminal liability for fraudulent trading arises whether or not the company is being wound up (s. 458 of the Companies Act 1985).

The intent to defraud creditors will be inferred if the company continues to carry on business and incurs credit when, to the knowledge of the directors, there is no reasonable prospect of the debts being repaid. In *Re Patrick and Lyon Ltd* [1933] Ch 786, Maugham J held at p. 790 that fraudulent trading connotes 'actual dishonesty involving, according to current notions of fair trading among commercial men, real moral blame'. It is important to distinguish here between acts of omission and commission. A director will be liable for fraudulent trading only if he took an active part in it and not where he fails to prevent it (*Re Maidstone Buildings Provisions Ltd* [1971] 1 WLR 1085). The court is required to find that the directors were acting dishonestly and not just that they were acting unreasonably (*Re L. Todd (Swanscombe) Ltd* [1990] BCC 125). The difficulty of establishing this has made the remedy of little use.

It is criminal conduct to incur credit without a reasonable prospect of satisfying creditors. In *Re White and Osmond (Parkstone) Ltd* (1960 unreported), the 'light at the end of the tunnel' approach was approved, that is, a belief that the company will be able to pay in future. Nevertheless, in *R v*

Grantham [1984] QB 675, the 'silver lining' test was disapproved, and the modern position appears to be whether the person charged *knew* that there was no good reason for thinking that funds would become available to pay a debt incurred when it became due or shortly thereafter.

So long as the fraud was perpetrated in the carrying on of a business, it does not matter that only one creditor was defrauded (*Re Gerald Cooper Chemicals Ltd* [1978] Ch 262).

The civil sanction
This consists of a compulsion to repay, restore or account for the money or property in whole or in part, plus interest at such a rate as the court thinks fit (s. 214 of the Insolvency Act 1986). The civil sanctions for fraudulent trading are the same as for wrongful trading (see below). In *Re Produce Marketing Consortium Ltd (No. 2)* [1989] BCLC 520, the court considered the question of the contribution a director should be ordered to pay under s. 214 of the Insolvency Act 1986. It was held by Knox J that the contribution was compensatory for the benefit of the general body of creditors. Nonetheless, Knox J concluded that it would be wrong to exclude entirely the director's culpability since the court has a wide discretion especially in the case of deliberate wrongdoing where, for example, there had been a failure to heed professional advice.

Only the official receiver or liquidator may apply under the civil remedy. In seeking such an order, the liquidator will have to balance various considerations, including the strength of the evidence against the director plus the cost, in terms of time and money, in pursuing such an order. There is a natural reluctance to throw good money after bad especially where the solvency of the director himself is questionable.

WRONGFUL TRADING

A new basis of civil liability was included in s. 214 of the Insolvency Act 1986 which introduced the concept of wrongful trading. The Cork committee, 1982, proposed the concept of wrongful trading in order to overcome the obstacles presented by the law of fraudulent trading, most notably, the requirement of proof of dishonesty which renders it extremely difficult for a liquidator to succeed in an application for the imposition of personal liability for fraudulent trading. The significance of the new section is that it does not require proof of intent to defraud creditors and, accordingly, the liquidator need only prove his case on a balance of probabilities and not to the criminal standard of beyond reasonable doubt.

There is no statutory definition of wrongful trading and the courts have been left with wide discretionary powers to formulate principles of liability. The right to make an application to the court under s. 214 is limited to the liquidator where the company has gone into insolvent liquidation. The basis of liability following insolvent liquidation will now be briefly considered.

Deemed knowledge of insolvent liquidation
The essence of wrongful trading is that the company continues to trade when

it was known, or ought to have been realised, by the director that liquidation was inevitable, or would appear to be probable to a reasonable person in the place of the director (s. 214(4)). It would appear that knowledge is not limited to facts subjectively known to the director because the provisions also postulate an objective test. The thinking of the courts regarding the standard of care was explained by Knox J in *Produce Marketing Consortium Ltd (No. 2)* [1989] BCLC 520 when he said:

> It is evident that Parliament intended to widen the scope of the legislation under which directors who trade on when the company is insolvent may, in appropriate circumstances, be required to make a contribution to [a company's creditors]. . . . the test to be applied by the court has become one under which the director in question is to be judged by the standards of what can be expected of a person fulfilling his functions, and showing reasonable diligence in doing so. . . . the general knowledge, skill and experience postulated will be much less extensive in a small company in a modest way of business, with simple accounting procedures and equipment, than it will be in a large company with sophisticated procedures. Nevertheless certain minimum standards are to be assumed to be attained. . . . [Wrongful trading], it was submitted [by counsel for the liquidator] is an enhanced version of the right which any company would have to sue its directors for breach of duty; — enhanced in the sense that the standard of knowledge, skill and experience required is made objective.

The balance sheet test of insolvent liquidation is utilised for the determination of the general issue of wrongful trading (s. 214(6)). In this respect, determination of the time at which deemed knowledge is acquired will be crucial because there can be no liability for wrongful trading in respect of acts or omissions before that time. This was an important issue in *Re Purpoint Ltd* [1991] BCC 121 since there were no meetings and no proper accounts and nothing, therefore, to assist the court in determining a date when the directors knew or ought reasonably to have known that there was no reasonable prospect of avoiding liquidation. The case concerned a phoenix company which had purchased the assets of its predecessor and started trading in January 1986. There was only one annual general meeting and no accounts or proper records were kept. The company had acquired property in 1986 on hire-purchase terms and creditors were already pressing for payment. However, trading continued, and in April 1987 the company acquired another car on hire-purchase. The company's director sought employment elsewhere and was offered a partnership from June 1987, but he would not be provided with a car. At the end of May, this director was told by the company's accountants that the company was insolvent and that he might be personally liable. The company ceased trading in November 1987 and was eventually wound up in May 1988 with debts in the order of £63,000. It was held that, at the latest, the director should have known that liquidation was unavoidable from the date of the professional advice in May 1987, although the evidence pointed to insolvency at a much earlier date. Given the absence of any proper records,

Vinelott J was prepared to impose a date at the end of 1986, on the basis that this was reasonable, and to hold that liability to contribute related to all the debts incurred from that time since there was no record of liabilities, and it was not possible to calculate how liabilities had increased by the continuation of trading after that date.

The prospect of avoiding insolvent liquidation must be reasonable in the sense that it is based on projections and financial information compiled on reasonable assumptions. Optimistic assumptions will not provide a defence unless there are reasonable grounds for which the assumptions are made.

There is a statutory defence to liability in s. 214(3) for a director who, after the time when he became actually or constructively aware that the company was destined to become insolvent, took *every step* with a view to minimising the potential loss to the company's creditors as he ought to have taken. From this it would appear that resignation is not necessarily a defence: he should seek to persuade colleagues of the unreasonableness of their conduct before resigning and/or persuade them to make an application for an administration order. This does not mean that the company should cease to trade when insolvent liquidation is inevitable because this, in itself, could constitute wrongful 'trading' since it may not constitute a reasonable step in minimising potential loss to creditors.

The person against whom the application is made was a director or shadow director at the relevant time Section 214 applies not only to directors but also to shadow directors (s. 214(7)). A person is a shadow director if he is a person in accordance with whose directions the directors of the company are accustomed to act except where advice is given in a professional capacity, for example, as an auditor (s. 251). The relevant criterion is the involvement in the day-to-day management of the company evidencing *control* of the company. As was evident in *Re MC Bacon Ltd* [1990] BCC 78, this entails a material risk for any bank which becomes too closely involved in the management of the company being monitored in a rescue situation. At present, there is no sufficiently precise test concerning the threshold of unacceptable interference except, to advise is one thing, to instruct and dominate is quite another (see *Re Maidstone Buildings Provisions Ltd* [1971] 1 WLR 1085).

It is unlikely that administrators or administrative receivers can be considered as directors because they act for the benefit of a creditor or creditors rather than for the members of the company. Nor can they be considered shadow directors since they *assume* the managerial function; they do not instruct the directors themselves.

PROSECUTION AND DISQUALIFICATION

Prosecution
Obligations are laid upon the liquidator in every winding up, except where the official receiver is acting, to report the discovery of evidence which indicates that any officer or member of the company has committed a criminal offence in relation to the company. The court may direct the liquidator to refer the matter

to the prosecuting authority (s. 218). It is the duty of the liquidator and every officer and agent of the company, past and present, to give the prosecuting authority, or the Secretary of State, all practicable assistance in connection with any criminal proceedings which are instituted by either of them (s. 219).

Disqualification

The application of stringent standards to the conduct of company directors was one of the cornerstones of the Cork committee report, 1982. The various statutory provisions relating to disqualification of directors are now consolidated in the Company Directors Disqualification Act 1986. Disqualification is defined in s. 1 of that Act as an order made by the court against a person whereby, for the period the order remains in force, that person may not, *without the leave* of the court:

(a) be a director of a company; or
(b) be a liquidator or administrator of a company; or
(c) be a receiver or manager of a company's property; or
(d) in any way, either directly or indirectly, be concerned or take part in the promotion, formation or management of a company.

The court's power to grant leave is an unfettered one and is exercisable either at the time the order is made or subsequently.

The court has a mandatory obligation to disqualify any director of an insolvent company whom it finds to be unfit (s. 6 of the Company Directors Disqualification Act 1986). The minimum period of disqualification is two years, the maximum 15 years. The operation of s. 6 is predicated upon two points: first, the person in question is or has been a director of a company which has at *any time* become insolvent; second, that his conduct as a director of that company, either taken alone or taken together with his conduct as a director of any other company or companies, makes him unfit to be concerned in the management of a company. Mere mismanagement is insufficient in determining unfitness; a breach of commercial morality or gross incompetence must be proved (see *Re Dawson Print Group Ltd* [1987] BCLC 601; *Re Douglas Construction Services Ltd* [1988] BCLC 397). In this respect, a distinction is drawn between collected taxes including national insurance contributions and income tax, with assessed taxes, such as corporation tax: a failure to pay the former is similar to misappropriation of trust assets since the money is deducted from employees' salaries with a view to transmission to the Inland Revenue. In this regard, a failure would amount to a breach of commercial morality (see *Re Churchill Hotel (Plymouth) Ltd* [1988] BCLC 341) in the sense that the Crown is an involuntary creditor (*Re Stanford Services Ltd* [1987] BCLC 607). General matters for determining unfitness of directors are included in sch. 1 to the Company Directors Disqualification Act 1986 to which the court *must* have regard. Unfitness is a concept of indeterminate meaning, even so, Lord Dillon in *Re Sevenoaks Stationers (Retail) Ltd* [1991] Ch 164 said that it must not be replaced by judicial paraphrase. It is a question of fact to be resolved by the court according to the particular circumstances before it.

The court has a discretion to order disqualification in certain circumstances, and the grounds are set out in ss. 3 to 5 and 8 to 10 of the Company Directors Disqualification Act 1986. Automatic disqualification applies where a person directly or indirectly takes part in, or is concerned with, the promotion, formation or management of a company where he is an undischarged bankrupt, or where as a result of his default in payment under a county court administration order the court revokes that order (ss. 11 to 12 of the Company Directors Disqualification Act 1986).

The available criminal penalties for contravention of a disqualification order are on conviction on indictment up to two years' imprisonment, or an unlimited fine or both, and on summary conviction, up to six months' imprisonment, or up to £2,000 fine or both (s. 13 of the Company Directors Disqualification Act 1986). Section 15 provides a formidable civil sanction in the form of the forfeiture of the protection of limited liability by the person(s) concerned.

The provisions for the disqualification of directors are regarded by the courts as available for the punishment of directors which includes shadow directors, that is, those in accordance with whose directions or instructions the board is accustomed to act (see *Re Tasbian (No. 3)* [1991] BCLC 792). The link between wrongful or fraudulent trading and disqualification is close. In *Secretary of State for Trade and Industry* v *Langridge* [1991] Ch 402, the nature of disqualification proceedings was at issue. In that case a company was declared insolvent on 22 April 1987. On 10 April 1989, the Secretary of State issued a notice of his intention to apply for an order under s. 6(1) of the Company Directors Disqualification Act 1986. That notice was served on the director on the following day. An application for disqualification of the director was then made on 21 April 1989. This was just within the two-year time-limit imposed by s. 7(2) of the Company Directors Disqualification Act 1986. The director applied to have the summons struck out on the ground that the notice of intention had not been served on him at least 10 days before the summons was issued (exclusive of the date of service) as required by s. 16(1) of the Act. He succeeded at first instance, but lost the appeal by a majority.

The outcome of the case revolved around the *nature* of disqualification and the importance of safeguarding the rights of the individual who was likely to suffer at the end of the day. It was held by the majority that the purpose of the Act was not penal but to protect the public by removing those unfit to be concerned in the management of a company. The difficulty with this approach is that if elimination of such directors were the only concern, the culpability of the directors, in the *mens rea* sense, would be irrelevant. It would appear that the dissenting judgment of Nourse LJ has more to commend as his lordship clearly identified the important penal consequences which may flow from the imposition of a disqualification order. An analogy was drawn between prosecutions and disqualification proceedings under the Road Traffic Act 1988 which provides a better analytical foundation for determining the length of disqualifications and also the amount of contributions made under ss. 213 and 214 of the Insolvency Act 1986. However, the approach of the majority was confirmed in *Re Samuel Sherman plc* [1991] 1 WLR 1070, where it was held that the power of the Secretary of State to seek disqualification under s. 8 of the Act was designed to protect the public.

PART 6   RESOLUTION OF COMMERCIAL DISPUTES

TWENTY-TWO
Dispute resolution machinery

It is inevitable that differences will arise between parties to a commercial contract. In large measure, this will reflect the fact that time is not static, so there may be labour disputes, shortages, the outbreak of war, price fluctuations, all of which point towards the fact that disputes cannot always be prevented. Even so, business people will often strive to prevent or take measures to minimise the likelihood of conflict, for example, through scrutiny of the credit ratings of debtors, a thorough investigation of suppliers and careful scrutiny of contractual terms. In addition, quality control mechanisms may be introduced, especially monitoring machinery so as to secure consistency of supply and quality during the contract period.

Little empirical data is available on the interrelationship, if any, between business practice and law. The standard works in this respect include contributions from Macaulay, 'Non-contractual Relations in Business' (1963) 28 Am Sociol Rev 45, and also from Beale and Dugdale, 'Contracts between Businessmen' (1975) 2 Br J Law Soc 451. It would seem from these studies that business people frequently do not use the law or legal planning when formulating a contract. They often reject the possible use of legal sanctions because of the presence of an 'occupational morality', that is, a flexible, informal approach is adopted which reflects the context of a *continuing* commercial relationship. In the Beale and Dugdale study of the contracts of sale or purchase made by engineering manufacturers in the Bristol area of England, buyers would order on forms drafted in the buyer's interests while sellers would respond on forms which favoured their interests. This is a course of proceeding which does not *necessarily* produce a legally binding contract because of the so-called 'battle of forms' where the negotiations may be analysed as a series of offers and counter-offers (*British Steel Corporation* v *Cleveland Bridge and Engineering Co. Ltd* [1984] 1 All ER 504; *Butler Machine Tool Co. Ltd* v *Ex-Cell-O-Corpn (England) Ltd* [1979] 1 WLR 401). The common law mirror-image rule of contract formation where the acceptance must correspond with the offer (*Hyde* v *Wrench* (1840) 3 Beav 334) makes

Dispute resolution machinery

printed forms matter since it encourages, or even forces parties receiving documents to read them carefully. Thus, as Beale and Dugdale conclude, merchants do pay attention to preprinted terms that may prove important or are 'unusual'.

A careful scrutiny of contract terms is essential so as to ensure that the agreement represents the intention of the parties where there are standard forms. It is unlikely that a supplier would make its preprinted form completely self-interested, not least because the buyer may go elsewhere. This explains the inclusion of a credit period which has featured in the retention-of-title line of case law (see chapter 12). Moreover, the buyer can always send back an acknowledgement form and the seller then has to take into account the possibility of a lost sale by dickering over the terms. Disputes can use up valuable resources in terms of finance and also managerial time which, again, may be illustrated by the retention-of-title line of case law where the incorporation of such a clause in the contract has played an important role in the enforcement process of such clauses. In this regard, the administrative receiver will often issue a questionnaire to a supplier who is claiming goods requiring the latter to document his trading history with the insolvent company. The questionnaire may require the production of standard terms and conditions of sale, and an indication of *who* at the insolvent company was aware of the terms and conditions of sale. These requirements will not be easy for suppliers geared towards the supply of new goods rather than a considerable research exercise through trading ledgers. Even if the questionnaire is duly completed, it may be argued that the person who signed the delivery slip confirming the supplier's standard conditions of supply did not have authority to bind the company in any case.

In the event of a dispute arising which cannot be prevented, there are a number of mechanisms available for resolution of the dispute ranging from informal settlements through to litigation. In this chapter, we shall consider some of the more common mechanisms available for dispute resolution.

LITIGATION

It is often said that business people prefer to avoid litigation if this is possible. Certainly, litigation may be slow and costly because even though a successful litigant will normally be awarded costs, he is unlikely to recover all his costs. More significantly, the privacy interest of the business will be prejudiced through litigation which may entail bad publicity, and may damage the existing commercial relationship and others as well. Be that as it may, in recent times, there has been a business litigation explosion which has significantly increased even relative to other claims. Thus, according to the Judicial Statistics Annual Reports, between 1975 and 1989, plaints for breach of contract in the county courts rose from 8,038 to 26,540, an increase of 230 per cent. Between 1975 and 1989, writs issued for breach of contract in the Queen's Bench Division rose from 4,172 to 8,640, an increase of 107 per cent. This increase in litigation may be explained as follows: first, the economic environment has become increasingly hostile over the last 15 years with greater competition which may sound in fewer 'repeat players', that is, continuity of business relationship has become less important in this competitive business environment; second, the increasing number of insolvencies has provided an impetus to discover 'legal solutions', for example, the *Romalpa* clause (1976); third, the 'occupational morality' referred to in the Beale and Dugdale study above has become more difficult to state in the present uncertain economic environment, that is, the boundaries between proper and improper business behaviour have increasingly been thrown into doubt; fourth, there is an increasing legal consciousness and litigiousness which has expressed itself in the phenomenal growth of commercial law firms and the expansion of the commercial bar.

The litigation process
Litigation involving a commercial dispute will normally be brought in the High Court which has jurisdiction over more serious civil cases. However, in terms of the volume of business, the county court is more important, a fact that is confirmed by the raising of the jurisdictional limits from £5,000 to £50,000 under s. 1 of the Courts and Legal Services Act 1990.

Commercial litigation in the High Court will be brought either in the Queen's Bench Division for breach of contract, or in the Chancery Division for disputes involving equitable rights. There are separate Companies and Patents Courts which form part of the Chancery Division. A special forum to resolve complex mercantile disputes was set up in 1895 by virtue of the creation of a 'list of commercial causes' in the Queen's Bench Division. Section 3 of the Administration of Justice Act 1970 gave statutory recognition to the Commercial Court as a constituent of the Queen's Bench Division. Most of the work of the Commercial Court is litigation in regard to carriage of goods by sea or air, transactions in the commodity market, and credit and security issues. Procedure in the Commercial Court is abbreviated and is manned by judges whose experience lies in the commercial side. The procedural rules in the Commercial Court have now been extended to the High Court and the county court in that they allow for the exchange of witness statements in advance of a court trial (see Civil Justice Review, *Report of the Review Body* (Cm 394, 1988)). Thus, Rules of the Supreme Court 1965, Ord. 38, provides that the court can order the statements of all witnesses who are to be called to give evidence to be exchanged by the parties.

In the course of the 1980s the volume of work in the Commercial Court was such that it caused delays, thereby negating one of the so-called advantages of the court which was to provide a forum for the speedy resolution of disputes. Under *Practice Direction (Commercial Lists: Manchester and Liverpool)* [1990] 1 WLR 331, the activities of the Commercial Court were streamlined by the creation of a new structure enabling the hearing of commercial actions in Manchester and Liverpool. At the same time, simplified procedures were introduced designed to encourage a more open approach to litigation. Hitherto, it was not necessary for a party to disclose the names of witnesses nor statements made, or details of evidence submitted. However, new rules came into force in 1990 which have altered the old restrictive position and it is now even possible, through a process known as discovery by interrogatories, to serve on the other party a written request to answer questions about his case by sworn statement.

Discovery is obviously crucial in the proceedings. Its scope has been greatly increased by the ability, in certain cases, to obtain an *Anton Piller* order for discovery *ex parte* (see below). This invites scrutiny of the wider pre-trial issues.

Procedural aids

A plaintiff may seek an injunction to prevent the defendant from taking steps which may prejudice the plaintiff. Typically, the defendant may seek to move assets abroad, or even dissipate assets which form the subject-matter of the dispute. Frequently, the plaintiff applies *ex parte* in the first instance, so no notice is given to the other side because speed is of the essence. However, in order to protect the defendant, the *ex parte* injunction will only be of short duration pending service of the application for an injunction and supporting evidence on the defendant. Section 37 of the Supreme Court Act 1981 enables the court to grant an interlocutory injunction to preserve the position until the trial or, alternatively, the court may discharge the *ex parte* injunction. The effect of an injunction is significant if the defendant chooses to disregard it since it will put him in contempt of court and make him liable to imprisonment. It should be noted that at the time of granting the interlocutory injunction, the plaintiff will be required to give an undertaking to the effect that, if he is unsuccessful in the full hearing, he will pay damages to the defendant for the loss suffered by the grant of the injunction.

The new form of injunctive relief emerged following the decision in *Mareva Cia Naviera SA* v *International Bulkcarriers SA* [1975] 2 Lloyd's Rep 509, and has become known as the *Mareva* injunction overturning the previous position in *Lister and Co.* v *Stubbs* (1890) 45 ChD 1. This is an order granted to restrain the defendants from disposing of assets in England outside the jurisdiction, and is an example of the importance of procedural law. In *Third Chandris Shipping Corporation* v *Unimarine SA* [1979] 1 QB 645, the Court of Appeal laid down the general principles for the granting of a *Mareva* injunction and how they should operate in practice.

(a) The plaintiff should make a full and frank disclosure of all matters in his knowledge which are material for the judge to know.

(b) The plaintiff should give particulars of his claim against the defendant stating the ground(s) for his claim and the amount, and fairly stating the points made against him by the defendant.

(c) The plaintiff should give some grounds for believing that the defendant has assets here. The court can order discovery and interrogatories for the purpose of ascertaining the existence and location of the assets to which the injunction can attach.

(d) The plaintiff should give some grounds for believing that there is a risk of the assets being removed before the judgment or award is satisfied.

(e) The plaintiff must give an undertaking in damages to cover the case of the granting of the injunction turning out to be unjustified.

It follows from the above guidelines that there is a heavy responsibility placed on the part of the plaintiff's legal advisers to prepare the evidence that will best testify to the claims made. This is especially the case where the *Mareva* injunction has extraterritorial effects. In *Derby and Co. Ltd* v *Weldon (Nos. 3 and 4)* [1990] Ch 65, the Court of Appeal confirmed the power of English courts to grant worldwide *Mareva* injunctions purporting to affect foreign assets as well as English (see *Babanaft International Co. SA* v *Bassatne* [1990] Ch 13; *Republic of Haiti* v *Duvalier* [1990] 1 QB 202).

The *Anton Piller* order is a more striking example of injunctive relief as it makes it possible for one party to a civil action to enter, search, and remove property from the premises of an opponent. In *Anton Piller KG* v *Manufacturing Processes Ltd* [1976] Ch 55, the Court of Appeal granted such an *ex parte* order and authoritatively established the central features of the new procedure. Essentially this is a power, exercisable *ex parte*, to deal with rogues who are not prepared to play the game of *inter partes* procedure honestly. The essence of the *Anton Piller* order is its surprise; it requires the defendant to admit representatives of the plaintiff on to his premises for the purpose of inspecting, and also seizing goods and documents which otherwise might be destroyed by the defendants if they had prior warning. Typically, the order is made where a manufacturer claims that a business rival was copying his ideas or infringing other intellectual property rights.

An *Anton Piller* order is only made in a case of necessity so as to ensure that justice is done. The court is concerned with three issues, namely:

(a) Is there a strong prima facie case?
(b) Is there a genuine risk that the defendant, if put on notice, might destroy goods or documents which he has in his possession and which could be used as evidence?
(c) Is the potential damage to the plaintiff likely to be very serious as a result of the defendant's actions?

There is no doubt that *Anton Piller* orders are dangerous and open to abuse. Indeed, concern has arisen that courts have been too ready to grant an order, and that the jurisdiction can be used oppressively (see *Universal Thermosensors Ltd* v *Hibben* (1992) *The Times*, 12 February 1992). Thus, trade secrets may be seized providing the plaintiff with an unfair trading advantage (see *Lock International plc* v *Beswick* [1989] 1 WLR 1268). Further problems have arisen concerning the ability of the defendant to rely upon the common law privilege against self-incrimination (s. 14(1) of the Civil Evidence Act 1968). However, in *Chappell* (1989) Eur Court HR, Series A, No. 152-A, the European Court of Human Rights upheld the granting of *Anton Piller* orders providing that they were not used oppressively and it was 'essential that this measure [an *ex parte* order] should be accompanied by adequate and effective safeguards against arbitrary interference and abuse'. Such measures would undoubtedly include the order being executed by the plaintiff's solicitor or an officer of the court, and the defendant being given time to contact his legal representative and to take appropriate steps to object to the execution of the order.

Dispute resolution machinery 465

The *Anton Piller* order and the *Mareva* injunction provide striking illustrations of the creative role of the judiciary. The drastic nature of the relief has led them to be described as two of the law's 'nuclear weapons' (per Donaldson LJ in *Bank Mellat* v *Nikpour* [1985] FSR 87 at p. 92). Such orders have a severe impact upon the defendant and any business carried on by him. It is for this reason that a *Mareva* injunction (asset freezing) is rarely appropriate against banks (see *Polly Peck International plc* v *Nadir* (1992) *The Times*, 24 March 1992). Certainly, at least in the case of *Anton Piller* orders, the time has come to put such orders on a clear statutory basis. In this respect, orders should be confined to their original role as wholly exceptional devices granted only after the most profound scrutiny. Even so, it presents a most useful procedural tool in commercial law.

It is worth noting by way of conclusion that there are other valuable procedural mechanisms available which may stimulate the early resolution of commercial disputes. These pre-trial procedures are normally conducted in London before a judicial officer known as a master, or outside the High Court in London before district judges. Thus, the plaintiff may apply for summary judgment under the Rules of the Supreme Court 1965, Ord. 14, so as to obviate the problem of procrastination on behalf of a defendant who has no real defence to the action. An alternative mechanism for speeding up the litigation process is through obtaining an interim payment under Ord. 29. In this situation, the defendant is required to make an interim payment on account of the damages if the court considers that the plaintiff is likely to succeed in the full trial. Undoubtedly, this mechanism does encourage negotiation and settlement. It will at least provoke the defendant to consider making a payment into court because, by doing so, the normal rule that the losing defendant must pay the contesting party's costs is modified. Thus, if the plaintiff recovers damages *less* than the sum which has been paid in, the plaintiff will be required to pay *all* the costs, at least from the date the money was first paid into court. Of course, the judge will not know of the payment in until after he has given judgment as such knowledge might prejudice the position of the defendant. In like fashion, a 'without prejudice' offer may be made to the plaintiff which avoids paying money into court but does not put the plaintiff at risk as to costs if he declines the offer.

ARBITRATION

In its traditional form, arbitration consists of an *agreement* to establish a private and domestic procedure for the resolution of existing or future disputes as an alternative to the use of courts. As Donaldson MR put it in *Northern Regional Health Authority* v *Derek Crouch Construction Co. Ltd* [1984] QB 644 at p. 670: 'Arbitration is usually no more and no less than litigation in the private sector'. During the second half of the 19th century, arbitration became institutionalised through the establishment of arbitration machinery and of general rules to govern its operation. Two important legal developments have institutionalised arbitration:

(a) The *Scott* v *Avery* (1856) 5 HL Cas 811 clause. A contractual provision purporting to oust the jurisdiction of the court is void as being contrary to public policy. There is, however, no objection to a clause which makes reference to arbitration a condition precedent to a right of action (litigation). The arbitral mechanism is established in anticipation of a subsequent action and not as an alternative to action.

(b) The legal system has lent the support of its coercive machinery to the awards of arbitrators so, if a party fails to comply with an order made by an arbitrator in the course of a reference, the High Court may extend the powers of the arbitrator and confer upon him power to treat the default in the same way as a High Court judge would in civil proceedings (s. 5 of the Arbitration Act 1979). Furthermore, there is more finality about an arbitral award compared with a judgment simply because High Court judgments may go to the Court of Appeal. Prior to the Arbitration Act 1979, there were frequent appeals from arbitrators' awards by applications to the High Court for arbitrators to state a case under s. 21 of the Arbitration Act 1950. The latter section was repealed by s. 1 of the 1979 Act. Nowadays, an appeal can be made to the High Court on a question of law arising out of the award, and then only if the other party agrees or the court grants leave. Leave is usually granted if the court considers that the question raised could substantially affect the rights of the parties. In *Pioneer Shipping Ltd* v *BTP Tioxide Ltd* [1982] AC 724, the House of Lords laid down guidelines as to the circumstances in which the court would exercise its discretion to grant leave to appeal from an arbitrator's decision. The court will decline in commercial cases to grant leave if it considers that the question is unique and is unlikely to occur in other cases, unless the arbitrator's decision is plainly wrong. Where the arbitral decision may involve a number of cases, for example, the interpretation of a standard-form contract, the court will be more ready to grant leave, although there must be a strong prima facie case of error. The court may require an arbitrator to give reasons or clarify reasons, but only if one of the parties gave notice to the arbitrator before the award that a reasoned award was required. Apart from these appeals against the award, the court may remove an arbitrator for misconduct, for example, failing to conduct the proceedings in accordance with the principles of natural justice.

The commercial context of arbitration

The present-day position is that arbitration is firmly established as the most utilised adjudicative mechanism in commercial life. It has been estimated that London arbitration bodies handle over 10,000 disputes per annum, a figure that embraces consumer as well as commercial transactions, and national as well as international transactions. The members of the London Maritime Arbitrators' Association based at the Baltic Exchange, the world's leading freight market, account for some 3,000 or 4,000 arbitrations each year. Indeed, 70 per cent of the world's maritime arbitrations involving shipbroking or chartering disputes each year are held in London. A large proportion of arbitrations involve international sales transactions which sometimes involve the Grain and Feed Trade Association (GAFTA). At the same time, the development of consumer protection has necessitated the utilisation of alternative means to litigation for the resolution of such disputes. Thousands of these which would otherwise flood the courts or fail to be resolved, and which deal with disputes as various as claims for defective houses under the NHBC scheme, disappointing holidays under the ABTA scheme, insurance claims, negligence claims against solicitors under the Solicitors' Arbitration Scheme are dealt with speedily and economically by arbitration. The Office of Fair Trading has encouraged arbitration as a public service.

Commercial arbitration in commodity transactions is no longer dominated by quality disputes. 'Physical' arbitrations have now often given way to 'technical' arbitration, that is, arbitrations on contractual points. Factors which have generated technical disputes for arbitration include price and currency fluctuations, the sudden imposition of export or import restrictions and the involvement of State trading companies whose governments are sometimes short of foreign exchange.

The commercial preference for arbitration over trial in a court of law is that arbitration is quicker and less expensive. However, the decisive virtue of arbitration is that the adjudication process is undertaken by arbitrators who have personal knowledge and experience of the trade in which the dispute has arisen, so they have the requisite technical expertise and a detailed grasp of commercial practice. This point is borne out by the reception given to s. 4 of the Administration of Justice Act 1970 which authorised Commercial Court judges to accept appointment as arbitrators in commercial disputes. The idea was that commercial disputants would appreciate the opportunity to dispense with the formality and publicity of an ordinary trial while nevertheless securing the juridical expertise of a judge. The scheme has not yet proved attractive as it is not frequently used. One explanation for this, especially since the statutory procedure is comparatively inexpensive to use, is that judge arbitrators cannot be relied upon to have the intimate familiarity with the trade or the market which characterises the professional or semi-professional arbitrator. Indeed, some arbitrators have considerable experience and international reputation, so in some cases, oral evidence may be dispensed with, leaving the arbitrator to resolve the dispute on written reports and his own inspection at the place in question, together with his own experience and skill. If the parties are unable to agree on an arbitrator, the matter can be referred to the president of some professional body to make an appointment, for example, the Chartered Institute of Arbitrators. This provides a striking contrast to litigation where the parties seldom know the name of the judge until the day before the trial. In this vein, the greatest real advantage in arbitration is the fact that the tribunal is *consistent*. The tribunal hearing the interlocutory application in an arbitration will be the same tribunal which hears the final substantive case.

The cost of arbitration should be less than litigation if only for the fact that the hearing takes less time, and is also undertaken at the place which is the subject-matter of the dispute. Costs are at the discretion of the arbitrator, so he can penalise parties who persist in adopting procedures which, in his view, are unhelpful and a waste of time. The taxation of the costs can be either by an arbitrator or by the High Court or, in appropriate cases, by a county court. If the taxation is by the arbitrator, this can take place very soon after the publication of the award. In the courts there is often very considerable delay in getting costs taxed. Awards of taxed costs, like the awards themselves, are enforceable in the High Court or in the county court. Interest accrues on an award as in the case of a judgment in the High Court (s. 20 of the Arbitration Act 1950). A further improvement which should cut down delay is provided by s. 103 of the Courts and Legal Services Act 1990 which repeals the courts' power under s. 12(6)(b) of the Arbitration Act 1950 to order discovery in arbitration. This is seen by arbitrators to be a very significant improvement, enabling them to keep a tight rein on the progress of arbitration.

Arbitration: a superior alternative to litigation?
It is simplistic to maintain that arbitration consists of nothing more than a superior alternative to litigation. There are some real difficulties associated with the process of arbitration which cannot be ignored. The English arbitrator adjudicates in the shadow of the law, notwithstanding the terms of the arbitration agreement; the dispute must be resolved *in accordance with the law* and not *ex aequo et bono*. This may explain the courts' interference with the finality of arbitral awards despite this being in the spirit of s. 1 of the Arbitration Act 1979 (see *Antaios Cia Naviera SA* v *Salen Rederierna AB* [1985] AC 191). The courts have been hostile to 'equity clauses' which provide that the arbitral tribunal shall decide as *amiable compositeur*, thereby, prejudicing the ability of the arbitrator to use his skill and expertise to address fully the issue in hand. An example of this phenomenon can be seen in *Overseas Union Insurance Ltd* v *AA Mutual International Insurance Co. Ltd* [1988] 2 Lloyd's Rep 63, where the law was summarised as follows:

> ... the effect of such provision is [i.e., an equity clause in an arbitration agreement which extends the liberty of the arbitrator by freeing him from his duty to apply the strict rules of law] is not clearly settled as a matter of law. The former view that they cannot displace the need for arbitrators to apply the law (*Czarnikow* v *Roth, Schmidt and Co.* [1922] 2 KB 478; *Orion Cia Espanola de Seguros* v *Belfort Maatschappij voor Algemene Verzekgringeen* [1962] 2 Lloyd's Rep 257) has been supplanted to some extent at least by more recent judgments: *Eagle Star Insurance Co.* v *Yuval Insurance Co. Ltd* [1978] 1 Lloyds Rep 357 per Lord Denning MR at p. 361 and Robert Goff LJ at p. 363, and *Home Insurance Co.* v *Administratia Asigurilor de Stat* [1983] 2 Lloyd's Rep 674. To what extent the clause has this effect is, in my respectful view, unclear from the later authorities. Although the clause may entitle the arbitrators 'to view the matter more leniently' ([1978] 1 Lloyd's Rep at p. 363) than a court would do, I am doubtful whether they can embark on any other inquiry than what the law requires, namely, finding the natural and proper meaning of the words used, in the particular context. ... the equity clause does however emphasise that commercial arbitrators may draw upon their own experience and knowledge of commercial matters without formal proof.

In *Eagle Star Insurance Co. Ltd* v *Yuval Insurance Co. Ltd* [1978] 1 Lloyd's Rep 357, the Court of Appeal unanimously viewed the inclusion of an equity clause in a commercial arbitration agreement as legally unobjectionable and enforceable. Somewhat irreconcilably, in the subsequent case of *Home and Overseas Insurance Co. Ltd* v *Mentor Insurance Co. (UK) Ltd* [1990] 1 WLR 153, Parker LJ in the Court of Appeal had no hesitation in accepting the submission that a clause which purported to authorise commercial arbitrators to settle a dispute referred to them according to what they deemed to be fair and reasonable, rather than in accordance with settled principles of law, would be legally invalid and unenforceable. The position is uncertain and tends to undermine the main purpose of the Arbitration Act 1979, namely, to make England an attractive centre for the settlement of transnational commercial disputes by arbitration. It should be noted that the Arbitration Rules of the United Nations Commission on International Trade Law (UNCITRAL) contain specific provision on the matter of equity clauses in commercial arbitration agreement. Under the UNCITRAL Model Rules, an arbitral tribunal is permitted to decide a dispute referred to it as an *amiable compositeur*, or to decide such dispute *ex aequo et bono* as long as the parties have expressly authorised it to do so, and the law applicable to the arbitral procedure permits this.

The power of the law to control arbitrators remains so that s. 23(1) of the Arbitration Act 1950 provides that 'Where an arbitrator or umpire has misconducted himself the High Court may remove him'. The court's powers over arbitration proceedings were altered and extended by the 1979 Act. There is now, for the first time, a right of appeal on any question of law arising out of an award made on an arbitration agreement (unless excluded by a valid 'exclusion agreement'), but only by consent of all parties or with leave of the court; the court may not grant leave unless it considers that the determination of the question of law could affect substantially the rights of the parties and it may attach conditions to the grant of leave, for example, the provision of security for the amount claimed. The effectiveness of an exclusion agreement is restricted in the case of 'domestic' and 'special category' arbitration agreements (ss. 3 and 4 of the Arbitration Act 1979). In addition to the right of appeal, there is jurisdiction in the High Court (save where there is a valid exclusion agreement) to determine any question of law arising in the course of the reference, but only with the consent of the arbitrator or of all the parties. This replaced the old special case procedure under s. 21 of the Arbitration Act 1950. The repeal of the old law in this regard is somewhat unfortunate, at least insofar as domestic arbitration is concerned, because it represented a useful method of reviewing the law of arbitration. Appeals by case stated meant that complicated questions of law could be formulated by parties involved in arbitration and submitted to the court for a decision. Accordingly, a body of precedent was created ensuring a degree of certainty in future decisions, and one unfortunate consequence of s. 1 of the Arbitration Act 1979 is that this has been removed from arbitration *in England and Wales*.

A major difficulty associated with arbitration was the issue of arbitral delay. This arose from the fact that an arbitrator could not, unless he had specific authority derived from the rules governing the particular arbitration, dismiss a claim for failure to pursue it. The particular mischief here was recognised by the Mustill Committee, *Report on Delay: Striking out Claims in Arbitration* (1988) at para. 1:

> Where a claimant in an arbitration has delayed his claim to such an extent that a fair hearing of the dispute is no longer possible there should be a statutory power to terminate the reference, or to strike out the claim. The committee has further unanimously resolved that the power should be conferred on the arbitrator rather than the court.

The recommendations of the committee were adopted under s. 102 of the Courts and Legal Services Act 1990 which gives arbitrators a statutory power to dismiss a claim for want of prosecution (compare *Bremer Vulkan Schiffbau und Maschinenfabrik* v *South India Shipping Corpn Ltd* [1981] AC 909; *Paal Wilson & Co. A/S* v *Partenreederei Hannah Blumenthal* [1983] 1 AC 854).

It is often suggested that one of the greatest advantages of arbitration over litigation is the privacy of the proceedings from the public gaze. Even so, it has become common for arbitral awards to be published in legal and professional journals although an attempt is made, at the same time, to protect the anonymity of the parties. The status of such reports is uncertain as they do not bind other arbitrators. In a consumer arbitration context, the anonymity of the proceedings might be a positive disadvantage for the consumer: publicity for a consumer dispute may impose pressure on a business to settle the case. Clearly, there is potential for abuse, and it is for this reason that the Consumer Arbitration Agreements Act 1988 polices the enforceability of a compulsory arbitration reference in a consumer agreement. Such an agreement under s. 4 of the 1988 Act will only be enforceable where the consumer agrees in writing to the reference to arbitration after the dispute has arisen, or if the consumer has actually submitted to arbitration, or if the court makes an order allowing the arbitration agreement to be enforced.

In *Shearson Lehman Hutton Inc.* v *Maclaine Watson and Co. Ltd* [1988] 1 WLR 946, it was said that a party to litigation is protected by the implied undertaking not to use discovered material except for the purpose of the action, even though that material had been read in court. However, the parties to a private arbitration may be ordered by the court in separate proceedings to reveal documents that were the subject-matter of their private dispute to a third party unconnected with the dispute. This will be a material factor when consideration is given to the balancing of the relative merits between arbitration and litigation, particularly for disputants considering arbitration which will involve discovery of sensitive documentary material.

The main advantages of arbitration over litigation may be summarised as follows: the difficulty of appeal; the privacy of proceedings; the ability to determine the procedure to be adopted. It should be noted that the non-adjudicative settlement of disputes will be maximised where adjudication is at its costliest — but the cost of arbitration is, in the broad sense, lower than litigation because it is generally quicker, cheaper, more expert and apparently does not preclude the disputants from doing business again. Nevertheless, in more recent years, alternative dispute mechanisms have emerged which will now be examined.

ALTERNATIVE DISPUTE RESOLUTION MECHANISMS

We have already noted some of the problems associated with litigation such as inexorable delay and expense. Arbitration presents a genuine alternative to litigation simply because both processes produce judgments or awards which are binding upon the parties and are enforceable. Other methods of resolving disputes have emerged but these are firmly based upon the agreement of the parties and, in the absence of this, the parties will remain in conflict, the dispute unresolved, and the liability will still be outstanding.

A feature of late 20th-century consumer law has been self-regulation. Indeed, the Director General of Fair Trading has encouraged trading associations to introduce codes of practice which have quasi-legal status under the Consumer Protection Act 1987. The pivotal role of the ombudsman has been confirmed as an appropriate mechanism to redress grievances and has certainly expanded from the original ombudsman who, as the Parliamentary Commissioner for Administration, was created to deal with complaints by citizens of maladministration against government departments and agencies. Local government, the insurance industry, banks and building societies, all have ombudsmen. The Courts and Legal Services Act 1990 provides for the appointment of a Legal Services Ombudsman who may investigate complaints made against an authorised litigator, advocate, licensed conveyancer or registered foreign lawyer. The main difficulty here, as in all ombudsmen arrangements, is that the ombudsman has no direct authority to order compensation and can only make a recommendation, as distinct from an arbitrator who can make an award.

Alternative dispute resolution (ADR) mechanisms which have their provenance in the USA have gained increasing recognition in the UK especially following the establishment, in 1991, of the Centre for Dispute Resolutions (CEDR), a non-profit-making organisation supported by industry to promote ADR. In the mid 1970s, ADR developed in the US when concern over the 'pathology of litigation' within American society was at its highest. A number of companies' lawyers in the US got together and set up the Centre for Public Resources upon which the CEDR is modelled. The aim is to promote private resolution of disputes without resort to expensive litigation. The most common techniques employed are mediation and the mini-trial. Mediation consists of the introduction of a third party into a dispute so as to seek a settlement. The mediator acts as a sort of conduit pipe where communication has broken down, or is fraught with difficulties. Mediation was used recently in the USA in resolving a long dispute between IBM and Fujitsu concerning a copyright infringement. The resolution included an award dealing with Fujitsu's past use of IBM software and also a framework for the resolution of outstanding issues and future disagreement. Crucially, mediation enabled a settlement of a commercial dispute without destroying continuing business relationships.

The mini-trial usually consists of a short presentation of the issues by each party's house lawyer in front of senior executives from each side who are unconnected with the actual dispute. There is normally a neutral chairman, perhaps a retired judge, a lawyer respected by both sides as an expert in the field. Following the presentation which must take place within a strict timetable, the executives retire and try to negotiate a settlement. They approach the problem as commercial people in the knowledge that they may win or lose, that enormous sums are at stake, and considerable wastage of time and undesirable publicity will result from litigation. If they fail in their negotiations, the chairman may be asked for his views as to the likely outcome of any ensuing litigation, after which, the executives may make another attempt at settlement. If they agree, the terms of the settlement are incorporated in a written document and is enforceable as an aspect of contract law. Perhaps the most significant commercial dispute which has been settled by this mechanism in recent times in the USA was Borden's $200 million trust suit against Texaco.

ADR is predicated upon negotiation and private settlement. It will, therefore, not be suitable where there is a novel or difficult point of law involved which needs a court ruling. Nevertheless, there is a momentum in favour of ADR and some businesses include in their standard terms that disputes, where possible, should be settled by ADR. This is not surprising since a high proportion of civil litigation is, in any case, concluded by compromise and all ADR does is expedite this settlement process.

TWENTY-THREE
Reform and codification of English commercial law

CODIFICATION

The codification of English commercial law is often portrayed as a panacea in that it will promote certainty in commercial transactions. However, the codification process does present real difficulties in that statutes tend to codify the past and, furthermore, it is impossible for a drafter to anticipate every future contingency. At the same time, legislation is bifocused in the sense that some laws are intended to provide specific instructions about particular conduct whilst other legislation may be more broadly rule-making, that is, providing guideposts for reasoned decision-making by the judges. The English Sale of Goods Act 1893 is drafted in the latter style as was the US Uniform Sales Act 1906 and, as such, they constitute an open-ended restatement of common law sales principles. In contrast, the Bills of Exchange Act 1882 and the US Uniform Negotiable Instruments Law contain detailed commands about the determination of negotiability. The US Uniform Commercial Code (the UCC) continues both patterns as its different articles have markedly divergent styles. Thus art. 2, the sales provision, was drafted by Professor Llewellyn and is characterised by statements of principle and presumptive guidelines, whereas. art. 9, which deals with personal property security interests leans heavily to positivist prescription of rules that dictate outcomes.

The draftsman who was responsible for the codification of early 20th-century US sales law, Professor Williston, basically disapproved abandonment of the generalisation and inclusiveness which he considered characterised the Uniform Sales Act and its replacement by far greater particularisation of rules. The learned draftsman indignantly pointed out that the UCC eschewed language honoured by legal usage. What Williston considered a 'seamless web', for example, the concept of title, the Code draftsmen saw as a 'tangled web' better boldly jettisoned where necessary than tinkered with. With this in mind,

Professor Llewellyn rejected title precisely in order to replace an over-broad category with a number of smaller categories. As a realist, he reacted against the Willistonian attempt to derive all rules of sales law from a few 'universally applicable' general principles. In his endeavour to replace artificial distinctions with functionally based distinctions, Llewellyn searched for narrow categories based upon commercially significant type-fact patterns. Even with regard to the values of codification, Williston disagreed sharply with Llewellyn. Williston considered the UCC as being unwise and iconoclastic, and he favoured piecemeal amendment over comprehensive codification.

There are at least three different types of codification and these may be conveniently set out as follows:

(a) Complete comprehensive codes, e.g., Bentham's approach as discussed below.
(b) Institutional comprehensive codes, i.e., stating rules as general principles in a generalised area of law like the French *Code civil*.
(c) Partial comprehensive codes dealing with a particular subject like the Sale of Goods Act 1893.

We shall now proceed to consider the above categories in the light of the English experience of codification of (especially) commercial law.

THE ENGLISH EXPERIENCE OF CODIFICATION IN COMMERCIAL LAW

The interaction of legislation and the common law under Anglo-American Uniform Acts and 'codes' is a comparatively recent phenomenon. In England, the codification movement in the Benthamite sense climaxed and then dissipated in the 19th century. The idea of Jeremy Bentham was to codify the 'entire field of law — a field a little less extensive than the whole field of human action' (Bentham, J., *Papers Relative to Codification and Public Instruction*, part 2, 1817, p. 40). No source of law except the codified enacted law would continue to exist and he urged the 'complete extirpation of the common law'. Bentham equated the code with the whole corpus of law which the courts would simply apply, reducing the judicial role to one of mere application of the law. In this respect, the role of the judge would be to obey instructions in the code itself. From this it would appear that Bentham's conception of codification anticipated the annihilation of both pre-existing case law and common law methods of reasoning.

Although Bentham did influence early 19th century attempts at partial codification, there was considerable scepticism about the superiority of any code in solving the problem of uncertainty in any field of law. On the criminal law side, there was an ambitious attempt to provide a unitary criminal code but this foundered, as did Lord Westbury's attempt to provide separate digests of statute and case law. An historical explanation for this failure may be that, in England, the monarchy's early establishment of a centralised administration of justice and with it a unified national law contrasted sharply with the

Continental position. The common law was part of the historical heritage of England and attempts to expunge any part of it were difficult politically. It is significant that in India, as part of the common law world, codification was a vehicle for the superimposition of the common law over native law.

The rational theory of law espoused by Bentham was itself imperfect. He attempted to treat the law as an exact science and exclude history as a vital element in the development of his scientific body of laws. Thus, the advocates of codification in England in the late 19th century favoured *limited* codification where the benefits of a code were seen in terms of being a classificatory reference rather than a methodological technique in amending the law. The 19th-century English commercial codes (the Bills of Exchange Act 1882; the Partnership Act 1890; the Sale of Goods Act 1893; the Marine Insurance Act 1906) were enacted then not to reform substantive law but rather to 're-form' its shape and organisation. Such codes were influenced by lawyers, the major English personalities being Chalmers who produced a digest of the law of bills of exchange in 1878 having been encouraged to produce this code by Sir Farrer Herschell who became Solicitor-General (1880–5) and later Lord Chancellor (1886 and 1892–5).

The Bills of Exchange Act 1882 itself was unique among all previous attempts at codifications proposed during the 19th century in that its drafting was sponsored by the Bankers' Institute, and by the Associated Chambers of Commerce. Commercial interests were also involved with the passage of the Partnership Act 1890 and the Marine Insurance Act 1906. The Sale of Goods Act 1893 differs in that there was a much lower level of commercial involvement. No commercial pressure group actively interested itself in the matter to a significant extent. It would appear that a significant factor which precluded Parliamentary inertia with respect to the Sale of Goods Bill was that in 1892, Lord Herschell became Lord Chancellor again, and in that position he was able to guide the Bill on to the statute book.

Following the passage of the Bills of Exchange Act 1882, the Association of British Chambers of Commerce (ABCC) attempted to move a comprehensive commercial code. In 1885, Lord Chancellor Selborne received a deputation from the ABCC but his lordship's advice was to stick to piecemeal codification, and even for this he could not promise government help. This initiative reflects a concern for a systematic exposition of commercial law principles as seen on the Continent. In this respect, the French Commercial Code had by 1879 been in operation for 75 years, while the German Code was completed during 1856–61. Some believed that the issue of English codification was a question of nationalism. Codification was also perceived as a way of promoting uniformity of commercial law in the Empire, thereby tightly binding the overseas possessions to the UK.

The general principles of the laws of commerce and business were well-settled in England which provided the impetus for codification. The codes were mere declarations of the common law. Solutions were to spring from a deductive application of statutes and not from inductive synthesising of *ratio decidendi*. At the same time, parity between the statute and the common law was ensured since the major premise, the code provision, was itself no more than a restatement of a common law principle. Furthermore, if no code provision precisely accommodated the facts which composed the minor premise of any case, the major premise could be amended, or a supplementary one could be found by searching among the common law.

One important factor underlying the codification movement was the quest for certainty. Claims were made of the Bills of Exchange Act 1882 that it reduced litigation, but these were made in the euphoria of the immediate post-Act scenario. In fact, in no case did codification have the observable effect of reducing the amount of reported litigation on points of law. Moreover, because Chalmers saw codification as an improvement in the form of the law then resurrection of old authorities is easy. Thus, in *Cehave NV v Bremer Handelsgesellschaft mbH* [1976] QB 44, the Court of Appeal considered that it was the intention to restate the pre-existing sales law, and this intention translated itself into a canon of statutory interpretation. Additionally, insofar as codification was seen as a way of promoting certainty in the sense that it constituted a mechanism for circumventing the formality, cost, and slowness of the judicial system, tools of alternative dispute resolution, especially arbitration, have developed as a semi-private dispute-settlement mechanism. Although Chalmers recognised the importance of legal certainty, he never talked about the other things business people might need from the legal system such as cheaper and quicker administration of justice, adjudication by people with commercial expertise, a more secure legal status for commercial usage.

A significant impetus to the codification movement was the effect of Bentham's critique on the common law. After Bentham, it could no longer be denied that the common law was judge-made, and the judicial process was deprived of its traditional legitimation that judges simply found the law. The underlying approach of the codifying movement in reforming the law stressed the *mechanistic* nature of legal reasoning as essentially a syllogistic exercise. It was the language of the code which would now form the major premise. As Lord Herschell said in *Bank of England* v *Vagliano Brothers* [1891] AC 107 at p. 145:

> The law should be ascertained from interpreting the language used instead of, as before, roaming over a vast number of authorities in order to discover what the law was.

At the same time as codification was seen as a starting-point for *finding* and *applying* traditional common law rules, Lord Herschell continued at p. 145:

> I am of course far from asserting that resort may never be had to the previous state of the law for the purpose of aiding in the construction of the provisions of the code. If, for example, a provision may be of doubtful import, such resort would be perfectly legitimate.

An important question which arises out of the above analysis concerns contemporary judicial attitudes to the English commercial codes. One method of investigating this question is by reference to the retention of title clause which provides a current and relatively self-contained line of case law.

Judicial attitudes: the *Romalpa* experience

In chapter 12 we were concerned with the question whether the arguments adopted by the judges were 'sound' as a matter of law. In this section we will focus only upon the *form* of the judgments adopted. We shall not attempt to assess the calculability or predictability of the decision-making in the cases since this would require an investigation of cases that never got to court, as well as cases at trial level. The analysis will be confined to the reported cases, the most significant being appeal cases. It is important to emphasise that the 'opinion style' in the Court of Appeal might be different from the lower courts simply because there are fewer authoritative constraints here, especially since the House of Lords has not *fully* considered these clauses. The subject-matter of the cases has, in the main, consisted of raw materials or semi-finished goods. All of the cases have a strong mercantile presence where both parties can be identified as being a trader, or a dealer, or a company/partnership. The most important factor is the prominence of the bankruptcy/insolvency of usually the buyer. This reflects the difficult economic circumstances in which we now live, as well as the lowly position of the trade (unsecured) creditor on the insolvency of its customer. The prominence of bankruptcy as a factor precipitating litigation can be seen in the early 19th-century sales case law where the extent of the stoppage *in transitu* doctrine figures highly (see chapter 6). In a sense, the *Romalpa* line of case law follows this tradition. The recognition of a retention of title clause entails the extension of the rights of recall of the seller beyond stoppage *in transitu*.

The use of precedent figures highly in the *Romalpa* case law. The greatest level of abstraction is where the circumstances or facts surrounding the precedent (i.e., either an authoritative example or a statement of principle) are substituted into the protasis of a rule, although the apodosis may or may not be articulated. This phenomenon can be illustrated by Robert Goff LJ in *Clough Mill Ltd* v *Martin* [1985] 1 WLR 111 who, when setting the scene for his judgment, identifies the principle but with no accompanying apodosis at p. 113:

> This appeal is concerned with what is sometimes called a 'retention of title clause' but more frequently nowadays a '*Romalpa* clause'.

The methodological presupposition of argument from precedent involves reconciliation of the cases and this is tacitly presupposed in the *Romalpa* line of cases. Thus in *Borden (UK) Ltd* v *Scottish Timber Products Ltd* [1981] Ch 25, Bridge LJ distinguishes the *Aluminium Industrie Vaassen BV* v *Romalpa Aluminium Ltd* [1976] 1 WLR 676 case at p. 38:

> It seems to me that there is a certain very clear distinction between that case [*Romalpa*] and this.

Often the methodology seen is analogical, i.e., precedents figure as examples to be followed or distinguished. The account given of each precedent may be long and circumstantial, and the issue is one of accepting or rejecting the analogy offered by, for example, highlighting the differences or similarities. Thus in *Hendy Lennox (Industrial Engines) Ltd* v *Grahame Puttick Ltd* [1984] 1 WLR 485 at p. 492, Staughton J in distinguishing *Borden (UK) Ltd* v *Scottish Timber Products Ltd* says:

> There are passages in the judgments of the Court of Appeal in *Borden (UK) Ltd* v *Scottish Timber Products Ltd* which, if taken out of context, might suggest that an unpaid seller cannot lawfully retain proprietary rights in goods delivered to a buyer, whether or not those goods have been used or altered in a manufacturing process. But the whole dispute in that case was about chipboard, or the proceeds of sale of chipboard; it was not about the resin which the plaintiffs had sold to the defendants and which the defendants had used to make chipboard.

Sometimes a principle emerges through mutual reconciliation of the cases. This phenomenon is evident in Vinelott J's approach in *Re Peachdart Ltd* [1984] Ch 131 at p. 139:

> In *Romalpa* the second part of the title retention clause . . . was relied on to support the implication of a power for Romalpa to sell the unused aluminium foil as agent for the vendor. But the question whether the vendor could claim to be entitled to or to a charge on mixed or manufactured goods was not in issue. That was the question in issue in *Borden (UK) Ltd* v *Scottish Timber Products Ltd*.

Axiomatic arguments are also evident in the *Romalpa* case law. This is where a legal statement is not supported by authority as the position is considered too well-established to require this. An example of this phenomenon can be seen in both *Aluminium Industrie Vaassen BV* v *Romalpa Aluminium Ltd* and *Borden (UK) Ltd* v *Scottish Timber Products Ltd* where there is no specific mention of the property-passing provisions, namely ss. 17 and 19 of the Sale of Goods Act 1979. Occasionally, precedents are considered superfluous, as seen in Buckley LJ's approach in *Borden* when in his discussion of tracing principles there is no mention of *Re Hallett's Estate* (1879) 13 ChD 696. The axiomatic statement is a representation of the law as how it is. In contrast, Bridge LJ at p. 41 in *Borden* uses a suppositive argument founded in 'common sense' to suggest that a certain proposition cannot be the law on the basis of *reductio ad absurdum*:

> Suppose cattle cake is sold to a farmer, or fuel to a steel manufacturer, in each case with a reservation of title clause, but on terms which permit the farmer to feed the cattle cake to his herd and the steelmaker to fuel his furnaces, before paying the purchase price. . . . the goods have been consumed. . . . I find it impossible to draw an intelligible line of distinction in principle which would give the plaintiffs a right to trace the resin into the chipboard in the instant case.

Reform and codification of English commercial law

Undoubtedly, an important feature of the *Romalpa* case law is the influence of the Sale of Goods Act. This is pertinent in the light of Chalmers's view of codification as providing the major premise in a syllogistic exercise. For example, the property-passing provisions in ascertained goods are to be found in ss. 17 to 19 of the Act:

MAJOR PREMISE: Property passes by agreement (ss. 17 and 19) and unless a different intention appears s. 18 applies.
MINOR PREMISE: A different intention does appear.
CONCLUSION: Section 18 does not apply.

This approach is illustrated by Oliver LJ's judgment in *Clough Mill Ltd* v *Martin* [1985] 1 WLR 111 at p. 121:

> Nor is there any conceptual impossibility or even difficulty in the notion, which is commercially familiar, of a seller of goods retaining a power of disposition and the legal property in goods after delivery to the buyer. Section 17(1) of the Sale of Goods Act 1979 provides... 'Property' is defined in section 61(1)... Reservation of a right of disposal is specifically dealt with by section 19, subsection (1) of which provides...

A certain amount of 'translation' of the language used in the different agreements is evident in the case law which is often supported by appeals to common sense and business purpose reflecting the commercial context. Perhaps the most dramatic example of this can be seen in Vinelott J's judgment in *Re Peachdart Ltd* [1984] Ch 131. In the *Romalpa* case itself the business-purpose argument was used to imply an agreement to retain title on subsale of the aluminium foil.

It is clear from the *Romalpa* line of case law that the same types of argument appear in each of the cases. What emerges is a combination of meta-authoritative, authoritative (or formal) and non-authoritative (or informal) arguments. Axiomatic precepts are examples of meta-authoritative arguments in the sense that they are understood to be law so well-settled that no authority need be cited in their support, whereas merely authoritative arguments proceed from precedent or statute. Non-authoritative arguments on the other hand proceed from 'common sense', suppositious examples. On the whole, argument from statutory text and precedent takes precedence over the other types of argument. From this it would appear that the judicial style in this instance as a response to an English commercial code (the Sale of Goods Act 1979) is formal.

CODIFICATION: A VEHICLE FOR REFORM?

The interaction of legislation and the common law under Anglo-American uniform Acts is a comparatively recent phenomenon. In contrast, civilian lawyers have been debating for centuries the relationship between enacted and other sources of law. The civilian code is seen as the primary authoritative source of law in the sense that it is an ideological expression which recognises the power of the centralised State as the unique originator of the law. This demonstrates the essential difference between the civilian and common law traditions. Ever since Justinian, civilians have developed and refined techniques for extending the scope of rules beyond their literal wording principally through *a fortiori, a pari,* and *e contrario* reasoning. This approach was necessitated under a Continental tradition which assumed codes to be gapless because, theoretically, civilian courts merely apply the written law. Of course, as a practical matter, prior decisions are indispensible to the civilian lawyer on points of interpretation of the written texts.

There is a critical difference between codified and case law systems on the basis of the relative priorities accorded to judicial decisions. In England, the courts traditionally have been institutions commanding great respect whilst civilians looked to the legislative bodies as the protectors of freedom and liberty. This was not considered necessary nor desirable in the Anglo-Saxon tradition. Although the civil method clearly recognises the existence of sources of law in addition to codified texts, its strict hierarchical arrangement of these sources just as clearly prescribes that every effort must first be made to reach a legal decision upon the basis of the rules and principles contained within the four corners of the relevant code. Civilian interpretative methodology applicable to codes reinforces the supremacy of enacted law as the primary source of law. This explains Professor Llewellyn's approach to the UCC when he anticipated that it would be a 'case law code', but insisted that the only part of precedent that should stand for future decisions is that which could be justified as a matter of reason, that is, a reference to *'jurisprudence constante'* rather *than stare decisis* (see Llewellyn, K., 'A Realistic Jurisprudence — The Next Step' (1930) 30 Colum L Rev 431).

The great virtue of the UCC is not that it is a perfect commercial code but that it demonstrates that the task of codifying commercial law is at least possible. The great English commercial codes drafted in the 19th century no longer adequately serve the needs of modern business. Furthermore, the European dimension can no longer be ignored. It may be that the peculiar mix of civilian and common law methodologies evident in the UCC will provide a model for the process of reform and harmonisation of commercial law within the European Community. In this regard, it is well to recall the approach of Chalmers who did not seek after an impossible perfect code as this would deter the application of a legal initiative that was within reach.

Select Bibliography

ARTICLES AND BOOKS

Adams, J. (ed.), Essays for Clive Schmitthoff (Professional Books) (1983).
Allan, D. E., 'Credit and Security: Economic Orders and Legal Regimes; 33 *ICLQ* 22, (1984).
Allan, D. E., 'Stock-in-Trade Financing, 2 *Tasmania UL Rev* 382, (1967).
Allcock, B., 'Restrictions on the Assignments of Contractual Rights', 42 *CLJ* 328, (1983).
Ames, J. B. 'The Disseisin of Chattels, 3 *Harv LR* 23, 313, 337, (1890–90).
Atiyah and Summers, *Form and Substance in the Anglo-American Law,* OUP (1988).
Atiyah, P. S., *From Principles to Pragmatism,* OUP (1978).
Atiyah, P. S., *Promises, Morals and Law,* OUP (1981).
Atiyah, P. S., *The Sale of Goods* (8th edn.), Pitman, (1990).
Baird, D. G., 'Notice Filing and the Problem of Ostensible Ownership', 12 *JLS* 53, (1983).
Baird, D. G., 'Standby Letters of Credit in Bankruptcy', 49 *Univ of Chicago LR* 130, (1982).
Baird and Jackson, 'Corporate Reorganization and the Treatment of Diverse Ownership Interests', 51 *Univ of Chicago LR* 130, (1984).
Baird and Jackson, 'Fraudulent Conveyance Law and its Proper Domain', 38 *Van LR* 829, (1985).
Baird and Jackson, 'Information, Uncertainty, and the Transfer of Property', 13 *JLS* 299, (1983).
Baird and Jackson, 'Notice Filing under the UCC', *JLS* 53, (1983).
Baird and Jackson, 'Possession and Ownership: An Examination of the Scope of Article 9', 35 *Stan LR* 175, (1983).
Baird and Weisberg, 'Rules, Standards and the Battle of Forms, 68 *Virginia LR* 1217, (1982).
Beale and Dugdale, 'Contracts Between Businessmen', 2 *British Journal of Law and Society* 451, (1975).

Bell, A. P., *Modern Law of Personal Property in England and Ireland*, Butterworths, (1989).
Calabresi and Melamed, 'Property Rules, Liability Rules and Inalienability: One View of the Cathedral', 85 *Harv LR* 1089, (1972).
Calligar, D. M., 'Subordination Agreements', 70 *Yale LJ* 376, (1960).
Chafee, Z., 'Equitable Servitudes on Chattels', 41 *Harv LR* 945, (1928).
Chalmers, M. D., 'An Experiment in Codification', 2 *LQR* 126, (1886).
Chalmers, M. D., 'Codification of Commercial Law', 19 *LQR* 10, (1903).
Chalmers and Guest, *On Bills of Exchange, Cheques and Promissory Notes*, (14th edn.), Sweet & Maxwell, (1991).
Coogan, P. F. 'Is There a Difference Between a Long Term Lease and an Installment Sale?', 56 *NYULR* 1036, (1981).
Coogan, P. F., 'Leases of Equipment and Some Other Unconventional Security Devices', *Duke LJ* 909, (1973).
Coogan, P. F., 'Outer Fringes of Article 9 of the UCC', 79 *Harv LR* 229, (1965).
Coogan, P. F., 'Public Notice under the UCC and other Recent Chattel Security Laws including "Notice Filing"', 47 *Iowa LR* 289, (1962).
Davies, I. R., 'Continuing Dilemmas with Passing of Property in Part of a Bulk', *JBL* 111, (1991).
Davies, I. R., 'The Reform of Personal Property Security Law', 37 *ICLQ 463*, (1988).
Davies, I. R., 'Transferability and Sale of Goods', 7 *Legal Studies* 1, (1987).
Derham, S. R., *Set-off*, OUP, (1988).
Diamond, A. L., 'Equitable Relief for the Purchaser of Hire Purchase Goods — A Rejoinder, 21 *MLR* 199, (1985).
Diamond, A. L., 'Hire Purchase Agreements as Bills of Sale', 23 *MLR* 399, 516, (1960).
Epstein, R. A., 'Notice and Freedom of Contract in the Law of Servitudes', 55 *S Cal LR* 1353, (1982).
Epstein, R. A., 'Possession as the Root of Title', 13 *Georgia LR* 1221, (1979).
Epstein, R. A., 'Security Transfers by Secured Parties', 4 *Georgia LR* 527, (1970).
Farrar, R. A., 'Why Restrain Alienability?', 85 *Columbia LR* 970, (1985).
Farrar, J. H., 'Contracting Out of Set-off', 120 *NLJ* 771, (1970).
Farrar, J. H., 'Floating Charges and Priorities', 38 *Conv (NS)* 315, (1974).
Farrar, J. H., 'Public Policy and the *Pari Passu* Rule', *NZLJ* 100, (1908).
Farrar, J. H., 'World Economic Stagnation put the Floating Charge on Trial', 1 *Co Lawyer* 83, (1980).
Ferguson, R. B., 'Legal Ideology and Commercial Interest: The Social Origins of the Commercial Law Codes', 4 *British Journal of Law & Society* 18, (1977).
Fletcher, I., *The Law of Insolvency*, Sweet & Maxwell, (1990).
Gilmore, G., *Ages of American Law*, Yale Univ Press, (1977).
Gilmore, G., 'Commercial Doctrine of Good Faith Purchase', 63 *Yale LJ* 1057, (1954).
Gilmore, G., 'Formalism and the Law of Negotiable Instruments', 13 *Creighton LR* 441–461, (1979).

Gilmore, G., 'Good Faith Purchase Idea and the UCC: Confessions of a Repentant Draftsman', 15 *Georgia LR* 605, (1981).
Gilmore, G., 'Purchase Money Priority', 76 *Harv LR* 1333, (1963).
Gilmore, G., *Security Interests in Personal Property*, New York, (1965).
Gilmore, G., *The Death of Contract Law*, Little and Brown Co., (1974).
Gilmore, G., 'The Difficulties of Codifying Commercial Law', 57 *Yale LJ* 1341, (1948).
Goode, R. M., *Commercial Law*, (rev. edn), Penguin, 1992.
Goode and Simonds, (eds), *Commercial Operations in Europe*, Sijthoff, (1977).
Goode, R. M., *Hire Purchase Law and Practice*, Butterworths, (1970).
Goode, R. M., *Legal Problems of Credit and Security*, (2nd edn), Sweet & Maxwell, (1988).
Goode, R. M., 'Is the Law too Favourable to Secured Creditors?' 8 *Can Bus LJ* 53, (1983).
Goode, R. M., 'Lender's Labyrinth' 112 *SJ* 772, (1968).
Goode, R. M., 'Ownership and Obligation in Commercial Transactions', 103 *LQR* 433, (1987).
Goode, R. M., *Payment Obligations in Commercial and Financial Transactions*, Sweet & Maxwell, (1983).
Goode, R. M., *Principles of Corporate Insolvency Law*, Sweet & Maxwell, (1990).
Goode, R. M., 'The Concept and Implications of a Market in Commercial Law', *LMCLQ* 177, (1991).
Goode, R. M., 'The Modernisation of Personal Property Security Law', 100 *LQR* 234, (1984).
Goode, R. M., 'The Right to Trace and its Impact on Commercial Transactions', 92 *LQR* 360, (1976).
Goode, R. M., 'Twentieth-Century Developments in Commercial Law, 3 *JLS* 283, (1983).
Goode and Ziegel, (eds) *Hire Purchase and Conditional Sale: A Comparative Survey*, (1965), Toronto.
Guest, A. G., 'Accession and Confusion in the Law of Hire Purchase', 27 *MLR* 505, (1964).
Guest, A. G., 'Hire Purchase Equipment Leases and Fixtures', 27 *Conveyancer* 30, (1963).
Harding and Rowell, 'Protection of Property versus Protection of Commercial Transactions in French and English Law', 26 *ICLQ* 354, (1977).
Herman, S., 'Excerpts from a Discourse on the Code Napoleon by Portalis and Case Law', 18 *Loy LR* 23, (1972).
Herman, S., 'Llewellyn the Civilian: Speculations on the Contribution of Continental Experience', 56 *Tul LR* 1125, (1982).
Jackson, T., 'Bankruptcy, Non-bankruptcy, Entitlements and the Creditors' Bargain', 91 *Yale LJ* 857, (1982).
Jackson, T., *The Logic and Limits of Bankruptcy Law*, Harv Univ Press, (1986).
Jackson, T., 'Translating Assets and Liabilities to the Bankruptcy Forum', 14 *JLS* 23, (1985).

Kennedy, P., 'Form and Substance in Private Law Adjudication', 89 *Harv LR* 1685, (1976).
Kerr, M., 'Modern Trends in Commercial Law and Practice', 41 *MLR* 1, (1978).
Khurshid and Matthews, 'Tracing Confusion', 59 *LQR* 78, (1979).
Kripke, H., 'Law and Economics: Measuring the Economic Efficiency of Commercial Law in a Vacuum', 133 *Univ of Pennsylvania LR* 929, (1985).
Landes and Posner, 'Private Enforcement of Law', 4 *JLS* 1, (1975).
Lawson, F. M., 'Passing of Property and Risk in Sale of Goods — A Comparative Study', 65 *LQR* 352, (1949).
Levmore, S., 'Monitors and Freeriders in Commercial and Corporate Settings', 92 *Yale LJ* 49, (1982).
Lingard, *Bank Security Documents*, (2nd edn), Butterworths, (1988).
Llewellyn, K. N., 'A Realistic Jurisprudence — The Next Step', 30 *Col LR* 431, (1930).
Llewellyn, K, N., 'First Struggle to Unhorse Sales', 52 *Harv LR* 873, (1939).
Llewellyn, K. N., 'Through Title to Contract and a Bit Beyond', 15 *NYULQ* 159, (1938).
Mann, F. A., 'On Interest, Compound Interest and Damages', 101 *LQR* 30, (1985).
MacLeod, J., *Consumer Sales Law*, Butterworths, (1989).
McKendrick, E., *Commercial Law and Fiduciary Duties*, OUP, (1992).
O'Donovan and Phillips, *The Modern Contract of Guarantee*, Butterworths, (1985).
Oditah, F., *Legal Aspects of Receivables Financing*, Sweet & Maxwell, (1991).
Palmer, R. L., 'Lord Mansfield's Commercial Law and Adam Smith's Wealth of Nations', *Commercial LJ* 99, (1983).
Pennington, R., *Corporate Insolvency Law*, Butterworths, (1991).
Pennington, R., 'Fixed Charges Over Future Assets of a Company', *Butterworths Banking and Financial LR* 177, (1987).
Pennington, R., 'The Genesis of the Floating Charge', 23 *MLR* 630, (1960).
Pennington, R., 'The Retention of Title to the Sale of Goods under European Law', 27 *ICLQ* 277, (1978).
Richardson's Guide to Negotiable Instruments, (ed. James), (8th edn), Butterworths, (1991).
Rickett, C. E. F., 'Different Views on the Scope of the Quistclose analysis, English and Antipodean Insights', 107 *LQR* 608, (1991).
Rodiere, R., 'Code Civil and Modern Procedures of Payment', 50 *Tul LR* 577, (1976).
Rose, C. M., 'Crystals and Mud in Property Law', 40 *Stanford LR* 577, (1988).
Rosenthal, A. J., 'Negotiability — Who Needs It?', 71 *Columbia LR* 375, (1971).
Rubin, P., 'Common Law and Statute Law', 11 *JLS* 205, (1982).
Rubin, P., 'Why is the Common Law Efficient?', 6 *JLS* 51, (1977).
Rutherford and Todd, 'Section 25(1) of the Sale of Goods Act 1893: The Reluctance to Create a Mercantile Agency', 38(2) *CLJ* 346, (1979).
Salinger, F. R., *Factoring Law and Practice*, Sweet & Maxwell, (1991).

Sauveplanne, (ed.), *Security over Corporeal Movables*, North Holland, (1974).
Sauveplanne, 'The Protection of the Bona Fide Purchase of Corporeal Movable Objects', *YB Int Inst for the Unification of Private Law* 50, (1961–62).
Schmitthoff, C., *Commercial Law in a Changing Economic Climate*, Sweet & Maxwell, (1981).
Schwartz, A., 'Security Interests and Bankruptcy Priorities: A Review of Current Theories', 10 *JLS* 1, (1981).
Schwartz, A., 'The Case for Specific Performance', 89 *Yale LJ* 271, (1979).
Schwartz, A., 'The Continuing Puzzle of Secured Debt', 37 *Van LR* 1051, (1984).
Schwartz and Scott, *Commercial Transactions: Principles and Policies*, Foundation Press, (1982).
Scott, H. S., 'Risk Fixes', 91 *Harv LR* 737, (1978).
Scott, M. F., 'Some Recent Problems in Applying the Rule in *Clayton's* Case', 6 *Australian Lawyer* 111, (1966).
Scott, M. F., 'The Right to Trace at Common Law', 7 *UWALR* 463, (1965–66).
Scott, R. E., 'A Relational Theory of Secured Financing', 86 *Col LR* 901, (1986).
Sealy, L. S., 'Fiduciary Relationships', 21 *CLJ* 69, (1962).
Sealy, L. S., 'Risk in the Law of Sale', 31 *CLJ* 225, (1972).
Simpson, A. W. B., 'The Analysis of Legal Concepts', 80 *LQR* 535, (1964).
Smith, T. B., *Property Problems in Sale*, Sweet & Maxwell, (1978).
Smith, T. B., 'Retention of Title: Lord Watson's Legacy', *SLT* 103, (1983).
Smith, T. B., 'The Common Law Cuckoo: Problems of "Mixed" Legal Systems', *S African LR* 147, (1956).
Spry, I. C. F., 'Equitable Set-offs', 43 *ALJ* 265, (1969).
Steeg, M. S., 'When is a Security not a Secured Right?', 39 *Tul LR* 513, (1965).
Steffen, R. T., and Danziger, F. S., 'Rebirth of the Commercial Factor', 36 *Col LR* 745, (1936).
Swartz, E. M., '*Bona Fide* Purchasers Revisited: A Comparative Inquiry', 42 *Boston Univ LR* 403, (1962).
Sykes, E. I., 'Bills of Sale and Other Puzzles', 3 *Univ of Queensland LJ* 152, (1957).
Taylor, A. M., 'Goods on Sale or Return and the *Nemo Dat* Rule', *JBL* 390, (1985).
Tepora, J., 'Reservation of Title as Security and in Administration of Property', 29 *Scandinavian Studies in Law* 213, (1985).
Terrebonne, A., 'Strictly Evolutionary Model of Common Law', 10 *JLS* 397, (1981).
Tollison, Willett and Sweeney, 'Market Failure, the Common Pool Problems and Ocean Resource Exploitations', 17 *JL and Econ* 179, (1974).
Trakman, L. E., *The Law Merchant: The Evolution of Commercial Law*, Rothman, (1983).
Tribe, L., 'Constitutional Calculus: Equal Justice or Economic Efficiency?', 98 *Harv LR* 592, (1985).
Tunc, A., 'English and Continental Commercial Law', *JBL* 234, (1961).

Tunc, A., 'The Not So Common Law of England and the US', 47 *MLR* 150, (1984).
Weinberg, H. R., Markets Overt, Voidable Titles and Feckless Agents: Judges and Efficiency, 56 *Tul L Rev* 1, (1981).
Weinberg, H. R., 'Sales Law Economics and the Negotiability of Goods', 9 *JLS* 569, (1980).
Wood, P. R., *English and International Set-off*, Sweet & Maxwell, (1989).
Wood, P. R., *The Law of Subordinated Debt*, Sweet & Maxwell, (1990).
Ziegel, J. S., 'Legal Problems of Wholesale Financing of Durable Goods in Canada', 41 *Can Bar Rev* 54, (1963).
Ziegel, J. S., 'Legal Problems of Canadian Personal Property Security Law', 31 *Univ of Toronto LJ* 249, (1981).

Index

ABTA scheme 467
Acceleration clauses 5
  finance leases and hire contracts 302–4
Acceptance
  bill of exchange 208
  in contract of sale 169–72
    express acceptance 169
    inconsistent act 169–70
    lapse of time 170–1
    part acceptance 171–2
  in contract of supply 172–4
    rejection 173–4
    total failure of consideration 173–4
  duty 160–1
  goods which prove to be defective 180
Accessio 40–2, 315
Accession *see* Property interests creation
Adjuntio 40–2
Administration order 403–15
  administrative receivership and 416
  avoidance of 411
  creditor protection 413–14
  discharge 415
  effect 408–11
  legal form 411
  lightweight floating charge 404–6
  moratorium over affairs 408
  notification duties 407–8
  objections to 404–6
  petitioners 403–4
  power to make 406–8
  see also Administrator
Administrative receivers 415–21
  administrator compared 419–20
  appointment 415
    validity 416–21

Administrative receivers – *continued*
  disposal of property 420–1
  duty of care 416, 417
  effect of receivership 416
  functions 416
  liability 418–19
  powers 417–19
  removal 416
  set-off right 433
  statement of affairs 415
  termination of agency 419
Administrator 403
  administrative receivers compared 419–20
  creditor protection 413–14
  disposal of property 420–1
  general duties 414–15
  notification duties after appointment 407–8
  powers 411–15
  set-off right 433
  termination of office 415
  veto on appointment 404
  see also Administration order
Advance factoring 233
Advertising "puffs" 66
Affixation 15, 41
Agents
  agency of necessity 136
  apparent authority 136–7
  consensual model 136
  gratuitous agency 136
  mercantile agent
    definition 139–40
    disposition with consent of owner 141
    disposition in course of business 140–1

Agents – *continued*
　　emergence of　139–41
　　notional agency　149
　　retention of title clauses　274–9
　　"business efficacy" test　277
　　commission agent　276
　　establishment of relationship　275–7
　　fiduciary relationship　277–9
　　proceeds clauses validity　274–9
　　unauthorised dispositions　135–7
　　usual or presumed authority　136
Alternative dispute resolution (ADR)
　　mechanism　471–2
Anton Piller order　464, 465
Appropriation　52–5
　　conditional　55
　　meaning　53
　　unconditional　53–4
Approval sales　351–2
Arbitration　465–71
　　ABTA scheme　467
　　Chartered Institute of Arbitrators　467
　　commercial context　466–8
　　cost　467–8
　　delay　469–70
　　Grain and Feed Trade Association　466
　　litigation compared　468–71
　　London Maritime Arbitrators' Association　466
　　NHBC scheme　467
　　Scott v *Avery* clause　466
　　Solicitors' Arbitration Scheme　467
　　UNCITRAL model rules　469
Artificer's lien　323
Ascertainment *see* Identification
Assets, distribution *see* Distribution of assets
Assignment
　　priority *see* Priorities
　　securitisation of receivables　255–6
　　theory　439
　　see also Credit factoring
Assize of Bread and Beer (1256)　84
Association of British Factors and Distributors　232
Attornment　33–4
Auction sales
　　formalities　75–6
　　liability of auctioneer　76
　　mock auctions　76
　　reserve price　75
Automated teller machines　210, 211, 217, 226–7
Available market rule　130–1

Back-to-back arrangements　234
Bailment　58–9, 107, 323, 324
　　commodity procession　272–3

Bailment – *continued*
　　field warehousing　271–2
　　finance leases　295
　　Romalpa context　270–4
　　sub-bailment　313–14
Balance sheet test　400, 401, 456
Bank Giro System　225–6
Bank notes　191
Bankers' liens　321
Banks
　　automated teller machines　210, 211, 217, 226–7
　　banker definition　211–2
　　banker-customer relationship　212
　　　termination　216–17
　　CHAPS　225
　　cheque guarantee cards　214
　　collecting bank liability　221–4
　　combining accounts　213
　　Committee of London Clearing Banks　221
　　customers' duties
　　　due care　215
　　　inform bank of forgeries　215
　　　negligence avoidance　215–6
　　definition　211
　　disclosure　214–15
　　duties
　　　confidentiality　214–15
　　　public policy restraints　213
　　　repayment　212–14
　　EFTPOS systems　211, 226–7
　　factoring participation schemes　233–4
　　opening accounts　223–4
　　paperless payment orders　225–7
　　paying bank　219–21
"Battle of forms"　66
Bearer bonds　191
Benedict rule　247–8
Bentham, Jeremy　474–5, 476
Bill of exchange
　　acceptance for honour　208
　　acceptor　191
　　addressed by one person to another　193
　　alterations　200
　　cheques and　210–11
　　complete　199–200
　　consideration requirement　198–9
　　cost of finance　189
　　defect in title　200–1
　　discharge　209
　　dishonour notice　200, 208
　　documentary bill　188–9
　　drawee　191, 192
　　drawer　191
　　endorsement　192, 207–8
　　　in blank　197

Index   489

Bill of exchange – *continued*
   notice of dishonour   208
   special   197
  fictitious payee   195–6
  forged signatures   202–7
   estoppel   203
    negligence   204
    representation   203
   liability
    accommodation party   206
    transferor of bearer bill   206–7
    see also statutory estoppel
   material alteration defence   207
   statutory estoppel
    acceptor's liability   205
    drawer's liability   205–6
    endorser's liability   206
   statutory protection   205
   unauthorised   204–5
  function   188–9
  historical development   187–8
  holder   192, 197
  holder in due course   199–201
   need for holder   199
  holder for value   198–9
  liability on
   capacity   201–2
   delivery   201
  negotiation   196–7
  non-existing payee   195–6
  noting bill   208–9
  overdue   200
  parties   191–2
  presentment
   for acceptance   207–8
   for payment   208
  presumption of value and good faith   201
  protesting   208–9
  screen-based transfers   209
  signatures   193–4
   forged *see* forged signatures
   minors   201–2
   partnerships   202
   unauthorised   204–5
  sum certain in money   194
  time payable   194
  to specified person or bearer   194–5
  trade bill   189
  transferability   197–202
  unconditional order   192–3
  validity requirements   191–6
  in writing   193
  see also Negotiable instruments
Bills of lading   35, 191, 323, 324
Bonds
  bearer bonds   191
  medieval bond   187

Bonds – *continued*
  performance bonds   187, 387–8
  syndicated bond facilities   390
Bulk factoring   234
Buyers in possession   151–7
  "agreed to buy"   151
  documents of title   152
  Factors Act   153–5
  innocent buyer   155
  innocent owner   155
  notice requirement for good-faith purchase   152–3
  Sale of Goods Act   155–7

Cancellation
  duties following cancellation   78
  right   77
Cash flow test   399, 410
Catzman Committee   368
Caveat emptor   84, 91
Caveat venditor   84, 92
Centre for Dispute Resolution   471
Cestui que trust   251
CHAPS   225
Charge card payment   163
Charges
  mortgages and   342–3
  non-registration of registrable charge   452–3
  register of   253
  sale transaction compared with   348
  see also Fixed *and* Floating charges
Chartered Institute of Arbitrators   467
Chattel mortgages
  legislation   59
  pledge and   319
Cheque guarantee cards   214
Cheques
  bank's duty to pay   212–14
  bills and   210–11
  clearing system   218–19
  collecting bank liability   221–4
  countermanding   213
  crossings   217–18
  definition   191
  due care duty in drawing   215–17
  endorsement   192, 221
  informing of forgeries   215
  legal regulation   217–24
  paying bank and true owners   219–21
   common law defences   219
   restitutionary principles   220
   statutory defences   220–1
  presentation   219
  travellers' cheques   219, 224–5
  see also Banks; Bill of exchange
Choses in action   16, 190

Choses in action – *continued*
  assignment 45
  definition 45
Clearing House Automated Payment System (CHAPS) 225
Codification 472–80
  English commercial law 474–9
  France 475
  Germany 475
  reform through 479–80
  Romalpa clause 477–9
Comfort letters 376–7
Commercial law
  contract sanctity 4–5
  conveyancing principle 10–12
  customs 13–14
  good faith 5–6
  inalienability of human organs or blood 13
  market place principle 14
  meaning 3–4
  "muddy rules" 4, 6
  negotiability principle 12–13
  principles 4–14
  priorities *see* Priorities
  realist school of jurisprudence (US) 3–4
  security interest creation 6–9
  usage 13–14
Committee of London Clearing Banks 221
Commixtio 38–40
Commodatum 295
Common carrier's lien 322
Compulsory winding-up 421–4
Condition, breach 178–80
Conditional sales 151
  contracts 60
Confusio 38–40
Connected persons
  floating charges 449
  preferences 447
Consequential losses 180–2
Consideration, total failure of 173–4
Consignment sales
  non-possessory security 351–2
  retention of title and 273–4
Constructive possession 23
  immediate 23
  qualified 23
Consumer Credit Act 1974
  ambit 61–2
  terminology 60–1
  see also Credit
Consumer protection
  securitisation of receivables and 254
  see also Product liability
Contract
  appropriation 52–5

Contract – *continued*
  bailment 58–9
  conditional sales 60
  conditions 66, 67
  definitions
    choses in action 45
    goods 45
    parties 45
    price 46
    sale 44
    seller 45
    transfer of property 45–6
  deliverable state 50–1
  disclaimer after insolvency 427–8
  exchange 55–6
  exclusions 68–9
  formalities 74–8
    auction sales 75–6
    regulated consumer credit agreement 76–8
  formation *see* Formation of contract
  free-gifts 56–7
  frustration 72, 73–4
  goods *see* Goods
  hire *see* Hire contract
  hire-purchase 60
  implied terms *see* Formation of contract
  impossibility of performance
    initial impossibility 71–3
    perishable goods 72–3
    specific goods 72
    subsequent impossibility 73–4
  intention 48–55
    ascertaining intention rules 49–55
    unconditional contract 50
  liability limitation 68–9
  mistake doctrine 63–4
  open-price 46
  part-exchange 56
  privity 113, 296–9
  property and 18
  reliance on description 88–9
  repudiation 427
  rescission 65, 132–3
  risk *see* Risk
  sale contract 44–55
  sanctity of 4–5
  severable, repudiation of 82
  supply for consideration other than money 55–60
  supply of goods and services 57–8
  termination, payment duty 163
  terms *see* Formation of contract
  trading stamps 57
  unconditional 50
  waiver doctrine 69–70
  warranty 66, 67

Index 491

Conveyancing principles 10–12
"Cooling-off" period 77
Cork Committee 341, 342, 392, 393–4, 402, 403, 407, 416, 423, 429, 435, 441
Corporate insolvency
  administration order *see* Administration order
  administrative receiver *see* Administrative receivers
  asset distribution *see* Distribution of assets; Priorities
  claims *see* Distribution of assets; Priorities
  collective proceedings 396–7
  creditors 396
  culpability 395
  disclaimer of contracts 427–8
  disclaimer of onerous property 427
  distribution of assets *see* Distribution of assets
  fact and status 391–2
  historical development 392–4
  liquidation *see* Winding-up
  objects of law 394–5
  personal and corporate compared 392–3
  pre-insolvency entitlements 395–6
  principles 395–7
  protection of public 395
  reform 393–4
  social and financial implications 394–5
  statutory trust 396–7
  tests for 398–401
    balance sheet test 400, 401, 456
    cash flow test 399, 401
    inability to pay 400–1
  transactions before *see* Transactions
  voluntary arrangements 402–3
Counterclaim right 241
Credit
  "cooling-off" period 77
  debtor-creditor agreements 61
  debtor-creditor-supplier agreements 61
  efficient credit hypothesis 9
  extortionate credit transactions 448–9
  factoring *see* Credit factoring
  fixed-sum 61
  regulated consumer credit agreement
    cancellation right 77
    duties following cancellation 78
    finance lease 315–17
    formalities 76–8
  restricted-use 60–1
  revolving credit plans 8
  running-account 61
  sale and loan on security 62
  unrestricted-use 60–1

Credit – *continued*
  see also Consumer Credit Act 1974; Credit factoring; Late payment of debts; Securitisation of receivables
Credit card payment 163, 164
Credit factoring 231–3
  accounting function 231–2
  advance factoring 233
  approved and disapproved invoice 240
  arrangements 237–47
    ad valorem duty 238–9
    assignment prohibition 242–5
    assignment taken subject to equities 240–1
    back-to-back 234
    counterclaim 241
    mistaken payment by obligor 246–7
    notice 239–40
    scope 242
  assignment with recourse 233
  back-to-back arrangements 234
  bank participation schemes 233–4
  bulk factoring 234
  clients suitable for 232–3
  commercial factor 234–5
  credit control function 232
  estoppel 137–9
  maturity factoring 233
  "net amount of invoice" 233
  old line factoring 233
  perfect client 233
  priorities 247–53
    Benedict rule 247–8
    charge conflicts 253
    Dearle v *Hall* rule 248, 249–52
    notice effect 252–3
    secret liens 247
  process 235–7
  recourse factoring 233, 351, 426
  set-off rights 241
Creditors
  administration order protection 413–14
  pari passu principle 396
  transactions defrauding 451
Crops 15
Crowther Committee 247, 251, 286, 351, 365, 368
Crystallisation of charge 340–2
Currency market 14
Custom 13–14
  implied conditions 107

Damages *see* Remedies
Dearle v *Hall* rule 11, 248, 249–52, 440
Debts *see* Credit factoring; Late payment of debts; Securitisation of receivables
Declaration of solvency 421

Delay
  arbitration 469–70
  damages for late delivery 179
Deliverable state 50–1
Delivery 79–84
  acceptance 79–80
    duty of 160–1
  actual custody 79
  damages for delay 179
  instalments 82–3
  non-delivery damages
    sale 174–7
    supply 178
  possession 79
  repudiation and 82, 83–4
  time of 79–80
  wrong quantity 80–2
Delivery warrant or order 35
Deposits, finance leases 295
Depositum 295
Description
  exclusion of requirement 89–91
  identity and attributes 86–7
  implied term of correspondence with 85
  meaning 85–8
  reasonableness test 90
  reliance on description 88–9
  samples 105–6
  supplies by 84–90
Deterioration 165, 167
  see also Perishable goods
Developing countries 9
Directors
  disqualification 458–9
  prosecution 457–8
  see also Fraudulent *and* Wrongful trading
Disclaimer of contracts 427–8
Disclaimer of onerous property 427
Dispositions
  administrative receivers 420–1
  administrators 420–1
  improper by non-owners 141–4
  mercantile agents
    in course of business 140–1
    with owner's consent 141
  unauthorised 135–7
  see also Distribution of assets
Dispute resolution 460–72
  alternative dispute resolution mechanisms 471–2
  arbitration *see* Arbitration
  litigation *see* Litigation
  mediation 471
  negotiation 472
  private settlements 472
  self-regulation 471
Disqualification of directors 458–9

Distribution of assets 395
  assets available 425–31
  belonging to third parties 428
  fresh start 425
  insurance 428
  assignment theory 439
  disclaimer of contracts 427–8
  disclaimer of onerous property 427
  insurance 428
  order of distribution 441–2
    ordinary creditors 442
    preferential creditors 441–2
    surplus 442
  pari passu principle 429–37
    British Eagle case 430–1
    exceptions 431–7
    mandatory nature 429–31
    market concept 430–1
    post-liquidation netting 431
    set-off *see* Set-off rights
    subordination and 438–9
  subordination 437–40
    proof 439–40
    security 440
    set-off and 438
Dividend warrants 191
Dock warrants 35
Documentary bill 188–9
Documentary letter of credit 122
Dominium 62
Dominus 243
Due diligence 119, 367
Duty to accept 160–1
Duty to pay *see* Payment duty

Efficient credit hypothesis 9
Electronic Funds Transfer at Point of Sale (EFTPOS) 211, 226–7
End-game 447
Equality in equity *see* Pari passu principle
Equipment Leasing Association 291
Equitable lien 185–6
Equitable mortgages, pledges and 319–20
Equity
  after-acquired property interest 328–31
  of original owner 147, 148
  retention of title clauses and 279–88
  tracing 281
  trust device 287–8
Estoppel
  agency *see* Agents
  apparent ownership principles 138
  automatic crystallisation of charge 342
  bill of exchange
    forged signatures 203
    negligence 204
    representation 203

Index 493

Estoppel – *continued*
  dispositions
    in course of business 140–1
    improper by non-owners 141–4
    with owner's consent 141
  Factors Acts 137–9
  mercantile agents *see* Agents
  negligence 144
  priorities 10
  proprietary 142
  representation requirement 142–4
  right to cure 144–5
Eurobonds 14
Eurocurrency deposits 14
Examination of goods 167–8
Exchange transactions
  contracts 55–6
  motor vehicles 159
"Exchange-product" theory 282
Exhaustion, ascertainment by process of 31–2
Extortionate credit transactions 448–9

Factoring *see* Credit factoring
Fairs 1
Field warehousing 271–2
Finance lease 289–317
  Consumer Credit Act 314–17
  contractual privity 296–9
  deposit 295
  growth of finance leasing 291–2
  legal problems 292–302
  lessee control 292
  lessor-lessee relationship 293–5
  meaning 290–1, 292
  minimum payment clause 311–12
  non-possessory security 350
  novation 293
  pledges 295
  regulated consumer credit agreement 315–17
  remedies
    acceleration clauses 302–4
    depreciation losses 310
    keeping lease on foot 302–4
    lease not kept on foot 304–14
    penalty clauses 311–13
    recaption 305
    repossession 305, 317
    repudiation 307–8
    repudiatory breach 308–10
    self-help 304–5
    third party interests 306–7
  subleasing 304
  subletting of goods 313–14
  termination 307–8, 310–11, 315–17
  rule against penalties 310–11

Finance lease – *continued*
  statutory implied terms 293–5
  supplier-lessor relationship 293
  supplier-lessor-lessee 296–9
  third parties 299–302
  unsafe products 300–2
First-in-line rule 15
First-in-time rule *see* Nemo dat quod (qui) non habet
Fitness for purpose 101–5
  communication of knowledge 102–3
  instructions and warnings 104–6
  knowledge 101–2
  reasonably fit 101
  reliance 103
Fixed charges 335–6
  floating charge and 338–42
Floating charges 336–8
  attachment of security interest 343
  connected persons 449
  crystallisation 340–2
    automatic 341–2
    estoppel 342
    partial 342
  fixed charge and 338–42
  invalidation 449–50
  juridical nature 337–8
  lightweight floating charge 404–6
  in personal property security law 343–5
  security interest, as 344–5
  winding-up and 449–50
Formation of contract
  "battle of forms" 66
  express terms 65–8
  implied terms
    correspondence with description 85
    finance leases 293–5
    fitness *see* Fitness for purpose
    merchantable quality *see* Merchantable quality
    quality *see* Quality undertakings
    samples 105–7
    supply and service contracts 105
  mirror-image rule 66
  misrepresentation 64–5, 66
  mistake doctrine 63–4
  mistaken identity 64
  parol evidence rule 65
  representation 64–6
  standard form contracts 66
France, Civil Code 474
Fraudulent trading
  civil sanctions 455
  criminality of conduct 454–5
Free gifts 56–7
  implied terms as to quality 93

Frustration
  contract 72, 73–4
  property passing and 28

General property guarantee 26–7
Gift vouchers 163
Good-faith 5–6
"Good-faith performance" 134–5
"Good-faith purchaser" 134
  notice requirement
    buyers in possession 152–3
    sellers in possession 149–50
  priority 10
Goods 16
  acceptance 160–1
  ascertained 48
  defective 179–82
  definition, sale contract 45
  examination of 167–8
  existing 46–7
  future 46–7
  future specific 47–8
  non-conforming 160
  perishable 72–3
    powers of sale 160
    time of payment 162
  "protected goods" rule 59
  rejection *see* Transferee rejection right
  specific 47, 49
  in transit
    risk 166–7
    stoppage *see* Stoppage in transit
  unascertained 47
    risk 165
Grain and Feed Trades Association 40, 466
Guarantees 374–90
  advance payment guarantees 388–9
  construction 375–6
  continuing 378
  counter-guarantees or bonds 389–90
  definitions 374–6
  general property guarantee 26–7
  illegality 383
  insolvencies
    of debtor 385–6
    of debtor and surety 386
    of surety 386
  legal presumptions 379–85
  limitation as to amount 378–9
  manufacturers' 112–13
  misrepresentation 382–3
  non est factum 383
  performance-based 387–8
  quasi-guarantees 387–90
  quiet possession guarantee 25–6, 27
  release of principle debtor 380–1
  release of security 381–2

Guarantees – *continued*
  repayment guarantees 388–9
  retention money guarantee 389
  rights of surety
    contribution 384
    indemnity 384
    recourse to security 384–5
    subrogation 385
  superguarantees 390
  surety and creditor 379–83
  surety and debtor 383–5
  suretyship contracts 376–9
    comfort letters 376–7
    construction 378–9
    forms of 377–8
  syndicated bond facilities 390
  undue influence 382
  variation of contract 380

Halliday Committee 343, 345, 368
Hire contracts 58–9
  remedies *see* Finance lease, remedies
Hire transactions, quality undertakings 92
Hire-purchase 151
  contract 60
  misrepresentation damages 133
  quality undertakings 92
  non-possessory security 350–1
Hire-Purchase Information plc 157
History 1–3
Human organs and blood inalienability 13

Identification 29–37, 281, 283
  accession where goods not separable 41–2
  ascertained goods 48
  ascertainment by process of exhaustion 31–2
  attornment 33–4
  common law position 32–3
  mistaken identity 64
  mixture of fungibles 40
  modern commercial context 29–30
  risk and unascertained goods 165
  sale contract 45–6
  symbolic possession 34–6
  unascertained goods 47
  see also Tracing
Impossibility *see* Contract, impossibility of performance
Inalienability of human organs or blood 13
Indemnity *see* Guarantees
Information, perfect 6–7
Injunctive relief 186
Innkeeper's lien 322
Innocent third party, supplier remedy and 132
Insecurity clauses 9

Index

Insolvency
  corporate *see* Corporate insolvency
  guarantees and   385–6
  personal and corporate compared   392–3
  property passing and   28–9
Instalment delivery   82–3
Instalment payment   8
Instructions, fitness for purpose   104–6
Intellectual property   16
Interest rate swaps   14
International Chamber of Commerce   2
International Institute for the Unification of Private Law *see* UNIDROIT
Investigation into company affairs   423–4
Invoice discounting   231

Jack Committee   191, 193, 194, 199, 204, 209
Joint Contracts Tribunal's standard form   389

Land, property in relation to   15–16
Late payment of debts   228–37
  credit factoring *see* Credit factoring
  dilemma of   228–9
  interest on   229, 230
  invoice discounting   231
  statutory relief   229
Leases
  finance *see* Finance lease
  net lease *see* Finance lease
  operating lease meaning   290
Letter of credit, documentary   122
Letters of comfort   376–7
Lex mercatoria   1–2
Liability
  administrative receiver   418–19
  product *see* Product liability
  suppliers' *see* Liability exclusion of supplier; Product liability
Liability exclusion of supplier   108–12
  "in course of business"   108
  "deals as customer"   108
  exemption clauses and UCTA   108–11
  limited contracting out   111–12
  reasonableness requirement   109–10
  statutory guidelines   110–11
Liens
  agents' liens   321
  artificer's lien   323
  Bankers' liens   321
  common carrier's lien   322
  created by usage   322
  equitable lien   185–6
  general liens   321
  innkeeper's lien   322
  non-possessory liens   323

Liens – *continued*
  particular liens   321–3
    created by contract   322
    created by statute   322
  pledge and   319
  possessory (common law) liens   320
  repairer's lien   307
  secret liens   247
  solicitors' liens   321
  stoppage in transit   35–6, 123–5
  unpaid seller's lien   122–3
Liquidation *see* Corporate insolvency; Winding-up
Litigation   461–5
  arbitration compared   468–71
  discovery   463
  injunctive relief   463
    Anton Piller order   464, 465
    Mareva injunction   463–4, 465
  procedural aids   463–5
  process   462–3
Locatio et conductio   295
London Maritime Arbitrators' Association   466

Malicious tampering   117
Manufacturers' guarantees   112–13
Mareva injunction   463–4, 465
Market overt   145–6
Market place principle   14
Market rule   130–1, 175, 176–7
Maturity factoring   233
Mediation   471
Medieval bond   187
Mercantile agents *see* Agents
Merchant courts   1, 2
Merchant law (*Lex mercatoria*)   1–2
Merchantable quality
  determination of   97–8
  durability   96–7
  excepted defects   98–9
  finance leases   294
  fitness *see* Fitness for purpose
  implied obligation of   93–101
  merchantability and quality   95–6
  price   96
  purpose   94–5
    quality and   99–101
  samples   106–7
  see also Quality undertakings
Mere "puffs"   66
Minerals   45
Mirror-image rule   66
Misrepresentation   64–5, 66
  guarantees   382–3
  supplier remedies against   133
Mistake doctrine   63–4

Mistaken identity   64
Mixture of fungibles *see* Property interests creation
Monitoring   6–7, 9
Mortgages
  charges compared   342–3
  chattel mortgages   59, 319
  equitable, pledges and   319–20
  sale transaction compared with   348
Motor vehicles   157–9
  exchange transactions   159
  Hire-Purchase Information plc   157

Negligence, estoppel and   144, 204
Negotiability principle   12–13
Negotiable instruments
  good-faith transferee   190
  "holder"   189
  insolvency of debtor   386
  negotiability   190–1
  payment by   163–4
  transfer   190
  see also Bill of exchange
Nemo dat quod (qui) non habet   10, 60, 134, 135, 190, 283
net lease *see* Finance lease
New York State Information and Intelligence Service   371
NHBC scheme   467
No available market   176–7
Non-acceptance damages   129–32
Non-delivery damages
  market rule   176–7
  measures   175–6
  no available market   176–7
  sale   174–7
  supply   178
Non-possessory security   327–57
  after-acquired property interest   328–35, 353–4
  Bills of Sale Acts 1854–1891   332–5
  equity   328–31
  legislative response   331–5
  consignment sales   351–2
  finance lease   350
  fixed charges   335–6
  floating charges   336–8
  hire-purchase   350–1
  purchase-money security interest   254–7
  recognition   333
  recourse credit factoring   351
  retention of title   346–54
  scintilla temporis doctrine   355–6
  Scottish law   346–7
  super purchase-money security interest   356–7
  Twyne's Case   327

Non-possessory security – *continued*
  unconventional devices   346–57
Novation   255
  finance leases   293

Off balance sheet financing   254
Official Receiver   423
Old-line factoring   233
Onerous property, disclaimer of   427
Open price contracts   46
Operating lease   290
Ostensible ownership   358–65
  English response   359–65
  registration under US law   365–9
Overreaching *see Tabula in naufragio* doctrine
Ownership   19–20
  apparent   138
  ostensible   358–65
  possession *see* Possession
  see also Property

Paperless payment orders   225–7
Pari passu principle   9
  creditors   396
  distribution of assets   429–37
    British Eagle case   430–1
    exceptions   431–7
    mandatory nature   429–31
    market concept   430–1
    post-liquidation netting   431
    set-off *see* Set-off rights
    subordination and   438–9
Parol evidence rule   65
Part payment   162–3
Part-exchange transactions   56, 159
Payment duty
  method   163–4
  part payment   162–3
  termination   163
  time of payment   162
  see also Late payment of debts
Payner Committee   393
Performance bonds   187, 387–8
Performance-based guarantees   387–8
Periodic payment transactions   350
Perishable goods   72–3
  powers of sale   160
  time of payment   162
Personal Identification Number (PIN)   226
Personal property security interests
  Canadian filing   369–73
  English filing system   360–1
Pignori acceptum   295
PIN   226
Pledge   138, 318–20, 323–4
  chattel mortgages   319
  delivery to third party   325–6

Index 497

Pledge – *continued*
  equitable mortgages   319–20
  liens   319
  pignori acceptum   295
  powers of sale   326
  transaction form   320
  trust receipt   325–6
PMSI *see* Purchase-money security interest
Possession   19–20, 20–9
  buyers in possession *see* Buyers in possession
  concept of   323–6
  constructive   23, 323
  control required   23
  factual   323
  French Civil Code   21–2
  German Civil Code   21–2
  giving up   324
  nature   23–4
  ostensible ownership   358–65
  quiet possession   25–6, 27, 294
  sellers in *see* Sellers in possession
  symbolic   24, 34–6
  title and   20–1
    see also Title
  trust receipt   325–6
  see also Possessory security
Possessory remedies   19
Possessory security
  delivery to third party   325–6
  lien *see* Liens
  pledge *see* Pledge
  powers of sale   326
  termination of interest   326
  see also Possession
Preferences   446–8
  powers of court   448
Preferential creditors   441
Price
  action for, by supplier   127–8
  merchantability and   96
Priorities
  administrative receivership   419
  Dearle v *Hall* rule   11, 248, 249–52, 440
  estoppel   10
  factoring *see* Credit factoring, priorities
  first-in-time rule *see* nemo dat
  good faith purchaser   10
  nemo dat   10, 15, 367
  no knowledge of prior interest   12
  ordering   10–12, 441–2
  overreaching *see* tabula in naufragio doctrine
  tabula in naufragio doctrine   11, 249
  tacking further advances   11
  variation of rules by agreement   11–12
  without fault loss or subordination   12

Privity of contract   113
  finance leases   296–9
Product, definition   114–15
Product liability
  burden of proof   116
  Consumer Protection Act   113–18
  criminal liability   118–20
  damage   115–16
  defences   116–18
  development risk   117
  "due diligence" defence   119
  finance leases   300–2
  general safety requirement   118–19
  product   114–15
  reliance on representation   300
  safety regulations   119–20
Promises to pay   191
Promissory notes   188, 191, 224
Property
  affixation degree   15
  choses in action   16
  classification of rights   16–17
  disclaimer of onerous property   427
  first-in-line-rule   15
  goods   16
  growing crops   15
  identification *see* Identification
  immovables   15
  intellectual property   16
  interest creation *see* Property interests creation
  land and   15–16
  movables   15
  nature of rights   17–18
  nemo dat principle   10, 60, 134, 135, 190, 283
  ownership *see* Ownership
  passing
    frustration   28
    identification   45–6
    insolvency of party   28–9
    intention   48–55
    risk   28
    security-of-property principle   29
    tenancy in common   37
    third party claims   29
    tracing rights   29
  possession *see* Possession
  real   15–16
  rights *in rem*   17
  security of   134–5
  title undertakings and   27–8
  transferable rights   18
Property interests creation
  accession   40–2, 315
  affixation   41

Property interests creation – *continued*
  goods identifiable but not separable 41–2
  at common law 37–43
  creation of new thing 42–3
  mixture of fungibles 38–40
    with consent 38–9
    identification 40
    without consent 39–40
  specificatio 42–3
"Protected goods" rule 59
Purchase-money security interest 254–7
  registration, English law 364
  scintilla temporis doctrine 355–6
  super 356–7

Quality undertakings 84–5, 90–3
  agent use 92
  all goods supplied 93
  containers 93
  damages for defects
    sale 179–80
    supply 180
  fitness *see* Fitness for purpose
  hire and hire-purchase transactions 92
  merchantable quality *see* Merchantable quality
  supply in course of business 91–3
Quasi-guarantees 387–90
Quiet possession 294
  guarantee 25–6
  right to sell and 27

Rational theory of law 475
Realist school of jurisprudence (US) 3–4
Receivables securitisation *see* Securitisation of receivables
Recourse factoring 233, 351, 426
Registration of charge 452–3
Registration of security interests *see* Security interest registration
Regulated consumer credit agreement
  cancellation right 77
  duties following cancellation 78
  finance lease 315–17
  formalities 76–8
Rejection *see* Transferee rejection right
Reliance
  on description 88–9
  fitness for purpose 103
Remedies
  finance leases *see* Finance lease, remedies
  hire contracts *see* Finance lease, remedies
  supplier's *see* Supplier remedies
  transferee's *see* Transferee remedies
  transferors' 126–7
Repair obligation 51

Repairer's lien 307
Repudiation 82, 83–4, 427
  severable contract 82
Resale right of unpaid seller 125–6
Rescission 65
Restitutio in integrum 65
Restitution 186
Restitutionary principles 18–19
Retention right 122–3
Retention of title clause 7, 258–88
  agency 274–9
    "business efficacy" test 277
    establishment of relationship 275–7
    fiduciary relationship 277–9
    proceeds clauses 274–9
  "all-liabilities" 357
  Andrabell Ltd 264–5
  Armour v *Thyssen Edelstahlwerke* 267–8
  bailment 270–4
  Bond Worth 260–1
  Borden (UK) Ltd 261–2
  Clough Mill Ltd v *Martin* 265–7, 268–9
  codification and 477–9
  consignment sales 273–4, 351–2
  contractual formulations 269
  equity and 279–88
  Hendy Lennox 263–4
  identification 268–70
  non-possessory security 346–54
  Peachdart Ltd 262–3
  Romalpa case 259–60
  tracing 281, 282–3
  trust instruments 279, 287–8
Right to sell, quiet possession and 27
"Ripple effect" phenomena 386
Risk 3, 164–7
  aversion 8
  deterioration 165, 167
    see also Perishable goods
  exposure 8
  fault relevance 165–6
  goods in transit 166–7
  late taking delivery 166
  property passing and 28
  unascertained goods 165
Romalpa clause *see* Retention of title clause

"Safe" defined 118
Safety *see* Product liability
Sale
  on approval 351–2
  common law powers 159
  conditional 60, 151
  contract *see* Contract
  mortgage transaction compared with 348
  powers, possessory security 326
  statutory powers 159–60

Index 499

Sale of Goods Act supplier remedies *see* Supplier remedies
Samples 105–7
Sanctity of contract 4–5
Scintilla temporis doctrine 355–6
Scottish law *see* Halliday Committee
Securities and Investments Board 14
Securitisation of receivables 253–7
  assignment 255–6
  economic advantages for issuers 254
  legal impediments 254
  novation 255
  stamp duty 254
  sub-participation 255, 256–7
  transfer of original debt 254–7
  transferable loan certificate (TLC) 255, 257
  transferable loan facility (TLF) 255
  transferable loan instrument (TLI) 256
Security
  interest *see* Security interest; Security interest registration
  non-possessory *see* Non-possessory security
  possessory *see* Possessory security
  sale and loans on 62
Security interest
  attachment of 343
  facilitation of creation 6–9
  floating charge as 344–5
  monitoring 6–7, 9
  perfect information 6–7
  registration *see* Security interest registration
Security interest registration
  Canadian law 369–73
    chattels 370–1
    errors in documents or registration 371–2
    indexing methods 369–73
    knowledge 372–3
  English law 359–65
    Bills of Sale Act 1878 361–2
    Companies Act 1985 as amended 363–5
    notice filing 363
    other registers 362–3
    personal property security interests 360–1
    public notice 363
    purchase-money security interest 364
  pure race system 372
  United State law 365–9
Self-regulation 471
Seller remedies *see* Supplier remedies
Sellers in possession 148–51
  notice requirement for good-faith

Sellers in possession – *continued*
  purchase 149–50
  notional mercantile agency 149
  section 24 and 150–1
Set-off rights 431–3
  administrative receiver and 433
  administrator and 433
  debtor's 241
  debts must be proved 436
  insolvency and 432, 433–7
  mutual dealing taken place 436
  preferential debts 437
  subordination and 438
  sums of money due 436–7
  waiver of rights 435
Share warrants to bearer 191
Signatures
  bill of exchange 193–4
    forged *see* Bill of exchange, forged signatures
  minore 201–2
  partnerships 202
"Silver lining" test 455
Solicitors' Arbitration Scheme 467
Solicitors' liens 321
Specific performance 183–8, 330
Specificatio 42–3
Stamp duty
  factoring 238–9
  securitisation of receivables 254
Stamps, trading stamp contracts 57
Stock-in-trade financing 358–9
Stoppage in transit 35–6
  exercise of right 123–5
  notice of stoppage 125
  termination of right 124
  unpaid seller's right 123–5
Stratification theory 6
Subbuyer 168
Subordination
  distribution of assets 437–40
    pari passu principle 438–9
    proof 439–40
    security 440
    set-off and 438
Subrogation 245
  sureties and 385
Subsales, damages for loss of 176–7
Supplier obligations
  custom and usage 107–8
  delivery *see* Delivery
  fitness *see* Fitness for purpose
  liability *see* Liability exclusion of supplier; Product liability
  manufacturers' guarantees 112–13
  samples 105–7
  supplies by description *see* Description

Supplier obligations – *continued*
  supply and service contracts   105
  undertakings as to quality *see* Quality undertakings
Supplier remedies
  action for price   127–8
  misrepresentation damages   133
  non-acceptance damages   129–32
    available market   130–1
    loss of profit recovery   131–2
    mitigation of loss   132
    not available market   131–2
  personal remedies   127–33
  real
    contracts of supply   126–7
    Sale of Goods Act 1979   121–6
  repudiation   129
  resale   125–6
  rescission   132–3
  retention right   122–3
  special damage claims   128–9
  stoppage in transit   123–5
    exercise of right   123–5
    notice of stoppage   125
    termination of right   124
  termination and damages   129
  unpaid seller's lien   122–3
Suretyship contracts   376–9
  construction   378–9
  forms of   377–8
  letters of comfort   376–7
  see also Guarantees
Surrogacy arrangements   13

Tabula in naufragio doctrine   11, 249
Tacking further advances   11
Tampering with product   117
Tenancy in common   37
Third-party claims, property passing and   29
Title
  defects in, damages for   178
  documents   152
  implied title undertaking   24–5
  market overt   145–6
  one-lump title   3
  possession and   20–1
    see also Possession
  priorities *see* Priorities
  registration   24
  relativity of   24
  retention *see* Retention of title clause
  undertakings   24
    property and   27–8
  voidable   146–8
Tort
  damages in   182

Tort – *continued*
  property and   18
Tracing   29, 281
  administrative receivership   420
  common law approach   282–3
  equity approach   283–7
    fund appreciated in value   284
    fund dissipated   284–7
    several trust fund monies mixed   285–7
    subsequent additions to dissipated fund   285
  property passing and   29
Trade bill   189
Trading stamps   57
  payment   163
Transactions
  at undervalue   444–6
  avoidance   442–51
  defrauding creditors   451
  extortionate credit transactions   448–9
  preferences   446–8
Transferable loan certificate (TLC)   255, 257
Transferable loan facility (TLF)   255
Transferable loan instrument (TLI)   256
Transferee obligations
  delivery acceptance   160–1
  payment *see* Payment duty
  risk *see* Risk
Transferee rejection right   167–8
  acceptance in contract of sale   169–72
  acceptance in contract of supply   172–4
  examination of goods   167–8
  loss of right   168–74
Transferee remedies
  consequential losses   180–2
  damages action   174–82
    breach of condition or warranty   178–80
  non-delivery damages
    sale   174–7
    supply   178
  tort   182
  equitable   182–6
    injunctive relief   186
    lien   185–6
    specific performance   183–8
    specific restitution   186
Transferors' remedies   126–7
Transportation *see* Delivery
Travellers' cheques   219, 224–5
Trust instruments   287–8
  retention of title and   279
Trust receipt   325–6

UNCITRAL   2
Unconscionability   6

Index

Undervalue transactions 444–6
  orders affecting third parties 446
  powers of court 446
Undue preference 446–8
UNIDROIT 2
  Convention on International Factoring 1988 242, 245
  Convention on International Financial Leasing 293
United Nations Commission on International Trade (UNCITRAL) 2
Unjust enrichment 18–19, 279
Unpaid seller *see* Supplier remedies
Unsolicited goods 56–7
Usage 13–14
  implied conditions 107
Usufructory 243

Voidable title 146–8
Voluntary arrangements 402–3
Voluntary winding-up 421

Waiver 69–70, 435. 437
Warehouse keeper's certificate 35
Warehousing 271–2
Warnings, fitness for purpose 104–6
Warranties, breach 178–80
Winding-up
  compulsory 421–4
    consequences 423–4
    grounds 422
    petitioners 422–3

Winding-up – *continued*
  declaration of solvency 421
  directors
    disqualification 458–9
    prosecution 457–8
  dispositions after commencement of 451–2
  fraudulent trading 454
  investigation into affairs of company 423–4
  liquidator
    good faith 423
    information to Official Receiver 423
    qualifications 422
  non-registration of registrable charge 452–3
  transactions
    at undervalue 444–6
    defrauding creditors 451
    extortionate credit transactions 448–9
    floating charges 449–50
    preferences 446–8
  voluntary 421
  wrongful trading 455–7
  see also Corporate insolvency
Wrongful trading 455–7
  deemed knowledge of insolvent liquidation 455–6
  directors or shadow directors 457
  statutory defence 457

"Zero-sum game" 6–7